A COMPREHENSIVE APPROACH TO

Striking a Balance

EARLY LITERACY

FIFTH EDITION

Nancy Lee Cecil
CALIFORNIA STATE UNIVERSITY, SACRAMENTO

Susan Baker
CALIFORNIA STATE UNIVERSITY, SACRAMENTO

Albert S. Lozano
CALIFORNIA STATE UNIVERSITY, SACRAMENTO

Routledge
Taylor & Francis Group

LONDON AND NEW YORK

Library of Congress Cataloging-in-Publication Data

Cecil, Nancy Lee.
  Striking a balance : a comprehensive approach to early literacy / Nancy Lee Cecil,
California State University, Sacramento, Susan Baker, California State University,
Sacramento, Albert S. Lozano, California State University, Sacramento. — Fifth edition.
     pages   cm
  ISBN 978-1-62159-037-8 (print) — ISBN 978-1-62159-038-5 (ebook)   1. Reading
(Primary)—United States.   2. Literacy—United States.   I. Title.
  LB1525.C34 2015
  372.40973—dc23

                                                          2015014332

Photo Credits:
Front cover, top to bottom: Wavebreak Media Ltd/123RF, Tatiana Gladskikh/123RF, Wong Sze Yuen/123RF, Syda Productions/123RF *(background). Back cover, top to bottom:* Kyolshin/Dreamstime, stylephotographs/123RF, Syda Productions/123RF, Dmitriy Shironosov/123RF *(background). Page iii,* Roman Gorielov/123RF/123RF; *page v,* Jacek Chabraszewski/123RF; *page xv,* 123RF Limited/123RF; *page xix,* Borges Samuel/ 123RF; *page xxi,* Oksana Kuzmina/123RF; *page 1,* Dmitriy Shironosov/123RF; *page 7,* DigitalVision; *page 10,* Wavebreak Media Ltd/123RF; *page 15,* Hongqi Zhang/123RF; *page 18,* Tyler Olson/123RF; *page 24,* Kyolshin/Dreamstime/123RF; *page 31,* Cathy Yeulet/123RF; *page 35,* Antonio Diaz/123RF; *page 39,* Digital/Vision/123RF; *page 44,* PhotoDisk/123RF; *page 53,* Banana Stock/123RF; *page 59,* Hongqi Zhang/123RF; *page 62,* PhotoDisk/123RF; *page 68,* darko64/123RF; *page 77,* iofoto/123RF; *page 79,* Banana Stock/123RF; *page 92,* Thomas Perkins/123RF; *page 96,* doctorkan/123RF; *page 99,* forsterforest/123RF; *page 103,* Syda Productions/123RF; *page 107,* Wavebreak Media Ltd/123RF; *page 113,* Thomas Perkins/123RF; *page 115,* Juan Carlos Tinjaca Rodriguez/123RF; *page 123,* Wavebreak Media Ltd/123RF; *page 127,* Oksana Kuzmina/123RF; *page 132,* Hongqi Zhang/ 123RF; *page 145,* stylephotographs/123RF; *page 151,* Cathy Yeulet /123RF; *page 157,* Wavebreak Media Ltd/123RF; *page 158,* nyul/123RF; *page 172,* Dmitriy Shironosov/123RF; *page 179,* iofoto/123RF; *page 181,* Syda Productions/123RF; *page 201,* waldru/123RF; *page 207,* Nagy-Bagoly Ilona/123RF; *page 209,* Dmitriy Shironosov/123RF; *page 218,* Banana Stock/123RF; *page 224,* Syda Productions/ 123RF; *page 229,* Cathy Yeulet/123RF; *page 231,* Banana Stock/123RF; *page 234,* Alan Poulson/123RF; *page 238,* stylephotographs/123RF; *page 242,* phartisan/123RF; *page 253,* Wavebreak Media Ltd/123RF; *page 261,* bowie15/123RF; *page 269,* Wavebreak Media Ltd/123RF; *page 271,* Matthew Antonino/123RF; *page 275,* Petro Feketa/123RF; *page 286,* Cathy Yeulet/123RF; *page 299,* Jose Manuel Gelpi Diaz/123RF; *page 302,* Wavebreak Media Ltd /123RF; *page 305,* mocker/123RF; *page 309,* Tyler Olson/123RF; *page 313,* Pavel Losevsky/123RF; *page 315,* Anna Lurye/123RF; *page 324,* Tyler Olson/123RF; *page 327,* Wavebreak Media Ltd/123RF; *page 329,* Banana Stock/123RF; *page 331,* stylephotographs/123RF; *page 334,* stylephotographs/123RF; *page 336,* nyul/123RF; *page 405,* Alexander Ermolaev/123RF; *page 415,* belchonock/ 123RF; *page 439,* Tetiana Vitsenko/123RF; *page 443,* 123RF Limited/123RF.

Please note: The authors and publisher have made every effort to provide current website addresses in this book. However, because web addresses change constantly, it is inevitable that some of the URLs listed here will change following publication of this book.

First published 2015 by Holcomb Hathaway, Publishers, Inc.

Published 2017 by Routledge
2 Park Square, Milton Park, Abingdon, Oxon OX14 4RN
711 Third Avenue, New York, NY 10017, USA

Routledge is an imprint of the Taylor & Francis Group, an informa business

Print ISBN: 978-1-62159-037-8 (pbk)

Brief Contents

Striking a Balance

A Child Learns to Read 1

PROCESS AND PRODUCT

A Quest for Balance 15

MOVING FORWARD

Emergent Literacy 31

FROM BIRTH TO CONVENTIONAL LITERACY

Phonemic Awareness 59

THE SOUNDS OF OUR LANGUAGE

Phonics, Sight Vocabulary, and Fluency 77

WHY AND HOW

Spelling 107

A WRITER'S TOOL

Acquiring Word Meanings 127

THE BUILDING BLOCKS OF LITERACY

Contents

1 A Child Learns to Read   1

PROCESS AND PRODUCT

2 A Quest for Balance   15

MOVING FORWARD

Emergent Literacy   31

FROM BIRTH TO CONVENTIONAL LITERACY

Phonemic Awareness   59

THE SOUNDS OF OUR LANGUAGE

Phonics, Sight Vocabulary, and Fluency   77

WHY AND HOW

Spelling   107

A WRITER'S TOOL

7 Acquiring Word Meanings   127

THE BUILDING BLOCKS OF LITERACY

8 Reading Comprehension   151

MAKING SENSE OF PRINT

Writing–Reading Connections   179

RECIPROCAL PATHS TO LITERACY

Informational Text in the Classroom   207

READING AND WRITING TO LEARN

Large- and Small-Group Reading Strategies   229

CREATING A LITERATE COMMUNITY

Literacy and Technology in a Balanced Classroom   253

EXPLORING TODAY'S RESOURCES

Assessment of Early Literacy Development   275

INFORMING INSTRUCTION

Home as Partner   309

THE SHARED CONNECTION

15 The Early Literacy Classroom   327

ORCHESTRATING A COMPREHENSIVE PROGRAM

APPENDICES

List of Activities

9   Writing–Reading Connections

Also see the section "Writing Structures" (pp. 191–198) for writing activities

10   Informational Text in the Classroom

12   Literacy and Technology in a Balanced Classroom

14   Home as Partner

Preface

L
ike its predecessors, this edition of *Striking a Balance: A Comprehensive Approach to Early Literacy* fully explores a comprehensive program of balanced literacy instruction. In such a program, young children can learn the basics of cracking the code of reading and writing through systematic explicit instruction; in addition, with caring teachers and well-chosen strategies, they will enjoy learning to become literate through ample practice with authentic literacy experiences. The need for balance is especially critical in early literacy, and this edition continues to emphasize why both decoding (or word identification) and meaning making (or comprehension) act as the foundation of beginning literacy instruction. In keeping with the current consensus in the field of literacy, we believe that students are best served when they receive direct skill and strategy instruction in conjunction with motivating contexts for reading.

Exactly what needs to be "balanced" in early literacy instruction to provide a comprehensive program? This book highlights the need to offer instruction that focuses on the affective dimension of learning and on the cognitive dimension of early literacy. The book balances attention to reading quality literature for enjoyment and reading for information, and it balances narrative and informational writing. It stresses balancing time spent teaching reading and writing and time allowed for students to actually practice these skills. It recognizes the need to nurture the other language arts (speaking, listening, viewing, and visually representing) as valid alternative ways of receiving and expressing information, and it provides myriad opportunities to integrate these processes. The book underscores the importance of explicit instruction, modeling, and scaffolding coupled with the gradual withdrawal of teacher support to encourage student independence. It stresses spelling, vocabulary, and phonics skills, but always in the larger context of authentic literacy experiences. A comprehensive and balanced approach takes all aspects of literacy into account.

Since the prior edition was published, emphasis on aligning instruction with standards has continued to gather momentum, and the Common Core State Standards (CCSS) and state standards play an important role in many school districts across the country. Educators differ in their opinions about the content and implementation of educational standards; however, it seems that most educators recognize that standards do provide helpful roadmaps for instruction and that it simply makes sense to select teaching practices shown to be effective through replicable research. Thus, we have included in this book only strategies that are compatible with CCSS and the majority of state standards for the early grades. Additionally, the selected strategies and activities are limited to those found to be effective through empirical research.

The CCSS and related state standards reflect the essence of a truly balanced and comprehensive approach to literacy. Aimed at better preparing students for

21st-century college course work and career choices, the standards (and now this text) emphasize critical thinking and analysis, and they include a greater emphasis on reading and writing informational text. Such standards strive to teach students to research, document, explain, and defend ideas and information. *Striking a Balance* emphasizes a transactional approach to teaching, in which the teacher and students negotiate meaning collaboratively, rather than a transmission model, where the teacher simply tells students what skills should be learned. Since this has always been the underlying philosophy of this text, this edition is able to seamlessly integrate the CCSS and related standards with the critical thinking that they are designed to support.

In this fifth edition, we have expanded content addressing the needs of diverse learners. All classrooms are diverse. Some children come to school speaking home languages other than English; others are academically gifted. Other children experience a variety of physical and/or neurological challenges such as autism, cerebral palsy, or cognitive learning disabilities. Still others manifest behavioral challenges or health issues that affect their ability to learn. Nearly all of these students have academic, behavioral, physical, or social needs that require instructional adaptations within the early childhood classroom. While many of the instructional strategies offered in this text are effective for all learners, each content chapter now includes sections that focus exclusively on differentiating instruction based on the particular learning needs of today's diverse learners, with additional information threaded throughout the text.

Also new to this edition is the input of two coauthors, Dr. Susan Baker and Dr. Albert Lozano, both literacy professors at CSU, Sacramento, who specialize in the needs of English learners. Their combined experience and knowledge about second language acquisition and its impact on all facets of literacy bring a robustness to the many discussions of the needs of these learners.

Educators have access to a wealth of programs, techniques, and instructional strategies—online, in teacher workshops, and in a host of texts—targeting the needs of learners in pre-K through third grade. Choosing just the right resources can be challenging for all teachers, regardless of experience level. In text discussions, in marginal WWW features, and in the appendices, this edition offers information about a variety of effective options, selected based on research and teacher testimonials. These resources reflect the best literacy practices that align with the comprehensive, transactional philosophy of this text.

SPECIAL FEATURES

Some of this book's special features help readers understand new concepts and vocabulary. Other features are designed to foster reflection on and mastery of the material, and to encourage readers to try out ideas in the field. The following features are particularly noteworthy:

- **The book's revised and updated chapter on reading and writing informational text.** Research on informational text indicates that even young children enjoy this mode of discourse, and today's educational standards emphasize the need for greater emphasis on it. This chapter gives teachers the tools to introduce students to informational text early in their academic lives, which will prepare them to succeed in later encounters with content area material.

- **"In the Classroom" feature.** Each chapter begins with a vignette in which readers observe an authentic classroom setting and see how a practicing teacher handles the subject addressed in the chapter. These small glimpses of literacy instruction build background and trigger the reader's prior knowledge about the chapter's topic. Throughout the chapter and in some of the activities, we refer to the vignette and help the reader connect chapter concepts and real classroom instruction.

■ **Activities.** Most chapters include activities designed for use in the classroom. These specific procedures allow readers to put the chapter's ideas and strategies into practice, either in their field placements or future classrooms.

■ **Questions for Journal Writing and Discussion.** Questions at the end of each chapter help readers reflect on and internalize key chapter ideas. These questions are suitable for response in journal form and for stimulating lively discussion.

■ **Suggestions for Projects and Field Activities.** This section makes the connection between research and theory and real classroom practice. At the end of each chapter, the reader is offered several suggestions for surveying, interviewing, or observing local classroom teachers to compare strategies presented in the chapter with actual practice. Other activities ask the reader to try out a strategy or activity with a small group of primary school children. These activities will be useful as assignments for students in their field placement experiences.

■ **Case Examples.** To help readers further apply chapter concepts, these boxed features provide a close look at a teacher's instructional practice or efforts to address an individual student's learning needs.

■ **A concluding chapter on "orchestration," or putting it all together.** In the final chapter of the book, we provide an intimate view of the urban classroom of an exemplary first-grade teacher who demonstrates many of the procedures, strategies, and ideals presented in the rest of the book. The reader receives a valuable perspective on how a seasoned teacher makes decisions about classroom climate, materials, and room arrangement, and how to best utilize the limited available instructional time.

■ **Glossary.** An extensive book-end glossary is included, allowing readers to review vocabulary they've encountered throughout the text (key terms are bolded in text and appear in the book's margins).

■ **Appendices.** This valuable section of the text includes references for children's literature by genre, teacher resources for early literacy, a variety of literacy checklists and other informal assessment tools for classroom use, and a list of widely used commercial evaluation instruments. An additional appendix describes almost 100 websites of special interest to literacy teachers.

■ **Ancillaries.** A PowerPoint presentation and an Instructor's Manual are available to adopters of this text. The Instructor's Manual provides several valuable tools: each chapter offers a summary of key concepts, a list of key vocabulary, suggestions for in-class discussions and activities, and a range of assessment devices, including objective and subjective questions.

■ **A companion website and study guide: www.routledge.com/cw/cecil**
Available to students, this site offers features such as chapter objectives, key concepts review, questions and projects, teaching activities, and relevant website links.

Acknowledgments

many outstanding professionals, friends, family members, and former students have helped us bring this vision to fruition. As before, we would like to thank the extraordinary primary teachers who graciously allowed us to attend their classrooms and share the amazing ways they are balancing skills-based and holistic instruction to teach children to joyfully read, write, and think. The voices of many of these fine teachers permeate this book. We especially wish to thank Maria Ramon, Janet Rodgers, Rita Lehman, Linda Bernard, and Maria Oropeza, the classroom teachers who allowed us to observe how they bring to life the concept of a comprehensive literacy program. We also wish to extend a special thanks to the Phase I and II students in San Juan Center for reading the manuscript and providing suggestions.

Present and prior reviewers of the manuscript offered critical feedback that we welcomed and incorporated into the final book. We are grateful for their help. Our sincere thanks to Sherron Killingsworth Roberts, University of Central Florida, for her insightful and constructive comments at various stages of the project's creation. We also want to thank the reviewers of this edition for their assistance: Marcie Belgard, Washington State University–Tri-Cities; Krystal Bishop, Southern Adventist University; Linda Chapa, University of Texas–Pan American; Maggie Chase, Boise State University; Carl Ferguson, California State University, Monterey Bay; Jameha Gardner, Athens State University; Linda Jukes, St. Vincent College; Andrea Karlin, Lamar University; Holly Lamb, Tarleton State University; Peggy Mason, Lakehead University; Rita Meadows, The University of South Florida; Michael Mott, The University of Mississippi; Lynda Robinson, Cameron University; Wilma Robles-Melendez, Nova Southeastern University; Jennifer Sennette, Texas A & M–Commerce; Bweikia Steen, Trinity Washington University; and Margaret Voss Howard, Salem State University.

Finally, our continued thanks to reviewers of earlier editions for their help: Merry Boggs, Maureen P. Boyd, Pamela Campbell, Lois Catrambone, Jeanne Clidas, Deborah Farrer, E. Sutton Flynt, Kathy Froelich, Jesse Gainer, Ingrid Graves, Dana L. Grisham, Stephanie A. Grote-Garcia, Susan Harnden, Jennifer Hathaway, Bonnie Henderson, T. Tana Herchold, Barbara Hershberger, Anita Holmes, Dee Holmes, Jennifer Lee Johnson, Timothy L. Krenzke, Stephen B. Kucer, Priscilla M. Leggett, Susan Davis Lenski, David Lund, Linda Marriott, Patricia Mulligan, Edward T. Murray, Judy Naim, Angela Raines, Kathy Rosebrock, Laura Schein, and Rebecca Swearingen.

During work on all editions of this book, everyone at Holcomb Hathaway, Publishers has been supportive and helpful beyond words. Editor Colette Kelly shared our vision of a balanced, comprehensive literacy program that creates readers who can read and who want to read.

From Nancy Cecil: I extend heartfelt gratitude to my husband, Gary, who was ever patient as I took time away from him and family activities to write and edit this new edition. Without his unceasing love, support, and unwavering belief in me, I would have given up long ago.

From Susan Baker: I am deeply grateful to Nancy Cecil for offering me this wonderful opportunity to learn from her about literacy practices and to develop my knowledge of the field. I would also like to extend my gratitude to my son, Max, for his patience while I worked on the revision of this book, and for his endless love of reading, his thought-provoking ideas, and his frank advice about what works and what doesn't in terms of teaching a love for reading and writing.

From Albert Lozano: First and foremost I would like to thank Nancy Cecil for giving me the opportunity to help with this edition. I've used this textbook since coming to Sacramento State and am honored to be able to put my name on this latest edition. I would also like to thank my family and friends for their support while I was working on this project. And finally, thanks to many of my former students who are now working as classroom teachers: Much of what I've learned about good literacy practices comes from what they've taught me.

About the Authors

NANCY LEE CECIL has had a rich and varied background in education, as an elementary school teacher and a literacy specialist in New York, urban Savannah, Georgia, and in the public schools in the U.S. Virgin Islands. As a result of these experiences, she is especially attuned to the needs of linguistically and culturally diverse children. Cecil received her doctorate from the University of Buffalo and currently teaches in the Department of Teacher Credentialing at California State University, Sacramento, where she was awarded the prestigious Outstanding Educator Award. She has written nineteen books on literacy, most recently *Phonemic Awareness and Music: A Feast of Rhyme, Rhythm, and Song,* and received the Teacher's Choice award for an earlier book, *For the Love of Language: Poetry for All Learners.* Cecil also has had many articles published in major literacy journals. She has spoken about literacy to groups of educators on local, national, and international levels.

SUE BAKER has taught in public schools at the kindergarten through high school levels in Soledad, Watsonville, and Los Angeles, California; Arlington, Virginia; and Mexicali, Mexico. She has worked primarily in bilingual settings with students who are English learners, and has taught literacy in English and Spanish. Baker earned her doctorate from Stanford University and currently teaches in the Department of Teacher Credentialing at California State University, Sacramento. Her research interests include the development of biliteracy, the use of culturally sustaining pedagogy in teacher education, and the fostering of teacher/parent relationships across social class, cultural, racial, and linguistic boundaries. She is currently the Principal Investigator for the CSU, Sacramento branch of the California Reading and Literature Project.

ALBERT LOZANO has been a third-grade bilingual teacher in San Bernardino, and has a Bilingual Crosscultural Language and Academic Development (BCLAD) credential and a Master of Arts degree from California State University, San Bernardino, and a doctorate from Stanford University. He teaches courses on elementary literacy, English language development (ELD), and specially designed academic instruction in English (SDAIE) in the Department of Teacher Credentialing at CSU, Sacramento, as well as thesis writing and education research in the Graduate and Professional Studies in Education program. His current research focuses on the effectiveness of credential programs in preparing teachers to instruct English learners; fostering the oral English proficiency of English learners; and helping to develop bilingualism/biliteracy.

A Child Learns to Read

PROCESS AND PRODUCT

focus questions

What are the fundamental processes of reading?

Why is it important for teachers in the field to understand all aspects of the reading process?

How is reading defined by researchers and practitioners in the field?

in the classroom

lthough this vignette is titled "In the Classroom," in actuality the learning-to-read process begins long before 4-year-old Lydia ever enters school. She has developed certain concepts about the function of print from the numerous signs in her urban environment and by observing how readers in her home interact with books, magazines, newspapers, and other reading material. For example, when she sees her older brother scan the fast-food menu and then order a hamburger and fries, she is discovering that those black squiggles carry meaning. When she asks her mother to write her name and her mother sounds it out in front of her, she observes that words are composed of a string of letters and that those letters are composed of sounds that hold meaning.

When she snuggles in her grandma's lap and "reads" the fairy tale she has memorized after hearing it nearly a hundred times, Lydia demonstrates her understanding that many words together can tell a story. She asks for a second story and Grandma complies. She puts a chubby finger on the words as Grandma says them. Lydia is again revealing her understanding of the matching of spoken and written word.

Lydia knows a lot about reading, but can she actually read?

WHAT IS READING?

t first glance, it would hardly seem worth the trouble to answer the basic question of what reading is because, in a sense, everybody knows perfectly well what it is: most people do it in one form or another every single day! Reading is:

- devouring a book from cover to cover.
- exploring the repair manual so you can fix your (car, computer, dishwasher).
- looking at a tweet.
- following a blog.
- discovering a message found floating in a bottle off the coast of Kauai.

But true definitions underlie all intellectual endeavors. Definitions contain assumptions that determine future educational activities. In other words, what teachers do to teach beginning reading will be determined, in large part, by what they believe reading is.

To define reading, we must know exactly what is involved in this activity that sets it apart from other similar activities. It is not enough, for example, to define reading as "a thought-getting process," because we can get thoughts just as easily from a lecture, a conversation, or a film. To put it another way, there are many similarities between reading a printed page (whether the printed page appears on paper or on an electronic screen) of difficult text and hearing the same text read to us by another person. The issue of comprehension is paramount for both reader and listener.

No one would deny that a major purpose of reading is to get information or enjoyment of some sort from the written words. But since we get information in the same way from spoken words, the purpose of getting information does not define reading in a way that distinguishes it from engaging in conversation. As soon as we understand this point, the problem of definition begins to resolve itself. If we see that meaning is a function of the relationship between the language and the receiver, we might then ask how the written words (which we read) are related to the spoken words (which we hear). If a language composed of sounds carries the meanings, then what is writing? Writing is a device, or a code, for representing the sounds of a language in visual form. The written words of a language are, in fact, just symbols for the spoken words, which are sounds.

So reading, then, becomes the process of turning these printed symbols back into sounds again whether or not audible vocalization of the sounds actually occurs. The moment we say this, however, some reasonable soul is bound to ask, anxiously, "But what about meaning? Can we propose to define reading as just deciphering the words without regard to the meaning?"

The answer is yes, but only partly. **Reading** is, first of all, the mechanical skill of turning the printed symbols into the sounds of our language. Of course, the reason we turn the printed words into sound—in other words, the reason we *read*—is to get at the meaning. We decode the printed symbols to get what the author is attempting to *say*, and then, more importantly, we make some meaningful connection to the world as we know it (Pearson, 1993).

■ reading

But there is even more to it than that. Reading entails both reconstructing an author's message and constructing one's own meaning using the words on the page as a stimulus. We can think of it as a transaction, or an exchange, among the reader, the text, and the purposes and context of the reading situation. A reader's reconstruction of the ideas and information intended by the author is somewhat like a listener's reconstruction of ideas from the combination of sounds a speaker makes. An artist creates a masterpiece that means one thing to him and a host of different things to different admirers of his piece. Likewise, the reader, like the listener, may create meanings that are different from those intended by the author. What a reader understands from the reconstructed and constructed meanings depends on that reader's prior knowledge, prior experiences, maturity, and proficiency in using language in differing social contexts (Afflerbach, Pearson, & Paris, 2008).

In addition to these traditional descriptions of what reading is, other considerations arise from the ubiquitous new technologies of the twenty-first century. Educators now talk about **new literacies** (Kist, 2005; Kress, 2003) that consist of ways not only to read and write but also to view and visually represent texts in new and exciting ways—especially texts related to technology. These texts are often in electronic rather than conventional printed paper format and can be viewed on many devices, such as computers, mobile devices, tablets/e-readers, and interactive whiteboards. They may also use a variety of enhancements, including video and/or audio clips, computer graphics, and digital photos. This type of reading and writing has many unique characteristics, including the way it is organized and discrete features that allow students to interact with the text. These new literacies will require students to be proficient in the six language arts (reading, writing, speaking, listening, viewing, and visually representing); in accessing and synthesizing information from a variety of sources—especially the Internet; and in evaluating the information's accuracy, relevance, and authenticity (Castek, Bevans-Mangelson, & Goldstone, 2006).

■ new literacies

THEORIES OF READING ACQUISITION

two theories regarding how we learn to read are at the heart of the question about how reading should be taught. Each of these theories offers us important insights about how students think about reading.

Nonstage Theory

The earlier theory is a **nonstage theory,** which holds that unskilled and skilled readers essentially use the same strategies to figure out unknown words. This theory, revisited by Goodman in 1997, posits that readers use predictions based on

■ nonstage theory

the context of sentences, as well as the letter–sound correspondence, to determine unknown words. They depend mostly, however, on the grammar (syntax) and semantics (underlying meaning) to decipher the message. In this process, the reader uses strategies to sample and select from the information in the text, makes predictions, draws inferences, confirms or rejects, and regresses when necessary to make corrections in reading. Visual and aural features of the words—the **graphophonic information**—are used as necessary. Such a theory suggests that certain apparent "errors" that students make while reading, such as saying the word *dad* for the key word *father*, offer observers an actual "window into the child's brain"; such **miscues** are not errors at all, according to the theory, but merely deviations from text, occurring because the child is trying to make sense of print.

■ graphophonic information

■ miscues

Stage Theory

A seminal study by Juel (1988) indicated that unskilled and skilled readers use different strategies to unlock or decipher unknown words. Unskilled readers become "stuck" with strategies such as guessing or trying to memorize every new word and therefore are not as successful as learners who have internalized a wide range of helpful strategies. The **stage theory** holds that children go through three stages in acquiring literacy: During the first stage, the *selective cue stage,* children might use only the context of surrounding words and illustrations to predict possible meaning for unknown words or might focus on limited components of words to decode them; for example, recognizing only the first and last letters in words. At the second stage, the *spelling–sound stage,* they listen for known sounds and letters to determine the meaning of new words. When children have arrived at the final stage, called the *automatic stage,* they have reached the fluent or automatic level of reading. At this sophisticated stage, they almost subconsciously scan every feature of a word and compare it instantaneously to patterns with which they are familiar. Very little mental effort needs to be directed toward decoding unknown words, and most of the reader's attention can be focused on obtaining personal meaning from text.

■ stage theory

CUEING SYSTEMS

Perhaps in an attempt to better understand just how literacy happens, some researchers then suggested that four systems make communication possible: (1) the grapho-phonological system, (2) the syntactic system, (3) the semantic system, and (4) the pragmatic system. Skilled readers must use all four systems at once as they read, write, listen, and speak (Clay, 1991). These **cueing systems** help children create meaning by using language in a way that most English speakers accept as "standard." Effective teachers of beginning literacy are aware of these systems and model and support students' use of them in all areas of communication. The four cueing systems are described briefly in the following sections.

■ cueing systems

The Grapho-Phonological System

There are roughly 44 to 48 sounds (or **phonemes**) in the English language, and children learn to pronounce these sounds in many different combinations as they begin to speak. Teachers support experimentation with how these sounds correspond to letters (**graphemes**) by teaching children how to use temporary or experimental spellings to sound out words; modeling how to pronounce words; calling attention to rhyming words and alliterations; and directly teaching other decoding skills, such as showing how to divide words into syllables. For example,

■ phonemes

■ graphemes

by pointing out the rhyme scheme in "Twinkle, Twinkle, Little Star," the teacher shows children how the words *are* and *star* have similar ending sounds but different beginning sounds.

The Syntactic (Sound Stream of Language) System

The syntactic system, which includes but is not limited to grammar, governs how a language is structured or how words are combined into sentences. Teachers support this cueing system by showing students how to combine sentences; add affixes to root words; use punctuation and inflectional endings; and write simple, compound, and complex sentences. To begin, a teacher might use the nonsensical group of words, "boy fell the down," to show students the importance of order in language. Further, a teacher might show students how to combine the two sentences "The boy fell down" and "The boy was not watching where he was going" to become "The boy fell down because he was not watching where he was going."

The Semantic System

The major components of the semantic system are meaning-making and vocabulary. An even smaller unit of meaning-making is the **morpheme,** the smallest unit of meaning in English words, highlighted when we use the *s* to make *cats* plural, or the prefix *re* to make *do* into *redo*. Teachers support the semantic system by providing meaningful literature and relevant reading topics; focusing students' attention on the meanings of words; discussing multiple meanings of words; and introducing synonyms, antonyms, and homonyms. For example, a teacher might explain to students that although they already know the meaning of the word *change*, in math we use it very differently when we "make change." In the intermediate grades, teaching students dictionary skills, in context, also supports this system.

■ morpheme

The Pragmatic System

The final cueing system is pragmatics, which addresses the social and cultural functions of language. People use language for differing purposes, and how they speak or write is determined partly by their purposes and intended audience. Teachers can support the use of this cueing system by showing students how different forms of language are appropriate for different situations. For example, a teacher might discuss how playground language differs in form and content from that of a shared experience in class, or how we use different language for giving directions and for conducting a pretend dialogue with a prince.

THE READING PROCESS

The act of reading is composed of two basic parts: the global reading process and the reading product. By *process* we mean a movement toward an end that is accomplished by going through the necessary steps to crack the code and construct meaning from what the author has said. These aspects of the reading process ideally combine to produce the reading *product*.

Skills Used in the Reading Process

Clearly, the beginning reader has many available options for figuring out unknown words. Some of these—such as random guessing—are more inefficient than others. Learning to read, then, involves sorting through a cafeteria of problem-solving choices and discarding those that are ineffective for the situation, while selecting those that allow for success. To make maximum progress, the beginning reader must acquire three closely related skills at approximately the same time (Clay, 1991):

- using letter–sound relationships
- acquiring a sight vocabulary of immediately recognized words
- gaining meaning from context

Using letter-sound relationships

phonics ■

Some experts believe that the most immediate goal of early reading instruction is teaching children **phonics**—how to "crack the code" by associating printed letters with the speech sounds they represent and helping them to immediately apply this knowledge to meaningful text. Every word in spoken English can be represented by selecting among only 26 different letter symbols. In general, letters and letter combinations stand for the same speech sounds in thousands of different words. Although there is not a perfect one-to-one correspondence between written/printed letters and the speech sounds they represent, learning to decode depends on a true understanding of the sound–spelling relationship of the English language (Moats, 1995).

For children to become proficient spellers and fluent readers, they must master the helpful skills of "sounding out" words, using their knowledge of the sound–spelling relationship in a real reading context. The child says to herself (very quickly and unconsciously), "I know that this word says *baby* and this word says *bed*." Then, pointing to the *b,* she asks herself, "I wonder if it makes the /b/ sound every time?" The child is giving herself a brief lesson in phonics; she is also using excellent inductive reasoning, but many children need to have these sound relationships pointed out to them directly. After children have learned two or three sound–spelling correspondences, such as the sounds for *b, a,* and *t,* a skilled teacher can then teach the students how to blend these sounds into words. The teacher next demonstrates how to move sequentially from left to right through spellings so that students can sound out or say the sound for each spelling. To be most effective, it seems, phonics should be taught to students formally by teachers trained in how to blend and segment sounds and in the appropriate order to teach phonics skills.

Acquiring a sight vocabulary

sight vocabulary
words ■

Many words used frequently in the English language cannot be easily sounded out or decoded, such as the words *the, give, come, to, was, could,* and *once,* to name just a few, because they do not follow any phonics rule (Cunningham, 2009). Such words appear so often in English speech and writing that it would seem wasteful for a child to even try to sound out these words each time they are met. Therefore, such words must be taught whole, using what has been called the *whole word* or *look–say method.* These words are known as **sight vocabulary words**—words that children should recognize about as quickly as they recognize their own names. The repetition of these words many times, in many different ways, fixes them in the child's memory. With enough repetition, recognition of the words then becomes automatic and instantaneous. When children couple their knowledge of these words with their expanding decoding skills, they will be able to read simple sentences and stories without undue frustration.

predictable books ■

For early readers, one of the most appropriate methods of teaching sight words, as well as general concepts about the written word, is through the use of *shared reading* with *big books* (see Chapter 3), especially familiar texts and **predictable books** that have rhyme, rhythm, and repetition, designed to allow children to learn the words by chiming in with their guesses (Clay, 1991). Motivational big books with repeated word patterns are ideal resources for helping children memorize sight words. **Big books** are those with considerably larger-than-usual format, suitable for reading aloud to a small group of students as they sit cross-legged on the floor. Encouraging **tracking**—having students point to words as they are read—while using such materials is also valuable. Tracking fosters awareness of printed text as well as understanding of and familiarity with differing grammatical phrases.

■ big books

■ tracking

Gaining meaning from context

When a child is reading for meaning, the **context** (the surrounding information in the sentence) in which an unknown word is met can often be useful in suggesting what that word might be. At times, only a few words could possibly complete the sentence. For example:

■ context

> The girl went swimming at the _____.
>
> The hungry boy walked to the _____.
>
> The girl _____ when she won the prize.

In the first example, probably fewer than a dozen words could logically be inserted in the blank space (swimming pool, pool, pond, park, lake, river, ocean, YMCA). If the child possesses rudimentary phonics skills and the word begins with a *p,* the child can further narrow the possibilities. Some choices would also be less logical than others, depending on what has happened in the story prior to this sentence, allowing students to make an "educated guess" as to what the word might be. When students are shown how to use context to aid them in narrowing the possibilities of an unknown word, they have another strategy at their command.

Authors use a number of devices to provide contextual clues that help readers determine the meaning of new words and difficult concepts. One of these is to incorporate a description/ definition in the text (Heilman, 2005).

> The [swan] swam in the pond. This [bird] was bigger than any of the other birds in the water.

Other contextual techniques for deciphering unknown words include comparison or contrast and the use of synonyms or antonyms.

> The apple was very [small]. No one but the new boy wanted the apple, because it was so [little].

Solving the pronunciation of the unknown word is made easier by (1) the meaning of the complete sentence in which the word occurs and (2) the meaning in the surrounding sentences.

The preceding approaches to figuring out new words (letter–sound relationships, sight vocabulary, and context) are probably not of equal value in learning how to read, although each is necessary to some degree. Research clearly shows that overemphasizing prediction from contextual clues for word recognition can be counterproductive, possibly even delaying the learning process

Is teaching children how to "crack the code" the most immediate goal of early reading instruction?

if it is stressed above trying to analyze words by their sound–spelling components (Stanovich, 1992). On the other hand, too little or too much phonics instruction may contribute to the failure to learn to read (Stahl, 2001; Vadasy, Sanders, & Peyton, 2006).

Additionally, it must be kept in mind that individual students may benefit from and rely on one method more than others, although some approaches, such as pure memorization by the form of the word, have limited usefulness beyond the earliest stages of learning how to read. It seems clear that automatic, fluent reading would *not* be the result if a child had to go through a series of trial-and-error approaches in which all three approaches were tried out every time a new word was encountered! Efficient readers tend to use all three methods of word recognition instantaneously and simultaneously, lending even more support to a balanced approach to reading instruction in which all strategies are employed (Bissex, 2004; Eldredge, 1995).

Characteristics of the Reading Process

Those new to the field of literacy will have realized by now that the act of learning to read is a much more complex endeavor than they may have previously believed. The next section will explore some of the fundamental characteristics of the nature of reading to help provide a clearer picture of what is involved in the reading process.

Reading is a holistic process

decoding ■

Reading is not the sum total of the discrete skills that we have students practice in order to teach them to read; rather, reading is a holistic process whereby the various subskills, such as **decoding**, finding the main idea, and locating important details must be integrated to form a smooth, coherent whole. The subskills, though crucial, must be applied to the act of reading by a competent teacher.

If we want children to be thinkers, we must structure our instruction toward active participation in the search for meaning. Students must be given time every school day to read material that is on their own level and that is of interest to them. Students at all grade levels must also be read to. Teachers who read to students and give them the opportunity to discuss and wrestle with ideas and concepts are providing a sophisticated model of the kinds of thinking they must do when reading on their own. Finally, if we want students to become lifelong readers—whether they are reading simply to enjoy a great story or to figure out how to make a flambé or construct a model plane—we must offer them ample time to read for enjoyment without always insisting on written or oral accountability for everything that has been read (Serafini, 2011/2012).

Reading is a constructive process

We have come to think of reading as the construction of meaning from text. As readers interact with the text, meaning is being constructed in their minds. The meaning does not lie on the page but in the mind of the reader. Readers use what is in their heads and what is on the page and construct a meaning based on a fusing of the two forces.

Teachers must be aware of the constructive nature of the reading process so that they can help students develop the necessary tools to participate in this meaning-building process. This can be accomplished by providing an opportunity for students to display a wide range of thinking about what they are reading.

Asking an abundance of open-ended questions—those for which there is no single "right" answer—encourages and validates students who are struggling to make their own meaning from text.

Reading is a strategic process

Good readers use different strategies, depending on their purposes for reading and the difficulty of the material. The purpose of reading may be purely for entertainment, to memorize a poem, or to discover how to put together some object. Having these different purposes leads us to read in different ways, depending on the nature of the task (Rosenblatt, 2005).

Teachers need to teach students to set their own purposes for reading and then check to see that their purposes are being met. Teachers can teach students to think about their own thinking (**metacognition**) by modeling various strategies as they read aloud to students. They can also do this by discussing how reading rate and strategies change according to the type of reading that is being done.

■ metacognition

Reading is an interactive process

Finally, we have come to think of reading as a process in which readers interact with the text while tapping into their own experience in order to construct meaning. What readers bring to the activity in terms of prior knowledge of content, structure, and vocabulary determines how well they will be able to derive a rich meaning from the text. We have all had the experience of reading something about which we had little or no background knowledge. When this happens, we soon realize that although we may know most of the words, we cannot make sense of the material. We do not have the content knowledge that we need to construct a valid meaning to take with us from the reading. To illustrate this point, I often ask my preservice students, who consider themselves "avid readers," to read the following paragraph from an accounting text:

> As suggested by Thomas, all allocation methods must be based upon some concept of a distribution of benefits expected to be received by using an asset over time (its net revenue contribution each period) or else the allocation must be arbitrary and thus meaningless as a measure of a rational concept of income. However, Thomas also suggests . . . that rarely would it be possible to measure either the *ex ante* or *ex post* net revenue contributions in the several periods during the use of an asset, because of the many interactions of the production functions or inputs in the production and other operating processes of a firm.

Upon completion of the preceding paragraph, a quiz reveals that my students with little background in accounting have achieved minimal comprehension of the paragraph and admit that if this were their daily reading fare, they would soon dislike the reading process.

As teachers, we must provide activities that activate, access, and build on the knowledge of the students with whom we are working. One way to do this is by showing video excerpts or pictures or by reading short informative passages about the study topic. Another way is to simply brainstorm with the group to elicit what the children know about the topic. For example, if the selection to be read is about koala bears, the teacher asks the students to raise their hands and tell the group anything they know about the animals—information the teacher writes on the board. What one student contributes often triggers a response in other students. This process helps bring to the surface everything the students know about the topic and also provides information for those who may know little or nothing about it. The students are now able to attach new information to known information. They are ready for the active search for meaning.

Reading and writing are synergistic processes

Reading and writing have long been considered related activities. They have been treated by educators as essential ingredients of the literacy "pie" (Langer & Flihan, 2000). In fact, the image of a pie, with its separate slices, is an apt illustration of how the various similar and yet discrete aspects of literacy relate. Both reading and writing are meaning-making activities. When one engages in either reading and writing, meaning is in a constant state of becoming; likewise, language, syntax, and sentence structure are all involved as the text is coming to be in the head of the reader or the text is coming to be on the paper of the writer. Finally, most current research on reading and writing processes indicates that reading and writing are related activities of language and thought that are shaped by usage (Shanahan, 2008). That is, the structures and strategies that readers and writers use to organize, remember, and present their ideas are for the most part identical in reading and writing; however, the structure of the message and the strategies used to deliver it can be somewhat different depending on the purpose of the reader or writer.

The Reading Process and Learners Who Are Diverse

In preparing to teach, new teachers must first and foremost consider the heterogeneous garden of learners before them. Students come to class from diverse cultural, ethnic, racial, economic, and linguistic backgrounds. They may offer a variety of challenges, such as autism, hearing and/or visual impairments, emotional disturbances, language impairments, learning disabilities, and orthopedic impairments. Students bring to their schools rich experiences to share and high expectations to be met by their teachers. Their own humor, folktales, dances, music, family traditions, and ways of looking at the world can enrich the learning experiences of ALL students and their teachers. All students can learn to celebrate diversity when their teachers model and promote acceptance of differences and are responsive to the positive qualities that make each learner unique.

Diversity can play a role in the process of assessing to determine special education services for children who require them. For example, teachers must be aware of the child's first language but also of the child's home language. How will the teacher gather assessment information about a child who speaks three languages but is just learning English?

In the past, children with disabilities were often inappropriately placed in separate and/or special classes based on the result of standard assessments given in English. When working with students who are English learners, teachers must be sure that the assessment used is measuring the disability, if present, and not the child's English language skills. The Individuals with Disabilities Act (IDEA, 2004) states that assessment must be provided in the child's home language and that for all children with disabilities, the teacher must adapt content, methodology, or delivery of instruction to meet each child's specific needs (Sec. 300.26[b][3][ii]). The current text proposes

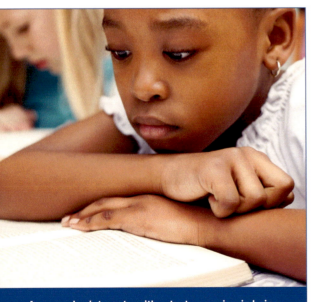

As a reader interacts with a text, meaning is being construed in her mind. The meaning does not lie on the page but in the mind of the reader.

many strategies to address these diverse needs to ensure that *all* children have access to the reading process (Cohen & Spenciner, 2008).

THE READING PRODUCT

the reading *product* should always be meaningful because it is some form of communication—the reader's transaction with the writer's printed ideas (Rosenblatt, 2005). A wealth of knowledge is available to people today because we are able to read what others have written in the past. Americans can read about events and accomplishments that have occurred at other times in other parts of the globe. Knowledge of great discoveries does not have to be laboriously passed from person to person by word of mouth; such knowledge is freely available to all who read.

As well as being a means of communicating generally, reading is a means of communicating specifically with friends and acquaintances who may or may not be nearby. A note read by a child can tell him his mother has gone shopping, or it can inform a babysitter whom to call in an emergency. An email from a teacher can alert parents to events and issues.

Reading can be a way of sharing another person's insights, joys, sorrows, or creative undertakings. Being able to read can make it possible for a person to vicariously visit places she has never visited before, to take advantage of bargains and discounts, or to avoid disaster by heeding warning signs. It is difficult to imagine what life would be like without this vital means of communication!

The rich form of communication described here depends on comprehension, which is affected by all aspects of the reading process. Being able to decipher the code and put sounds to the symbols is essential, but comprehension involves much more than turning the symbols into the appropriate sounds; the reader must derive meaning from these symbols and in some way connect them to experiences or impressions from his own life. Some students may be able to read a passage and pronounce all the words beautifully and still have no idea what they have just read, or they may understand the words but lack the ability to relate the ideas to anything that has happened in their own lives.

Teachers who understand that all aspects of the reading process have an effect on the comprehension of written material will be better able to survey students' reading progress and, as a result, create sound instructional programs based on their needs. Poor performance related to any aspect of the reading process may result in a less-than-satisfactory reading ability or an inability to learn to read at all. The following conditions suggest that a child is at risk for poor performance in reading:

1. The child does not see the symbols or letters on the page; he may not be able to recognize them.

2. The child has developed confusions or incorrect associations between a number of sounds and letters; incorrect recognition of words will result, and comprehension will be lessened.

3. The child has little experience with or knowledge of the topic about which she is reading; she will have less comprehension of the passage than one who has had a rich background in the topic.

The bottom line for teachers, then, is to ensure that students are given an abundance of **explicit,** or direct, **instruction** on the graphic symbols or letters that represent the sounds of our language so that they can begin to build a strong association between the letters and the sounds they make. Additionally, to achieve

■ explicit instruction

the greatest transaction between author and reader, any decoded message must have some connection to the child's life and experiences. Therefore, the teacher must determine whether students have the necessary background information and knowledge to understand any given material; if this is not the case, the teacher must provide the background by other means, such as discussion, pictures, or video excerpts, to ensure adequate processing. Finally, the effective teacher must be sure to provide an abundance of literature of all genres, representing diverse cultures, and appealing to a wide variety of interests. These books should span all ability levels in the classroom. Then she must be sure to allow time for students to read and respond to these books in myriad ways.

SUMMARY

Learning to read is a complicated, rather miraculous process, and for most children, it does not happen without at least some explicit instruction. Because few of us as adults can accurately remember how we managed to accomplish this feat, we are hard-pressed to provide any earthshaking insights into how it is done. Understanding how children learn to read is further complicated by the fact that whenever we observe a teacher instructing a child in reading, we are seeing only one tiny piece of an ongoing process, and even then we cannot see what is really taking place within the reader. Moreover, if we were to watch a particular child as she reads silently, all we can do is try to guess what is going on in her brain from the behaviors she is showing us at the moment; however, if we were to be a fly on the wall in a classroom where this same first-grader was struggling with her burgeoning reading ability over several months, we might get a better overview of the child's perspective of this intricate process. We could listen to and observe the set of strategies she uses to read aloud and how she responds to what she has read, observe how the teacher facilitates the process, and watch as literacy blossoms.

What we do know is that the act of learning to read does not always occur naturally; it may be arduous and time-consuming or quick and immediately gratifying, and we know that it will not be exactly the same for any two youngsters. For some children, much learning about how to read has occurred before they enter school, through supportive interactions in a literate environment where they have been frequently read to and where evidence of the importance of print is everywhere. But it would be wrong to assume such exposure is enough.

Although some children learn to read at home prior to direct school instruction, many children with the same exposure do not. Sometimes formal instruction is needed for children to put together the observations they have made through their experiences with print. For children who have had few experiences with print, exposure to a print-rich environment in school is not enough. Most children require explicit instruction in letter–sound relationships in order to figure out unknown words, they must build a basic sight vocabulary of words they recognize immediately, and they must decide on a method of extracting meaning from unknown words through context and other clues. Equally important, they need to understand how to construct meaning by connecting an author's message to their own experiences. They need to be able to strategize how they will adjust their reading and thinking to the demands of the task at hand. Finally, they need to be supported in their use of the four cueing systems that make communication possible and will allow them to create meaning through socially shared situations.

Because we care about them, we give children affection, attention, exercise, and nutritious things to eat; we try to teach them to be polite, good-natured, thoughtful, and fair. We do these things because we believe it is the best way to start them on their way to healthy, happy lives. We must do as much with reading. When a child has learned how to construct his own meaning from text, he soon enters into a considerably richer world—one where he is able to communicate with all sorts of people he may never even meet. He is able to discover a new dimension of ideas, facts, and opinions that may take him anywhere he wishes to go.

questions FOR JOURNAL WRITING AND DISCUSSION

1. What is your definition of reading? How do you think your understanding of reading will affect the methods you choose to teach your students to read?

2. How would you explain the difference between "reading process" and "reading product" to a parent or any person who is not in the education profession? Why might it be important to distinguish between the two concepts?

3. What are your memories of learning to read? Write a list of everything you can recall about initial instruction, favorite books, successes, difficulties, and how you managed to "crack the code." Solicit help from parents, older siblings, and relatives to help reconstruct your early literacy experiences. Why might such memories be important to your teaching?

suggestions FOR PROJECTS AND FIELD ACTIVITIES

1. Try to teach recognition of two words—*they* and *elephant*—to a child who has not yet learned to read and write. Record and compare the difficulties the child encounters with the two words. Which word was easier for the child to remember? Why do you think this was so? What strategies do you feel were most successful in helping the child to remember the words?

2. Talk to two first-grade students. Ask the students what reading is and what kinds of things they think they must do to read successfully. Administer An Early Reader's View of the Reading Process (found in Appendix E) to one of the students. What new insights did you gain about how this child views the reading process? Share this information with your college class.

▶ see appendix E

3. Observe a child who is in the early stages of learning to read. Ask the child to read several sentences aloud. What are some difficulties the child encounters? What do you think the child needs to know to be more successful? Make two columns on a sheet of paper, one labeled "Practice" and the other "Explicit Instruction." Try to determine what skills would best be developed through each of these modes.

A Quest for Balance

2

focus questions

What is the history of reading instruction in the United States?

What are the key issues in phonics and whole language instruction?

How can classroom teachers combine the elements of both approaches to create a rich and balanced, comprehensive literacy program for *all* learners?

How can a balanced, comprehensive literacy program address the goals of standards, including the Common Core State Standards for the English Language Arts?

mrs. Johnson, a first-grade teacher in Illinois, uses a holistic approach to literacy instruction with her beginning readers. Her students spend much of the school day sharing quality children's literature and tend to remember many new words after being engaged with them numerous times through print that is displayed everywhere in the classroom. Mrs. Johnson's students leave her classroom at the end of a year with a deep appreciation for reading and writing. By contrast, Mr. Ruiz, down the hall, teaches his young learners the names and sounds of each letter of the alphabet. The students spend many hours practicing these sounds so they can immediately sound out unfamiliar words. Mr. Ruiz explains that his pupils love to read because they are empowered by their ability to figure out many words quickly. The two colleagues spend the year comparing notes on beginning reading and discussing which approach is more effective for their students; finally, they agree to disagree. The same practices and discussions are occurring in schools across the country.

INTRODUCTION

this is an exciting time to be a teacher of literacy. We now have more conclusive evidence about what can be considered "effective literacy instruction" than at any other time in history. Over the last 20 years, national panels in the United States have completed a greater number of reports about best practices in reading than have been produced in any prior decade (National Institute of Child Health and Human Development, 2000; Sweet & Snow, 2003). Moreover, the Common Core State Standards (CCSS) have been developed to provide a clear, understandable, and consistent road map to help teachers address what students at each grade level are expected to know and be able to do (IRA, 2012). Most states have adopted the standards or modified their state standards to reflect some of the goals reflected in the CCSS.

This body of knowledge did not evolve without challenges. For years, people debated the relative effectiveness of various reading methodologies. A look into the history of reading instruction in the United States will help to shed light on where we have been and where we are now.

THE HISTORY OF EARLY LITERACY

much of the history of early literacy has involved ongoing discussions about two issues: the use of a skills-based versus a more holistic approach to early literacy instruction and the best way to standardize instruction.

Skills-Based vs. Holistic Approach

Few educational issues have engendered as much dialogue as the ongoing discussions over a *skills-based* versus a more *holistic* approach to early literacy instruction. Such dialogues have quite a history. As long ago as 1844, Horace Mann, considered the "father of public education," wrote a report criticizing schools that implored teachers to adopt a rigid decoding approach to teaching reading.

For decades afterward, popular thinking among educators appeared to move back and forth between a **skills-based approach,** akin to phonics instruction, and a **holistic approach** that was more meaning-centered, as stressed in the whole language philosophy. By the 1950s, a strong skills-based (or phonics) movement

skills-based approach ■
holistic approach ■

gained momentum. This was due in part to the publication of a widely circulated book called *Why Johnny Can't Read* (Flesch, 1955), in which Flesch took teachers to task for abandoning traditional phonics instruction in favor of the then popular **look–say method,** which was more meaning based and required students to use the context alone to figure out words they did not know. Flesch claimed the reason students were doing so poorly in reading and writing was that they had not been taught that every letter of the alphabet had at least one corresponding sound. Once that was understood, he contended, every child could easily read and spell every word by simply sounding it out.

- look–say method

In the 1960s, however, a movement came along de-emphasizing decoding and discouraging overreliance on the use of **basal readers,** the set of leveled textbooks most commonly used to teach reading. Teachers had begun noticing that although students were proficient at decoding, they did not seem to understand what they were reading, nor did they seem to enjoy the activity. The "new" movement, christened the **whole language philosophy** by the National Council of Teachers of English (NCTE) in 1978, stressed a pedagogy that moved from a narrow focus on isolated subskills to one that encouraged teachers to look at reading more holistically, as a part of the total communication process (Beck & Juel, 1995).

- basal readers

- whole language philosophy

When the whole language movement was predominant in American schools in the 1980s, many educators assumed that learning to read was a "natural" process, much like learning to talk—a set of skills that most children acquire with no direct tutoring and with apparent ease, if not joy. The concomitant practice, therefore, was to create a literacy-rich environment in early childhood classrooms, filled with plenty of signs, books, posters, captions, and language play. Some extreme proponents of whole language expected that reading would simply flourish in a natural way, in the same way that children learned to speak by being spoken to and having their first words and phrases elaborated upon. In truth, some children *do* learn to read in this way—with plenty of print-rich stimulation but no direct instruction. The downside of this approach to learning to read is that many children were not always successful at cracking the code and often needed more direct instruction. While many whole language teachers provided direct instruction via explicit mini-lessons on phonics components that were lacking, others did not.

Science offers compelling reasons why so many young children failed to learn to read using a purely whole language philosophy. The National Institute of Child Health and Development (NICHD) has studied normal reading development and reading difficulties in children for 35 years. NICHD-supported researchers have studied more than 10,000 children, published more than 2,500 articles, and written more than 50 books that present the results of 20 large-scale longitudinal studies and more than 1,500 smaller-scale experimental and cross-sectional studies. Some children were studied for 15 years, others for at least 5 years (Fletcher & Lyon, 2002).

In 2000, the National Reading Panel (NRP) added another scientific voice to the discussion. They issued a report in response to a congressional mandate to help parents, teachers, and policy makers identify key skills and methods essential for reading achievement. The panel was charged with reviewing research in reading instruction, focusing on the foundational years between kindergarten and third grade, and identifying methods that were consistently associated with reading success. In addition to identifying effective practices, the panel identified five essential components of early reading success, tagged "the Fabulous Five":

1. *Phonemic awareness*: the ability to hear and identify sounds in spoken words
2. *Phonics*: the relationship between the letters of written language and the sounds of spoken language

3. *Fluency:* the capacity to read text accurately, quickly, and with expression

4. *Vocabulary acquisition:* the words children must know to communicate effectively

5. *Comprehension:* the ability to understand and gain meaning from what has been read

(*Note:* The state of Florida recently added oral language to the five components, changing from "the Fabulous Five" to "the Sensational Six.")

The work of the NRP challenged educators to consider the evidence of effectiveness when teaching the five components as they make decisions about the content and structure of programs designed to promote early literacy. In 2001, the No Child Left Behind (NCLB) Act mandated that all students show progress in the five components identified by the NRP.

Some leading literacy experts, however, believe that the NRP missed an important opportunity to clarify and enumerate the kind of instructional conditions that lead to effective reading development. When the panel failed to discuss the lack of relationship between phonics instruction and reading comprehension beyond first grade (Allington, 2004; Garan, 2004; Krashen, 2004), they may have overemphasized the importance of systematic and explicit phonics instruction to the exclusion of providing ample opportunities for students to practice comprehension strategies through extensive reading.

Regardless of the method of reading instruction, children benefit from a literacy-rich environment at school and at home.

The results of such in-depth research-based approaches have impacted the way we teach beginning reading. We know from research that reading is a language-based activity. We also know that reading does *not* always develop naturally, and for many children, specific decoding, word recognition, and comprehension strategies must be taught explicitly and systematically. The evidence also strongly suggests that teachers can foster reading development by providing young children with explicit instruction in concepts about print, age-appropriate vocabulary, the structure of the English language, phonemic awareness, phonics, and spelling skills. Indeed, the scientific research suggesting that learning how to read is *not* a natural process is so overwhelming that it caused Keith Stanovich (1994) to write, "That direct instruction in alphabetic coding facilitates early reading acquisition is one of the most well-established connections in all of behavior science" (pp. 285–286). Note that in this scenario, the teacher is key and must plan effective instruction.

Although the reforms described here mandate "scientifically based" reading instruction, scientific research *does* support the importance of extensive reading (Krashen, 2004), together with an instructional emphasis on reading comprehension (Pressley, Duke, & Boling, 2004), to maximize reading comprehension development.

Standards-Based Education

Besides the controversy surrounding the best ways to teach literacy, educators have extensively discussed the best ways to standardize instruction and determine what

standards ■   students should be required to know at any given grade level. **Standards** are broad curricular goals containing specific grade-level targets or benchmarks. Standards, as they underpin the curriculum, stipulate what the state or district wants students to know and be able to do as a result of schooling.

Standards-based education reform in the United States began with the publication of *A Nation at Risk* in 1983. Education reform in the United States since the 1980s has been largely driven by the setting of academic standards for what students should know and be able to do. These standards can then be used to guide all other system components. The standards-based education (SBE) reform movement calls for clear, measurable standards for all students. Rather than norm-referenced rankings, a standards-based system measures each student against the concrete standard. Curriculum, assessments, and professional development are aligned to the standards.

A nationwide set of standards, now adopted by 45 states and the District of Columbia, has been in the works since at least 2008. Around that time, a task force composed of governors, corporate chief executive officers, and experts in higher education was formed to create uniform standards for all states to ensure that students in the United States would have an internationally competitive educational system. The Common Core State Standards Initiative, headed by the National Governors Association Center for Best Practices (NGACBP) and the Council of Chief State School Officers (CCSSO), has had input from teachers, civil rights groups, English learners, and the College Board, among others. The group's efforts led to the Common Core State Standards (CCSS), which lay out what every student should know and be able to do by each grade level (Kendall, 2011) to ensure that all students are college and career ready in literacy by no later than the end of high school.

The CCSS apply to English language arts, math, history, social studies, and science. The standards for English language arts are composed of strands, anchor standards, and grade-level standards. The strands consist of language, reading, writing, and speaking and listening. The anchor standards are organized to complement grade-specific standards. The domains for the grade-level standards are (1) Reading: Literature, (2) Reading: Informational Text, (3) Reading: Foundation Skills, (4) Writing, (5) Speaking and Listening, and (6) Language (NGACBP & CCSSO, 2010). As students move through their academic career, they are expected to meet each year's specific grade-level standards, retain or further develop skills and understandings mastered in previous grades, and proceed steadily toward meeting the more general expectations described by the anchor standards (Calkins, Ehrenworth, & Lehman, 2012).

Literacy practitioners know that the process of becoming literate requires more than phonemic awareness, phonics, fluency, vocabulary, and comprehension. At its core, reading is a meaning-making endeavor. As an alternative to skills-based instruction, which emphasizes skills out of context—to the detriment of meaning, purpose, and enjoyment—the present text supports a more balanced, comprehensive approach to literacy instruction. The CCSS for English language arts have taken a step toward more intensive teaching of meaning-making, or critical thinking, in literacy. The key shifts in focus have been summarized in the following way (NGACBP & CCSSO, 2010, www.corestandards.org/other-resources/key-shifts-in-english-language-arts/):

- Regular practice with close reading of complex texts and their discipline-specific academic language (e.g., having students becoming familiar with content-area words not common in normal conversation, such as *conversion* or *differ*)
- Reading, writing, and speaking supported by evidence from both narrative and informational text
- Encouraging students to gain knowledge through the reading of much more factual text

In addition, the CCSS suggest that teachers use half informational text and half narrative text until the fifth grade, although some educators fear that self-expression and study of literary forms such as poetry may be neglected using these guidelines (Esolen, Highfill, & Stotsky, 2014).

APPROACHES TO TEACHING READING

Parents and caregivers of children in schools, other interested citizens, and many new to the field of education may read about the different approaches used to teach reading and form an opinion without understanding the underlying concepts. Many are not quite sure what is meant by terms such as *phonics, holistic, balanced,* and *comprehensive.* It may be helpful to further explore these concepts.

Comprehensive literacy instruction is a complex concept. We all know how difficult it is to maintain a balanced diet in our fast-food society; so it is with a balanced approach to literacy. Balanced literacy instruction must take into account many continua, including authenticity of instruction—how many real-life applications are included—and the teacher's level of assistance, as dictated by students' needs. Balance in curricular control takes into account how much input the students and others are granted in deciding on the curriculum. Balance in classroom talk considers how much of the talk is teacher directed. Balance also needs to be considered when selecting materials: for example, the amount of fiction versus nonfiction text that is used and the blend of predictable and decodable texts. Advocates of balanced instruction recognize that effective literacy instruction is multifaceted, rather than based on one position (e.g., phonics) or another, and that it addresses all of the criteria mentioned. Figure 2.1 compares three views of literacy instruction: (1) a heavily phonics, or transmission, approach; (2) a transactional, or more holistic, approach that employs many of the elements of the whole language philosophy; and (3) a comprehensive approach that combines the important facets of *both* approaches.

Phonics Instruction and the Transmission Model

The term *phonics* is much used but not always entirely understood—especially by those not directly involved in literacy education. From as early as the Greek and Phoenician civilizations 3,000 years ago, most approaches to early literacy instruction in alphabetic languages have included letter sequences and how such sequences corresponded to speech patterns (Mathews, 1966). Such methods, focusing on sound–symbol relationships, are what educators generally refer to as phonics.

transmission model ■
    Phonics instruction has sometimes been associated with the **transmission model** of instruction. In other words, when using this model in its strictest sense, teachers assume the responsibility of directly "transmitting" information, such as the knowledge of letter sounds and symbols, to their students through explicit instruction and systematic teaching of the code that is the foundation of the English alphabet. Other approaches using transmission include rote instruction of sight words and memorization of lists of word families, such as words containing "oi": *voice, noise, moist,* and so forth. Such instruction is also frequently called *skills-based,* as its emphasis is on presenting the smallest parts of our language—the letters and sounds—in isolation, often long before showing children the whole picture of how enjoyable the reading act can be.

Over the years, phonics instruction has been perceived negatively because of additional unfortunate practices that included more drills on isolated skills than

| figure 2.1 | A comparison of three views of literacy instruction. |

PHONICS	HOLISTIC	A COMPREHENSIVE APPROACH
(Skills-Based, Transmission Model)	(Meaning-Based, Transactional Model)	(An Interface Between the Best of Both Stances)
Emphasis on product	*Emphasis on process*	*Emphasis on process and product*
Language broken into bite-sized pieces (letters and words)	Language is kept whole in connected text	Direct, explicit phonics instruction completed by end of primary grades
Skills in sequence taught directly	Phonics often taught incidentally	Skills and strategies modeled alone and in context
Phonics taught up to third and fourth grades	Strategies modeled in context	Phonics based on internal structure of words
Word families used for memorization	Real literature used; often no basal text	Skills based on need per assessment
Teacher makes curricular decisions	Literature study groups	Decodable text used for phonics instruction; predictable text for comprehension
Reading groups based on ability; inflexible	Predictable books and big books used for incidental phonics instruction	Quality literature for listening comprehension
Traditional basal texts with controlled vocabulary	Children choose recreational reading material	Free reading time with choice
Emphasis on decodable text	Shared and guided reading for instruction	Shared and guided reading with embedded phonics instruction
Discussion questions from teacher or basal text	Paired reading	Emphasis on spelling as a key to phonics
Sight words memorized by children	Drama, poetry, and songs used for enjoyment	Word walls, word building, word sorting, word hunts utilized
Directed reading of basal text for instruction	Writing topics chosen by children	Writing workshop
Writing topics chosen by teacher	Writing workshop	Direct, explicit instruction in comprehension strategies
Worksheets for reinforcement of skills	Journals used for response to literature	Drama, poetry, and songs used for phonemic awareness and enjoyment
Workbooks used for response to basal text	Discussion questions come from children	Journals for personal writing and literature response; logs for content areas
Traditional spelling programs	Children encouraged to "invent" spelling	Writing as experimentation with sound–letter relationships
Growth is quantitatively measured (formal assessment)	Growth is observable (informal assessment)	Experimental spelling and instruction in correct spelling
		Flexible grouping systems
		Paired reading, buddy reading, and dyad reading
		Assessment based on measurement and observation (informal and formal)

were necessary and worksheets unrelated to real reading (see Figure 2.2), often to the distress of children who were already proficient readers. Phonics instruction has also been criticized when it has focused on the teaching of a litany of abstract rules, too many of which have limited application in our language and are lost on very young children who can memorize the rules but have little idea what they actually mean.

figure	2.2	An early workbook activity.

Source: *Your Child Can Learn to Read* by Margaret McEathron. New York: Grosset & Dunlap, 1952.

The positive role of phonics instruction

Researchers and educators seeking a balance have long been interested in the positive role that the appropriate amount of phonics instruction can play in early literacy. Many studies have been conducted to determine the value of direct instruction in the sounds and letters of the English alphabet when integrated into a total, literature-rich program.

In a project funded by the U.S. Office of Education Cooperative Research Program in First-Grade Reading Instruction, two prominent researchers, Bond and Dykstra (1967), published the results of a landmark research study involving first-grade classrooms and the literacy methods employed by the teachers. In many ways, this study was the first of its kind to support the notion that a balance between phonics and a meaning-based approach may represent ideal literacy instruction. The results of the study suggested that approaches to reading that included, but were not limited to, a form of systematic phonics instruction were somewhat more effective at producing high word recognition performance in learners than other methods used in the study. The data from the study also indicated that emphasizing meaning and a connection to children's lives produced greater gains in reading achievement. In addition, writing instruction was found to promote literacy acquisition, or the ability to read, write, and speak. Perhaps the most unexpected finding of the study, however, was that the crucial factor in teaching a child to read was not the *method* that was used but that instruction was delivered by a committed and competent teacher.

In *Becoming a Nation of Readers*, a report by the Commission on Reading in the 1980s, phonics instruction was still being advocated:

> The purpose of phonics instruction is to teach children the alphabetic principle and to help young readers recognize patterns in the English language. The ultimate goal is for these two processes to become operating principles so that young readers consistently use information about the relationship between letters and sounds to assist in the identification of known words and to independently figure out unknown words. (Anderson, Hilbert, Scott, & Wilkinson, 1985, p. 73)

The commission continued by stating that children then need to immediately practice reading the new words they have encountered in meaningful context (Anderson et al., 1985). The work of these researchers suggests that the transmitting of phonics could be followed by use of a transactional instructional strategy, using student-centered group discussion of the reading material. This report also seemed to offer an early nod toward a balanced, comprehensive approach in literacy instruction.

Current leading educators advocate a "less is more" approach suggesting that teachers offer small doses of direct, systematically taught phonics instruction in the primary grades only to children who need this structure to make sense of print. Many students come to school with a wide repertoire of word-unlocking skills gained from much experience with and exposure to print. Such educators urge teachers to teach a wide range of comprehension strategies, limiting the teaching of phonics generalizations to those that are the most useful and consistent. Instead of having students memorize phonics generalizations, teachers are encouraged to help students discover the recurring spelling patterns in English words. They also encourage teachers to share an abundance of quality children's literature. Under the CCSS as well as many state standards, teachers are being urged to encourage young children to listen critically to more challenging texts than previously, and to begin to read and respond to more difficult texts, both informational and narrative, starting in the second grade, although the foundational skills in the earlier grades provide much scaffolding to allow them to do so (IRA, 2012). We know now that balance in the teaching of reading is possible only when the teaching of skills does not become an end in itself, but rather a means to an end: reading for personal meaning, acquisition of information, and enjoyment.

Holistic Instruction and the Transactional Model

There have been many terms for and definitions given to holistic approaches throughout the literature on literacy, without a consensus about what such terms actually encompass. Whole language, the most recent manifestation of a holistic, meaning-based approach, was not an approach or a practice at all, but rather a perspective or philosophical stance. Whole language teachers were focused not on transmitting knowledge to their students but rather on negotiating with students about their individual ideas concerning what they were reading and writing. Reading was offered not in stilted basal readers but in high-quality children's literature. Whole language teachers believed, too, that reading occurs in the brain of the child rather than on the page, as proponents of skills-based instruction seem to suggest. Indeed, whole language as a transactional, child-centered model elevates students to "collaborators in the quest for knowledge" (Goodman, 1986).

Later, this whole language philosophy began to be recognized as a holistic way of teaching that, unlike phonics (which teaches the sounds of letters and words and then introduces stories), would first get students interested in great literature and then proceed to the parts. Goodman (1986), often considered the father of the whole language movement, argued that skilled reading involves gaining meaning from the context of whole passages rather than simply reading words as individual entities. Readers, according to this view, sample just enough text to get meaning from a passage.

Holistic instruction has also often been associated with the **constructivist model of learning** (Au, 1997). This perspective encourages students to "actively construct their own understandings of text material" through experimentation with words. With this model, the teacher continually observes how each child thinks about reading by listening to the child's oral reading. For example, José

■ constructivist model of learning

The constructivist model of learning is learner-centered—focused on the child's experience, background, and understanding of the world.

makes wild guesses about words based solely on the way they look and sound; this practice tells the teacher that José thinks reading is little more than word-calling. Brea, on the other hand, constantly rereads sentences in a story saying, "That doesn't make sense!" revealing that she sees reading as meaningful but may need help in acquiring specific decoding skills.

In transactional, holistic approaches, quality children's literature is more commonly used for instruction than basals. Literature often takes the form of predictable books. The stories are often read to students using big books. The intent of this exposure to quality literature is not only to increase children's motivation to read but also, through its superior story structure, to provide an excellent model for children's own writing. Students are encouraged to write about topics of their own choosing by using temporary writing or **experimental,** or *temporary,* **spelling**—a kind of sounding out of new words that is now one of the language arts grade-level standards for the CCSS. For example, CCSS.ELA-Literacy.L.1.2.e requires students to "Spell untaught words phonetically, drawing on phonemic awareness and spelling conventions" (NGACBP &

experimental spelling ■ CCSSO, 2010, p. 26). This experimentation with words is supposed to help children learn to decipher the sound and letter relationships of the English language.

Finally, free choice in activities emphasizing reading, writing, listening, speaking, viewing, and visually representing, together with ongoing **authentic assessment,**

authentic assessment ■ are important aspects of a transactional, holistic approach to literacy. Authentic, ongoing assessment includes observation and analysis of oral reading to determine how students are thinking about reading, what strategies they are employing, and which ones might need to be taught. Such assessment practices are considered superior to standardized tests because they are individualized and can be interpreted by a teacher who can see the performance in light of *all* the child's strengths and

portfolio ■ needs. Authentic assessment sometimes includes a **portfolio** that contains many samples of the work the child has done over time, selected in tandem with the student (Clay, 1990).

A Quest for Balance: A Comprehensive Approach

A comprehensive approach to literacy includes the best elements of a transactional (holistic) and a transmissive (phonics) approach to literacy instruction. Both of these approaches have much to offer for the beginning teacher of young children. The authors of this book believe that the two can be used together to create a dynamic, synergistic program. Research supports the notion that instruction from a committed teacher who can integrate a program of explicit, systematic phonics into a curriculum rich with quality literature, easily decodable text, a variety of leveled texts, and meaningful writing experiences will result in children who not only know how to read but do so willingly, beyond the classroom doors (Tompkins, 2014). Most reading educators and classroom teachers have long agreed that instruction in phonics is vital in learning how to decode automatically and that incorporating the basic elements of a holistic, meaning-based program with such instruction will increase children's enthusiasm toward reading (Wink, 2005).

Effective teachers tend to see new movement in literacy, such as the trend toward a comprehensive approach, not as a pendulum swing but as a positive spiral in which they acquire exciting new research-based information about implementing best literacy practices each time the focus shifts. Echoing this belief, Goodman (1997) muses, "When people talk to me about cycles and pendulum swings, it helps me remember that progress is rarely in a straight line and that knowledge takes a long time to be accommodated, absorbed, and put to work" (p. 596).

Adding support to the comprehensive approach to literacy is the fact that current thinking on phonics instruction is not as extreme as once perceived. Most phonics proponents today support *streamlined phonics,* in which children are helped to become independent, automatic decoders but are not inadvertently discouraged from reading by an overabundance of worksheets, drills, and abstract rules with little application. Current thinking suggests that efficient phonics instruction that is systematic and explicit gets children decoding quickly so that they can soon turn their attention to more important and enjoyable reading tasks (Wink, 2005). Indeed, it appears that the question is now not *whether* to teach phonics but *how* best to teach phonics, within a literature-rich classroom that also stresses background knowledge, comprehension strategies, and an enormous amount of reading (Combs, 2010; Jalongo, 2013). The CCSS underscore this notion, with a strong emphasis on rigorous reading and thoughtful, evidence-based writing, with the underlying skills taught as a means to an end.

Stahl (1992) offers nine guidelines for "exemplary phonics instruction" to be used in tandem with other more holistic, meaning-based methods. He urges that such balanced instruction should do the following:

- build on a child's rich background in how print functions
- build on a foundation of sound awareness (phonemics)
- be clear and direct
- be integrated into a total reading program
- focus on reading words rather than memorizing rules
- include the study of beginning sounds and ending sounds
- include practice with sound–symbol relationships through writing
- develop word recognition strategies by focusing on the internal structure of words
- develop automatic word recognition skills quickly so that children can devote their attention to meaning and enjoyment, not individual words

There is even more reason to believe that current thinking on reading instruction has evolved from the philosophy first articulated by Goodman in the 1960s. The CCSS do *not* give teachers the specific instructional strategies to help students meet the standards (Allen, 2012), but rather rely on the expertise of each teacher to select these strategies according to the needs of their students. This book offers a variety of strategies with the goal of addressing standards for English language arts. Toward that end, it advocates a comprehensive program of broad early literacy curricula that would include phonemic awareness, phonics and word study, rich literature-based activities, a variety of comprehension strategies, and multiple, varied writing opportunities. Specifically, such a comprehensive perspective would include the following (Pearson, Raphael, Benson, & Madda, 2007):

- a wide range of reading materials, both informational and story-based, in a variety of genres, on many developmental levels in English and the other languages and cultures of the students in the class
- direct teaching of concepts relating to print

- explicit instruction in the concept that words are a series of speech sounds
- cueing systems, including graphophonics, semantics, and syntax
- explicit instruction in the strategies that skilled readers use
- critical thinking strategies
- a flow of reading, writing, listening, speaking, viewing, and visually representing activities
- vocabulary development
- extensive opportunities to write for many different purposes in many different genres
- instruction in strategies that good writers use
- reading fluency through encouragement of wide reading at each student's independent reading level
- thorough and ongoing assessment to ensure that instruction is compatible with individual needs

A comparison of three views of literacy instruction (refer back to Figure 2.1) shows how a comprehensive program might be a selection of the best elements of both educational philosophies used to create Mrs. Ramon's first-grade program (outlined in depth in Chapter 15).

On a personal note, through visits to hundreds of primary-grade classrooms over the past few years, I (author Nancy Cecil) have observed that many extraordinary teachers in the field now use and have *always* used phonics skills instruction within a transactional framework. With certain groups of students, such teachers stress one approach more than others, and for some students, they find it is best to use one approach exclusively. These dedicated professionals believe that this long-standing pedagogical dialogue will cease only when teachers are treated as knowledgeable authorities regarding their students. They must be allowed to decide, based on the individual needs in their classroom, which instructional methods are most appropriate (Bialostok, 1997).

BALANCE AND TEACHING TO STANDARDS

As discussed earlier, the standards movement has also had an impact on education. In most school districts, today's teachers are asked to teach to standards set by their state or district. Teachers often ask how addressing standards, including the CCSS, can lead to a balanced, high-quality literacy program. The answer has to do with commitment. To value and use something in the teaching profession, educators must first understand what it is and what it can mean for them and their students, and then commit to doing it.

Historically, curricula in schools have been driven by many influences. Usually an administrator, a committee of teachers, or the principal has chosen the textbooks for a particular grade or subject. Teachers then used the textbook as their resource for delivering instruction. In essence, this gave publishing companies the main responsibility for researching and establishing what is important for students to know and be able to do. Many teachers used the adopted basal reader as their blueprint for teaching literacy (see Figure 2.3). This dependence often made teachers feel compelled to teach page by page; rather than teaching according to true learning goals, some teachers felt their goal was to race to finish the basal reader by the end of the school year. The published basals might have been of excellent quality and based on national standards, but there was an inherent problem with this scenario: although it established consistency within a district's curriculum, such an approach led to an emphasis on uniform materials, which sometimes resulted in a "cookbook" approach to teaching literacy. Teachers were sometimes left out of the important process of having input into, ownership over, and a thorough understanding of the decisions about the skills and knowledge their particular students needed.

State and district standards have proved problematic because there are many differences in student expectations between states and even between districts in the same states. The quality of the standards has varied widely from state to state. The Common Core State Standards represent an attempt to establish a set of core national standards for education.

As stated earlier, the CCSS include specific goals, organized by grade and subject. For example, by the end of kindergarten, children are expected to be able to decode simple words with CVC (consonant, vowel, consonant) and silent /e/ patterns and to know by sight most of the high-frequency words. As another example, fifth-grade reading standards expect students to be able to explain how similes and metaphors give meaning and rhythm to a poem. By the fourth and fifth grade, students are expected to read books like *Alice's Adventures in Wonderland* and *The Black Stallion*. By ninth and tenth grades, students are expected to be reading William Shakespeare and John Steinbeck or the equivalent (*Sacramento Bee*, 2010).

One concern being expressed by teachers and other practitioners is that students won't be able to learn at their own speed and according to their own individual development under a set of national core standards. "Once, schools gave youngsters a chance to learn how to read according to their own development. Now, a child who still can't read by the end of first grade is in deep trouble from which it can be hard to emerge," a second-grade teacher recently lamented to me. She added that most standards, including the CCSS, tend to focus on basic literacy and math, ignoring other essential subjects like the arts and physical education.

Skeptics also worried that national standards might result in a "lowest common denominator" approach, but this appears not to be the case. The CCSS, with some exceptions, have been well received nationally. As advocates for a comprehensive approach to literacy, we, the authors of this book, believe that the more recently developed literacy standards, including the CCSS and most other state standards, represent a substantive improvement over earlier standards. Specifically, they address ongoing concerns in the following areas (adapted from IRA, 2012):

- Teach early, systematic foundational reading, writing, listening, and speaking skills simultaneously.

- Engage students in critical reading of high-quality texts in grades 2–12; earlier, engage them in listening to higher-level texts.

- Teach students research-based reading comprehension strategies and how to apply them.

- Develop students' vocabulary all day, in all subjects, using both word-solving strategies and the teaching of individual words.

figure 2.3

An excerpt from a basal reader, 1966.

swing

Here I go, Mark.
See me go up in the swing.
I like this swing.
I like to go up.
I like to go down.
Come on, Daddy, come on.

Source: Outdoors and In by M. O'Donnell and B. H. Van Roekel. California State Series. Sacramento: California State Dept. of Education, 1966.

- Engage students in writing in response to their reading.
- Provide teachers with professional development in teaching students how to write and to read a variety of text types.
- For special needs populations, vary the amounts and types of instruction provided to ensure success, and monitor student learning and then adjust and supplement instruction accordingly.

The task placed before literacy teachers today, then, is to be aware of the standards for the grade level they teach and to employ a wide range of instructional strategies, materials, and methods to ensure that all students meet the established learning goals. Again, a balanced, comprehensive approach of imparting the skills of literacy and offering many opportunities to use those skills appears to be the optimal way to meet the learning targets set by such standards.

THE IMPACT OF TECHNOLOGY ON LITERACY

finally, a phenomenon is occurring that must be acknowledged in any text addressing the issue of comprehensiveness in literacy instruction. Electronic devices have become integral tools in U.S. classrooms and culture (Felvegi & Matthew, 2012). As the focus has shifted away from an almost exclusive use of story-type reading to using more informational text for early readers, the way most people in this country read and obtain their information has changed: they spend time online that was previously spent in more traditional reading pursuits.

Integrating Literacy and Technology

http://ctell.uconn.edu/ cases.htm

Reading at Risk (National Endowment for the Arts, 2004) decries a decline in the number of books that adults are reading in their leisure time. According to this report, fewer than half the people surveyed reported that they read any literary works at all for pleasure in a year's time. However, Vogt (2004) implored teachers to think more broadly about the possible implications of the findings of this report. Does "reading" entail only reading of "literature"? With desktop, laptop, and/ or tablet computers in most homes, schools, and businesses, children and adults spend much time interacting with vast amounts of information online. Also, reading online and using the embedded links often encourages readers to move beyond the original article they are seeking and explore related articles, blogs, videos, chat responses, and so forth. Reading on the original topic, therefore, may be enhanced by the very nature of online resources, exposing the reader to multiple versions of, reactions to, and interpretations of the original article. The Internet and its ability to expose ("link," if you will) readers to broader resources may lead to a populace with more reading experience, whose comprehension of any topic they are exploring becomes broader, richer, and deeper.

SUMMARY

Unlike a purely political debate or any such hypothetical argument pertaining to abstract ideas and theoretical outcomes, the ongoing dialogue about how we should teach our nation's children to read is concrete and crucial and involves the very core of our future. Educators who have taken sides on this issue have done so with candor and a good deal of questioning, observation of students in classrooms, and a heavy dose of soul searching. Most teachers do not take their tasks lightly; the ultimate mission of teachers is, after all, to challenge, assist, and encourage each child in their charge to become a good reader, responding to text in meaningful ways, both for enjoyment and for gaining knowledge. With the constant enhancement of knowledge about literacy instruction, we are more than ever realizing the best practices needed to reach these goals. We have learned that fluent reading requires a basic understanding of the sounds and symbols of our alphabetic language. We are heeding the substantive body of research suggesting that early, systematic phonics instruction that moves from decoding text to abundant opportunities to read, write, and share ideas can help teachers accomplish their goals of teaching every child to read.

The charge of the teacher of this millennium, then, is to become a wise diagnostician and to provide excellent literacy teaching and intervention for each child. Every child can learn to read and write. The path to literacy may begin with the presence of explicit, systematic phonics instruction and include instruction in phonemic awareness, fluency, vocabulary, and comprehension, but always in the context of a print-rich environment that invites children to explore the world of literature and information while enjoying the thrill of penning their own ideas to be eagerly shared with others. The real question is not whether systematic skills instruction should be part of the total program; research continues to support the inclusion of such instruction for beginning readers. More appropriate questions appear to concern how much skills instruction students should receive and under what conditions, and how such instruction can be integrated into a program rich with literature and meaning while addressing standards mandated by the district or state, including the Common Core State Standards. This book is an attempt to answer those key questions.

questions | FOR JOURNAL WRITING AND DISCUSSION

1. Discuss in your own words the current issues involving the relative merits of phonics and a meaning-based approach to literacy instruction. How would you explain both approaches to the parents of a primary-age youngster? How might you convince them that an ideal program can contain elements from both perspectives?

2. Describe what you remember about your own early reading experiences. Would you characterize the instruction you recall as meaning-based, phonics, or a combination of the two?

3. React to the often-heard statement, "In education, the pendulum constantly swings back and forth from a meaning-based approach to a phonics approach to literacy instruction." What do you think is the impetus for such change? Would you characterize the cyclical changes as static "swings" or as progressive "spirals" toward better literacy instruction?

suggestions | FOR PROJECTS AND FIELD ACTIVITIES

1. Scan current literacy journals such as *The Reading Teacher* or *Language Arts* for articles on prevalent practices in early literacy instruction. Visit the website for the Common Core State Standards or the standards for your state. Summarize your findings and report them to your class. How do the issues raised relate to the issues addressed in this chapter? How do the literacy journals respond to the government mandates on teaching reading?

2. Observe three different first-grade teachers instructing their students in beginning literacy. How might you characterize the methods they are using? In what

ways are these educators responding to recent changes in educational methods? How do the educators describe the approaches they are using? What are their reasons for making the choices they did?

3. Survey several older adults in your area. Ask them how they think literacy is being taught in the local schools. From where have they obtained their information? Ask them what their recollections are about how they were taught to read. Do they believe that the methods used when they were in school were superior to those used today? What conclusions can you draw from this survey?

Emergent Literacy

FROM BIRTH TO CONVENTIONAL LITERACY

focus questions

What are the stages of language acquisition?

What are some of the literacy-related concepts that come into play when children from birth to kindergarten share in literacy experiences?

How is *emergent literacy* defined, and how does this differ from reading readiness?

What are the key components of emergent literacy that help determine whether a child will be successful in learning to read and write?

What are the major influences on children's early literacy development?

How can parents and teachers best foster the development of emergent literacy?

How do the Common Core State Standards impact emergent literacy education?

What are some research-supported emergent literacy interventions for children with special needs?

What are strategies to use with students who are in the early stages of learning to read and write while learning to become fluent in speaking English?

not all plums ripen on the same day, nor are all children able to formally read and write in the same month, year, or day. Just observe three-and-a-half-year-old Sam, on an errand with his mother. "Oh, there's Walmart!" exclaims Sam, as his mother drives into the parking lot of the local discount store. "Hey, there's a car just like ours!" he continues. "It says 'C–h–e–v–r–o–l–e–t'! Does that say 'Chevy,' Mommy?" Later, at home, Sam scribbles on a sheet of paper and informs his mother that he has written a letter to his cousin in Denver. His mother smiles approvingly and admires the child's "writing." Sam's mother feels confident that her child is showing real signs of being ready to learn to read and write.

In another part of town, in the local elementary school, 5-year-old Bronson squirms at her desk as the kindergarten teacher, Mrs. McNeil, points out letters in the alphabet. An active yet shy child, Bronson is busy daydreaming about climbing her favorite tree and is fiddling with the plastic dinosaur she has secreted in her pocket. Her parents worry because, although her older brother and sister caught on quickly to literacy activities, Bronson has never seemed to enjoy being read to, nor has she asked how to spell her name. She seldom uses a pencil or crayons and seems to shun any activity requiring fine motor skills.

Can Mrs. McNeil help Bronson become literate along with her classmates, and can she kindle the enthusiasm for learning of her younger contemporary, Sam? Yes. Is Bronson destined to fail at reading and writing? No. We now know that literacy is an active process that can be developed at the child's own rate; it is not something that happens spontaneously with time, like the aging of fine wine!

INTRODUCTION

reading is a learned set of strategies. For many individuals, it is *not* a spontaneous development (Adams, Treiman, & Pressley, 1997). Children who fall behind in reading at an early age—kindergarten and first grade—have tended to fall further behind over time (Fletcher et al., 1994). In fact, this phenomenon is so common that it has been given a name, "The Matthew Effect," adapted from the biblical book of Matthew, where he states that the rich get richer and the poor get poorer (Stanovich, 1986). Such a finding contradicts the once prevalent notion that children begin to learn to read only when they are "ready." But the good news is that most children do not need to lag behind at all in literacy acquisition. There are prerequisite experiences with literacy from which all children—especially children like Bronson—can benefit.

Awareness of language patterns and how sounds go together in the English language can and should be fostered through enjoyable language activities because such awareness is not innately developed (Grossen, 1997). Beginning at birth, virtually every early learner is ready for positive experiences with spoken and written language. Focusing their attention on sounds, print, words, ideas, and conversations in a playful way can help preschool and kindergarten children to develop the background they will need to decode or unlock unknown words. However, if the children who fall behind do not begin to become aware of sounds in language and are not offered experiences with literacy through active listening and oral reproduction activities, they are likely to fall further behind as the demands of reading become more and more complex.

LANGUAGE ACQUISITION: AN OVERVIEW

emergent literacy   **t**he first stage of **emergent literacy** occurs long before formal reading or writing takes place. Literacy begins with the child's first utterances, as language miraculously begins to support the child's ability to think. A child's first words are among the most frequently documented joys of parenthood. The language acquisition journey, beginning in the womb and continuing throughout a child's school years, is also well documented and appears to follow a similar course regardless of linguistic group. In today's multilingual classrooms, a child's second-language acquisition appears to follow the same path. Like spelling development, which will be explored in Chapter 6, language development can be broken down into a series of stages that tend to be associated with specific age levels: prebirth, infancy, the holographic stage, the telegraphic stage, preschool to fluency, and primary school.

The stages of language development will be discussed here, with the caveat that the descriptions are to be accepted solely as guidelines, because variation in language acquisition is typical. Awareness of guidelines for language acquisition is important because when a child's speech development seems to vary significantly from the norm, it is vital that that child be evaluated by a speech and language expert. (Federal law mandates that school districts provide such service at no cost to parents.) Another reason for the importance of understanding first-language development is that, as mentioned earlier, second-language acquisition appears to follow the same stages.

Prebirth

Even in the womb, infants experience and process a vast array of sensory stimuli that promote neurological development in the brain. Of all these neural sensations, response to the mother's voice is the most apparent (Locke, 1993).

Infancy

From birth through about 9 to 18 months, infants set the stage for later speech through a series of speech production–like utterings. At first the infant cries, burps, and makes other reflexive responses that are often called "vegetative." At around 2 months, the infant becomes more interactive and responds to attention with pleasurable sounds, an activity called *cooing*. By 6 months, the infant is making more specific sounds with the mouth, lips, and throat and is beginning to "babble." Gradually, between 9 and 18 months old, infants begin to imitate sounds heard around them, as if they were speaking their own language, often using appropriate rhythm, phrasing, and intonational patterns, although no meaningful words are uttered. This vocal activity is referred to as *nonreplicated babbling*. At the same time, children at this age often imitate real words and phrases that they hear, but again, with little or no understanding of the speech. This parrot-like speech behavior is called *echolalia*.

The Holographic Stage

Children move from babbling to authentic speech when they first grasp the concept of the function of speech: to communicate. Occurring at about 12 months, this is referred to as the **holographic stage**. They begin with the traditional "first word," which often represents a person, animal, or pet that captures their interest. For many months they use only one word to represent a whole concept, idea, or complete thought. For example, "kitty" might mean the child sees his pet, or it might mean he is acknowledging any one of a dozen furry animals that live on his street; similarly, "up" might mean "I want you to pick me up," or "The plane is up in the air." According to Vygotsky (1986), with new opportunities, the words' meanings begin to acquire more and more depth.

■ holographic stage

The Telegraphic Stage

telegraphic stage ■   Children in the two-word **telegraphic stage** (occurring at about 12 to 24 months) can perform an amazingly greater repertoire of communicative acts with the simple addition of one more word. They can describe objects and actions ("bad dog"), identify locations ("daddy bye-bye"), and suggest who is doing what ("birdie fly"). Children in this stage have learned some important functions of language, according to Halliday (1975), and can now use it to request something ("Brittany cookie!"), to express interest ("pretty baby!"), and to provide information ("my toy!").

Preschool to Fluency

Children between 2 and 5 years old generally experience a "language explosion." They begin to speak in whole sentences and phrases and can negate sentences ("She is not my friend anymore"). They use language to ask questions beginning with *why, how,* and *who.* They interrupt less often and take turns in conversation. Meaning becomes clearer as the child learns to add the morpheme *–ed* to a verb and suddenly refer to events that occurred in the past, and to indicate quantities by adding *–s* to the end of words. Also, at this stage children recognize when they have not been understood and rephrase their utterance to ensure that their meaning has been communicated.

Primary Grades

By the time children whose first language is English enter kindergarten, they can use, to a greater or lesser extent, all the linguistic constructs in the English language. The greatest communicative skill that separates school-aged children from younger children is their ability to use the passive voice ("The dog was put in the kennel while we were on vacation").

    Between ages 5 and 8, the focus on communication is enhanced by a growing appreciation for the ability to communicate as its own reward, which explains

metalinguistic ability ■   why children of this age often find riddles and puns so hilarious. The term **metalinguistic ability** refers to conscious awareness of the sound, meaning, and practical nuances of language. This ability to evaluate a well-formed sentence, recognize an alliteration, or appreciate a well-told story is manifested during this period of the child's early schooling.

LITERACY'S BEGINNINGS

many fortunate children have literacy encounters very early in their lives, beginning as early as infancy or as toddlers. Although not all infants and toddlers are involved in literacy experiences with their families, most preschoolers acquire foundational literacy concepts that support later formal understanding of reading, writing, speaking, listening, viewing, and visually representing. At least five crucial literacy-related concepts about books can result when children from birth to kindergarten age share literacy experiences, such as listening to books read to them by parents or caregivers or sharing stories or information on a tablet or computer (McGee & Richgels, 2011):

- Reading is enjoyable.
- Books and other reading materials should be handled in special ways.
- Story and book sharing, whether traditional or electronic, involve a routine.
- Illustrations represent real things.
- Printed words have meaning.

Reading Is Enjoyable

Probably the most critical concept that children learn as they are read to while sitting on the lap of a beloved parent or caregiver is the idea that reading is a pleasurable experience. This "lap reading" activity can be one of the most emotionally pleasing activities for children. It often builds fond associations that are remembered for a lifetime. Because this activity involves the adult's total concentration, the activity epitomizes quality time; thus children often choose lap reading over playing with favorite toys.

Books Should Be Handled in Special Ways

Even babies learn important concepts about print (see the discussion and Figure 3.1 later in this chapter) by having books read to them. They quickly learn how to hold a book right side up and how to help turn the pages. They see that books are handled with respect and that pages are turned carefully with eager anticipation as to what will be found on the next page. They also begin to understand that books contain stories and are not just for turning pages.

Even very young children learn important concepts about print when caregivers read to them.

Book and Story Sharing Involve a Routine

Very young children and those who read to them often develop a shared reading routine. Children may initiate a bedtime story, for example, by finding a book they would like to hear and bringing it to their parent or caregiver. Nestled in the arms of the adult, they learn to focus their attention for a prolonged period of time. As the book is being read, the child learns to show her knowledge by answering the question "What is that?" or pointing to objects suggested by the adult. Older children respond to specific questions about characters in the book.

Illustrations Represent Real Things

Well before children can decipher words and sentences, they become aware of the representational nature of the illustrations in reading materials. Young toddlers begin to see that pictures are symbols for real objects and actions with which they are familiar. Children learn, for example, that the apples they see in a favorite book are not real apples, but that they suggest apples and even have the same name.

Printed Words Have Meaning

Another decisive outcome of early reading-together routines is the nascent understanding that printed words carry messages. This understanding is the foundation of children's fluency with later comprehension strategies that, as proficient readers, they will use with ease. Young children begin to use visual cues, including written language cues, to make meaning. When they share books and other reading materials with adults, they attempt to understand the words they hear and the visual symbols they see. Although infants do not look at print and read it as an adult does, they try to figure out what is going on as the adult reads aloud or talks about the pictures in a story.

READING READINESS: A RETROSPECTIVE

acquiring the preceding literacy-related concepts is perhaps the first step toward becoming aware of and interested in books. The following sections explore how children emerge into early readers and writers.

reading readiness ■

In the past few decades, the most pervasive definitions of **reading readiness** have included (a) being ready to profit from reading instruction beyond the most basic level (Dechant, 1982); (b) readiness to learn to read, as distinguished from a general readiness to learn (Reutzel, 1992); and (c) having the cognitive ability to meet the specific demands of reading tasks (Ausubel, 1959).

In the early 1950s educators believed that children had to reach a certain level of intelligence—a mental age of 6.6—and develop nonreading skills such as perceptual–motor skills and large motor coordination before they could learn to read (Durkin, 1966). According to this view, children were not ready to begin reading until they had been instructed in the prerequisite reading abilities, also referred to as "readiness activities." Many parents were amazed when their child was miraculously able to "read" important words such as *McDonald's* or *Target* without having been formally taught them!

This concept of a formal reading readiness period was accompanied by the related belief that literacy should be taught only in formal school settings. Parents were cautioned not to try to teach their children to read at home, lest the children develop bad habits that would later have to be "untaught" by teachers. It was also believed that writing instruction should occur only after children had learned to read.

These beliefs of the early 1950s resulted in the pervasive idea that early childhood was a time during which a specific set of readiness skills should be taught as a prelude to "real" reading (Teale & Sulzby, 1986a). Accordingly, reading readiness tests were developed to assess children's readiness abilities, and reading readiness programs with workbooks full of perceptual–motor activities (e.g., "Draw a line from the dog to the bone") became popular, although they often had little or nothing to do with reading. Kindergarten and the beginning of first grade were devoted to these kinds of prerequisite skills. Writing activities were postponed until even later, often second or third grade. Such beliefs persisted in many school settings (and they persist in a few), mostly fading with the dawning of the whole language movement. Teachers began to see that readiness was not a simple matter of aging. They found they could help children become ready to learn how to read and write by building on the language background their learners already possessed and by providing a print-rich environment and language-play activities (Clay, 1991).

Since the 1970s, the paradigm of a time of "reading readiness" has been largely discarded because preschoolers have demonstrated that, well before any formal instruction, they can engage in many activities involving literacy, including retelling stories and scribbling as well as recognizing environmental print (Morrow & Gambrell, 2011).

OVERVIEW OF EMERGENT LITERACY

although the term *reading readiness* has been used for a long time, more recent research has gradually concluded that such a model is inadequate for studying how a young child becomes literate. The term *emergent literacy* represents a profound change in how we look at early literacy. Whereas we once defined reading readiness as the prereading period that extends from birth to the time when a child begins to recognize and read words, the term *emergent literacy* proposes that literacy begins at birth and continues throughout life (Reutzel & Cooter, 2014).

Use of the Term *Emergent Literacy*

In 1966, New Zealand researcher Marie Clay introduced the term *emergent literacy* to describe the behaviors seen in young children when they use books and writing materials to imitate reading and writing activities, even though they cannot read and write on a functional level. Since then, an extensive body of research has expanded the understanding of emergent literacy. According to current research, children's literacy development begins long before children start formal instruction in elementary school (Beaty & Pratt, 2011; McGee & Richgels, 2011; Morrow & Gambrell, 2011; Mullis, Martin, Kennedy, & Foy, 2007). This development is expanded through social interactions with caring adults and exposure to literacy materials, such as children's storybooks (Clay, 2000). It proceeds along a continuum, and children acquire literacy skills in a variety of ways and at different ages. Moreover, instead of reading preceding writing, as educators once believed necessary, abundant evidence shows that children's skills in reading and writing develop at the same time and are synergistic rather than sequential (Morrow & Gambrell, 2011).

This new way of thinking about early literacy supports the notion that very young children, even as young as 2.5 years old, come into early childhood education with a rich yet diverse background of language experiences, including recognizing written symbols and a variety of prewriting efforts from their home and neighborhood; for example, most children entering kindergarten can read *something*, such as their names and commonly encountered words such as *Coke*, *Target*, and *Toyota*. With effective strategies and routines in place for small-group work, this foundation can be used to formally develop literacy in pre-K and kindergarten (Hayes & Creange, 2001). Ollila and Mayfield (1992) stress that emergent literacy includes language awareness that stems from children's active participation in communicating with those around them. This new concept of literacy places every child on a continuum of readiness in all components of the language that springs from the child as a result of environmental stimulation. This stage of emergent literacy is said to last until children begin to formally read and write, when they become "beginning" readers and writers.

Literacy, in this current model, embraces not only reading, listening, speaking, viewing, and visually representing, but also writing. During the period when literacy is emerging, children learn to understand and generate words, follow directions, draw and interpret pictures, perceive differences in sight and sound, and acquire a curiosity about how things work. Although such behaviors are related to literacy acquisition, they tell us little about exactly when a given child will begin to formally read and write.

WWW

Activities for Letter Recognition

www.starfall.com

Key Components of Emergent Literacy

Perhaps a more constructive way to look at emergent literacy is to examine its key components as well as commonly held myths about what constitutes readiness for formal and informal literacy instruction. By developing a better idea about what factors need to be present in children's preliterate development, we are better able to develop a curriculum that assists children in early literacy acquisition. In the literacy acquisition literature over the past 70 years, the following factors have been most frequently discussed in association with early reading and writing success; revisiting such a list sheds some light on what factors educators once emphasized as compared with current thinking on how a child becomes literate:

- intelligence
- chronological age
- gender
- interest in language
- phonemic awareness

Intelligence

Because learning how to read and write are such complex tasks, it would seem obvious that high intelligence would be correlated with early success in literacy. Research has shown, however, that although some intelligence appears to facilitate progress, a bright child may not necessarily succeed at the task earlier than a child with average intelligence. Research by Bond and Dykstra (1967) found only a small relationship between reading ability and intelligence. Spache and Spache (1985) discovered that intelligence may be a modest predictor of reading success, but only for children at the extremes; in other words, for those with very high or very low intelligence, there is a positive relationship between intelligence and later success in reading. Finally, a review of reading readiness research by Torrey (1979) indicated that although many early readers who read before kindergarten did well on intelligence tests, the intelligence of most early readers fell into the average and below-average range. These studies suggest that although high intelligence may be helpful to reading readiness, it is not a deciding factor in predicting which children will do well in early literacy acquisition.

Chronological age

As far back as the 1930s, researchers were attempting to determine if there was an ideal age at which to begin reading instruction. In a classic study, Morphett and Washburn (1931) looked at the mental ages of children in first-grade reading programs. These researchers found that children who had reached a mental age of approximately 6.5 did well in beginning reading instruction, whereas those who had not yet reached that level generally experienced more problems. Unfortunately, many educators misinterpreted these results to mean that the *chronological age* of 6.5 was the ideal age to begin reading instruction; thus, educators began to consider delaying early reading instruction for all children until they had reached the age of 6.5. In fact, the study had only indicated that a child who is functioning at the cognitive, or intellectual, level of a child 6.5 years old would probably succeed at learning to read—whether that child was 4, 7, or even 10 years old.

Later studies suggested that many children learn to read successfully whether they are taught as early as age 5, as occurs in Japan, or as late as 7 or 8, as occurs in Denmark and Finland (Harris & Sipay, 1990). These researchers further concluded that many children appear to read successfully regardless of chronological age on entering school, and that age is, by itself, an inadequate predictor of success in early reading.

Gender

Numerous fallacies surround the differences in linguistic competence between boys and girls. "Girls grow up faster than boys do," chirped a once-popular singing group. Educators, too, once believed that boys tended to have a delayed start in general readiness and therefore had more problems learning how to read than their female counterparts. Other research suggests that these widely held views may have been misleading (Downing & Thomson, 1977). A landmark study by Dale Johnson (1973) supports a different conclusion. This investigator studied the reading prowess of early readers in the United States, Canada, Nigeria, and England. In most respects, in Nigeria and England the boys tended to score higher in tests of initial reading achievement than the girls. On the other hand, in Canada and the United States the girls scored higher on the same tests. Based on these findings, Johnson concluded that the girls' relative reading superiority in English-speaking countries may have more to do with how they are acculturated and taught than with their native abilities or natural proclivities toward linguistic success. Recent brain research may offer new perspectives on the differences between boys and girls when acquiring early reading proficiency (Gurian, 2009).

Interest in language

Interest is perhaps as important as any other factor in determining when a child is ready to succeed at formal literacy instruction. Because it is not as objectively measurable as, for example, chronological age, interest is a quality that must be assessed by someone who is around the child in many different situations and has a chance to observe the child's interaction with her environment. Questions and comments such as "What does that word say?" or "How do you spell my name?" or "Please read me a story!" or "Can I tell you a story I made up?" are all examples of a child with a clear interest in and curiosity directed toward beginning the tasks involved in literacy acquisition (Cecil, 1994b).

Interest is an important factor in determining when a child is ready to succeed at formal literacy instruction.

Besides being motivated to begin the reading and writing processes, children must have enough confidence to believe that they have a fair shot at succeeding, and they must be emotionally strong enough not to become unduly frustrated when encountering a word or concept that they cannot easily figure out. Coupled with interest, they must also have an attention span that allows them to attend to literacy instruction and practice for an extended period of time (Pflaum, 1990). Finally, interest in literacy must be carefully fanned by initiating activities that challenge but do not frustrate. Such activities must reach children at their current level by using their existing knowledge to bring them one step closer to becoming literate.

Teachers and caregivers play a major role in encouraging curiosity and interest and developing confidence about reading success.

Phonemic awareness

The ability to speak clearly and express ideas articulately has long been associated with emergent literacy. Thirty years of research into the reading success of early readers indicates that phonemic awareness plays an even larger role in this relationship than was earlier believed. While the terms *phonological awareness* and *phonemic awareness* are often used interchangeably, there is a slight distinction between them. **Phonological awareness** is the recognition that speech is made up of a variety of sound units that can be segmented into larger "chunks" known as syllables. **Phonemic awareness** is a division of phonological awareness that refers to a child's ability to manipulate, classify, and listen to each speech unit, or phoneme, in order to distinguish words with differing meanings made from them.

■ phonological
   awareness
■ phonemic awareness

For children to succeed at reading, especially in reading programs where phonics plays a large role, phonemic awareness is *the* most crucial component of emergent literacy (Adams, 1990)—a more potent predictor than nonverbal intelligence, vocabulary, or listening comprehension. To be truly ready to learn how to read and write, children must have an awareness of sounds; that is, an understanding that we speak in a flow of words and that those words contain a sequence of sounds that can be represented by graphic symbols called letters. Later, children must not only be able to discriminate between the sounds of letters, such as /f/ and /v/, but they must also be able to segment, blend, and isolate sounds to manipulate them, or sound them out, into meaningful words (Cunningham & Allington, 2010).

The ability to hear, blend, and discriminate between sounds is also an important part of listening comprehension as well as a factor in helping children understand subtle differences in meaning related to stress, pitch, and intonation in speech (Pearson, 1985). For example, "I wouldn't buy *that* car!" (I'd buy a different model) has a slightly different meaning than "I wouldn't *buy* that car!" (although I might lease it). Another example of the need for accurate discrimination of distinct words is the two-word slang phrase "Jeet yet?" as compared with the four words contained in the query "Did you eat yet?"

rubber-banding ■   Finally, the ability to segment words, also called **rubber-banding,** is helpful as children begin to explore sound–spelling relationships (Calkins, 2000). An example of this occurs when 6-year-old Jessica is trying to sound out the word *man* and she stretches the word to *mmmmmmmaaaaaannnnnn* as she laboriously pencils the word onto her paper. Research by Roberts (1975) supports the notion that blending ability seems most necessary in readiness for sounding out words in reading, while the ability to segment sounds into words appears to facilitate early spelling.

Specifically, the following hierarchy of phonemic understandings appears to be necessary for children to experience a smooth transition into formal reading instruction (Juel, 1994):

- ability to distinguish between letter sounds
- ability to hear sounds in words
- ability to hear syllables within words
- ability to identify phonemes
- knowledge about how print works

INFLUENCES ON CHILDREN'S LITERACY DEVELOPMENT

Teachers and early childhood educators can promote young children's understanding of reading and writing by helping them build literacy knowledge and skills through the use of engaged-learning activities. Children's growth from emergent to conventional literacy, discussed next, is influenced by (1) their understanding of literacy concepts, (2) their developing cognitive skills, and (3) the efforts of parents, caregivers, and teachers to promote literacy, which are discussed subsequently.

Continuing Literacy Development

Children's introduction to literacy begins well before they enter school and continues into adulthood, if not throughout life. It used to be assumed that 5-year-olds went to kindergarten to be "readied" for reading and writing instruction, which would not formally begin until first grade. Today, researchers and practitioners believe that literacy acquisition begins at birth and should be fostered at every age. This view of literacy is explored in the following sections.

Emergent literacy

From as early as birth, children experience oral-language development and begin to build a foundation for later reading and literacy success. From 2 to 3 years of

Videos containing information for developing emergent literacy

Center for Early Literacy Learning, www.earlyliteracy learning.org/ta_pract_videos1.php

Offers several videos for parents and caregivers that support parent–child interactions for promoting language and literacy

ELLISA Project, www.youtube.com/watch?v=QpWUEuEpHCl

This video shows how to successfully teach emergent literacy to a diverse group of first-grade students.

Early learning links, www.nefec.org/erf/links/

Offers videos in targeted areas including language, vocabulary, and emergent literacy. Each component includes videos by leading literacy experts.

CLAS, http://clas.uiuc.edu/fulltext/cl03406/cl03406.html

Includes six emergent literacy training modules consisting of 60-minute recorded sessions and accompanying written materials

age, children begin to produce understandable speech in response to books and the written marks they create (Schickedanz & Casbergue, 2007). From 3 to 4 years of age, children show rapid growth in emergent literacy, as Marie Clay (2000) described it: they begin to "read" their favorite books by themselves, focusing mostly on reenacting the story from the pictures. Eventually, they progress from telling about each picture individually to weaving a story from picture to picture using language that sounds like reading or written language; for example, using the exact dialogue from the story: "'My! What big ears you have!' said Red Riding Hood, as she looked closely as her grandma."

At this time, children also experiment with writing by forming scribbles, letter-like forms, and random strings of letters (Beaty & Pratt, 2011). They also begin to use "mock handwriting" or wavy scribbles to imitate adult cursive writing. Letter-like forms or "mock letters" are the young child's attempt to form alphabetic letters; these forms of writing eventually develop into standard letters. When using various forms of writing, children maintain their intention to create meaning and often "read" their printed messages again, using language that sounds like reading (Jalongo, 2013).

Around age 5, children enter school and begin receiving formal literacy instruction. They continue to make rapid growth in literacy skills if they are exposed to literacy-rich environments. Children at this age continue to "read" from books they've heard repeatedly. Gradually, these readings demonstrate the intonation patterns of the adult reader and contain some of the language used in the book. Emergent readers are just beginning to control early reading strategies such as directionality, word-by-word matching, and concepts of printed language. They use pictures to support reading and rely heavily on their knowledge of language (Christie, Enz, & Vukelich, 2011).

Children's writing also develops rapidly during kindergarten. Just as children's reading acquisition does not occur in a linear path, children's writing skills also reflect an overlapping development. Children continue to use the variety of writing forms developed earlier, but they typically add random letter strings to their repertoire; in effect, they create strings of letters for their written messages without regard for the sounds represented by the letters (Combs, 2010). At this age, children plan their writing and discuss their plans with others. If encouraged, they begin to use experimental, or temporary, spelling. Whimsical spellings typically represent the most dominant sounds in the words, such as the beginning and ending sounds. Even though children begin applying phonetic knowledge to create invented spellings, there is a lapse in time before they use phonetic clues to read what they write. Often children try to recall what has been written or use a picture created with the text to "reread" instead of using the letter clues (Corgill, 2008).

In a synthesis of the research on emergent literacy, Gunn, Simmons, and Kameenui (2004) found that five areas of emergent literacy have implications for ensuring a match between a child's literacy background and classroom instruction:

- experiences with print to understand the purpose and function of print
- interactions with others who model language functions
- phonemic awareness and letter recognition
- family characteristics, such as attitudes toward education, academic guidance, rich conversations, and the amount of literacy materials in the home
- storybook reading, with accompanying adult–child interactions

To this we would add *informational text reading also accompanied by adult–child interactions.*

Conventional literacy

At some point during kindergarten or first grade, most children begin to move from emergent literacy into conventional literacy. This process is gradual and cannot be hurried, any more than a chrysalis can be hurried into a butterfly. Although all aspects of conventional literacy are developing during the emergent period, they become recognizable in conventional literacy. Educators working with young children—as well as parents and legislators—must keep in mind that there is no prescribed grade or age level for reaching conventional literacy. Emergent literacy and conventional literacy are not discrete stages but a continuum of learning that varies with the complexity of each individual's development and internal timeline (Combs, 2010). As children move into conventional literacy, they pass through different periods of development in their efforts to become successful readers, just as they did at the emergent level. Many traditional researchers use the terms *early, transitional,* and *fluent* to describe these periods of literacy growth.

early readers/writers ■ **Early readers/writers.** Most children at the first-grade level are or will soon become **early readers/writers.** They know how to use early reading strategies (such as predicting and using context to help decode new words) and can read appropriately selected text independently after a story introduction given by a teacher. Early readers begin to attend to print and apply the one-to-one correspondence of matching sounds to letters in order to read. They look at beginning and ending letters in order to decode unfamiliar words (Tompkins, 2015). Children in this early reading period also begin to attend to more than one source for cues while reading. Attention is paid to meaning cues, grammatical cues, and prior knowledge on a limited basis (Combs, 2010; Tompkins, 2015). These children recognize a small number of words on sight. In writing, children typically progress through five stages of invented spelling, ranging from writing the initial consonant sound of a word to using conventional spelling.

transitional readers/writers ■ **Transitional readers/writers.** Most children at the second-grade level are **transitional readers/writers.** They can read unknown text with more independence than can early readers. Transitional readers use meaning as well as grammatical and letter cues more fully. They recognize a large number of frequently used words on sight and use pictures in a limited way while reading (Corgill, 2008).

In writing, some children continue to use phonetic or invented spelling, but the spelling is easily readable. Sometime during children's development from early readers into transitional readers, their writing also begins to demonstrate characteristics of the transitional speller. Transitional spellers can apply spelling rules, patterns, and a variety of other strategies for putting words on paper (Corgill, 2008).

Fluent readers/writers. Children at the third-grade level typically are **fluent readers/ writers.** They can use a number of sources of information flexibly to read a variety of unknown texts. Fluent readers read for meaning with less attention to decoding and can independently solve problems encountered in the text (Christie, Enz, & Vukelich, 2011). If the reading materials are appropriately challenging, children's fluency (which includes automatic word recognition, rapid decoding, and checking for meaning) continues to increase (Corgill, 2008).

■ fluent readers/writers

Typically, writing develops into mostly conventional spelling, although children may use transitional and phonetic spellings to spell challenging or infrequently used words. Children at this stage write expressively in many different forms and use an increasingly rich vocabulary and more complex sentences. They often revise and edit their own work.

Understanding of Literacy Concepts

In addition to acknowledging children's developmental acquisition of decoding, comprehension, and writing skills, emergent literacy research emphasizes the changes in children's understanding of literacy concepts. As children have more experience with reading and writing, their understanding of the concepts of reading and writing expands and grows to fit their new knowledge. For instance, Combs (2010) describes categories of children's storybook reading from emergent through conventional reading. She notes that children eventually move from pointing and labeling pictures in a book, to "reading" a story through the illustrations, to telling the story using book language, and finally to reading conventionally using the text of a story.

An important transition occurs when children's "reading" of stories changes from sounding like oral language to sounding like written language. This transition demonstrates a change in ideas from thinking of reading as spoken words to understanding that reading is re-created from written text that uses words in special ways (Combs, 2008; McGee & Richgels, 2011). A similar shift in language can be observed in children's story dictation and in the rereading of their emergent writing (Jalongo, 2013).

Studies indicate that children's ideas about words are quite different from adults' concepts of words. There are differences between how an adult understands reading and writing and how a child understands reading and writing, according to McGee and Richgels (2011). As children progress into conventional literacy, however, their concepts of literacy gradually develop toward more conventional adult conceptualizations.

Developing Cognitive Skills

Because reading and writing are also thinking processes, emergent literacy must be considered in the context of children's developing cognitive skills. The constructionist theories of both Piaget and Vygotsky are relevant to the discussion of emergent literacy and help explain the cognitive concepts formed by young learners. Emergent literacy is partly discovered; children construct their own ideas about literacy as they actively participate in literacy activities (Piaget). Emergent literacy also is based on behaviors modeled and supported by adults (Vygotsky) that encourage children to change and refine their own ideas to more closely match conventional notions. One example of this interface between literacy acquisition and literacy instruction is the child's development of phonemic awareness (awareness that spoken words are made with individual sounds). By playing with language, such as rhyming or substituting sounds in words, some children develop phonemic awareness on their own, while other children require instruction from adults. Instruction may enable some children to use metacognition (the process of thinking about and regulating one's own learning) to achieve higher levels of sound awareness.

The Role of Early Childhood Educators, Parents, and Caregivers

The adults with whom children interact during the transitional years from emergent to conventional literacy play a crucial role in ensuring that children progress successfully in their literacy development. Children's literacy efforts are best supported by adults' interactions with children through reading aloud and conversation and by children's social interactions with each other (McGee & Richgels, 2011). Caregivers and educators must be knowledgeable about emergent literacy and ensure that children experience literacy-rich environments to support their development into conventional literacy.

Reading aloud to children and providing opportunities for them to react to and discuss the stories that they hear is critically important, especially during the preschool years. Reading aloud to children not only introduces them to the joy of reading but also helps them begin to develop in four areas that are important in later formal reading instruction: oral language, cognitive skills, concepts of print, and phonemic awareness. Development of these skills provides a strong foundation to support literacy development during the early school years (Sulzby & Teale, 2010).

Children who are frequently read to also develop background knowledge about a range of topics and build a large vocabulary, all of which assist in later reading comprehension and development of reading strategies. They become familiar with rich language patterns and understand what written language sounds like. Moreover, reading aloud to children helps them associate reading with pleasure and encourages them to seek opportunities to read on their own. Children also become familiar with the reading process by watching how others read, and they learn to understand story structure. Repeated readings of favorite stories allow children to develop a more elaborate understanding of these concepts. By revisiting stories many times, children focus on unique features of a story or text and reinforce previous understandings. In addition, rereadings enable children to engage in emergent reading (Sulzby & Teale, 2010).

Literacy-rich environments at home and at school are fundamental to promoting literacy and preventing reading difficulties. In literacy-rich home environments, parents and caregivers provide opportunities for daily reading, extended discourse (extensive talking or writing), language play, experimentation with literacy materials, book talk (discussion of characters, action, and plot), and dramatic play. In literacy-rich classrooms, teachers incorporate the characteristics of literacy-rich home environments, but they also use grouping for learning, developmentally appropriate practices, and literacy routines; in addition,

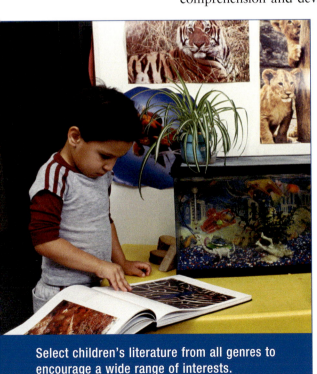

Select children's literature from all genres to encourage a wide range of interests.

they have classroom designs that encourage reading and writing (McGee & Richgels, 2011) through learning centers and engaged-learning activities.

Some children, unfortunately, enter elementary school without a strong foundation for literacy. The children most at risk for developing reading problems are those who begin school with less skill in language, less phonemic awareness and letter knowledge, and less familiarity with literacy tasks and underlying purposes (Beaty & Pratt, 2011). Research on family risk factors that contribute to children's reading difficulties, on adult–child interactions during story reading, and on delays in language development verifies that successes or struggles with reading can be observed early in a child's life. To help children develop emergent skills and overcome barriers to literacy, teachers may need to work with children individually and support and encourage parents and caregivers who participate in their children's literacy development. Schools also can use literacy intervention programs to minimize risk factors and support children in their literacy development.

Literacy development begins early in a child's life and forms a foundation for the acquisition of conventional literacy. Research consistently indicates that the more children know about language and literacy before they begin formal schooling, the better equipped they are to succeed in reading. Parents, caregivers, and teachers need to ensure that young children are exposed to literacy-rich environments and receive developmentally appropriate literacy instruction. Such environments and experiences have a profound effect on children's literacy development by providing opportunities and encouragement for children to become successful readers (Tompkins, 2015).

Developmentally appropriate practice (DAP), as defined by the National Association for the Education of Young Children (NAEYC), is "a framework of principles and guidelines for best practice in the care and education of young children, birth through age 8" (NAEYC, 2011). For a detailed description of the DAP framework, see NAEYC's *Position Statement on Developmentally Appropriate Practice* (NAEYC, 2009).

■ developmentally appropriate practice

GUIDELINES FOR SETTING UP A BALANCED, COMPREHENSIVE LITERACY PROGRAM FROM BIRTH TO PRIMARY YEARS

eachers and early childhood educators may choose from many evidence-based practices to ensure that *all* children have an enjoyable and successful journey into literacy. These practices are explored in the rest of this chapter. The following are general guidelines that teachers may use to set up a balanced and comprehensive literacy program from birth through the primary years.

- Use developmentally appropriate literacy practices that acknowledge children's development, interests, and literacy knowledge.
- Read to children daily and allow them to take turns "reading" the material to each other.
- Use a wide range of literacy materials in class. Allow children to experience a variety of children's books, magazines, newspapers, and online texts. Be sure to include all genres as well as fiction and nonfiction books, and include a wide variety of multicultural books.
- Take time to listen to children to determine their interests, language skills, and areas of need.
- Use children's home cultures and languages as literacy resources.

- Provide multiple rereadings of stories for pleasure and exploration. Invite children to join in the readings, honoring their emergent reading behaviors.
- Provide plenty of appropriate writing materials for children, including differing sizes and types of writing materials and surfaces (e.g., chalk, gel pens, lined and unlined paper, tablets, computers).
- Encourage children to compose stories and informational articles in emergent forms; provide opportunities for children to read, share, and display their writing.
- Provide writing experiences that allow the flexibility to use nonconventional forms of writing at first (invented or phonetic spelling), and over time move to conventional forms.
- As children begin to read conventionally, provide balanced reading instruction to teach skills and meaning and to meet the reading needs of individual children.
- Share ideas with parents and caregivers about creating an optimal environment to support young children's literacy development.
- Participate in professional development activities to learn and understand more about emergent literacy and appropriate teaching practices.

POSITIVE PRACTICES TO FOSTER EMERGENT LITERACY

In most primary classrooms teachers now encounter a heterogeneous garden of children with a multitude of abilities and language backgrounds as well as a diverse set of literacy experiences, such as having been read to and having sung songs. Some enter the classroom door with many such experiences; others will have had fewer activities directly related to language development in its many forms.

Although individualized instruction seems a logical solution to these diversities, such a course of action is not without a host of problems. Most children are social beings who enjoy interaction with other children their own age. Teachers should take an active stance in getting children ready to learn how to read and write, rather than simply waiting for them to become, magically, ready. Three of the factors previously mentioned—interest, development of concepts about print and books, and language experiences—are ones teachers can readily supplement in the classroom in a small- or large-group setting.

For early literacy experiences to flourish, a teacher must be sensitive to the physical environment of the classroom and a facilitator of learning. Such a teacher creates a print-rich environment and offers activities to provide a varied, motivational exposure to the English language. Such a teacher must also believe in the power of pre-K and kindergarten experiences to improve the developmental trajectory of children by teaching to what they already bring with them to the classroom (McGill-Franzen, 2005).

The CCSS for the language arts and reading outline what children should know and be able to do by the end of their first year of school, or kindergarten. These standards are directed toward fostering young children's understanding and working knowledge of concepts of print, the alphabetic principle, and other basic conventions of the English writing system. The standards set a goal for kindergarten children to become familiar with five aspects of literacy (NGACBP & CCSSO, 2010):

- *Print concepts.* Children must be able to demonstrate understanding of the organization and basic features of print.
- *Phonemic awareness.* Children must demonstrate awareness of spoken words, syllables, and sounds.

The CCSS and pre-K literacy education

Although the Common Core State Standards were designed for grades K through 12, the exclusion of pre-K from the standards does not mean that a child's early literacy development is insignificant or can be ignored. Far from it! Researchers and policy makers alike recognize that children's literacy development before kindergarten has a significant impact on their success throughout their later school years. Therefore, there has been a growing emphasis on pre-K and the need to align its standards and expectations with the K–12 CCSS. A high-quality pre-K experience will prepare children to meet the rigorous standards expected of them in kindergarten and, as a result, some states are already designing a pre-K curriculum that will help early childhood educators to do just that. For example, the state of Delaware has begun to define what types of experiences children should have before they enter kindergarten. The intention of this work is to help parents, day care providers, and early education instructors provide developmentally appropriate experiences that promote children's success in literacy in later school years. The state of New York has also focused on the prekindergarten years. In an effort to provide a clear, comprehensive, and consolidated resource for early childhood professionals, the New York State P–12 Common Core Learning Standards for the English language arts, literacy, and mathematics at the prekindergarten level was created. Among the five domains targeted, language and literacy standards are prominent (NYSED, 2011).

Although the rigorous standards of the CCSS have been largely perceived as a positive opportunity in most early childhood discussions as mentioned earlier, there has been some controversy about what the standards will mean to those involved with emergent literacy education. The NAEYC has created a position paper on its concerns about what the grade-level standards for grades K–3 will mean to prekindergarten education. The NAEYC has historically focused on the whole child and considerations of the larger social and cultural world in which the child lives. Although they are optimistic that providing consistent learning benchmarks for all children across the country will produce positive effects, there are also reservations. The focus on English language arts and mathematics, they believe, may put pressure on early childhood programs to neglect emphases that have long been their hallmark, such as social and emotional development and holistic approaches to learning. They have always emphasized the important role of parents, family members, and child care providers in helping children develop oral language and apprenticing toddlers into the world of literacy, as well as literacy events and functions. They are therefore concerned that connecting early childhood education with traditional K–12 education may exert a downward pressure of increased academic focus and more narrowed instructional approaches (NAEYC, 2013). Hopefully, ongoing dialogue will lead to heightened communication between early childhood educators and later elementary childhood educators to bring about a better understanding of how developmentally appropriate practices used before children begin formal literacy will help children become ready for the rigors and critical thinking necessary to be successful in their future academic lives.

- *Phonics.* Children should be able to know and apply phonics and word analysis skills in decoding words.
- *Sight word recognition.* Children should have a rudimentary sight vocabulary of words that are recognized automatically.
- *Reading fluency.* By the end of kindergarten, children should be able to read emergent-reader texts with purpose and understanding.

Chapter 4 offers a host of activities that can be used for direct, explicit instruction in phonemic awareness, while Chapter 5 presents activities for developing phonics, vocabulary, and fluency. The following section will allow teachers to build on what children already know to ready them for more formal reading and writing instruction.

Developing Concepts About Print

As children get ready for formal instruction in literacy, they need to develop some basic understandings of how print works in text; most of these concepts of print have often been mastered before entering first grade. What seems simple may sometimes bewilder children who have never been exposed to it. It is unlikely, for example, that a preliterate child will spot any patterns in a page of print if that child sometimes looks at it from right to left and at other times from left to right. The concepts about (Western) print listed in Figure 3.1 can be taught directly to children during read-aloud sessions (Clay, 2000).

To reinforce such concepts, teachers can use big books, posters, text posted on an interactive whiteboard, sentence strips in a pocket chart, songs, poetry, or any text that is large enough to share with children. Then before reading the text with children, the teacher can feign forgetfulness and ask children:

Who can show me . . .

where the cover of the book is?

which way is right side up?

where I should start to read?

where a word is?

where the end of the story is?

where a capital (or lowercase) letter is?

On a familiar text, some children may be ready to point to the words as they are read, establishing one-to-one matching of words to print.

Providing Direct and Vicarious Experiences

Providing an adequate background of experience is an integral part of cultivating emergent literacy. Because the child who is intellectually curious reaps the most from his experiences, teachers must take every opportunity to whet his curiosity about unfamiliar activities, ideas, and objects. A broad experiential background is necessary for literacy success because children must be familiar with the concepts and vocabulary they hear and see in written form to gain meaning from them. Indeed, experiences are the foundation for building concepts, and concepts are the foundation for building new vocabulary. Through their experiences children gain an understanding of ideas and concepts and then learn words that go with them. When they later begin to read, they better comprehend the text because they can relate their experiences to the symbols on the page.

figure 3.1   Concepts about print.

- Print carries meaning.
- Reading of print goes from left to right, top to bottom.
- Print goes from the left page, then proceeds to the right.
- Letters are the black squiggles on the page.
- A word is composed of letters and is surrounded by white space.
- Punctuation marks provide information about inflection and meaning.
- A book has a front and back cover, a title page, an author, and often an illustrator.
- A story has a beginning, a middle, and an end.
- A text can be factual.

Teachers, including preschool teachers, can help children build experiential backgrounds in a variety of ways. As they observe and talk with their students, they can see gaps in experience and find ways to fill them. Students can build experience through constructing mobiles and collages, cooking, playing with puzzles, identifying hidden objects, playing language guessing games, singing nursery rhymes, and marching to a Sousa tune. Teachers can invite resource people into the classroom or arrange field trips or virtual field trips on the Internet to places children have never visited.

During "calendar" or "news" time, children gain useful experience observing and discussing the weather, reciting the days of the week and months of the year, and establishing what to do in a fire drill, among other experiences. Because young children love to play, a hidden coin can be a language-learning experience for those studying English (they must repeatedly ask questions in complete sentences to determine who has the coin); a box becomes a concept-building game when children try to identify the position of an object placed on it, over it, beside it, or under it. Similarly, children can increase their understanding of the subtleties of vocabulary by responding to invitations to crawl, trot, dash, or stroll.

Experiences may be either direct or vicarious. Children usually remember direct experiences with actual physical involvement best, but such experiences are not always possible. For example, the ideal way to teach about the Laplanders in Scandinavia would be to climb aboard a plane, observe their lives, talk to them firsthand, and spend time in their homes. Because that is not feasible, vicarious experiences, such as television programs about the Laplanders, exhibits, a talk by someone who has been to Scandinavia, photographs, video excerpts, and online stories or articles about their lives will also promote concept and vocabulary development.

Interactive Story Writing

Interactive story writing is a logical extension of either direct or vicarious experiences and is an ideal vehicle through which to reinforce concepts about print. Such story writing can be planned and occur as an introduction to an experience, or it can be the spontaneous result of an experience (Tompkins & Collom, 2004). If the class writes a story after there has been a severe thunderstorm, the children should first discuss the event. By asking carefully selected questions, the teacher can encourage children to formulate valid concepts and to use appropriate vocabulary words. For example, the teacher might ask:

■ interactive story writing

> Who can tell me what the weather was like this morning?
>
> What kinds of things happen during a storm?
>
> How did the storm make you feel?
>
> Why might rain be important to us?

In response to a discussion generated by questions, the children then dictate sentences for the teacher to transcribe onto a chart. The resultant piece of writing might look like the one shown in Figure 3.2, composed by a group of second-graders. The story can be written on chart paper, a board, or an interactive whiteboard. Dictated pieces such as this provide an excellent precursor to later use of the language experience approach (see Chapter 9).

Perhaps the most important reason for writing stories in partnership with children, before they are able to write their own, is that they begin to grasp the critical concept that writing is a way to record speech. This awareness occurs as the teacher reads the story back to the children in the words they have just dictated. After repeated readings by the teacher, the children may be able to "read" the story too. The teacher may make copies of the story for the children to take home and share with their families. As a result of this repeated involvement with the story, chil-

figure	3.2	An interactive story.

THE STORM

This morning we didn't have any recess because there was a big storm.

There was loud thunder and bright lightning.

It rained very hard for a long time.

Some children were afraid of the noise.

The storm was scary, but the rain can be good.

We need the rain to make the flowers grow.

dren may learn to recognize some high-interest words (e.g., *storm* in the preceding story) and words that were used more than once (*we* and *there*). These understandings are further reinforced when seen in a number of different contexts.

Many literacy skills are reinforced through transcriptions; essentially, children gain a bird's-eye view of all the skills involved in literacy. Consider: Children watch as the teacher forms letters that make up the words and demonstrates how she sounds out the beginning letters. They begin to notice, as the teacher writes, that language consists of separate words that are combined into sentences. They see the teacher begin reading at the left side of the story and move to the right, going from top to bottom. They become aware that dictated stories have titles that tell about the most important idea in the story, and they see that each letter of the title is capitalized. They discover that sentences begin with capital letters and end with a punctuation mark. In addition to becoming familiar with the mechanical conventions of the English language, children develop their thinking skills as the teacher guides them to summarize and organize their thoughts. Finally, as the children recall the events in the order in which they occurred, they become aware of the importance of sequencing ideas.

Reading Aloud to Students: The Importance of Print and Books

Jim Trelease, author of *The New Read Aloud Handbook* (2006), travels around the country exhorting parents to read to their child for fifteen minutes a night to ensure later academic success. The reason he preaches this important message has much to do with emergent literacy: children who have been read to—early and often—develop important concepts about print. Advanced understanding of print allows children to identify the first and last word on a page, capital and lowercase letters, and the first and last letters of words—all excellent precursors to the reading process (Clay, 1972, 1993). In a family setting, these understandings are developed naturally through enjoyable exposure to print.

To build on children's knowledge of what is available in print, the teacher should choose a wide variety of reading materials to read aloud to students every day. Reading to children not only builds appreciation of literature and concepts of print; it also develops listening comprehension skills and understanding of various text structures (Beck & McKeown, 2007; Fisher, Flood, Lapp, & Frey, 2004).

When reading aloud to students, teachers share reading materials on a wide range of topics, capture children's attention, and engage them in deep thinking about texts and how one responds to literature (Dickenson, Hao, & He, 1995). Read-aloud materials should be challenging stories or informational texts that provide opportunities to talk about word meanings, to puzzle over characters' motivations, or to explore new concepts (McGee, 1998). Read-aloud materials can be chosen to reflect the cultures and ethnicities within the classroom and introduce children to other ones as well. Listening to books being read aloud provides children with opportunities to acquire new vocabulary, extend understandings about the world and themselves, and develop an awareness of story and informational text structures.

Researchers suggest that the most valuable aspect of reading aloud is that it requires children to make sense of ideas that are about something beyond the physical "here and now." The instructive verbal interactions teachers have with students during a read-aloud promote language development and the ability to handle ideas that do not concern the present moment. To optimize this benefit to children, the teacher can initiate **text talk** (Beck & McKeown, 2002), an approach to enhancing young children's ability to build meaning from text. Using this method, the teacher intersperses reading with open-ended questions and follows each story with direct attention to vocabulary. Such questions often begin by repeating and rephrasing the children's answers and then providing generic prompting such as, "What was that all about?" and "Can you tell me more about what you mean by that?" Text talk also includes rereading the relevant portion of text and then repeating the initial question, if a child's answers seem to be coming only from the pictures or her own background. This approach helps young children focus on the text language as the source for their answers to the questions and thus builds vocabulary and comprehension. *Caveat:* Too much text talk may disrupt comprehension of the story by interrupting flow and enjoyment.

■ text talk

For heightened enjoyment, use a variety of well-crafted picture books with large illustrations so that children can observe the action as well as hear what is happening. Big books are commercially available for this purpose. The box below offers guidelines for selecting a big book. Keep in mind, too, that online books with interactive whiteboard technology can be used effectively in a classroom for the same purpose.

At times the teacher may wish to choose stories with only pictures, or **wordless books** (see Appendix A), so that very young children have a chance to use their imaginations to help tell the story from their everyday experiences and from their experiences with other stories. Predictable books (see Appendix A) are other excellent options for reading aloud to children. These children's books, through their rhyme, rhythm, and repetition, allow children to participate in the reading and,

■ wordless books

> **see appendix A**

Selecting a big book to read aloud

The criteria for evaluating a big book are the same as the criteria used for selecting any children's book to be read aloud, with the addition of the following features:

1. The book should not be so large that it is difficult to hold on your lap with one hand and turn the pages with the other.

2. The print should be clearly distinguishable from the illustrations. In other words, it should be easy for the children to visually discriminate the units of print from the illustrations.

3. There should be a strong connection between the print and the illustrations; the children should be able to predict what the story is about from the pictures.

4. The print should be large enough to be seen clearly from the back of the group of children.

5. The text of the book should have specific instructional qualities, such as rhythm, a rhyming pattern, a particular phonic element such as an abundance of words beginning with "b," predictability enhanced by repetition, or informational content, and pictures that support comprehension.

with the teacher's help, associate the spoken words with the written ones, creating an understanding of one-to-one correspondence between oral and written words.

To acquaint English learners with language variety, the teacher should offer a variety of styles and structures, too. Remember that children do not need to understand every word that is read to them, especially when the text is supported by appropriate illustrations. As with infants acquiring a first language, hearing new words in familiar contexts helps children begin to construct new meanings.

It is important to select children's literature from all ethnic groups and all genres—fiction, nonfiction, prose, and poetry—to encourage a wide range of interests.

informational texts ■

Recent studies have shown that **informational texts** (see Chapter 10 and Appendix A) are surprisingly scarce in primary classrooms (Duke, 2000). Seek a variety of informational texts, as such material helps develop important skills and interest in informational reading and writing. Early in the year the teacher can survey students' interests, hobbies, special talents, and country of birth, and then choose stories and nonfiction pieces based on this information (see the interest inventory in Appendix E).

see appendix A ◁

see appendix E ◁

Finally, the teacher should also share reading materials that he especially enjoys, because pleasure and enthusiasm for reading and books is more effectively "caught" than "taught."

Sharing literature is the perfect experience through which to develop concepts about books and print, as they occur naturally in the material being read. Talking about literature with children can also help develop the ideas that the words should make sense, that readers are to be actively involved in thinking about what might happen next, and that the learner brings her own knowledge, ideas, and experiences to the text. Prereading discussions about a topic and what the children know about it, the author and illustrator, and what they predict the story might be about will set preliterate children on the road to comprehending text. The modeling of these behaviors by a proficient reader, the teacher, will encourage children to construct meaning as they begin to read. The following box offers a list of classic read-aloud books.

Classic read-alouds for young children

The following picture storybooks are "classics" that have withstood the test of time, offering countless children—and adults—enjoyable associations with literature.

Corduroy by Don Freeman
A stuffed bear is rescued from the department store shelf by a little girl who takes him home to be her friend.

From Seed to Plant by Gail Gibbons
A simple introduction to how plants reproduce, discussing pollination, seed dispersal, and growth from seed to plant.

Goodnight Moon by Margaret Wise Brown
Mother Rabbit settles her little one into bed through rhyme by saying good night to all the things in the bedroom.

Ira Sleeps Over by Bernard Weber
When he is asked to spend the night at his friend's house, a little boy must decide whether to take along his teddy bear.

Make Way for Ducklings by Robert McCloskey
This is the story of the city adventures of Mr. and Mrs. Mallard and their eight ducklings.

Sylvester and the Magic Pebble by William Steig
Sylvester makes a wish on a magic pebble and is unable to undo his wish and return home to his family. The story resolves when Sylvester is reunited with his parents.

The Very Hungry Caterpillar by Eric Carle
An egg hatches into a caterpillar that eats its way through several storybook pages before turning into a beautiful butterfly.

Using Drama

Informal dramatic activities create interest in language and stories, develop children's imagination, and allow them to use language to express their ideas and feelings. It is especially appropriate for use with those who are learning English, because the action involved supports and reinforces the words, making the meaning accessible for all such students.

Informal drama should be spontaneous and unrehearsed, with students assuming the roles of characters from real life or from stories they have heard. They are free to think, feel, move, react, and speak in accordance with their interpretation of the characters. The drama may begin with simple movements or actions in response to poems or songs the teacher reads ("'And the horses went clippety-clop, clippety-clop.' *Show* me what the horses did, boys and girls!"). Later, students may develop their interpretational skills by pantomiming stories, events, or actions after the teacher has read, such as pretending to be great white sharks after hearing *The Truth About Great White Sharks* or dancing the horrific monster dance in *Where the Wild Things Are,* when the "wild rumpus begins." Acting out stories not only helps build interest in stories but also develops understandings of the structure of stories. Students can progress to more sophisticated drama that more nearly resembles the entire story. As the teacher reads the story, the students must pay attention to the sequence of events, the personalities of the characters, the dialogue, and the mood of the story. Before the students act out the story, the teacher can help them review the sequence of events and characters by using a simple organizer such as the one shown in Figure 3.3.

As they act, the children can be encouraged to use appropriate vocabulary, enunciate clearly, and speak audibly. Puppets can be useful with shy children who are reluctant to speak themselves but are often willing to talk through a puppet. Props, such as masks, costumes, scarves, empty food containers, and cardboard boxes, help inspire dialogue. Children often want to act out the stories several times, with different children playing different characters each time. Each successive rereading allows for a deeper appreciation and understanding of the original story.

Dramatic play has many benefits, all prerequisite for learning in literacy. Because children need to carry on conversations, they are practicing their language skills. By interacting with other children, they are developing social and emotional

Props, masks, and simple costumes can help build interest in acting out stories.

figure	3.3	A simple story frame.

Somebody/	Wanted/	But/	So
Goldilocks	to sit	bears	she
	to eat	came	ran
	to sleep	home	away

play centers ■

readiness. The teacher can encourage children to use printed words as labels, such as street signs, character names, and package labels. Ambiguous props used in their play can also be labeled—for example, a ball becomes a "bowling ball"— and will later become words recognized on sight. **Play centers** such as the ones described in Figure 3.4 can also facilitate spontaneous dramatic play.

By listening attentively to each other, children begin to develop the auditory memory and discrimination necessary for phonemic awareness in an enjoyable package that effectively furthers their learning but seems like play.

EMERGENT LITERACY AND CHILDREN WITH SPECIAL NEEDS

recent decades have seen increased attention to early intervention for children at risk for learning disabilities. Many approaches to early literacy have been tried with varying degrees of success. Justice and Pullen (2003) synthesized trends and offered three strategies for emergent literacy interventions that were based on a body of empirical research: literacy-enriched play interventions, print referencing, and dialogic reading. Although each is a proven practice that would be helpful for *all* children, the strategies are especially effective for students with special learning needs.

Literacy-enriched play intervention. Many, if not most, preschool classrooms and child care facilities include play centers with themes, such as playing house and supermarkets (see Figure 3.4). Many studies have supported a conclusion that literacy skills can be accelerated by contextualizing literacy props into such centers. For example, magazines, shopping lists, and newspapers can contextualize language and how it functions in everyday life. Children's interactions in such centers can be heightened through adult mediation by the teacher scaffolding their interactions through elaboration of their play dialogue, or even through casual conversation about the content of the dramatic play.

figure **3.4** Examples of play centers.

GROCERY STORE	POST OFFICE
Empty cereal and other boxes	Mail boxes
Pretend money and coins	Stationery
Receipt book for purchasing items	Assorted writing utensils
Paper sacks for bagging groceries	Old stamps or stickers
Calculator or cash register that prints onto tape	Puppets
HOUSE	**FARM**
Puppets	Stuffed or plastic animals
Telephone	Large boxes or crates for barn
Cardboard boxes for furniture	Burlap bags for pretend feed
Clothing appropriate for different family members	Pails
Kitchen utensils	Plastic plants
Paper and crayons for making props	

Print referencing. When a teacher or caretaker is reading to a student or group of students, literacy skills can be taught naturally by integrating knowledge of print with the reading experience. When the teacher points out new orthological, or print, features or ones the students already know (e.g., "Oh—we know this letter! It's an 'm'"), asks questions about reading behavior (e.g., "Where do we begin reading on this page?"), or even models literacy by pointing to words or tracking, students with special needs will, over time, develop literacy knowledge.

Dialogic reading. Dialogic reading is a strategy of reading with children in a way that they are continually participating in the content of the text in much the same way as the reader is. The interaction in dialogic reading consists of asking open-ended questions, extending children's answers, repeating and elaborating on their comments, valuing their participation, and following their interests.

STRATEGIES FOR ENGLISH LEARNERS

Special consideration can be given to young students who do not have strong skills in oral English. According to Jalongo (2013), children who do not speak English need adequate preparation before they are taught to read in English. The ability to speak English provides the foundation for learning the alphabetic principle, the structure of the language, and the content of the material they are reading. If children cannot speak English, they can be taught to read and write in their own language while becoming proficient in English. If that is not possible, the initial instructional priority should be developing the children's oral proficiency in English (Jalongo, 2013). Formal reading instruction in English can be started after the child is adequately proficient in oral English.

Verbal scaffolding can be used with young children who are in the early stages of learning to read and write and who are learning to become fluent in speaking English. Verbal scaffolding is a strategy in which the teacher, aware of the child's particular level of English language development, uses prompting, questioning, and elaboration to help the learner progress to a higher level of English language proficiency, listening comprehension, and thinking. The following three instructional strategies are examples of verbal strategies appropriate for children at both early levels of second language learning and beginning literacy (Echevarria, Vogt, & Short, 2010).

Modeling phrasing and punctuation. By slowing their speech and using natural pauses as they would occur in written language, teachers can model how to speak in phrases or normal speech patterns using breaks between thoughts. Moderating the rate of speaking also allows the "wait time" young English learners need to process information in English.

Using contextual definitions. Children acquire much of the vocabulary used for speaking and for other forms of literacy when listening to modeling provided by proficient speakers of English, including the teacher. Providing helpful definitions in interactions with learners can help students acquire a meaning vocabulary in a natural way. Example: "I was exhausted—so very, very tired—after I finished raking the leaves yesterday." Or, "Tangerines, which are kind of like oranges but a bit sweeter, are one of my favorite fruits."

Elaborating on children's responses. Since communication is the purpose of language, a teacher must be careful to never overtly correct a student's pronunciation of an English word. Sometimes, however, the student has a correct response, but the word(s) are mispronounced or the syllabic stress is wrong. Instead of making the student self-conscious about her burgeoning use of English, the best practice is to repeat the student's response, while nodding affirmation, with the correct pronunciation and inflection. This way, the meaning of the child's response is validated while the learner is presented with another opportunity to hear the content modeled in Standard English.

SUMMARY

All young children—and everyone else, for that matter—are somewhere on the continuum of proficiency in literacy; therefore, the old question of *when* they will be ready to learn to read becomes irrelevant. The most current understanding of emergent literacy holds that children are emerging as literate people from birth and continue on this path throughout their lives. Success in literacy, then, depends on a constellation of interlocking factors—neither on wholly physical nor on totally intellectual maturation alone, although both of these realms seem to be at least minimally involved. Nor do modern educators believe that success in literacy is something to wait for passively, as educators tended to believe in the early 1950s; we now argue that literacy is a stage onto which a child can be gently guided—and even enticed—when the appropriate methods and activities are offered to that child.

Gender, home environment, and chronological age of children may not be the factors that most determine who will be literate and when. However, it is helpful to be aware of such factors to understand possible tangential reasons for certain inexplicable behaviors or lack of progress in early literacy acquisition. On the other hand, teachers must guard against preconceived expectations for children, based on gender or chronological age, home environment, or any other nonacademic aspects of the child's life that are not subject to change.

Fortunately, teachers of young children can influence their later literacy success by fostering awareness of sounds in language—phonemic awareness. They can affect other areas correlated with success in early literacy as well, such as background experience, interest in literacy, and language development. Teachers can fill in children's experiential gaps with appropriate real-life experiences or well-designed vicarious ones; they can incorporate language-rich activities such as transcription of stories, dramatic play, and reading aloud to children into their daily routines. Most of all, teachers have a crucial responsibility to fill their classrooms with plenty of opportunities for pupils to play and experiment with print and language in all their forms. With such print-rich and language-rich experiences at the beginning of their academic lives, children will find their path to formalized literacy instruction considerably smoother.

questions FOR JOURNAL WRITING AND DISCUSSION

1. Discuss the prevalent practice of "red shirting"—holding children back a year before sending them to kindergarten. What is your opinion of this practice? How might such a practice stratify our society along socioeconomic lines?

2. What might you say to parents of a kindergarten student who ask you what they can do at home to help their child become "ready to learn to read"? Explore some websites that discuss emergent literacy. (See Appendix C as well as the box earlier in the chapter with links to websites with videos for some suggestions.) Note the source: who wrote the information and for what purpose? Share the information you find with the class.

see appendix C

3. Schools often use a teacher's judgment in addition to the data derived from reading readiness assessments to decide whether children are ready to begin formal reading instruction. Do you think these two sources of data are equally reliable? Why or why not? What might be some advantages of each of these forms of evaluation? What might be some limitations?

suggestions   FOR PROJECTS AND FIELD ACTIVITIES

1. From the information in this chapter, create a checklist you might use to help determine if a student is ready to learn to read. Include such factors as language development, interest in reading, and understanding of the English writing system. For each of these main headings, create ways to evaluate each of the factors. For example, you might say for language development, "Asks many complex questions containing five or more words," or for interest in reading, "Listens attentively when read to" or "Often talks about books he has heard."

2. Spend time observing in a kindergarten class. Observe how oral language skills are enhanced. Observe how teachers and caretakers promote critical-thinking skills as they interact with the children in centers and other times.

3. Research the emergent literacy issues of a country outside North America. Find out the following: (a) When do children begin formal reading instruction? (b) What methods are used for instruction? (c) Are there any noticeable differences in achievement levels of boys and girls on standardized reading tests in later years? (d) If there is a discrepancy in test results between boys and girls, to what do educational practitioners attribute this difference? What do you think accounts for the difference?

4. Read a picture book to a child in preschool and observe what he seems to understand about the concepts of print. Record your observations using the Concepts About Print Assessment in Appendix E. For concepts with which the student seems unfamiliar, list several ways parents or preschool teachers can work with the child to help him become familiar with the concepts of print.

> see appendix E

Phonemic Awareness

4

focus questions

What is the relationship between phonemic awareness and phonics?

What motivational methods can teachers use to develop phonemic awareness?

Why is knowledge of phonemic awareness and the alphabetic principle so important to emergent literacy?

What are strategies to use when teaching phonemic awareness to English learners? To students with special needs?

the students in Mrs. Rodgers' kindergarten class are enthusiastically brainstorming all the foods they can think of while their teacher writes their responses on the board. For every favorite food mentioned, such as "hot dog," the students try to think of a nonsense rhyme that could go with it. "Rot hog!" Aaron exclaims gleefully, and the other students burst into a fit of giggles at this hilarious rhyme, quickly offering a "thumbs-up" sign to Aaron. Mrs. Rodgers grins as she writes the letters on the board, with the students helping her sound out the words. The students in Mrs. Rodgers' class enjoy this game immensely. They are oblivious to the fact that they are also engaging in an activity that encompasses important skills that will benefit their reading. First, creating the fun nonsense rhymes, an oral activity, is helping them tune in to the sounds in the English language and develop their phonemic awareness. And when Mrs. Rodgers writes on the board and sounds out the letters, she is preparing them to benefit from later phonics instruction.

INTRODUCTION

Until fairly recently, the teaching of decoding addressed mostly phonics, or the relationship between spoken sounds and individual printed letters or letter combinations. Now, greater emphasis is being placed on the understanding and teaching of phonemic awareness.

When preparing students to develop phonemic awareness, remember that phonemic awareness is a subcomponent of a larger phonological process, and that addressing both components is necessary. **Phonological sensitivity (PS)** is a term first used by Stanovich (1992) to describe the dual components of phonological processing: *phonological awareness* and *phonemic awareness*. As discussed in Chapter 3, phonological awareness refers to the ability to understand larger units of speech such as words, syllables, **onsets** (the sounds of a word before the first vowel, such as /k/) and **rimes** (the first vowel in a word and all the sounds that follow, e.g., /ar/; see Appendix F) (e.g., Anthony, Lonigan, Burgess et al., 2002; Anthony, Lonigan, Driscoll et al., 2003; Mott & Rutherford, 2012; Pufpaff, 2009), while phonemic awareness is the ability to hear, identify, and manipulate individual sounds—phonemes—in spoken words (National Institute for Literacy, 2001).

A multitude of studies indicate that phonological sensitivity develops on a continuum (Anthony, Lonigan, Burgess et al., 2002; Anthony, Lonigan, Driscoll et al., 2003; Byrnes & Wasik, 2009; Carroll, Snowling, Hulme, & Stevenson, 2003; Lonigan, 2006) and that success in phonological awareness ultimately helps develop students' phonemic awareness (Blachman, 2000; Bryant et al., 1990; Byrne & Fielding-Barnsley, 1993, 1995; Carroll et al., 2003). Pufpaff (2009) warns us that "insufficient attention is being paid to the developmental nature of phonological sensitivity skills in our efforts to identify and remediate early literacy difficulties among children" (p. 689) and provides an excellent table ranking studies of phonological sensitivity from least complex (phonological) to most complex (phonemic) skills. Although technically *phonemic awareness* is only one aspect of phonological sensitivity, the term is often used interchangeably with *phonological awareness*. This text uses the more commonly used term *phonemic awareness* to describe both sets of skills.

The focus in phonemic awareness is on hearing the sounds in words spoken aloud, and not on the letters or printed words. When children have developed awareness of the sounds in words, they can then use the sound–symbol correspondence to read and spell words (Gillon, 2007). A child who possesses phonemic

phonological
sensitivity (PS) ■

onsets ■
rimes ■

see appendix F

awareness can segment and manipulate sounds in words (e.g., pronounce just the first sound heard in the word *gap*), blend strings of isolated sounds together to form recognizable word forms, and so on (IRA Board, 1998). As should be clear from the preceding discussion, phonemic awareness is really an understanding of oral language. It is not the same as phonics. *Phonics* generally refers to knowing the relationship between specific printed letters (and combinations of letters) and specific spoken sounds (see Chapter 5). Phonemic awareness has been shown to be an important *precursor* to phonics and to the successful decoding skills critical in reading (Pressley, 2005). Moreover, children who receive instruction in phonemic awareness in kindergarten are better able to produce experimental spellings than those who are not (Tangel & Blachman, 1995). Studies have shown that the many children who lack experience with phonemic awareness activities often profit less from phonics instruction (Griffith & Olson, 1992).

Many researchers have studied the problems of the many schoolchildren who do not read at grade level (Fletcher et al., 1994; Hernandez, 2012; National Governors Association, 2013; Shaywitz et al., 1992; Stanovich & Siegel, 1994). Whereas most children learn to read regardless of the reading methods used by their teachers, reading has consistently been a problem for about 25 percent of children (Adams, 1990). Early facilitation in phonemic awareness may very well be the instructional component, when integrated into a program rich with language and text, that will enable educators to teach every child to read. Adoption of the Common Core State Standards has focused the attention of many educators on the use of informational texts, critical thinking skills, and writing. Nevertheless, the CCSS acknowledge the important role of phonemic awareness in learning to read and include standards that address these skills in the Reading: Foundational Skills domain for grades 1 through 3. For example, the standards for grade 1 (NGACBP & CCSSO, 2010, p. 15) require students to acquire the following skills:

> CCSS.ELA-Literacy.RF.1.2 Demonstrate understanding of spoken words, syllables, and sounds (phonemes).

> CCSS.ELA-Literacy.RF.1.2.a Distinguish long from short vowel sounds in spoken single-syllable words.

> CCSS.ELA-Literacy.RF.1.2.b Orally produce single-syllable words by blending sounds (phonemes), including consonant blends.

> CCSS.ELA-Literacy.RF.1.2.c Isolate and pronounce initial, medial vowel, and final sounds (phonemes) in spoken single-syllable words.

> CCSS.ELA-Literacy.RF.1.2.d Segment spoken single-syllable words into their complete sequence of individual sounds (phonemes).

THE IMPORTANCE OF PHONEMIC AWARENESS

To understand why phonemic awareness is important, first we must understand a bit about the nature of our language. Linguists describe four separate areas of functioning in the human language system: phonology (sounds), syntax (grammar), semantics (underlying meaning), and pragmatics (usage) (see Chapter 1). The component of phonology is central to eventual success in phonics. **Phonology** is the study of the sound patterns of a language. As we put our ideas into words, the phonological part of our language system assembles the proper sounds of those words in the appropriate sequence; in other words, our canine best friend is a dog and not a god, only because of the precise arrangement of sounds.

■ phonology

Some time ago, Isabelle Liberman and her colleagues (Liberman et al., 1974) suggested that the primary cause for difficulty in learning to read an alphabetic written

Teachers contribute to their students' phonemic awareness by spending a few minutes every day engaging children in stimulating oral language activities that explicitly emphasize the sequence of sounds in language.

alphabetic principle ■

language (as compared with an ideographic language with meaning-laden characters, such as kanji or Mandarin) is due to a lack of awareness of the phonology or sounds of the language. The English language employs the **alphabetic principle.** Any alphabetic writing system uses symbols to represent the sounds of a language. Readers must first understand that words can be divided into sounds and that the same basic set of letters can be combined in a variety of ways. Only then can a child understand that *lake* and *kale*, for instance, have the same letters but represent different words because the sequence of the letters—and therefore the sequence of the sounds—is different.

The ability to hear discrete speech sounds in individual words is elusive for many young children and remains undeveloped—even into adulthood—in a surprisingly large number of people. This is understandable when we consider that sounds are abstract, meaningless in isolation, and often influenced by context. (What does your mouth do when you say the /s/ in *see?* When you say the /s/ in *say?*) However, in the past 30-plus years a large body of research has supported a conclusion that the ability to segment words into individual sounds is an absolute prerequisite to learning how to read in an alphabetic symbol system such as English. Moreover, the degree to which emergent readers are aware of the individual sounds in spoken words often predicts future reading success. In fact, it has been shown to be a better predictor of reading success than intelligence, parents' educational background, visual or auditory perception, memory, or even eyesight (Blachman, 1991; Wagner, Torgeson, & Rashotte, 1994)! This predictive power has been demonstrated not only among English-speaking children but also among Swedish-speaking children (Lundberg, Olofsson, & Wall, 1980), Spanish-speaking children (deManrique & Gramigna, 1984), French-speaking children (Alegria, Pignot, & Morais, 1982), Italian-speaking children (Cossu et al., 1988), Portuguese-speaking children (Cardoso-Martins, 1995), and Russian-speaking children (Elkonin, 1973). In fact, phonemic awareness is a common underlying ability that transfers from one language to nearly every other language (Riches & Genesee, 2006).

THE COMPONENTS OF PHONEMIC AWARENESS

Phonemic awareness should be viewed not as one grand skill but as a continuum of understandings, ranging from simple to complex awareness of the sounds, or phonemes, of our language (Ball & Blachman, 1991; Byrne & Fielding-Barnsley, 1989). At the least complex of the spectrum, to be considered phonemically aware, children are able to discriminate whether words are the same or different and to appreciate, recognize, or produce rhymes. Intermediate skill occurs when children can blend sounds, for example, when they can segment the /m/ from the word *man*. One of the most difficult tasks in phonemic awareness is to isolate speech sounds. This task requires the child to tell the beginning, middle, or ending sound in the word *soap*, or to say the word *lake* without the /k/.

The actual hierarchy, from easiest to the most difficult, for phonemic awareness competence is shown in the following box.

Because phonemic awareness has been shown to be strongly related to success in beginning reading, it should be developed as early as possible in children—

Learning the Alphabet
with Music

*www.songsforteaching.com/
avni/alliterativebooks.htm*

The hierarchy of phonemic awareness competence

The hierarchy of phonemic awareness competence

1. **Awareness of words.** Child can tell which of two words is longer.

   EXAMPLE: *hamburger or cat*

2. **Ability to rhyme.** Child can rhyme simple one-syllable words.

   EXAMPLE: *What word rhymes with* pin?

3. **Ability to blend.** Child can put together an onset and an ending speech sound (rime) given by the teacher.

   EXAMPLE: */bl/ and /ack/. What would these two sounds be if they were put together?*

4. **Ability to segment into words and syllables.** Child can take apart compound words, put words into syllables, and break up a sentence into words.

   EXAMPLE: *What are the words in this sentence: "The boy went after the ball"?*

5. **Ability to identify beginning sounds (onsets).** Child can listen to a series of words and identify which has a target sound.

   EXAMPLE: *Which of the following begins like* baby—mud, lake, *or* ball?

6. **Ability to isolate.** Child can listen to a word and identify a target sound.

   EXAMPLE: *What is the first sound in* sat?

7. **Ability to delete.** Child can say a word after deleting a specific sound.

   EXAMPLE: *How do you say* pat *without the /p/?*

8. **Ability to segment words into phonemes.** Child can tell the sounds in a word in order.

   EXAMPLE: *What are the three sounds in the word* got?

9. **Ability to substitute and manipulate beginning phonemes.** Child can replace speech sounds with others.

   EXAMPLE: *Can you change the word* bake *by changing the first sound to an /m/?*

10. **Ability to substitute middle and ending phonemes.** Child can replace middle and ending speech sounds (rimes).

    EXAMPLE: *Can you change the word* cot *to another word by changing the middle sound to an /a/?*

---

preferably in their preschool years—through a variety of stimulating language activities (Foorman et al., 1998). These activities are not intended to replace children's interaction with meaningful oral and written language. Rather, the activities presented here are designed to supplement and enhance such experiences by providing a means of focusing children's attention on a critical aspect of the structure of their language—its phonemic base. Reading aloud to students, developing language experience charts, using predictable books for guided and shared reading, and journal writing are also invaluable reading experiences in a comprehensive early literacy program. These activities will be explored in later chapters.

Research suggests that phonemic awareness activities can maximize children's potential for a successful learning-to-read experience (Adams, Foorman, Lundberg, & Beeler, 1998; Cunningham, 2007). Therefore, teachers of young children should recognize the importance of contributing to their students' phonemic awareness by spending a few minutes every day engaging students in playful oral language activities that emphasize the sequence of sounds in language.

WWW

Phonemic Awareness
Games and Activities

www.readwritethink.org

DEVELOPING PHONEMIC AWARENESS

a useful way to plan phonemic awareness activities is to focus on the nature of the specific phonemic skill that needs to be developed. For example, an activity may require a child to merely listen to a poem or song, match words by sounds, isolate a word by sounds, blend individual sounds to make a word, substitute sounds within a word, or even break a word into its parts. Each of these tasks is a part of phonemic awareness, yet these tasks are not equally difficult, as indicated by the hierarchy in the preceding box.

The first task, then, is to determine which components of phonemic awareness the student needs to develop, based on the results of an assessment such as the Phonemic Awareness Assessment Device (see Appendix E). You can then provide experiences and activities to enhance the child's specific need.

see appendix E

General Guidelines

At this point, we discuss some general considerations for facilitating phonemic awareness. First, it is important to explain the task in which you want the students to be engaged through explicit instruction, adequate modeling, and demonstration. For example, if you want the students to listen for all the words that have the /m/ sound, first you must clearly say the *name* of the letter and then model how to say the /m/ *sound,* asking students to carefully watch your mouth. It is then helpful to pass out small hand mirrors to have students experiment with saying the /m/ sound and observing what they do with *their* mouths when producing the sound. Ask the students to share orally what their mouths do—in their own words. Demonstrate how to tell when the /m/ sound is heard in various words by giving some examples. The students will be more likely to succeed in this task as subsequent examples are given for practice.

Early Literacy Screening, Tools, and Activities

www.getreadytoread.org

Second, you must analyze the task to be performed and, initially, keep it as simple as possible. Are you asking the students to listen for syllables or sounds, and exactly which sound should the students be looking for and where in the word will it be found? Also, beginning with simple two- and then three-phoneme words will help reduce confusion: for example, rather than using a lesson that asks students to listen for the speech sounds in the words *blend, green,* or *brook* (which have blended consonants and other sounds that require more sophisticated discrimination), start with continuous sounds, such as those in *man, sat,* or *nut.*

From Research to Practice

Not every child needs intensive training in phonemic awareness. In kindergarten, children needing guidance in this area, for example, would be those who cannot rhyme and who don't recognize that *pat* and *pick* start with the same sounds. In first and second grades, children who cannot segment initial sounds or detect different beginning, middle, and ending sounds need additional help. On the other hand, children who already manifest phonemic awareness can be exposed to the phonics and decoding activities presented in Chapter 5.

For children who do need such assistance, many research-supported methods help develop the spectrum of phonemic awareness skills (Griffith & Olson, 1992; Yopp & Yopp, 2000). Initially, children should be exposed to poems and nursery rhymes, especially those in which the rhymes are the most obvious feature of the poem. At first, the poems should be read for enjoyment and understanding. Then, if the poems are recited with a great deal of emphasis on the words that rhyme, almost to the point of exaggeration, the children's attention will be drawn to that rhyme. Eventually the children should be able to generate their own rhyming words. Engagement in this type of activity should be accompanied by a good deal of humor and poetic license, as "hot dog" is rhymed with "rot hog" in the opening vignette of this chapter. Certain children's literature lends itself to this type of language play. Books such as *The Hungry Thing* by Jan Slepian and Ann Seidler

(1985), for example, engage children in rhyming while having a rollicking good time. Examples of additional appropriate books are found in Appendix A.

Many phonemic awareness activities can take the form of games or puzzles and can be used in an informal, relaxed setting. For example, students may be asked to identify pictures for which the beginning sound or the beginning consonant and vowel sound for the picture is the same. Given pictures of a pig, a pin, a pot, and a sun, a child would put the pig, pin, and pot pictures together or tell which picture doesn't fit and explain why on the basis of his perception of sound. When students can do this easily with pictures, they can often listen to just three or four words and tell which ones go together and which ones do not. This can evolve into selecting which middle sounds go together and which ones do not fit (mat, can, lap, bit) and then performing the same tasks with ending sounds (cup, map, lot, pep).

Another game would be to look for objects in the classroom or in magazines whose names begin with a certain sound. Extra challenge and interest can be added by going through the alphabet, finding one thing that starts with /a/, then /b/, and so on. You will need to specify the sound and, if it is a vowel, indicate whether it is long or short.

A similar game is "I Spy with My Eye," except instead of suggesting colors, the teacher declares, "I spy with my eye something beginning with /th/" or "I spy with my eye something ending with /k/," choosing word parts and sounds that the students can handle without too much difficulty.

Children also enjoy counting the number of syllables in words that are pronounced for them in exaggerated fashion. The names of children in the class provide personal examples for this activity. Counting with young children can be done in a variety of ways, such as tapping the table with a pencil, clapping each syllable, or noting the number of times their jaws move up and down as the word is said. It is always most difficult for children to count the syllable in a one-syllable word, as they often attempt to make discrete speech sounds into syllables, so it is helpful to warn them, "Here's a tricky one!"

As students become proficient with activities in which they are asked to recognize how the sounds in words differ, they are often ready to manipulate the sounds themselves. For example, you can give them a word to say (e.g., *bat*) and ask them to say it without the /b/. For children who have difficulty with this, you can begin with compound words, having them leave off one of the syllables, which is a phonologically easier task. For example: "Say *baseball*. Now say it without the *ball*." "Say *baseball*. Now say it without the *base*."

When the students become comfortable with manipulating the sounds in words, but before they have been taught the actual letters, you can begin to use colored markers or small pieces of paper on **sound boxes** (also referred to as Elkonin boxes; Elkonin, 1973) to represent the sounds (see Figure 4.1). Each different sound should be represented with a different color, but the same color does not always have to match a particular sound. For example, if you have red, yellow, green, blue, and purple markers, the word *map* may be represented by blue–green–red, red–purple–yellow, or green–blue–red, as long as each sound has a different color. A word like *pop*, using the same patterning, may be represented by green–blue–green, red–yellow–red, or blue–red–blue, as long as the beginning and ending colors are the same. Using this approach, students may be given problems to solve such as the following:

> If this says /go/, make it say /so/. (*Students should replace the first marker with one of another color.*)

> If this says /kite/, make it say /cat/. (*Students should replace the second marker with one of a different color; silent /e/ is not represented at this early stage. See Figure 4.1.*)

▷ **see appendix A**

WWW

Preschool Games and Rhyming Activities

www.mothergoose.com

■ sound boxes

figure	4.1	Sound boxes.

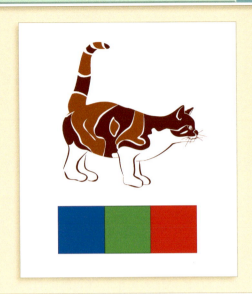

Eventually students can progress to deleting a sound:

If this says /man/, make it say /an/. (Students should remove the first marker.)

When students have learned the sounds and graphic representations (letters) for some consonants and a vowel, they can use letter cards or tiles for these activities, and they will have progressed to reading and spelling words. Sound boxes can also be used for activities that focus on phonemic awareness skills such as counting the number of words in a sentence or syllables per word. Additional activities for teaching phonemic awareness are presented later in the chapter.

PHONEMIC AWARENESS AND ENGLISH LEARNERS

teachers of English learners should be aware that some sounds regularly used in English are not part of other languages. In general, the sounds listed in Figure 4.2 are not part of the other languages' regular sound systems, although they may occur in certain dialects or at times only in the middle positions of words. These sounds are difficult for beginning speakers of English for two reasons. First, children have not had any practice recognizing these sounds or discriminating them from others; native English-speaking children have heard the sounds and have had practice discriminating them since infancy. Second, because children have not used these sounds before, they have had no practice pronouncing them. To help students in these language groups master these sounds in readiness for later phonics instruction, point out the discrepant sounds to the children, exaggerate their pronunciation, and help students learn to pronounce them through practice with repetition of each sound used in the beginning, middle, and end positions of words. Specifically, help non–English-speaking children become phonemically aware by using the guidelines shown in the box on the following page. Be consistent when using phonemic awareness–related terms; for example, avoid describing the same skill as segmenting, separating, and/or dividing, which may confuse English learners (McIntyre, Hulan, & Layne, 2010).

Although the sounds used in English may not be part of an English learner's home language, a plethora of research has shown that phonemic awareness in one language can be applied to a second language (Cisero & Royer, 1995; Comeau,

figure	4.2	English sounds not occurring in other languages.

LANGUAGE	ENGLISH SOUNDS NOT PART OF OTHER LANGUAGES							
Chinese	dg	th	v	z				
French	ch	ee	j	ng	oo	th		
Greek	aw	ee	i	oo	schwa			
Italian	a	ar	dg	h	i	ng	th	schwa
Japanese	dg	f	i	th	oo	v	schwa	
Spanish	dg	j	sh	th	z			
Native American (some dialects)	l	r	st					

Cormier, Grandmaison, & Lacroix, 1999), and that phonemic awareness in one language predicts reading ability in a second (Durgunoglu, Nagy, & Hancin-Bhatt, 1993; Lindsey, Manis, & Bailey, 2003; Quiroga, Lemos-Britton, Mostafapour, & Beringer, 2002). Activities such as using traditional Spanish songs and poems, Spanish tongue twisters (called *trabalenguas*), and Spanish read-aloud books will help their English reading ability; these findings are evidence of Jim Cummins's linguistic interdependence hypothesis, suggesting a transfer of skills between languages (Yopp & Stapleton, 2008).

Most teachers, however, will teach English learners phonemic awareness in English and are encouraged to use the activities described in this chapter with some enhancements. For instance, classroom teachers should become familiar with sounds that are not found in English learners' home language and conduct focus phonemic awareness lessons on those sounds. In addition, as much as possible use words that English learners are familiar with, or incorporate visual aids to make these new words comprehensible, which will increase English learners' English proficiency.

During these activities, teachers should also slow down the rate of pronouncing the words/sounds. As readers who have listened to a foreign language know, often it is difficult to decipher the gaps between words and sentences; trying to figure out the individual phonemes can be extremely difficult (Vaughn & Linan-Thompson, 2007). As several researchers (Anthony, Lonigan, Driscoll et al., 2003;

Helping non–English speakers

For Spanish speakers:

- Assess students' phonemic awareness in Spanish, not English.
- Allow students to do many language activities in Spanish.
- Continue to develop proficiency in Spanish.
- Help students see similarities in the two language systems.
- Use pictures that have the same sounds in both languages (e.g., *gato, cat*).

For non–alphabetic language speakers (e.g., Mandarin):

- Treat students as English speakers who are struggling to "hear" the sounds in English.
- Speak slowly and use lip, mouth, and tongue training in an active, fun approach.
- Intensify instruction three to four times a week, building on students' progress in oral English.

Articles for Teaching Phonemic Awareness to English Learners

www.readingrockets.org/ reading-topics/english-language-learners

www.colorincolorado.org

Mott & Rutherford, 2012; Pufpaff, 2009) remind us, teachers of English learners should include lessons on phonemic awareness that focus on word-level and syllable skills before moving on to phonemic awareness skills. An activity that helps students learn awareness of words is to read students a sentence aloud and then read it a second time with a word omitted; see if students can figure out what word was deleted. Clapping the number of syllables and repeating a word with a syllable replaced (e.g, *today —> tonight*) are two activities that will develop syllable knowledge (Mitchell, 2008). Encourage student practice in producing new sounds by modeling how to make these sounds and asking students to repeat the sound. Two excellent online sources for articles on teaching phonemic awareness to these students are Reading Rockets (for English learners) and Colorín Colorado (a bilingual Spanish–English site); web addresses are provided in the margin. For more information on phonemic awareness and English learners, see Peregoy and Boyle (2009).

PHONEMIC AWARENESS AND STUDENTS WITH SPECIAL NEEDS

today's classrooms may include students with an array of challenges and abilities, including severe learning disabilities, developmental disabilities, speech and language disabilities, and Asperger's syndrome. Thus, it is important that all classroom teachers be prepared to educate these students. Literacy instruction for students with special needs should include the vital skills, such as phonemic awareness, that are part of a balanced literacy program (Cohen & Spenciner, 2008; Durán 2006). Schnorr (2011) adds that some students with developmental disabilities may not demonstrate phonemic awareness before they begin reading. However, older readers will show knowledge of these concepts, indicating that these readers have acquired phonemic awareness by learning to read. Finally, research by Stevens and colleagues (2008) reveals that when provided with two daily periods of explicit phonemic awareness instruction as part of an integrated curriculum, students in K–1 special education did better on post-test assessments than did students who were not provided with this direct instruction.

Many phonemic awareness activities can take the form of games or puzzles and can be used in an informal, relaxed setting.

For students with special needs, many of the activities described shortly can be useful in building phonemic awareness. Problems can occur because of processing difficulties (auditory, language, or phonological) or memory or attention difficulties. Modifications for students with these special needs can be helpful, and Mitchell (2008) offers several suggestions. To focus on listening skills, teachers can play recordings of familiar songs or poems, and then play them again but occasionally replacing key words with nonsense words, which students can identify. Another listening activity is to sit students in a circle. The first person whispers a word or phrase to the next person, and this continues until the last person says the word out loud. These activities, along with the phonemic awareness activities described in the Phonemic Awareness Activities section, can be effective for students with special needs.

Studies have also focused on the use of naturalistic instruction, which incorporates structured and free play, to develop phonemic awareness (Culatta, Hall, Kovarsky, & Theadore, 2007; Hansen, Wadsworth, Roberts, & Poole, 2014). Research with students with reading problems (Snowling & Hulme, 2012) and language-related difficulties using computer-based auditory training (Loo, Bamiou, Campbell, & Luxon, 2010) provides further evidence of the positive role of phonemic awareness training; readers interested in learning more about this research should consult literature reviews by Al Otaiba, Puranik, Ziolkowski, and Montgomery (2009) and Gillon (2007).

PHONEMIC AWARENESS ACTIVITIES

The activities presented here are categorized into word beginnings, sound isolation activities, blending activities, and sound substitution activities. The list of activities in this chapter is by no means exhaustive. You may easily modify any of the preceding and following activities by choosing sounds that are developmentally appropriate for your students or discovering similar ways to draw your students' attention to the particular sounds in our language that they are ready to consider. You may also use the websites identified in Appendix C to access many other phonemic awareness activities.

> **see appendix C**

Rhyming

A C T I V I T Y

THE SHIP IS LOADED WITH . . .

(ADAMS ET AL., 1998)

Seat students in a circle. To begin the game, say, "The ship is loaded with *bugs.*" Then toss a ball or a beanbag to a child in the circle. That child must produce a rhyme (e.g., "The ship is loaded with *jugs*") and throw the ball back to you. Repeating the original rhyme, toss the ball to another child. Continue the game this way until students run out of rhymes. Then begin the game again with another rhyme (e.g., "The ship is loaded with *mice*").

When the students have become good at rhyming, each child can throw the ball to another child instead of back to you. The second child must then continue rhyming with the word suggested by the first child.

WWW

Rhyming Word Activities
http://teams.lacoe.edu/teachers/

> The ship is loaded with bugs. (*jugs, mugs, tugs, rugs*, etc.)
>
> The ship is loaded with mice. (*rice, lice, spice, dice*, etc.)
>
> The ship is loaded with cats. (*rats, bats, mats, hats*, etc.)

Word Beginnings (Onsets)

A C T I V I T Y

THE SOUND SONG

The lyrics to the following song are sung to the tune of "Mary Had a Little Lamb."

> Taco starts with /t/, /t/, /t/
>
> /t/, /t/, /t/—/t/, /t/, /t/
>
> Taco starts with /t/, /t/, /t/
>
> Other words do too!
>
> It has to start with /t/, /t/, /t/
>
> /t/, /t/, /t/—/t/, /t/, /t/
>
> It has to start with /t/, /t/, /t/
>
> The next word comes from YOU!

The class first sings the song together using a beginning sound chosen by you, and then you ask a volunteer to contribute another word that begins with the same sound. To add enjoyment and an extra challenge, the words can be themed, such as all food words or all boys' names or all flowers, and so forth. Finally, when students are adept at discriminating beginning sounds, ending sounds can be targeted using the same song.

PICTURE SORTS

Picture sorts allow students to create their own personal books or posters of objects that begin with the same sound. For instance, students can draw objects that start with the same sound as objects they have at home or find in the classroom. If you use learning centers, give students magazines from which they can cut and paste objects that start with the same sound (dentists' and doctors' offices are a good source for old magazines that otherwise would be thrown out). For English learners, the use of visuals will help them build not only their phonemic awareness but also their vocabulary. Picture sorts can be adapted to include pictures of objects that have the same vowel or ending sounds.

CHARADES

Create a 3 x 5 card file that contains pictures of children performing actions (verbs) for every beginning consonant sound (e.g., *bat* for /b/, *walk* for /w/, *wink* for /w/). Introduce these words using charades for each action and allow students to copy the actions. When several words and their actions have been introduced, include charades as part of your reading lesson routine. Distribute the cards to the students. (If they are unable to recognize their picture, help them identify it.) Invite each child to perform the charade indicated on the card while the remaining students try to guess the action by first stating the *word* being acted out, then the *beginning sound* of that word, and finally, the *name of the letter* that makes that sound. (*Note:* This is an effective phonemic awareness activity for English learners, who will increase their speaking vocabulary at the same time.)

ACTIVITY

Comparing and Contrasting Sounds

WHAT'S THE SOUND?

Students can be given a word and asked to tell what sound occurs at the beginning, middle, and end of that word. The following song, sung to the tune of "Old MacDonald," asks students to think about the placement of sounds in words.

BEGINNING SOUNDS

What's the sound that starts these words:
PAPER, PEN, and POUND?
[wait for a response from students]
/p/ is the sound that starts these words:
PAPER, PEN, and POUND.
With a /p/, /p/ here, and a /p/, /p/ there,
Here a /p/, there a /p/, everywhere a /p/, /p/
/p/ is the sound that starts these words:
PAPER, PEN, and POUND.

MIDDLE SOUNDS

What's the sound in the middle of these words:
RAIN, LAKE, and CANE?
[wait for a response]
/a/ is the sound in the middle of these words:
RAIN, LAKE, and CANE.

With an /a/, /a/ here, and an /a/, /a/ there,

Here an /a/, there an /a/, everywhere an /a/, /a/

/a/ is the sound in the middle of these words:

RAIN, LAKE, and CANE.

ENDING SOUNDS

What's the sound at the end of these words:

NECK, ROCK, and SEEK?

[wait for a response]

/k/ is the sound at the end of these words:

NECK, ROCK, and SEEK.

With a /k/, /k/ here, and a /k/, /k/ there,

Here a /k/, there a /k/, everywhere a /k/, /k/

/k/ is the sound at the end of these words:

NECK, ROCK, and SEEK.

Blending Sounds

SECRET LANGUAGE

Prepare a list of about 30 one-syllable words containing middle or ending vowels. The first 10 should have only two phonemes, or speech sounds (e.g., *go* or *me*); the other 20 should have three phonemes (e.g., *kite* or *chin*). Explain to the students that you are going to tell them some words in a secret language, and they must try to guess what you are saying. Then say the word in a stretched out manner (e.g., "ch—i—n"), and see if they are able to blend the word back into a whole unit. *Note:* It is sometimes helpful to use a rubber band to graphically illustrate how an item can be stretched out, then snapped back to its normal position and still be exactly the same thing.

Taking this activity to another level of difficulty, make another list of common one-syllable words two or three phonemes long. The words should sample a variety of sounds represented by different vowel and consonant combinations. Demonstrate once more how words can be segmented into their sound components, and then invite pairs of students to say each word in the secret language for their partners to guess, as you observe individual success with this task (Griffith & Olson, 1992).

WHAT AM I THINKING OF?

Tell the class you are thinking of an object or an animal. Give them a sound clue: segment each of the sounds of the word, articulating each sound slowly and deliberately. The students then must blend the sounds together to discover the animal or object you are thinking of. For higher motivation, and especially to make the game accessible to English learners, you may use picture cards, hiding them from the students; give the segmented clue and turn the picture around to allow them to check their answers. Finally, real toys or objects in a grab bag heighten suspense when you look into the bag and say, "I see a d—o—ll in here. Can anyone tell me what I am looking at?"

Substituting Sounds

SPEECH SUBSTITUTION CHANT

A voice projection exercise used by drama students makes an excellent activity to practice consonant substitution while reinforcing a variety of vowel sounds. For this activity, have the students stand up at their desks. The leader (the teacher, initially) presents a consonant sound or blend such as /d/. Then the students project, at the top of their voices, but without shouting,

Da day dee doe doo! [three times]

Another leader is chosen, who gives a different consonant sound (e.g., /ch/). The students chorus:

Cha chay chee cho choo! [three times]

For musical variety, the chant can be sung using one note, raising the note for every succeeding consonant, or a simple tune can be created for the chant.

Segmenting Sounds

A C T I V I T Y

WHAT'S THE SOUND?

Start with beginning sounds (onsets) that can be held for a long period of time, such as /m/, /s/, or /f/, or the parts of the syllable that follow the initial sound (rimes) that are very common, such as /-at/, /-ock/, or /-an/. Introduce the game by saying, "I am going to say some words. If you hear one that starts with /m/, show me a thumbs-up sign. If it starts with any other sound, show me a thumbs-down." Begin mostly with words that start with the target sound. Slowly introduce words with other initial or ending sounds. Have students then volunteer to contribute words that others either accept or reject.

Finish the game by showing students pictures of objects that have the target sound and invite them to help you make all the sounds (segment). Discuss similarities and differences in sounds. These pictures can be gathered into a file or bound into a class book.

BEGINNING, MIDDLE, END

This game, which is derived from *Words Their Way* (Bear, Invernizzi, Templeton, & Johnston, 2004) expands on the concept of phonemes in differing locations within words. First, write letters of a word on cards or sentence strips and place them on a pocket chart facedown. Tell the students the word (e.g., *hat*), then sing the following song to the tune of "Are You Sleeping, Brother John?": "Beginning, middle, end; beginning, middle, end / Where is the sound? Where is the sound? / Where's the *hhhh* in *hat*? Where's the *hhhh* in *hat*? / Let's find out. Let's find out." Then, have students come and pick where they think the sound is (e.g., where is the card with the /h/ sound?).

Manipulating Phonemes

A C T I V I T Y

(DEVRIES, 2015)

MOVING THE TILES

1. Cut seven 2 x 3 tiles from seven different colors of poster board. You can laminate the pieces so they can be used over a period of time.
2. Lay out three different colored tiles in front of the student (e.g., blue, red, and yellow). Assign a letter sound to the blue tile (e.g., the /b/ sound), another sound to the red tile (e.g., the short /a/ sound), and a third sound to the yellow tile (e.g., the /t/ sound).
3. Ask the student to say the word that the tiles make.
4. Remove the blue tile and replace it with a white tile, calling it the /f/ sound. Again ask the student to pronounce the new word. Do this activity first with three tiles and later add the fourth tile to form four-letter words.

The following are lists of suggested words. Note that the child is to replace the initial sound of each of the words in the list with the sound of the letter that is on top of the list.

S	M	B	P	H
pat	late	late (bait)	sat	sat
pit	neat	meat	meat	pit
neat	ball	call	ball (Paul)	meat
ham	bat	sat	bat	Sam
boar	bake	cake	ham	late
bake	fan	fill	bill	neat
ring	cart	sit	sit	ball
round	night	soar	cart	cart (heart)
right	round	turn	cup	fill
		pear	bear	farm
		wig	wig	fair
		site		night (height)

RECOMMENDATIONS FOR TEACHING PHONEMIC AWARENESS

phonemic awareness activities can be a first step toward literacy for many students, especially for English learners, who are just becoming aware of the sounds in a new language. Such activities enable students to become aware of the sounds that will later help them learn to decode; these activities must be motivational and appropriate to the developmental level of the learners. For this reason, we include the following suggestions to ensure that initial instruction in phonemic awareness becomes a joyful entree into literacy, especially for students who are at risk.

1. For younger students, do not accompany sound activities with visual cues if this combination seems confusing for them. Although evidence suggests that presenting sounds for words with their visual counterparts is more effective for children who already know the letters of the alphabet (Hohn & Ehri, 1984; National Institute for Literacy, 2001), students who have not yet reached this level of phonemic sophistication may be better served by concentrating just on the sound units alone (McCracken & McCracken, 1996; Yopp, 1995).

2. Make the lessons playful—a "treat," not a "treatment." Students will enjoy playing with language if the activities are presented by an enthusiastic, fun-loving teacher, rather than a "drill sergeant" bent on completing exercises and performing rote memorization as quickly and efficiently as possible.

3. Encourage social interaction wherever possible. Social interaction tends to heighten language development. Therefore, invite students to learn from one another by asking them to help each other. Provide many opportunities for students to turn to a neighbor and discuss their answers, work with letters and sounds in small groups, and participate in other team-building activities. Make sure the environment is absolutely safe, so there is never the fear of blurting out the "wrong" answer.

4. Invite students to experiment with language. When asking for rhyming words, beginning sounds, and other sound units, encourage students to manipulate the sounds and construct their own nonsensical and delightful words and humorous sounds. Demonstrate a sense of playfulness and wonder at the English language, which will be infectious among students.

5. Support the self-esteem of your students. If the phonemic awareness activities are conducted in group settings, some students will inevitably do better than others. Therefore, a cooperative, relaxed environment is mandatory—no "put-downs" from classmates allowed, *ever!* Also, students for whom hearing sounds is difficult should be given lots of support, demonstrations, and modeling to ensure that they, too, have a positive language experience. Above all, allow for individual differences and expect a tremendous amount of individual variation in hearing speech sounds. Although many students can achieve phonemic awareness by the end of first grade, not all students do so. In time, however, with continued motivational lessons and practice, most students become adept at this vital precursor to reading.

6. Do not overdo it. Research indicates that a teacher should spend no more than 20 total hours in phonemic awareness activities for the whole school year (Duke & Block, 2012; National Institute of Child Health and Human Development, 2000). Remember, phonemic awareness should be part of a balanced literacy program and not the main focus of instruction.

SUMMARY

Phonemic awareness is the bridge between spoken and written language. Some children construct this bridge for themselves without explicit instruction, but many others do not. Children who lack this bridge often find that written language remains a puzzle; they try to solve the puzzle for only so long before giving up on the task of learning how to read. It isn't too long before "I can't!" becomes "I won't!"

Experiences must always be provided so children can understand reading as an activity undertaken for enjoyment, new understandings, and information gathering. But, for that joyful activity to be accessible, learners must also be able to see how the sounds of the language are patterned into words. Extensive research over the past 30-plus years has supported the conclusion that phonemic awareness is the most important prerequisite to understanding the nature of the relationship between letters and sounds. Young children, therefore, must be exposed to experiences that invite them to blend sounds into words and to segment words into sounds before further instruction in the sound–symbol representations—phonics instruction—can take place.

Fortunately, this instruction need not be conducted through a series of repetitious workbook pages or unexciting exercises completed in isolation at the child's desk; rather, these activities can be highly motivational group activities accomplished through enjoyable language play and game-like tasks that are naturally appealing to students. Although many students come to school with much experience with language through a print- and language-rich environment in their homes, for others such activities may bridge a gap in their language development and ensure a bright future of success in attaining literacy.

questions FOR JOURNAL WRITING AND DISCUSSION

1. Explain how you would describe the difference between "phonemic awareness instruction" and "phonics instruction" to the parent of a child about to enter school.
2. Examine the scope and sequence of three basal readers used in area elementary schools. Determine which phonemic awareness activities are taught and

when. Describe how the three series differ. Based on your knowledge of phonemic awareness, discuss which you prefer and why.

3. The mother of a 4-year-old child asks you what she can do, besides reading aloud, to help her child become ready for kindergarten literacy instruction. What can you tell her? Visit some of the websites listed in Appendix C that are appropriate for phonemic awareness and parents. How could such sites encourage parents to help their children become ready for early literacy instruction?

suggestions   FOR PROJECTS AND FIELD ACTIVITIES

1. Look for a folk song, nursery rhyme, or camp song that would be suitable for developing a component of phonemic awareness in young children. Adapt the song as necessary. Teach the song to a small group of kindergarten children. What did you observe about the increased awareness of the identified sounds through this exercise?

2. Browse through some children's books in your local bookstore or library without first researching which ones are recommended in Appendix A of this book. With phonemic awareness in mind, identify those books that would help students develop awareness of sounds in our language. Write down the names of the books you have identified, and then compare them with the ones in Appendix A or other lists compiled by literacy professionals.

> see appendix A

3. Interview two kindergarten teachers. Ask them what activities they use to teach phonemic awareness to their students. If possible, observe several of these activities. How do they differentiate these activities for their English learners? Summarize your findings for your classmates.

4. Administer the Quick Phonemic Awareness Assessment Device in Appendix E to a child in kindergarten. From this assessment, determine which components of phonemic awareness the child has mastered and which he or she needs to develop. Then select three activities from this chapter and from one of the resources (Appendix B) or websites (Appendix C) to enhance the specific needs of the child.

> see appendix E

> see appendix B

> see appendix C

Phonics, Sight Vocabulary, and Fluency

5

focus questions

How does direct, systematic instruction in phonics fit into a comprehensive approach to literacy?

How should sight vocabulary be taught?

What are the key components of a model phonics program?

What is fluency, and how does it relate to comprehension?

What are the most important factors to keep in mind when teaching phonics to beginning readers? To English learners? To students with special needs?

in the classroom

gina has selected a book from the public library and is sitting cross-legged on the carpet, looking forward to the same enjoyment she has always experienced when she reads in class or when her grandmother reads to her. She puts a chubby finger on the cover of the book and tries to sound out the title: *The Laughing Cow*. Although she is able to sound out the word *cow* and knows the beginning sound for the word *laugh*, the peculiar spelling of the word *laugh* makes no sense to her. Gina scratches her head and discards the book, having just received a tiny dent in self-confidence in her burgeoning reading ability.

INTRODUCTION

Learning to read can be a bewildering experience for children, and teaching reading can be a confounding instructional ordeal for educators. Children become frustrated when they cannot easily figure out the words in a language that is not always user-friendly. The task is difficult, too, because figuring out new words is an undertaking entirely different from any of a child's other previous experiences.

Literature-loving educators, on the other hand, often become disenchanted with stilted early basal readers. They know that constructing meaning from written words is the whole purpose of reading, and yet the material they are asked to use to teach reading, given the limited number of words young children can recognize, is not nearly as exciting as *The Laughing Cow* in the preceding vignette. Many children come to school knowing the meanings of most of the words to which they are exposed, yet they still cannot read, because their young brains are still discovering patterns and analogies in sounds and words. Children grow as readers as they learn decoding strategies for identifying words that they do not immediately recognize; then they will be able to access the thousands of delightful children's books awaiting them in the public library.

The good news is that there is help for both teachers and beginning readers who need to accomplish these tasks together. To help students recognize words as quickly as possible, teachers can show them the relationship between visual cues (letters) and the speech sounds they represent. This is what the teaching of phonics is all about. After words have been identified and have been met many times, they can be recognized automatically, in much the same way that we automatically recognize an old friend or the dilapidated Honda driven by our next-door neighbor. Words that are automatically recognized become part of a child's **sight vocabulary,** and further strategies for identification are no longer required for those words. When a child arrives at this automatic stage with most of the words she encounters, we can say that he has "learned to crack the code." The child can then move on to more interesting reading tasks.

sight vocabulary ■

WHY PHONICS INSTRUCTION?

Two of the five essential elements in reading programs, according to the National Reading Panel, are phonics and fluency. Direct phonics instruction provides a path to fluent reading. Whereas phonemic awareness instruction focuses a child's attention on the way sounds are sequenced in a language, phonics instruction helps students associate letters with those sounds. The purpose of phonics instruction is to teach beginning readers which printed letters and letter combinations represent certain speech sounds heard in words. By themselves the letters are meaningless squiggles. They become meaning-bearing units only when the child applies and adheres to the system of signals. In applying phonics skills, or the system of signals, to unknown words, the reader blends a series of sounds dictated by the order in which particular letters occur in the printed word. When a child can do that, she can **decode** or unlock the code (Beck & Juel, 1995). Then, as the child writes her own ideas, she learns to listen to the sounds within words as they break up words to **encode** them. A child who listens to sounds and makes approximations as she writes will become a better decoder as she reads (Cunningham, 2012). A child needs this ability to arrive at the pronunciation of printed word symbols that she does not immediately recognize. If the child does recognize the word, however, she will not need to waste time puzzling over the speech sounds represented by the individual letters. Explicit instruction in phonics, then, can lead to fluent reading.

- decode

- encode

Proper use of phonics strategies is one of a number of ways a child may figure out words he does not immediately recognize (Blevins, 2006). Phonics instruction is concerned with teaching letter–sound relationships and patterns as they relate to learning how to figure out unfamiliar written words; such careful attention to the sequence of letters in words can also contribute to spelling ability (Shefelbine, 1995). Because English spelling patterns tend to be deceptive, a child sometimes arrives at only a close approximation of the needed sounds. The child may, for example, come upon the word *broad* and pronounce it so that it rhymes with *road* or pronounce *give* so that it rhymes with *five*—both reasonable analyses of these irregular words. If the child is taught to take a flexible attitude with the sounds, however, and if the child is reading for meaning, he will frequently go back and correct these errors. After several such self-corrections, the child will not repeat the same error with these words.

Phonics instruction has long been considered a useful tool in learning how to decode automatically so that students can begin to attend to more interesting reading tasks (Adams, 1990; Beck, 2006; McIntyre & Freppon, 1994; Stanovich & Stanovich, 1995; Vellutino, 1991). As in the case of native English speakers, phonics instruction has been found crucial to the reading success of English learners (Lasaux & Siegel, 2003). Moreover, a large body of evidence suggests that children who quickly develop efficient decoding strategies find reading enjoyable and thus read more; on the other hand, those who get off to a slow start in learning to decode words rarely catch up to become strong readers (Stanovich, 1986). In fact, Juel (1994) asserts that students who fall behind in first-grade reading have only a one-in-eight chance of ever catching up to grade level. As discussed in Chapter 3, Stanovich calls this phenomenon the "Matthew effect," in which skilled decoders get better and better through practice while poor decoders lag further and further behind. Although many teachers believe that students who fall behind will catch up in future grades, Clay (2000) concurs with Stanovich; through her own research and experience, she finds that a child's reading level compared with classmates at the end of first grade is pretty much the same level at which that child will be reading, relative to classmates, two years later.

Phonics continues to be misunderstood by many educators. The reason for this misunderstanding becomes clear when we look closely at the language. English spelling appears imperfect when we look at strange words like *might, cough, should, colonel, sleigh,* and *machine;*

The purpose of phonics instruction is to teach beginning readers which printed letters represent specific speech sounds heard in words.

Phonics Skills Chart

www.scholastic.com/teachers/
article/teach-phonics-skills-chart

indeed, it is challenging, for we use 26 letters to spell 44 to 48 different sounds in more than 250 different ways! This is only one side of the matter, however. If we look at all the words that are spelled regularly (such as these simple consonant, vowel, consonant, or CVC, words: *bat, cat, pat, mat; hit, bit, fit*) and set about organizing the irregular spellings into groups and patterns suitable for beginning readers (*could, would, should*), we find that it is not so bad after all. And if we begin instruction with the most regular words, it is not overwhelming for most students to master the exceptions when they are introduced one at a time and continually reinforced. The following statistics support this belief:

- Approximately 50 percent of English words are regular.
- Another 37 percent (like the word *could*) have only one sound that is represented irregularly, and this is usually close enough to connect the written letters and sounds with the actual word.
- The remaining 13 percent (like the word *ocean*) must be memorized as sight words.
- Even irregular words are stored in memory with the letter or letter pattern/sound correspondences (e.g., *light*).

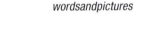

Word and Picture Activities

www.bbc.co.uk/schools/
wordsandpictures

This brings us to what may at first glance seem a startling contradiction: the "un-phonic" spelling of so many common words constitutes the strongest argument for beginning formal instruction with the regular phonics of English spelling! Why? Simply because if our spelling system is regular a good percentage of the time, it would seem logical to begin with the regular system before taking up the exceptions. When the child learns, at the beginning, one consistent pattern after another, she rapidly gains confidence in understanding the code. If we were to teach a dozen words only by using rote memorization or by the sight-word method, a child might still confuse *but* and *got,* but when he has been taught all the sounds of the letters, he understands why these series of letters spell each word. His recognition of the two words at a glance becomes easier than it would have been if he had memorized each word using only word configuration, without the benefit of previous training in letter sounds. The sight-word method of rote memorization may be appropriate for teaching only those high-frequency words that cannot be easily sounded out, sometimes referred to as "snurks" (see p. 85) or "outlaws."

BEGINNING PHONICS INSTRUCTION

the first few weeks of formal phonics instruction can have remarkable results. Through all the previous reading experiences the child may have had, she may have met many words she did not instantly recognize, and at various times she may have tried one or more of the following strategies:

- skipped the word
- asked someone
- guessed the word
- applied any phonics rules she knew
- sounded out the first letter and then guessed the rest of the word
- tried to figure out the word from the context

Clearly, the beginning reader has many available options for figuring out unknown words. Some of these—such as random guessing—are not always the most efficient choices. Learning to read, then, involves sorting through a cafeteria of choices and discarding those that are ineffective for the situation, while using others that allow for success. To make maximum progress, the beginning reader must acquire three closely related skills at approximately the same time, as discussed in Chapter 1:

- using letter–sound relationships
- acquiring a sight vocabulary of immediately recognized words
- gaining meaning from context

Beginning readers read words in four ways: by sight (memorization), by sounding out each letter, by **analog** (comparing patterns to ones already known), and by guessing from the context (Gaskins et al., 1997). Although there is not always a one-to-one correspondence between letters seen and speech sounds represented, learning to read is facilitated when a child understands the sound–spelling relationships in English.

■ analog

To illustrate how word learning works, let's focus on what the child gains by learning about spelling–sound relationships. Assume that the child has already been taught through phonemic awareness exercises or other early literacy activities to do the following:

- visually recognize the letters *m, k, a, r*
- visually recognize the inflection *–er*
- associate /m/ with the sound it represents at the beginning of the words *mat, man,* and *mud*
- differentiate the /m/ sound in *man* from the /p/ in *pan* and the /c/ in *can*

Phonics instruction then invites the student to become a "word detective," to think to himself in the following way when encountering the unfamiliar word *marker:*

> When I see the letter m I think of the /m/ sound because this is the same sound that begins the words *mat* and *mud*. It ends with an *er* just like *mother* and *father.* The middle of the word has an *ark,* just like the word *bark.* The word must be *marker,* a word I have heard before. Yes, it must be, because it's talking about art and drawing, so that makes sense.

Although this process may seem unreasonably slow and tedious, remember that such thoughts go through a child's mind much more quickly than we can read about the phenomenon. As subsequent instruction focuses on other sounds represented by medial vowels and vowel combinations, the child gains new skills that enable her to decode other unfamiliar words, with each mastered skill providing a greater degree of independence and **automaticity,** or fluency, in reading. The main point to keep in mind is the eventual goal of making the decoding process almost second nature so that students can expend much more of their time and energy thinking about and enjoying and/or learning from the material they are reading.

■ automaticity

Every new gain the student makes in learning to read will, with practice, transfer to future authentic reading situations. For instance, after several weeks of early instruction, a child will have encountered some words so frequently that he will recognize them instantly. Once this happens, he will never again puzzle over the speech sounds represented by those words. Similarly, with much exposure to reading words that incorporate new phonics patterns to which he has been introduced, he will be capable of detecting and using the pattern for other, similar words (Heilman, 2005).

APPROACHES TO SOUNDING OUT WORDS

esearch has shown that direct, systematic teaching of phonics elements is more effective than the "hit-or-miss" variety that was once taught only incidentally, when phonics elements were encountered in reading and writing situations (Shefelbine, 1995). With repeated modeling of the following process, students can learn how to sound out unfamiliar words using phonics. The teacher of emergent readers should start with one or two regular words (never snurks) that contain a targeted sound and model this approach several times every day, using this script or a similar one:

> Listen. When I say a letter, I'll say its sound. I'll keep saying its sound until I touch the next letter. I won't stop between sounds.
>
> [Example: *Sssssaaaaat* or *Mmmmmaaaaaannnnnnn.*]
>
> My turn to sound out this word.
>
> [Put a finger under continuous sounds for 1 to 2 seconds and under stops (sounds that are *not* continuous, such as /b/, /c/, /d/) for just an instant.]
>
> Now you sound out this word with me. Get ready.
>
> [Touch each sound, and say them with the students.]
>
> Your turn. Sound out this word by yourselves. Get ready.
>
> [Touch the word, and let students make the sounds.]
>
> [Encourage individual students to try it with new words.]

When students can blend two or three sounds to make a word, they are ready to tackle more difficult blending tasks through phonics and analog. Although such strategies should be modeled incidentally whenever new words are written on the board, they should also be taught directly by explaining the use of the following approaches:

- Make the first sound. Add the second sound. Put them together before adding the third sound.

  EXAMPLE: "p," "pa," *pan.*

- Make the first sound and add the rime or the string of letters that follows the initial sound in a word, usually starting with a vowel.

  EXAMPLE: "b," "oat," *boat.*

- Look at the rime first and put it together backward.

  EXAMPLE: "eam," "dr," *dream.*

- Identify the word parts you know.

  EXAMPLE: "re," "turn," "ing" equals *returning.*

- Ask yourself: What do I know about this word?

  EXAMPLE: *Appointment:* I know the word *point.*

- Ask yourself: Do I know any word that looks like this word or any part of it? Does this word make sense?

  EXAMPLE: *Glisten:* I know the word *listen* that looks like this word. Adding a *g* makes it *glisten.* That sounds right.

Following are two activities that will also help students learn to sound out words.

Sound Switch

A C T I V I T Y

(FITZPATRICK, 1997)

Gather two sets of large alphabet cards and a wall pocket chart (see Figure 5.1). Distribute an alphabet card containing one letter to each child. Place letters in a pocket chart to form a simple one-syllable word (e.g., *get*). Point to each letter in the pocket chart and have students say each sound. Then ask students to blend the sounds to form the word. Next invite volunteers to create new words by placing

| figure | 5.1 | A pocket chart. |

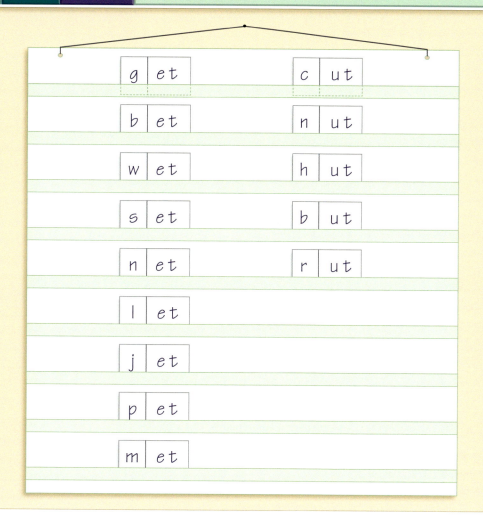

A pocket chart is a large, heavy paper, cloth, or plastic chart that has pockets into which words or sentences may be placed.

their letters over those in the pocket chart, such as placing the letter *b* over the *g* to form the word *bet*. Have students blend the new sounds together and decide whether the word is one they know (nonsense words are acceptable). Place a new one-syllable word in the pocket chart, and repeat the process.

Roll Call Variation

A C T I V I T Y

(STRUIKSMA & ZUNO, 2003)

This activity is designed to pique student interest by using their names in the lesson. Using a pocket chart and student names on sentence strips, bring your class to the front and take roll (first names). Then tell the students that you are going to play a "fun game" with their names. Select a subset of names (e.g., 6 to 10) and read them again; however, cover up the initial letter of names that begin with a consonant (e.g., David —> Avid), while reading names that begin with a vowel as is (Ashley —> Ashley). Then, using a letter students have been studying, place the letter in the front of the new names (e.g., Ravid, Rashley), allowing the students to blend the new names as a group.

When first introducing roll call variation, it may be wise to keep it simple. Blends that begin names (e.g., Brian) can be hard for students to hear, plus it can be confusing to know what to delete (e.g., *Br,* or just the *B?*), while names that start with irregular patterns (e.g., Thomas, Christina) could also be problematic. However, this can be a great opportunity for teachers to discuss the linguistic diversity that students bring to school. Analyzing names such as Joe (/j/ /o/) and Jose (/h/ /o/ /s/ /e/) will show students that all of their home languages (and phonemic skills) are valued in your class.

A SEQUENCE FOR TEACHING PHONICS

a phonics program consists of many concepts. In any systematic program, the skills must be arranged in a teaching sequence that allows the young reader to build confidently on what he already knows. Figure 5.2 presents one possible sequence for teaching phonic skills (Hendricks & Rinsky, 2007). Consult your district or state content standards to determine the sequence of skills that teachers in your area are expected to follow.

figure	5.2	A phonics sequence.

KINDERGARTEN

Begin phonemic awareness training during kindergarten and include sounds with and without letters, beginning with consonant sounds; introduce blending and segmentation skills; introduce a few high-frequency sight words; introduce onsets and rimes with a few short vowels. Start with the letters that are dissimilar, the most useful, and introduce the lowercase letters first. An acceptable sequence is:

m, t, a, s, i, f, d, r, o, g, l, h, u, c, b, n, k, v, e, w, j, p, y,

T, L, M, F, D, I, N, A, R, H, G, B, x, q, z, J, E

FIRST GRADE

Review consonants and vowels and letter combinations, and introduce useful rules: endings (*ing, er, s*), consonant digraphs (two letters that cannot be separated): *sh, ch, th, wh, ph;* blending and segmentation skills reinforced, frequently used sight words, the final "e" rule, consonant blends (two consonants that can be separated): *fl, fr, sl, sm, sn, sw, sc, sk, sp, sq, st;* then *bl, br, cl, cr, dr, gl, gr, pl, pr, tr, tw;* then *scr, spl, spr, str;* the "ed" ending; then vowel digraphs (*ai, ay, ee, ea, igh, oa, ow, ew, oo, ow, ou, oi, oy, au,* and *aw*), r-controlled vowels (*ar, er, ir, ur,* and *or*), transformations of open and closed syllables (*me* becomes *met; go* becomes *got*) and generalizations for "y" at the end of a word.

SECOND GRADE

Complete highest-frequency words; review and complete single-syllable phonics patterns, then generalizations for *c* and *g* at ends of words; silent consonant clusters: *kn, wr, gn, mb, ght, ng, nk, tch;* continue word parts (prefixes and suffixes, root words) and dividing words into word parts or syllables.

THIRD GRADE

Reinforce syllabication and word parts, and introduce word derivatives (e.g., *interrogative* comes from the word *interrogate*).

Source: Hendricks & Rinsky, 2007.

TEACHING SIGHT VOCABULARY WORDS

a s discussed previously, sight vocabulary is the group of words that the reader recognizes immediately, without having to decode. As students begin learning how to read, they must be taught some common sight vocabulary words known as **high-frequency words** at the same time they are learning how to decode. High-frequency words include *both* very widespread "snurk" words, such as *the,* that children are commonly confused by (see Figure 5.3) and should not attempt to decode while reading or "invent" while writing, and easily decodable words such as *but.* Approximately 50 percent of the words children see are from the 100 to 150 words in the high-frequency word group (see Appendix G). The larger the store of words a child can recognize immediately without analysis, the more rapidly and fluently he can read a selection (Burns, Roe, & Ross, 1999).

■ high-frequency words

> **see appendix G**

Become very familiar with a list of high-frequency words, such as Fry's List of Instant Words (see Appendix G), so that you can select meaningful words for classroom activities. Plan activities that focus directly and repeatedly on the words, introducing one or two new words each day and reinforcing them through games, daily stories, and "words of the week." Incorporate new words into reading and writing activities on successive days for review. Each week, the cumulative list of words should be reviewed.

Abstract words are usually more difficult for children to learn than concrete words, especially for English learners. It is important, therefore, to help students associate these words with something meaningful. For example, when teaching the word *of,* one might provide pictures of a piece *of* pie or a box *of* cookies and label the pictures. The students would then be asked to do one of the following activities:

WWWW

Reading Games

www.adrianbruce.com/ reading/games.htm

■ find or draw their own pictures and label them
■ chant or cheer the word (e.g., *of! of! of!*)
■ write the word

Finally, four or five words would be selected from the reading each week and added to a **word wall** or bulletin board in the classroom (see Figure 5.4). A word wall or word chart is a listing of high-frequency words that are of interest to students or are being studied in a reading lesson. These words can be connected by meaning, patterns, or sounds or can simply be words that students hear and want to know how to spell. Such words usually follow a specific pattern in their beginning sound (onsets), vowel sounds, or ending sounds; other times they are words related to some topic under study. This collection of words can be alphabetized or placed under the corresponding letter of the alphabet. The words should be prominently displayed on the wall or on a bulletin board so that the students may add to the list whenever they think of an appropriate word, and the words may also be used for reference during writing activities. These words should be practiced a

■ word wall

figure	**5.3**	Common snurks (sight words) for early readers.

give	woman	word	the	saw	there	what
love	work	of	any	laugh	walk	some
great	to	was	choose	because	does	pear

| figure | 5.4 | A word wall inspired by discussion of the five senses. |

TASTE	SEE	SMELL	FEEL	HEAR
sweet	dirty	flowery	smooth	squeaky
yummy	round	nasty	rough	loud
sour	pretty	stinky	slimy	soft
yucky	red		dry	
	nice		bumpy	

few minutes each day at the beginning of a word lesson by having the students (1) stretch them out and read them together, (2) chant or cheer them three times, and/or (3) write them in isolation and context. Also, all words with the same spelling patterns should be starred (Cunningham & Cunningham, 2002).

There is more than one way to set up a word wall, but it should contain these features:

- The wall used should be the wall the students can see most easily when they write.
- The word wall should be dynamic. New words should go up and old ones should come down on a regular basis.
- Easily confusable words (e.g., *that, what*) can be placed on different colors of paper.
- Students should be encouraged to use the word wall as a resource when they are trying to sound out a word.
- The word wall should be referred to several times as students are reading, writing, speaking, and listening.

The following is a list of activities involving these word walls that should be used on a daily basis (Cunningham, 2013):

- Ask students to use the word wall to find a word that rhymes with the word you say.
- Write the first letter you are thinking of on the board. Say a sentence, leaving out a word that begins with that letter. Have the students find the word on the word wall, and then chant the answer together.
- Dictate a simple sentence using word wall words.
- Play "Be a Mind Reader." Give several clues to the word you are thinking of. Clues should be based on the meaning or function of the word or on the phonic elements. The first clue is always, "It's one of the words on the word wall." Each clue should narrow down the possibilities until the last clue has been given and every student can guess the word.

A MODEL PHONICS PROGRAM

d irect phonics instruction with decodable text is an essential component of a reading and writing program during the early grades, but it is also important that students be involved in authentic reading, writing, speaking, and listening activities as they acquire the tools for cracking the code. Without this rich glimpse of literacy, phonics instruction is often ineffective (Freppon & Dahl, 1991). Effective teachers use direct, systematic (explicit) but also indirect (embedded or implicit) methods to impart knowledge about decoding words (Mesmer & Griffith, 2005). For example, teachers may use short **minilessons** (5–8 minutes) (see Chapter 9) to introduce specific concepts, skills, and phonics generalizations in a systematic way. Lessons can also take advantage of the **teachable moments** that can crop up in any print-rich classroom during the day, providing indirect instruction in decoding through vehicles such as language play, story writing, the language experience approach (see Chapter 9), or word walls. In general, an effective phonics program consists of all the components described in this section (Stahl, 1992; Trachtenburg, 1990).

■ minilessons

■ teachable moments

Phonemic Awareness

Teachers reinforce understanding of the way sounds form words in our language by having students who need this reinforcement segment words into their component parts or sounds and by having them blend sounds into words through activities in which they try to discover how to sound out new words. These skills underscore the need for mastery of the subskills of phonemic awareness.

Useful Phonics Generalizations

Teachers teach the phonics concepts, patterns, and generalizations that have the most consistency and utility in helping students decode and spell unfamiliar words. It is best to teach these rules by *showing* students the pattern and having *them* tell what is analogous about the words through word sorting activities (Ehri & Robbins, 1992). Eighteen phonics generalizations that have been shown to be most useful to students are presented in Figure 5.5 (Baer & Dow, 2013; Clymer, 1963).

Whole–Part–Whole Instructional Sequence

To make sure students get the phonics support they need and also understand how these skills are useful to them, teachers use the reading of a chart with a poem or a very short story using controlled language (the first whole), followed by the teaching through direct instruction of the phonics generalization in isolation (the part), and then have students apply these elements immediately into **decodable text** or text that incorporates all the elements with which students are familiar (the second whole). For example, the following brief poem (original source unknown) is used to illustrate the phonics generalization silent *e* (the first whole):

■ decodable text

> I hang around the ends of words,
> So silently I sneak.
> But, oh the magic I perform,
> To make the long vowel speak!
>
> I hang around the end of words
> And I am not to blame
> 'Cause I just like to pinch the vowel
> And make him say his name.

After reading the poem with the class, the teacher creates a list with the students of words from the poem that include a long vowel sound, and asks the students if they notice any patterns in the words (the part). Students notice that some (not all) of the words that end with silent *e* also include a long vowel sound. This is an important discussion, as students should be led to realize that silent *e* is a generalization, not a rule, and that one example is that some words that include a long vowel sound use a vowel team, as opposed to the silent *e*. Sight words—such as *come* and *love*, which end with an *e* but do not include a long vowel sound, should also be discussed. Direct instruction for the students providing practice in applying the silent *e* generalization would follow.

After the discussion of the poem, the teacher guides the students in the reading of a decodable book that focuses on the silent *e* (the second whole). Further discussion of the generalization and the need for flexibility takes place during the reading.

Coaching

Coaching can be the key to success in helping a child learn to sound out new words (Clark, 2004). For example, if a child is unable to decode the word *reptiles,* the teacher can coach by providing the following cues:

- Cover up the *s.*
- The ending is a part of a word family you know *(–ile).*
- The first *e* makes a short sound.
- Break the word into two parts *(rep* and *–tiles).*
- What kind of animals are snakes and crocodiles? Think about the first part of the word *(rep).* What word would make sense here?

In all cases, to coach effectively the teacher needs to ensure that students have the appropriate background knowledge and vocabulary.

Minilessons

Teachers can use brief (10–12 minutes), directed lessons to concisely present concepts about phonics generalizations (e.g, one of the 18 presented in Figure 5.5) and skills to students who, through observation and other forms of assessment, appear to require it. They can then offer opportunities for students to apply these new skills in reading and writing situations. Here is an effective minilesson structure:

WWW

Phonological Awareness,
Phonics, and Sight Word
Scope and Sequence Chart

*https://www.collaborative
classroom.org/sites/default/
files/media/pdfs/sipps/sipps_
beg_sands_3rd_ed.pdf*

1. Connect a new generalization to known information, such as other phonics generalizations.
2. Provide direct instruction on the unfamiliar generalization.
3. Have students practice the new generalization.
4. Have students apply the generalization in their reading and writing.

The SIPPS (Systematic Instruction in Phonological Awareness, Phonics, and Sight Words) program provides a useful scope and sequence of such lessons.

Application of Phonics Skills

Through a variety of enjoyable activities such as word play, journal writing (see Chapter 9), word sorts (see Chapter 6), the building of word walls, rhyming books (see Appendix A), and sound matching exercises (see Chapter 4), students reinforce what they are learning about phonics concepts and generalizations.

Use of Different Types of Literature

WWW

Online Stories for Phonics

www.theideabox.com

Three types of literature (predictable texts, high-quality trade books, and decodable texts) are necessary for an effective early literacy program, although predictable texts should not be used in phonics instruction.

figure   5.5   Eighteen useful phonics generalizations.

1. An *r* gives the preceding vowel a sound that is neither long nor short. *(car)*

2. Words having double *e* usually have the long *e* sound. *(meek)*

3. In *ay* the *y* is silent and gives *a* its long sound. *(say)*

4. When *y* is the final letter in a word, it usually has a vowel sound. *(baby)*

5. When *c* and *h* are next to each other, they make only one sound. *(chair)*

6. *Ch* is usually pronounced as it is in *kitchen, catch,* and *chair,* not like *sh.*

7. When *c* is followed by *e* or *i,* the sound of *s* is likely to be heard. *(ceiling)*

8. When the letter *c* is followed by *o* or *a,* the sound of *k* is likely to be heard. *(coat)*

9. When *ght* is seen in a word, the *gh* is silent. *(light)*

10. When two consonants are side by side, only one is heard. *(running, hymn)*

11. When a word ends in *ck,* it has the same last sound as in *look. (clock)*

12. In most two-syllable words, the first syllable is accented. *(monkey, lion)*

13. If *a, in, re, ex, de,* or *be* is in the first syllable in a word, it is usually unaccented. *(begin, decide)*

14. In most two-syllable words that end in a consonant followed by a *y,* the first syllable is accented and the last syllable is unaccented. *(baby)*

15. If the last syllable of a word ends in *le,* the consonant preceding the *le* usually begins the last syllable. *(table)*

16. When the first vowel element in a word is followed by *ch, th,* or *sh,* these symbols are not broken when the word is divided into syllables and may go with either the first or second syllable. *(teacher)*

17. When there is one *e* in a word that ends in a consonant, that *e* usually has a short sound. *(bed)*

18. When the last syllable is the sound /r/, it is unaccented. *(runner)*

Predictable texts. **Predictable texts** contain much rhyme, rhythm, and repetition and are used to teach concepts of print and English grammar and to provide an enjoyable language experience when read to young children. Although they have a critical role in a balanced reading program, *they should not be used for direct phonics instruction.* With such texts, students delight in trying to predict or "guess" words, thus delaying the acquisition of important phonics skills. (See Appendix A for a list of predictable books suitable for beginning readers.)

■ predictable texts

▶ **see appendix A**

High-quality trade books. High-quality **trade books** are used to build academic knowledge K–12, to build vocabulary, and for enjoyment. A variety of both fiction and nonfiction trade books should be made available to students. In early literacy instruction, to encourage listening comprehension and enjoyment, teachers should always read such literature aloud and discuss it (see Appendix A). While such books do not build phonics knowledge per se, they provide motivation for students to learn phonics so they can access such books themselves.

■ trade books

Decodable texts. **Decodable texts** are small, beginner-oriented books used to immediately apply phonics elements that have just been taught and need practice. They provide novice readers with easy textual experiences because they contain plenty of repetition and fewer complex patterns than trade books (Cole, 1998). Good decodable texts also use many high-frequency words that become sight words (see Appendix A).

■ decodable texts

Teachable Moments

Teachers often give spontaneous phonics lessons as they engage students in literacy lessons (prompted by questions the students ask about strange words or alliterative sounds), as they model how to spell the words that come up in brainstorming sessions leading to writing activities, and as the students themselves embark upon writing.

GENERAL SUGGESTIONS FOR PHONICS INSTRUCTION

a few important constraints should always be considered when planning a phonics lesson. Such behaviors and practices are compatible with exemplary phonics instruction. Although some have been mentioned briefly earlier in the chapter, they are worth discussing here.

Make sure children possess the necessary prerequisites in phonemic awareness for the letter–sound correspondence being introduced. If students cannot hear the sequence of sounds in words, training in phonics will be a frustrating and futile experience for them. Therefore, careful assessment of the phonemic awareness abilities of each learner is vital to any successful phonics program (see phonemic awareness assessment devices in Appendix E). Students who are deficient in this area may be regrouped and should receive further individualized phonemic awareness training.

see appendix E

Always base phonics lessons on knowledge students already have about print. Children come to school with a variety of language and literacy backgrounds. Some have a wide repertoire of rap songs they can chant; others have heard the entire collection of Dr. Seuss books. Being aware of the background knowledge of your learners can be an important way to connect, create discussions, and begin instruction (Stahl, 1992).

Focus students' attention on detecting patterns, not memorizing rules. The human brain is a detector of patterns, not an applier of rules (Cunningham, 2012). Phonics rules are abstract (e.g., "*i* before *e* except after *c*") and although children may memorize them, true application involves a stage of development beyond that of most young children. Therefore, a phonics lesson should help students learn to flexibly apply generalizations, for example, by directing students' attention to the letter sequences and combinations that are similar to ones they already know and to the ones in the words being introduced.

Knowledge of phonics may be developed by the use of inductive learning of phonics generalizations through analogy. Using this strategy, after ensuring basic understandings in CVC-type words, you will present words without pronouncing them, and then ask students to pronounce the words, using their knowledge of similar appearing words. A combination of inductive and deductive phonics learning strategies as opposed to simply deductive strategies shows promise in increasing student motivation (White, 2005).

Provide plenty of opportunities for students to experiment with printed words through use of experimental spelling. Experimenting freely with the way sounds and letters go together in our language is an excellent way for students to reinforce their understanding of and familiarity with the alphabetic principle and how it works (Stahl, 1992). The Common Core State Standards support the use of invented spelling in the lower grades and do not specify that students should be able to correctly spell grade-appropriate words until fourth grade. For example, for first grade, CCSS.ELA-Literacy.L.1.2.e specifies that students "Spell untaught words phonetically, drawing on phonemic awareness and spelling conventions" (p. 26) while for grade 4, CCSS.ELA-Literacy.L.4.2.d requires students to "Spell grade-appropriate words correctly, consulting references as needed" (p. 28) (NGACBP & CCSSO, 2010).

Be sure that teaching of new letter–sound correspondences is done explicitly and clearly. In direct and clear phonics instruction, you will isolate a particular sound or combination of sounds and show the student how the sound is associated with a particular letter or combination of letters. Such instruction also includes first showing the student exactly how to blend those sounds by modeling and then guiding the child's practice.

Provide immediate practice with newly taught letter–sound correspondences through decodable text containing the new letter patterns. Like any other skill that is being learned, automatic application of phonics skills will not flourish without consistent practice. Therefore, students should be given immediate practice reading materials containing words with the new phonics elements to which they have been introduced. To the extent possible, avoid stilted, contrived decodable material that is limited in motivational appeal (e.g., The fat cat sat on the mat). Also, use quality children's literature for reading aloud to students and for building listening comprehension many times throughout the day.

Focus on achieving sight vocabulary skills so students can soon concentrate on comprehension and enjoyment. Teach students strategies to use when encountering an unknown word; these strategies were delineated earlier in this chapter. Also, show students what you do when you encounter a new word by modeling chunking, use of affixes, and comparing patterns in the unknown word to patterns in known words. Also, teaching some high-frequency words as sight words will add to students' arsenal of words they do not have to sound out and will help them sound out unfamiliar words through analogy as their skills grow. When you teach sight words to English learners, the sight word must be part of the student's oral-language repertoire, or its meaning must be taught to the English learner at the time of instruction (Helman & Burns, 2008).

Integrate phonics instruction into a total, joyful reading program. Phonics instruction is only a small part of reading instruction, and, for many, the least exciting part at that. Phonics should never be considered a goal in itself, but rather a functional *means* to a goal. The ultimate goal of reading instruction should always be to allow students to easily decode the words they encounter so they can not only begin to read for academic purposes but also experience the joy of a most worthwhile pastime (Adams, 1991). An exemplary reading program includes not only phonics instruction but also a variety of strategies for reading and writing and motivational activities associated with outstanding children's literature, so students will want to pursue reading far beyond the classroom doors. Readers who struggle often do not perceive reading as a meaning-making endeavor, and instead see reading as a task-based activity—perhaps reflecting the reality that these readers are often bombarded by an array of phonics activities as opposed to a balanced literacy program focused on deriving meaning from text (Brown, 2010).

   The CCSS clearly signal the place of phonics instruction within the larger English language arts curriculum: Foundational Skills in Language Arts are not outlined until after the Reading Standards for Literature and Reading Standards for Informational Text, thus communicating that Foundational Skills are not prerequisites to other components of the CCSS English Language Arts standards but rather need to be taught in concert with them (IRA, 2012).

CASE EXAMPLE

Mrs. Rodgers teaches a phonics lesson

Although the sequence shown earlier in Figure 5.2 tells *what* to teach *when,* it gives very little information about *how* to structure a phonics lesson. This case study explains how to orchestrate a phonics lesson by describing how one first-grade teacher, Mrs. Rodgers, designs a typical reading lesson that includes an exemplary phonics component. She is aware that phonics instruction is one small but essential part of a first-grade language arts curriculum, and she makes sure that students accomplish all aspects of her state grade-level standards, including the listening comprehension and oral-language development standards.

1. Reread yesterday's story from a chart or from a decodable book *(1–2 minutes)*

Students read chorally or in pairs the short story that was introduced on the preceding day. That story allows students to apply a new letter–sound combination immediately in a real reading situation. This repeated reading of the story affords deeper comprehension for the students and a chance for the teacher to revisit the story for differing purposes. Mrs. Rodgers briefly asks the students comprehension questions to assess their understanding of the story, being careful to ask both literal and inferential questions.

2. Learn a new letter–sound combination *(1 minute every other day)*

Mrs. Rodgers writes the new letter–sound combination /sp/ on the board with a directional arrow underneath. She points under the letters and pauses. Then she moves her finger under the letters and says the sound. Then she says, "I'll say it again," and repeats the sequence. Next she says, "Now say it with me." She points under the letters and pauses. She says, "Ready?" as she quickly moves her finger under the letters. The students say the blend with her. Then she says, "Your turn." She repeats the process while the students look at the letter–sound combination and say the sound.

3. Review activity *(2 minutes)*

These first-graders have finished learning about each of the short vowel sounds; they can now identify and write each one. Mrs. Rodgers shows the students pictures of the following five items to remind them of the short vowel sounds: half an apple, yellow Jell-O, an inch of licorice, a lollipop, and bubble gum. (Each student was given one of each of these food items to eat when they were originally introduced.) The students cheerfully chant the names of each of these food items, exaggerating the vowel sounds in each case. As the food items are shown and the names called out, Mrs. Rodgers asks the students to help her sound out the words as she writes them on the board. For each sound, the students then brainstorm some other words that contain these sounds.

4. Oral blending and segmentation *(2–3 minutes)*

Mrs. Rodgers leads this activity in a direct yet playful way. The activities in this part of the lesson are carefully sequenced and require a great deal of support for the students. Using a cake-mixing analogy, Mrs. Rodgers again introduces the consonant blend *sp.* She has written each of the two letters on small squares of white construction paper. She takes the *s* paper and drops it into a bowl, as the students watch and make the /s/ sound; she does the same for the *p* paper. She then pretends to "stir" these two consonants, telling the students to "stir and say" the sounds. Then she dramatically plucks a third paper from the bowl that contains both the letters *sp.* The students say /sp/. The teacher has graphically demonstrated that a blend is two consonant sounds blended together. Students then practice the blending by holding their arms in a bowl shape on their desks. With their writing finger, they then trace each consonant inside their "bowl." They then pull their finger across the letters, combining, or blending, the sounds. Mrs. Rodgers then invites them to "stir and say," and they make the /sp/ sound several times (see Figure 5.6).

5. Instruction in blending *(2–3 minutes)*

Blending is considered the "heart and soul" of any phonics instruction. Students must be taught how to blend sounds by seeing and hearing the blending process modeled explicitly. Mrs. Rodgers has several words written on her pocket chart in the reading corner of her classroom. These words, for encoding and decoding, include *spot, spin, sped, spill,* and *spam.* She says the words aloud, slowly and deliberately, while showing them to the students. Then she writes the onsets on the

Spelling 6

A WRITER'S TOOL

focus questions

Why is it important for classroom teachers to be able to identify the stages of spelling development in their students?

Describe some ways that teachers can support children's spelling development.

How can experimental spelling be used to help students understand the alphabetic principle?

Chrissy, a child in the third month of first grade, has just drawn an elaborate picture of a princess in an ornate ball gown surrounded by a swarthy prince, an adoring fairy godmother, and a lake full of swans. Ms. Sullivan, after offering profuse praise for the effort Chrissy put into her creation, asks the child if she would like to label the characters in her picture. Chrissy shakes her head vehemently, sighing, "I don't know how to write. Can you write it for me?" Ms. Sullivan smiles and urges, "Just have a go. What is the first sound you hear in *Cinderella?*" Chrissy scratches her head and hisses *S–s–s* and then laboriously pens an *s* and, later, an *n*. Chrissy is well on her way toward discovering that English writing is an alphabetic system in which letters are used to indicate speech sounds and, subsequently, meaning. She is just beginning to learn how to spell—and how to read and write.

Chrissy and very young children like her are engaged in experimental spelling, which, when carefully analyzed, can tell teachers much about the developmental stages of writing and how beginning readers and writers develop important aspects of the English sound system.

LEARNING AND APPLYING SPELLING SKILLS

because of limited instructional time and a curriculum crowded with critical content, young teachers often question the value of teaching spelling in today's classrooms. Is spelling an antiquated subject given the use of spell checkers and the public's seeming indifference to misspelled words? Does spelling still have a place in the curriculum, or is it an anachronism compared with the intense focus on other literacy skills considered more crucial?

There is a synchrony in learning to read, write, and spell. Development in one area generally coincides with advances in the other two areas. All three evolve in stage-like progressions that share important conceptual dimensions (Bear, Invernizzi, Templeton, & Johnston, 2012). Studies support a significant link between writing, spelling, and reading development (Graham & Hebert, 2010). Moreover, the Common Core State Standards (CCSS) as well as other state and district standards call for the same spelling goals for students as those that have been in place for many years. For example, the CCSS appropriately connect spelling to writing. One of the anchor standards for Language (CCSS.ELA-Literacy.CCRA.L.1) requires students to "Demonstrate command of the conventions of standard English capitalization, punctuation, and spelling when writing" (NGACBP & CCSSO, 2010, p. 25), and CCSS. ELA-Literacy.L.2.2D requires that students be able to "Generalize learned spelling patterns when writing words," for example, *tough* and *rough* (NGACBP & CCSSO, 2010, p. 26).

Noting exactly how children learn to spell is instructive. Children give evidence of learning to spell by advancing through a sequence of increasingly complex understandings about the organizational patterns of words. Although memory is involved, children learn by progressively inferring the principles by which English words are spelled. A growing body of research has revealed that knowledge of letter patterns, or orthographic knowledge, develops as a process in children and that this development is reflected in their errors or experimental spelling (Reed, 2012). Research also suggests that children also use early spelling experimentation to "break the code" of reading (Gentry, 2004).

Just as reading comprehension is enhanced by an ability to recognize words quickly and accurately, students' writing is also supported by proficiency in spelling. Along with instruction in the writing process (see Chapter 9), students must be taught letter formation and stage-appropriate spelling skills in order to produce longer, more detailed pieces of writing. Moreover, research suggests that children can develop correct spelling more quickly if spelling skills are taught beginning in first grade in authentic writing contexts (*Every Child a Reader*, 2000).

Children who are taught spelling explicitly and systematically, and who are also invited to apply their skills in a variety of writing contexts, learn to spell more quickly and accurately than children who are simply given random lists of words to memorize by rote. Additionally, systematic instruction in the following has been found to create more efficient spellers (Gentry, 2008):

1. sound syllable segmentation ("con-tam-in-a-tion")
2. sound–symbol association or **sound mapping**—matching letters and letter combinations with sounds ("Open: /o/ /p/ /e/ /n/.")   ■ sound mapping
3. spelling patterns ("Hmmm, *glisten* and *listen* have the same patterns!")

THE STAGES OF SPELLING DEVELOPMENT

In learning to communicate in written form, a child generally goes through five basic **developmental spelling stages** (discussed below) in roughly the same sequence, despite differences in educational background, although children often achieve elements of two or more of these stages at any one time. However, the rate of progress through the stages varies from child to child. Children first string letters together at random. Then, when they have discovered the alphabetic principle, they begin to "sound out" words. Finally, they progress to one-syllable spelling patterns, syllable combinations, and the spelling of meaningful word parts, or *morphemes* (Bear et al., 2012).   ■ developmental spelling stages

A quick assessment device called the "Monster Test" can help teachers determine the approximate developmental spelling stage of their learners (see Appendix E for this and other spelling assessment materials).   ▶ **see appendix E**

Researchers have used various hierarchies to describe the stages children go through as they learn to spell. The next sections present two ways of looking at the developmental stages of spelling. To familiarize you with these two distinct views, Figure 6.1 compares how the stages of spelling are discussed in the literature, each focusing on differing components of spelling.

Gentry's Stages

According to Gentry (2008), children go through the following stages when learning to encode: precommunicative, prephonetic or preliterate, phonetic or letter-name, transitional or within-word, and conventional spelling or syllable juncture stages.

The precommunicative stage

The initial stage of spelling development is called the **precommunicative stage** and occurs about the time the child learns the alphabet and discovers that words are composed of letters, although the child may have little or no concept at this time of exactly which letter stands for which sound. In this stage, the young child strings scribbles, letters, and letter-like forms together without any knowledge of associated phonemes, and the writing may proceed from top to bottom and right to left, or even randomly across the page. A child at this stage might compose a story about an elephant, and to our eyes, the story will be virtually unintelligible and look something like the writing shown in Figure 6.2(a).   ■ precommunicative stage

| figure | 6.1 | Stages of spelling development: Two views. |

Gentry (1985, 2006)	Bear, Invernizzi, Templeton, and Johnston (2012)
PRECOMMUNICATIVE STAGE	**EMERGENT SPELLING**
Learning the alphabet	Random letters
Scribbles and letter-like forms	Mostly upper-case letters
Mostly unintelligible	Learning directionality
PREPHONETIC STAGE	**LETTER NAME–ALPHABETIC SPELLING**
Alphabetic principle	Alphabetic principle known
Left-to-right orientation emerges	Short vowels and consonants appear
One letter used for dominant sounds	Abbreviated spellings
PHONETIC STAGE	**WITHIN-WORD PATTERN SPELLING**
Refinement of earlier stage	Long vowels and r-controlled words
Basic spelling patterns and families	More complex vowel and consonant patterns
Many sight words known	Awareness of homophones
TRANSITIONAL STAGE	**SYLLABLES AND AFFIXES SPELLING**
Most words spelled correctly	Inflectional endings applied
Aware of visual aspects of words	Can spell multisyllabic words
Vowels in each syllable	Know common affixes
CONVENTIONAL STAGE	**DERIVATIONAL RELATIONS SPELLING**
Mastered English orthography	Aware of Greek and Latin roots
Have a spelling consciousness	Examine etymologies of words
Can apply rules of orthography	Can spell related forms of words and alternative spellings

The prephonetic, or preliterate, stage

prephonetic stage ◼ The second stage of spelling development is called the **prephonetic stage** and evolves when the child begins to understand the alphabetic principle that letters have certain sounds that form words. About this time, too, the child becomes aware of the left-to-right orientation of the English language. This stage is somewhat like the stage in very young children's language acquisition when they use one word to symbolize a whole idea or concept, such as "Up!" to mean "I would like you to pick me up, Daddy." Similarly, in this stage, one letter—usually the most dominant sound—is used to represent the entire word. In the previously addressed story about an elephant, a child in this more advanced stage might represent the word *elephant* with an *L* because the name of the letter *L* sounds most like the beginning of the word *elephant*. The story might look like the writing in Figure 6.2(b).

The phonetic, or letter-name, stage

phonetic stage ◼ The third stage, the **phonetic stage,** is in many ways a refinement of the earlier prephonetic stage. Children continue to use letter names to represent sounds, but at

| figure | 6.2 | Sample illustrations of the stages of spelling development. |

(a) Precommunicative stage.

(b) Prephonetic, or preliterate, stage.

(c) Phonetic, or letter- name, stage.

(d) Transitional, or within-word, stage.

this more advanced stage, they also use consonant and vowel sounds for each spoken syllable. Although certain vowels and silent letters may be omitted, the child seems to have become aware of some of the basic spelling patterns and families in the English language through the visual attention afforded by reading. She may also have memorized some sight words. Now the story about the elephant could look like the writing in Figure 6.2(c).

The transitional, or within-word, stage

The fourth developmental spelling stage, the **transitional stage,** occurs when the child can come close to the spelling of various English words, usually about third grade. Many words are spelled correctly, but irregular words that have not been directly taught still cause confusion. At this stage, children are exposed to a wide range of reading experiences, and they are aware of visual aspects of words that are not detectable to the ear. Vowels are correctly placed in each syllable, and common English letter sequences such as the *ai* in *pain* and *rain* begin to emerge correctly in the child's writing. At this stage the elephant story would look something like the writing in Figure 6.2(d).

■ transitional stage

The conventional spelling, or syllable juncture, stage

When children have mastered the basic principles of English orthography, we say they have arrived at the **conventional spelling stage,** meaning that most words are spelled correctly, as the name implies. Children in this stage are aware of syllables but may still incorrectly spell vowels in the schwa position (e.g., *elavate* for *elevate*). At this stage, children are developing a **spelling "conscience,"** or a concern for spelling all words correctly, as well as a **spelling "consciousness,"** meaning they can generally tell if a word they are trying to spell "looks right." Additionally, children learn how to spell homonyms and contractions and become adept at doubling consonants and adding affixes to words; they also learn that there are alternative spellings to certain words.

■ conventional spelling stage

■ spelling "conscience"
■ spelling "consciousness"

Bear, Invernizzi, Templeton, and Johnston's Stages

Bear, Invernizzi, Templeton, and Johnston (2012) view the stages of spelling development as emergent spelling, letter-name alphabetic spelling, within-word pattern spelling, syllables and affixes spelling, and derivational relations spelling; these run parallel to Gentry's stages, with some unique observations (see Figure 6.1).

Emergent spelling

The greatest range in expression is found in this earliest of stages. Much like Gentry's precommunicative stage, 3- to 5-year-old children in this phase of spelling development generally make random marks anywhere on a page, usually using uppercase letters. While there may be some letter–sound matches, such children are just learning how to make letters and realizing that drawing and writing are two different processes.

figure 6.3 Example story by a child in the within-word spelling phase.

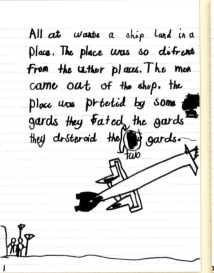

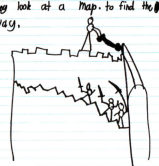

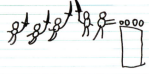

Letter-name–alphabetic spelling

At this point, 5- to 7-year-old children are learning the alphabetic principle—that letters represent sounds—and beginning to apply this principle to "sound out" words they are trying to write. Initially, such spelling includes only the surface sounds in the word, as in the prephonetic stage where *L* may represent *elephant,* but as they begin to progress through this stage, they hear and use more short vowels, as well as blends and digraphs, as they learn about them.

Within-word pattern spelling

In this stage, according to Bear et al. (2012), at about ages 7 to 9, children become aware of long vowels, *r*-controlled words, and more complex consonant and vowel structures, such as *tough, piece,* and *boil.* They can spell most one-syllable short vowel words with ease. Often overgeneralization occurs: *caught* becomes *catched,* and *mouse* becomes *mowse.*

Syllables and affixes spelling

At about ages 9 to 11, children begin to use the process of "chunking" to break apart multisyllabic words in order to spell them. As a result of reading and formal instruction, they also learn about inflectional endings, such as *–ed, –ing,* and *–s,* as well as how to double consonants or drop the final *e* before adding an inflectional ending, such as in the words *getting* and *racing.*

Children can learn to spell fairly easily if they are initially encouraged to experiment freely with the way print works.

Derivational relations spelling

Instead of entering a conventional stage, as in Gentry's model, children at this stage are still working on specific aspects of our orthographic system in this final stage. They begin to explore the ways that words with similar meanings are spelled when they are derived from the same root or base word, such as *sanitary* and *sanitize.* They are also learning about morphemes and Greek and Latin roots and how the etymology of certain words affects their spelling (e.g., the word *bazaar,* from Turkish, or *pasteurize,* after Louis Pasteur.

OBSERVING EXPERIMENTAL SPELLING

When children are first beginning to write, it is best to encourage them to do experimental spelling—to invite them to sound out words they don't know, without asking them to necessarily spell them correctly. At this early phase in emergent literacy, teachers need to be resolute about *not* showing children how to spell each word, or students will not develop the strategy of making a first attempt, thus losing important opportunities to experiment with sound–spelling relationships. Because learning how to spell involves problem solving, all students should be encouraged to listen for all the sounds of a word as they say it slowly. Then they should be encouraged to picture the word in their minds; attempt a first spelling, perhaps trying it several ways; and then check its correctness with a resource (Routman, 2000).

Observations of experimental spellings in early writing can show teachers much about children's knowledge of sound–spelling relationships. These observations can also demonstrate how knowing the names of letters can sometimes be a slight hindrance as well as a help, which we shall see in a later discussion. Additionally, teachers begin to understand how coupling this experimentation with systematic instruction in the visual patterns of our language, starting in the first grade, helps students become adept at using the structural patterns of the English language to learn to spell words correctly.

Children's spellings in the following examples illustrate six important concepts about how children attempt to sound out words they wish to spell.

We see from observing children's experimental spelling that knowing letter names helps children spell when the word contains a long vowel sound. For example, a child will spell words with long vowels in the following ways:

mak for *make*	*kit* for *kite*	*tigr* for *tiger*

The vowels are spelled correctly because they are spelled the way the name of the letter sounds. On the other hand, short vowels, such as those in the words *bad, hot,* and *win* are more problematic for children if they are trying to spell them based solely on their knowledge of the names of the letters in the alphabet. A beginner's spelling of these words is often *bed, hit,* and *wen,* respectively, because experimental spellers use the vowel name that is closest to the sound in the word when spoken.

When children attempt to sound out words with certain consonant blends, such as *dr* and *tr*, they often represent these sounds with the letters *jr* or *ch* because the sounds are somewhat similar. The way words such as *dress* and *try* are pronounced sheds light on why this may be so: A sophisticated speller is aware of how such blends *look* in relation to their sound. Beginning writers, however, are concentrating on what their mouths and tongues are doing as they sound out a word slowly, and these sounds tend to cause a slight friction at the front of their mouths as they articulate the words. Children generate their own rules for these sounds based on their pronunciation; later, with instruction, their focus changes to the similarity of the phonetic features of the beginning sounds to other words they know. Sophisticated writers learn this through instruction in English spelling patterns and how words are supposed to *look*.

Especially at the earliest stages of experimental spelling, children tend to represent /t/ in the middle of words with a *d*. Again, this outcome of experimental spelling underscores that children pay attention to what they *hear* in the word as they articulate it slowly: *butter (budder),* therefore, is often spelled *budr* by early writers, while *matter (madder)* would be sounded out *madr,* because American English does not clearly articulate these middle sounds. As soon as the child sees and understands the difference between the way we say such a word and the way it is represented, he then consistently incorporates this knowledge into subsequent spellings of words with the consonant *t* in the middle of the word.

Early spellers tend to exclude the first letters of certain consonant pairs that are blended in their mouths. The words *can't* and *won't*, for example, are generally spelled *cat* and *wot* in experimental spelling because the nasal sound produced when they say the /nt/ sound in these words causes their tongues to stay in only one place—in the front of their mouths. Since they do not need to *move* their tongues when they say each of these sounds, they tend to believe they need only one letter to represent both sounds. Again, they are focusing on what they *hear* and experience and are usually not yet aware of how such words *look*.

The ways early writers represent the final letters that signify past tense, plurals, and third-person singular vowels are very consistent. Proficient readers and writers understand that we add *–ed* to the ending of a word to indicate that the action happened in the past, whether the *–ed* is pronounced as a discrete syllable or not. Young children have no such knowledge until this visual reality is pointed out. We know, for example, that *wanted* contains a final *–ed* to indicate that the *wanting* occurred in the past, but we realize that *hoped* also terminates with an *–ed* even though it sounds like a /t/ at the end of a one-syllable word. Children using experimental spelling sound out such words as *hopt, laft,* and *stopt.* Similarly, words with plurals commonly represented by the letter *s* would be spelled with the sound that is more prominently heard: *sez, stayz,* and *criz.*

In general, children are remarkably consistent in their use of the patterns they have devised in their experimental spellings. This is similar to the overgeneralization that occurs when children are learning their first language. They unconsciously detect the pattern they must use to change the original word when forming a past tense, noticing that *pat* becomes *patted* and *want* becomes *wanted.* They overgeneralize this pattern, however, devising *runned* for *ran* and *goed* for *went.* Likewise, it becomes clear from observing children's initial attempts at spelling that when children devise rules to govern how they will construct words according to their sounds, they tend to follow them routinely.

Children move beyond experimental spelling into predicting spellings on the basis of extensive knowledge—knowledge gained through experience with and instruction in how language works—and by noticing the similar patterns or analogs of the words they meet. The following Case Example offers a report of one student's (Tommy's)

CASE EXAMPLE

Tommy's perspective on experimental spelling

M.G. ROMEO, 1995

Our school's parent survey indicated that several parents remained unconvinced about the benefits of invented [experimental] spelling in their children's writing.

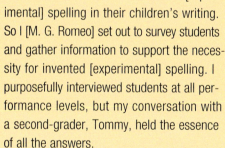

So I [M. G. Romeo] set out to survey students and gather information to support the necessity for invented [experimental] spelling. I purposefully interviewed students at all performance levels, but my conversation with a second-grader, Tommy, held the essence of all the answers.

"Tommy, what strategies do you use when you want to write a word, but you're not sure how to spell it?" I asked.

"I sound it out or ask the kid next to me," answered Tommy confidently.

"Good. But what if all the words you wrote had to be spelled correctly—you couldn't sound them out and the kid next to you didn't know how to spell them either?"

"Oh, I know what you mean," said Tommy. "Then I use different words, like in my journal. I can't spell 'because,' so I write 'it is' instead. Like I write 'My favorite sport is baseball. It is fun' instead of 'because it is fun.' Get it?"

"Yes, I do—that's a good strategy. So baseball is your favorite sport, huh?" I asked, making conversation while I jotted down Tommy's response.

"No, it's soccer, but the kid next to me can't spell soccer."

Undaunted, I pressed on. "So, what if you were all alone in the room with no one to ask how to spell a word?"

"You mean like if I had to stay in for recess because I had messed around all morning and didn't finish my work?" asked an obviously experienced Tommy.

"Yes, like that."

"And there was no one to ask, right?" He wanted to be sure.

"Right," I answered, "no one. And you can't sound it out. What would you do?"

Tommy thought for just a moment and then said, "Then I would write, 'I do not like sports.' I can spell all that."

perspective on spelling and how it would have helped him in the writing process if his teacher had emphasized written expression, including experimental spelling, over correct spelling.

UNDERSTANDING OUR ALPHABETIC SYSTEM

ood spelling is more than a literary nicety or icing on the editorial cake. Poorly developed spelling knowledge hinders children's writing, disrupts their reading fluency, and even interferes with their vocabulary development (Adams, Foorman, Lundberg, & Beeler, 1998; Read, 1986). Although it is appropriate to encourage beginning readers, such as Chrissy in the opening vignette, to use experimental spellings to express their written ideas, programmatic instruction in correct spellings should begin in first grade and continue across the school years (California Department of Education, 1996). In addition, children—as well as many adults!—need to be guided to develop a robust conscience about and consciousness of correct spelling in all their written work.

Research suggests that written composition and reading are enhanced by mastery of the component skills of spelling, just as reading comprehension is supported by mastery of fluent word recognition (Gentry, 2006). Fluent, accurate letter formation and spelling are associated with children's production of longer and better-organized compositions (Berninger et al., 1998). Word usage, handwriting, punctuation, and capitalization, as well as spelling, are the necessary conventions of written expression that must be taught alongside strategies for composing. Children learn these skills more readily if they are taught explicitly from the first grade onward and applied within the context of frequent, purposeful writing assignments (Graham et al., 1997).

Children can learn to spell fairly easily if they are initially encouraged to experiment freely with the way print works. With guidance, children soon discover that all 44 or so phonemes in the English language can be represented by letters or groups of letters. With this understanding and further teaching in the common patterns found in English spellings, children eventually become literate (Tangel & Blachman, 1992, 1995). The word *discover* is used advisedly, however, because children do not learn how print works simply by learning the alphabet, then the letter sounds, and then that English is an alphabetic system (Gentry, 2006). Although early educators believed there was little more to spelling than that, spelling research suggests that to become good spellers, children must understand the phonemic nature of speech by being shown that (1) we speak in a flow of individual words, (2) each word is composed of a number of sounds, and (3) the sounds of speech are expressed graphically in a specific left-to-right sequence (McCracken & McCracken, 1996).

Because one of the initial challenges for teachers is to develop children's phonemic awareness and knowledge of basic letter–sound correspondences, activities designed to meet these goals should begin with short, regular words such as *man*, *but*, and *can*. Because the major goal of these early sessions is to develop the kind of strategizing necessary for good spelling, these lessons should be enjoyable and exploratory. They should also model the processes literate people use to generate the spelling of words and to make logical guesses when they are stumped by unknown spelling patterns. Gradually, the focus of these spelling lessons should be expanded to more complex spelling patterns and words, moving from pattern to pattern and from two- and three-letter words through consonant blends, long vowel spellings, and so on (Gentry & Gillet, 1993). The real challenge is to instill in students an understanding of the underlying logic and regularities of a system that, in many cases, can be highly illogical and irregular, as illustrated by the piece in Figure 6.4, written by a child in early second grade.

An effective spelling program, then, is one in which teachers help students explore and understand the patterns and useful generalizations about the complex relationships within and between words, helping them apply these concepts to each new spelling encounter (Henderson, 1995; Zutell, 1996). Moreover, an informed, developmental analysis of children's efforts as they begin to write will show teachers how to match the features of words to be taught to the students' readiness to discover them.

A program with these components would be similar to the one described in the following section.

SUPPORTING SPELLING DEVELOPMENT

for children in the early phonetic/early letter-name stage, formal instructional strategies should include activities that draw students' attention to the beginning, end, and middle of words, in that order. Whenever possible, children should be involved in spelling the same words they are learning to read.

figure   6.4

A second-grader's experimentation with print.

Early Phonetic/Early Letter-Name Stage

The following strategy from Moats (1995) is especially good for introducing new words to students needing help discerning individual sounds.

1. The teacher pronounces the word: *bat.*
2. The students repeat the word, hearing their own voices and feeling the articulation: b–a–t.
3. The students say the word, sound by sound; after identifying each sound, they say the name of the letter that represents the sound and then write the letter as it is being named on individual chalkboards or tablets: *b* /b/; *a* /a/; *t* /t/.
4. The students read back, orally, the word they have written: *bat.*

Sound–symbol correspondence can be reinforced on subsequent days using the following activities:

Word hunts. Using the beginning, ending, or middle sound being studied, have the students go around the room searching for other words or objects that begin with the same sound. For example, for the /b/ sound they might find the words *Bill, boat,* and *by.* Write these words on the board as the students contribute them and help to sound them out.

Picture sorts. Place picture cards among the students and set up one or two pictures as examples of the beginning, middle, or ending sound being studied. Have the students take turns coming up and placing their cards with the appropriate example, saying the word as they do so. Make a list of the words, with the students helping to sound them out.

Word-building activities (Cunningham & Cunningham, 1997). Have the students use paper or tile letters to form words. Read a word slowly (e.g., *in*), stretching out each sound. Ask the students to stretch the word out using their imaginary rubber bands. Students are required to listen for beginning, middle, and ending sounds; to

Ideas for meaningful spelling lists

- A series of words containing a specific phoneme
- Any of the dozens of common spelling patterns: *oo* words, words that end with *y* or *ey*, compound words, words with double consonants, words that contain the pattern *ough*, and so on
- Words from the decodable text that is being used for reading instruction
- Words with similar meanings: *paper, newspaper, wallpaper, papered*

- Words that have related roots: *photo, photographer, telephoto*
- Words from units of study: *whale, ocean, tadpole, waves*
- Common words we use all the time: *it, the, when, my, little*
- Place names: *Sacramento, California, Ohio, Canada*
- Any other grouping that will provide related words for sorting

notice letter patterns; and to discover how capitalization is used in words as they manipulate letters and sounds through the following example sequence:

| in | is | it | hit | sit | nit |
| tin | tins | Tim | this | thin | things |

A pocket chart can be used to highlight words for all students to see, and an interactive whiteboard can be used for students to manipulate letters. As students work through several lessons, each using a different combination of letters, they begin to internalize common word patterns, letter blends, and digraphs.

Cut, paste, and label. Create a large poster headed with one or more pictures of things with the same beginning, ending, or middle sound being studied. Give students magazines, catalogs, scissors, and paste. Have the students, in small groups, find pictures of items with the same target sound, cut them out, and paste them on the poster. As the words are said, write them on the board, asking the students to help sound them out.

Phonetic/Late Letter-Name and Within-Word Stage

As students advance to the phonetic/late letter-name and within-word phases, generally in late first grade through third grade, more systematic spelling is conducted throughout the week and includes different activities for each day, based on a teacher-selected spelling list. An excellent resource for such grade-level-appropriate lists is *Teaching Spelling* (Henderson, 1995). However, many teachers question the use of commercial lists to teach spelling (especially when the words chosen from lists are unrelated to the words students are seeing in their reading and using in their writing), as research on experimental spelling suggests that spelling is ideally learned through copious reading and writing (Gentry & Gillet, 1993; Wilde, 1992). Words chosen should *always* be those that students can already read, particularly those that students use, but misspell, when writing. Initially, sorting by sight and sound is the most helpful. More ideas for appropriate spelling lists are included in the box above.

Transitional/Syllables and Affixes Spelling Stage

As children enter the transitional/syllables and affixes spelling stage, some who have had no previous trouble mapping sounds in words become confused when they begin to encounter words with more than one syllable. Distinguishing where one word part or chunk ends and the next chunk begins seems overwhelming to them. Before these larger words appear, such children are usually successful with sound–symbol strategies that fit common spelling patterns, such as CVC, one-syllable words (*cat*), or words with a silent *e* (*gate*). But multisyllabic words cannot be sounded out as one entity, and not all children automatically say each syllable as they are spelling each chunk. In such cases, the following instructional strategy must be directly taught.

Spelling in Parts (SIP) (Powel & Aram, 2008), uses sound, visual, and meaning strategies. It can be used to help students break multisyllabic words into smaller chunks to make spelling much easier.

Spelling in Parts (SIP)

ACTIVITY

(POWEL & ARAM, 2008)

1. The teacher models the SIP strategy on the board, demonstrating how she would say and spell the word continent. She discusses the meaning of the word.

2. The teacher says the word continent and has the students say the word and distinctly clap each syllable.

3. The students divide the word into chunks as they pronounce each chunk: /con/ti/nent/.

4. Then, on paper, students write the parts one at a time, leaving a space between the parts, as the teacher checks that the division between chunks is acceptable.

5. The students circle any syllables that may be problematic (e.g., the /i/ sound is a schwa and sounds like a /u/).

6. They "take a picture" of the problematic word part within the word to help them keep a permanent visual memory of the word feature.

7. From memory, students say and write each syllable.

8. Students check their spelling against their initial spelling of the word and repeat the process if necessary.

A Possible Week's Study Plan*

Fresch and Wheaton (1997) devised an effective week's study plan, as we will discuss next.

Monday: Pretest

Select a spelling sound, pattern, or rule that you feel students are ready for, based on the spelling assessment. The pattern might be as simple as the short /a/, or as complex as words that have the /k/ sound. All the words you choose will contain this pattern. Select 15 or 20 words that have this pattern or sound for the pretest, such as the following list containing variations of the /k/ sound:

like	think	king	kind	cake
car	call	back	book	pack
bike	kitten	lock	walk	talk

Administer a pretest created from these words, and have students proofread and correct their own attempts. Then display another slightly more difficult list of 15 to 20 words (fewer words for spellers who are struggling) containing the sound or pattern:

ticket	camp	nickel	kangaroo	cape
ache	cabin	kingdom	cattle	school
Canada	camel	Kansas	camera	market

Have students choose words from this list to study in place of any words spelled correctly in the pretest or, if they are exceptionally skilled spellers, create their own lists based on the spelling concept in the lists (Hong & Stafford, 1999). Alternatively, some students who consistently score above 80 percent on the pretest may develop individual contracts with you regarding either specific words they wish to learn to spell or words they have recently needed for writing stories, reports, letters, or other written pieces (see the next section, "Contract Spelling").

Then have the students copy their individual word lists three times. One list is sent home to be shared with parents, a second is stapled to the child's writing folder for future reference, and the third is cut up into individual word cards for later sorting activities.

Tuesday: Word sort

Ask students to use their ears, eyes, and brains to sort out their word cards, either individually or in small groups. Such focused, small-group work on word patterns enhances spelling and aids in reading development (Invernizzi, Abouzeid, & Gill, 1994; Schlagel & Schlagel, 1992). Initially, the students use their ears to listen to the sounds in their words, and they sort the words by the sounds they have in common, if different sounds are included in the list. Then, they use their eyes to detect other patterns with your help, as you move from group to group offering assistance. Next, tell students to underline the letters that make the specific sound (e.g., /k/) in each word. Finally, ask students to use their brains to draw some conclusions, either orally with preliterate students or in written form, about what they have discovered. One pair of students came up with the following list and set of generalizations from their list:

k	**c**	**ch**	**ck**
kingdom	cape	ache	ticket
Kansas	Canada	school	nickel
kangaroo	camera		
market	camel		
	camp		
	cattle		
	cabin		

"There are four different ways to make the /k/ sound. You can spell it *k, c, ch,* and *ck.* The most common way seems to be *c,* followed by *k.* The least common seems to be *ch; c* never seems to come at the end of a word; *ck* never seems to come at the beginning of a word; *ck* is never spelled *kc.*"

Now the whole class comes together to share their findings. Sort the words using a pocket chart, overhead, or interactive whiteboard. Model how you would sort the words, thinking through your decisions aloud. Have the students add their insights and generalizations to yours, explaining the bases for their conclusions.

Write all generalizations on chart paper and post them in the room for future reference and for periodic review.

Wednesday: Word hunt

To allow students to apply the generalizations or rules they encountered on Tuesday, give pairs or small groups of students 10 or 15 minutes to search through printed or written material and come up with other words that conform to the generalizations. Later, reconvene the students as a whole group to share their lists and create a new word wall that is kept visible and updated by students throughout the day as they find other words that fit the pattern.

Thursday: Using the words in context

The ability to remember how to read and write a specific word comes from understanding its meaning in context. Therefore, you will ask students with rudimentary writing skills to create brief sentences—and as they grow in literacy, even stories, poems, riddles, or other text—using their individual word lists. Then ask them to highlight all the spelling words in the piece. They will read the post-test words (see Friday's activity) directly from this written material.

To help students write their words in context, teach them a set of strategies for figuring out what to do when they can't spell a word. Some strategies will be more efficient when students are composing their text; others will be more useful when they are editing. While they are writing, they should learn to take a guess by sounding it out; teach the following strategies and then post them for students to reference during any writing activity:

- Say the word to yourself very slowly; really stretch it out so you can *listen* for the different sounds.
- Think of the beginning sound and write down the letters that make that sound; for help with the beginning sound, think of a word you know that begins with that sound.
- Think of the middle sound and write down the letters that make that sound.
- Think of the ending sound and write down the letters that make that sound.
- Look at the word carefully and see if it looks right. Read it back to yourself out loud and make sure you are able to read it even if it isn't correct.
- Always write *something*, even if it's just one letter, so you can remember the word you wanted.

After they have completed a rough draft, students even at the earliest stages need to get into the habit of editing their writing for spelling. Therefore, you should also teach the following strategies and post them for reference.

BEFORE FINISHING A PIECE OF WRITING:
- Circle or underline the words you are unsure of.
- Check the spelling of the word, using your personal dictionary, a word wall, a class list, or a proofreading buddy.
- If you still can't find the word, ask your teacher.
- Make the corrections you need.
- Recopy the piece and read it again.

Friday: Paired post-tests

Have students give a final post-test to each other in pairs by reading the highlighted words from the contextual material written on Thursday. Pairs may correct each other's post-tests or request that you do so. Students scoring below 80 percent are targeted for future minilessons (see Chapter 5) with the week's spelling patterns. You can retain the lists, writings, and post-tests to provide valuable assessment information about each child's spelling growth.

CONTRACT SPELLING

contract spelling ■

an alternative approach to spelling instruction for all spellers is **contract spelling** (Hoskisson & Tompkins, 2001), whereby students have a written agreement with the teacher each week to learn specific words. Students who select the words for their spelling program have a special engagement in their own learning. If they are encouraged to select words from their own writing needs, they can see the purpose for their spelling list; the motivation to succeed is thus heightened.

For this approach, have students keep a list of their own spelling mistakes and challenges from each week's writing. This becomes the master list from which the child selects a certain number of words, depending on the child's age and ability, to study for the next week. You and each participating child negotiate the appropriate number of words to select. Then the child takes a pretest on the words (these can be administered by you or a spelling partner), fills out a spelling contract on the words, studies the words during the week, and takes a final test to see how well the contract has been met. This information provides the foundation for the new contract the following week (see Figure 6.5).

| figure | 6.5 | A sample spelling contract. |

Name: Carmen R.   Grade: 3

Week: Sept. 8–12

SPELLING CONTRACT

Number of words spelled correctly on the pretest: 8

Number of words to be learned: 2

Total number of words contracted: 10

1. personal
2. beautiful
3. curious
4. obvious
5. mascara
6. popular
7. women
8. beginning
9. sincerely
10. receive

STRATEGIES FOR ENGLISH LEARNERS

english learners may participate successfully in spelling instruction if they are developmentally ready, are learning to read in English, and understand the meanings of the words they are being asked to spell. English learners who are also learning to read in a language other than English may most comfortably participate in spelling instruction by doing so orally, if they wish. The primary focus should be on comprehending spelling vocabulary and developing awareness of English sound patterns and specific spelling patterns.

English learners who are only participating orally should not be required to take formal spelling pre- and post-tests; however, they may be asked to demonstrate knowledge of the meaning of spelling words by drawing pictures of the word or providing brief explanations of the word's meaning.

The strategy described in the "Think, Pair, Share" activity can be helpful in the spelling acquisition of all students—but particularly for English learners.

English learners may participate successfully in spelling instruction if they are developmentally ready.

Think, Pair, Share

ACTIVITY

THINK

Students look at the spelling list (or, for younger children, listen as someone reads the words) and consider what they know about each word. They may write down their ideas, draw pictures, use gestures, or use any means to show what they are thinking.

PAIR

Students sit in pairs facing one another. One child chooses a word to share with the partner and completes the following sentence: "Something I know about [the spelling word] is that . . ." Students may share drawings, and if their partner speaks the same home language, that language may be used.

SHARE

Students regroup into linguistically heterogeneous small groups and, in English, share and build on the knowledge they acquired in the pairs. They may repeat the pair activity by changing their sentences to "Something I learned from my partner about [the spelling word] was . . ." or they may do a different activity such as a word sort or a word hunt and discuss their findings in the group. They may also choose to enter the words that reflect the concepts they have been studying for the week into a word study notebook, in columns.

CONSIDERATIONS FOR STUDENTS WITH SPECIAL NEEDS

becoming conventional spellers is often difficult for students who have reading and writing disabilities because spelling involves memorization, phonemic awareness, phonics, and editing. For such students, the development of writing fluency and the expression of ideas should be emphasized over a concern for correct spelling; you should also be aware of activities that can make the act of putting letters to sounds easier for students who struggle.

Reflecting on Spelling

You can help students become more aware of their spelling by inviting them to think about the words that pose difficulty for them and consider the strategies that they use when attempting to spell unfamiliar words. After students write a draft, ask them to note on a corner of the page any words they think they may have misspelled. They can then log these words in a special place for future reference. You can further this strategy by helping students to identify a pattern in the errors in their spelling in their drafts. Prompting students to reflect systematically on their spelling in this manner can help them to become more strategic spellers (Sipe et al., 2002).

Word Lists and High-Frequency Words

Provide word lists when studying content areas such as science or social studies. Place the lists in students' notebooks, tape them to their desks, or add them to word prediction software if used. Word prediction software (e.g., Co:Writer or Word Q 2) is an assistive technology that helps by filling in the word the user intends to type based on the first few keystrokes.

Word lists can also be grouped into word families. A word family is a group of words that have some of the same letter combinations, such as *ei* or *er*. Word families can be taught using games such as Concentration or Word Bingo. Finally, some students benefit from the use of the kinesthetic strategy of Spelling Rainbow, in which students outline the configuration of a troubling word in a first color, while spelling the word, then use a second color to outline it again, and so forth.

see appendix G

Teach words that are used frequently (see Figure 5.3 and Appendix G), or a list of the "spelling demons," rather than words from commercialized spelling books, for students who have extreme difficulty with spelling. Shorten lists to memorize to a minimum number attainable for the child's success each week. Finally, have students create illustrations for words, form sentences on cards using these words, and create their own word banks and personal dictionaries with the words that they find difficult (Cohen & Spenciner, 2008).

Portable Keyboards

Many students who have reading and writing disabilities or challenges experience greater success and can craft their ideas more easily when composing on computers or tablets, which reduce the need for neat handwriting and include spell checkers. Although not every classroom has computers for every student, portable smart keyboards, such as AlphaSmart, CalcuScribe, and QuickPAD, are inexpensive and lightweight, run on batteries, and can access wireless networks. Students can carry them from school to home as they work on writing assignments.

PRACTICES TO AVOID

Certain questionable practices in the instruction of spelling have been around since the one-room schoolhouse. In spite of volumes of research disclaiming some of these practices, some teachers still use the same unsubstantiated teaching formulas used generations ago. Because these dubious practices continue to some degree, most books on spelling feel the need to mention activities teachers should avoid. The following practices are not recommended, because they yield nothing of value and may hinder normal spelling development (Gentry, 1981).

AVOID:

- *requiring students to write out their spelling words repeatedly.* Writing the words three times appears to be the optimal number for retention; all else is counterproductive, and time would be better spent on other applied writing activities. Moreover, practice doesn't always make perfect; if the word is misspelled ten times, practice has most likely made the error permanent.

- *correcting spelling mistakes for students.* Students learn much more by paying careful attention to the exact sequence of letters they have confused so they can write it over correctly. A small check in the margin of the line where there is a misspelled word should be enough to call students' attention to a spelling mistake.

- *having students unscramble strings of letters to find words.* This is an unusually poor practice because it frustrates the visual recognition that is the most important skill students can develop for spelling. Word searches are also poor exercises, as the diagonal and right-to-left placement of words reinforce poor orientation skills, especially in beginning readers.

- *lowering grades on written work solely because of poor spelling.* When students are writing drafts and getting their ideas down, they are in the creative stages of writing. At this stage, always respond only to what the writer has to say. Later, when students have had a chance to edit their work, the spelling can be addressed.

- *giving weekly spelling bees.* Spelling bees are enjoyable for students who are naturally good spellers, but they provide limited practice for those who are experiencing problems in spelling. Moreover, the "good" spellers tend to get most of the spelling reinforcement, whereas the poorer spellers, who could use the practice, get little but a bruised ego.

- *spending more than 10 to 15 minutes a day on spelling instruction.* Good spelling is an important convention of writing, but it is only a small part of what makes a child literate. Thus, you should actively engage students in analyzing and categorizing words and identifying generalizations for a few minutes every day; spend much more time applying that information to meaningful writing experiences.

- *giving very difficult content-related words as spelling lists,* rather than as vocabulary words that are important to know in order to understand a particular topic. Give students only words whose meaning they already know.

SUMMARY

The purpose of spelling is to allow writers to communicate more effectively, so writing is the best way for children to learn how to spell. To become good spellers, then, children need to write a lot, and that means they have to begin by using experimental spelling. During the primary years, students' abilities to spell lag so far behind their abilities to communicate that if they could not initially experiment with new spellings, they simply could not write at all. However, it isn't enough to tell children to use experimental spelling; teachers need to show them how to use strategies to sound out new words, thus helping them discover important concepts about sound–spelling relationships in the English language. By observing and analyzing their experimental spellings, teachers can then determine which new concepts about print their students are ready to incorporate into their spelling.

Learning how to spell is not about merely memorizing words anymore; a more sensible approach to the teaching of spelling is now based on several premises: Children must be taught about print and how it works, and they must be shown strategies that are used by competent spellers. They must be taught the symbols used to represent each sound. They must also be guided to discover common spelling patterns and the generalizations that apply to many words. Most importantly, they must be given numerous opportunities to use their spelling in meaningful and varied writing activities. With a burgeoning spelling consciousness that alerts them when a word is not spelled correctly, and a spelling conscience that makes them *want* to spell correctly, young children will be well on the road to effective written communication.

questions FOR JOURNAL WRITING AND DISCUSSION

1. Describe in your own words the stages of spelling development in young children. Explain how being aware of these stages might help a teacher plan an appropriate spelling program for each learner.

2. In your own words, list the six concepts that can be derived from observing children's experimental spelling. Discuss how knowing letter names can be both a help and a hindrance to young children at the initial phases of writing.

3. The mother of a first-grader asks you why the teacher allows her child to misspell so many words in draft writing. What explanation do you offer her?

suggestions FOR PROJECTS AND FIELD ACTIVITIES

 see appendix E

1. Administer the "Monster Test" (see Appendix E) to three first-grade students. From their responses, what stage of spelling development would you say each child is in? List what each child already knows about how print works. What do you think each child needs in order to progress toward the next stage?

2. Develop a list of 15 spelling words based on similar or contrasting visual or sound aspects. Invite a small group of second-grade students to sort the words and then make statements about their findings, as demonstrated in this chapter. Present your findings to your classmates.

3. Observe a spelling lesson taught to primary-age youngsters. Through discussion with the teacher and your direct observation, answer the following questions:

   ■ What strategies are students being taught about how to spell new words?

   ■ How are students being taught about common patterns that occur in words?

   ■ How is new knowledge of spelling applied in real writing situations in this classroom?

Acquiring Word Meanings

THE BUILDING BLOCKS OF LITERACY

focus questions

What is the most important way children acquire new words? How should this information guide classroom practice?

What factors comprise an effective meaning vocabulary acquisition program?

What are the two types of meaning vocabulary instruction, and when should each be used?

What are guidelines for making vocabulary acquisition more accessible for English learners? For students with special needs?

What requirements do the Common Core State Standards include regarding vocabulary acquisition?

ecause words are the building blocks of sentences and thus all reading and writing activities, a classroom in which both teacher and students enjoy playing with and discussing new words is most conducive to literacy acquisition. In one such classroom, when seven-year-old Maria chirps, "That story was so *um—memorable,* Ms. Komar!" the teacher and the students are visibly enchanted with this sophisticated new word. They immediately stop what they are doing to comment on the meaning of the word after Ms. Komar profusely congratulates Maria on using such a fine word. The teacher then enlists the students to help her sound the word out as she pens it with a black marker on a large word wall chart toward the front of the room. This prominent chart has been created for just such a purpose: to provide a tangible reminder of the group's love of words and to reinforce new words as they are discovered either through class discussion, as in this example, or through content reading, recreational reading, or other media.

INTRODUCTION

Vocabulary development has been widely researched, and in the past 20 years, a number of studies have examined the impact of vocabulary knowledge on student achievement. One major conclusion of these studies is that the interdependence between reading achievement and vocabulary knowledge is very strong (Beck, McKeown, & Kucan, 2013; Graves, 2006; Mitchell & Brady, 2013). As a result of this vocabulary acquisition research, three main implications for instruction have come to light:

- Children understand a wide range of vocabulary.
- There is a significant difference between the vocabulary knowledge of high- and low-achieving students.
- A sustained focus on oral and written vocabulary acquisition in the reading/ language arts program as well as programs in other content areas such as mathematics, science, and social studies is crucial.

Several researchers have offered evidence that strongly links vocabulary deficiencies to academic failure in high-risk youngsters in grades 3–12. Although the research does not support a conclusion that any single method of teaching vocabulary is better than others, many comprehensive vocabulary acquisition programs have produced positive results (Dixon-Krauss, 2002; Nilsen & Nilsen, 2003; Rosenbaum, 2001). Therefore, teachers should incorporate daily vocabulary acquisition activities into their literacy programs (Herrell & Jordan, 2006) as well as their programs in the other content areas.

WHY ACQUIRING A MEANING VOCABULARY IS IMPORTANT

meaning vocabulary ■

Meaning vocabulary is just what the term implies—a child's understanding of the meanings of words. It is first acquired through the child's total orallanguage experiences and therefore begins to form before the child enters school. In kindergarten, before children know how to read, they gain their meaning vocabulary primarily through listening to and retelling stories, songs, and poems, and by having adults or older children help them focus on the meaning of new words. As children become literate, their vocabularies are enhanced through explicit instruction and independent reading. By the end of third grade, students ideally can decode any word in their meaning vocabulary.

The meaning vocabulary of children grows at an astonishing rate—by some estimates about 3,000 words a year, or approximately 7 to 10 new words per day (Nagy & Herman, 1985). To master such a large number of words, children acquire this new vocabulary both inside and outside school. Although many teachers suppose that their students learn most new words through their explicit instruction, students actually learn a great deal of vocabulary through informal means, such as through conversations with adults, being read to, and exposure to print in their environment (including online). Educational television, especially, has a positive effect on vocabulary acquisition (Wright, Huston, Murphy, et al., 2001). The number of new words children can acquire from reading, of course, depends on exactly how much they read, and that amount can vary tremendously. Research indicates that a fifth-grader achieving at the 90th percentile in reading on standardized tests reads about 200 times more than does a 10th percentile fifth-grade reader (Nagy, Herman, & Anderson, 1985)! Moreover, capable readers have larger vocabularies and more strategies for figuring out new words than children who read less often (McKeown, 1985).

Written language places greater demands on children's vocabulary knowledge than does everyday spoken language. If children do not continue to develop vocabulary rapidly, they will be ill-equipped to handle the extensive vocabulary demands of fourth-grade content-area subjects, such as science and social studies. This problem is compounded for children for whom English is not the home language. Therefore, a swiftly growing vocabulary is indispensable for growth in every area of reading. Although the proportion of difficult words in text is the single most powerful predictor of text difficulty, a reader's general vocabulary knowledge is the best predictor of how well that reader understands text (California Department of Education, 1996). This is undoubtedly why Nagy (1988) asserts that increasing the volume of students' reading of both informational and narrative text is the most important thing a teacher can do to promote large-scale vocabulary growth. Both research and the CCSS underscore the importance of students reading informational text. Research supports the relationship between vocabulary development and the reading of informational text, finding that incidental vocabulary acquisition is higher when reading informational text than narrative text (Shokouhi & Maniati, 2009). Beginning with kindergarten, the CCSS call for increased reading of informational texts as well as literature (NGACBP & CCSSO, 2010).

The CCSS also make a case for the proficiency in **academic language** (words commonly used in educational contexts across the disciplines) and **domain-specific vocabulary** (vocabulary specific to a content area) and broad vocabulary knowledge not only in the language arts but also in content areas such as mathematics, social studies, and science (NGACBP & CCSSO, 2010). In a departure from previous standards, students are asked to collaborate with other students to solve problems and to explain their thinking, all necessitating an emphasis on domain-specific and academic vocabulary. In addition, high-stakes assessments aligned with the CCSS require students to justify their decision making in solving content-area problems and thus to have control of a wide array of domain-specific vocabulary and each discipline's specific language practices in order to meet the performance demands of these assessments.

- academic language
- domain-specific vocabulary

Given the tremendous number of words that students should learn, choosing which vocabulary to teach is challenging. Beck, McKeown, and Kucan (2013) offer a helpful framework for dividing vocabulary into three broad tiers:

1. Tier one includes common words that children tend to already know when they come to school—for example, *baby* and *ring*.

2. Tier two encompasses words that are academic in nature and can be used across disciplines, such as *coincidence* and *principles*. Words that are specific to what we "do" with language, or language functions, such as describing, comparing, and analyzing, also fall into tier two. Therefore, words and phrases such as *on the other hand, similarly,* and *however* are examples of tier two words.

3. Tier three is reserved for words that need to be understood only during the study of certain school subjects; for example, the words *mitosis* and *sorghum* are rarely transferrable across disciplines or even other units of study (domain-specific).

Beck and colleagues suggest that a focus on tier two vocabulary is most efficient, and that teachers should identify and teach tier two vocabulary purposefully and consistently to their students.

PRINCIPLES OF EFFECTIVE VOCABULARY DEVELOPMENT

To foster proficient readers and writers, teachers must do everything in their power to expand children's vocabulary. Research suggests that explicit instruction in vocabulary, using a variety of approaches, can lead to an enriched vocabulary as well as an increase in reading comprehension for children (Boulware-Gooden, Carreker, Thornhill, & Malatesha, 2007; Kamil, 2004; Nelson & Stage, 2007). Moreover, this finding holds true both for those who have difficulty reading (Ebbers & Denton, 2008; Kennedy, Lloyd, Cole, & Ely, 2012) and for English learners (Schmitt, 2008; Calderón, Slavin, & Sanchez, 2011).

In addition, children can acquire the extensive vocabulary they need for complex tasks if they have access to good literature and well-crafted informational texts on many topics. Moreover, they must be actively engaged with the reading material and have many opportunities to transfer and apply newly acquired words in different, meaningful ways. Especially in the early grades, children need numerous opportunities to gain meaning vocabulary through oral-language development. This can take place through group reading (see Chapter 11), teacher-directed group reading activities, and read-alouds and by applying new vocabulary through motivational writing activities shared with classmates. Also helpful for acquiring meaning vocabulary are extensive discussions, listening and thinking activities, and oral asking and answering of open-ended questions. The following box provides additional suggestions for vocabulary learning.

Additionally, students need to be encouraged to read widely at home and at school and given plenty of opportunities to do so.

Teacher behaviors that enhance vocabulary learning

LINK	Relate students' past experiences with present ones.	CLARIFY	Add examples, illustrations, or descriptions.
ELABORATE	Add more information about familiar content or suggest rewording of the content.	QUESTION	Stimulate thinking about terms through questioning.
INPUT	Introduce new vocabulary and reinforce through constant use.	RELATE	Show how new words compare with those children know.
CONNECT	Tie new words to the activity or vice versa.	CATEGORIZE	Group new words, ideas, and concepts.
		LABEL	Provide names for concepts, ideas, and objects.

Motivating Students to Read Independently

Independent reading is one of the most essential factors in acquiring new meaning vocabulary. Moreover, children who read the most also read at higher levels and score the highest on formal and informal assessments (California Reading Association, 1996). Because independent reading is so pivotal for the reading success of all students, every classroom of every school should enact a plan for motivating them to read inside and outside the classroom.

To encourage reading at home, you should communicate with parents. Inform them that for 10 to 15 minutes every evening, their children are expected to read—with the help of a caregiver for children at the preliterate level—independently as soon as they are able. (*Note:* For students whose home language is not English, reading in the home language with parents, and then independently, should be encouraged.) A classroom library with a variety of materials on many topics on many reading levels is a priority; the students should be able to check out these materials and take them home.

Students can also read on their own during independent work time in the classroom—for example, as another small group is receiving reading instruction or after they have completed one activity and are waiting for another to begin (National Institute for Literacy, 2001). Students can keep personal progress charts so that you can check reading interests and growth; offer incentives for specified numbers of books, articles, or other textbooks read. Encourage students to read a variety of genres, including informational texts, which often contain a greater range of academic as well as domain-specific vocabulary than narrative texts.

Also plan structured time during the instructional day in which students read independently, to help students build their stamina for and interest in independent reading. Students need instruction on how to read independently and apply the reading strategies they are learning in class to their independent reading; these strategies include monitoring their comprehension, adjusting their reading rate given the complexity of the text and other factors, and choosing books that are "just right."

This kind of book selection is a challenging but crucial skill for students to acquire if we hope to encourage independent reading. One useful strategy for teaching this skill is the "five-finger strategy" (Rogers, 2008):

1. Choose a book that you think you will enjoy.
2. Read the second page.
3. Hold up a finger for each word you are not sure of or do not know.
4. If there are five or more words you did not know, choose an easier book.

This strategy builds independence in book choosing and provides you with visual confirmation that students are using the skill, as they hold up their fingers while reading a page of the book they have chosen. The video listed in the margin shows the five-finger strategy being modeled by older students who are English learners.

For further evidence as to whether a book is "just right," teach students questions to ask themselves as they begin reading. These questions include the following (Rogers, 2008):

- Do I understand what I am reading?
- Are there fewer than five words on the second page that I don't understand?
- When I read it aloud, can I read it smoothly?
- Do I think the topic will interest me?
- If most of your answers were "yes," this will be an easy book to read independently by yourself.

Five-finger Strategy

*www.colorincolorado.org/
multimedia/experts/video/
prentice/strategies/*

Teachers should attempt to build upon the vocabulary students already have when introducing new reading material.

Many digital resources encourage wide reading, including online magazines and journals that publish high-interest articles for children. A few of these are shown in the margin. These websites can be made available for wide reading during school or shared with caregivers so that students can access them at home.

Listening to the Teacher Read

There may be one more great reason to read to your students, no matter what their grade level. Listening to text has been found to have a significant effect on vocabulary acquisition. Because primary students have limited word recognition capabilities, they usually comprehend stories at a higher level of sophistication when they listen to proficient readers read than when they read themselves. Reading to children, then, may have an even more powerful effect on their vocabulary than their own reading. This relationship is well supported in the research (Beck & McKeown, 2007; Blachowicz & Fisher, 2010). Kindle (2009) proposes that teachers should identify four or five words per read-aloud for in-depth instruction and should identify the type of vocabulary each word is: a new label for a familiar concept or a label for a new concept. Strategies vary for teaching various types of vocabulary, and teachers can adjust their instruction according to the type. For example, a strategy for teaching new labels for already-known concepts is providing short, student-friendly instruction *during* the read-aloud. A strategy for words that are new labels for new concepts is to teach them *before* the read-aloud, linking the new label and concept to related already-known labels and concepts. Then, during the read-aloud, provide a short definition when the word is encountered. To enhance vocabulary gains even more, take a few minutes after reading aloud to discuss interesting words students heard and their meanings and then invite the students to use the word in a sentence related to their own lives; for example, "I was *benevolent* when _____," or "I would rather be described as *benevolent* than *generous* because _____" (Beck, McKeown, & Kucan, 2013).

Other Factors in Vocabulary Development

Activities besides extensive reading are conducive to vocabulary acquisition. The most successful vocabulary-enhancing activities are those that are significant to all students and involve active engagement with words taken directly from their reading. Activities that teach children how to determine the meaning of unknown words themselves (Blachowicz & Lee, 1991; Rasinski, Padak, Newton, & Newton, 2011) are preferred over traditional methods demanding that children memorize dictionary definitions of commercial lists of arbitrarily chosen words and then use them in sentences (Blachowicz, 1987).

A number of other key strands must be present in a reading program that seeks to increase meaning vocabulary. As discussed earlier, above all, to foster vocabulary development, children should be read to as much as possible from a wide variety of quality narrative and informational material. Teachers must also attempt to build on the vocabulary children already have whenever introducing new reading material. For example, if students already know the word *knife*, it is then easy to build on that knowledge to teach them the word *saber*. Students should be shown strategies for figuring out the meanings of words they encounter in text and encouraged to apply such strategies independently. Finally, studies by Stahl (1983) and Stahl and Fairbanks (1986) suggest that building background knowledge prior to reading is simply not enough to help students overcome limited vocabulary knowledge; these researchers encourage teachers to teach new words directly by showing students how to use context and other strategies to understand complex concepts.

TYPES OF VOCABULARY INSTRUCTION

formal meaning vocabulary instruction for young children is of two main types with two different purposes. In the first type, the teacher provides explicit instruction that helps students acquire new vocabulary words. In the second type, teachers help students develop vocabulary-building strategies they can use on their own during noninstructional, independent reading times. Both types of meaning vocabulary instruction will be explored in the following sections.

Explicit Instruction in Meaning Vocabulary

The vocabulary-enhancing effect of reading can be significantly expanded, especially for English learners and struggling readers, when the teacher takes time to explain directly the meaning of unknown words (Biemiller & Boote, 2006; Hui-Tzu, 2008). This section explores ways teachers can provide direct study in meaning vocabulary for five different instructional situations (Graves, Watts, & Graves, 1998):

Vocabulary Instruction
www.vocabulary.com

1. Learning new words that represent new concepts (e.g., students come to grips with the new concept/word *culture*)

2. Clarifying and enriching the meanings of known words (e.g., students learn how *shed* differs from *cabin*)

3. Learning new words for known concepts (e.g., students know what *rain* is and now learn the word *precipitation*)

4. Moving words into students' speaking vocabularies (e.g., students know the meaning of *selfish* but have never used the word)

5. Learning new meanings for known words (e.g., students know the word *change* but not *to make change* as in money)

Learning new words for new concepts

Learning a new word and a new concept at the same time is a complex task but is best accomplished by comparing both the concept and the word with those that are already familiar. The following activity, creating a **word map** (Duffelmeyer & Banwart, 1993), will be useful in this regard and adds an extra layer of clarification for English learners.

■ word map

A Word Map

A C T I V I T Y

1. Define the new word and concept by pointing out its special characteristics. For example, "Spring is a season of the year when it begins to get warm and flowers begin to bloom." Show a very short video (under 1 minute) or a couple of still photos from online sources that depict spring.

2. Describe what the new word is like and what it is unlike: "In spring, it is getting warm and it is often breezy and everything seems new. It is not snowy or freezing cold; it is not like winter." Show a very short video or a couple of still photos that show "nonexamples" of spring.

3. Give examples of the concept and explain why they are examples: "Spring is in March, April, and May. These are the months when it begins to warm up and buds come on the trees."

4. Give nonexamples of the concept and explain why they would be poor examples: "December, January, and February are not examples of spring because it is usually very cold in those months and all the flowers have died."

5. Continue to show examples and nonexamples of the concept and ask students to explain why each was chosen: show a picture of a warm spring day with light green everywhere; show another picture of the middle of winter with snow and trees devoid of leaves.

6. Ask students to find examples and nonexamples and to explain their choices.

Use words and brief descriptions from your discussions with the students to create a word map (also called a word web) similar to the one shown in Figure 7.1.

Clarifying and enriching the meanings of known words

semantic maps ■ **Semantic maps** (Johnson & Pearson, 1984), a type of graphic organizer, are important vehicles for helping students integrate related information and develop additional words for the same concepts (see Figure 7.2). Keep maps on separate sheets in a central location so that students can return to them, add to them, and refer to them over time. Such reinforcement has been found to be particularly important for English learners (Anderson & Roit, 1998). The steps outlined in the activity on the following page are a guide that can be adapted for individual purposes.

| figure | 7.1 | A word map (also called a "word web"). |

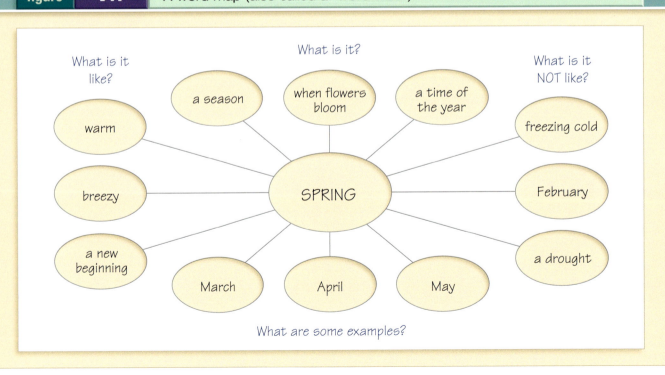

A Semantic Map

1. Choose a key word from a book, story, or passage students will soon be reading.

2. Write the word on a chalkboard, whiteboard, or large sheet of chart paper.

3. Ask students to think of as many words as they can that are related to the word, as you list them in broad categories. (*Note:* You may want to add any important words that have been overlooked.)

4. Lead students in a discussion of the broad categories and invite them to help you label them. Some words may fit into more than one category.

5. When the map is completed, discuss the categories (such as those for dishwashers in Figure 7.2) and focus attention on those that will be highlighted in the passage to be read.

6. After the reading of the passage, revisit the map and augment it with new words that were not mentioned in the original map making.

figure   7.2   A semantic map for *dishwasher*.

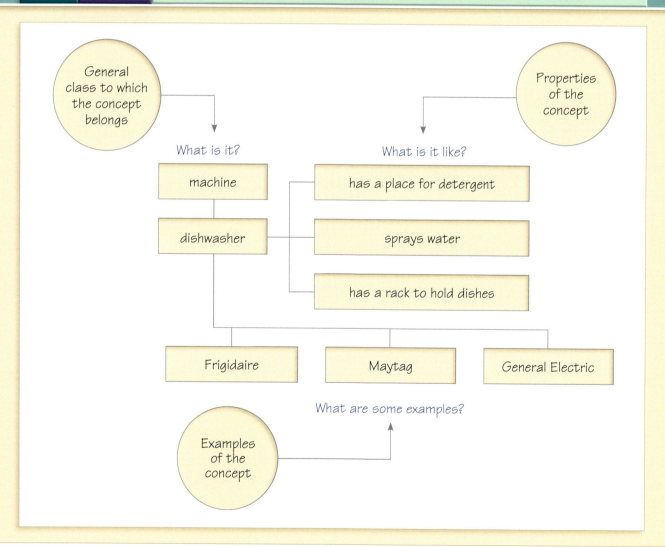

context–relationship
procedure ■

Learning new words for known concepts

When students are already familiar with a concept but are acquiring a new word to go with their existing meaning base, a method called the **context–relationship procedure** (Aulls & Graves, 1985) can be used to help students integrate the new word into their meaning vocabularies. The steps of this procedure are outlined in the following activity.

Context–Relationship Procedure

ACTIVITY

1. Write the word (e.g., *precipitation*) on the board for students and pronounce it for them. Have the students look at the word as they say it several times.

2. Present a paragraph on the board, or on individual copies, in which the word is used three or four times. Read it with the students.

   EXAMPLE: The newspaper said there was a chance of *precipitation*. Everybody got out their umbrellas to prepare for the rain. *Precipitation* can mean more than just rain. It could be snow or sleet or hail. *Precipitation* means that there will be something wet coming down from the sky.

3. Ask students a question such as the following:

   Precipitation means: A. wet weather   B. an earthquake   C. sunshine

4. Read the possible definitions and ask students to choose the best one. Discuss the answers given.

5. Read the word and its definition once again.

Moving words into children's speaking vocabularies

Encourage students to expand their speaking vocabularies, or the words they use in oral language, by recognizing and praising appropriate word usage in the classroom and by providing plenty of time and support for word play, which prompts children to experiment with words of their own choosing. The following activity fosters the development of expanded speaking vocabularies.

Semantic Gradient

ACTIVITY

1. Allow small groups of students to choose two known words with opposite meanings, such as *good/bad*, *hot/cold*, or *run/walk*.

2. Have the students put one of the words toward the top of a sheet of paper and the other toward the bottom.

3. Through small-group discussion about word meanings, have students think of words that would fit, meaningwise, between the two words, and other words that might fit above and below the words. Stress that there are no right or wrong answers.

   EXAMPLE (2nd grade):   perfect
   excellent

   good
   okay
   naughty
   mischievous

   bad
   terrible
   evil

4. Ask students to share their lists and to explain why they placed the words where they did by giving examples of how they would use the words in sentences.

Learning new meanings for known words

Many words in the English language are **polysemantic,** having multiple meanings. The word *fast*, for example, has many different meanings, such as *abstain from eating* when used as a verb, *rapid* when used as an adjective, and many more meanings when used as a noun or an adverb. If a new meaning for a word does not represent a difficult concept, you can teach it simply by discussing with students their current understanding of the word's meaning, presenting the word's new meaning, and then noting the similarities and differences when the word is used in this new way. If the new meaning is more complex, however, the method outlined in the following activity, ideal for informational text, may be more helpful.

■ polysemantic

Possible Sentences

ACTIVITY

(STAHL & KAPINUS, 1991)

1. From an upcoming reading assignment, choose several key words that might be difficult because they are used in an unfamiliar context.

    EXAMPLE: *change, spend, left*

    Choose a few additional words with which the children are already familiar.

    EXAMPLE: *boys, ball, bat, buying*

    Write these words on the chalkboard, whiteboard, or Smart board, or use paper with a document camera.

2. Provide short definitions for the difficult words or encourage any students who know the words to define them. For English learners it is helpful to provide known synonyms for the new words.

3. Ask students to make up sentences using the words in *possible sentences* that might be in the passage they are about to read.

4. Write the sentences the students suggest on the board. Read them together.

5. After the reading of the passage, revisit the sentences the students have written and decide if they could or could not be true based on new information from the passage.

6. If the sentences could not be true, have students help you revise them to make them true.

    EXAMPLE: The boy will change his bat into a ball. (could not be true)

    The boy has change left after buying a ball. (revised)

Strategies to Enhance Independent Meaning Vocabulary Growth

Because, as noted earlier, children by some estimates learn as many as 3,000 words a year, you cannot teach every new vocabulary word individually. Therefore, you must also explicitly teach strategies to help students become independent word learners through avenues such as the following, which will be explored next:

■ using the context

■ using word structure, or morphology

■ using the dictionary

- figuring out unknown words
- developing an appreciation for words

Using the context

Arguably the best independent vocabulary-enriching strategy is to use the surrounding information or *context* in a sentence to predict the meaning of an unknown word (see also Chapter 1). Context clues, however, take a variety of forms. Sometimes the word is defined in the sentence (e.g., "When someone *exchanges* something, they trade it for something else"), or it may be defined later in the paragraph. At other times synonyms or antonyms are used, or examples give the reader an idea of the meaning of the word (e.g., "The boy *exchanged*, or traded, the ball for a bat"). You may find a *think-aloud* strategy (see Chapter 8) helpful for modeling how to use context clues. The steps in the following activity provide a guideline.

Using the Context Think-Aloud

ACTIVITY

Sentence: *Carla wants to keep her candy, but José wants to exchange his for a new toy.*

1. Write the sentence on the chalkboard, whiteboard, or Smart board, or use the document reader.
2. Read the sentence aloud, sharing how you think through the problem, as in this example:

   "I wonder what *exchange* means? Let's see; the sentence says that Carla wants to keep her candy, but José wants to exchange his. It also says José wants a toy instead. The *but* must mean that José wants to do something different from keeping the candy. When I get something I don't like, I take it back to the store and trade it for something I do like. Maybe that is what José is going to do. I guess *exchange* must mean trade."

3. Provide other unknown words in context and ask student volunteers to verbalize their context usage strategies for the rest of the class or in small groups.

When there is not enough contextual information for children to determine the meaning of an unknown word, the following activity teaches them to make informed guesses about a word's meaning when they are reading independently.

Contextual Redefinition

ACTIVITY

(TIERNEY, READENCE, & DISHNER, 2005)

1. Select two or three unknown words to be pretaught.
2. Write several sentences for each word with enough clues provided for students to guess the meaning of the word. Try to use different strategies such as definitions, synonyms, and antonyms. If the actual text has enough clues to expose the meaning, use that.

   EXAMPLE (1st grade): The boy had played baseball all day long. His arms and legs were very tired. He went to bed early. The boy was *exhausted.*

3. First present the words in isolation. Pronounce the words for the students and have them repeat the words. Then ask the students to guess what they think the words might mean.
4. Then present the words in context, using the sentences you have created. Read them aloud for the students and have them discuss what the meanings might be from the words around them.

5. Finally, to help the students see the value of contextual information, guide them in a discussion of the difference between trying to guess the meanings of words in context and in isolation.

Using word structure, or morphology

Morphology is the study of the aspects of language structure related to the ways words are formed from **prefixes, root words,** and **suffixes** (e.g., re-heat-ing) and the ways in which words are related to each other. Knowing the meanings of common **affixes** (prefixes and suffixes) and combining them with meanings of familiar root or base words can help children discover the meanings of many new words. For example, if students know the meaning of *heat* and also know that the prefix *pre–* means *before,* they can conclude that the word *preheat* means to heat the oven *ahead of time.* Likewise, students can often determine the meaning of **compound words** by combining the meanings of the component parts: *dollhouse* means a house for dolls. Even the earliest readers can be taught to use word parts as they discover that the simplest, most basic structure of a word, the morpheme, can change the meaning of a word: *dog* with the addition of an *s* becomes more than one dog. In fact, the CCSS require students beginning in kindergarten to use affixes "as a clue the meaning of unknown words" (CCSS.ELA-Literacy.L.K.4.B, NGACBP & CCSSO, 2010, p. 27).

Students can be made aware of the value of word structure through the following activities.

- morphology
- prefixes
- root words
- suffixes
- affixes

- compound words

Divide and Conquer

ACTIVITY

(RASINSKI ET AL., 2011)

Begin with a list of words that share the same prefix or suffix (e.g., *preheat, preview, preread*). Post the list on a chart or interactive whiteboard, read the words out loud, and ask the students to choose one or two words and make an educated guess as to their meaning. Then ask them to speculate on the affix's meaning (e.g., *pre–* means "before"). Have students discuss the parts of the words and break the words into meaningful parts. Continue as a whole class until students understand how to break the words apart into prefix and root. Have students complete their analysis of the words on the chart, as well as provide a personal definition for each of the words.

Word Hunts

ACTIVITY

(BEAR, INVERNIZZI, TEMPLETON, & JOHNSTON, 2004)

1. As you introduce a new prefix or suffix, prepare several flip strips. To create a flip strip, print root words on the front left-hand side of colored strips of construction paper. On the back, print the suffix so that when the paper is folded, a new word appears (see Figure 7.3). Give the flip strips to the students to practice making words using each affix.

2. Using magazines, books, and newspapers, invite students to search for words that have the same structural feature, such as the prefix or suffix that was introduced. For example, students might search for all the words they can find with the suffix *–ful.* Provide a time limit.

3. Students write their words in a special word study notebook.

4. Following the word hunt, bring the students back together and record on the board or on chart paper all the words that were discovered.

5. Discuss the meaning of each word with the students. Have them verify that it contains the focus structural element, in this case *–ful.*

| figure | 7.3 | Flip strips for suffixes. |

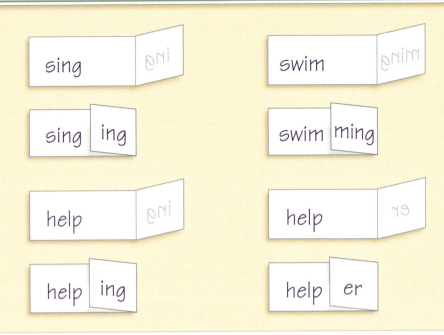

6. Words that did not contain the element should be put in a "miscellaneous" column, studied closely, and discussed to discover other patterns and word features.

Using the dictionary

The use of the dictionary must be taught in a way that leaves students with a positive attitude toward this important tool. Teaching dictionary skills should begin in kindergarten and proceed through the primary grades until students know and understand the components of a dictionary and can use them effectively. In kindergarten and first grade, the basic concept of a dictionary can be taught using a picture dictionary either online or in book form. As soon as they have some knowledge of the alphabet, students can begin to learn how to locate words or pictures, based on beginning sounds; they can then make picture dictionaries of their own. Older students, or more advanced readers with rudimentary dictionary skills and the ability to alphabetize, can coin their own words with some initial direct teaching of the common word parts shown in Figure 7.4. The "Class Dictionary" activity that follows allows them to coin words in a creative way. Personal or class picture dictionaries can also be created for domain-specific vocabulary used in a content area (e.g., math or science).

Class Dictionary

ACTIVITY

1. Over several weeks, introduce each of the word parts in Figure 7.4 with example words for each.

2. Conduct a word hunt as new parts are introduced, if the part is a common one (e.g., "re" versus "hydr").

3. Put students in small groups and ask them to form three new words by combining a prefix, a root, and a suffix in new ways.

figure	7.4	Common word parts.

	PREFIXES	ROOTS	SUFFIXES
1.	auto (self)	graph (writing)	mania (madness for)
2.	anti (against)	phon (sound)	phobia (fear of)
3.	tele (far)	hydr (water)	itis (inflammation)
4.	bi (two)	therm (heat)	ist (one who)
5.	dia (through)	meter (measure)	ic (pertaining to)
6.	con (together)	dic (say)	ism (condition of)
7.	trans (across)	vit (life)	able (able to)
8.	re (again)	port (carry)	ment (state of)
9.	in, im, un (not, in)	pen, pun (punish)	er (one who)
10.	pre (before)	vert (turn)	ion, tion (act of)

4. Instruct each group to define each of their new words by considering the meanings of each element. (*Note:* Tell the students the definitions can be humorous or serious.)

5. Encourage a spokesperson for each group to share each of their new words with the other class members and to ask them to guess the meanings of the new words from their own knowledge of the components.

6. Have each group make an illustration to accompany each of their new words. For example, see the sketch illustrating *autohydrable* (adj., capable of bathing oneself).

7. As a whole class, help students alphabetize all the words and put them into a printed and bound class dictionary.

As an alternative, have students create their drawings using a free drawing program (see the website shown in the margin for some suggested tools). Then using presentation software, a teacher together with the students can add words to their pictures and create a digital dictionary that can be posted on the class website or displayed on an interactive whiteboard.

You can also use online word reference tools to help students build dictionary skills and aid their vocabulary development (Dalton & Grisham, 2011). E-books typically include brief definitions of words that can be accessed via mouseover. In addition, teachers can download free word-reference tools that students can access while reading online text.

Suggestions for Free Drawing and Painting Tools

www.educatorstechnology.com/ 2012/07/15-free-awesome- drawing-and-painting.html

Autohydrable—a child's illustration.

Figuring out unknown words

When students read independently, they need a general strategy to unlock the meaning of unfamiliar words they encounter. Getting children into the habit of using such a strategy is not easy, but with a careful introduction and much guided practice, it can be accomplished. The following activity is based on the work of Graves (1986) and has been adapted for beginning readers.

Learning New Words

ACTIVITY

Teach the following procedure by explaining the process and then use a think-aloud to model the steps (see Chapter 8). Offer constant guided practice as students attempt the procedure themselves.

1. When you come to a word you don't know, read to the end of the sentence or paragraph to decide if the word is important to your understanding. If the word is unimportant, just keep reading.

2. If the word *is* important, reread that sentence or paragraph. Try to use the other words around it to figure out what the word means.

3. If the other words are not helpful, look for roots, prefixes, or suffixes that you know.

4. Try to sound out the word. Is it a word you have heard before?

5. If you still don't know the word, ask someone to tell you what it means or ask an older person to look it up for you in the dictionary.

6. Once you think you know the meaning of the word, reread the text and see if it makes sense.

Another activity illustrates the kind of child-centered instruction that encourages independence as well as vocabulary development. Watson (1987) suggests allowing students to select the words that are the focus of instruction. This includes domain-specific vocabulary in content-area lessons. In addition, his technique provides you with an informal assessment of how well the students are reading.

Reader-Selected Vocabulary Procedures (RSVP)

ACTIVITY

1. Give students several strips of paper to use as bookmarks. The strips are cut from letter or notebook paper and are two to three inches wide and three to five inches long.

2. Instruct the students to read as usual, but when they come to a word they do not know and it interferes with their comprehension, they are to place the bookmark there and continue to read. Encourage students to continue reading until they reach the end or come to a logical stopping point.

3. At the end of the independent reading time, ask students to go back to the place where they have placed their markers. Have them choose the one or two unknown words that *most* affected their comprehension.

4. On their bookmarks, have students write down the words and the sentences in which they came across the word and hand them to you.

5. You can use the bookmarks to organize future instruction around the vocabulary problems the students have identified. Students who are having similar problems can be grouped together for small-group instruction planned by you.

Developing an appreciation for words

Teachers who truly find the study of language fascinating can pass this excitement on to their students by constantly directing their attention to words or phrases they find effective in literature, media, online, discussion, or informal conversation (Lane & Allen, 2010). For example, while reading a poem to her class, one teacher stopped when she came to "a plethora of pink poppies" and had the students say it with her. She pointed out the alliteration of the sounds, allowing children to observe how the beginning letters "exploded" on their tongues. Then she eagerly explained the meaning of the words *plethora* and *poppies* to her pupils, who were thrilled to acquire such exciting new vocabulary.

A more direct way of imparting an appreciation for words is to have students collect words and then write them on cards to be stored in their personal word banks or shared on word walls (see Chapter 5). As a precursor to reading a Halloween story, for example, students can participate in a brainstorming session to generate "scary" words. Similarly, you can encourage students to accumulate "pretty words," "animal words," "summer words," "Arabic words," or words specific to any topic they are studying in a content area, increasing students' domain-specific vocabulary.

Technology can also help with vocabulary appreciation through the use of on-screen captions and captioned television programs. Sentences corresponding to the words spoken in videos can be presented onscreen, allowing students to see the words contextualized by the action. Many captioned videos, such as *Reading Rainbow* programs, can be obtained from video distributors or educational publishers (Tompkins, 2014). A captioned television broadcast can also be an excellent prereading activity to introduce new vocabulary and build background in an enjoyable way. Online sites for vocabulary building abound; some are high-quality and some are not. Two that provide thoughtful vocabulary-learning games are noted in the margin.

Another way to foster students' appreciation for words is to use the following activity, orally for preliterate children and in written form for beginning writers. This activity is especially suitable for classrooms with linguistically diverse children because it provides them with synonyms to words that are used often in oral language but are not descriptive or precise (e.g., *good, nice, walk, run*).

Vocabulary development in the content areas

As mentioned, the CCSS signal the need for teachers to include vocabulary development strategies in all content areas, not simply in the language arts. Fortunately, many of the vocabulary development strategies used in language arts can be used across the content areas. For example, words that have one meaning in English and associated but different meanings in mathematics can be studied explicitly, using vocabulary development activities such as creating possible sentences, semantic maps, and word dictionaries, "comparing words in English with their counterparts in the language of math" (Pierce & Fontaine, 2009).

WWW

Captioned Videos

www.readingrainbow.com/classic-series

Vocabulary-Learning Games

www.vocabulary.co.il

www.vocabulary.com

Word Aerobics

ACTIVITY

1. Write a simple sentence on the board. This sentence should contain only a subject and a simple verb or predicate.

2. Read the sentence to the students and then ask them to repeat the sentence.

    EXAMPLE: *The man ran.*

3. Ask the students to think about how they could make the sentence more vivid and precise by answering questions such as, "Where was the man going?" "What does he look like?" "Why was the man running?" "Is there another word that describes more specifically what he looked like or what he was doing [e.g., sprinting, loping, trotting, etc.]?"

4. Invite students to think of a revised sentence that would give the reader a more vivid, precise mental picture.

   EXAMPLE (2nd grade): *The tall, thin man ran after the gray cat.*

5. Encourage students to share their revised sentences. Discuss how adding descriptive words and phrases helps create a richer mental image for readers.

Note: This activity can be made accessible to English learners by allowing those who are just beginning to speak to simply repeat the original sentence; more proficient English learners can use one describing word; others can add more complex phrases.

STRATEGIES FOR ENGLISH LEARNERS

English learners come to our classrooms with a wide variety of language levels and vocabulary knowledge. All must struggle, to some degree, with academic language—the vocabulary routinely found in written text but less commonly in everyday conversation. Many English learners lack enough academic language in both their home language and English to be successful with the more complex tasks of reading formal texts (Beck, McKeown, & Kucan, 2008). Some general guidelines for making vocabulary acquisition more accessible to English learners, especially when much academic language is involved (Blachowicz & Fisher, 2010), are presented in the following section, with examples of how to use them.

Activate the Schema of the Learners

English learners often know a word or concept being taught in their own language but are not familiar with the English word(s) for it. In order to tap into their schema, you can teach English learners who are native speakers of Romance

cognates ■ languages to identify **cognates**—words with similar spellings and meanings across languages—between English and their first language. *Romance languages* refers to a group of languages such as Spanish, French, Portuguese, Italian, and Romanian that derive from Latin and thus may share cognates in some cases. It is important to explicitly teach students to draw on their knowledge of their first language in looking for cognates, as students will not do this automatically (Jiménez, 1997). You do not have to know a Romance language to help students study cognates; many websites, including Colorín Colorado, provide lists of exact cognates (e.g.,

false cognates ■ *hotel/hotel*) and **false cognates,** words that sound alike and may seem related but have quite different meanings (*embarrassed* versus *embarazada*, meaning "pregnant" in Spanish). Other sites, such as Angelfire, enable users to check whether a word has a cognate in English or in Spanish. Encourage students to determine

Colorín Colorado

www.colorincolorado.org/ educators/background/ cognates/

Angelfire

www.angelfire.com/ill/ monte/findacognate.html

whether the unknown word is a cognate using these online resources. Or a context clue in the sentence may also reveal a cognate. Consider this example sentence: "A *settlement* is usually a small *community* of people who have recently moved there." Students who speak Spanish will recognize that *community* is a cognate for *comunidad* in Spanish and conclude that a "settlement" is a community (Montelongo, Hernández, Herter, & Cuello, 2011). Students should also be cautioned to not make assumptions and to look out for false cognates (e.g., the Spanish word *bizaro* means "gallant" and not "bizarre"). False cognates are not common but can cause confusion.

Calderón and colleagues (2005) adapted Beck and McKeown's three tiers of vocabulary introduced earlier to encompass four tiers for Spanish-speaking English learners.

1. Tier one is made up of basic words and basic cognates.

2. Tier two encompasses all tier two words from Beck and McKeown's work minus the obvious cognates, which have been recategorized as part of tier one. In a departure from the original hierarchy, tier two words also include **homonyms**—words that are pronounced the same but have different spellings—which are challenging for Spanish-speaking English learners because they occur infrequently in Spanish.

   ■ homonyms

3. Tier three comprises less obvious cognates such as *disappear* and *desaparecer*.

4. Tier four consists of words that are content-specific, or the same vocabulary as in Beck and McKeown's tier three.

This reworking of the three-tiered system allows you to tailor vocabulary instruction more closely to the needs of Spanish-speaking English learners, by far the largest English learner population.

In addition, **realia,** such as pictures, brief video clips, or objects, can be helpful when introduced in tandem with the new word or concept to build new associations with the English words (Silverman & Hines, 2009). Another way to activate prior knowledge is to have English learners consider what they know about the words to be presented. Cull some words that will be in the passage to be read and then ask students, in pairs, to think about the words, discuss them, and put them into three groups: (1) "I know this word and can tell you what it means," (2) "I know something about the word," and (3) "I have never seen this word before." This activity helps English learners monitor their own knowledge, and working with a native English speaker also encourages discussion about the meanings of the words.

■ realia

Focus on Understanding

Although comprehension should be the main focus of any literacy lesson, it is more immediately pressing for English learners simply to get the gist of any passage rather than read it fluently with prosody and appropriate speed. Instructional activities such as dyad or paired reading (see Chapter 8), which ask students to summarize the paragraph a partner reader has just read or to illustrate their understanding of the paragraph if they are not fluent speakers, focus the attention squarely on reading for meaning. For English learners with some proficiency, an activity called "probable passages" can be used (Cecil & Pfeifer, 2011). In this pre-reading activity, thoroughly introduce 15 key words from a passage, pointing out any decoding issues and using realia to explain the meaning. Then, invite students to create a possible story using the story grammar or frame (the Structured Listening Activity in Chapter 8, p. 161, offers a story frame) and the 15 words. Through the use of this scaffolding device, English learners can write a story using the new vocabulary, and because the words are relevant to the gist of the story, the resultant piece usually closely predicts the author's story the students will read.

It is never too early to begin to encourage children to guess and hypothesize about new words based on what they do know.

Scaffold Vocabulary Usage

Parents of infants and toddlers often unwittingly prop up their child's language with some artful scaffolding to teach them new vocabulary through elaboration. When the

10-month-old, using telegraphic speech, exclaims, "Up!" with both arms extended, the mother might respond with something like, "Oh, you want me to pick you up in my arms and carry you for a while," increasing the child's vocabulary acquisition in the most natural of ways. Similarly, teachers who respond to the emerging language of children at the early stages of English acquisition through elaboration extend their English vocabulary. For example, since you are the model of standard English in the classroom, you need only to repeat early English learners' rudimentary messages in standard English, without correcting or criticizing them, to increase their vocabulary knowledge. For example, you can respond to "My dog, he be name Frisco," with an accepting nod that immediately acknowledges the content of the message. Then you can offer a restatement in standard English, adding elaboration and a question: "Your dog is named Frisco? That is a great name for a dog! Who thought of that name?" Alternatively, having students echo-read passages modeled by you and reading predictable texts and inviting students to join in on repeated lines are other productive ways to scaffold English vocabulary usage in the classroom.

Use Multisensory and Multimedia Approaches

When too many words are not comprehensible to English learners in the early stages of second language acquisition, students are left feeling disconnected to what is going on in the classroom. To rectify the situation, bridge the gap by sheltering, providing meaningful contexts for the words and concepts that are being introduced. In addition to pictures, film clips, charts, and graphs, you can also use gestures, charades, and pantomime in providing **sheltered instruction** to get concepts across. For any verb that is being taught, actions can make it instantly accessible to all. For example, in one second-grade class, when students got to the part of the text where "the lemmings become *exhausted* from all the swimming," the teacher turned to the class and said, "*Show* me 'exhausted'!" and led them in demonstrating just how an exhausted lemming might appear.

sheltered instruction ■

Graphic novels and comic books are another way to help scaffold new vocabulary for students by simultaneously showing the action that is being discussed. Books in audio and/or video format also can support the reading of books for young English learners. Some programs read the book while highlighting the text and then invite the student to read along. Finally, charts of multiple-meaning words, created with the students, can be helpful to English learners. Such charts might have the multiple-meaning word in the center of the chart, with the various meanings around it, including a sentence with each meaning, and a visual representation of each meaning (see Figure 7.5).

Provide Opportunities to Share Home Language

It is important for all the students in a class to honor each child's home language, hear it spoken, and understand that many English learners are already able to speak fluently in languages that others in the class, and perhaps even you, do not speak. To respect the fact that learning a second language is difficult and to develop empathy for the challenges the English learner faces, you can offer many opportunities for English learners to share their languages with classmates. At the beginning of the school year, determine the home language spoken by each student and allow each English learner to teach the rest of the class a few common phrases, such as "Good morning!" and "How are you?" in their native tongues, along with a favorite song, poem, or rhyme. This practice instantly elevates the status of each English learner. Additionally, encourage English learners to code-switch, or

| figure | 7.5 | Multiple-meaning word chart. |

A piece of jewelry we wear on our fingers or toes: She wore a giant emerald ring on her index finger. Noun.

When lots of people or animals or plants or other things make a circle around something: There was a ring of trees around the shaded spot. Noun.

RING

The sound that a bell or an alarm makes: The alarm rang so loud that I practically jumped out of my pajamas. Verb.

An area in the shape of a circle in which there's a performance: The cowboy ran out of the rodeo ring when the bull began to chase him! Noun.

write in either language, when they are doing dialogue journals (see Chapter 9). Finally, an effective writing practice is to use the universal language of poetry to allow students to intersperse words from their home languages and, as they share their poetry with their classmates, to invite them to explain what the words mean through charades, pantomime, art, or other means.

Focus on the Functional Use of Language

"Skill and drill" classrooms, where endless worksheets are completed in isolation, are not places where language learning naturally occurs; second language acquisition happens much more quickly when language is used to communicate for authentic reasons that are important to the language learners. Having students participate in literature circles (see Chapter 11), engaging them in collaborative learning where they are talking about what they are doing, and creating classrooms where students are encouraged to ask classmates when they do not understand something are all examples of instances where language is used purposefully. You can teach the various functions of language more formally in the classroom as well. For example, when students are reading content-area texts with much new vocabulary, they can use structured language frames to practice domain-specific vocabulary as well as specific language functions. For example, an upcoming unit may require students to understand the concept of a "habitat." You then determine an appropriate language function to use for the concept, such as compare/contrast or description. First, give the students a simple explanation of each word: "A habitat is a place where something lives." Then provide a sentence frame to help the students practice, in pairs, the new vocabulary with an important language function: "The _____ (habitat) of a bird is a tree, *while* the _____ (habitat) of a deer is _____ (the forest)." English learners can use the appropriate frames with the new vocabulary before, during, and after the unit to increase language skill and vocabulary knowledge (Donnelly & Roe, 2010).

VOCABULARY DEVELOPMENT FOR STUDENTS WITH SPECIAL NEEDS

Students with learning disabilities do not learn vocabulary in the same manner as students who do not have learning disabilities (Baumann, Kame'enui, & Ash, 2003). While strategies that work well for mainstream students have also been found effective with students with special needs, you need to use methods above and beyond those used with mainstream students. These methods include giving students multiple opportunities supported by visuals and direct teaching of vocabulary definitions, as well as providing written or rebus-type (pictorial) learning strategies that students can use to figure out the meaning of unknown words (Dexter, Park, & Hughes, 2011). In addition, teachers of students with special needs should offer a limited number of new vocabulary words and make vocabulary instruction a regular daily part of instruction (Kennedy et al., 2012).

Technology is also an effective tool for teaching vocabulary to students with special needs. You can create *e-word walls* using a presentation program to integrate pictures and spoken language for learning vocabulary. These are helpful in teaching students along the autism spectrum, who often need both auditory and visual information in order to effectively internalize new vocabulary (Narkon, Wells, & Segal, 2011). The e-word wall also allows you to personalize the visuals used to learn the vocabulary (for example, using a photo of the student's family, or the voice of a family member stating the definition of the word).

A variety of apps have been tailored to teach vocabulary to students with special needs (Palmer, 2013). For example, the Sosh app helps students who struggle with social skills to simulate working step-by-step through difficult social situations, thus giving them the concepts and vocabulary they need to self-regulate during those situations. Such terms for metacognition include *regulate, reason,* and *relate.* Another app, Symbol Support, translates words into pictures or symbols, providing visual clues for difficult vocabulary. This app is helpful for students with cognitive disabilities. Finally, ConversationBuilder provides vocabulary for use during day-to-day conversations in a number of social situations. This app is helpful for students with special needs who struggle breaking into or holding conversations, as it allows them to memorize and practice vocabulary words and phrases needed to relate to their peers and others.

MODIFYING TRADITIONAL APPROACHES

many activities purporting to develop students' vocabulary accompany most basal readers, but they are not always effective or appropriate. With a few adjustments, however, these approaches can often be made more constructive. Here are some ideas to keep in mind when following basal manual instructions for introducing new meaning vocabulary:

1. Begin instruction with what the students already know. Instead of telling students the meaning of words they may not know, first ask them, "What do you know about these words?" It is never too early to begin to encourage students to take risks by guessing and hypothesizing about new words, based on what they do know.

2. Use as many senses as possible when introducing new words. Instead of always *telling* students the meanings of new words, have the class act out action words ("*Show* me exhausted!") and sing, draw, or demonstrate other words ("This is how you pirouette!"). Also, don't forget the old saying, also true in vocabulary acquisition, that a picture is worth a thousand words—especially for second language learners, who especially need a visual context for the word.

3. Give students meaningful opportunities to use their new words. Using only the strategy of providing definitions before reading a story or reinforcing new words with workbook pages does not markedly increase meaning vocabulary unless students actually use the words introduced. The words must be used in daily conversations and writing to become part of the students' permanent knowledge.

4. Encourage students to teach each other. Sometimes students are better able to explain new words and concepts to each other than a teacher or a glossary is. Because young students think concretely, they can often present examples of the word that will help others who are not relating the word to anything they already know. This strategy is helpful with students who are English learners.

5. Model curiosity about words and good dictionary habits. For students who are not yet ready to use a dictionary, observing a respected adult musing, "I wonder what that word means?" and then looking it up and sharing the meaning with the class would be an excellent introduction.

SUMMARY

Children learn to identify words in order to develop reading fluency and to understand the meanings of words as they add approximately 3,000 words to their vocabularies every year. This chapter has focused specifically on meaning vocabulary and what we know about how it is acquired and how it grows in beginning readers.

Effective meaning vocabulary development strategies include reading aloud to children, helping them appreciate words, encouraging wide reading experiences and application of new words, presenting strategies for independently figuring out new words, and explicit teaching of vocabulary and vocabulary-related skills. The ultimate goal of all vocabulary instruction should be to inspire students to become independent word collectors who enjoy acquiring new words. Such learners become the students who comprehend best and thus read the most, entering into a self-perpetuating cycle of success.

Learning the meanings of many new words is unquestionably an integral part of a balanced comprehensive literacy program for early readers. The more numerous the reading, writing, listening, and speaking experiences young children have, the more they will come into contact with intriguing new words. It is through precisely such experiences that the meaning vocabularies of children grow, just as it is through the excitement of reading and writing that they blossom into readers and writers.

questions   FOR JOURNAL WRITING AND DISCUSSION

1. Think back to your own early schooling. Do you remember having to look up definitions for vocabulary words? Do you feel you benefited from that experience? How will you teach vocabulary differently?

2. Design and discuss an ideal classroom environment in which meaning vocabulary acquisition could flourish. What, if anything, would you change in your design if you had many English learners in your classroom? Students with special needs? Why?

3. How would you explain your approach to vocabulary instruction to parents of your students? Pair up with another member of the class and role-play,

presenting your explanation to a parent. Change roles and attempt to make a similar explanation to a teacher who believes only in having students memorize definitions.

4. How would you explain to a parent of an English learner the value of reading to his child in the home language?

suggestions   FOR PROJECTS AND FIELD ACTIVITIES

1. Construct a board game that requires players to respond with synonyms or antonyms when they land on certain spaces or draw certain cards. Include examples of cognates in English and Spanish. Demonstrate the game to your classmates, asking them to role-play primary-age students, or use the game with second- or third-graders in a regular classroom or tutoring setting.

2. Ask three 5-year-old students, three 6-year-old students, three 7-year-old students, and three 8-year-old students to tell you the meanings of the following words: *ask, tell, sister,* and *girl.* Record their responses. Were there differences in the children's abilities to give precise definitions for the words? Discuss your findings with your classmates. Repeat the activity with a range of English learners.

3. Select several new terms encountered in this chapter. Decide which ones could be defined, or partially defined, using the context or word parts. Teach these words to a small group of your classmates using one of the vocabulary development activities in this chapter.

Reading Comprehension

MAKING SENSE OF PRINT

focus questions

How is reading comprehension currently defined by reading researchers and practitioners? How does such a definition inform instruction?

What strategies do skilled readers employ to help them construct meaning from text?

What special challenges do English learners and students with special needs face in achieving reading comprehension?

What are some components of an effective program for teaching reading comprehension?

even-year-old Tiffani reads the words slowly and deliberately to the teacher: "Bobby will go to the party if his sister cleans her room." Tiffani is able to pronounce each of the twelve words in the sentence perfectly. Moreover, since English is her first language, she has probably known the meaning of each of the individual words in the sentence for several years. But Tiffani reports, after reading this sentence, "I get it! The sister went to the party while Bobby cleaned his room!" Mr. Nguyen is rather surprised at this misinformed interpretation of the sentence, but he probably shouldn't be. Simply being able to read the words on a page does not ensure that Tiffani or other beginning readers like her will necessarily understand what they are reading.

Early readers like Tiffani need to be taught directly how language works within the context of a sentence, paragraph, and book. They also need support in acquiring specific strategies that skilled readers use to fully comprehend what they are reading. Then they need plenty of opportunity to use those strategies freely under the watchful eye of a competent and caring teacher.

WHAT IS COMPREHENSION?

comprehension ■

Comprehension is the construction of meaning and is the ultimate goal of exemplary, comprehensive reading instruction. Proficient readers, and beginning readers too, construct meaning by making connections—by integrating what they already know about a topic with what they encounter in print. As they establish meaning, skilled readers also use their knowledge about the structure of the text they are reading—*informational* or *narrative*, folktales or historical fiction—to make predictions about what they expect to discover. They also use problem-solving strategies to monitor their thinking and interpret the meaning of the text (Israel & Duffy, 2008).

Reading comprehension begins as *listening* comprehension in preschool and prekindergarten. Young children can be taught to listen analytically and to practice the same thinking skills that will help them unlock text meaning once they reach automaticity in decoding. However, instruction in listening comprehension should continue throughout the grades, with students practicing and mastering more sophisticated listening comprehension skills over their educational careers.

If a student can decode the words in a text but, like Tiffani in the opening vignette, cannot understand what those words mean, is the child actually reading? Research suggests that she is not, for reading must be both purposeful and active in the construction of the intended meaning of the text. To comprehend, a reader must have a specific purpose for reading, whether it is to find out how to fold an origami swan, to discover where the robber hid the gold, to learn about math, or simply to enjoy. A reader must also be actively engaged in thinking as she reads, using her experiences in the world and her knowledge of specific words and the way language works to make sense of the text and receive the author's message. Finally, when a reader does not understand a sentence or paragraph, she needs to be aware of it and know how to resolve the problem (National Institute for Literacy, 2001).

In comprehensive literacy instruction, comprehension is now seen as an interactive process. Meaning and content are embedded in the text, but each reader or listener also brings particular knowledge and personal ideas to the reading/listening task; comprehension occurs when the reader or listener thinks critically, makes meaning by coming to grips with the text, and collaborates and negotiates with the author's meaning toward an understanding of both the text and the writer of the text (Sweet & Snow, 2003). The discerning teacher, then, assumes the role of coach, encouraging the trial and error that accompanies fledgling meaning-making and also moderating unsuccessful attempts without discouraging the student.

The Common Core State Standards as well as many state standards have raised expectations regarding comprehension. Students are now expected to understand a text on three levels, as described in Figure 8.1 (Shanahan, 2012). The three levels—key ideas and details, craft and structure, and integration of knowledge and ideas—appear as organizing heads for the Anchor standards for reading as well as the grade-level standards for reading literature and reading informational text.

The emphasis on the levels of understanding means that teachers must go well beyond what was asked of students by previous state standards as well as by most previous curricula to help students engage in the processes that enable deep understanding of text meaning at all three levels. This challenge is critical, as it will allow all students to engage in text "uncovering" and discussion at higher levels that, for the most part, were previously asked only of students in advanced placement and gifted classrooms.

figure	8.1

Three levels of text comprehension as emphasized by the CCSS as well as many state standards (Shanahan, 2012).

1. What did the text say? (literal and inferential understanding of key ideas and details)

2. How did the text say it? (writer's craft and text structure, or the decisions the author made that affected meaning and tone?)

3. How does the text connect to other texts in terms of meaning and value? (integration of knowledge and ideas)

AN IDEAL CLIMATE FOR CRITICAL THINKING

In an ideal classroom climate for thinking and comprehending in a comprehensive literacy program, students' faces are alive with excitement and every hand is up because every child's imagination is churning and producing ideas about the reading material at hand. Young minds are being stimulated and challenged, and many questions are asked for which there are no right or wrong answers. Immediately upon entering such a classroom, an observer notices how questions and answers proliferate, many of them initiated by the students themselves. Classrooms that embody this kind of enthusiastic interchange strengthen the spirit of children and spark the flames of curiosity. In such classrooms, students respect their own thoughts and ideas and the thoughts and ideas of others; they are open to new experiences and ways to figure things out. Such a classroom climate is most conducive to nurturing readers who feel up to the task of negotiating meaning with texts.

The term **critical literacy,** which has been found to enhance reading comprehension, describes practices that guide students to interact with texts in powerful ways (Labadie, Wetzel, & Rogers, 2012). These practices include helping students do the following:

■ critical literacy

1. interrogate common assumptions mirrored in the text to discover stereotypes that may be present in a reading.

2. recognize various points of view about an event or issue presented in a piece of text.

3. reveal social justice issues suggested in a text.

4. take action to address a social justice issue, after conducting inquiry on the issue. (Lewison et al., 2008)

Such practices, because they engage the reader deeply in understanding text and empathizing with characters, enhance reading comprehension (Literacy GAINS, 2009). To access lesson plans using critical literacy practices, visit the website in the margin.

Critical Literacy Lesson Plans

www.rethinkingschools.org/index.shtml

A critical, collaborative, language- and text-rich instructional environment is beneficial for all students but particularly for English learners. For example, many students from Latin cultures are accustomed to working together for the good of the community, a process that is encouraged in their families (Rothstein-Fisch & Trumbull, 2008). They are therefore likely to be comfortable working in small cooperative groups where a group goal is required. And because English learners often struggle with the academic language used in many textbooks (Vacca & Vacca, 2010), cooperative classroom environments where students help one another through rich conversations about the tasks at hand are not only desirable but also necessary for their success.

One way to foster students' willingness and ability to think critically and to comprehend is for the teacher to remove any factors that block—in herself or in her students—the willingness to accept new ideas. To do this, the teacher must in some cases eradicate ingrained patterns of behavior in herself, such as the tendency to evaluate all answers students give to questions. In other cases the teacher may need to take more of a direct role than usual and provide students with some rudimentary background knowledge to enable them to think about what they are reading (Cecil & Pfeifer, 2011). Specifically, the teacher–coach in a classroom conducive to thinking and comprehending must consider the following factors, among others: knowledge, think time, and praise.

Knowledge

schema ◼

For students to think about what they are reading, they must have some background knowledge of the topic being considered. This is sometimes called a **schema**—the background of expectations, knowledge, attitudes, feelings, and predictions an individual may hold about a topic. Clearly, students cannot critically examine a topic if they know nothing at all about the subject. For example, a teacher may wish to introduce an informational piece about snakes with a critical question such as, "Why are snakes important to us?" Although this seems to be an excellent open-ended question, it may be a poor first question to introduce the piece, for many children may not have enough background knowledge about snakes to formulate an answer. By contrast, after the teacher reads students an article about snakes, shows excerpts of videos about snakes, shows pictures of different species of snakes, and discusses them with the class—all excellent prereading strategies—students are more able and eager to respond to the original question, backing up their ideas, thoughts, and opinions with facts gleaned from the information they have just received. These activities have helped students create a schema or recall background they already had. Helping students acquire a knowledge base is often a first step in the total process of comprehending text.

Think Time

Thinking through comprehension strategies takes time. Unfortunately, it is often the students who are quick thinkers or vociferous who respond in class to critical-thinking questions, thus getting most of the practice in such skills. Moreover, students from various cultural groups, such as some Southeast Asians, may have been taught at home to be unfailingly polite and even self-effacing, and they may often be overshadowed by more assertive students. A pattern can be quickly established in the classroom: The teacher demonstrates a comprehension strategy and follows up with a critical-thinking question. Six "eager beavers" have their hands in the air or shout out the answer before the others have even had a chance to consider the question. The other students notice that if they delay raising their hands, the quicker, more assertive students answer and the slower thinkers, or less forthcoming youngsters, are not held accountable for thinking. To increase the engagement level for all students, the teacher should provide as much "think time" as necessary for every student to think through an answer to a critical-thinking question. A further strategy is to ask students to "turn and talk" their response, so that all students get a chance to share their thinking. Students can be strategically paired so each is with a student at a different level of English language proficiency.

Praise

A strong (perhaps overly strong) praise response is exemplified by a teacher who responds to a child's answer with, "That's exactly the right answer! Excellent job!" A more tempered response, such as, "Yes, Kay, that is one way to think about the boy's problem," acknowledges the child's thinking rather than the response, and also keeps the window open for different responses by other members of the class.

The use of robust praise is sometimes appropriate—as when working with very young students, second language learners who are just emerging from their **silent period** (the period during which they are faced with a new language and are not speaking but are developing receptive language skills), students with special needs, or when asking a question of factual or low-level recall, such as, "Raúl, what was the name of the little boy's dog?" On the other hand, when the goal is to have students think critically or creatively about text, the teacher should temper strong praise to student responses because teacher praise can become the reason students volunteer answers, rather than for the mere sharing of their ideas. The goal should be to help students discover intrinsic sources for their motivation as well as to produce more extended and meaningful talk. Overly strong praise tends to encourage conformity and short "known" answers, causing students to depend on the praise-giver for the worth of their ideas, rather than on themselves and their own satisfaction with their thinking.

■ silent period

READING STRATEGIES FOR COMPREHENDING

r *eading comprehension strategies* are among the skills proficient readers use to gain personal meaning from literature. Good readers and writers are *always* in the process of creating meaning. They select from appropriate strategies, monitoring their understanding as they read (or listen, in the case of prereaders) and refining that meaning as they encounter new information in the text.

Essential Strategies to Teach

Essential comprehension strategies, discussed next, include the following (Tompkins, 1997):

- making predictions
- tuning in to prior knowledge
- visualizing
- making connections

- monitoring understanding
- generalizing
- evaluating
- asking and answering questions

These strategies must be adapted for early readers and, as mentioned earlier, may involve listening rather than reading. The activities later in the chapter will offer ideas for incorporating and modeling these strategies.

Previewing and making predictions

Proficient readers (and listeners) make mental predictions, or calculated hunches, about what might happen next in the text they are reading. Their hunches are based on what they already know about the topic, what they know about the literary structure the author is using (e.g., is it narrative or informational text? a fairy tale or an autobiographical event?), and what they have learned thus far in the text. As skilled readers continue, they tend to confirm or nullify their previous hunches, according to new understandings that occur. In the case of informational text, effective readers often preview text to get an overview of what information will be covered, looking through it to see if it matches their expectations.

Tuning in to prior knowledge

Proficient readers (and young listeners) consider what they already know about a topic before they begin reading, and then they assimilate the new information by integrating it with their prior knowledge during the reading process. Such background knowledge may include, but is not limited to, knowledge of the text structure the author is using, familiarity with the literary genre, and the reader's vocabulary and knowledge about the topic. This prior knowledge constitutes a schema for the topic, with which further learning will need to be reconciled.

Visualizing

Proficient readers tend to create pictures in their mind's eye as they read and listen to text, especially text containing elaborate imagery or well-developed story characters. Placing themselves in the story as the main character—imagining themselves facing the same trials and tribulations as that character—helps them appreciate, remember, and internalize the story that is unfolding before them (Wilson, 2012). (See the Case Example on visualizing on p. 158.) The experience of mental vision is so personal and intense that readers skilled in this strategy are often disappointed when they see the film version of a story they have read, because the film frequently pales by comparison with what occurs in their rich imaginations.

Making connections

Proficient readers tend to personalize whatever they are reading and hearing by relating it directly to their own lives. They categorize events according to their own sets of experiences and compare story characters to people they know. Experienced readers also compare what they are reading to other literature they have read. Making connections can extend even further when the skilled reader compares books written by the same author or various versions of the same tale or event.

Monitoring understanding

Proficient readers continually check their understanding as they read, making sure the content conforms to what they already know and to new knowledge gained during the reading itself, and assuring themselves they haven't missed something. Therefore, skilled readers often make frequent regressions or go back and reread a sentence or passage to check that they initially "got it right." Monitoring understanding is a two-step process: students have that "aha" moment in which they realize their understanding has been interrupted, followed by the realization that now they must do something about their lack of understanding, such as go back and reread. Such monitoring occurs, for example, when a skilled reader is reading an unstimulating text late at night and suddenly realizes that not a word has been understood—a phenomenon to which most of us can relate!

Generalizing

Proficient readers tend to remember important ideas and information they discover throughout a text and bring them together to draw conclusions. Such conclusions then form the "big picture" of the reading material; such a strategy is the basis on which skilled readers are able to summarize what they have read or to articulate the main idea in informational text and separate it from the supporting details. Generalization is also the basis on which readers are able to identify particular underlying themes in literature.

Evaluating

Proficient readers and listeners reflect on and form personal opinions about the texts they encounter; they internalize the meanings certain works have held for them, review ideas frequently, and evaluate what they have read compared with other texts and what they had hoped to gain from the text. Such opinions and reflections about text are not transmitted to the student by a teacher but emanate directly from the child's own thinking about the personal transaction with the material.

Even the youngest readers benefit from comprehension strategies such as making predictions and connections and tuning in to prior knowledge.

Asking and answering questions

One of the most valuable ways proficient readers/listeners construct text meanings is by asking and answering important questions about the text as they read. They know the difference between "thinking" questions and "locating information" questions, and they can later reflect on the caliber of the questions they have asked themselves.

Teaching the Use of Comprehension Strategies

Teachers must explicitly teach reading comprehension strategies, as often students do not pick them up on their own (McLaughlin, 2012). Unfortunately, teachers do not always spend enough time ensuring that students have mastered critical comprehension strategies. An ethnographic study of 43 third-grade classrooms found that teachers spent an average of little more than a minute per day on comprehension strategy instruction (Connor, Morrison, & Petrella, 2004), whereas far more time is spent on individual decoding skills in most primary classrooms. Flynt and Cooter (2005) suggest deciding on key comprehension strategies, such as those discussed earlier, and then spending at least three weeks introducing and reinforcing them in minilessons, an approach they call "marinating." Researchers have attested that children must be taught, directly, what each comprehension strategy is, how and when to use such a strategy, and the circumstances under which they should use it. The teacher should first model each strategy, and then the students should receive guided practice in applying the strategy, and finally students should use it independently with feedback from the teacher (Duffy, Roehler, & Hermann, 1988) (see the Case Example for a description of explicit teaching of a comprehension strategy). Although introducing the strategies one by one is useful initially, teachers must model using the strategies in concert with each other, just as proficient readers do. Think-alouds during read-alouds are especially effective for modeling the use of reading comprehension strategies.

CASE EXAMPLE

Jane Waskeiwitz teaches visualizing

Explicit teaching begins

"Today we are going to learn another way readers think DUR-ING reading. It's called 'visualizing.'

"One way good readers visualize during reading is to make pictures in their heads," she continues. "I'm going to show you how, and then it will be your turn. I'll start with one word."

Jane pulls out a card with the word *dog* printed on it and places it beside the word *image* in the pocket chart. Jane then begins her think-aloud.

"I know this is the word *dog.* When I read *dog,* I can make an image in my head of a dog. The dog I see has reddish fur that is long and silky. He is about this big [she holds her hand about three feet from the floor]. He has flop-py ears and brown eyes. I also have a smell image, because this dog needs a bath!" The kids giggle, and several put their thumbs up.

"Jerry, what are you thinking?" she asks.

"I guessed it is Chester," he says.

"Me, too," says a girl with her thumb up.

"You are right. I was thinking about my dog," Jane says.

"He's a golden retriever," a boy adds knowingly.

Jane explains: "I want you to notice HOW I was thinking about the word *dog.*" The students seem puzzled. "What were the *visual* images I made in my head?" she coaches.

"You said he was reddish and had brown eyes." A boy responds to the category of color.

"I did have that in my brain image," Jane says. "What else?"

"You said he was silky. That is texture," explains a girl.

"Size! You showed us how big he is," exclaims a boy.

"You could have showed us his shape," adds another boy.

"You are absolutely right, Joshua," Jane says. They are on a roll, and now there are hands up all over. Jane takes another minute to allow students to share and then proceeds.

"Okay, I did the image making in my head, and now it is your turn. I have a new word to read. When I show the card, just read it in your mind, not out loud." Jane shows a card that has the word *cat.*

Scaffolded practice

"You can close your eyes, if you like. I'll give you suggestions, and you try to make the image in your head. First, make a pic-ture of a cat. Imagine it any color you want." Jane pauses. "Now think the shape of the cat. In your head draw a line around its body like we do with shapes in art prints." She pauses again. "Now visualize how the cat's fur feels, the texture."

Some students are squinting. Others have covered their eyes with their hands. Some are looking up.

"This is our first try. Let's see how you did. Find your Study Buddy and tell each other about your images. Start with whoever is A for this week, and I'll cue you for Person B. Begin."

Text use and independent practice

Jane takes the book *Millions of Cats* from the chalk tray and reads aloud the first sentence. She then does a think-aloud to model her image making. The students then have a go at it and share with their partners. Jane then continues reading without showing any of the pictures, stopping several times for students to share their own mental pictures. These include specifics about the setting, characters (an old man and woman), and more cats.

There is a recess break, and when the students return Jane asks them why they think making images in their heads would help them be good readers. The students reiterate how it is fun and add how it makes them think more. One says it would help them remember ideas. Jane writes down the children's comments on sentence strips and adds them to an ongoing bulletin board labeled "What Good Readers Do." Now it is time for Daily Engaged Independent Read-ing (DEIR), and Jane reminds students to use all their good reader strategies and to use a sticky note to mark one place in their books where they try visualizing.

Adapted from C. Cornett. (2010). *Comprehension First: Inquiry into Big Ideas Using Important Questions.* Scottsdale, AZ: Holcomb Hathaway.

Of all the strategies, monitoring comprehension is the foundation strategy for students to understand and use. For preliterate students, teachers should focus on the monitoring of listening comprehension during read-alouds. Teachers should model the other strategies during think-alouds as "fix it up" strategies when comprehension breaks down. While teachers must use an appropriate amount of instruction so that reading strategy skills are mastered, research shows that extended practice of reading strategies is not necessary, and time is better spent on other important language arts areas such as vocabulary development and analysis of writer's craft (Willingham and Lovette, 2014).

The CCSS as well as many state standards signal the importance of teaching students to use reading comprehension strategies across the subject areas (NGACBP & CCSSO, 2010). For example, many of the strategies can be taught using text from the mathematics content area (Halladay & Neumann, 2012). Students can be taught to monitor their own understanding of word problems or to make connections with prior learning (e.g., ask students, "How can our solution to yesterday's problem about tree-growing rates help us understand how to solve today's problem?"). Likewise, such strategies can be taught explicitly while reading from a science textbook, which often lends itself to an examination of how to use text features such as captions and headings to better understand content (Bryce, 2011).

Fountas and Pinnell (2006) offer helpful lists of teacher prompts that correspond to specific reading comprehension strategies. Students can be taught to use these prompts independently to help them focus on text meaning. Teachers model using the prompts during minilessons to help students understand how to process text at various levels, including "thinking within the text" (literal meanings), "thinking beyond the text" (including inferring and predicting), and "thinking about the text" (including analyzing and critiquing the text). Such prompts are helpful as they provide models of "what good readers do" that are specific to understanding text. For example, a prompt that students can use to help them understand a passage of text at the literal level would be "Good readers understand how to use the features of nonfiction texts to help them find information." An example of a prompt that students can use to help them comprehend text at a deeper level would be "Good readers understand that some information is stated, and some is found 'between the lines.'"

When teaching comprehension strategies, note that while students must be aware of the strategies and how to use them, discussion of the strategies should not distract students from the meaning of the text, but rather help them discern text meaning (McKeown, Beck, & Blake, 2009). In other words, it is more helpful for you to model prompts you ask yourself to help process a text. Here is an effective prompt: "As I read, I notice how the author uses words to make the reader feel a certain way. In this book, the author (Viorst, 1987) used the words 'terrible, horrible, no good, very bad,' repeating words that make us feel sad." A less effective prompt, "What comprehension strategy did you use here?" may sidetrack the student on a discussion of strategies rather than focusing on the meaning of the text.

INSTRUCTIONAL ACTIVITIES FOR TEACHING COMPREHENSION

Students do not learn to comprehend text just by doing a lot of reading. Teachers must help students learn how to comprehend by explaining comprehension strategies and then explicitly demonstrating how proficient readers gain meaning using those strategies. Moreover, teachers must provide authentic reading experiences in which students can apply those prompts and strategies (Block & Pressley, 2007). The activities offered in this section incorporate the comprehension strategies discussed in the preceding section. Activities are designated for use during prereading, reading, or postreading, as appropriate. The activities can begin with students as early as kindergarten, when no written response is requested. Written responses can be included as soon as children have the writing proficiency to answer the questions, but oral responses should always be an option. Oral discussions during the activities, accompanied by pictures, objects, or other visuals, have the added benefit of allowing English learners to listen to the way others are thinking, practice their academic language orally before being asked to use it in writing, and participate as they feel comfortable. Teachers may also visit the websites identified in Appendix C for other activities designed to foster reading comprehension.

see appendix C

As stated earlier, when teaching reading comprehension strategies, teachers should first explain the process involved in using the strategy and then model it for students. They should explain that strategies are used in concert with each other, and have differing purposes. Then teachers can work with students on activities such as the ones in this section for practice using strategies such as the Directed Reading–Thinking Activity for predicting, the Knowledge Chart for accessing background knowledge, and so forth.

Directed Listening–Thinking Activity and Directed Reading–Thinking Activity

ACTIVITY

A GUIDED READING ACTIVITY (see Chapter 11)

The objectives of directed listening–thinking activities (DLTAs) and directed reading–thinking activities (DRTAs), originally developed by Stauffer (1969, 1980), are to improve comprehension by having students focus on a book or passage and to make predictions about it based on textual features. The DLTA and DRTA are some of the most commonly used approaches to a listening or reading comprehension lesson; most basal readers more or less follow this format. Although they can be conducted in various ways, the steps include the following:

Prereading

1. Direct the children's attention to the title of the passage and ask them to predict its content. After the students have volunteered their predictions and the reasons for their responses, ask a preselected group whether they agree or disagree and why.

During Reading

2. Read or ask a student to read several sentences and ask the students what they think the story is about, based on this new information.
3. Direct the children's attention to vocabulary or phrases that are especially relevant to the meaning of the text. Ask them to use these words to hypothesize what the piece is about.
4. Ask them to look at pictures, graphs, and figures and make more predictions based on this new information. Prompt for demonstration of other standards-based skills and thinking, such as noticing how characters change or how characters' actions contribute to plot development.

Postreading

5. Ask the students to remember or reread the text to confirm or negate their predictions and hypotheses. Discuss findings. Summarize the piece as appropriate.

Structured Listening Activity (SLA)

A C T I V I T Y

■ structured listening activity

For preliterate children, comprehension can be enhanced in an enjoyable way through a **structured listening activity** (SLA) that establishes the story line with visuals, allowing even preschool children and non-English-speaking students to participate in the telling and retelling of a story. In this sense, it is a good example of sheltered instruction. Here are the steps to be followed:

1. Draw or trace, color, or cut out felt visuals of each of the main characters and props to set the story you have chosen to read to the children, for example, *The Gingerbread Boy.* Display these visuals on a flannel board or an interactive whiteboard (see Figure 8.2).

Prereading

2. Introduce the key concepts in the story (e.g., "Have you ever run away from anyone? Why?").

During Reading

3. Read the story once with the visuals. Reread the story, focusing children's attention on the visuals that support the events in the story.

Postreading

4. Ask the students to retell the story with the help of a chart such as the one shown in Figure 8.3. Help them fill in this chart.
5. Ask for volunteers to retell the story while other students manipulate the visuals. (*Note:* Non–English speakers may be encouraged to retell the story in their home language.) Use the story frame (Figure 8.3) to assist in the retelling.

| figure | 8.2 | Flannel board depicting the ending of the story *The Gingerbread Boy.* |

OTHER PROPS:

Grandmother
oven
bird
rabbit
cat
horse
happy gingerbread boy
house

figure	8.3	Story frame for retelling.	

Somebody	Wanted	But	So
Gingerbread Boy	to run & play	a fox came	he got eaten

Dyad Reading

ACTIVITY

dyad reading ■   **Dyad reading** is a form of paired oral reading (also called "buddy reading" or "say something") that reinforces the important comprehension strategies of summarizing and questioning. The activity consists of the following format:

1. Select two students to demonstrate the activity. One reads a paragraph aloud. (With younger children, this can be reduced to one sentence.)
2. As that student reads, the other student listens carefully and then summarizes (orally or in writing) what was in the paragraph. For variation, the second student may simply quickly sketch what was read, then describe the picture.

Postreading

gradual release
of responsibility ■

3. The reader creates critical comprehension questions to ask the listener. In a **gradual release of responsibility** ("I do," "we do," "you do") process, first model the creation of these questions, then, after time, co-construct them with the students; when you see that the students are ready, they create the questions independently.
4. Encourage students to discuss the answers and, where there is disagreement, to refer to the paragraph to support their answers.
5. Call for students to change roles with succeeding paragraphs.

When students appear ready to practice this activity independently, divide the class into pairs or groups of three. (*Note:* In a threesome, a student who is an English learner or a nonreader can get the gist of the passage simply by listening to it being read and then summarized. If this strategy is used, the pair of students needs to be coached to include the English learner or nonreader in the conversation, as appropriate, perhaps asking questions such as "Can you say the summary in your own words?" or "Can you describe the picture in your own words?" If the English learner or nonreader is not included in the conversation, there is a danger that he will become disengaged.)

Story Prediction

ACTIVITY

Story prediction can be used as a written adaptation of the DRTA to help students develop elaborate predictions about the basal reader or trade book stories they will read (Buckley, 1986). For this activity, pair students or divide the class into small groups. Then follow this sequence:

Prereading

1. The partners or members of the group leaf through the illustrations in the story in order. Then each partner or group member takes a turn carefully describing what is happening in each illustration. After each illustration is described, the next student in rotation predicts aloud what will happen in that part of the story.

2. After all the illustrations in the story have been discussed in this way, each student writes a story predicting what will happen in the story according to what was described in the illustrations. (Younger students can record their predictions.)

3. The partners or group members share their stories with the rest of the class and discuss their opinions about the accuracy of each prediction.

During Reading

4. The partners or group members take turns reading the story aloud (or silently) to check their predictions. (For younger students, you may read the story.)

Postreading

5. The partners or group members compare the actual story with their predictive stories and discuss, as a group, who they think came closest to the actual events in the story.

Think-Aloud

A C T I V I T Y

■ think-aloud

A **think-aloud** is one of the most effective ways a teacher can model all the effective comprehension strategies a fluent reader uses to gain meaning from the printed page. You may use this activity in the following way:

1. Beforehand, make copies of the text passage that will be demonstrated or prepare it for a projector or interactive whiteboard.

Prereading

2. After looking at the cover or the title and the illustrations in the passage, ruminate aloud as to what the passage might be about, and what you are basing your predictions on.

During Reading

3. Read the passage aloud as the students track. Continually organize images by explaining the passage after every sentence or paragraph.

4. Answer aloud such questions as the following:

    "What am I reminded of here that I already know?" (tapping prior knowledge)

    "What are some ways I can get help understanding unfamiliar words and/or ideas? When do I notice that I am not understanding what I'm reading, or my mind is wandering?" (monitoring understanding)

    "What does this remind me of in my own life?" (making connections)

5. After modeling the reading of several paragraphs in this fashion, invite students to add their own comprehension/problem-solving tactics and personal impressions by reading succeeding passages in pairs.

Think-Aloud Mysteries

A C T I V I T Y

(SMITH, 2006)

For struggling readers, you can use "think-aloud mysteries" (Smith, 2006). In this think-aloud variation, a small group of students work together to identify the "mystery" solution as they read a short passage that you have written beforehand on sentence strips. They look at one sentence at a time and participate in a think-aloud discussion about what "evidence" is provided in each strip. From this evidence, they offer predictions and hypotheses. Initially, you may guide them using typical higher-level comprehension questions. Figure 8.4 shows a partial example (adapted from Smith, 2006) of a think-aloud mystery in which a teacher helps her students identify "hail."

figure	8.4	Sample think-aloud mystery on weather.*

Suddenly I could hear it making noise pounding on the roof of the house.

Teacher: What do you know from your experience that does that?

Student: A storm.

Teacher: Good.

Thunder boomed and lightning flashed.

Teacher: Anything else?

Student: Oh, yeah, still thundering and raining.

Teacher: Yes, I like your noticing details like that.

* * *

I could see something bouncing onto the sidewalk and gathering into little white piles.

Student: Still thundering and raining . . .

Teacher: Well, what are those white piles?

Student: Huh? [rereads] Hah. Snow!

Teacher: Really? What does it say besides "white piles"? Is there another clue?

Student: Gathering . . . bouncing? Let's see what the next sentence says.

Teacher: Good thinking! Keep your mind thinking while you read more. This next one might really throw you.

It was summertime, but cold bits were falling from the sky.

Student: Oooh, so it was raining?

Teacher: What makes you think so? Does that fit with what you read right before?

Student: Uh huh.

Teacher: But you said "snow" right before.

Student: Oh, man, snow.

Teacher: Okay, let's review what we've read so far. So you have a storm. What else do you have?

Student: Ice.

Teacher: [laughs delightedly and reads next sentence.]

I've heard that sometimes it could get the size of golf balls or break car windshields.

Student: Oh, I know it . . . but I can't get the word out for it!

Teacher: What's it like?

Student: Hail!

Teacher: You think?! All right, let's see . . .

* * *

*This example includes only some of the sentence strips and student interaction from the original.

Source: Adapted from L. A. Smith (May, 2006). Think-Aloud Mysteries: Using structured sentence-by-sentence text passages to teach comprehension strategies. *Journal of Adolescent & Adult Literacy, 49*(8) (764–773). Reprinted with permission of the Interrenational Reading Association via Copyright Clearance Center.

Reciprocal Teaching

A C T I V I T Y

(PALINCSAR & BROWN, 1986)

reciprocal teaching ■ The **reciprocal teaching** activity has been found to foster comprehension by helping students actively monitor their thinking (Rosenshine, Meister, & Chapman, 1996). During this question-generating activity, you demonstrate how the students can monitor their reading comprehension, observe their thinking process while reading, and determine when they are successfully comprehending and when they are not. Then ask the students to attempt the same activity on their own, offering them feedback on their performance. The procedure contains five subcomponents—reading, summarizing, questioning, predicting, and clarifying—and is conducted as follows:

1. As the students track, read a paragraph from a passage of text aloud.

2. Model how the paragraph might be summarized. Focus on the main ideas in the paragraph, include the topic sentence, and point out that a summary should be no more than one-third of the original paragraph.

3. Ask the group an important question about the paragraph, one that focuses on the key issues. Solicit other questions from the group.

4. Predict aloud what might be expected in the remainder of the passage. Solicit other predictions from the group.

5. Think aloud about any clarifying information that might be helpful to understand the paragraph more completely. (*Note:* This step is not always necessary for well-written paragraphs that are appropriate for the reader's skill.) Solicit other ideas about what information might be needed.

Students can be prompted, after modeling, to conduct reciprocal teaching on their own, in small groups (Stricklin, 2011). With the help of props and sentence starters, students conduct small-group discussions based on their predictions, clarifications, questions, and text summaries. In planning for reciprocal teaching, it would be helpful for teachers to refer to the CCSS Speaking & Listening standards (NGACBP & CCSSO, 2010) or their state standards for guidance on the target skills and strategies for their grade level.

The Knowledge Chart

ACTIVITY

You can use the knowledge chart (also called K-W-L: "Know, Want to Know, Learned") to show children how to access their background knowledge or their schema for a topic through guided questions; you can then help students identify the new knowledge they gained by reading and place the knowledge on a chart. Modeled after a procedure developed by Ogle (1986), the **knowledge chart** is intended to be used before and after reading or listening to a selection containing factual material. The procedure goes as follows:

■ knowledge chart

Prereading

1. *Knowledge.* Ask the students, "What do you know about [the topic]?" Record all responses in the first column of a large sheet of chart paper under the heading "What We Know" or "Knowledge."

2. *Questions.* Ask, "What would you *like* to know about [the topic]?" Record the students' responses in the second column of the chart paper under the heading "Questions We Have."

Postreading

3. *New knowledge.* After the reading of the selection, ask, "What have you learned about [the topic]?" Help the students revise the knowledge from the first column, answer the questions from the second column, and list new facts not considered prior to the reading. Place these entries in a third column labeled "What We Learned."

4. *Research.* Distribute student-initiated questions from the second column that have not yet been answered to students interested in researching the answers. Help them find more information on the topic. This information may be added to the chart in a new column, as in Figure 8.5.

5. *Evaluation (optional).* Ask a provocative question that will lead students to a personal evaluation of the topic, such as "How did this selection change your feelings about [the topic]?" Place new appreciations in a column labeled "How We Feel Now" or "Evaluation."

| figure | 8.5 | Knowledge chart on lemmings. |

LEMMINGS				
What we know	Questions we have	What we learned from research	What we learned from reading	How we feel now
little animals live far away	What do they eat? Good pets? How big? In zoos? Where do you get one?	eat leaves and bugs too wild 4 or 5 inches not in zoos found in Norway	Lemmings drown themselves. No one knows why. Scientists think to keep population down or instinct.	We think it's an interesting mystery!

Experience–Text Relationship

ACTIVITY

experience–text relationship ■

Students are not always able to relate their own experiences to a topic before read-ing about it, even though such a skill is indispensable for adequate comprehension and that background must be brought to bear at all phases of the reading process. Thus, the activity **experience–text relationship** (Au, 1979), which helps students make their past experiences an integral part of reading, can enhance comprehension for a wide range of learners. Using Au's method, you ask questions about passages that are difficult for the students because of inadequate background, attempting to fill in the experiential gaps. Through your questioning, cueing, and prompting, the students are better able to integrate features of the text with their existing experiences. The activity is composed of three phases: (1) an experience phase for eliciting existing background; (2) a text phase for determining what students are deriving from the text; and (3) a relationship phase in which students compare their own experiences with what they have just read. The activity proceeds as follows:

Prereading

1. *Experience.* Ask the students questions about experiences they have had or ask them to share knowledge they have that is related to the selection they are about to read or hear.

During Reading

2. *Text.* After all the students have had an opportunity to share their knowledge or experiences, have them read or listen to short passages of the selection (usually a paragraph or a page at a time), asking them critical-thinking questions about the content after each section is read. Listen for responses that reveal lack of understanding due to differing worldviews or lack of experience with the topic. Add necessary background to correct misunderstandings. This can be in the form of personal anecdotes, pictures, questions, and/or discussion.

Postreading

3. *Relationship.* Attempt to make connections for students between the content of the selection, as discussed in the *text* phase, and their own experiences and knowledge, as shared in the *experience* phase.

Question–Answer Relationships

A C T I V I T Y

■ question–answer
relationships

Question–answer relationships (QARs) (Raphael, 1984) help students enhance their comprehension by helping them answer a range of questions and understand each question's relationship to the text, the author, and themselves (see Figure 8.6). With this strategy, students ask themselves, "Where would I find an answer to this question in the text?" and use the hierarchy of questions and answers described below to help them decide.

Literal question *(type 1)*

The answer is "right there." This tells the student that the answer to the question is easy to find in the text. In fact, the exact words in the question are contained within the text.

Inferential question *(type 2)*

The answer can be found if you "think and search." This tells the student that the answer is in the text, but two ideas will have to be brought together; that is, the words used in the question may be a bit different from the words used in the text, so the answer will be a bit harder to find.

figure 8.6   Question–answer relationships (QARs).

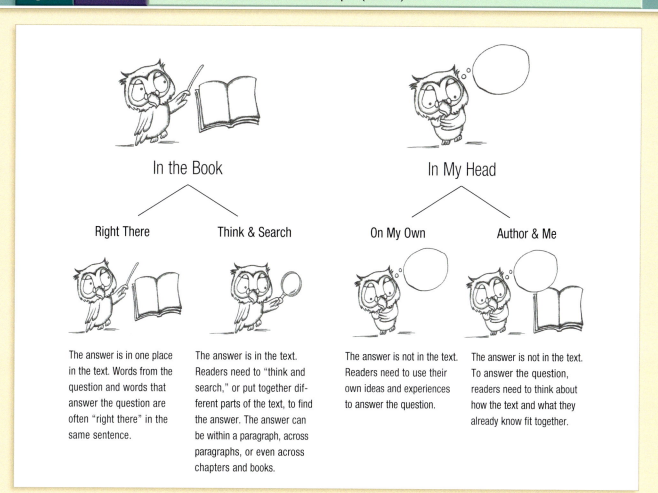

Source: T. E. Raphael. Teaching question–answer relationships, revisited. *The Reading Teacher, 39*(6),516–522, via CCC. Reprinted with permission.

Critical question *(type 3)*

The answer is in the mind of "the author and you." The answer is not directly stated in the story, but if readers bring their own ideas to the text and combine them with the opinion the author seems to hold, they will be able to answer the question. There are several possible answers.

Creative question *(type 4)*

The answer has to be determined "on your own." The student won't find a direct answer to the question in the text. There is no right or wrong answer to the question; it must emanate from the child's imagination or from information he already has about the topic. There are many possible answers.

The following outlines how students can be guided to incorporate the use of these questions to boost their own comprehension:

Earth Adventure Activities

www.missmaggie.org

Prereading

1. Give students four passages with questions for which the question types have already been determined.

2. Using the first passage, model how the answers to each question might be found in the text by identifying the appropriate QAR.

During Reading

3. Read the second passage aloud to students. Ask the questions aloud and ask volunteers to explain which kind of question is being asked and how they would find the answer in the text.

During/Postreading

4. Divide the class into small cooperative groups. Ask them to read the third passage, answer the questions, and identify the appropriate QARs.

5. Have students follow the same procedure individually, as the teacher goes around the classroom offering assistance as needed.

COMPONENTS OF A SUCCESSFUL COMPREHENSION PROGRAM

a review of the research offers classroom teachers consistent findings identifying the key factors in setting the stage for a successful comprehension-based reading program. Fielding and Pearson (1994), synthesizing the findings of research on reading comprehension, suggest the following practical guidelines for teachers:

- Devote a large block of time to actual text reading.
- Engage in close reading of text.
- Provide opportunities for reading in a social setting.
- Give students access to plenty of children's literature.
- Provide opportunities for personal response to text.
- Consider the language and culture of all learners.

Devote a Large Block of Time for Actual Text Reading

As a rule of thumb, students should have more time during the school day to practice reading than the combined total allocated for learning about, talking about, or writing about what they are reading. In a truly balanced reading program for primary grades, this is true even for the most fledgling, beginning readers. This is especially necessary, given the expectations of the CCSS and aligned state standards.

According to Teachers College, "students must be reading great quantities of text if they are to reach the expectations of the Common Core" (Reading and Writing Project, 2010, unpaged). Such time for reading can be built into the curriculum by having students read on their own during independent work time in the classroom—as another small group is receiving directed reading instruction, for example, or after they have completed one activity and are waiting for another to begin (National Institute for Literacy, 2001).

Encourage Greater Comprehension

www.bookadventure.com

To ensure that such practice translates into enhanced comprehension, however, students should be given some choice about what they read. They should also be provided with reasons to reread some materials to increase fluency, and the material offered should be appropriate in difficulty—that is, not so difficult as to be frustrating but not so easy that nothing challenging is encountered (Fielding & Pearson, 1994). See Chapter 7 for a discussion of teaching students to select "just right" books.

In the past, the most able readers, because of their ability, were given far less specific, isolated comprehension strategy instruction and were allotted more time to read than other, less able readers. Today researchers are speculating on whether that discrepancy might have caused an even wider gap between the able and less able readers (Anderson, Wilson, & Fielding, 1988).

From this research, it seems clear that students should be provided with plenty of time during the day to practice reading. Reading material should include texts that are easily decodable so that students can apply recently learned decoding strategies to text. Free time to select from a wide variety of trade books appealing to differing interests and encompassing all independent reading levels in the class should also be a prominent part of the reading program. Classroom libraries should include texts on subjects in which students are interested, to pique student interest in reading and motivate them to read more and more widely. Enhancing students' intrinsic motivation to read is crucial, and students who are intrinsically motivated to read (as opposed to extrinsically motivated, through rewards such as prizes or pizza parties) have higher levels of reading competence (Schiefele et al., 2012).

To create classroom libraries that include books that reflect students' interests, you can learn about students' interests through interest surveys, literacy histories, and sharing interviews with classmates (McLaughlin, 2012). Additionally, explore the wide variety of informational texts now available for young readers. Research suggests that later difficulties with informational reading and writing may be avoided by early experience with such material (Duke, 2000). Finally, demonstrate the use of the compendium of strategies by reading aloud high-quality children's literature that, although above the decoding level of many of the students in the class, can still be used effectively to spur interest and enhance comprehension.

Engage in Close Reading of Text

Close reading has a long history, but has recently regained popularity as an activity that supports reading comprehension at the levels mandated by the CCSS (Fisher & Frey, 2012). The Introduction to the English Language Arts Standards states that the ELA/literacy standards "are designed to prepare students for life outside the classroom" and "include critical-thinking skills and the ability to closely and attentively read texts in a way that will help them understand and enjoy complex works of literature" (www.corestandards.org/ELA-Literacy/Introduction). While close reading has been used most often at the high school level, it is making its way into elementary school practices as well.

Close reading involves the multiple reading of short texts with the goal of understanding the text at three basic levels (Figure 8.1). A main goal of close reading is to teach students to read text and achieve all three levels of understanding independently. To do this, after briefly building background and helping students make personal connections to the main aspects of the text, you need to go well beyond asking surface-level questions to modeling and teaching questions that students can ask themselves about any text. To help young students approach the first level of understanding, Boyles (2012/2013) suggests that they be taught to ask themselves the following questions as they read:

- What is the author *telling* me here?
- Are there any hard or important *words*?
- What does the author want me to *understand*?
- What seems important here?
- Is there anything that could have been explained more thoroughly for greater clarity?
- Is there a message or main idea? What in the text led me to this conclusion?

After gaining a literal and inferential understanding of the text, through a first reading and careful questioning by the teacher, and increasingly, by the students themselves, a second reading is done to explore writer's craft, with teacher questioning. See Figure 8.7 for suggestions teachers can ask about the writer's craft.

After discerning and discussing the effects of writer's craft and structure on the meaning of the text, close reading focuses on locating the text within the "big picture" of literature and the reader's life. Questions such as the following can be modeled through think-alouds and taught to students to help them gain independence in reaching this level of text analysis.

- What did you take the story to mean from the main character's point of view? Another character?
- What did the story mean to you? What does it say about how you live your life?
- Do you know other stories like this? How were those stories similar and different?
- Which stories did you like best? Why?

The steps to planning a close reading lesson vary greatly from the planning required when using most traditional textbooks and accompanying teacher's guides adopted prior to the CCSS. Steps to creating a close reading lesson are as follows (Shanahan, 2012):

1. Select a high-quality short text that is worth reading and rereading.
2. Read the text.
3. Analyze why the text may be difficult for students to understand (e.g., vocabulary, sentence structure, text structure).
4. Create text-dependent questions—those that require students to read closely and provide evidence for their oral or written response from the text—for all three levels or steps of the close read. For an excellent resource on creating text-dependent questions, see *Text-Dependent Questions* (Fisher & Frey, 2015).
5. *Optional:* Create a post-reading activity involving writing that is engaging, authentic, and creative.

These activities may include a Socratic Seminar (a dialogue among students using open-ended questions), a student-led investigation, a presentation, or a debate. See Fisher and Frey (2015, Ch. 5), for further ideas.

figure 8.7	Craft techniques and related questions for close reading.

CRAFT TECHNIQUE	POSSIBLE QUESTIONS
Imagery, including comparisons: ■ Similes ■ Metaphors ■ Personification ■ Figurative language ■ Symbols	What is being compared? Why is the comparison effective? (typically because of the clear, strong, or unusual connection between the two) What symbols are present? Why did the author choose these symbols?
Word choice	What word(s) stand out? Why? (typically vivid words, unusual choices, or a contrast to what a reader expects) How do particular words get us to look at characters or events in a particular way? Do they evoke an emotion? Did the author use nonstandard English or words in another language? Why? What is the effect? Are there any words that could have more than one meaning? Why might the author have played with language in this way?
Tone and voice	What *one* word describes the tone? Is the voice formal or informal? If it seems informal, how did the author make it that way? If it's formal, what makes it formal? Does the voice seem appropriate for the content?
Sentence structure: ■ Short sentences ■ Long sentences ■ Sentence fragments ■ Sentences in which word order is important ■ Questions	What stands out about the way this sentence is written? Why did the author choose a short sentence here? (for example, so it stands out from sentences around it, for emphasis) Why did the author make this sentence really long? (for example, to convey the "on and on" sense of the experience) Why did the author write a fragment here? (for example, for emphasis, to show a character's thoughts) Based on the order of the words in this sentence, which word do you think is the most important? Why? What was the author trying to show by placing a particular word in a certain place?

Source: Nancy Boyles. (December 2012/January 2013). Closing in on close reading. *Educational Leadership, 70*(4). Retrieved from www.ascd.org/publications/educational-leadership/dec12/vol70/num04/Closing-in-on-Close-Reading.aspx. Used with permission via CCC.

Provide Opportunities for Reading in a Social Setting

Students, especially English learners, learn best when they can talk about what they are doing and learn from each other. Besides enhancing their knowledge by adding sensory input and vocabulary development provided by oral discussion, social reading is more enjoyable for most students. Reading in a social setting also allows students to practice speaking and listening skills they have learned in school; for example, the CCSS call for students to "Participate in collaborative conversations with diverse partners about grade 1 topics and texts with peers and adults in small and larger groups" (NGACBP & CCSSO, 2010, p. 23).

Children's Literature
Web Guide

www.people.ucalgary.ca/~dkbrown

Leave time for rich, personal discussion of text—the kind of voluntary conversation that is most significant to children.

A continuum of reading configurations should be used in classrooms across the grade levels, including (1) *shared reading* (see Chapter 11), in which the teacher is prominent and models through think-alouds and other strategies, and (2) *guided reading* (see Chapter 11), in which the teacher is less prominent and assesses and supports small groups as they carry out the skills and strategies modeled during read-alouds and shared reading. Reading comprehension skills are enhanced when teachers use small-group instruction because they can better fine-tune instructional decisions based on formative assessments of students' reading skills (Connor et al., 2011). Other collaborative approaches include dyad reading (discussed earlier), simple partner reading, and echo reading, with students repeating the lines the teacher reads. When students begin to possess a degree of fluency and independence, they can move toward small, independent discussion groups or literature circles where they are in charge of sharing their personal reactions to text.

Give Students Access to Plenty of Children's Literature

Quality children's literature is a necessity in beginning literacy instruction. Literature does much more than merely teach children how to read; it also contributes to language development, stimulates the senses, provokes emotional response, and exposes children to a variety of thoughts and ideas (Jalongo, 1988). Although decodable texts are essential for use in reinforcing phonic elements and decoding skills, children's literature is the ideal vehicle for modeling comprehension strategies for students. The primary classroom should be stocked with picture books or books that use both pictures and text to tell the story; award winners, such as the Children's Choice and Newbery Medal winners; informational texts and books; predictable books containing phrases that children can easily anticipate, such as rhyming patterns, repeating verses, or cumulative verses; and big books, oversized versions of favorite children's books suitable for sharing in small groups. Many books with pictures can also be found online. Besides being used for modeling by teachers, such literature can be used for browsing during free reading time and can be recorded for individual read-alongs.

Provide Opportunities for Personal Response to Text

Not so long ago, teachers often became so concerned with assessing comprehension and completing the lists of comprehension questions provided at the end of each basal reader story that little time was left for rich, personal discussion of text—the kind of voluntary conversation that is the most significant to children. Eeds and Wells (1989) call these two contrasting types of discourses the difference between a "gentle inquisition," a barrage of mainly factual, assessment-oriented questions about text, and "grand conversations" that ask students to reflect on the personal relevance of the text, much as adults are invited to do in the intimate setting of a book club. Such conversations are vital to developing a genuine love for reading and have the added value of elevating the classroom climate to one of a "community of readers" (Hansen, 2001).

To act on this suggestion, do not limit yourself to factual-type questions, and allow plenty of time for critical and creative questions for which there is no one "correct" answer and for which every student has an opportunity to voice an opinion (e.g., questions on the upper level of Bloom's taxonomy). It is also helpful to create provocative questions about text for which you yourself do not have an answer, thereby assuring that you will not be "fishing" for the response you have in mind or that is provided by the basal instructor's manual. Moreover, set aside adequate time for sharing journal reactions to literature in small interest groups where the atmosphere is safe and conducive to personal conversations about text.

Students can also share responses about books they are reading using a variety of electronic dialoguing techniques. Using a computer, students can write their thoughts and feelings about their books and send them to students in other classrooms, to older students, or to preservice students at a university. Using blogs and wikis (see Chapter 12), students can be instantly connected to audiences around the world.

Consider the Language and Culture of All Learners

There are great differences in how rapidly and how well children learn to speak English. When students who are struggling with English are asked to comprehend text in their second language too soon, they can become frustrated and confused. Such students can be encouraged in a supportive classroom where instruction provides for and celebrates differences. You may find it helpful to use a variety of predictable texts, multisensory teaching, and repetition to improve comprehension strategies. Most important, create a language-rich environment and provide many opportunities for cooperative interaction with English-speaking students (see the accompanying box).

To support English learning, incorporate specific language objectives into content-area lessons to accommodate second language learners. Such students can benefit from objectives that incorporate functional language use, such as how to request information, present opinions, negotiate meaning, and provide detailed explanations. Higher-order thinking skills, such as articulating predictions or hypotheses, stating conclusions, summarizing information, and making comparisons, can be tied to language objectives as well (Echevarria, Vogt, & Short, 2010).

You can also improve comprehension in all learners by offering a variety of multicultural reading material that reflects the prior knowledge and background of the diverse learners in the classroom (Wiseman, 1992). For example, supply classroom literature that represents a wide range of values, lifestyles, customs, and historical traditions. An example of an effective comprehension activity that encourages multicultural awareness for all students is to compare folktales, such as *Cinderella* with its African counterpart, *Mufaro's Beautiful Daughters* (Steptoe, 1987) or the Chinese *Lon Po Po* (Young, 1990) with its European counterpart, *Little Red Riding Hood*.

Special considerations must be made for students who are learning English as a second language in order for them to fully comprehend, and think critically about, the materials you present. The goal should always be to present quality literature with engaging illustrations; however, consider these additional key elements (outlined by Vardell, Hadaway, & Young, 2006) when matching English learners with books to ensure that they have the best chance to comprehend:

Is the language accessible? English learners, especially at the initial stages of language acquisition, benefit from predictable books with simple sentences, simple language patterns, and repetitive text. The reader should not be overwhelmed by too many words on a page.

Is a variety of text genres available? Students for whom English is a second language will benefit by being exposed to a wide variety of writing styles, topics, genres, and patterns of text organization. While this is true of *all* students, it is crucial for those becoming familiar with the way English text is structured.

Are the illustrations accessible? When students do not have full command of English, the text must be supported and made comprehensible by the illustrations.

Selecting multicultural children's literature

For Preschool through Grade 4

To develop positive attitudes about people of all cultures, students need many opportunities to read and listen to quality children's literature that presents accurate and respectful images from a variety of cultures. Unfortunately, relatively few children's books are written from the perspectives of racial and cultural minorities; some that are available include negative racial and cultural stereotypes as well as inaccurate factual information. Therefore, it is helpful to consider the following criteria when selecting quality literature for young children (Temple, Martinez, & Yokota, 2011):

Does the book show physical diversity? For example, one popular children's book shows many pictures of Chinese people of all ages—all of whom are drawn to look exactly alike, depriving children of an understanding of the rich diversity of Chinese faces.

Are the illustrations authentic without being stereotypical? Every race and culture has positive features that can be highlighted in positive ways. Unfortunately, illustrations may accentuate negative stereotypes.

Do the author and illustrator present the culture authentically? There are many misperceptions of cultures, and a quality book is often written and/or illustrated by a member of the culture and presents an accurate portrayal of the essence of that culture.

Is the culture shown to be multidimensional and nonstatic? A quality multicultural children's book shows a wide array of facets of life and ways that culture can change for the racial or cultural group being studied.

Does the author integrate cultural details in a natural way? Stories including other races and cultures should avoid misrepresenting diverse people as overly exotic or "quaint."

Are the details historically accurate? Much research is needed in selecting informational text and historical fiction because they are great ways for students to pick up factual information, but they must be accurate for the time period portrayed.

Does the book reflect on awareness of the changing status of women? In the United States as well as the rest of the world, women are increasingly in positions of power. This status should be reflected in the text, to include the portrayal of female characters taking active—not only passive and domestic—roles.

Are nonwhite characters shown as equals of Anglo characters? Too often, while a text may include racial diversity, the nonwhite characters are seen in subservient roles or seem to need the Anglo characters to solve problems for them.

Does the author avoid offensive vocabulary? While there may be appropriate times for racially offensive language that was used historically (as in *Huckleberry Finn*), such language is rarely necessary to the integrity of the story, and is never appropriate for younger readers.

If dialect is used, does it have a real purpose and appear genuine? Nonstandard English can be confusing for young children, yet a children's book set in St. Croix would be inauthentic without the characters speaking in a Cruzan dialect. Use of a dialect is appropriate if it makes the characters appear more genuine and if the dialect is truly one that the characters would use.

Some exemplary children's books that contain positive portrayals of cultural diversity are Sherley Anne Williams's *Working Cotton,* which illustrates the hardworking life of a migrant family; Stephanie Stuve-Bodeen's *Babu's Song,* which depicts a loving relationship between a child and her grandmother; Pat Mora's bilingual text, *The Bakery Lady,* which describes close family relationships as they prepare food for the Feast of the Three Kings; and the photographic essay *Hoang Anh: A Vietnamese American Boy,* by Diane Hoyt-Goldsmith, which shows the daily experiences in the life of a Vietnamese American child and his family.

Abundant high-quality illustrations provide cues to help English learners discern the meaning of the text. *Note:* Consider comic books and graphic novels in your classroom library as genres of reading material in which the text is often fully supported by the illustrations. For example, comics on superheroes (Spider-Man, Batman, Wonder Woman) and folklore and fairy tales such as *Little Lit: Folklore and Fairy Tale Funnies* (Spiegelman & Mouly, 2000) and *The Big Book of Grimm* (Factoid Books, 1999) can make good additions to your classroom library.

Is the content accessible? When students already have a schema or background knowledge about a topic in their own language, the comprehension of that topic is supported and easier for them to understand.

See the box on the previous page for a discussion of selecting multicultural children's literature.

IMPROVING COMPREHENSION FOR ENGLISH LEARNERS

ccording to August, McCardle, Shanahan, and Burns (2014), a variety of approaches are effective for improving English learners' listening and reading comprehension. One effective strategy in enhancing English learners' comprehension is enriched book environments (Koskinen et al., 2000). Instructional conversations coupled with literature logs also been bolster rates of comprehension for English learners (Saunders & Goldenberg, 1999). Liang, Peterson, and Graves (2005) found that two complementary approaches used in tandem enhance English learners' comprehension. The first approach includes heavy scaffolding before, during, and after a reading, including activating and building background knowledge (before the reading), teacher questioning about key concepts and events (during the reading), and an extension activity coupled with discussion of the text (after the reading). The second approach focuses on short interactive conversations accompanied by open-ended writing activities based on the text. The researchers found that while both approaches are effective, they are most effective when used together. Research on prekindergarten English learners found that showing brief video clips of the content of a reading before engaging in reading aloud can enhance these children's comprehension of the text (Roberts & Neal, 2004).

Interventions that focus on phonics instruction are also effective in bolstering English learners' rates of comprehension but not as effective as interventions focused on meaning-making. Both types of interventions, however, enhance comprehension, further supporting a balanced literacy approach (August et al., 2014).

Here are additional specific suggestions for improving comprehension of English learners:

- Build English vocabulary and language knowledge through oral language development activities.
- Teach phonics skills in English.
- Use multisensory materials, such as e-books, videos, DVDs, pictures, audio recordings, and other supports.
- Preview key vocabulary by conducting a "picture walk" before a text is read aloud.
- Guide students who are literate in their first language to create a bilingual dictionary to record new vocabulary.
- Assess and build background information about the content of a text before it is read.
- Conduct teacher-led discussions about the similarities and differences between English learners' lives and those of the characters in the text, and clarify any parts of the text that may be unclear to your English learners.
- Use gestures and body language.
- Speak slowly and enunciate clearly.
- Use longer pauses between phrases and sentences.
- Use much repetition and review.

- Use short sentences and simpler syntax.
- Use fewer pronouns.
- Use bilingual books.
- Exaggerate intonation, especially when introducing phonemic elements.
- Use high-frequency vocabulary.
- Use fewer idioms and slang terms.
- Maintain a low anxiety level.
- Emphasize cooperative learning.

READING COMPREHENSION AND STUDENTS WITH SPECIAL NEEDS

Certain teacher interventions can be helpful for students with special needs who struggle with reading comprehension. For example, for students with learning disabilities, it is important to explicitly teach and model reading strategies, as well as "fix-it" strategies when meaning breaks down. In addition, students with learning disabilities achieve at a higher level when taught using small groups as opposed to one-on-one tutoring by the teacher (Stanberry & Swanson, 2009). Other effective strategies for these students include teaching them to use semantic maps and graphic organizers as they read as well as how to identify the main idea. Teaching structures such as reciprocal teaching have also been found effective in helping students with learning disabilities acquire reading comprehension skills (Gajria, Jitendra, Sood, & Sacks, 2007). Finally, these students struggle more than students who are non–learning disabled in discerning the "story grammar" of a piece of narrative text. Therefore, students with learning disabilities should to be taught how to use story grammar to comprehend narrative text. Visual story maps together with teacher think-alouds about story grammar, conducted while reading aloud, have been found effective with students with learning disabilities (Stetter & Hughes, 2010).

Students along the autism spectrum especially struggle with understanding narrative text, given that many have difficulties interpreting social situations and inferring character intent and motivation. A number of interventions help these students comprehend narrative text, including priming their background knowledge, creating visual maps of the story structure, creating a goal structure map to help them infer character motivations (see Figure 8.8), and drawing "emotional thermometers" (see Figure 8.9) to aid them in intuiting character emotion (Gately, 2008). When using each of these visuals, students need to cite the text that showed them that the character had certain goals or felt a certain way.

Students who are hearing impaired may also struggle with reading comprehension. These students may have a limited vocabulary, weak topic knowledge, and a slow reading rate. They also may lack motivation and fail to monitor comprehension as they read. Thus, it is important to implement research-supported techniques for students with hearing impairments to promote growth and improvement. Such supports may include explicit comprehension strategy instruction, teaching of story grammar, modified DRTA with an emphasis on teacher questioning about the text, activating background knowledge, and use of well-written, high-interest text (Luckner & Handley, 2008).

SUMMARY

Learning to sound out words through phonics and other word-unlocking strategies is certainly a fundamental skill, but if this component of literacy

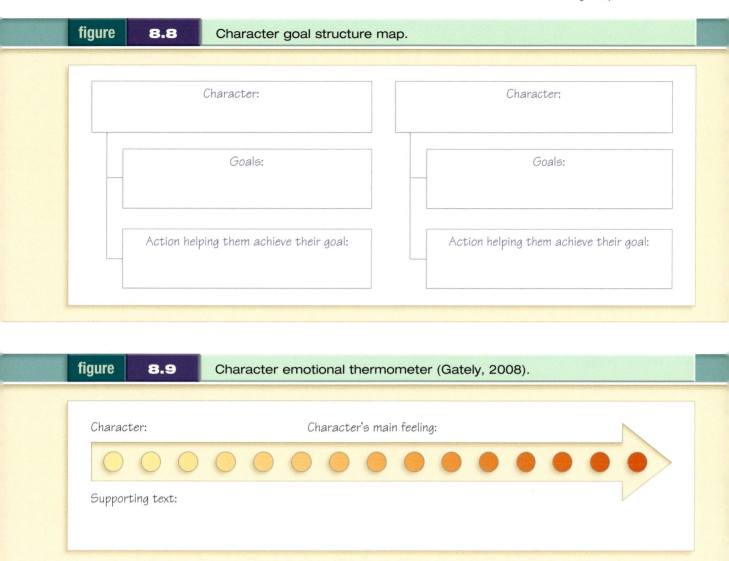

figure **8.8**   Character goal structure map.

figure **8.9**   Character emotional thermometer (Gately, 2008).

has been accomplished, can we then say a child has learned to read? No. Control of phonics is necessary but is not sufficient to constitute learning how to read. For real reading to occur the student has to be simultaneously constructing meaning from the words that have been decoded; that meaning must then be assimilated into the child's worldview. This meaning-making is a complex and arduous process best consummated through a program that offers guidance in specific comprehension strategies and many opportunities to apply them with quality literature and decodable text. The teacher in such a program becomes a coach who is there to model, guide, and provide feedback to learners.

Proficient readers possess strategies from which they choose to interact with text and construct meaning. These strategies must be directly taught to developing readers through modeling, guided instruction, and plenty of independent application with actual text. Additionally, readers must be given the opportunity to share their personal responses to text with each other in a variety of social settings. For English learners, give special consideration to making a variety of genres available and to ensuring that the texts and illustrations are accessible.

A literacy program myopically focused on meaning-making to the exclusion of instruction in decoding skills may create a rich literacy environment that is, inadvertently, inaccessible to many learners; on the other hand, a program lacking in ways to derive personal meaning from text may well create learners who can read but who choose not to do so. For a literacy program to be truly comprehensive, it must enable learners to decode text, but it must also offer them guidance in strategic reading and ample opportunity to read for meaning and enjoyment.

questions   FOR JOURNAL WRITING AND DISCUSSION

1. What is your definition of reading? In what way will your definition determine the importance of comprehension instruction to your total reading program?

2. Think about what you do when you read. What comprehension strategies did you use as you read the beginning of this chapter? Make a list of the strategies you can identify. Then spend several minutes reading a novel or other narrative text. Make a second list of the strategies you used with the narrative text. Compare the two lists. Are there major differences? Why?

3. Consider the English learners and students with special needs in your classroom. Which of the reading comprehension activities outlined in this chapter would be especially effective for *your* English learners and special needs students, and why?

4. The parent of one of your students visits your classroom. She expects to see a lot of silent workbook activities. Prepare an argument that you might give to this parent, who wonders why you allow so much time for students to read self-selected material and discuss it in small groups.

suggestions   FOR PROJECTS AND FIELD ACTIVITIES

1. Select one of the comprehension activities outlined in this chapter. Find a selection from a primary basal reader that would be appropriate content for such a strategy. Teach the activity to a small group of your classmates. Discuss their reactions.

2. Plan a reading comprehension activity tailored to support your English learners, taking into account strategies and techniques that are helpful for these students. Assess the students' level of comprehension after the activity. Was comprehension aided, compared to that gained from past activities?

3. Conduct the same activity, or another of your choice, with a small group of third-grade students. What problems did they have with the lesson? What did they like about using the strategy? Discuss your findings with your class.

4. View two close reading lessons: one conducted by a respected practitioner (on DVD or online) and one in a classroom at your teaching site. Take notes and compare the two lessons against the criteria for close reading lessons outlined in this chapter.

5. Observe the reading lessons in a primary classroom for an entire week. Make a list of all the activities the teacher and the students engage in during the week and note the time spent on each. How much time was spent on direct teaching of comprehension strategies? What percentage of total teaching time was spent on teaching comprehension compared with time allotted for the application of these strategies or actual reading by the students? What might you decide to do differently in your own classroom?

Writing–Reading Connections

RECIPROCAL PATHS TO LITERACY

focus questions

What are appropriate writing goals for primary-grade students? How can these goals be achieved for every child?

How can writing workshop be used to help young children learn about print and see themselves as authors?

How can a writing program be structured so that students write about topics that are interesting to them and write stories that are personally meaningful?

In what ways can teachers use modeling and writing structures to encourage emergent writers to acquire the conventions of written language?

How can "reading to write" and "writing to read" strategies be used to nurture young students' emerging literacy skills?

In what ways can students be supported to be effective writers across genres, and use specific text features strategically to make their writing meaningful, purposeful, and effective?

even-year-old Maria turns to her trusted friend, Josh, to get some objective feedback about her current writing ideas.

"I'm thinking of writing a story about three frogs or maybe about when my dog ran away," Maria declares, showing Josh a paper full of half-formed ideas. "Which one do *you* think I should write about?"

Josh looks up from his own writing and asks Maria what exactly she has to say about the frogs. Maria ponders this for a moment. Then she replies that she really doesn't know much about frogs but that she's read lots of stories that contain three animals, although not necessarily about frogs. Abruptly, Josh poses an insightful question.

"Well, what about your dog running away? Was that a big deal?" "Oh, yes!" replies Maria, her face clouding over with the memory.

Maria begins to tell Josh a woeful tale about a recent time when her dog, Puppy, jumped the fence; the family had thought the dog was gone for good. Josh listens intently and then shrugs; Maria has answered her own question, and both students suddenly realize it.

Talking about her writing before she puts pen to paper has provided Maria with a kind of mental rehearsal for her writing and a clearer picture of what she really wants to write about.

INTRODUCTION

Like the students in the preceding vignette, most students in the primary grades come to school with excitement and enthusiasm for learning. They tend to be highly motivated and interested in engaging in the reciprocal communicative skills of reading and writing. Their image of being "grown-up" and attending school includes involvement in authentic literacy activities such as those they have seen all around them. Most of these young children have probably picked up the idea that they would be learning to write as soon as they entered school.

Farnan, Lapp, and Flood (1992) suggest that early attempts at writing are perfect opportunities for children to experiment with print and extend their understanding of text; Richgels (1995) claims that early writing provides children with invaluable practice with phonics skills, such as blending sounds into words and segmenting words into parts. Research in emergent literacy has found that writing—if much experimentation is encouraged—can play a pivotal role in children's learning to read. Rather than developing *after* reading, as educators once assumed, we now know that writing accompanies young children's growing interest in naming letters and reading print. Early-grade teachers would therefore benefit from putting research into practice by accommodating young children's wishes to quickly read and write, providing them with immediate opportunities to participate in real writing along with their initial reading instruction.

The need for students to be proficient writers has never been greater. After many years in which reading instruction often eclipsed writing instruction, students' voices are being heard once more in the classroom in the form of student writing. This shift in focus is due partly to increased emphasis placed on writing by the CCSS and many state standards. The CCSS also introduce a focus on text structures, some of which were not previously emphasized, including writing opinion and argumentation. For example, CCSS.ELA-Literacy.W.1.1 states that students be able to "Write opinion pieces in which they introduce the topic or name the book they are writing about, state an opinion, supply a reason for the opinion, and provide some sense of closure" (NGACBP & CCSSO, 2010, p. 19). In addition, the

CCSS place a greater emphasis on having students write informative/explanatory texts and participate in shared research and writing projects using technology. CCSS.ELA-Literacy.W.3.8 requires students to "Recall information from experiences or gather information from print and digital sources; take brief notes on sources and sort evidence into provided categories" (NGACBP & CCSSO, 2010, p. 21). The CCSS as well as many state standards also emphasize students' written engagement with universal messages and text meanings, rather than calling for simply a reflection on their own experiences, as in the case of the personal narrative genre. Students are asked to write a greater number of brief pieces in addition to well-developed research pieces that are longer than required by previous standards, meaning that students will be simultaneously required to focus on brevity and increase their writing stamina (Allyn, 2013).

WRITING GOALS FOR EARLY READERS

mergent literacy depends on much more than providing a print-rich environment and then allowing children to "go to it naturally," although such advice is sometimes appropriate. But literate models—teachers, parents, siblings, or caregivers—must also demonstrate the "how-to's" of writing. As will be explored in Chapter 11, read-alouds, shared reading, and guided reading lessons provide excellent opportunities for discussing writing. Students can explore what makes writing boring or interesting, how authors select words that make readers feel a certain way, how authors make their writing personally meaningful to readers, and so on. Such talk empowers students to see authors as real people and to realize that they, too, can be authors.

With these ideas in mind, the following suggested literacy goals are appropriate for fostering the reading–writing connection in kindergarten through third-grade students, with some appropriate for prekindergarten students. Prekindergarten students' literacy instruction, however, should focus on listening and speaking, and engaging in interactive read-alouds, rather than on writing instruction. While even prekindergartners can engage in writing workshop, they should not be pressured to write words or sentences until they are ready, which may not happen until kindergarten. Simply drawing pictures to communicate their thoughts during writing workshop is appropriate for prekindergarten students.

Students in grades K–3 should be encouraged to develop the following:

1. Oral-language fluency for all students, native English speakers as well as English learners.

2. An awareness that writing is constructing meaning with thoughts and speech in written form.

3. A positive, confident, and conscientious attitude toward writing and its conventions as aids that help readers better understand an author's message (spelling, punctuation, and so forth).

4. An awareness and appreciation of self as writer, and as a communicator of messages, stories, and information that is personally important and meaningful.

5. An awareness and appreciation of self as collaborator and evaluator in the writing process.

Early-grade teachers must provide opportunities for their students to participate in authentic writing experiences.

Education Northwest

http://educationnorthwest.
org/traits/traits-and-
common-core

6. An interest in personal, meaningful writing and experimentation within a widening variety of structures and genres.

7. The ability to identify and use the key features that define high-quality writing (i.e., the 6 +1 writing traits), including ideas, organization, voice, word choice, sentence fluency, conventions, and presentation. For details about the 6+1 traits and the relationship between the traits and the CCSS, visit the Education Northwest site. The site also includes samples of annotated student papers, scored through the lens of the 6+1 traits.

8. Skills in using technology in researching, writing, and publishing texts.

9. An awareness that writing can promote change through increased awareness of self and of social realities and problems and that it can be used as a way to help organize to solve social problems at the individual, classroom, school, community, and societal levels.

The remainder of this chapter is devoted to program attributes and positive practices designed to help teachers reach these early literacy goals.

WRITING WORKSHOP

writing workshop ■

Writing workshop (Calkins, 2000) is the best way to organize the teaching of writing and an ideal vehicle through which students can apply the steps of the writing process (discussed next). You can teach students how to complete the activities during each stage of the writing process; the students can then practice what they have learned during the writing workshop. The workshop can alternate between two main structures: *open writing* and *genre study*. When these writing workshop formats are alternated throughout the year, students can experiment freely with their writing (during the open format) and learn the essential features of written genres and produce their own samples of that genre (during genre study).

Open Format Workshop

The open format may appear loosely structured, but it requires much planning and organization as well as an ongoing, authentic assessment on the part of the teacher (Engel & Streich, 2009). An open-format writing workshop for the primary grades can roughly follow this suggested structure (see Figure 9.1 for an alternate structure): Each session begins with a 5- to 12-minute minilesson to demonstrate a procedure, concept, or skill—such as using vivid words—that you have noticed that most students are ready to learn. Part of the minilesson includes reading of an anchor text that models the new skill. After direct instruction, students engage in a 2- to 3-minute partner practice of the new skill. The rest of the workshop is devoted to writing with students working through the stages of the writing process, including prewriting, or brainstorming topics, as well as filling graphic organizers specific to the genre in which students are writing, followed by drafting, revising, and editing. These steps are described in detail a little later in this chapter.

During writing time, you will circulate, asking questions, providing support, taking anecdotal notes on the students' writing, and providing one-on-one conferences with students. Encourage students to apply the skill learned during the minilesson, as appropriate. Students provide peer revision of each other's work and keep their written work, in various stages of completion, in writing folders. The session ends with sharing time when students read their pieces to small groups, or to the whole group, and request feedback. Application of the new writing skill is discussed and shared as well during this time.

figure   **9.1**   An alternate suggested format for writing workshop.

Minilesson (5–8 minutes)

This is a short lesson focused on a single, narrow topic that the students need, chosen by the teacher based upon skills outlined by grade level standards and her observation of the children's daily writing. The teacher may see a need only in certain students and invite just them to meet for the lesson.

Status of the class (2–3 minutes)

This is a brief survey by the teacher to find out what each child is working on as well as what stage of the writing process each is in.

Writing time (15–20 minutes) (writing process)

The children write, choosing topics from their writing folder. The teacher conferences with individual children.

Sharing (5–10 minutes)

Children read what they have written and seek specific feedback from an audience (whole class, small groups, or partners).

Genre Study Workshop

Unlike the open format, the genre study format has a specific beginning, middle, and end, as students study and practice writing the individual genres. Genre study has been used successfully in Australia for a number of years (Gibbons, 2002) and is gaining popularity in the United States, especially since it effectively supports the goals of the CCSS. It simultaneously addresses the CCSS Reading Standards' focus on author's craft and the skills needed to achieve the Writing Standards, such as writing routinely over both shorter and longer time frames and writing opinion and informational/explanatory texts as well as narrative texts (NGACBP & CCSSO, 2010). Genre study can be broken into following steps, but the steps are fluid and can be combined depending on the proficiency of the students:

1. *Inquiry.* At the beginning of a genre study, you read aloud or have the students read examples of the focus genre (e.g., an informational text). Then lead the students in an inquiry-based process of identifying the features of the focus genre. This process should focus on standards (CCSS or state) specific to the genre. For example, in an informational text workshop, lead the students in an analysis of the credibility and accuracy of the author's sources.

2. *Modeling.* After brainstorming a list of the text features as well as examples of each, begin the modeling portion of the workshop. In this step, you model the creation of a piece of text in the focus genre using a think-aloud process. Your creation of a piece of text should model not only the technical features of writing but also the personal meaning of the text as well as the purpose of the genre (conveying information, entertaining, communicating an important message such as a moral). The steps you model are the same as in the writing process for open writing workshop.

3. *Shared writing.* In this step of a genre study, you and the students go through the steps of the writing process together and co-create a piece of text in the target genre. The fact that the text should be personally meaningful should be an important criteria for this step of the process as well.

4. *Collaborative writing.* In this step, pair students strategically (e.g., an English learner with a student with a high level of English proficiency) to write a text piece in the target genre. This step should be used judiciously depending on students' collaboration skills, and should be used only to co-create very short pieces of text.

5. *Independent writing.* In the final step, students independently create their own piece of text, following the writing process, in the target genre. This can be a brief piece of writing, or a longer piece, depending on the purpose of the writing.

Genre studies can focus on genres required by the CCSS and many state standards, such as opinion, narrative, or informational/explanatory text, as well as subgenres such as song lyrics, recipes, or poetry. While you can focus writing workshop on a certain genre, during genre study it is important that students choose their own topics within the genre; for example, if students are learning how to write an opinion piece, they may choose to write a piece about their favorite book by an author or their favorite class field trip of the year.

THE WRITING PROCESS

writing process ■

as stated earlier, through writing workshop, students apply the steps in the **writing process,** an effective approach widely used in classrooms and by many professional writers. The process reflects the premise that writers write best when they write frequently, for extended periods of time, and on topics of their own choosing. The writing process describes a set of stages in which a writer engages in activities designed to solve certain problems unique to a particular stage. This problem-solving approach makes the writing process more effective than traditional approaches that focus merely on the completed product. A final product in traditional writing programs is often simply a second draft consisting of a recopying of the piece that fixes the teacher's red-pen corrections.

The writing process and methods of teaching writing have evolved over the years, but two beliefs have remained consistent: (1) the creation of a piece of writing is a developmental process that takes place over a period of time, and (2) writers engage in differing activities depending on their stage of development. The writing process can be introduced to emergent writers as early as kindergarten.

During writing workshop, students work through the following stages of the writing process over a period of several days or, sometimes, weeks (Graham et al., 2012; Peha, 1996). These steps are iterative and sometimes overlap with each other; for instance, there is often overlap between the sharing and revising stages.

- prewriting
- sharing
- editing
- drafting
- revising
- publishing

Prewriting (Exploring the Topic)

In this initial stage, students think, plan, talk, and take rudimentary notes about a topic or story about which they feel passionate. Many activities qualify as prewriting activities. Some of the most helpful activities for young children are conversations with a friend about the topic, reflecting, drawing, brainstorming, visualizing personal experiences, and jotting down notes. Have students brainstorm a list of topics, experiences, and story ideas (in different columns on a piece of paper) to keep in their writers' notebook to refer to throughout the year. Such a list can begin as a class brainstorming, from which the students can start their own lists.

writing prompts ■

Another way of igniting the thinking process is to offer creative or reflective **writing prompts** or motivational ideas to inspire the students and get their imaginations churning. For example, you might offer a sentence such as "When I opened my front door, I saw a cute puppy just sitting on my doorstep," and ask students, orally, to add some ideas to turn the sentence into a story. Another prompt might be to brainstorm a "What if?" question with the students—for example, "What if everyone looked exactly alike?" or "What if we could talk to animals?" or "What if we were invisible?" An example of a prompt for an opinion piece might be "What is your favorite recess activity? Why is it a good recess activity?" and for an informational piece, "What do you think your classmates would want to know about sharks?" You can also provide prompts to help students tap into and write about personal experiences, for example, "Close your eyes and visualize a favorite activity, special family moment, or a time when you learned a new skill." Such prompts, followed by much oral discussion and subsequent brainstorming, make most students eager to write.

Drafting (Getting Ideas Down)

During the drafting stage, formal writing begins. Very young children usually write single-draft compositions, adding words or squiggles to accompany drawings they have made. (See Figure 9.2.)

The Institute of Education Sciences argues that students should be introduced to keyboarding in first grade and be able to type as fast as they can write by hand by the end of second or third grade (Graham et al., 2012). Because it doesn't require the substantial fine motor coordination needed to handwrite, keyboarding their writing in a word processing program allows students to focus on their ideas. As a result, they tend to write more and enjoy seeing the professional-looking results. Indeed, when students type as opposed to handwrite, the volume of sentences and number of words increase (HW 21 Community, 2012), and students who use word processing spend more time revising their work (Warschauer, 2008). When using programs designed for early writers, such as *First Writer* or

| figure | 9.2 | A young writer's draft. |

Bank Street Prewriter, students can more easily revise and edit rough drafts and receive the added bonus of a clean copy every time. Most programs include tutorial lessons ideal for independent small-group work after an initial introduction by the teacher. See Chapter 12 for more information on using technology in writing.

During the drafting stage, the emphasis is on expressing ideas, never on spelling or handwriting. It is vital at this stage to respond to what the students have to say with positive oral comments or, with older students, written ones. As in the prewriting stage, emergent writers must be given sufficient time and encouragement to engage in risk-free exploration of their subject matter.

When students are drafting their compositions, you need to be aware when students are experiencing writer's block so you can provide suggestions, such as the following, to get them beyond the block (Kucer, 2010):

1. Brainstorm possible ideas and jot them down on paper. Select one of the ideas and try it out.
2. Reread what you have written so far and see if an idea comes to mind.
3. Skip ahead to a part where you know what you will write about. Come back to the problem later.
4. Write it as best you can and return later to make it better.
5. Write it several different ways and choose the one that you like the best.
6. Write whatever comes into your mind.
7. Talk about it/conference with a friend.
8. Read other texts to get some ideas.
9. Stop writing for a while and come back to it later.

It may be helpful to introduce the chart shown in Figure 9.3 to the students and then to display it prominently in the room.

---

figure   9.3   Writing steps.

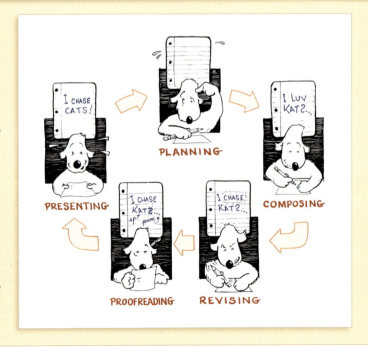

1. Choose a topic. *(Planning)*
2. Discuss your writing with a partner in a comfortable place. *(Planning)*
3. Write down all your ideas for your piece. *(Composing)*
4. Share your writing with a partner, with the class, or with your teacher. Ask your partners questions about your writing. *(Sharing)*
5. Use what your partner says to help you add information, get rid of information, or change words or ideas. *(Revising)*
6. Reread your piece. Correct mistakes you find. *(Proofreading)*
7. Read your piece to the class, a share group, or a partner. *(Presenting)*
8. Store your writing in your folder. Later you may decide to publish it.
9. Choose a new topic and begin again.

Sharing (Pre-revising, Getting Feedback)

Sharing is an integral part of writing workshop because children are social and want continual feedback on their hard work. Such sharing should happen *during* the writing process and not after, so that students can take the valuable advice they are offered and use it to revise their work along the way. However, the feedback need not always come only from you. Writing partnerships of wisely chosen pairs of students can help students to talk constructively and think more deeply about their writing in a social and motivational way (Hsu, 2010). Instead of you answering all questions, providing all the advice for revising, and offering all the support, students can learn, with careful instruction in the use of response guidelines, to critique and provide revision suggestions to each other. The sharing phase should occur during and after each draft. In their role as writing partners and, effectively, as peer editors, students possibly learn as much about writing as they do when creating their own pieces.

Teach students to respond to each other's writing in a way that is constructive, helpful, and tactful. Introduce the guidelines for responding shown in Figure 9.4 and model them several times with anonymous writing (from other classes or previous years) so students can see which messages are helpful for revising and which ones are not. A blank checklist based on these guidelines is provided in Appendix E. You can easily enter this checklist into a free online survey creator such as SurveyMonkey, so students can share feedback electronically. With careful teacher modeling and oversight, students can also use Google Docs to revise and edit each other's writing.

You can also use editing forms called Praise, Question, and Polish (PQP) with directions for students to use routinely when reviewing their partner's writing for the purpose of revision (see Appendix E). Model your questions and comments as coming from their responses as readers, not writers, so as to emphasize that they write for an audience. PQP uses these three steps:

1. *Praise.* First find something positive and specific to say about the piece. ("I really liked the beginning of your piece. It really grabbed my attention and made me want to keep reading.")

Survey Monkey
www.surveymonkey.com

> **see appendix E**

---

figure	**9.4**	Guidelines for sharing writing with a peer editor.

1. Ask a partner to listen to your writing.

2. Move quietly to a comfortable place where you can talk in 6" (tiny, inside) voices.

3. Ask your partner questions such as the following:

   - Do you think the opening "grabs" you?

   - Is there any part I should throw away?

   - Did I use any "tired" words?

   - What is the best part of my writing?

   - Is there any part you didn't understand?

   - Do I need a different ending?

   - Are there any sentences I should combine or separate?

   - What do you like best? Why? Least? Why?

4. Return to your seat and decide which, if any, of the suggestions you will use.

2. *Question.* Tell the author something that is not clear in his or her piece. ("When I read this it wasn't clear to me how Josh felt when his dog ran away. How can you show that?")

3. *Polish.* Suggest a way the author can make the piece even better. ("When I was reading and saw that you described the shark as "scary" I didn't get a vivid picture in my mind because you've used the word *scary* over and over again. Can you think of another word to describe the shark that will paint in my mind the picture you want of the shark?")

When you engage a student in a writing conference, it is a conversation with a clear purpose—revision—and a predictable structure. A "conversation" is the best lens through which to view the task of talking about writing (Anderson, 2000). Listed in Figure 9.5 are a few examples of questions you might ask during an author–teacher conference.

figure	9.5	Guidelines for conferencing for revision (teacher).

General Opening Questions

To begin the conference, ask a few general questions to encourage students to talk about their writing.

- What can I help you with?
- How do you think you are doing? (probe for evidence—e.g., "why?" "Tell me more . . .")

Genre-Specific Questions

Most teacher questions should be genre-specific. For example, if a student is writing an informational/explanatory text, the teacher might ask:

- How can you learn more about this topic or event?
- When I read this I wanted more information about _____. Your purpose is to inform, and I didn't feel informed as a reader about this part/subtopic.
- When I read this I saw that you said your topic was interesting, but as a reader, I have to be convinced that your topic is interesting. How can you convince me?
- What interesting facts have you provided about your topic?
- I found this part confusing because . . .
- When I read this part, I wished that I had more information about . . .

If a student is writing a narrative, questions and comments might include:

- When I read the ending I felt like it ended the same way as a lot of other stories, and I didn't feel very excited. How could you make your ending fit better with your story?

- When I read this I thought, "This doesn't sound how people really talk."
- When I read this I couldn't picture this setting (e.g., the forest, the apartment building). Can you provide a few more specific details so I can form a picture in my mind?

If a student is writing an opinion piece, comments might include:

- Tell me more about why you liked this book; it is not clear to me why you liked the book.
- What reasons did you provide for your opinion?
- When I was reading this I didn't know your piece was ending, and I was surprised, but without the "good" surprised feeling.

Questions That Address Standards

When looking for areas in which to provide feedback about writing, look at your grade-level standards for writing. For example, under the CCSS, students in grade 2 are expected to "Write narratives . . . [that] include details to describe actions, thoughts, and feelings" (CCSS.ELA-Literacy.W.2.3; NGACBP & CCSSO, 2010). Therefore, if a student is writing a narrative, teacher questions during conferencing could include:

- What is your character feeling right here? Don't *tell* your reader, *show* your reader by describing your character's actions. For instance, if your character is nervous, maybe you could write that he tapped his fingers on the table while he was watching the movie. What else could the character do to show how he was feeling?

Revising

Do not introduce this stage until students have learned the importance of changing their piece to meet the needs of their audience. This stage is more formalized than the sharing stage in that after the completion of the first draft, a structured conference will take place with you and, possibly, a small group of students. Students must understand that the purpose of revision is to improve the quality of the message, so that their audience fully understands what they are communicating. If students are not writing about topics that are personally meaningful, however, they will not be motivated to revise. At first, to revise, emergent writers simply reread their writing to see that they have included everything they wanted to say, check that their writing includes the pieces from their prewriting notes or graphic organizer, and make very few changes. As they gain more experience, they begin to make changes to clarify their writing and add more information to make it complete.

At this point students can read their piece aloud to a small group or the whole class and receive feedback. As stated earlier, students need to be taught how to give constructive, concrete feedback, based on grade-level expectations. Listening as a reader, not as a writer, should be modeled (e.g., "This part was not quite clear" versus "I would add more detail here"). (See the section on sharing and Figure 9.4.) Model the process for offering such advice multiple times before students complete the process on their own, probably beginning around the middle of first grade. Typical questions to ask during revision sessions (outlined in the section on conferencing for revision) can be written on a chart to provide support.

Editing (Making Corrections)

The editing stage is also played down until emergent writers have learned conventional spellings for many words and have acquired a rudimentary understanding of punctuation and capitalization rules. (The CCSS as well as your state or district standards should provide guidance about when this should occur.) To introduce editing, help students by showing them a grade-appropriate editing checklist, and then make a couple of corrections by putting a line through the error and writing the correction in pencil above the child's writing, eventually progressing to just a check in the margin of the sentence. As students become more fluent, encourage them to use an editing checklist (see Figure 9.6 for an example) to make more of their own corrections. Eventually, allow students to read each other's compositions and check for errors, again using an editing checklist, to help them begin to devel-

figure	9.6	Editing checklist.

☐ I have read my piece out loud.

☐ I have sounded out words or asked someone for help with spelling.

☐ Every sentence begins with a capital letter.

☐ Every sentence ends with an ending mark.

☐ I have capitalized names of people and the pronoun "I."

☐ I have checked my spelling.

op a spelling and writing conventions consciousness (see Chapter 6). As you are teaching the editing process, keep reminding students of the purpose for editing—to help the reader read the writer's important ideas and messages more effortlessly (correct spelling) and with the right expression (punctuation).

Publishing (Polishing for Presentation)

Kindergartners and first-graders usually do not recopy their writings, but sometimes you may type the final copy for the student, editing it and putting it into conventional form (Forseth & Avery, 2002). Students receive their piece polished and ready to read to others. When their writing is of "publication" quality, students then share their writing and show their drawings to the other students, often in a special chair labeled and set aside for writers, commonly called the "author's chair" (Graves & Hansen, 1983) (and, possibly, online to groups of offsite students). You and the students sit in the chair to share books and other texts they have read and written; this is the *only* time anyone sits in the chair. Specifically, you can teach students the steps shown in Figure 9.7 for publishing and sharing.

One of the most motivational ways for students to publish their individual or group writing is by putting their work into a presentation or book. Simple booklets/presentations can be created using technology, or constructed by folding a sheet of paper into quarters, like a greeting card. Students write the title on the front cover and use the three remaining sides for their composition and accompanying drawings. Students can also make booklets by stapling sheets of writing paper together and adding covers from construction paper or wallpaper from old sample books. Book covers can be laminated. Figure 9.8 shows a sample of an early first-grade class's literature-response book in traditional format and using presentation software.

Starting no later than third grade, students compose independently using technology, and students even younger enjoy creating presentations using kid-friendly software, such as Kid Pix. As mentioned earlier, students' writing is improved through the use of technology for a variety of reasons. By fourth grade, according to the CCSS and many state standards, students should be taught how to integrate multimedia into their writing, and judge when its inclusion is useful to aid comprehension (NGACBP & CCSSO, 2010).

Using technology to help students publish their writing will increase student motivation as well as enhance the quality and variety of their writing. Websites

WWW

Kid Pix
http://kid-pix.soft112.com

Lucidpress
www.lucidpress.com

Book Creator
www.redjumper.net/
bookcreator/

Fotobabble
www.fotobabble.com

Write a biography
www.bellinghamschools.org/
sites/default/files/BIO/
Biomaker.htm

figure	9.7	Publishing steps.

1. Decide which of your writings you would like to publish.

2. Share your writing with a partner, with the class, or with your teacher. Begin by telling what your piece is about, where you are in the process, and what help you need from the listener.

3. Change your writing if you need to by adding something, getting rid of something, or changing something.

4. Edit your writing for spelling, capitals, punctuation, and correct words.

5. Prepare the paper for your final copy.

6. Add pictures. Rewrite the piece in your best handwriting, or type it.

figure **9.8**   Sample of a class literature-response book or presentation.

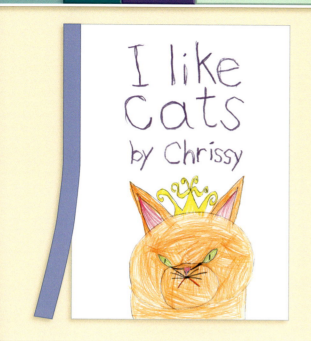
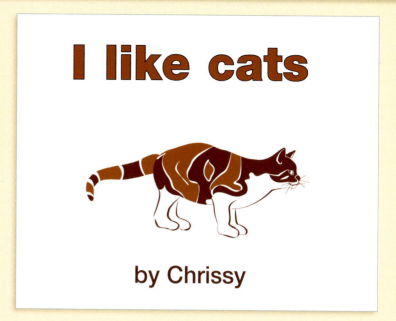

such as Lucidpress.com offer digital templates for newspapers and flippable books that students can use to create published-quality text. Students can use the templates collaboratively by sharing them through Google Docs. Also, a number of apps have been created especially for student publishing, such as Book Creator for the iPad, which students can use to create their own e-book in a variety of formats (e.g., photobook, manual). Their published e-books can then be shared digitally with others. The app Fotobabble allows students to create narrated picture books with photos they have taken themselves or pictures they create. Students then compile the photos or pictures, or both, then record a narrative to accompany their visuals, thus creating a published-quality narrated piece of text.

WRITING STRUCTURES

as explored earlier, students must realize that there are various text genres, each with its own specific structure. For young students, though, this realization takes time, modeling, and explicit instruction. For example, while most teachers expect children to begin school with some awareness of narrative or story structure, as a result of being read to and seeing hundreds of stories on television and in movies, many primary-grade youngsters have only a partially developed sense of story. Teaching students about narrative structure using *story frames* can directly improve their reading comprehension as well as their writing ability (Spiegel & Fitzgerald, 1986). Moreover, providing a literacy scaffold for writing poetry or other patterned pieces (see the activity on page 193), or a prompt for opinion pieces, or a template for informational writing (see Chapter 10) allows students, particularly English learners and struggling writers, to reach a higher level of achievement than is possible *without* the structure (Peregoy & Boyle, 2013). Journal writing and class newspapers are other tools that can serve as prompts to student writing. These structures should leave room for students to make their writing personally meaningful and not be overly prescriptive.

Story Frames

story frames ■ **Story frames,** also called story grammars, are structured templates that can be used orally as early as prekindergarten to help students understand story structure. Use the following steps to encourage story writing and improve comprehension through the use of the prepared structure:

1. Read students a well-formed story, either pointing out the elements that are usually found in a story (i.e., setting, main characters, problem, solution, and ending), or, as in genre study, using inquiry to help students discover the elements on their own.

2. Write a story with the students, using the board. Provide the structure for them, but have them fill in the blanks with what they remember from the story, using a story frame such as the one illustrated in Figure 9.9.

3. When the story is complete, read it to the students and then ask for volunteers to read sentences.

4. Give the students a blank story frame and invite them to write their own original stories. You may want to brainstorm with the whole class to help get them started and then do an original story as a class (see Figure 9.10).

| figure | 9.9 | A basic story frame. |

(Story Title)

Once upon a time in (setting) there lived a (main character). (S)he was very (description) and always liked to (character's favorite activity) . One day (character) wanted very much to (goal) . But there was a problem. The problem was (problem) . So (character) tried and tried and finally (how the character resolved the problem) . The story ends when (resolution and ending) .

| figure | 9.10 | Example of a story written by a second-grade class using the story frame in Figure 9.9. |

Petey the Lion

Once upon a time in a tiny village in Texas there lived a very strange lion named Petey. He was very shy and quiet and always liked to run and hide when the other lions roared. One day Petey wanted very much to play with the other lions. But there was a problem. The problem was that they didn't like Petey because they thought he was a coward. So Petey tried and tried and finally showed them he wasn't a coward. He saved the life of a baby lion cub who was drowning. The story ends when Petey is playing with the other lions. Now they like him because he is no longer shy but mighty.

With very young children, oral and drawing activities can be substituted for the written aspects of this activity. See Chapter 10 for a discussion of applying the concept of "frames" to informational text.

Literacy Scaffolds

For struggling writers, especially those for whom English is a second language, writing prose and poetry can be overwhelming, even frightening. This fear can be alleviated with additional structural support. **Literacy scaffolds,** which are temporary frameworks for narrative or informational writing and somewhat looser in structure than story frames, enable all students to succeed in writing prose and poetry. With a structure provided, students can formulate their ideas in ways that might be difficult, if not impossible, without the framework. Literacy scaffolds offer easy-to-follow patterns or "formulas" for writing, so students can focus on their ideas rather than the mechanics of capitalization and spelling. These scaffolds should be removed as soon as students no longer need them. Offer these scaffolds as an option so that students with greater ability and more proficiency with the English language are not restricted by their use.

■ literacy scaffolds

Many repetitive patterns, such as those found in published poems or songs, can be turned into literacy scaffolds. The following activity is an example of a simple literacy scaffold and the steps for employing it (Cecil, 1994a). A variation using another type of framework, a predictive web, follows.

A Simple Literacy Scaffold

A C T I V I T Y

1. Have the students listen to "These Are a Few of My Favorite Things" from *The Sound of Music.*
2. Have them recall the singer's favorite things as they are listed on the board.
3. Invite them to brainstorm their favorite things and add them to the list.
4. For each of the favorite things, ask the students if they can think of a "downside" to it; for example, gentle rain is nice, but thunderstorms can be scary.
5. Provide each student with a photocopied sheet containing the following scaffold:

   I Like

   I like ice cream .

   But I don't like to eat ice cream in the wintertime .

   (Repeat as often as desired.)

6. As a class, write a group piece that includes a response from each child. Read the group effort chorally.
7. Have the students write their own "I Like" pieces.

Imagine What Happens!

A C T I V I T Y

Select a picture book such as *The King, the Cheese, and the Mice* (1965) by Nancy and Eric Gurney. Read the story aloud and stop at the most exciting point. Ask students to predict what might happen next, using a "predictive web" such as the one shown in Figure 9.11 to predict the story's ending.

Invite students to use one of the brainstormed ideas or one of their own and write (or draw for preliterate children) their version of the ending of the story. Allow students to read or tell about their original endings. Finally, read the author's ending and compare it with the students' predictions.

figure   9.11   Predictive web for *The King, the Cheese, and the Mice.*

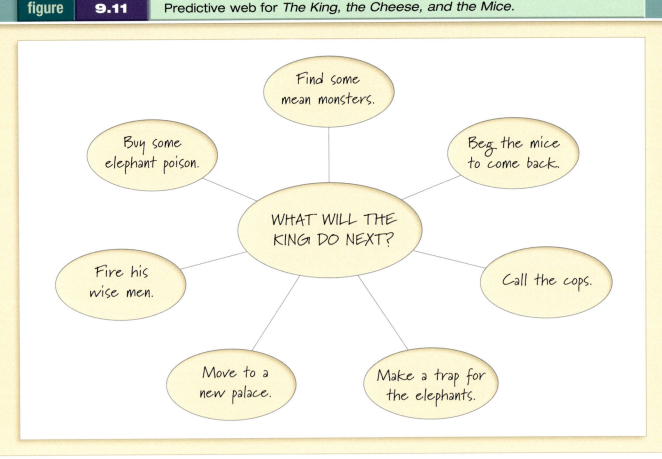

patterned stories ■
Students also enjoy writing **patterned stories** based on texts such as *Fortunately* (1993) by Remy Charlip. Cumulative stories like John Burningham's *Mr. Grumpy's Outing* (2001) and *Mr. Grumpy's Motorcar* (1976) and Ed Emberley's *Drummer Hoff* (1972) offer writing models for students. Additionally, folktales such as *Chicken Little* and *The Little Red Hen* provide repetitive phrases that can be emulated (Tompkins, 1997). As another example, *Rosie's Walk* (1971), by Pat Hutchins, provides a frame that can be used by teachers to talk about "juicy" words, words that evoke a precise meaning or feeling, as opposed to boring or overused words. Expanding on the frame in Figure 9.12, students can brainstorm "juicy" words to describe a teacher's walk across a schoolyard (e.g., the "vast" playground, the "towering" jungle gym), and then create a story emulation using their new vocabulary (Graham et al., 2012).

Prompts for Opinion Pieces

As stated previously, the CCSS and many state standards emphasize that students, even young students, should be able to write pieces in which they state an opinion and give reasons for their opinion. You can encourage students' writing in this format by using a prompt, such as "If you could wave a magic wand, what would you change about . . . ?" For example, ask your students, "If you could wave a magic wand, what would you change about our school?" Then brainstorm a list of issues about which your students may have strong opinions, such as the order of events in the day, school lunches, school uniforms, student use of technology,

figure   9.12   Sample story emulation of *Rosie's Walk* with first-grade students.

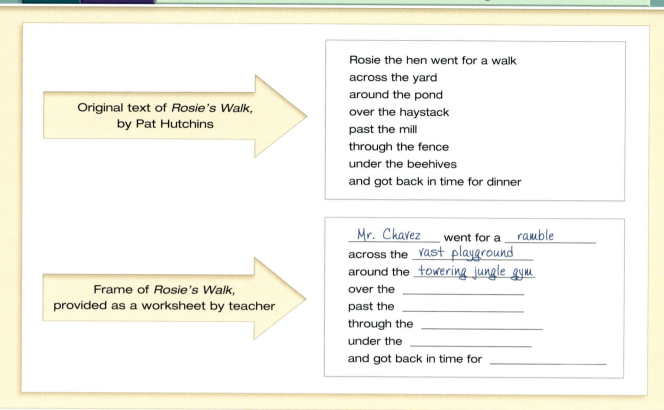

Original text of *Rosie's Walk*,
by Pat Hutchins

> Rosie the hen went for a walk
> across the yard
> around the pond
> over the haystack
> past the mill
> through the fence
> under the beehives
> and got back in time for dinner

Frame of *Rosie's Walk*,
provided as a worksheet by teacher

> ___Mr. Chavez___ went for a ___ramble___
> across the ___vast playground___
> around the ___towering jungle gym___
> over the _____
> past the _____
> through the _____
> under the _____
> and got back in time for _____

Source: Adapted from Graham, S., Bollinger, A., Booth Olson, C., D'Aoust, C., MacArthur, C., McCutchen, D., & Ollinghouse, N. (2012). Teaching elementary school students to be effective writers: A practice guide (NCEE 2012–4058). Washington, DC: National Center for Education Evaluation and Regional Assistance, U.S. Department of Education. Retrieved from http://ies.ed.gov/ncee/wwc/publications_reviews.aspx#pubsearch

or the amount of time at recess. Once a list has been brainstormed, have the students vote on which issue they would like to learn more about, and try to change. The first step is for students to weigh in on the issue, and to be clear where they stand on it. To do this, students should write an opinion piece, stating the issue or problem, and then their opinion about why the issue is problematic. For example, students could expand on opinions such as the following: "Our school lunches are not good. I believe that they are bad because they taste bad, and most of the kids throw their lunches away." By second grade and above, students can start to conduct surveys and interviews, collect information from textual sources about the issue, and use their data to write information reports about the issue. Students can then use both their opinion writing and the informational reports to effect change, through actions such as presenting to the teacher, principal, or school board.

Journal Writing

Classrooms typically allow time for students to engage in some amount of intimate oral communication in the early grades. But until recently, there was no place in the literacy curriculum of primary grades for personal writing, leaving a large void in this mode of communication. Journal writing provides the opportunity for personal expression as well as valuable writing practice. Three of the journal-writing techniques used in elementary schools seem well suited for emergent writers and will be explored here.

Dialogue journals

dialogue journal ■

In a **dialogue journal,** you and the student can carry on a written conversation about any topic of interest to the child. By making written comments in the margins of a notebook in direct response to the child's words, by asking questions, and by providing positive written feedback in response to what the student has written, you help the student grow as a writer. The frequent writing that occurs in dialogue journals helps promote students' writing fluency, and reading your comments provides valuable reading experience and builds a relationship between you and the student.

code-switch ■

Children just beginning to speak and write English or students who speak a nondominant dialect of English can be encouraged to write in their home language or to **code-switch** by using both English for words they know and their home language or dialect for words or grammatical structures they haven't yet acquired in standard English. (It is important to note that students often use code-switching strategically, and it does not always reflect lack of vocabulary or grammatical knowledge.) You may provide sentence starters for English learners, which they can elect to use, or not (Cox, n.d.). Such starters could include the following:

> Today I *will, feel, need, want, saw, heard, played*
>
> I *want to, wish I had, went to, used, read, wrote, watched*

For more ideas on how to use dialogue journals and a list of recommended children's literature that simulates the journal format, visit the website in the margin.

For preliterate students, the dialogue journal can be used with pictures interspersed with letters, and eventually words, as the student learns them. You can initially ask the student to tell about the pictures. Then transcribe above the picture exactly what the student composes, carefully modeling the sounding out of words until gradually the student begins to use experimental spelling to write down ideas (Cunningham & Allington, 2010; Isabell, 2010).

For some young children, delayed fine motor coordination can make forming tiny letters in straight lines difficult and painstakingly slow, thus hampering their interest in writing. Their ideas may flow many times faster than their ability to capture them in print. This was the case for 7-year-old Ethan, who took 30 minutes and two large sheets of paper to write a piece about a fictional car he created (see Figure 9.13). Although writing practice fosters dexterity for such students, the

WWW

Journal Writing

www.readingrockets.org/ article/journal-writing

---

figure 9.13 Ethan's composition.

Ethan's piece translation:

The Ferrari Palato has a manual transmission with a 10 cylinder, turbo, V-8 engine, auto seat move, with leather seats.

teacher may wish to occasionally transcribe the child's ideas to ensure that frustration with the mechanics of writing does not squelch enthusiasm for composing. Also, teaching students keyboarding skills enables them to use word processing programs to more quickly write down their ideas; this can motivate students for whom lack of motor skills is a continuing concern (see Chapter 12).

Reading response journals

Young children become interested in literature, for the most part, to the degree that it affects them. You can solicit personal responses to reading by asking students to write in a **reading response journal** a first reaction to something they have read, saying whatever they like without correction (with the exception of simply "I liked it" or "I didn't like it"). Alternatives to traditional book reports in journal format can include responding to a quotation from the book, questioning the author, continuing the story, or writing another version of the story from another character's point of view (Sweeney & Peterson, 1996). Another alternative is for students to respond by expressing their opinion of the text with the reasons for their opinion.

■ reading response journal

This type of journal is an ideal vehicle for personal expression, often called **expressive writing.** Students can write fluently without fear of criticism, because they are not burdened with the task of polishing their writing for another reader. Journal writers are free to answer the question, "What did I really think of that?" as they read, think, and write.

■ expressive writing

You can adapt reading journals for early writers' use by providing **sentence stems** that ask questions designed to connect what they have read with their own experiences. For example, you can use the following questions after reading a story to prompt journal writing:

■ sentence stems

1. This character is like me because _____.

2. I like/dislike this character because _____.

3. This story reminds me of _____.

4. If I were _____, I would have _____.

5. I would like the story to have ended this way _____.

6. I liked when the author used the word _____ because it made me really be able to see _____.

Learning logs

For content-area material, students can begin to crystallize their understandings via a **learning log.** This activity requires that students write in their journals immediately after a content-area subject lesson, such as social studies. Their journal entry would then include the following:

■ learning log

■ a summary or examples of what they understand has been presented or read

■ a summary or examples of what they do *not* understand about what has been presented or read

■ questions they have about what has been presented or read

■ a personal reaction to what has been presented or read

These logs can be interactive if you respond to them regularly, answering students' questions and directing their attention to important concepts. Figure 9.14 shows examples taken from the mathematics learning logs of a third-grade class. The teacher answered the students' thoughtful questions in the margins of the log.

| figure | 9.14 | Examples from third-graders' learning logs. |

How is multiplication like addition?	You are adding, but you're doing it much more quickly.
How do I know when to divide?	Look for the word "each."
What problems should I watch out for when I am borrowing?	Be sure to cross out the old number and put in the new one so you're not confused.
Why do I need to know the times tables when I have a calculator?	You may not always have a calculator with you!

Class Newspaper

Students can be highly motivated to write when they are allowed to choose (1) the structure or genre in which they will write and (2) the content that they will write about. One way to accommodate these choices is to create a class newspaper. The newspaper can be created in hard copy or online, or both, and then shared with parents, the school, and community members. To prepare students for newspaper writing, you can teach minilessons on the major structures found in newspapers: editorials, book reviews, reports of local news, cartoons, and human-interest stories (Wetzel, Peterson, Weber, & Steinback, 2013). Once students understand these structures and have explored and analyzed anchor texts representing each text structure, they can begin to create their own pieces, following the writing process steps.

In newspaper writing, encourage students to use their writing to promote change. For example, students might write about challenges they identify within their own school (e.g., bullying, lack of library time), researching the problem and presenting possible solutions. They can use phones or tablet computers to provide photographs or videos (for online newspapers) to accompany their stories.

THE LANGUAGE EXPERIENCE APPROACH

language experience approach (LEA) ▪

The **language experience approach (LEA)** is well suited for modeling beginning literacy because it uses students' own language as writing material, and it can be used with students as young as prekindergarten. Later you can transcribe the LEA charts and have the students read them—thus graphically illustrating the connection between the communication processes (Ashton-Warner, 1965; Lee & Allen, 1963; Stauffer, 1980). Because the language patterns are determined by students' own speech and the content is determined by their own experiences, students easily remember the text of these stories, and they are eager to read them again and again. While the approach is powerful it should not be overused, as having students write their own stories about what is important to them, using their own experimental spelling, is crucial to their development as writers.

This approach, which stems back to the story and sentence methods of reading instruction that were popular around the turn of the twentieth century, is an ideal way for teachers to demonstrate the interrelatedness of reading, writing, listening, and speaking. It also provides readers and writers who are struggling with accessible high-interest texts. Students watch you *write* down their story on chart paper or an interactive whiteboard as they *speak*. They *listen* as you read the story, and finally they *read* the story themselves. This helps students realize that (1) what they experience can be talked about; (2) what they talk about can be written down; and (3) what they write can be read. It also helps students grasp the idea that written language often has the same purpose as oral language: the communication of meaning (Allen, 1976; Hall, 1981). As you take dictation, you can also demonstrate the conventions of written language: that it proceeds from left to right and from top to bottom, that words have spaces between them, that the first word in a sentence is capitalized, and so forth. The stories can also be illustrated, allowing opportunities for viewing and visually representing. The chart pages can be bound together, creating monthly "books" that students can read during open reading time. You can take a daily picture of the LEA chart to get an electronic copy, creating an updated presentation of the LEA that is available to students to read on a classroom computer or tablet.

Steps in the LEA

Language experience compositions can be composed using a chart and chart paper (see Figure 9.15) or an interactive whiteboard by groups of students or individuals, and they are ideal for English learners because of the many senses being used simultaneously. The format is the same in either case and includes the following steps (Cecil, 1994b):

1. Provide a stimulus for discussion and writing.
2. Conduct an oral discussion about the stimulus.
3. Brainstorm about the stimulus, creating a word bank.
4. Help students compose the passage.
5. Read the passage aloud; reread several times.
6. Recruit students to read individual sentences.
7. Have the students name the passage.
8. Conduct a minilesson.
9. Duplicate the passage either in print or digital form, and have students provide their own illustrations and reread the passage at home.

Provide a stimulus for discussion and writing

The stimulus for writing or discussion is usually a concrete object or a current event, but it can encompass anything that all members of the group have recently experienced. That the object or experience has been witnessed by all students ensures that English learners will benefit from the later discussion and composing. A language experience story could be written about a snowman made at recess, a seasonal thunderstorm, a television program that everyone happened to see, a story the class just enjoyed listening to, chocolate pudding that all have enjoyed eating, or a garter snake brought in by one of the class members. The most important criterion is that the subject has captured the interest of the students and they would now like to talk, write, and read about it.

Conduct an oral discussion about the stimulus

Oral discussion is a natural bridge between the sensory stimulus and reading and writing about it. After the stimulus has been experienced, encourage the sharing of thoughts and ideas about it. If the LEA is to be based on a shared classroom expe-

| figure | 9.15 | Making a language experience chart. |

1. Use regular 24" x 16" (or larger) ruled chart paper, oak tag, or posterboard.

2. Keep a 2" margin on both right and left sides, and a 3" margin on the top of the paper.

3. Use short one-line sentences for beginners.

4. Do not divide a word or phrase at the end of a line.

5. Invite children to illustrate the piece—at the top, bottom, or even the sides of papers—but do not let pictures break up a sentence.

6. Use manuscript writing, with crayon, lettering pen, or felt-tip marker.

7. "Pack" together the letters of each word, leaving the space of an "o" between words.

The Snake

Robert brought a snake to school.
The snake was green and skinny.
Robert let us hold him but some children were scared.
We thought he would be slimy but he wasn't.
He was dry! We hope the snake enjoyed being in school!

rience, take pictures of the experience and share them with the students during the discussion before the LEA, on a smart TV or interactive whiteboard. Visuals of the experience coupled with a discussion will help English learners' vocabulary development better than a discussion devoid of visual support. Your role is that of an interested facilitator who positively and nonjudgmentally responds to comments and paraphrases what may be unclear.

Brainstorm about the stimulus

This step gives students the opportunity to think critically and creatively about the stimulus and provides words and phrases for the word bank that will be helpful in writing the passage. Guide the students into categorizing the responses. If, for example, the class were writing a language experience story about a garter snake that a student has brought to class, the brainstorming might proceed as follows:

Associations (nouns). "What kinds of things do you think of when you think of a snake?" *(poison, rattles, grass)* "Why?" *(after each response)*

Description (adjectives). "What words could we use to tell about a snake? How does it look, smell, sound, feel?" *(skinny, slimy, scary)*

Actions (verbs). "What do snakes do?" *(slither, crawl, bite)*

Reactions. "How do snakes make you feel? Why?" *(scared, like running away, curious)*

Similarities (synonyms). "What are some other things that are kind of like snakes? How?" *(worms, spaghetti, sticks)*

Differences (antonyms). "What are some things that are very different from snakes? How?" *(Elephants, because they are big and snakes are small. Note: Almost any answer is acceptable here if students can offer a reasonable explanation for their choice.)*

Phonological awareness element. "What are some words that rhyme with snake?" *(bake, make, take)* or "What words begin like snake?" *(snail, snow, snore)*

The responses to the group brainstorming are written or projected prominently on the board, interactive whiteboard, or chart paper as the students help you sound out the words according to their current knowledge.

Help students compose the passage

Referring to the words on the board, suggest that the students write a passage about the stimulus. (*Note:* The word *story* is studiously avoided so that the piece can be written in either informational, opinion, or narrative format.) Ask for a beginning for the piece and solicit suggestions and continue until students run out of ideas. Finally, request an ending and invite students to illustrate the piece. A typical second-grade piece might look like the one shown earlier in Figure 9.15.

During the dictation phase, accept the students' ideas verbatim; however, if students offer an unclear sentence or incorrect grammar, paraphrase the sentence correctly, keeping the meaning intact by asking a question such as "Do you mean . . . ?" This approach, diplomatically employed, can assist an English learner's transition to standard English in a positive way.

Read the passage aloud

Follow the dictation with several readings of the passage, each reading in a different manner. First, read the passage aloud to the students while they follow along, phrase by phrase, to avoid stilted word-by-word reading. You may then echo-read, or have students repeat every line after you model it. Then point at each word and deliberately exaggerate the left-to-right progression and the return sweep to the next line while students read the passage chorally. English learners and less able readers are thereby participating in the reading experience by being "fed" the words they hear around them, avoiding the usual embarrassment that can occur with oral reading when not every word is known. Plus, they are able to hear the syntax, rhythm, and cadence of the new language repeatedly.

Recruit students to read individual sentences

When all students have read the entire story, recruit students to read each individual sentence, thereby focusing the students' attention on the sentence unit as part of the passage. Also, reinforcement is being provided for high-frequency words as well as new ones.

Have students name the passage

Determining the main idea of a paragraph is one of the most difficult comprehension skills. However, with daily

Children want to write, to create their own texts in order to make meaning.

practice in selecting the titles for language experience passages, students can soon grasp the idea of homing in on one general thought that conveys the central idea in the passage. Solicit several nominations of titles for the passage, followed by a short discussion of why one title does a slightly better job of summarizing the main idea than another. For example, you may want the students to see, through another rereading, why "The Snake" is a more appropriate title for the second-graders' story than "Our Pets," which was also offered.

Conduct a minilesson

Describing the relationship between illustrations and text is an important as identified by the CCSS. For example, CCSS.ELA-Literacy.RL.1.7 requires students to "Use illustrations and details in a story to describe its characters, setting, or events" (NGACBP & CCSSO, 2010, p. 11). Once you have led a class discussion and helped the students compose the language experience passage, you can lead a discussion about the use and purpose of illustrations. This discussion is best led in conjunction with the read-aloud and study of grade-appropriate trade books that clearly show the relationship between illustrations and text. For example, narrative anchor texts that include illustrations about the story elements—the setting, characters, problem, and solution—are useful to read aloud to the students, accompanied by the creation of a "noticing chart" about the illustrations. Likewise, an anchor text that includes illustrations about the main ideas of an informational text can be studied and a "noticing chart" created to describe the relationship between the text and the illustrations. Point out, for both narrative and informational anchor texts, that the author and illustrator make purposeful decisions about the content of the illustrations, and that the illustrations indicate to the reader what is important in the story.

Once anchor texts have been read and analyzed for the relationship between their illustrations and the text, students can start to apply their knowledge of that relationship to decisions about what to illustrate in their language experience (LE) passage. Refer to the "noticing chart" for narrative and informational text and ask which genre fits that day's LE passage the best. Once the students have identified the genre of the passage, ask them which text elements in each are likely to be illustrated (e.g., setting, characters, or in the case of informational text, specific information). With your help the students can identify the elements of their LE passage that should be illustrated, and either you can create a quick sketch on the chart next to the elements, or the students can create their own illustrations and cut and paste them onto the chart.

Duplicate the passage

You can carefully duplicate each passage that the students write in this manner, with space for a personal illustration, so that each student has a copy to reread at home and a copy to compile into a collaborative class book, or class slide presentation. The digital presentation can be posted on the class website and shared with the class's community of family and friends. Review passages often with students to reinforce phonics elements, high-frequency words, and new vocabulary. Students will also be proud and eager to read their books to other classes or to create recorded read-alongs for students needing more reinforcement. Every so often, revisit the passage to allow for further rereadings and review.

Variations on the Basic LEA (Salinger, 1993)

You can use the following group writing activities to vary the standard language experience lesson just presented. Note that interactive writing can also be used (see Chapter 3).

Morning message. Each day, write a brief **morning message** about the day's weather and upcoming events and record it on a chart or using presentation software. Sometimes the students may dictate the message. This chart provides a model for the students' own daily writing in their journals.

■ morning message

Digital morning message (Labbo, 2005). Using creativity software such as Kid Pix, which supports brainstorming, illustrating, and drafting a writing piece, write the morning message digitally. While individual students dictate the sentences, model using the keyboard to type the students' message. The students then listen and follow along as the voice synthesizer on the computer reads each sentence. Finally, the students read the message chorally, led by you or the class leader of the day.

Individual dictation. For beginning writers, you may take **individual dictation** from each student and record his work in a small notebook. Transcribing a caption for artwork falls into this category.

■ individual dictation

Sentence strips. Record transcriptions on long strips of paper or index cards and cut the **sentence strips** into word cards. Students use these word cards to create sentences at their desks or in pocket charts. Encourage students to copy their sentences into a notebook.

■ sentence strips

Word bank. Students request individual words from you and keep them in a **word bank** to study on their own, play games such as word sorts with, swap with friends, and so forth. Frequently review the words with students and discard the ones they cannot read. This strategy complements the sentence strip strategy. Write words on sentence strips, attach them together using a metal ring, and hang them on hooks on the wall. In this way, students can grab their "word banks" and read them daily to other students, classroom visitors, and so on, adding a new word (of their choice) each day. The words can also be put on word walls for whole-class use.

■ word bank

Content-area use. Using LEA strategies, keep records of the students' work in content areas such as science and social studies. Observations of experiments, field trips, and even math activities lend themselves to this approach.

ONLINE EXPERIENCES FOR LITERACY AND LEARNING

many researchers suggest that the Internet is the major vehicle through which literacy and learning will take place (Hartman et al., 2005), and technology is redefining what it means to be literate. Young people need to be critical thinkers about what they read in text as well as critical producers and consumers of electronic messages (Rhoades, 2013). Thus, you must fully integrate new technologies in teaching students to love literacy and learning. Motivational online writing experiences in the classroom can create positive attitudes toward literacy and learning and also develop strong—and increasingly valuable—technology skills.

Castek, Bevans-Mangelson, and Goldstone (2006) offer several ways to make the reading, writing, and technology connection through use of the Internet:

WWW

BookPALS Storyline
www.storylineonline.net/

Read Along Stories and Songs
*www.rif.org/kids/readingplanet/
bookzone/read_aloud_stories.htm*

1. Have students read or listen to literature online. For example, through the Screen Actors Guild Foundation, many actors have volunteered to read exceptional picture storybooks such as *Thank You, Mr. Falker* (Polacco, 1998) on a streaming video at BookPALS Storyline. Young students can explore and respond to the read-along stories on the RIF Reading Planet website.

2. Add informational websites to your study of literature. For example, a third-grade class reading *How I Spent My Summer Vacation* (Teague, 1997), a story about a boy who is captured by cowboys, can deviate from the usual personal essay response and instead visit teacher-provided informational links to sound and photo displays of cowboys, rodeos, Western geography, and so forth. (Appendix C includes examples of informational websites.)

3. Have students join virtual book clubs. For example, students can participate in discussions, ask questions, and post comments on their favorite books on sites such as the Scholastic STACKS site (or search "children's online book clubs").

4. Encourage students to become online authors. The work of revising and editing may become more enjoyable when students know their polished work will be read by a larger audience. As an example, Launchpad allows students to create and present their writing online, as well as read the books of other children from around the world. Through this participation, students make deep reading/writing connections and develop positive attitudes toward the Internet as a vehicle for reading and writing. As an added bonus, they also learn about other cultures. See Chapter 12 for additional suggestions for online literacy experiences.

see appendix C

Scholastic STACKS
*www.scholastic.com/kids/
stacks/index.asp*

Launchpad
www.launchpadmag.com

WRITING AND STUDENTS WHO ARE ENGLISH LEARNERS

According to Goldman (2014) six high-leverage practices emerge from the research as crucial for helping English learners achieve success with writing skills. These practices are as follows.

1. Teach genre writing as a process. Teach students how to write through a study of written genres, as outlined earlier in this chapter.

2. Build on students' background knowledge. Validate students' background knowledge and link new concepts about writing to students' existing knowledge. In addition, create writing assignments that connect with issues in the students' communities.

3. Model writing for and with students. Using a think-aloud approach, model writing for specific purposes. Also, co-create with English learners written products through a guided-practice approach, helping students draw connections between language features and accomplishing purposes through writing.

4. Develop their academic oral language. Teaching the use of extended oral discourse to accomplish purposes helps students practice and control the academic language they need in order to write effectively. This academic language goes beyond discrete vocabulary to the use of extended, connected language needed to accomplish specific purposes, such as describing, crafting arguments, and explaining.

5. Teach vocabulary and grammar explicitly and in context. Teaching discrete vocabulary and grammar points is crucial to nurturing English learners' success in writing. Academic vocabulary should be taught explicitly and assessed regularly. Provide direct and indirect feedback on writing in the form of written comments and mini-lessons on language use and grammar points.

6. Publish and celebrate writing using technology. Teaching students to publish their writing is crucial for increasing student motivation for writing. Research shows that when students write using technology, both their process and written products are of higher quality than those of their peers who do not use technology to write.

WRITING FOR STUDENTS WITH SPECIAL NEEDS

Students who have learning disabilities and struggle with reading also often struggle with writing, especially informational writing (Abadiano & Turner, 2004). It is often helpful to teach these students to use reading to unlock writing skills, and vice versa. For example, if the student is struggling to decode a word while reading, tell her, "Think about how you say words slowly in writing. That will help you in reading" (Anderson & Briggs, 2011).

Writing workshop has been found to be successful with students with special needs (Fu & Shelton, 2007). Students in special education are receptive to the *process approach*, which allows them to approximate "correct" writing and receive peer and teacher feedback on their writing, as opposed to a *product* orientation, which can be isolating and cause stress in students with special needs.

Students with dyslexia struggle with skills across the literacy spectrum, including writing (International Dyslexia Association, 2012). It is difficult for them to juggle the overlapping cognitive tasks necessary to compose text, such as keeping a focus on a topic while at the same time choosing the appropriate words to communicate thoughts about that topic. The "talk to write" process is helpful with students with dyslexia; it involves asking students to talk through their thoughts for writing, and repeating the process again and again until the structure and words that will be used in their writing become clear in their mind (Wilson, 2012). Once the students are clear about the structure and words that they will write, the writing process can begin.

Students who are deaf or hearing impaired face a number of challenges in learning how to compose text. Compared with students without hearing impairments, these students use shorter sentences, fewer clauses, and less precise vocabulary in their writing (Wolbers, 2008). In addition, students who are deaf often struggle with organization of text and with applying text features appropriate to text genre. Because these students struggle with both the lower-order skills of writing (conventions, syntax, etc.) and the higher-order skills (text organization), teachers of students who are deaf must use balanced literacy strategies. Morning message balances the modeling and teaching of written conventions with text structure and is effective in teaching these students (Wolbers, 2008). Genre study, in which students are explicitly taught and practice text structures is also effective in teaching students who are deaf to compose text (Wolbers, Dostal, & Bowers, 2012). These practices are especially effective because they target areas that students who are deaf struggle with, such as application of writing conventions, using precise vocabulary, and identification and application of text structures.

SUMMARY

before they began school, most children scribbled on sidewalks, newspapers, and even wallpaper with chalk, crayons, lipstick, pencils, pens—*anything* that would make a mark. The child's mark said, "I am." Whereas in reading children create their meaning from a given text, in writing, children create their own texts in order to make meaning—at first for themselves, and then for other readers. Children *want* to write. They want to write the first day they enter school.

School is merely where the beginning of children's *formal* literacy instruction takes place. The writing process for emergent writers has already begun with the child's drawing pictures, and it continues with scribble writing, a precursor to the developmental spelling stages that lead to conventional writing. Guided by teacher modeling and inspired by provocative ideas, a fertile imagination, and the freedom to experiment with print, students soon learn to express their own thoughts and feelings in their own language. They gradually evolve into conventional writers and quickly realize the power of the written word to make their thoughts visible to others, graphically illustrated by one little boy's intercepted note to his classmate that proclaimed, "I luv yuw!"

questions FOR JOURNAL WRITING AND DISCUSSION

1. How many ways do you think spoken language can be used in a primary classroom to provide a foundation for writing activities? Make a list and share it with your class.

2. Consider the importance of providing emergent writers with appropriate feedback and encouragement during the process of drafting a piece of writing. Do you or your classmates remember receiving this kind of encouragement? Discuss.

3. Which activities are effective in teaching young English learners to compose text? Students with special needs?

4. Review the suggestions offered in this chapter for connecting reading, writing, and technology. Which of these do you feel you would be most likely to implement in your classroom? Why? Discuss these suggestions with a small group of your classmates. Rate each according to the benefits in the following areas:
   - Amount of writing practice gained.
   - Amount of reading required.
   - Motivational appeal to students.
   - Level of computer and online practice afforded.

suggestions FOR PROJECTS AND FIELD ACTIVITIES

1. Interview two students at different primary-grade levels to determine how much writing they say they do in class and how they feel about the writing and themselves as writers.

2. Obtain permission to teach a language experience lesson to a small group of primary-grade youngsters. Bring in a toy or another object to use as a stimulus for discussion, brainstorming, and writing. Follow the steps in this chapter to teach the lesson. Share with your classmates what worked well, what you would do differently next time, and what you learned about the students' ability to compose.

3. Collect and evaluate a writing sample from a typical English learner in your placement classroom. How does the writing differ from that of a student in your placement classroom who is fully English proficient? Given your analysis of the English learner's writing sample, select and carry out one of the scaffolding techniques outlined in this chapter, collect another writing sample from the same student, and reassess the student's writing. Did you find improvement in the English learner's writing? If so, why do you think the student improved? If not, what might explain the lack of improvement?

4. Observe a writing workshop over one week. Ask the students to show you their favorite pieces. Ask them to tell you what they are learning about writing. Finally, ask the teacher what she has learned about each of the writing skills of the students in the class through this process. Share your insights with your college class.

Informational Text in the Classroom

10

READING AND WRITING TO LEARN

focus questions

Why is informational text important?

How will the use of informational text change with the adoption of the Common Core State Standards?

What makes informational text challenging?

What instructional practices can help students with informational text?

How can instruction in the structure of informational text help students succeed in writing using this mode of discourse?

When several of Mrs. Shreve's second-graders come into the classroom on Monday morning chatting about a film they have seen about sharks over the weekend, the teacher decides to use the children's interest to create a lesson on reading and writing informational text. The next day Mrs. Shreve asks her students, "So . . . what do you know about sharks?" The students eagerly write their answers on sticky notes and place them on the board. Then, as a class, they organize their facts and place them under categories they have identified, including "where they live," "what they eat," "different kinds of sharks," and "behavior." From this list Mrs. Shreve invites the students to create questions, which will serve as their purpose for reading and locating information.

When Hadley asks the popular question, "Do *all* sharks attack people?" the children's eyes widen with curiosity. The teacher, seizing the moment, shows the students how to locate this information in the table of contents (under shark attacks) and the index of an informational book about sharks she has brought for them. She turns to the pages listed and reads the information aloud, modeling how to extract the information that will address the question the student has asked. The teacher then helps the students explore other informational texts about sharks she has amassed from the library and online resources in order to help them answer such questions as, "What are baby sharks like?" "How big are sharks?" and "What are some other interesting facts about sharks?" This reading activity continues as a writing activity over the next several days in which pairs of students use an introduction, a body, and a conclusion in the writing process to create an informative piece explaining what they have learned about sharks. Included in their paper is a diagram showing the parts of a shark with appropriate labels. They proudly read their pieces aloud to their sixth-grade buddies. Then they publish them in the school newspaper.

WHY INFORMATIONAL TEXT IS IMPORTANT

a goal of the Common Core State Standards is to prepare students for career and college readiness, and thus it is imperative—even in the primary grades—that teachers prepare students by using a greater percentage of informational text and guiding students to an appreciation of strategic reading and writing in this genre (NGACBP & CCSSO, 2010). Because of the widespread adoption of and alignment of many state standards to the CCSS, the reading and writing of informational text has increased in primary-grade classrooms across the country. The grade-level standards beginning in kindergarten for English/language arts include Reading Standards for Informational Text (NGACBP & CCSSO, 2010, pp. 13–14). Likewise, the grade-level standards for writing require students to begin writing informational/explanatory text as early as kindergarten (NGACBP & CCSSO, 2010, p. 19).

The state and national standards' emphasis on informational text parallels a trend prevalent in the National Assessment of Education Progress (NAEP) report, also known as the Nation's Report Card. The 2009 NAEP report suggests that by fourth grade, 50 percent of texts students encounter should be informational; these percentages increase to 55 percent in eighth grade and 70 percent in eleventh (National Assessment Governing Board, 2007). Although educational experts and practitioners have previously called for more informational texts to be used in primary classrooms (Moss, 2005), they were still rare in many primary classrooms. Early readers were previously steered toward narrative text almost exclusively (Duke & Bennett-Armistead, 2003; Palmer & Stewart, 2003). Publishers are now responding quickly to this focus, and quality informational texts have become available for young readers in increasingly accessible reading levels.

Incorporation of informational text can be a positive endeavor (Calo, 2011; Cowan & Sandefur, 2013; Mantzicopoulos & Patrick, 2011; Marinak & Gambrell, 2009). Informational text requires much more than simply acquiring the facts; students must learn *how* to learn by rapidly analyzing the truth and relevance of the information they consume (Rasinski, Padak, & Fawcett, 2010). Other reasons for teaching young students to read and write informational text include the following:

Most literacy activities that students will do in their later years in school and beyond will involve comprehending informational text. We live in an increasingly informational world. An expanding focus of U.S. schooling is to develop citizens who can read, write, and critically evaluate informational text and discuss the information they find (Duke, 2000). If we value the ability of young readers to deal effectively with this genre, they must be directly taught the necessary foundational skills—and the earlier the better (Moss, Leone, & Depillo, 1997). Moreover, with much reading and research occurring online, students must learn to access information quickly, sort through volumes of text, and analyze and evaluate the information (Schmar-Dobler, 2003).

Informational literacy helps students learn content. In the past, educators believed that first children learned to read and then, in the intermediate grades, they began to read to learn. By using informational text, learning to read and reading to learn can occur simultaneously (Guillaume, 1998). Furthermore, some evidence suggests that students who have more exposure to informational text have an advantage in achievement in science (Bernhardt, Destino, Kamil, & Rodriguez-Munoz, 1995) and other content areas. For some students, engaging with informational text may be the most efficient path to overall literacy. Mohr (2006) found that girls also enjoy informational texts, while Yopp and Yopp (2006) found that boys tend to read more informational texts at home. In fact, some have argued that increasing informational texts can help address the gap in reading between boys and girls (Freedmon, 2003; Jones, 2005). More research on if and why a difference in preference for informational texts exists between boys and girls is needed. However, these books can be beneficial, especially for boys and readers and writers who struggle (Caswell & Duke, 1998). Often such students prefer the concrete nature of the straightforward, factual material in these texts.

Informational literacy can be as motivational to students as narrative format, if not more so. Although, as was previously stated, informational text has *not* been found in abundance in most primary classrooms in the past, mounting evidence shows that young children do enjoy—and sometimes prefer—informational text (Caswell & Duke, 1998; Palmer & Stewart, 2003; Pappas, 1993). Indeed, in a series of studies, Kamil (1994) found that although libraries had the same proportion of fiction and nonfiction books, children checked out a greater number of informational books than storybooks.

Exposure to informational literacy can help students think clearly and critically. Research, digital skills, and computer literacy skills are finding their way into the earlier grades, and students are increasingly asked to organize

Informational reading and writing help students to learn content.

and display their work in PowerPoint and similar media formats. By third or fourth grade, students are now expected to read and analyze a great amount of material and then write about what they have read in a clear and logical way, integrating several sources and including their prior knowledge (Cazden, 1993). Additionally, although much helpful information may be gleaned from online resources, students must also learn to evaluate and discard much questionable content. Instruction in and exposure to informational literacy can help young children engage in the kind of critical thinking and research necessary to build meaningful knowledge bases and can foster an ability to think analytically in all the content areas (McMath, King, & Smith, 1998; Parkes, 2003).

WHY INFORMATIONAL TEXT IS CHALLENGING

Informational text has been long overlooked as a learning genre for early readers and writers for many reasons. Prominent among these is the perception that informational text is dry, boring, and difficult and that in order to capture the fancy of beginning readers, teachers must resort to the more appealing storybook or narrative structure. Textbooks, in particular, are thought to be especially difficult for students to read. In truth, many students who have no difficulty reading basal reader and trade book stories often *do* have more trouble with informational text. However, this difficulty appears to have less to do with motivational factors and more to do with the reader's lack of understanding of the structure and lack of appropriate strategies to comprehend such text (Pages, 2002).

The challenges inherent in informational text include the following:

- dense content contained in minimal text, resulting in a need to reduce reading rate
- visual aids (graphs, charts, tables, and the like) that contain much information
- unfamiliar technical terms
- a variety of organizational styles

Fortunately, many instructional strategies may be used to address the challenges presented by informational text. These will be discussed in the remainder of this chapter.

PRINCIPLES OF USING INFORMATIONAL TEXT

The ability to gain knowledge from text is indispensable in our age of exponentially expanding information and access to information both current and from the past. From an early age, students must learn to understand the discrete languages of disciplines such as history, science, and mathematics. They also must develop critical-reading abilities to begin to think the way historians, scientists, and mathematicians think. They must understand the information that is being presented to them and be able to evaluate it as well (Moss, 2005). Certain pedagogical tools, discussed next, will help you tailor instruction to the interests and capabilities of young children (Richgels, 2002) and thus allow this learning to occur more efficiently.

Use Text Features for Previewing

Most teachers in the early grades begin a shared reading lesson by going over elements of the text; students are asked to identify the cover, author, illustrator, and so on. Instruction like this should also be done with informational books and textbooks to teach students about features that will help them understand these texts. Some elements to focus on include the following.

Table of contents. Teach students that informational texts often have a different purpose—to inform—than a story or narrative. As a result, informational texts are also structured differently than narratives. You can begin these discussions by talking about the table of contents. Preview the table of contents to show students that informational texts are written to discuss specific topics and frequently are not arranged chronologically like many stories are. For example, *Oceans: Dolphins, sharks, penguins, and more!* (Rizzo, 2010) has chapters on whales, jellyfish, and sea otters. These chapters tell students where these sea animals live and what they eat. Also point out these chapters can be rearranged without a loss of continuity; the chapter on sea otters can be read before the one on jellyfish, and the chapter on sea otters will still make sense. Teaching students the difference between facts versus plot and that the whole text need not always be read to meet a learning goal will help them with learning about specific content.

Headings. Show students how to use the headings and subheadings to create questions about the text. Headings outline key elements about a topic; teach students to scan headings to find specific information.

Glossaries. Often informational texts use technical, domain-specific vocabulary that may be unfamiliar to many students. However, many texts present these key words in bold or italics and provide definitions in the *glossary*, which if used can increase student comprehension. Introduce students to the glossary and instruct them how to locate the text's highlighted words in the alphabetical glossary.

Index. Many informational texts provide readers with an *index* providing the page number(s) where key concepts are discussed. Show students how to use an index as they learn to look for specific concepts related to a topic. Also point out the difference between an item discussed across multiple sequential pages (e.g., pp. 10–20) as opposed to mentioned on a series of nonsequential pages (pp. 10, 20, 22).

Sidebar text. Another technique that informational authors use is to include important information in sidebars. These brief passages are sometimes used instead of a glossary to define key vocabulary, but they can also be used to connect content with other books or list websites related to a topic.

Photos with captions. Previewing informational texts also includes showing students that the pictures and captions can help them understand the subject.

Illustrations. Authors also may use pictorial representations to illustrate important concepts. These illustrations can convey important details that students should not overlook, e.g., an illustration of photosynthesis or the plant life cycle.

Graphs and charts. Authors also use graphs and charts to give their audience important details. Show students various kinds of graphs and charts and explain how to read pie graphs, line graphs, area graphs, and bar graphs (both vertical and horizontal). For the primary grades, create a graph on a topic relevant to the class (e.g., favorite foods) and present the same information in different ways, or compare how the same information is presented graphically in various texts.

Preview and review questions. Many informational texts and textbooks include questions at the beginnings and/or ends of chapters designed to aid student comprehension. A question at the beginning of the chapter can alert readers to upcoming content, while the same question at the end can help their review and summarization skills. Teach students that answering questions such as these will improve their understanding of the material.

Teach students directly and early how to preview informational text using the text features through the use of study-skill methods. These methods will help them succeed later, when they encounter a higher percentage of, and more complex, informational text in the content areas. Other ways that you can preview these texts for your students include the following:

- Model and provide guided instruction in hypothesizing what the chapter/book/article will be about, based on the title and introductory paragraph.
- Teach students how to incorporate prior knowledge on various topics. Explain how reading the summary and previewing the questions and other tools at the beginning and end of a chapter can tell them much about what will be important in the text.

Swanson and colleagues (2011) suggest that along with previewing, teachers instruct students in generating questions, finding the gist, and writing summaries. All of these skills will improve student comprehension. Teachers may use the following activity with students, along with a grid based on Figure 10.1, to preview an informational book. A student guide for previewing an informational text is shown in Figure 10.2.

Expectation Grid

A C T I V I T Y

(DEVRIES, 2015)

The expectation grid combines reading, writing, viewing, and visually representing. With the class, preview the chapter title, headings, subheadings, photos, graphics, and other elements described earlier. For example, what do the headings and subheadings tell us about the chapter? What information do the photos and graphics provide? Have the class decide what the main topics are and draw a diagram like the one in Figure 10.1; if possible, draw it in such a way as to link it to the content. This activity works well in the primary grades when using an informational big book. The details are then added as the students read the passage.

figure 10.1   Sample expectation grid.

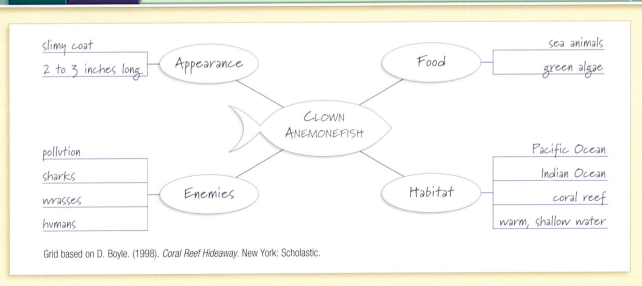

Grid based on D. Boyle. (1998). *Coral Reef Hideaway.* New York: Scholastic.

figure   10.2   Student guide for previewing informational text.

Name _____   Date _____

Partner's Name _____

Title of book/article _____

STEP 1.   Read the title and introduction of the book/article.

From the introduction, what do you think this book/article will be about?

_____

_____

_____

STEP 2.   Look at the photos or diagrams in the book/article.

What do the illustrations tell you about the information in the book?

_____

_____

_____

STEP 3.   Read the headings and subheadings.

What are two things you will find out by reading this book/article?

_____

_____

_____

STEP 4.   Read the book summary.

What are two things you should have learned when you finish this book/article?

_____

_____

_____

STEP 5.   Think about the information you wrote for Steps 1–4. Finish this sentence:

I think this book/article will be about

_____

_____

_____

Adapted from *Direct Instruction Reading,* 4th ed. (2003), by D. Carnine, J. Silbert, E. Kameenui, & S. Tarver. Upper Saddle River, NJ: Prentice Hall.

Establish an Authentic Context and Purpose for Reading

Ensure that young children's experiences with informational text are authentic and purposeful to them. Do this by modeling how informational texts can be used to help them find answers to many of their common questions, such as "Why do cats purr?" Furthermore, show students how such text can help them find certain bits of information ("What are gills?") even if they cannot read the entire text. Finally, demonstrate to students how informational text often contains pictures and other graphics that can be used to support presentations and discussions; for example, a map of the habitat of different frogs in the world can be copied to help show this concept more expediently than several paragraphs of explanation. Likewise, pictures of different types of frogs can add motivational appeal to a presentation on frogs.

Use in Conjunction with Other Forms of Text

Avoid using informational text in isolation. Information can be gleaned from many sources besides textbooks. All kinds of environmental print—from signs to recipes and labels—carry information that can help students access this genre of print. Also, morning message routines that are typical in primary classrooms—where the weather, lunch information, and other events of the day are reported—can be used to provide a schema for informational text. In addition, the Internet can expand the information on the topic presented in the book. Studies involving English learners (Proctor, Dalton, & Grisham, 2007) and students with special needs (Palumbo & Loiacono, 2009) indicate that the use of technology can foster understanding of these texts. The Library of Congress website contains information on many topics appropriate for young students. Show students how to compare information found online with that in the book. During this process, you can teach critical-thinking skills as you help students learn about biases and evaluate the accuracy of the information. Such instruction is vital in our highly technological world. However, Malloy and Gambrell (2006) underscore the challenges of teaching about the Internet: "As educators, we need to commit to preparing students for their technological journey . . . [one] toward literacies that grow and change more quickly than we can keep up with them. But by learning together, teachers and students can become fully literate in every sense of the word" (p. 484). The websites listed in the margin can supplement and enhance information found in informational texts.

Finally, an informational book can be paired with a narrative text containing information about a topic being studied in a content area such as science or social studies (e.g., *The Wall*, about the Vietnam Memorial, can provide motivation, background, and "color" for the lessons). Using the parallel genres, or a narrative and an informational text, can also create an opportunity for you to compare and contrast the two differing ways of presenting information (Richgels, 2002). These **twin texts,** sometimes referred to as paired books, lead students from fiction into nonfiction by pairing related books, one of fiction and one of fact. An authentic way to introduce content material, twin texts form a bridge from reading stories to understanding content from all areas of the curriculum (Camp, 2000).

The next section explores strategies for teaching students how to gain information and enjoyment from informational text.

TEACHING YOUNG STUDENTS TO READ INFORMATIONAL TEXT

Young children are usually very curious about the world around them. Observe any primary classroom, and it becomes clear that primary youngsters are continually asking questions about how the world works. Young children enjoy

Awesome library

www.awesomelibrary.org/ student.html

U.S. Library of Congress

www.americaslibrary.gov/

twin texts ■

learning new things and exploring facts—if the factual information is presented in an accessible and supportive way. Certain instructional strategies implemented by the teacher can provide successful experiences with informational text that will help students feel more strategic and confident with informational text. Such successful experiences and effective instruction can lead to enjoyment of and proficiency with informational text.

Teacher Think-Alouds

The most expedient way to familiarize young children with informational text is for the teacher to read aloud excellent examples of such text and to point out how such text differs from narrative text in both genre and organization. Figure 10.3 offers a simple comparison of narrative and informational texts.

Such read-alouds can be conducted in a "think-aloud" manner, with the teacher addressing the specific organizational patterns and "wondering" out loud why the author may have chosen to use a particular structure. The reading can be followed by a discussion and critical appraisal of the content. Pages (2002) suggests that teachers start such informational read-alouds with books they themselves enjoy and that they provide background information on the subject to build a knowledge schema before reading, by bringing in artifacts, dramatizing events, sharing current newspaper articles on the topic, and so forth. The following activity will help students explore background information and make predictions about what they will

| figure | 10.3 | Important distinctions between narrative and informational text. |

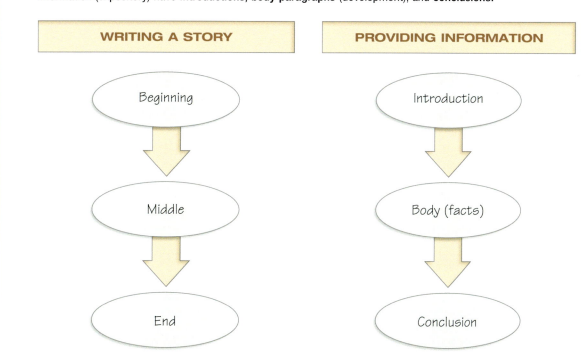

To help you understand the differences between writing a story and providing information, consider the following terms. When I write a story (narrative), I need a **beginning**, a **middle**, and an **ending**. But papers that share information (expository) have **introductions**, **body paragraphs** (development), and **conclusions**.

WRITING A STORY	PROVIDING INFORMATION
Beginning	Introduction
Middle	Body (facts)
End	Conclusion

Background research on
different topics

www.smithsonianeducation.org

see appendix A

read. Over time, reading informational texts aloud not only familiarizes students with the organizational styles but also helps them learn content and new vocabulary related to the topic (Bortnem, 2008; Cummins & Stallmeyer-Gerard, 2011; Duke, Bennett-Armistead, & Roberts, 2003; Kraemer, McCabe, & Sinatra, 2012; May, 2011; Pappas et al., 2012; Yopp & Yopp, 2006). Also, teachers may encourage parents to select informational texts to read to, and with, their children. Appendix A offers a wide variety of informational texts that would be suitable for this purpose.

Making Predictions from Artifacts

ACTIVITY

(ELLERMEYER & CHICK, 2007)

1. Using an informational picture book (for example, *This Is the Ocean* by Kersten Hamilton), choose artifacts to represent the book and place them in a shoebox. In this case, for example, you might place a toy fish or shark, a miniature umbrella, a picture of a rain cloud, and a map showing the names of the oceans.

2. Cover the picture book you selected with brown paper, so students can't see the title or cover. Show students the wrapped book and tell them you will give them some hints about what it is about. Show one artifact at a time from the shoebox and ask students to guess what it might represent in the story. Guesses can be documented on chart paper or the board.

3. After predictions have been made for each artifact, unwrap the book, read the title, and show the cover. Students can again make predictions about each artifact. List these guesses beside the first predictions.

4. Read the book, reminding students to listen for the way each artifact is used in the story. Discuss each artifact, documenting its real purpose in a third list. Have students discuss how close their predictions were to the real purpose of each item.

5. Discuss how people need water to drink and grow food, what people can do to reduce water use, and the history and culture of a group that lives near water.

6. Artifacts can be used to make predictions in any subject area. For example, *Snowflake Bentley* by Jacqueline Briggs Martin would be a good choice for the science classroom.

Explicit Instruction of Organizational Patterns

Once students have become familiar with the basic differences between narrative and informational text, you can explicitly show students the major expository text patterns that authors use when writing informational text. Armed with a schema of the different organizational structures authors can use, students will usually find it much easier to comprehend the informational material being presented. Following are common text patterns used by authors of informational text.

Question and answer. Content area discussions may use this pattern: the author begins with a question and then answers it in the body of the paragraph.

Description/enumeration. With enumeration, an author states a concept and then elaborates on it (DeVries, 2015). Words such as *for example, in addition,* and *finally* may be used to help the reader follow the facts or ideas. The author's intent is to describe in such a way that the idea is best understood.

Sequence or chronology. When time or order is relevant, particularly in content areas such as history, authors may use numbered lists and outline ideas using words such as *first, next, then, after that,* and *finally* to signal the use of sequence or chronology. Sequence may also be used for science experiments, instructions, or the presentation of occurrences that require a number of ordered steps, such as an explanation of how to make bread.

Cause and effect. One of the most difficult patterns for young readers, the cause-and-effect pattern, is used to show how one event or fact happens because of another event or fact. Science and social studies texts often use this text pattern and signal the use of such a pattern with words such as *because, as a result,* and *therefore.*

Comparison/contrast. When two or more ideas, people, animals, facts, or events have both similarities and differences, a common way to portray them in informational text is to compare and/or contrast them. Such a treatment of text can be identified through such words as *however, on the other hand, by contrast, but,* and *whereas.*

When introducing informational text patterns to young children, the following sequence for instruction may be used (adapted from Tompkins, 2002):

1. Introduce the organizational pattern (e.g., comparison/contrast or sequence) by explaining when and why writers would choose this particular structure.
2. Point out the **transition words** or key words associated with a structure (e.g., *because, therefore, as a result—comparison/contrast; first, next, after that—sequence*), and share an example of text using these *signal words.* (See Figure 10.4.)

   ■ transition words
3. Model ways students can determine text structures when transition words are *not* used (e.g., look at the table of contents and headings).
4. Introduce a graphic organizer for the pattern, such as an expository frame.
5. Read aloud a section of a book illustrating the text structure.
6. Ask students to listen for and identify the transition words in the selection.
7. Using a whiteboard or projector, have the class complete a graphic organizer illustrating the pattern type.
8. Ask students to work in pairs to locate an example of the structure in other informational books.
9. Have students create a graphic organizer for their informational book.

figure	10.4	Transition words associated with various expository text patterns.

SEQUENCE	ENUMERATION	CAUSE/EFFECT	COMPARISON/CONTRAST
First	To begin	Because	Alike
Second	First	Hence	Different
Next	Second	Therefore	Similarly
Then	Also	As a result	In contrast
Last	In fact	If/then	But
Before	For example	Consequently	However
After	Most important		Although
Finally			

A brief minilesson about counting, for example, can help reader comprehension of an informational book.

Minilessons

One way to address the major challenges of reading and comprehending informational text is through minilessons. For example, to address the issue of dense content in a science textbook, you may do a short lesson on using different reading rates for different purposes; the beginning vignette of this chapter presents a teacher showing students how to find just the needed information from informational sources. You can explain the use of topic sentences by providing examples of interesting introductions, such as those containing provocative questions, quotes, anecdotes, and so forth. Likewise, note the importance of visual aids, and show students how to gain important information from them. Explain unfamiliar technical terms—especially multimeaning words that are used in a differing context—with abundant examples, such as the word *change*, which has different meanings when used in math (*make change*) or everyday situations (*change your clothes*). Show examples of different organizational styles for informational text and discuss them with students.

Other Instructional Strategies for Informational Text

Many other instructional strategies can be used to help students understand and learn from the unique aspects of informational text. Here are a few other specific suggestions for helping students become involved in (and excited by) the many forms of knowledge they will encounter:

- Discuss the content of the text and organize the information using a language experience chart, semantic webbing, KWL chart, or another form of graphic organizer. (See Chapter 8.)

- Read several different informational books on the same topic. Point out how different authors look at the same topic in different ways; for example, one author might address a frog's life cycle while another may focus on the different types of frogs and where they are found.

- Compare fiction and informational works on a single topic such as dolphins. Discuss how each genre treats the subject matter differently. See Figure 10.5 for an example comparison of informational and narrative passages.

- Use the strategy of retelling. The activity on the following page offers steps for retelling.

Web-Based Digital Poster

www.glogster.com

After giving students instruction in these strategies, you can begin guiding them into an area emphasized in the CCSS and many state standards: *research*. For example, beginning as early as kindergarten, the CCSS requires students to "Participate in shared research and writing projects" (CCSS.ELA-Literacy.W.K.7, NGACBP & CCSSO, 2010, p. 19). Assign research topics related to grade-level content and construct a class KWL chart. Then, using multiple informational texts as well as appropriate websites, students can complete the "L" (what we learned) part of the KWL chart, collaborating in small groups. Remind students that not all informational texts need to be read from cover to cover, unlike the story structure that is usually found in narratives. In addition, using informational text in a research project enables you to review the specific elements of an information text, such as the table of contents and indexes that were discussed when previewing

| figure | 10.5 | Example passages for contrasting informational and narrative writing. |

GIVING INFORMATION
(Explaining)

The dolphin may look like a fish, but this friendly sea creature is really a mammal. First of all, dolphins have lungs just like we do. They must come to the surface of the water to breathe and get oxygen from the air. Fish can take oxygen from the water. Like other mammals, dolphins have backbones and are warm blooded. Finally, they nurse young dolphins on milk just like a cow might nurse a calf. The dolphin's stream-lined body and its big, strong tail might resemble a fish, but don't be fooled; it's definitely a mammal.

TELLING A STORY
(A Narrative)

I was excited to see the dolphins, my favorite animal.

"Go closer to the tank," my father said.

I looked into the water and saw the beautiful animals swimming together. Someone was feeding them fish.

"I wish I could swim with the dolphins," I said.

"Maybe someday you will," said my father.

Just then one of the dolphins swam close to us and suddenly we were as wet as could be! We laughed and laughed.

informational text. Finally, research projects and presentations, whether done via an in-class slide presentation or a web-based digital poster, can motivate student learning of content-based topics and provide opportunities for collaboration.

Retelling Informational Texts

ACTIVITY

(MOSS, 2004)

- Involve students in prereading activities such as KWL, brainstorming, or problem solving. Also, encourage students to predict what the text might be about and to predict the order of the text by looking at the table of contents or previewing other aspects of the text.

- The text should then be read aloud by you or silently by the students. You can also make the text come alive with props, pictures, and examples of concepts within the story.

- Invite students to create charts, fill out graphic organizers, and use other visual aids from the text to help them retell important points of the text. Completing a graphic organizer such as the one shown in Figure 10.6 can help a student remember facts about a topic—for example, the habitat, enemies, appearance, and physical capabilities of a box turtle.

- Ask students what they can remember about the text, and list their responses on the whiteboard. Provide scaffolds and prompts, such as pictures or questions,

figure 10.6 Graphic organizer: description or enumeration.

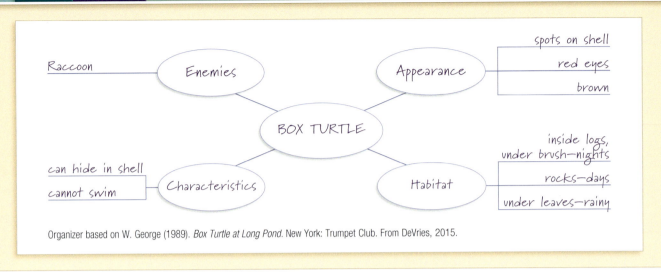

Organizer based on W. George (1989). *Box Turtle at Long Pond.* New York: Trumpet Club. From DeVries, 2015.

to help students recall the text. Example questions include the following: What did you find out first? What did you learn after that?

- Reread the text or have students reread the text, this time searching for information missed during the first retelling. Add any additional information to the list of previously generated student responses.

- Encourage students to make personal connections between their lives and the concepts within the text. If appropriate, you may also record these ideas on the whiteboard.

WRITING INFORMATIONAL TEXT

Informational writing is often called "expository writing" and generally concerns itself with explaining an idea, an object, or a process. The informational paragraph or essay presents a certain amount of information about a topic. The major purpose of the mode of discourse is to explain or inform, to tell readers something they may not know, and to tell them in a way that they will understand.

Given appropriate instruction in the structure of informational text and a topic they find interesting, students are fully capable of coping with the complex organizational challenges of writing informational text. Indeed, children as young as first and second grade can be successful in writing informational text (Read, 2005). As stated earlier, the CCSS requires students beginning in kindergarten to write informational/explanatory text (NGACBP & CCSSO, 2010, p. 19).

Structuring Informational Writing

Instead of having, loosely, a beginning, a middle, and an end as is found in narrative structure, the informational paragraph has a somewhat more rigid organization and is usually organized according to one of the patterns (question and answer, enumeration, cause and effect, or comparison/contrast) discussed in the last section. Essentially, all informational writing has three main parts to it that students can be taught to include when creating an informational piece. Each piece of informational writing must contain the following:

- *A topic sentence that clearly tells what the piece is going to be about.* This sentence is the idea statement that tells the reader the reason that the piece is being written. *Example:* Insects differ from spiders in several ways.

- *Examples, evidence, and explanations.* The essence of any informational piece is in the details. The topic sentence has been given, and now the writer must elaborate and make a case for the claim by citing evidence or offering an explanation or by providing examples, reasons, or facts, depending on the organizational structure being used. Using the preceding example, in the paragraph on the difference between insects and spiders, a possible supporting sentence might be, "First, insects have six legs while spiders have eight." The phrases are connected together by *transition words* that hold the paragraphs in the piece together. *First, second, finally, on the other hand, nevertheless,* and *in a similar way* are all examples of words and phrases that help the reader realize that a transition to a new idea is occurring.

- *A conclusion.* The informational piece is usually tied together with a conclusion that reminds the reader of the topic sentence. Because information has been given in the examples, evidence, or explanations, the conclusion is stated slightly differently than in the original topic sentence. For example, "It is easy to tell an insect from a spider because of the many differences between them."

Instructional Strategies for Writing Informational Text

Expository text frames

Primary-grade children's knowledge of expository structures—content organized around a main idea and supporting details—usually lags far behind their knowledge of narrative structures. This is because almost all students have had less exposure to expository passages and also because the structure of expository text tends to be more complex (Duke, 2000; Englert & Hiebert, 1984). Using **expository frames** can help students understand expository structure by providing a systematic way to write about content material they have read. It is also an effective way to introduce young children to expository writing (Cudd, 1990).

■ expository frames

Expository frames, analogous to story frames that introduce students to narrative structure, provide a scaffold for creating different ways to organize text. They can be used to review and reinforce specific content and to familiarize students with the different ways authors organize informational material. In effect, the frames serve as bridges that help ease the often difficult transition from narrative to expository reading and writing.

By the second semester of first grade, most students can begin working with content-area expository frames that are organized sequentially. The sequential pattern appears to be one of the easiest structures for students to recognize and use in their own writing and is a skill taught and reinforced regularly in basal texts. Moreover, such text structures have been found to increase the comprehension of English learners (Anderson & Roit, 1998). At this point, students are already familiar with transition words, such as *first, next, then,* and *last,* that are used as transitional devices within sequential paragraphs. See Figure 10.4 for additional examples of transition words.

To ensure informational in completing expository frames, begin instruction with a prewritten informational paragraph rather than a blank frame, as in the following activity (Cudd, 1990). Having students create their own texts on topics of interest, using their knowledge of expository structures, is a great way to connect the reading and writing of informational text.

A C T I V I T Y

Using Expository Frames

A C T I V I T Y

1. Write a simple paragraph about a topic that lends itself to sequential ordering, using the transition words *first, next, then,* and *last*.
2. Copy the sentences on sentence strips.
3. With the class, review the topic and logical sequence of events.
4. In a pocket chart, have the students arrange the sentences in correct order.
5. Read the completed paragraph together.
6. Have the students reorder the paragraph on their own and paste it on construction paper in paragraph form.
7. Invite the students to illustrate the details or some important part of the paragraph.

Gradually introduce a sequentially ordered expository frame for the students to complete independently, as in Figure 10.7.

Other frames using different organizational models, such as cause/effect patterns, problem/solution patterns, and comparison/contrast patterns, are also helpful for assisting students in writing expository text. Figure 10.8 is an example of a comparison/contrast pattern, and Figure 10.9 is an example of an enumeration pattern.

| figure | 10.7 | A child's expository frame for sequence. |

Setting the Table

In order to set the table, you need to go step by step. First, you must _get knives, forks, and spoons_. Next, you need to _put napkins under the forks_. After this, you _get glasses of milk for everyone_. Last of all, _you give everybody a plate of food_. When you are finished, _you eat dinner!_

| figure | 10.8 | A child's expository frame for comparison/contrast. |

(Title)

Comparing Insects with Spiders

Insects differ from spiders in many ways. First, insects _fly while spiders don't_. Second, insects _don't spin webs but spiders do_. I think the easiest way to tell an insect from a spider is _to count the legs. A spider has eight legs. An insect only has six_.

figure	10.9	A child's expository frame for enumeration.

Trees are useful in many ways. For example, _____
_____.

Also, _____.

In addition, _____.

Finally, _____.

Strategies for choosing a topic

It is often easier for young children to choose a topic for informational writing than for narrative writing (Read, 2005). They are less likely to feel that "I don't know what to write about!" with so many different topics to explore. Students enjoy researching and then writing about their discoveries in a wide variety of topics, including wild and domestic animals, cars, other countries, volcanoes, and planets. You can show how to use the Internet effectively for researching a topic by leading the students on scavenger hunts. Two sites appropriate for young students are Education World's Scavenger Hunt and Internet Treasure Hunts for ESL Students. However, for informational writing that requires no research, it is sometimes helpful to offer an interesting topic with a prescribed organization for students to follow. The following informational writing activity does just that.

WWW

Scavenger hunts

www.educationworld.com/ a_curr/curr113.shtml

Treasure hunts for ESL students

http://iteslj.org/th

Writing Persuasive Pieces

A C T I V I T Y

Have students use real or hypothetical situations to create a four-paragraph, persuasive essay. As a class or individually, students can come up with topics that are important to them and create essays that have an authentic purpose. These real topics can include the following:

- persuading the principal to buy library books
- asking for more or different playground equipment
- convincing the school that more computers and/or software are necessary
- explaining why a book is your favorite (and why others should read it)
- persuading your teacher to take a field trip to . . .
- persuading the school about the pros or cons of having a school dress code

As an alternative, you may also present students with hypothetical situations that can provide the kind of rich stimuli that help students turn their fantasies into colorful informational text. Every so often, pose one of the following situations, or similar ones, to the class:

- What if you could have three wishes?
- What if you could be invisible?
- What if we could talk to animals?

An Internet scavenger hunt will excite readers about researching a topic.

- What if you could read people's minds?
- What if there were no television?
- What if there were only one kind of food?
- What if we could fly?
- What if everyone looked exactly alike?
- What if you could have everything you wanted?
- What if people got younger, not older?
- What if people could live forever?

Put two columns on the board, one for "Advantages" and one for "Disadvantages." Ask students to brainstorm some advantages to the chosen situation and then some disadvantages. Write down every new suggestion.

Invite students to write a persuasive essay with the following format:

- Paragraph 1: Introduction to the topic
- Paragraph 2: Real topics: reasons to support the proposition; Hypothetical situations: advantages of the situation
- Paragraph 3: Real topics: reasons not to support the proposition; Hypothetical situations: disadvantages of the situation
- Paragraph 4: What the student believes, with a goal of "persuading" the reader to also believe that it would, for example, be good, or bad, if . . .

Have students work together to peer-edit their pieces. Publish the essays in a class book or post them on a class website.

Writing workshop

Writing workshop (discussed in Chapter 9) is an effective tool for helping young writers explore the complex organizational structures of informational text. As mentioned earlier, children as young as first and second grade can be successful in writing informational text, given the appropriate instruction. As an example, Read (2005) conducted a study of first- and second-graders in a writing workshop environment. She found that when children were allowed to write on topics of their own choosing and were invited to write collaboratively, they worked out content problems aloud and provided feedback to each other regarding the organization of the content as well as the conventions of print. See Chapter 9 for information on conducting a writing workshop.

STRATEGIES FOR ENGLISH LEARNERS AND READING AND WRITING INFORMATIONAL TEXT

Several studies that incorporated the use of informational and/or expository texts with English learners suggest that different ways of engaging with these texts may be necessary. García (1998) indicates that the strategies students used to comprehend expository texts were influenced more by genre than text language, while Jímenez, García, and Pearson (1996) report that bilingual students had more difficulty with Spanish expository texts than either Spanish narratives or English expository or narratives, which could have been due to a lack of exposure. Langer, Bartolomé, Vásquez, and Lucas (1990) wrote: "Neither the mode of recall nor the language seemed to be as important as the genre in determining where the students experienced the greatest difficulty: they had greatest difficulty in building envisionments, hypothesizing, and utilizing the structure when they were reading reports, and they also recalled less information with less depth and breadth afterward" (p. 451).

Instructional texts, while difficult for all learners, can be extremely difficult for English learners. Ogle and Correa-Kovtun (2010) identified five components that teachers of English learners should consider when using informational text:

1. Have students read informational texts at their instructional or independent levels daily.
2. Provide students with regular opportunities to talk with peers about the texts.
3. Encourage students must ask and answer their own questions.
4. Focus students on factual *and* higher-order thinking knowledge.
5. Provide students with guidance of these text types.

In order to scaffold English learners into reading informational text, Ogle and Correa-Kovtun (2010) propose that teachers use a routine for independent reading called Partner Reading and Content, Too (PRC2).

Partner Reading and Content, Too (PRC2)

ADAPTED FROM OGLE & CORREA-KOVTUN (2010)

ACTIVITY

Lasting 20–30 minutes each day, PRC2 consists of the following steps:

- Partners preview the whole book during their first engagement with the text.
- For each two-page spread, both partners first read the two pages silently to get a sense of the text. Then each partner rereads the page closest to him and prepares for his performance read. He also selects or prepares a question to ask his partner, either from a prepared question sheet or a question written using questioning approaches with which he is familiar (e.g., thick and thin questions or Bloom's taxonomy; Blachowicz & Ogle, 2008). One important method to help comprehension is QAR (question–answer relationships; see Chapter 8).
- Each partner reads a page or section orally and then asks her question of the listening partner; partners then talk about the page of text, providing them an opportunity to gain ownership of any academic or domain-specific vocabulary and concepts.
- Partners switch roles—reader and listener—as they read section by section.
- Each partner adds words to a personal vocabulary notebook at end of PRC2.

A website that provides teachers with excellent resources for helping English learners with informational text, with specific connection to the CCSS, is provided in the margin.

WWW

Resources for Informational Text and English Learners

http://blog.colorincolorado. org/2013/02/13/teaching-informational-text-to-ells/

INFORMATIONAL TEXT AND STUDENTS WITH SPECIAL NEEDS

Teachers who have students with special needs should focus their efforts on providing additional scaffolding when using informational text, such as providing a *graphic organizer*. For example, an analysis of three fifth-graders with reading disabilities found that these students did not have trouble with decoding or word meaning. Their troubles were due to slow reading and *understanding informational text* (Vaughn & Edmonds, 2006). Ozmen (2011) reported positive effects when using graphic organizers. He used graphic organizers with five students diagnosed as intellectually disabled. Students were provided with graphic organizers to help them recall information from compare-and-contrast essays both before and after reading; four of the students reported that using graphic organizers after the reading was more effective. However, all five students shared that these organizers helped organize information, which can be problematic for students with special needs.

Graphic organizers are one of two scaffolds shown to help students increase their comprehension. Vaughn and Edmonds (2006) also used *collaborative strategic reading* (CSR), a multicomponent intervention that includes elements of reciprocal teaching (see Chapter 8). This intervention includes a collaborative component as students are placed in small heterogeneous groups based on reading ability or behavior. In these groups, students use *strategic reading*, which focuses on four strategies:

- previewing
- click and clunk (monitoring comprehension by identifying difficult words and concepts and addressing those issues)
- finding the gist of the text
- wrap-up

In the wrap-up portion, students are encouraged to compose and answer an easy question, a hard question, and a harder question, and a CSR learning log is kept by individual students or the group to document progress.

Comprehension of informational text can also be increased for students with special needs by using intense QAR instruction (Kinniburgh & Baxter, 2012; see Chapter 8 for a discussion of QAR). A study of 40 students, 20 of whom were classified as typical language and 20 as language impaired, showed that the ability to understand informational text was related to the ability of students to paraphrase information (Gillam, Fargo, & St. Robertson, 2009). When using informational text, teachers of students with special needs should spend more time getting students to *talk* about what they've read.

SUMMARY

The use of informational text with primary-age youngsters is a widely discussed topic among researchers and practitioners. Educators realize that learning to read and reading to learn can occur at the same time; therefore, both narrative and informational texts can be presented to children much earlier than previously thought. Also, the advent of technology and the wide use of the Internet make it crucial for students to be able to read content material and critically evaluate many informational sources.

Assessments of literacy achievement are beginning to reflect the new focus on informational text, as are state and national standards for the language arts.

In the past, instruction in the primary grades may have reflected an underestimation of the ability of young children to read, comprehend, and produce informational text. Though many challenges must be addressed when students read and write informational text, teachers can help students to work through these challenges using modeling, minilessons, and direct teaching of organizational patterns. When teachers present students with a wide variety of instructional experiences with informational text, evidence suggests that the students will succeed. Moreover, including informational text allows students to read about topics of personal experience or interest, which may enhance their desire to become lifelong readers, a goal of any solid reading program. Informational text can also be used as a great resource for topics that occur in content areas such as science and social studies. However, teachers should not drastically increase time spent with informational text at the cost of attention paid to narrative text. As with most issues in literacy, it is not a matter of choosing one genre or the other, but rather achieving a *balance* of the two. With confidence from their successes in both genres, students will be highly motivated to read and write about the interesting facts and events in the world around them.

questions   FOR JOURNAL WRITING AND DISCUSSION

1. Explain, in your own words, why informational reading and writing are important in the primary grades. Prepare a role-play with a classmate where one of you is a parent of a student in your class and the other is the teacher. Through the role-play, defend your choice of spending a large portion of your classroom requisition money on informational texts for your classroom library.

2. Review the instructional strategies in this chapter for helping students to learn from informational text. Which ones do you think would be most helpful for second language learners? Why? Which ones would be most helpful for students who prefer narrative text and have little or no experience with informational text? Why?

3. Choose a piece of informational literature from Appendix A. Read the text carefully and make a list of all the challenges the text might present to native English speakers and another list for challenges to English learners. Read the story to your classmates and then share the list. Have your classmates add to your list. Discuss what makes such text challenging.

> see appendix A

suggestions   FOR PROJECTS AND FIELD ACTIVITIES

1. Plan a reading lesson for a small group of early readers. Select an informational text from Appendix A or another one with which you are familiar. Choose an instructional strategy from the chapter that you feel would best help students to cope with the unique aspects of the text. Write a short reflection statement sharing your feelings about how the strategy helped students respond to the textual demands of the book.

2. Create a reading lesson using parallel genres, or twin texts, to compare and contrast two different ways to present information. For example, obtain a copy of an informational book such as *Valentine's Day Is . . . .* by Gail Gibbons. Find a corresponding narrative text, such as *The Night Before Valentine's Day* by Natasha Wing and Heidi Petach, and use it to provide motivation, background, and "color" for the lesson. Or, use Appendix A to select another informational book and find a narrative text on the same topic to create the lesson.

> see appendix A

3. Visit three websites suggested in Appendix C to support informational reading and writing. Choose one that you particularly like and find an informational text for which the website information would be helpful. How might the website information be used to support the text?

> see appendix C

4. Read the K–2 standards for reading information text and writing information text. Create a list of questions you have about how to best incorporate pedagogical strategies to help students achieve these goals.

11

Large- and Small-Group Reading Strategies

CREATING A LITERATE COMMUNITY

focus questions

How can shared reading be used to model effective reading strategies?

How can teachers use guided reading to help students construct personal meanings from text?

How can the practices of shared and guided reading be kept exciting for both the students and the teacher?

t he students are sitting cross-legged on their carpet squares in the back of Mr. Kohl's first-grade classroom, eagerly awaiting the second reading of *The Three Billy Goats Gruff.* Prior to the first reading of this story, students scanned the colorful illustrations of the oversized book and made predictions about what they thought was happening on each page. Several students made comments about similar stories they were reminded of, and one little girl shared that her uncle owned a pygmy goat—much to the delight of the other learners. Mr. Kohl took the opportunity afforded by the story to introduce the students to the /tr/ blend and pointed it out each time it was encountered, as the goats went "trip, trap, trip, trap" across the bridge three times. By the third time the goats reached the bridge, the students were rhythmically and enthusiastically chanting the words "trip, trap, trip, trap" with Mr. Kohl as he pointed to them in the story.

On this day, the day of the second reading of the story, the students brainstorm some ways they might talk to the troll and convince him they really should be allowed to cross the bridge. As the story is read aloud this time, the students turn to each other after every page and take turns summarizing in their own words what has happened on that page. Occasionally, the teacher stops the reading, points to a word, and asks, "What is this word? Can anyone raise a quiet hand and tell me?" Eighteen small hands shoot up, and one student is called upon to tell Mr. Kohl that the word is *bridge;* they have seen the word over thirty times now, and they can all recognize it. Mr. Kohl then asks the students to think of some other words that begin with the same blend, the /br/ sound. He writes their answers carefully on the small writing board *(brag, broken, broccoli, brick)* as the students help him sound out the words.

(Later in this chapter, we'll visit another teacher using *The Three Billy Goats Gruff* for a *shared reading* experience.)

INTRODUCTION

I n a comprehensive approach to literacy, teachers use a variety of instructional strategies, from reading aloud to minilessons, to modeling what fluent readers do, and to gradually releasing to students the responsibility for reading and constructing meaning (Pearson, 1993).

Mr. Kohl is using *shared reading* with his students, a technique useful in modeling reading for students, by reading a book aloud and ultimately inviting the students to join with him. In this chapter we will explore how this strategy, and a similar one requiring more student independence, *guided reading,* can be used to blend comprehension strategies and beginning phonics instruction with strategies that engage the reader in the printed word. Both pedagogical methods are forms of mediated reading instruction in which the teacher, through modeling and explicit instruction, demonstrates how proficient readers decode and gain meaning from text.

SHARED READING

shared reading ■

T he mediated reading activity known as **shared reading,** or the *shared book experience,* was developed by Holdaway (1986) as a means of introducing early readers to the use of favorite books, raps, chants, rhymes, and poems in a highly motivational way. In shared reading, all students can see the text. Shared reading is often done with a big book, and all students can participate in reading, learn important concepts of how print works, and get the feel of the fluency and smoothness of reading without the possibility of error, because the teacher is doing the decoding for them. The teacher reads with fluency and expression and eventually invites the learners to read along. Each reading situation is a relaxed, social one, with emphasis on appreciation of the text. Shared reading is also an excellent technique for allowing students to identify sight words, because it stresses the external features and sounds of individual words while it maintains a focus on meaning. Integrated with a direct and explicit phonics program (see Chapter 5), such a technique can ensure that students not only know *how* to read but also thoroughly enjoy doing so.

The use of the mediated strategy of shared reading is ideal for a teacher wishing to balance meaning-based and skills-based instruction. Through shared reading, the teacher models for students how proficient readers "get" the message the author is trying to communicate and then shows how it can be related to one's own life experiences. It represents the second step in the gradual release of responsibility model in that first the teacher models the reading and then the students participate in subsequent rereadings. Such mediated reading instruction also uses modeling to show how proficient readers sound out words or use context or word analogies to determine the meaning of unknown words. It is based on the extensive body of research that suggests that young children become accomplished with language through the synergistic processes of talking, listening, experimenting with written language, and interacting with the various language models in their environments (Clay, 1991). These studies found that young children who have learned to read at home before coming to school generally accomplished this task by having their favorite books read aloud to them over and over in a relaxed, joyful atmosphere (Baghban, 1984; Bissex, 2004). Holdaway's (1979) procedure capitalizes on the natural learning processes of young children and builds on their innate curiosity to help them grow into literacy. Many teachers and researchers have used this procedure to engage students of various ability levels and backgrounds in reading (Bridge, Winograd, & Haley, 1983; Harlin, 1990).

Purposes for Shared Reading

Shared reading builds on children's natural desire to read and reread favorite texts, imitating and re-creating the intimacy of sitting on a parent's lap listening to a story. Moreover, abundant research supports the effectiveness of shared reading when used with many language-minority populations (Anderson & Roit, 1998). Au (1991) suggests that such reading doesn't have to be simply random rereading, however. Rather, each time a text is reread with the teacher, it can be for an entirely different purpose, although always with the central aim in mind: to extend, refine, and deepen a child's abilities to decode text and construct meaning. Following are six major purposes for shared reading and rereading text (Cooper, 1997):

- to develop print concepts
- to reinforce decoding skills in the context of authentic text
- to explore language

Shared reading builds on children's natural desire to read and reread favorite books.

- to think creatively
- to improve comprehension skills through listening
- to foster an appreciation for reading

Developing print concepts

Students at the emergent literacy stage are developing crucial concepts about print through shared reading. Children learn about the conventions of our language—words, letters, sentences, punctuation—as they are discussed in the context of the story being read. For example, in the introduction of *The Three Billy Goats Gruff* story (Stimson, 1993), you might point out how quotation marks were used whenever one character talked to another, or how a capital letter always began a sentence (see Figure 11.1).

Reinforcing decoding skills

Another advantage of this strategy is that it reinforces students' decoding skills in the context of authentic text. With teacher guidance, students learn to figure out unfamiliar words using the various cues provided in the language of the text—context, structure (prefixes, suffixes, inflectional endings), and recurring patterns or phonic elements. Learning to decode involves rereading texts with numerous examples of the exact element to which the students have recently been introduced through explicit instruction. For example, through the reading of the fairy tale, the students

---

figure	11.1	Excerpt from *The Three Billy Goats Gruff.*

Suddenly, *up* popped the ugly troll! "Who's that trip-trapping over *my* bridge?" he roared.

"It's only me . . . the littlest billy goat Gruff," said the frightened goat in a tiny voice. "I'm off to the meadow to eat the green grass."

"Then I'm coming to gobble you up!" roared the troll.

Source: Joan Stimson, *The Three Billy Goats Gruff.* Illustrated by Chris Russell. Loughborough, UK: Ladybird Books, 1993. Used with permission.

were ready to learn the *tr* blend. The teacher pointed out this phonic element in the story, exaggerated it, and asked the students to think of other words beginning with the same sound. Rereading then helped students reinforce that learning.

Exploring language

Through shared reading, students are continually engaged in exploring language. By examining unusual or repetitive language patterns, you guide the students in developing a greater appreciation for language while learning about structure and cues that will help them construct meaning. Often the language pattern can serve as a basis for students to then write a new story. For example, in *The Three Billy Goats Gruff*, students explored the language pattern created by the goats tramping across the bridge. They were invited to use the blends they had been studying to make new sounds the goats might have made, using a similar language pattern: The goats went "hip, hop, hip, hop," or the goats went "clip, clop, clip, clop."

Thinking creatively

A fourth by-product of shared reading is that students develop the ability to think creatively. At times, you will urge listeners and readers to jump far beyond what an author is saying to formulate original ideas. When this happens, the author's words serve as a trigger that often ignites a new train of thought; students may momentarily stop listening to what an author is saying to ruminate on their own exploding ideas. They may ask themselves, "What can I do with this information? What does this mean in my life? Where can I go with this? What would I do if I were in this character's shoes?" The result of thinking about such questions is often a unique personal invention or a totally original idea.

Improving comprehension skills

Another benefit of shared reading is that students' comprehension skills constantly evolve through intent listening. You begin by reading the text to the group, inviting the students to chime in if they know words or phrases, and asking them to make predictions or to listen for a specific purpose. Sometimes you will encourage students to summarize sections of text by recounting them to another classmate, as occurred in Mr. Kohl's second reading of *The Three Billy Goats Gruff*. At other times, you may ask students to think about the motivation of characters, enumerate episodes in the story, guess outcomes, or share what the text reminds them of in their own lives.

Appreciating reading

Above all, through shared reading students develop an appreciation for reading. The primary reason for a young child to read is, after all, to construct personal meaning; if the child acquires the skill of reading but doesn't care for reading, that child will soon fall into the category of *aliterate*, or one who *can* read but chooses *not* to. Therefore, when you read aloud, use methods that encourage students to enjoy texts and to become excited about them. During shared reading, talk about the illustrations, the characters, things that happened in the story, things the students liked or didn't like, and how certain events or characters made them feel. All these activities help students form an appreciation for the characters and events in the text. Texts may be reread many times for this purpose alone. In fact, this appears to be the primary reason that most students choose to reread any story. Informational texts are also excellent choices for shared reading. Shared reading with informational text provides a good opportunity for teachers to model how to comprehend unfamiliar academic and domain-specific words and phrases and to model critical-thinking skills, both emphasized in the CCSS and many state standards.

Procedures for Shared Reading

Carefully chosen stories or informational texts in big-book format (see Chapter 3) are perfect for engaging very young children in critical and creative thinking. Stories from quality children's literature (try Caldecott Award winners or Children's Choice selections) or literature-based basal readers usually have an easily discernible structure that teaches students what to look for when they encounter a certain structure in their independent reading. Such stories should grab the imagination of young children and stimulate a range of feelings. If wisely chosen, they provide an enjoyable association with reading. Shared reading is an equally effective way to model for students how to read informational texts. First, discuss the structural features that distinguish informational texts from narratives (see Chapter 10). Subsequent shared readings could include reading and looking for specific information in the text, creating a summary of the reading, and comparing stories and informational text on similar topics. A major emphasis of the CCSS and many state standards is to make sure students support their answers with evidence from the text; students should "use relevant evidence when supporting their own points in writing and speaking, making their reasoning clear to the reader or listener, [and] constructively evaluate others' use of evidence" (NGACBP & CCSSO, 2010, p. 7). Shared reading activities are a good time to model this skill.

Many educators break the shared reading activity into several related parts: (1) a "warm-up" activity where familiar nursery rhymes, chants, and songs are read and sung, using large print as a guide; (2) introducing the reading selection ("into" the text, or *before* reading); (3) reading and responding to the text ("through" the text, or *during* reading); (4) rereading the text one or more times for various purposes; and (5) extending the text ("beyond" the text, or *post-reading*). The time frames for each of these elements are flexible and can be adapted, shortened, or lengthened, as you see fit or as time allows (Peetoom, 1986). See the accompanying Case Example for a detailed look at the procedures as we join a shared reading experience in Mr. Jimenez's classroom.

CASE EXAMPLE

A shared reading experience in Mr. Jimenez's classroom

It's Wednesday morning in Mr. Jimenez's kindergarten classroom. They have just finished a choral reading of a poem from *Poetry Works! The First Verse Complete Set* (1998). Following this warm-up activity, he intends to introduce the book *The Three Billy Goats Gruff* (1993), by Joan Stimson and illustrated by Chris Russell, to his students in a shared reading activity.

"Into" the book: Introducing the text

In Mr. Jimenez's class, the introduction of a text in a shared reading activity meets with a joyous sense of anticipation—beginning with focused attention to the cover. Mr. Jimenez reads the title and asks the students what they think the book might be about. He discusses the author and illustrator and tells the students about any other familiar texts the author and illustrator may have created.

Next, Mr. Jimenez gets the students excited about reading the book by showing a few selected pictures to "whet the children's appetite." This is called a **"picture walk"**; he shows each of the pictures, and the students tell what they think is happening in each one. He asks **predictive questions** that encourage students

to think about what is going to happen, thus constructing text. The following are examples of predictive questions he may ask:

"Who do you think are going to be the main characters in this story? What do you think is going to happen to them?" (anticipating; predicting)

"Where do you think the goats are going?" (inferring from cover clues)

"What do goats usually eat? Where do they usually live?" (activating prior knowledge)

"Does anyone know what goats' feet are called?" (assessing prior knowledge)

"What kind of sound do you think their hooves make?" (inferring, to prepare students to hear the words *trip, trap*)

Mr. Jimenez records the students' predictions on the board to refer to later. This introduction can take anywhere from 3 to 20 minutes (see Chapter 8 for more information on developing appropriate questions). *Note:* When Mr. Jimenez reads the shared reading text for the first time, he can record it. Students could then work at a listening center to listen to the story again while tracking along.

"Through" the book:
Reading and responding to the text

In this phase, Mr. Jimenez reads the book aloud to the students as they are gathered around him, holding it so they can see each page clearly. He runs his hand or a pointer along each line of print so that the students develop a sense of the left-to-right orientation of English text and also match speech to print. He invites the students to join in, but for the initial reading, many will just listen.

The first reading is often rather quick, to allow students to get an overview of the story. Mr. Jimenez reads with enthusiasm, modeling the fluency of a proficient reader, yet stopping often to ask predictive questions and to field students' comments and reactions about the text.

At the conclusion of the text, he asks open-ended, prompting questions designed to get students engaged in discussion about the story:

- "How did your predictions match what actually happened in the story?"
- "What was your favorite part of the story?"
- "What did the story remind you of in your own life?"
- "Who was your favorite character? Why?"
- "Which billy goat do you think you are most like? Why?"

- "How did the story make you feel?"
- "What would you have done if you were a billy goat trying to get across the bridge?"
- "How would the story have been different if it had been told from the point of view of the troll?"

Rereading and revisiting
the text for various purposes

Mr. Jimenez returns to the story and does a second reading, this time encouraging the students to join in, especially with rhyming and repetitious parts. After the second reading the students spontaneously exclaim, "Let's read it again!" which certainly means they have enjoyed the story and having been participants in it. If time permits, Mr. Jimenez will do another reading, because when students are excited about reading, a lifelong love is being kindled.

He may wish to select a variety of purposes for revisiting the story. Students may now be ready to reflect on it in a more individual way. The method Mr. Jimenez uses to encourage responses may vary according to the nature of the story or the wishes of individual students. Some suggestions to elicit reflective responses (but by no means an exhaustive list) are as follows (Hennings, 1992):

- Tell a classmate about a favorite part.
- Retell the story to a partner.
- Write a sentence about the story in your journal.
- Draw a picture about the story with a caption.
- Draw and/or write about a favorite character.
- Explain why you didn't like a certain character.
- Prepare a skit of your favorite scene in the story.

The story can also be revisited to help students visualize the relationships among the story's characters. A **literary sociogram** (Butler & Turbil, 1986; see Figure 11.2) can be used to help students better understand the relationships between story characters and see the differences in feelings that one character may have from another. Mr. Jimenez employs this device by asking students parallel questions about characters. For example, when reading the story *Little Red Riding Hood,* he asked: "How did Mother feel about Red Riding Hood? What evidence do you have?" and "How does Red Riding Hood feel about Mother? What evidence do you have?" After writing down students' responses on arrows, the class discussed why the pairs of characters may have had differing feelings toward each other.

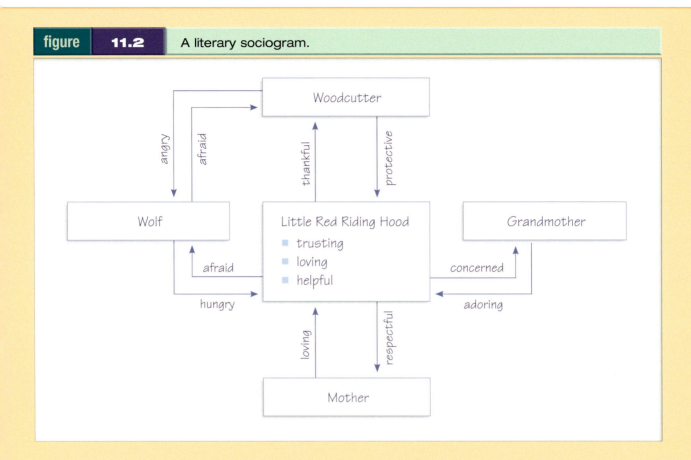

figure 11.2   A literary sociogram.

In another session, *The Three Billy Goats Gruff* may be revisited to help students make contact with their feelings through those of the characters. For example, Mr. Jimenez might ask the students:

"How do you think the last billy goat felt when he was left all alone? Have you ever felt that way?"

"Why was the troll so upset that the goats were going over the bridge?"

"What are some other things the billy goats might have done to keep the troll from being angry?"

"How would you have felt if it had been your bridge?"

In yet another session, Mr. Jimenez used *masking devices* (described later in this chapter) to isolate individual words and focus students' attention on the details of the words. For example, he masked off several words, starting with the blend *tr,* helping the students discover that these words all start with the same sound. Mr. Jimenez uses oral cloze activities, in which he deliberately omits words in the story and pauses for the students to supply the missing words, for promoting prediction and contextual analysis skills:

EXAMPLE: Now, there was a _____ over the river, and under this bridge lived a very fierce and ugly _____.

Yet another revisiting of the text might be for the purpose of encouraging students to compare and contrast the present story with another one they have read in the past; for example, Mr. Jimenez used a Venn diagram (see Figure 11.3) to have students compare and contrast the story *The Three Billy Goats Gruff* with the story *The Three Little Pigs.* This device of two overlapping circles allows students to view graphically the similarities and differences between two stories or ideas.

"Beyond" the book: Extending the text

The extending phase is another chance for students to respond to the text; with extension activities, however, oral, visual, or written creative expression is the primary focus. Such activities may take place in a small group, or they may be individual efforts and include such experiences as skits, puppet shows, murals, painting, or the creation of a class book from individual statements students have written about the story. Extended activities for Mr. Jimenez's class after several readings of *The Three Billy Goats Gruff* might include the following:

- Singing a song about goats that includes hand actions.

- A dramatization of the story using student-created props.

- A flannel-board retelling of the story with felt cutouts.

- A group-written poem using the rime from goat—*oat*.

- A tempera paint mural showing the events in order.

- A retelling using three sizes of masks for the goats and three different voices.

- An activity where one student plays the part of the troll and fields questions from other classmates about his motivation.

- Creating another adventure with the same characters.

- Asking a story character some questions.

- Having students explain what they would have done at a particular point in the story if they were the character.

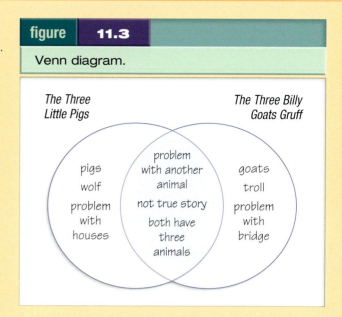

figure   11.3

Venn diagram.

The Three Little Pigs — *The Three Billy Goats Gruff*

pigs
wolf
problem with houses

problem with another animal
not true story
both have three animals

goats
troll
problem with bridge

GUIDED READING

guided reading is a small-group reading activity similar in many ways to shared reading. In guided reading, however, students usually decode the text independently, silently or aloud, and emphasis is often on skills such as answering or asking questions, making predictions, or summarizing what they've read (Fountas & Pinnell, 1996). Guided reading, done with leveled books at students' instructional level, has been shown to be a positive part of a school's literacy program (Fisher & Frey, 2007). The Directed Reading–Thinking Activity (DRTA) (see Chapter 8) is an example of a guided reading activity (Guastello & Lenz, 2005; Schwartz, 2005).

Guided reading is initially teacher-led (later done independently) and conducted in small groups, giving students the opportunity to develop as individual readers while they participate in a socially supported activity. At the early stages of reading development, students use their fingers to finger-point read. Finger-pointing involves students in **tracking,** or indicating an understanding of the one-to-one correspondence between spoken and written words (Reutzel, 1995). At the conclusion of each section, the students stop and discuss with the teacher the answers to their questions or predictions. At each stopping point, the teacher allows and encourages students to respond to what they have read. The teacher is then able to observe each child's processing of new text. By taking notes on each learner, the teacher becomes aware of what further instruction each student requires. The teacher must continually gather assessment data, monitor groups, and adjust instruction.

- guided reading

- tracking

Purposes for Guided Reading

Guided reading is an ideal strategy for several reasons. Guided reading is an opportune time to individually assess students, for example, by conducting running records, fluency tests, and so forth. In addition, guided reading is useful when small groups of students need additional support in constructing meaning from text, either because of the text's difficulty or because of the students' limited experience or

scaffold ■

ability. This approach also allows the teacher to adjust the level of modeling needed for understanding or to **scaffold** according to the students' needs (see Chapter 9). For example, students might read a story about a boy going into a cave or read an informational text about caves. After a brief before-reading survey, you might realize the students have limited backgrounds for this text; most have never been in a cave. Using a scaffolding technique, you would "walk" the group of students through the text, offering helpful information about caves along the way (e.g., "Caves have pieces of limestone hanging down that look kind of like icicles. They are called stalactites"), checking their understanding at every point with probing questions (e.g., "But *why* do you think the boy's hands were trembling as he entered the cave?") and clarifying concepts as needed.

Guided reading is ideal for use in *literature-based units*. Using this alternative to a basal reader, students read aloud group-selected literature in small groups, and you demonstrate comprehension strategies, clarify misconceptions, introduce new vocabulary, and take advantage of "teachable moments" to discuss any other instructional issue that may arise. The small-group arrangement also gives you a chance to observe individual students reading orally, providing an opportunity for informal diagnosis of decoding skills and monitoring comprehension (Tompkins, 2006).

When children are excited about reading, a lifelong love is being kindled.

Because of its flexibility, guided reading is a powerful tool; do not overuse it, however. You can relinquish some control by providing more support at the beginning of the reading and gradually releasing the responsibility to the students as they become more confident with the reading of the story. With guided reading, you can control the amount of scaffolding you provide in the following areas:

1. the types of questions asked before reading and during discussion
2. the amount of text students read at any one time
3. the type of discussion held between reading sessions
4. the number of comprehension strategies modeled by you via think-alouds (see Chapter 8)

When maximum support is needed, for example, you can direct the discussion to underscore a specific fact or idea; then, as students have grasped the idea, decreases the direction and let the students take more responsibility by carrying out and directing their own discussion with a partner.

The Role of Questioning in Guided Reading

Questions play a vital role in guided reading and should always go beyond simply asking students to restate what they have just read. By responding to provocative questions that help them get an overall mental picture, students begin to understand how to construct meaning from text (Beck, 1984; Durkin, 1990). Many of the questions asked should be open-ended—not answerable with a simple "yes" or "no"—and should require critical thinking by the student that is supported with evidence from the text. Allow plenty of time for all students to formulate a response. During guided reading, questions should meet the specific criteria discussed next. See Figure 11.4 for examples of each.

figure	11.4	Typical questions for guided reading.*

BEFORE READING	
Narrative text:	Why might [the main character] want to run away from home?
	Have you ever wanted to run away from home? Why or why not?
Informational text:	Why are trees important to us?
	What would the world be like without trees?

DURING READING*	
Narrative text:	What made the boy realize that he cared about his family?
	Why do you think they welcomed him home and were not angry?
Informational text:	From what you have read, what are some other ways trees are important to us?
	Why are loggers cutting down the trees?

AFTER READING*	
Narrative text:	What would you now say to a friend who says he wants to run away?
	What are some other ways you can solve a family problem?
Informational text:	Why are there fewer trees in our cities?
	How can we take better care of our trees?

*Students should provide evidence from the text to support their answers when appropriate.

Before reading. Questions posed to students *before* the reading of the text should guide students' attention to the key concepts or the most important ideas in the piece to be read. In narrative text, these ideas may include the plot, the theme, the main character, the problem, or the main events. In informational text, students' attention should be focused on the major concept(s) to be presented.

During reading. Questions asked *between* sections of the text should bring together ideas discovered in the reading and are designed to build relationships among facts and ideas. Students need to be taught to support their answers with evidence.

After reading. Questions asked *after* the reading of the text should be designed to help students internalize narrative text by identifying with the main characters or events in the story and, thus, to grow in appreciation of the reading experience; for informational text, the final questions should be created to help students apply the new information to their own lives. Again, students should be taught to use specific evidence from the texts they read.

Leveled Texts

In order to ensure that students are being taught at their appropriate reading level (see Chapter 13), teachers use leveled books such as those published by Rigby, Scholastic, and the Wright Group for instruction in guided reading. **Leveled books** tend to have subtler differences in the difficulty between levels than more traditional "grade-leveled" texts (Fountas & Pinnell, 1999; Schulman & Payne, 2000).

■ leveled books

Research on a program for students with special needs, Concept-Oriented Reading Instruction (CORI), revealed that leveled text, in conjunction with explicit instruction and motivation support, helped students increase their achievement in word recognition speed and reading comprehension (Guthrie et al., 2009). Using these texts, teachers may group students according to their individual instructional reading level. The level of each text is determined by the following criteria:

- length of words
- number of words
- size of font and layout
- difficulty of vocabulary and concepts
- predictability and pattern of language
- complexity of language and syntax
- word frequency (how "rare" a word is in comparison to all words in a given word bank)

Figure 11.5 shows books with guided reading book lists, and Figure 11.6 lists publishers of leveled books used in guided reading.

---

figure   11.5   Books with guided reading book lists.

Fountas, I., & Pinnell, G.S. (2000). *Guided Reading: Good first teaching for all children.* Portsmouth, NH: Heinemann.

Fountas, I.C., & Pinnell, G.S. (2013). *The Fountas and Pinnell leveled booklist, K–8 (2013–2015 ed.).* Portsmouth, NH: Heinemann.

Fountas, I., & Pinnell, G.S. (2001). *Guiding readers and writers, Grades 3-6: Teaching comprehension, genre, and content literacy.* Portsmouth, NH: Heinemann.

Schulman, M.B., & Payne, C.D. (2000). *Guided Reading: Making it work.* New York: Scholastic.

---

figure   11.6   Publishers of leveled books.

Celebrations Press, www.celebrationspress.com

Creative Teaching Press, www.creative teaching.com

Houghton Mifflin, www.eduplace.com

McGraw-Hill, www.mheonline.com

National Geographic, www.national geographic.com

Newbridge Educational Publishing, www.newbridgeonline.com

Sadlier-Oxford, www.sadlier-oxford.com

Scholastic, www.scholastic.com

Scott Foresman, http://books.atozteacherstuff. com/leveled-books

Sundance, www.sundancepub.com

Source: DeVries (2015).

Procedures for Guided Reading

In a guided reading session, students are placed into small groups (4 to 6 students). These groups may include students at similar reading levels or students who need instruction on a specific skill (more shortly). In guided reading, you will continually assess, monitor, and adjust the groups. You will typically sit at a table with the guided reading group in front of you, making sure you can see the rest of the class (a kidney-shaped table is great for this). You should have immediate access to an easel with chart paper, a whiteboard, or a pocket chart to use for direct instruction. Guided reading often takes about 15 to 20 minutes, which varies according to grade level, lesson focus, and whether students require more or less time.

Guided reading lessons include five main parts: (1) the new text or story orientation, (2) the oral or silent reading of the text, (3) story retelling or summarizing the content of an informational reading, (4) a "grand conversation" between you and group members and/or explicit instruction on a phonics or reading comprehension component, as needed, and (5) follow-up activities. As with shared reading, guided reading should be considered flexible and can be expanded, condensed, or modified to meet group needs and teacher time constraints.

New text orientation

Before introducing the new text or story, link any new ideas or difficult concepts to the students' prior experience, through a discussion, a visualization of what they are about to read, a video excerpt, or any other technique that will help students, especially English learners, relate to the text.

Then hold up the book and show the cover, read the title, and briefly talk about the main idea of the book. Covering the text, "walk through" the book, discussing the pictures, providing an opportunity for students to make predictions about the text, asking key questions (as discussed earlier), and introducing some of the vocabulary and language structures found in the text—so that students will not find them troublesome when they are reading it independently. With an informational text, this book walk includes instruction about the text features (see Chapter 10). These books are written to provide facts, and students should be taught to make predictions about what they will learn by looking at the pictures and captions, graphs, and headings and subheadings.

Depending on the children's developmental levels, begin the first reading while the students track with their fingers. Later, gradually relinquish responsibility for the first reading to the students by sharing the reading role and then fading into the role of supporter.

Oral/silent reading

When the students are ready to read independently, give each student a copy of the text. In some cases, you will have a large edition of the book, or a big book (see Chapter 3), or an e-book for display on an interactive whiteboard (see Chapter 12), and the students will have smaller versions of the same text. Discuss with students the title, author, and illustrator. Until one-to-one correspondence is established, allow students to point to the words as they read. Repeating the key concept they are to look for, direct them to read individually at their own pace. While the students are reading, work with them on an individual basis in the following ways:

1. With children at the very early reading level, check for evidence of, and/or prompt for, directionality and one-to-one matching of spoken to printed word. Example: "Who can find the word *is* on this page?"

2. When students have mastered the preceding skills, check for evidence of, and/or prompt for, self-monitoring of understanding ("No, that doesn't make sense"), the ability to search through the repertoire of decoding skills, accuracy, and self-correcting behavior. How students read, whether orally or silently, will depend on the lesson focus. You may want to work on decoding or fluency skills, which means students will read aloud. Another guided reading group, however, may need instruction only on a reading comprehension strategy and will read to themselves. Silent reading has proven to be beneficial for struggling third graders (Reutzel, Petscher, & Spichtig, 2012) and can help improve reading fluency (Rasinski et al., 2011).

Retelling/summarizing

Students then retell what they have read—to you, to their peers, or to a partner. (See p. 219 for the activity "Retelling Informational Texts.") Typically, you will say, "Can you tell me (or a partner) about what you have just read?" Sometimes you will probe, or further explore, students' answers by asking specific questions to prompt recall. You may take notes during this phase to record language facility and comprehension of individual students. While many students have prior experiences with retelling events (e.g., "Teacher, guess what happened?"), guided reading is also a good time to model how to *summarize* information. Being able to understand the "gist" of a story or informational text is an integral part of reading comprehension in strategies such as reciprocal teaching (see Chapter 8). In fact, CCSSS.ELA-Literacy.CCRA.R.2 requires students to "Determine central ideas or themes of a text and analyze their development; summarize the key supporting details and ideas" (NGACBP & CCSSO, 2010, p. 10). To help young students meet this goal, incorporate the skill of summarizing into guided reading sessions.

Grand conversation and/or explicit phonics instruction

grand conversation ■

Help the students internalize and appreciate what they have just read through a **grand conversation.** As in any adult book club, appreciation of a book is best created by asking open-ended questions and allowing students to say what they liked or disliked, what they found humorous, what "grabbed" them, and so forth. Set a conversational tone by starting with an open-ended question (e.g., "Would you have chosen Leslie for a friend? Why or why not?") and encouraging students to ask questions of and respond to each other for the sheer joy of discussing their feelings about the book. Your role, then, becomes that of facilitator, ensuring that all who want to respond are heard—not just the most vociferous.

For students who need it, you may do an additional minilesson (5 to 7 minutes) on some aspect of phonics or structural analysis development that you deems necessary. Such a lesson may be conducted before the piece is read, to increase reading independence, or after, to reinforce patterns that have been introduced previously. This lesson may include (1) letter/sound association, or focusing students' attention on certain beginning or ending sounds found in the story; (2) word chunks or word patterns, or briefly drawing students' attention to a word chunk used in the story, such as a specific blend, ending, or rime; or (3) reinforcement of high-frequency

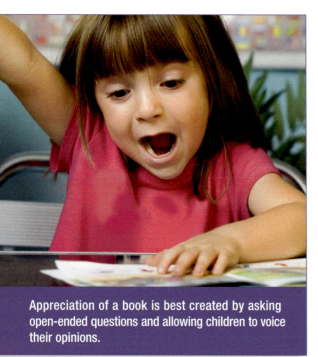

Appreciation of a book is best created by asking open-ended questions and allowing children to voice their opinions.

words, or picking several repeated words from the story and asking students to find, frame, and say them.

Follow-up

The most appropriate follow-up activity to a guided reading lesson is to invite students to take the finished text home to demonstrate their reading ability to parents, caretakers, or siblings. Such a follow-up not only provides needed practice but also promotes increased confidence and fluency for beginning readers.

Classroom management during guided reading

One of the most common questions that teachers have about guided reading is not about the small group they are teaching, but rather, "What do I do with the other students?" If you are going to lead a guided reading session, you must provide meaningful activities that will engage the other students. Some teachers want the rest of the class all doing the same activity; other teachers, however, allow students to rotate through different "centers" while students engage in different literacy activities. The following is a list of strategies that you incorporate into language arts instruction while conducting a guided reading session. To avoid stopping a guided reading session to get students back on task, ensure that students know exactly what to do if they complete an activity. In other words, students should have more work than they can finish.

Writing center. A writing center is a perfect way to emphasize the reading–writing connection. For instance, during a guided reading session students not involved in the current reading group can write using any of a variety of formats to reinforce and extend new concepts from their reading, such as writing a letter after reading a book featuring letters. Writing centers can include writing letters to friends and family, poems, essays on a current class topic, or written responses to expository prompts. One appealing feature of a writing center is that it can be low maintenance; if students have access to writing supplies and supporting materials (e.g., word walls, posters depicting the writing process), you will be able to concentrate on the guided reading group.

Listening center. As this chapter has discussed, shared reading is an excellent way for learners to listen to models of fluent reading, and a *listening center* can also be effective in this regard. When possible, schools can purchase books with corresponding audio versions so that students can listen at their own pace. In addition, you can record yourself reading poems, stories, plays, or texts that are related to what the class is studying (e.g., books on planets) that encompass a variety of levels. Students can also record themselves reading their favorite texts and read along with their own recording. Many primary classrooms use recordings to accompany favorite books. At listening posts, students follow along by tracking with their fingers to commercially made or teacher/volunteer-made recordings. Although the focus is on reading for enjoyment, repeated listenings and rereadings of favorite stories aid fluency, develop sight vocabulary, and deepen comprehension (Routman, 1995).

A listening center can be helpful for English learners and students with special needs who are experiencing difficulty reading and require extra support. Listening centers can also be great for students reading above grade level; too often teachers don't provide these students with challenging materials, and having texts available for them at the appropriate reading level is a great motivating and instructional strategy.

Classroom library. Every textbook on literacy argues that the goal of good reading instruction is to create lifelong readers who read not only to prepare for colleges and careers but simply for the enjoyment of reading; a well-stocked class library is a great way to achieve this goal. A library with books on a variety of topics and at various reading levels can be a place where students spend time doing what you want them to do: read. You can connect a library with other centers such as the writing center as students fill out a log/summary of what they have read in the class library.

GROUPING FOR INSTRUCTION

S tudents can be placed in temporary, small, homogeneous groups for guided reading instruction based on their knowledge, skills, interest, instructional reading level, and experience. Although students should come together for whole-group reading many times during the day, sometimes it is helpful to group small numbers of students who can read at about the same level and to meet with them three to five days a week. With ongoing assessment of their abilities, these groups should be fluid and frequently changed. To avoid the stigma of low-ability groups, maintain other heterogeneous groups during the day for reading aloud, shared reading, discussion groups, writing, and other activities.

The following flexible grouping systems each have a place in a comprehensive literacy program:

- leveled groups
- skill groups
- literature circles
- pairs (buddy reading)
- peer-editing groups
- cooperative groups

Leveled Groups

Conduct a guided reading lesson for a homogeneous group of five or six students who are reading at about the same instructional level, which means they're reading texts of the same readability level with 90 to 94 percent accuracy (with comprehension). These leveled groups use texts that are slightly above students' reading level and often focus on areas such as fluency or reading comprehension; provide instructional support with the goal of increasing students' reading ability. This practice also helps avoid frustrating a struggling reader or holding back a capable reader from appropriately challenging material.

Skill Groups

Form small skill groups when several students are having a problem with a specific skill or strategy and need reinforcement in that area. For example, if several students are having problems with the *ain* word chunk or pattern that was introduced in the day's guided reading lesson, form a temporary skill group composed of those students and provide a brief minilesson on words containing *ain*. The group lasts only until the skill is mastered.

Literature Circles

As students grow in independence, set aside time during the day when students with the same reading interest—for example, those interested in mysteries, horse stories, or the books of Judy Blume—come together to read and discuss those texts. Such reading groups can evolve into writing groups as students decide to

More about literature circles

Beginning around the second grade, you can organize litera-ture circles for readers using the following series of activities.

Select books. Prepare text sets with five or six titles cor-responding to the independent reading levels of the students in the class, gathering five or six copies of each book. Read the blurb on the back of the book cover to garner interest in each of the books and then ask each student to sign up for the first and second choices, to allow you to select which choice is closer to the reading level of the student.

Form literature circles and assign roles. Have students get together and create a schedule for discussing each chapter or section of the book within the time limits you set. They choose discussion roles, which rotate with each chapter or section. Students may not know how to conduct themselves in literature circles or how their discussions can enhance each other's understanding of the text. Conduct minilessons addressing what each role entails and routinely debrief the discussions with students to ensure their success (Daniels & Steineke, 2004). For younger children, five roles are suggested:

- **Discussion leader:** Creates two or three critical-thinking questions about the reading that cannot be answered within the text. Such questions may address personal reactions to what was read or questions about why the events occurred.
- **Word detective:** Chooses three or four words from the reading, learns as much as possible about the words,

and teaches them to the others in the group by acting them out, by illustrating them, or by another means chosen by the student.

- **Artist:** Draws a picture, sketch, diagram, or cartoon, or finds clip art that is related to the chapter. The group discusses how the illustration is related to the text.
- **Summarizer:** In a one- or two-minute statement, sum-marizes what the reading was about, focusing on the main ideas of what was read.
- **Jewel finder:** Locates one or two sentences in the reading that were especially interesting, funny, sad, or important.

Independent reading and role preparation. Have students read the assigned parts of the book independently at home or using partner reading. Then they complete their assigned role in preparation for the group meeting.

Book discussion. Have students come together and discuss their chosen book, usually beginning with the summary and the discussion leader. Unlike more conventional book groups, where a vociferous individual may dominate the discourse, every student in the literature circle has a voice in the discussion because every student has a role to perform.

Book share. When the books have been completed, ask students from each circle to do a book talk, PowerPoint, or some other presentation to interest their classmates in the book they just read.

write letters to the author or add an epilogue to the text. Students in the groups can decide to do *readers theater* (explained in Chapter 5), puppet shows, or murals using the text as inspiration. Literature circles can be temporary or permanent but often last as long as activities related to the chosen book do.

Pairs (Buddy Reading)

Because children are social beings, they often enjoy reading aloud to one anoth-er. Such partnerships can be formed between cross-age "reading buddies," pairing a sixth-grader from another class with a first-grader, or between friends getting together to take turns reading. Also, pairs of students can participate in dyad reading (see Chapter 8) for the purpose of improving listening and summarizing skills.

Peer-Editing Groups

When students are writing during a writing workshop or in response to a piece they have read during guided reading, peer editors can offer helpful advice (see

Chapter 9). In groups containing no more than two or three students, each student is both writer and editor. As writer, the student obtains feedback on parts of her writing that may not make sense. As editor, the student can offer suggestions for improvement in style and word choice and calls attention to mechanical errors that may have been overlooked in self-editing. Peer editors also provide feedback on the content of the writing, such as if there are any confusing parts in the writing or if more detail is needed. The students in these groups are rotated in order to obtain different feedback from many editors during the school year.

Cooperative Groups

To foster a collaborative atmosphere in the classroom and to avoid the stigma of low-ability groups, cooperative groups are ideal; they also foster language acquisition for English learners. Assign students to four- or five-member groups mixed in ability (there may be one high achiever, one low achiever, and two average achievers per group), gender, and primary language. Focus on teaching a social skill and assign specific roles as discussed earlier for each group member so everyone participates in some capacity. Present a lesson to the entire class and then ask students to work on follow-up material (workbook pages, spelling words, word sorts, posters) in groups. The students help one another because each is invested in the achievement of the other members since everyone gets credit for the work done by the group.

OTHER PRACTICES FOR GROUP READING

To keep group approaches for early reading instruction fresh and exciting for both yourself and the students, you can integrate the following six techniques and tools into group activities. Other reading activities can be explored on the websites identified in Appendix C.

see appendix C

- masking
- music
- multimedia packages
- pocket charts
- word walls
- cloze activities

Masking

masking ■

When you want students to focus on a particular word or word part, an ideal way to do this is by **masking,** using a sliding frame or stick-on notes to call attention to just that part of the word (see Figure 11.7). Usually masking takes place during repeated readings and not during the initial reading of a book. For example, if you are reading a story to focus on decoding a specific phonic element, such as the *br* blend, use the masking frame to call attention to that particular letter–sound relationship. Then ask the students to think of other words that begin with that sound.

Music

In a 2004 letter to all U.S. school superintendents, former secretary of education Rod Paige wrote, "the arts are a core academic subject." He reminded us of the signifi-

figure   11.7   Masking device.

DEMONSTRATION SIZE:

1. Starting from the folded edge of a file folder, cut an 8.5 x 6 inch rectangle.

2. Using the remnants of the file folder, start at the fold and cut a 1-inch-wide strip that runs from the fold all the way across the folder.

3. Remove a 2 x 7 inch rectangle from the center of #1. Start cutting at the open edge so the fold remains completely intact.

4. Slide the 1-inch strip over the open ends of the "U" shaped section and staple as indicated.

5. Slide the thin strip back and forth to adjust the frame to the size of the word or letter you are working on.

INDIVIDUAL STUDENT SIZE:

Follow the previous directions with the following changes in dimension:

- The original rectangle cut from the fold should be 5 x 2 inches.

- Remove a .75 x 4 inch rectangle from the center of the 5 x 2 segment.

- Cut a strip .5 x 3 inches, beginning at the fold.

- Staple or tape open edges.

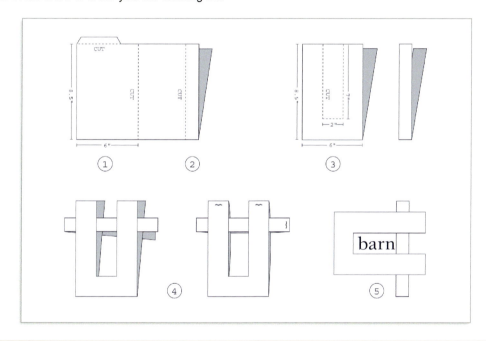

cant role the arts can play in academic achievement. Music, as one of the fine arts, is no exception and can enhance literacy in a multitude of ways (Paige, 2004).

Carefully selected lyrics can be placed on chart paper in large black letters, with repeated or high-frequency words in color or highlighted. The lyrics can be sung (to the original tune or one with which all are familiar) or chanted. When songs, poems, chants, and raps are chosen for their rhyme, rhythm, repetition, or cumulative sequence, music brings the reading and rereading of text to new heights of motivation (Cecil & Lauritzen, 1994). Young children never seem to tire of singing a catchy tune; thus, songs selected for their patterns can familiarize children with high-frequency sight vocabulary. Songs can also be used to reinforce phonic elements in an enjoyable way, as in the "Old MacDonald" adaptation mentioned in Chapter 4. See the box "Linking Literacy and Lyrics" for more information.

Integrate Music with Literature

www.rockhall.com/education

Linking literacy and lyrics

Music can be used to reinforce print in many ways:

1. Teach students a song by singing the song once (with or without accompaniment) and then inviting the students to sing along with you. Discuss the meaning of the song and any special words that may be unfamiliar to the students. Add motions or drama as appropriate.

2. Link the song to print. Write the lyrics to the song on chart paper. Read the lyrics, inviting the students to join in. Reread the lyrics, with the students reading each word as you point to it.

3. Build phonics skills and reinforce sight vocabulary. Point out words that appear more than once. Select one or two phonic elements or patterns to work with. Have the students find all words with the same pattern, begin-ning sound, ending sound, vowel sound, and so forth. Use sentence strips and word cards for matching and sequencing activities.

4. Create new activities based on the song lyrics. Cover words on the song chart and encourage students to brainstorm some new words to fill in the blanks, for example:

> "Mary had a little cat, her fur was black as night."

> Change the pattern of the song, the main character, the outcome, and so on.

Reprinted with permission of the publisher, Teaching K–8, Norwalk, CT. From K. Barclay and T. Coffman (1990). "I Know an Old Lady: Linking Literacy and Lyrics." Teaching K–8, May, 47–51.

Multimedia Packages

Sometimes books and media are sold together, allowing you to motivate students to sing while repeatedly reading the lyrics, all of which increases fluency (see Chapter 5). One example of such a package is a book of John Denver's "Country Roads," adapted and illustrated by Christopher Canyon (2005) and accompanied with a CD of John Denver's music. The colorful pictures of the journey, coupled with the music, stimulate students' interest (while adults get nostalgic hearing an old favorite). The book and its CD are perfect for shared reading or a community sing with the whole school. Visit the website in the margin for excellent collections of e-books for children, such as Aesop's Fables and Clifford Interactive Storybooks, as well as chapter excerpts and educational resources for teachers.

Drs. Cavanaugh Educational Technology

http:drscavanaugh.org

Pocket Charts

The use of pocket charts (as discussed in Chapter 4) can help develop students' ability to decode words; they also aid in building students' sight vocabulary. Print selected words from a story on cards, or print sentences from the story on sentence strips. Then have the students "rebuild" the story using the words or sentence strips (McCracken & McCracken, 1986).

Word Walls

As discussed in Chapter 5, a word wall or word chart is a listing of high-frequency words that are of interest to students or are being studied in a reading lesson. Display the words on the wall or on a bulletin board so that students can add to the list whenever they think of an appropriate word and so they can use them for reference during writing activities. Practice these words a few minutes each day at the beginning of a word lesson by having the students (1) stretch them out and read them together, (2) chant or cheer them three times, and/or (3) write using them in isolation and in context. During center rotations, a word wall or word chart can be used by partners who discuss the meanings of the words as the partners "read the room." Additionally, all words having the same spelling patterns can be starred (Cunningham & Cunningham, 1997).

Cloze Activities

A **cloze procedure** is often used when assessing student ability to understand vocabulary in a content area. Present a paragraph in its entirety and have students read the passage. On a subsequent page, the paragraph is given again but this time certain words in the paragraph (e.g., every fifth word) are deleted. The deleted words are printed above the paragraph, and students need to put the words back into the paragraph, thereby demonstrating an understanding of the words. In an instructional cloze procedure, words or parts of words are blocked out, and the reader uses clues within the text to predict what might complete the blocked portion. You can use this technique, orally or on a recording, during a repeated reading to help students develop sight vocabulary, to practice their use of prediction for decoding unfamiliar words, and to help them construct meaning using all the cueing systems (Cecil, 1994a). A cloze activity is especially helpful for students who are just learning English. Students can build their knowledge of English syntax as they guess what type of word could fit in the blanks. For example:

■ cloze procedure

> I had a cat
>
> And I named him Buffy.
>
> His eyes were coal black
>
> And his fur was so _____. (fluffy)

SMALL-GROUP READING AND ENGLISH LEARNERS

One of Goldenberg's (2008) conclusions in his review of the reports from the National Literacy Panel (August & Shanahan, 2006) and the Center for Research on Education, Diversity, and Excellence (Genesee, Lindholm-Leary, Saunders, & Christian, 2006) was that instruction that was effective for English-only students should also be implemented with English learners. Thus, as supported by more recent studies (Chaaya & Ghosn, 2010; Soto Huerta, 2012), guided reading can be an effective method of instruction of English learners. Peregoy and Boyle (2013) suggest that guided reading is especially effective with these students because of the teacher scaffolding and smaller groups.

LARGE- AND SMALL-GROUP READING AND STUDENTS WITH SPECIAL NEEDS

The inclusion of students with special needs in mainstream classrooms means that you must be able to differentiate instruction and teach students of various reading and skill levels. Whole-class instruction, which happens in shared reading, is great for modeling a skill for the entire class. Guided reading, however, can be effective with students with special needs because you can provide direct instruction and support for students in small groups. Gillam, Fargo, and St. Robertson (2009) found, for example, that students' ability to paraphrase was related to how well they understood informational text. Because guided reading is always in small groups, you can focus more attention on modeling, providing individual feedback, and allowing students to practice the skill of paraphrasing in a setting that tends to be less stressful than in front of an entire class. The ability to give students specific modeling, feedback, and guided practice is also evident in the success of CSR (Vaughn & Edmonds, 2006), described in Chapter 10.

Guided reading was also an integral part of a program at an elementary school with a classroom for 11 students with autism spectrum disorder (ASD). The program, Living in a Functional Environment (LIFE), focused on helping students with functional skills and incorporated the guided reading approach used by Fountas and Pinnell (1996). The teacher differentiated instruction to fit student needs; some students were at a low-functioning level and were working on activities to help their knowledge of the alphabet, while others were involved in higher-level reading practices such as alphabetizing sight words. A full year of the program resulted in 6 to 24 months of growth on reading measures, and the teacher reported that students began to show confidence with unfamiliar books and started checking out books from the library, considerable growth for LIFE skills students. "Thus, these findings suggest that guided reading can serve as a successful reading intervention for students with ASD" (Simpson, Spencer, Button, & Rendon, 2007, p. 7). Key to this success was the teacher's ability to differentiate instruction, which is at the heart of guided reading.

Moreover, Chapman, Greenfield, and Rinaldi (2010) found that students with special needs preferred small and one-on-one instruction, while Shepard and Uhry (1997) indicated that students who received instruction in phonemic awareness, letter–sound associations, and guided reading made substantial progress in sight-word reading, nonword reading, and spelling. Incorporating guided reading was also effective in developing social skills in three students identified as having problems in this area (Miller, Fenty, Scott, & Park, 2011).

Other studies confirm that guided reading can be effective with students diagnosed with autism (Simpson, Spencer, Button, & Rendon, 2007), students who are deaf (Schaffer & Schirmer, 2010); students with dyslexia (Shepard & Uhry, 1997); and students having problems with social skills (Miller, Fenty, Scott, Park, & Lee, 2011). The inclusion of students with special needs in mainstream classrooms requires you to adjust to students' needs, and guided reading is an important and effective strategy to make this happen.

MAKING TEXT ACCESSIBLE FOR ALL LEARNERS

Although enabling students to become independent, silent readers is the desired goal of reading instruction, many less-able students and those for whom English is a second language may need extra support or scaffolding to actually read a text by themselves. Mediated reading methods, with their provisions for reading to students and repeated readings, are ideal techniques for providing this support; the following are additional ways to make difficult texts more accessible to less-able readers (Guillaume, 1998; Tompkins, 2006).

Selective Pairing

Pairing an able reader with a reader who is less skilled makes the task of reading more sociable but also more accessible for the less-able reader. If low comprehension is also a problem, you can use dyad reading (see Chapter 8), asking students to summarize sentences or paragraphs and make predictions.

Online Books

Increasingly, stories can be found online to help students explore and appreciate literature and also develop positive attitudes toward technology (Castek, Bevans-Mangelson, & Goldstone, 2006). Students can visit Storyline, an online series of streaming videos, where they can enjoy pieces of wonderful literature read aloud by such actors as Betty White, James Earl Jones, and Elijah Wood. The site includes classic storybooks such as *The Polar Express* (Van Allsburg, 1985) and *Knots on a Counting Rope* (Martin & Archambault, 1997). For more on e-books, see Chapter 12.

Echo Reading

For text with a limited number of words, students can "echo" the text as you read and points to the words while the students repeat them. Such a strategy helps reinforce one-to-one correspondence and is especially appropriate for big books, where all students can see and follow along.

Building Background

Often a text is difficult for some students simply because they have limited background knowledge or prior experience with the topic. If an informal survey of readers suggests this may be the case, you can build background by reading a simpler text, providing hands-on experiences, showing a short video excerpt, discussing the topic, brainstorming ideas about the topic, or bringing in objects that relate to the topic before the text is read.

Delaying Independent Reading

If many activities related to the text have occurred before the initial reading of the text, or if the text has been read aloud first, students will be much more familiar with new words and concepts before they are expected to decode them. In other words, students may need to hear more read-alouds and engage in more shared and guided reading experiences before reading independently. These steps in the gradual release of responsibility must be done thoroughly before students are ready for independent reading.

Encouraging a Variety of Responses

Although school life primarily centers on thoughts and ideas, you should also encourage expressions of emotions and feelings in reading. For difficult reading material such as science or social studies, for example, a teacher who elicits the expression of feelings may notice resultant changes in attitudes, curiosity in science, or the ability to look at historical events from another's point of view—all of which would encourage a deeper engagement with the text.

SUMMARY

 BookPALS Storyline
www.storylineonline.net

Information on museum subjects
www.si.edu/kids

Links for thousands of subjects
www.kidsclick.org

The goal of a truly comprehensive approach to reading instruction should always be to create young learners who are able to decode fluently, interact meaningfully with text, and read willingly for the sheer enjoyment of the activity. Listening to stories and conversing about them paves the way for the later reading of stories with insight and appreciation. By reflecting before, during, and after listening, students learn how sophisticated readers process text. A comprehensive approach also creates students who learn information from reading and are eager to read more about real-world concepts. Using both stories and informational texts will help accomplish this goal.

Shared reading and guided reading, two group-reading practices combining appreciation for literature with decoding and constructing meaning from text, are ideal vehicles to meet the goals of an effective reading program for early readers. As shown in this chapter, you can use shared and guided reading to teach specific phonics skills, practice fluency, help students ask and answer questions, or simply share a stimulating story or information text with young learners—learners who are taking giant steps toward becoming literate human beings. The Common Core State Standards and aligned state standards emphasize finding evidence in text, using informational texts, and teaching critical-thinking skills. Shared and guided reading are two mediated strategies that can help you in these areas. Fountas and Pinnell (2013) remind us that although guided reading has been positive, we must continue to improve these instructional methods in order to develop students to their fullest potential.

questions   FOR JOURNAL WRITING AND DISCUSSION

1. How can shared reading and/or guided reading be used to expand each of the following?
   - oral language
   - phonemic awareness
   - phonics acquisition
   - literature appreciation

2. Predicting what will happen in a story has been found to ensure more engagement with the story and increased comprehension on the part of the learners. Why do you think this is so?

3. How do the similar conversational approaches of shared and guided reading compare with the methods of reading instruction of which you are currently aware? How do they differ from instruction you received when you were learning to read?

4. How can you structure activities so that all students are engaged during guided reading? Are there additional activities that you can have students do while you are conducting a guided reading session?

suggestions   FOR PROJECTS AND FIELD ACTIVITIES

1. Plan a shared or guided reading lesson for a small group of early readers. Record their responses to the lesson. Write a short reflection statement sharing your feelings about student involvement with the lesson.

2. Using the same group of students as in Question 1, read them a story "straight," without using predictive strategies, picture sharing, or any thought-provoking questions. Instead, ask only literal questions requiring factual recall, such as "What was the name of the main character?" What differences in student engagement with the story do you notice between the two lessons?

3. Observe a primary teacher who is conducting two readings of the same story with the same group of learners on successive days. What differences do you notice in the questions the teacher asks during the second reading? In what other ways is the instruction different? Do the students appear to be bored during their second encounter with the text? Why or why not?

Literacy and Technology in a Balanced Classroom

12

EXPLORING TODAY'S RESOURCES

How has the increased use of media in the classroom changed how teachers must think about literacy instruction?

What are some ways that technology can augment a writing workshop?

How are *visual literacy* and *multimodal literacy* defined and how can they be incorporated in the classroom?

How can the Internet and online resources be used in the classroom as a potent source for informational reading and writing?

How can online communities enhance written communication and connect readers and writers across the globe?

How can English learners be supported in learning to use technology, and how can their content learning be enhanced by using technology as a teaching tool?

How can technological devices become effective learning tools for students with special needs?

nterest in writing in Ms. Lambating's second-grade class has changed dramatically this year with the introduction of four new computers and four tablets, all with online access, to replace older, slower equipment. The teacher smiles and shakes her head as little Quanim uses Kid Pix to create a drawing of two fierce sharks of different species in an empty rectangular box and then adds text below, recounting the differences between the two. A reluctant writer only weeks ago, Quanim now thoroughly enjoys using her imagination to connect the information she found online to an exciting picture she has created. Without the constraint of her usual labored handwriting, which is large and unfocused, she has become much more prolific, as her thoughts turn almost magically into descriptive details, using her growing keyboard skills. Meanwhile Todd, Brittney, and José are collaborating on their wiki, responding to the latest episode of *Ben 10,* which they will immediately publish and link to several of their favorite *Ben 10* websites. To their great delight, a class of *Ben 10* fans from Connecticut has read their previous entry and commented enthusiastically. The trio is eager to respond to them and post their newest ideas. Several other students in the class are reading e-books on tablet computers and responding to the readings in personal digital response journals. Finally, at another computer, Jerome is preparing his latest poem for publication. Another erstwhile reluctant writer, he has recently become fascinated with writing poetry, especially after he learned to justify his phrases and select just the right font—and clip art—to make his poetry look polished and professional. Jerome has proudly kept all his poems in a folder and is preparing to publish a book of his poetry on his own poetry blog for a wide audience to read and, he hopes, respond to.

INTRODUCTION

echnology and education go hand and hand, offering exciting possibilities for transforming how children experience literacy. In fact, the Internet is the current generation's defining technology for literacy (Coiro & Dobler, 2007). Hancock (2008) suggests that in today's classrooms the Internet and other forms of instructional technology offer a "new dimension for reader response research" (p. 108), as students incorporate digital literacies with the more traditional literacies of paper, pencil, and textbooks. Encouraging and teaching young children to use technology in addition to traditional learning tools is crucial to prepare students for further education and for the challenges of our increasingly high-tech world. Indeed, the International Literacy Association (ILA, formerly the IRA), the bastion of all methods of instruction related to text, recognizes the need for a broadened concept of literacy encompassing new literacies. The ILA supports the ranks of those who believe that teachers have a crucial responsibility to integrate these literacies into the classroom, as literacy learning more often involves online resources and computers (IRA, 2002). A central tenet in the Common Core State Standards is the importance of learning how to use technology to further literacy skills. For example, according to the CCSS, third graders must be able to "Use text features and search tools (e.g., key words, sidebars, hyperlinks) to locate information relevant to a given topic" (CCSS.ELA-LITERACY.RI.3.5; NGACBP & CCSSO, 2010, p. 15).

The reality of the "digital divide," the gap in access to technology between middle-class families and low-income families, is also a powerful argument to support use of technology in the literacy classroom. When you integrate current technologies in your teaching, it gives all students access to technology and tools that they may not have at home (Common Sense Media, 2011). Moreover, classroom use of technology allows all students access to engaging narrative and informational text that is often missing in textbooks, which often are written with middle-class students in mind.

Numerous case studies in the research literature document how profoundly various forms of technology can enhance early literacy in classrooms whose teachers embrace a social constructivist and transformative approach to teaching, and the effects are particularly significant for low-income and minority students. Studies show that properly guided collaborative use of computers in early elementary classrooms can contribute to prosocial behavior, including positive peer interactions, increased vocabulary, mutual enjoyment, and a heightened understanding of the nature and function of written language when producing and using texts (Van Scoter, 2008). Further, a study of two elementary schools in impoverished neighborhoods (Warschaur, Grant, Del Real, and Rousseau, 2004) examined how technology-supported teaching practices can lead to enhanced learning when supported by a schoolwide commitment:

> Both schools make highly effective use of technology to promote academic literacy among their students, resulting in sophisticated student products, highly engaged learners, and high standardized test scores in relationship to school demographics. The keys in both cases are a schoolwide commitment to excellence, equity, and development of classroom communities of inquiry. Technology is used to apprentice students into academic literacy through promotion of independent reading, support for language scaffolding, involvement in cognitively engaging projects, and student analysis and creation of purposeful texts in a variety of media and genres. (p. 535)

Integrating technology use into the classroom can also strengthen connections between school and home. You can use technology to communicate with parents about literacy practices and advise families how to build digital literacy skills at home (NAEYC and Fred Rogers Center, 2012).

Finally, technology offers a powerful tool for literacy assessment, giving you effective tools to document students' literacy growth and achievement. With students, you can generate digital portfolios of students' written work as well as videos of presentations and media creations, to be shared during parent conferences. In addition, students can maintain and use such portfolios to gauge their own growth using rubrics and other self-assessments based on literacy and technology-use standards (NAEYC and Fred Rogers Center, 2012).

Although robust use of instructional technology in support of literacy learning may still be the exception rather than the norm in some schools (Project RED, 2011), there is, in principle at least, little dispute at the policy level about the need to realign school curricula to promote and take advantage of emerging and evolving literacies. Most educators and legislators realize that we have moved from a print-dominated literacy landscape to one where various forms of electronic communications are a routine component of literacy development (Leu et al., 2005).

The remainder of this chapter focuses on the potential for positive synergy between literacy and technology that can occur when teachers take an expanded view of literacy for inquiry learning that incorporates technology with the literacy skills of viewing and visually representing and with reading, writing, listening, and speaking. Indeed, technology lends itself well to literacy learning, providing a flexible venue in which students can seamlessly integrate reading, writing, listening, speaking, viewing, and visually representing to a greater degree than was possible with traditional print texts (Walsh, Asha, & Sprainger, 2007).

We first define and explore visual literacy and its capabilities. We then discuss a number of ways to use technology as a tool to enrich all aspects of literacy learning. Finally, we identify tools and resources for using technology in teaching literacy to our youngest learners.

VISUAL LITERACY

visual literacy ■

Visual literacy includes (1) viewing, or the ability to comprehend and interpret images and icons, video, photographs, graphs, charts, maps, and any other form of visual content, and (2) visually representing, or the ability to create these visuals. Children in the United States are inundated by visual and auditory media daily. Children from preschool to third grade watch as many as 30 hours of television and online videos in an average week—and often spend additional time playing video and computer games. Though in some cases children's viewing may be excessive, they learn much through viewing and visually representing from a very early age, and doing so can provide support for learning English as a second language (Krashen, 2004). Moreover, many viewing and visually representing experiences are integral parts of teaching literacy throughout the curriculum. Such experiences can help children to view critically as they explore media literacy in film, video, and television as well as literacy in the visual arts and dramatic productions (Cox, 2008). If young children are bombarded with visual and auditory stimuli on a daily basis, the literacy curriculum must be used to teach them how to critically sift through it all, helping them build a foundation of fundamental thinking skills along the way. The following sections deal with viewing and visually representing as they relate to technology.

Viewing

Children should have positive experiences with quality children's films just as they do with quality children's books. Students can be encouraged to respond to films and other video and visual content just as they do to literature, through written responses, drama, discussion, art, and other media forms. Mirroring the "into, through, and beyond" model for guided reading (see Chapter 11), you can provide the necessary instruction for the previewing, viewing, and postviewing phases.

Before viewing a video with students, do the same kinds of "intro" activities that you generally do before presenting a new book. Always watch the video before showing it to students, checking it for appropriateness of theme and vocabulary and reflecting on how the concepts in the video can be extended through discussion. Identify a purpose for viewing and write it on the board, along with several initiating questions for students to keep in mind and to guide their thinking as they view the film.

While viewing a video, occasionally pause it to point out an important occurrence or an especially confusing part. You may want to "think aloud" about how you interpret the clip and to share personal connections you have made. You can then ask for individual reactions from the students as well.

In the postviewing phase, students can talk about the video in small groups or using a "think, pair, share" activity (see Chapter 6). The students' responses should be the basis for planning further discussion, drawing, writing, drama, or other multimedia activities.

Because young people spend so much time watching television and online videos, teachers must help them develop the critical-thinking and media literacy skills necessary to analyze what they are watching. To do this, you can ask students to keep double-response journals about television programs they watch and online video sites they visit frequently, with the summary of a program or video in one column and their critical response to it in the other. See Figure 12.1 for an example of such a journal. Encourage students to consider whether what happens online or on television is different from what, in their experience, happens in real life. Small share groups who have watched the same programs and videos can discuss their reactions. Guide students to use Venn diagrams to contrast original books with their adapted television shows or movies or videos with the same theme or subject. Finally, invite students to watch television and online advertisements and alert them to examples of the following tactics, used mainly by advertisers of products targeted to young children:

- Lots of happy children (friends don't come with the toy)
- Magic (you have to make the plane fly yourself)
- Size distortions (dolls and toy cars are not that large)
- Purposely vague disclaimers (all sold separately; in specially marked packages; batteries not included; some assembly required)
- Testimonials (A popular teen singer uses it . . . [or does he?])

figure 12.1   Sample of a double-response journal.

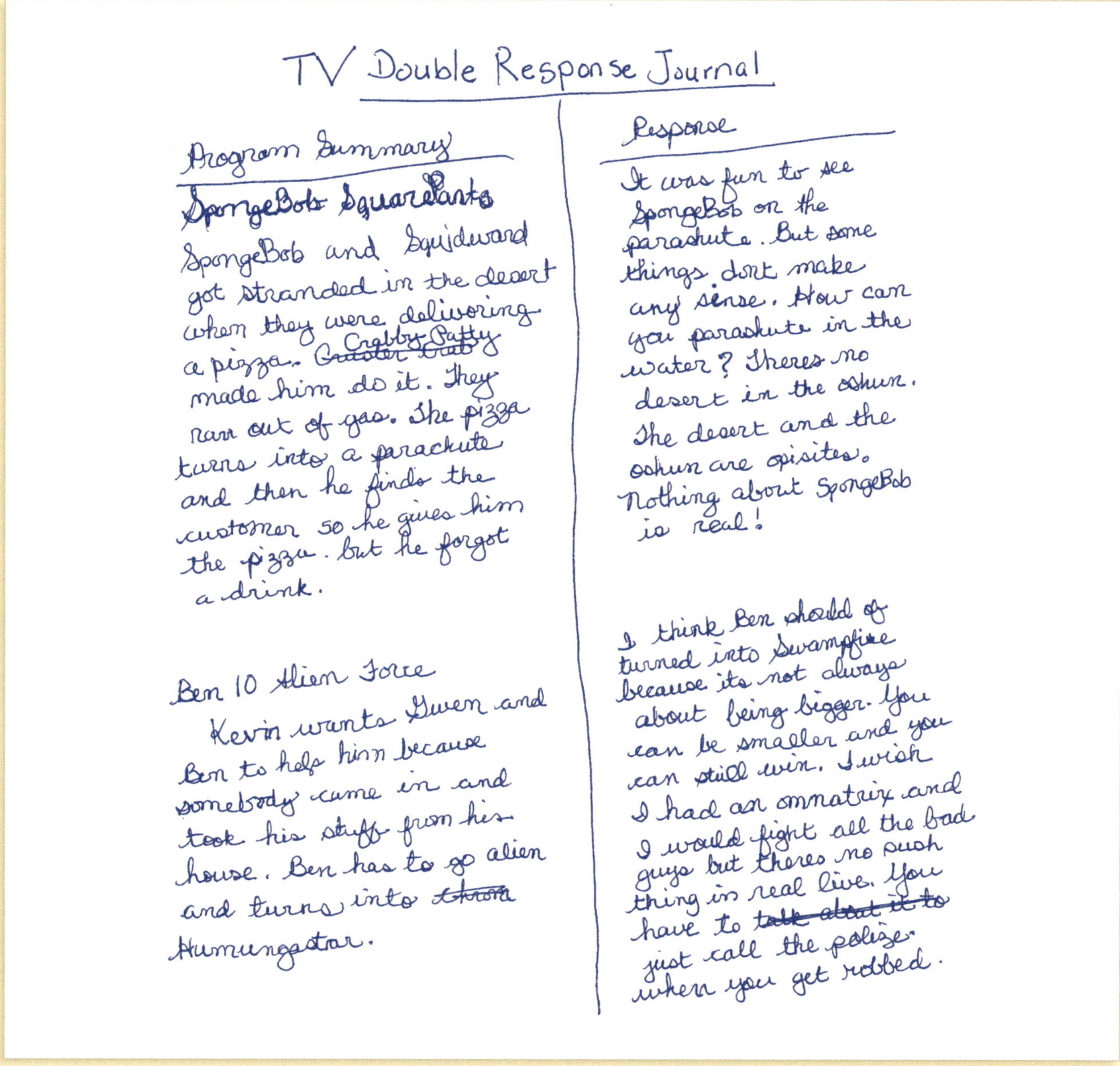

TV Double Response Journal

Program Summary

SpongeBob SquarePants

SpongeBob and Squidward got stranded in the desert when they were delivering a pizza. Crabby Patty made him do it. They ran out of gas. The pizza turns into a parachute and then he finds the customer so he gives him the pizza. But he forgot a drink.

Ben 10 Alien Force

Kevin wants Gwen and Ben to help him because somebody came in and took his stuff from his house. Ben has to go alien and turns into Humungasaur.

Response

It was fun to see SpongeBob on the parachute. But some things don't make any sense. How can you parachute in the water? Theres no desert in the oshun. The desert and the oshun are opisites. Nothing about SpongeBob is real!

I think Ben should of turned into Swampfire because its not always about being bigger. You can be smaller and you can still win. I wish I had an omnatrix and I would fight all the bad guys but theres no such thing in real live. You have to just call the polise when you get robbed.

Information about Drawing
and Graphics Software

*http://graphicssoft.about.com/
od/softwareforkids/*

Creating Multimedia Projects

www.mackiev.com/kidpix/

Visually Representing

Drawing, painting, and other graphic arts have historically been used in the primary classroom to help students visually represent their thoughts and ideas and to extend literacy projects in motivational ways. Indeed, creating visual representations is a crucial skill in the Common Core State Standards. CCSS.ELA-Literacy. CCRA.SL.5 states that students will be able to "Make strategic use of digital media and visual displays of data to express information and enhance understanding of presentations" (NGACBP & CCSSO, 2010, p. 26). Such visual representations can be created via technology. Kid Pix, which is available in a 3-D version, and similar software allows students to create multimedia works of art by pasting, drawing, altering, and animating them with easy-to-use tools. This software is also useful for creating projects, charts, and presentations. In some classrooms, such vehicles for visually representing are combined with the more traditional technologies of video and photography. Information on drawing and graphics software for children can be found at the website in the margin.

Photography, using either a smart phone or digital camera, can enhance young students' written pieces about what they find interesting (their baby sister, a soccer game, a family outing). For younger children, a tutorial for camera usage, including such components as how to hold the phone or camera, appropriate lighting, and composition, will help them feel successful. Young students can also learn how edit, sharpen, and add effects to their photographs when they use software such as Kid Pix, and third-graders and above can use Adobe Photoshop Elements. Once students edit the photographs and write captions about them, they can photo-illustrate their written pieces. The finished pieces can then be published in a slideshow format discussed later in the chapter, on a class website or blog, or in a laminated book to be read to younger classes in the school. In the content areas, students can use photography to take pictures of specific topics of interest (e.g., flowers, cars, food, places in the community, or animals) and then research the topics online. The result can be a photo essay on their chosen area or a topic being studied in science or social studies.

Young students can also create live-action films with a phone or digital video camera, including documentaries of real events as they occur, original dramas, or the telling of stories, or docudramas, which combine real events with fiction.

Creating a Video

A C T I V I T Y

After students have been shown the basics of handling the digital camera, flip camera, or phone, walk them through the following steps for producing media (adapted from Cox, 2008):

1. *Getting an idea.* Encourage students to get ideas for creating their own videos from books they have read, people who have inspired them, or content that fascinates them.

2. *Organizing.* Have students clarify their vision by brainstorming, by using a graphic organizer such as a cluster or web, or by using software such as Kidspiration.

3. *Storyboarding.* A helpful way to plan action is by sketching each image with three, six, or nine sequential squares, and then folding paper accordingly, with tentative narrative or dialogue underneath (see Figure 12.2). The document "Create" (accessible online) provides helpful tips on how to teach students to storyboard as a step in producing video.

4. *Producing.* Students use the storyboard to direct live actors to dramatize the story or event.

figure   12.2   Sample storyboard.

5. *Editing.* Students shoot the story or event in sequence and edit it in the camera. (This step is complex, and younger children are likely to require teacher assistance.)

6. *Presenting.* Students play their video for classmates, other classes, parents, and community members, with posters and e-vites announcing the viewing. The video can then be posted to a class wiki or website.

The website "Picture This" provides in-depth tips for teachers on how to incorporate the making of videos into the curriculum.

Picture This

http://picturethis.sdcoe.net/

TECHNOLOGY APPLICATIONS FOR LITERACY LEARNING

You can choose from numerous ways of incorporating technology in students' literacy learning as they write, read, research, and communicate and collaborate electronically.

Writing Electronically

Word processing and desktop publishing may be among the most widespread uses of computers in literacy because they provide such positive supports to the fundamental literacy skill of writing (International Society for Technology in Education, 2007), making print instantly legible and professional looking, as the students in the opening vignette of this chapter demonstrate. For this to happen, young students should spend some of their computer literacy time learning keyboarding skills and using word processing programs.

Although keyboarding skill is not a prerequisite for writing on the computer, it does help make writing more fluent and less frustrating for young students. Just 10 or 15 minutes' practice a day using keyboarding software, as the students in Ms. Lambating's class do, can help students develop the skills they need. Students are then more easily able to get their ideas down and revise them; moreover, they are motivated to write longer, more detailed pieces because the work is not as slow and painstaking.

Students become fluent writers when they are given many opportunities to practice writing for many purposes. Landauer (1995) captured the potential of computers as tools for writing when he described the computer as a kind of "power tool for the human mind" (p. 137). By removing the fine motor concerns associated with writing in longhand, computers used for writing and composing have the exciting capacity to enhance and extend their users' abilities to create and produce their ideas more fluently.

A variety of computer tools are available, and when used effectively, each tool has the potential to support writing fluency development. Writing also requires repeated reading, and writing electronically provides an interesting alternative interface in which students can experience text. Using the computer, students can compose more rapidly as they construct knowledge by creating informational reports and narratives using word processing programs and computer graphics and creating presentations using applications such as Kid Pix, PowerPoint, Prezi, Photo Story, Sound Slides, or Glogster.com. Expressing knowledge through stories, reports, or slideshows requires thinking about the important ideas involved in a concept and then skimming and scanning through resources to find material that supports the concepts or arguments the students are attempting to make; moreover, such activities provide powerful opportunities to teach the thinking skills that are essential for determining the validity and authority of websites.

Even the youngest students can write electronically. You can take dictation from younger students using word processing programs—another application of the language experience approach (see Chapter 9). Young students can brainstorm ideas and record them on graphic organizers using software such as Kidspiration. Copies of a composition can be printed for the students' revising, and then a final draft can be edited and printed for illustration with clip art or freehand art. Finally, students can experience the process of bookmaking.

Brainstorming and Organizing Software

www.inspiration.com

SurveyMonkey

www.surveymonkey.com

A variety of word processing programs, desktop publishing programs, and graphics packages support students who are involved in a writing workshop (Tompkins, 2014). Some of the most suitable for increasing writing fluency are Kid Works II, Kidwriter Gold, and MacWrite Pro. Students can revise and edit their rough drafts much more easily when they use such word processing programs, and they can then print out neat, final copies without the "busy work" of constant recopying. With desktop publishing, students can create professional-looking newsletters, pamphlets, and even books for the classroom library. Students who are proficient at word processing will be eager to write more prolifically. Indeed, research on word processing and writing shows that students' attitudes toward the fluency and length of writing can be improved, and revising made faster and easier, when students use word processing (Klein & Olson, 2001). With increased practice, increased fluency in writing naturally ensues.

The scenario described in the box on the next page demonstrates what a writing workshop can look like when writing is enhanced with technology (adapted from Barone & Wright, 2009).

Ms. Pfeifer's class writes electronically

Every day, the students in Ms. Pfeifer's class do digital Quick Writes, short extemporaneous drafts, about a topic she provides or one of their own choosing (see Figure 12.3). The Quick Write files are saved in folders for each child. Today, in writing workshop, Ms. Pfeifer asks her students to browse through their folders and to select a Quick Write that they deem worthy to complete, using the writing process. They then use the software program Inspiration to brainstorm and organize their narrative or informational pieces. Students revise their piece with teacher guidance, adding needed details and cutting extraneous information, so as to create a written piece that is concise, precise, and interesting. Revising text is easy because students learn to cut and paste using Inspiration, and also use the built-in thesaurus to select just the right words to express their thoughts more powerfully. After they proofread the pieces themselves and add needed details, the spell and grammar check helps them to edit their work. When they are satisfied with their piece, a peer editor reads, evaluates, and offers feedback electronically, via email or through Ms. Pfeifer's specially designed online survey posted on a free online survey creator. Finally, after several revisions, students pick their favorite font, add art and photographs if appropriate, print a copy of their work, and post it on the classroom writing bulletin board for all to see and admire. Ms. Pfeifer also posts the students' final pieces on the class website and shares them with the whole class via an interactive whiteboard.

figure	12.3

Landon's Quick Write draft, grade 1.

I had a hard time getting to scool today. It rained last night and the road was all floded out. My Granma said were going to be late so I disited to use my super powers. I flied up to Mars and got help from an alien. He was the strongis alien. I took him back to earth with me and we piked up are car and brang it to shool. All the kids wer yelling and high fivng me because I was a hero at lest to my granma.

Creating Multimodal/Hypermedia Projects

Once students have basic keyboarding skills and can find information online, they can use computers to make multimodal/hypermedia projects of their newly discovered information.

Communicating in the twenty-first century will require students to be literate in multiple modes of communication, including the ability to read, produce, and interpret text, graphics, images, sound, and videos. To help students develop **multimodal literacy,** you can assign students multimodal projects, such as digital storytelling. Adams (2009) defines digital storytelling as a technique that "mixes still images (photos or artwork), voice narration, and music, to tell a personal narrative, recount a historical event, or instruct" (p. 35). She states, "Kids are drawn to technology. They also love a good story. Combining the two can be a powerful educational tool" (p. 35).

■ multimodal literacy

Digital Storytelling

A C T I V I T Y

(ADAPTED FROM DEVRIES, 2015)

For this activity, students use a presentation program such as PowerPoint, Soundslides, or Photo Story.

- To create digital stories, students begin by writing a story or informational piece. The text later will be used as the narration for the digitalized version.

- After the text is complete, the author decides how it will be divided into scenes or subtopics and which photo or illustration is needed to depict each scene/subtopic in the script. (For planning, sketches of these illustrations can be used in a storyboard similar to the one in Figure 12.2.)

- Students then find or create photographs, video clips, or illustrations, or use clip art, to complement each page of text. Any illustration that is created by hand is scanned so that it is in digital form.

- Next, the student records the text, using expressions that will convey the mood and action or emphasize an important point and that will captivate the listeners.

- After the text is recorded without any errors, the student is ready to make the "video." Some students may want to enhance their video by adding appropriate music and/or sound effects just like a real movie. The next step is to add a title frame, transitions between frames, and rolling credits, citing all the sources for their clip art, photographs, and so on.

- Finally, the student publishes his work by inviting peers to watch his digital story either online or on an interactive whiteboard.

The creation of podcasts provides another opportunity for students to use technology in engaging ways to achieve literacy goals (Kervin & Mantei, 2010). In creating podcasts, students listen to "anchor" podcasts that are chosen for their high quality as well as engaging content. Students then create their own podcasts using software (for example, GarageBand 3) to record the oral text. To extend the project, students can choose to create "vodcasts" (oral and visual texts) and embed visuals such as photographs, other art, or videos to enhance the meaning of the podcast.

hypermedia projects ■

Hypermedia projects, like multimodal projects, combine text, graphics, audio, and video, but they also include hyperlinks in the presentation. Because the presentation includes links, the complete presentation may not be viewed in a linear sequence. Having students complete hypermedia projects using presentation software is highly engaging. These projects can be used for learning throughout the curriculum as well as for literacy, as students learn to use research, writing composition skills, oral language, and visual representation and to select content (Garthwait, 2001). For example, students can read and discuss informational texts, create a KWL chart, research facts online, plan and write up a series of slides—each containing some information on the topic—add sound and interesting links, and then put all the information together using one of the programs mentioned previously.

Creating such projects can be highly motivational for students, who become engaged in adding colorful backgrounds, different fonts, and even music or voice-over narration. The results are aesthetically pleasing slides that can be displayed on the computer or an interactive whiteboard or printed out and displayed on a bulletin board, or they can be published in book form. See Figure 12.4 for an example with a hyperlink to a video showing large carousels. Moreover, when students create such projects collaboratively, they have participated actively in every facet of literacy learning and acquired new informational content.

A further creative activity involving literacy and technology is guiding students to create their own web pages (Kervin & Mantei, 2010). Software programs and websites such as Weebly and Bravenet help young students create web pages. The website WikiHow introduces easy-to-use web hosts for these students. In creating their own web pages, students can begin with a literacy-based "big question" such as "What makes writing good?" and purposefully design a page that includes links to documents, other web pages, and other media projects such as slide presenta-

Student-created Websites

www.weebly.com

www.bravenet.com/

www.wikihow.com/Create-a-Free-Website-(for-Kids)

Teacher-created Classroom Website

http://classpages.i-s-d.org/grade5/

figure	12.4	Sample hypermedia project on carousels.

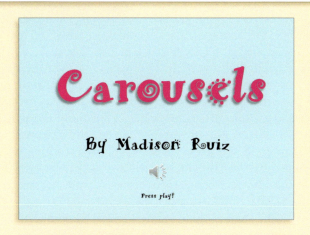

There are lots of kinds of horses on carousels. Some are jumping and some are standing.

There are more animals than horses. They can be tigers or elephants or other animals.

Here is a video of a big carousel. It has two stories.

tions or podcasts that aid users in their understanding of "the big question." For an example of a teacher-created classroom website with student-created video presentations and math projects, visit the website in the margin.

Online Reading and Researching

Although online reading involves some of the same strategies as reading in closed environments, such as book reading, it also requires readers to use other strategies. In fact, the National Institute for Literacy (2008) argues that "technology-handling" skills needed for effective use of technology are analogous to and just as important as concepts of print with printed material. Strategies essential for effective reading of online text include the following:

- having prior knowledge of website structures and online search engines
- self-regulating or directing choices about where to go and in what sequence and how long to spend among the various reading pathways
- understanding and effectively interacting with new kinds of text, including interactive charts, maps, diagrams, and videos, as part of the reading experience (Coiro & Dobler, 2007)

Some of these strategies can be introduced to beginning readers as they are learning how to find information online.

Evaluating websites

The CCSS clearly signal the importance of students' abilities to evaluate the credibility and usefulness of websites. CCSS.ELA-Literacy.CCRA.R.7 requires students "to evaluate content presented in diverse media and formats, including visually and quantitatively, as well as in words" (NGACBP & CCSSO, 2010, p. 10). One way to help young students become more directed in their use of the Internet is to show them how to evaluate websites. Teachers and students can use the Internet as a potent resource for doing fascinating research—one that provides instant access to almost anywhere: museums, libraries, governments, schools, and other places all around the world (Henry, 2006). As we all know, however, not all websites are equally worthwhile. Teachers must distinguish between good and poor websites and help students learn how to select appropriate ones. Harris (2010) provides an effective way to assess websites critically based on their credibility, accuracy, reasonableness, and support. He calls this evaluation technique the CARS Checklist, and it can be adapted for use with young students (see Appendix E). The steps include asking the following questions:

see appendix E

> C: *Credibility.* What is the authority of the author? What are her credentials? Is there evidence that peers have judged the site positively? Does the piece exhibit correct grammar and spelling?
>
> A: *Accuracy.* Is the site current, with updated information? Is the information easy to understand, and is it complete? Does the author acknowledge other viewpoints or possible controversies?
>
> R: *Reasonableness.* Does the author present a fair and objective point of view? Does the author appear concerned with the accuracy of the facts presented or with promoting a point of view?
>
> S: *Support.* Does the author provide documentation for his ideas? Are all sources listed? Are there other resources on this topic with similar information? Are these sites mentioned or linked?

Teach students to evaluate websites by showing them both good and poor websites, according to the preceding criteria, and using a think-aloud approach to demonstrate how they can be judged. After a lesson on discerning fact from opinion in text, you can then apply the same principles to information on websites. Show students how to check websites for currency and to look critically at the author's credentials using child-friendly examples: is a high school student the best source for information about nutrition? Finally, students can compare information in text to that found on the website. Any discrepancies can lead to rich discussion.

Teaching website navigation

Once students have learned to evaluate websites, show them how to navigate efficiently within a site. This will help them develop knowledge of website instructions and get beyond the random clicking and superficial skimming that often occurs when young children read online. Following is an activity to help students navigate websites.

Website Exploration

A C T I V I T Y

(ADAPTED FROM CORNETT, 2010)

Steps for teaching how websites are structured and how to navigate a site include the following:

1. Point out the title of the page and the title of the website in the margin at the top of the window.

2. Model a think-aloud about how to scan menu choices. Hold the mouse pointer over the navigational topic menus that often appear down the left frame or across the top of the window, but don't click them. Use them to help students get a big picture of the information within the site.

3. With the help of students, predict where each of the major links may lead.

4. Explore interactive images, such as animations (images that change as the mouse pointer is held over them), pop-up menus, and scroll bars that may show additional levels of information within the site.

5. Check author and date. Identify who created the site and when it was last updated. Click a homepage button labeled "About This Site" to get this information. If it is not available, consider what this indicates about the site.

6. Try out any electronic supports such as an organizational site map or internal search engine.

7. Decide whether information you need will be found at the site, and if so, explore further. If not, return to search results.

8. If you stay on the site, decide which areas to explore first.

Finding information online

Introducing students to use the Internet as a source of information should be just a different, nonprint way to engage them in the process of constructing meaning and reading critically. Just as teachers must plan, guide instruction, and assess using books and discussions, so must they plan classroom experiences for finding information online with the same strategies and goals in mind. A *WebQuest* is an activity designed to help students locate information on the Internet.

WebQuest

A C T I V I T Y

Use a WebQuest, an Internet-based inquiry activity, to direct students to various online sites that present information on a particular topic. You may design a WebQuest around any of the topics covered in the informational books listed in Appendix A or any other text on a topic in which students have expressed interest.

see appendix A

Note: Because of the dynamic nature of online resources, selected websites may disappear over time. Thus, always offer plenty of sites from which to choose.

- Present students with a compelling problem or question. If you have used a knowledge chart (see Chapter 8) with students when reading the informational text, you and the class can choose questions from the "Questions we have" column that were not answered in the book for the quest.

- Prepare a list of websites that will provide students with information to answer the question/problem.

- Explain that during the quest, students will find information from a number of websites, which they will then need to synthesize.

- Have them record the information in response to the initial question or problem.

- Students then share their findings with the class, and you can lead a discussion about resolving any discrepancies in the information provided by the various sites.

See Figure 12.5 for a sample WebQuest on frogs in conjunction with *Frogs* (Gibbons, 1994). In this example, the class chose the discovery of the life cycle of the frog as their compelling question.

figure   12.5   A WebQuest for grades 2 and 3.

A FROG'S LIFE

INTRODUCTION

Have you ever wondered how a frog goes from an egg to a full-grown jumping animal? You are a famous scientist who is very interested in frogs, and your job is to research the life cycle of a frog. Then you draw pictures of the life cycle of frogs and, finally, make an origami super-frog. Have fun on your mission!

THE TASK

After reading the book *Frogs* by Gail Gibbons, you will work with a group of 2 to 3 people to do the following:

- discover a description of the life cycle of a frog
- create pictures of the 4 stages in a frog's life cycle and label the stages
- make an origami superfrog

RESOURCES

- computer and access to the Internet
- *Frogs,* by Gail Gibbons (1994). New York: Holiday House.
- two blank pieces of paper, one divided into 4 sections
- Internet sites about the life cycle of frogs
- Internet site for making an origami superfrog

PROCESS

Follow these steps to complete your quest:

1. As a class we will read *Frogs,* by Gail Gibbons.

2. I will divide you into groups. With your group, research these sites for information about the life cycle of frogs:

   www.EnchantedLearning.com/subjects/amphibians/Frogprintout.shtml

   www.tooter4kids.com/Frogs/life_cycle_of_frogs.htm

3. Using one of the blank sheets of paper, evaluate the websites to determine whether the information on the sites will be accurate and unbiased by answering these questions:

   - Who created the site? (Is the person an expert in the field or just someone interested in the topic?)

   - What is the purpose of the site? (If the site is created to promote a product, can the same information be found on any other site?)

   - Can the same information be found in classroom library books or on any other site(s)? (Always check "facts" from websites by comparing to other sites or resources.)

(continued)

figure   12.5   Continued.

4. After reading the information, get a blank piece of paper and divide it into 4 equal squares. (*Note:* Students can create text and pictures digitally and present them sequentially in a slide presentation.)

5. In the top left square of your paper, draw a picture of the first stage of a frog's life cycle. Label the stage by writing a sentence(s) about what happens in the first stage.

6. In the top right square of your paper, draw a picture of the second stage of a frog's life cycle. Label the stage by writing a sentence(s) about what happens in the second stage.

7. In the bottom right square of your paper, draw a picture of the third stage of a frog's life cycle. Label the stage by writing a sentence(s) about what happens in the third stage.

8. In the bottom left square of your paper, draw a picture of the fourth and final stage of a frog's life cycle. Label the stage by writing a sentence(s) about what happens in the final stage.

9. Go to this website to play a game about the life cycle of a frog:

   www.sheppardsoftware.com/scienceforkids/life_cycle/frog_lifecycle.htm

10. Make an origami jumping frog by following the directions at the site below:

   www.origami-fun.com/origami-jumping-frog.html

EVALUATION

You will be evaluated by your teacher on the following:

1. Did you find the answers to the three questions in item 3 to evaluate the websites for accuracy and credibility?   YES   NO

2. Are the stages of a frog's life cycle in the correct order?   YES   NO

3. Did you label each stage with the correct information?   YES   NO

4. Did you demonstrate a knowledge of a frog's life cycle?   YES   NO

5. Did you work cooperatively with members of the group?   YES   NO

6. Is your handwriting legible?   YES   NO

7. Did you follow all directions?   YES   NO

CONCLUSION

Congratulations, scientist!! You have completed your assignment successfully. Have fun playing with your origami jumping frog!

Created by Meghan Hickey, Fall 2000 as an independent study project at Bowling Green State University, Bowling Green, Ohio. This WebQuest is part of the CRC Internet Resources WebQuest Children's Literature web page at www.bgsu.edu/colleges/library/crc/page38731.html

Communicating and Collaborating in Online Communities

With increasing access to the Internet, online discussions are becoming more common as a means for teachers to encourage written communication and learner engagement (Hamilton & Cherniavsky, 2006). Effective communication and collaboration between students using technology is a key skill needed to achieve the Common Core State Standards. CCSS.ELA-Literacy.CCRA.W.6 states that students will be able to "Use technology, including the Internet, to produce and publish writing and to interact and collaborate with others" (p. 18). Meeting the needs of almost any context and user, digital communications are available in many formats, including email messages and texting, message board discussions, wikis, blogs, and social networking sites. Wikis and blogs, in particular, are now finding their way into elementary classrooms more frequently. They require no knowledge of programming, and they are simple to set up using free software with easy-to-use templates. They have the added bonus of being accessible to anyone anywhere in the world.

Figure 12.6 shows the similarities and differences between wikis and blogs so you can make decisions about the relative usefulness of each for your instructional purposes.

Wikis

A wiki is a useful collaborative writing tool—a website where the pages can be changed and instantly published using only a web browser. Pages are automatically created and linked to one another. The uses for K–3 classrooms, for both the teacher and the students, include the following:

FOR TEACHERS:

1. **Class activities.** The teacher can inform families about class activities by creating a calendar of events, and upload newsletters and circulars that often get lost in backpacks.

figure	12.6	Comparing a wiki and a blog.

WIKI	BLOG
A group of interlinked pages appears, each with its own authorship.	Distinct, dated entries are made of news, commentary, notes, or personal reflections.
Suited for collaborative writing; many children can edit each piece.	Suited more for individual authoring; it can also be collaborative.
Wikis are written according to content or any desired order.	Written in reverse chronological order; newest entry is at top.
Children can edit the posts of others.	Only the blogger can edit his or her own post.
Most entries are anonymous.	Usually children sign their names after each entry.
More like a discussion board—others can "talk" about an entry.	Others, such as teacher or peers, can comment on entries—even from a distance.
Previous versions of a post can be saved and retrieved in case of a mistake.	Blogs have no automatic saving function of previous posts.

2. **Organizing events.** Members of a faculty committee can work together remotely on the planning of events such as book fairs or sports events.

3. **Curriculum planning.** Worksheets, lesson plans, units, and links to resources can all be shared on a wiki.

FOR STUDENTS:

1. **Whole class projects.** Students can each create a certain number of pages related to a research project and link those pages to their classmates' work.

2. **Collaborative writing.** Students can work together to create a story or information piece.

3. **Pen pals.** Students can connect to classes in China or India on an international project or simply write to individual pen pals from other countries or states and share information about their culture, history, geography, and climate.

4. **Group projects.** Small groups of students can collaborate on reports and presentations without having to be physically present.

You can find more information about setting up a wiki by searching for "setting up a class wiki."

Blogs

A blog, by contrast, comes from a combining of the terms "web" and "log." A blog is an online journal that may contain personal reflections or comments, book reviews, and often hyperlinks or other websites provided by the author. In simplest terms, a blog is an online diary, posted so that readers across the globe may read and respond to what the blogger has to say. To begin classroom blogging, two good sites are Kidblog and Edublogs; they provide free blogs for teachers and students with helpful video tutorials.

A blog is perhaps one of the best online tools for encouraging students to express themselves in written form. Blogs provide a unique space for sharing personal opinions, where online communities can converse with one another about any conceivable topic. Often, students dislike writing because it is such a solitary pursuit; the interactive nature of blogging creates enthusiasm for communicating in written form, because it closely resembles a written conversation—with immediate feedback—unlike written composition, with its usual time lag. Also, blogs can give students an understanding of the meaning of personal voice. As students explore their own thinking and learning, their distinctive written voices tend to emerge. As their own voices emerge, the conversation and the thinking behind it become richer. Finally, just as a blog is an excellent way to motivate students to write, it also provides motivation for revising and editing: many others may read and respond to the student's musings. A worldwide audience is an unparalleled motivator for students to try to do their most polished and professional work.

Blogs can also develop higher-order thinking (Zawilinski, 2009). As online readers gather information to solve a problem, they often need to analyze information, critically evaluate, synthesize content across multiple texts, and communicate with others using blogs, email, wikis, or other communication vehicles (Leu, 2007). Also, although

WWW

Blog Setup Sites

www.kidblog.org

http://edublogs.org/

Used effectively, the Internet provides access to museums, libraries, schools, and other places all around the world.

blogs are often used to report classroom news, to showcase writing or art projects, or to respond to literature, special *mirror blogs* allow students to reflect on their thinking or about lessons or content that have been introduced.

The entire class can use a blog to discuss a text they are reading, or students can post entries on their individual blogs about their interests and outside reading. Other students can visit these posts to gather ideas for new texts to read and to discover new online resources that can provide information about the text and the author. As students gather and share online information about a text or topic, they must synthesize various resources, including other classmates' posts. Blogs can be used for the following purposes:

1. *Autobiographical writing.* Students share their personal thoughts in diary or journal format.
2. *Interactive journals.* Students write their thoughts and ideas or respond to the teacher's prompts.
3. *Book reviews.* Students post comments about a book the whole class, or another class in another school, is reading.
4. *Expressive writing.* Students post their prose or poetry and/or constructively critique each other's work.
5. *Digital portfolios.* Students record a body or term of written work by uploading all their documents and images.
6. *Multimedia presentations.* Students add images and sound to their blog entries (Kajder & Bull, 2003).

Interactive Reading: E-Books

Reading fluency and engagement can be enhanced in an enjoyable social context using paired reading—with students doing several readings of the same text and offering feedback to one another. E-books can play a similar role, and they may be instrumental in improving automatic word recognition and providing a "digital language experience approach" that reinforces fluency and the link between written and oral language (Labbo, Eakle, & Montero, 2002).

Many e-books offer students the ability to self-select the amount of assistance they want, thus increasing individual control over the learning environment as they choose for themselves where and when they need help (Larson, 2008). For example, when students come to a word or phrase they do not know and provide a definition, they can click the text to have the computer read it for them, removing the burden of decoding and figuring out the meaning of an unknown word, allowing for more fluent reading on subsequent attempts. Ultimately, students have more energy to consider the meaning of—and to reap enjoyment from—the text.

A further use of e-books is to help you differentiate instruction and provide a wider range of opportunities for all students to interact with text. Children develop literacy skills at their own rate, in their own time frames. Most teachers deal with students on many different developmental reading levels. While the same level of basal reader is often used to teach all the students in a class, you can benefit from e-books as valuable alternative resources to engage students in successful reading at all levels.

Although the features offered by e-books vary, almost all contain audio and graphic animations that allow the characters to talk and seemingly come to life through the use of "hotspots" that produce animation, sound effects, or other features when a child clicks them. Most also invite students to highlight an unfa-

Reading and writing workshops and technology

The inclusion of technology can greatly enhance reading and workshops. Tablet computers are especially useful for streamlining reading workshop tasks and making them more authentic. According to Erin Klein (see the marginal website), class sets of iPads or other tablets can be used for "just in time reading responses" while students are engaged in independent reading. Writing workshop can also be facilitated by using an app such as Padlet, in which students can publicly post their progress through the writing process. Then you can move students' postings to create groups of students in the same writing stage so to aid peer coaching and editing. Apps such as Answer Pad turn tablet computers and smart phones into clickers, allowing you to formatively assess literacy knowledge and skills during reading workshop minlessons. For more information on using technology in reading and writing workshops, visit Erin Klein's website.

Reading and writing workshops also can be enhanced through the use of interactive whiteboards, smart TVs, and document readers. Instead of traditional writing surfaces using chalk or colored markers, you can now use your computer to connect with students for instruction that allows everyone to participate. These devices are especially useful because they can project an image of the object being studied (e.g., a plant, math manipulatives) or a piece of student writing, without the necessity of making photocopies or transparencies. In addition, you (or the student) can mark directly on the piece of text (e.g., a piece of student writing, or a photocopied article or story) in order to model a target skill. Thus, you can easily model text annotation and text revision using such devices, and can scan the image under the reader for later use—to post on a class website or embed in a PowerPoint presentation. For ideas on how to use a document reader in the elementary classroom, see the website in the margin.

miliar phrase or listen to a reader pronounce a word for them (Lefever-Davis & Pearman, 2005). Some e-storybooks read the entire book aloud for students, providing an individualized read-aloud with which the student can track along, using the mouse. Use caution, though, in selecting e-books, as some hotspots may be distracting and actually mitigate the effectiveness of the e-book experience (Zucker, Moody, & McKenna, 2009). Also, choose e-books that target students' emerging literacy needs, such as decoding and questioning (Roskos, Brueck, & Widman, 2009).

WWW

Technology in Reading and Writing Workshops

www.kleinspiration.com

Document Readers

www.edtechnetwork.com/ document_cameras.html

Choosing Technology Applications

As we have explored throughout this chapter, technology offers great potential to enhance literacy instruction. Software programs and technology-supported learning activities can promote deep understanding when they build on students' prior knowledge and permit learners to control their own learning. Such tools can also motivate students to engage in extensive reading and writing and help them acquire new vocabulary by communicating with others online (Cummins, Brown, & Sayers, 2007). However, technology should *not* be used merely for its own sake, simply because it is *there*, nor is technology always the best tool for every classroom literacy activity. Any technology use should directly support the literacy goals that you have already established. Moreover, you must be familiar with available software programs and know how to integrate them effectively with the currently used literacy curriculum. Finally, any software used must be developmentally appropriate in order for it to

An interactive whiteboard can be used in a myriad of ways to engage and motivate learners.

Reviews of Educational
Software

www.superkids.com

positively impact students' learning. As the National Association for the Education of Young Children (2012) cautions, "With a focus on technology and interactive media as tools—not as ends in and of themselves—teachers can avoid the passive and potentially harmful use of noninteractive, linear screen media that is inappropriate in early childhood settings" (p. 8). Reviews of educational software are available online at the site listed in the margin. Additionally, we suggest that you ask the following questions when choosing technology applications (adapted from Labbo, Leu, & Kinzer, 2003):

- Does it serve the intended purpose? For example, if it claims to improve fluency, can you see that students' fluency is actually improving?
- Can students use it independently, or will you need to work with them to facilitate?
- Are there so many sight and sound distractions that students will become overstimulated and lose the literacy focus?
- Does it offer students an opportunity for free choice? (This can be part of the motivation for using technology.)
- Does it use humor? Children tend to prefer these programs and use them more frequently.
- Does it align with literacy goals, district benchmarks, and state or national standards for literacy?
- Does it address students' individual literacy needs?
- Does it contribute to an overall unit theme or project?

see appendix E

See Appendix E for a form for evaluating technology applications based on this list.

TECHNOLOGY AND ENGLISH LEARNERS

english learners need to have access to the latest technology and be taught to use it. Indeed, the new California English Language Development (CA ELD) Standards mandate that these students be technologically adept. English learners comprise a population for which technology can be an especially helpful tool for learning both content and English language skills. The beauty of technology is that it can be made equally accessible to *every* learner, much to the surprise of some teachers who may believe that English learners are "too busy learning English and content material to be receptive to adding bells and whistles," as one teacher recently shared with us.

While teachers must take into account the background knowledge of all students when introducing technology, it can provide much-needed support in composing text, vocabulary building, reading comprehension, and a myriad of other literacy-related skills that English learners may need. Recent research focusing on the attitude of English learners toward learning as a result of the use of technology has been promising. In traditional classrooms, English learners often are unable to follow grade-level curriculum and participate fully in learning for two or three years after starting to acquire English. As a result, such students often receive rote instruction addressing low-level skills, such as phonics, vocabulary acquisition, and word pronunciation (LeLoup & Ponterio, 2003). Alternatively, the Internet can give recently arrived immigrant students, who may have high levels of previous schooling, access to texts in the primary language. In many cases, this allows students to remain on grade level in the content areas while they acquire English skills.

In addition, a study by Meskill & Mossop (2000) shows encouraging patterns of engagement and investment in learning with the use of technology-supported instruction. English learners in the classrooms they observed were able to participate in classroom activities to the full extent of their intelligence and imagination:

> [The students'] finished work, whether a word-processed, desk-top published document, an animated story, a multimedia presentation . . . was consistently a source of great pride and, among peers and family members, great admiration. . . . Learners' achievements extended from moment-to-moment successes in editing their work or making decisions to demonstrating to the larger school and community what they could do with technology. . . . The ESOL children became adept at using technology in their classes and school. (p. 589)

The website Colorín Colorado provides helpful tips on teaching English learners to use technology and lists technology tools that are especially useful for helping English learners gain access to core content and English.

Technology Tips for English Learners
www.colorincolorado.org/educators/technology/ells

TECHNOLOGY AND STUDENTS WITH SPECIAL NEEDS

For students with physical or learning disabilities, technology can be a helpful learning aid. Tools such as eye-gaze devices, which allow students with physical challenges to compose text, do research, and communicate with others, and closed-captioning devices and videoconferencing for individuals who are hearing impaired offer access to content and allow students with special needs to be increasingly included in mainstream classrooms (Hayes, 2013). Technology can provide much-needed support for the learning of literacy skills by these students. E-books with text-to-speech capabilities, speech recognition software such as Dragon NaturallySpeaking, and Livescribe Smartpens, which record speech and writing, support the literacy needs of students with special needs in both special education and mainstream classrooms.

Tools for Transcription
www.nuance.com/dragon/index.htm
www.livescribe.com/en-us/solutions/learningdisabilities/

TEACHER PROFESSIONAL DEVELOPMENT

Teachers are offered a myriad of opportunities for learning about how technology can support their teaching of literacy. Websites such as The Teaching Channel and Read, Write, Think offer lesson plans and videos of effective literacy teaching. Especially exciting are the possibilities of free MOOCs (massive open online courses) for teachers, offering sustained high-quality instruction in literacy pedagogy that is rarely offered through in-service programs available at school sites.

The Teaching Channel
www.teachingchannel.org

Read, Write, Think
www.readwritethink.org/professional-development/

SUMMARY

When integrated into a balanced and comprehensive early literacy program that includes plenty of high-quality literature to foster reading and writing enjoyment, technology can be a powerful resource for teachers. Word processing programs and multimedia tools can be used to energize writing workshops, while the Internet provides a plethora of ways to research and critically read about almost any topic students can imagine. Online communities such as blogs and wikis can be used to connect learners to other readers and writers across the globe, both as live audiences and as learning resources. Literacy skills such as fluency and reading rate can be enhanced through the introduction of e-books and programs that give learners autonomy over the amount of help they need. Carefully chosen technology applications can offer teachers a high level of differentiated instruction for learners and the tools to engage them in all facets of literacy. All learners, including English learners and students with special needs, can benefit from these technologies. Finally, pedagogy resources, such as tablet computers, can make the delivery of instruction more interactive and the creation of new literacy activities and assessments easier.

Although nothing will ever replace excellent explicit instruction from an adept and dedicated teacher, technological tools can be valuable resources in the early elementary classroom, if chosen wisely and integrated effectively into the literacy curriculum. Perhaps the best reason to use technology to increase literacy skills is the high level of motivation and investment that students bring to literacy tasks completed using technology. Its use in the primary classroom can complement and extend traditional literacy learning and enhance student engagement while helping to prepare students for life in the twenty-first century.

questions FOR JOURNAL WRITING AND DISCUSSION

1. If you were given $1,000 to spend on classroom materials or resources, would you buy technology or spend it in other ways? Justify your response by comparing how you might use technology with how you would use other types of materials (e.g., book sets) or resources (individual whiteboards).

2. Consider the educational possibilities of technologies other than computers, such as digital cameras, tablets, video cameras, and smart phones. How might you use these technologies to enhance your students' literacy development?

3. If you had a recently arrived English learner in your classroom, how would you use technology to (a) make your content more accessible for your English learner, (b) help your English learner learn English?

4. Compare a writing workshop conducted with word processing software and a writing workshop without such resources. List five ways that word processing software can make writing more appealing for students. Finally, create a written argument addressed to a school board with the goal of convincing them that computers and word processing software are necessary for the success of your writing program.

suggestions FOR PROJECTS AND FIELD ACTIVITIES

1. Try out a popular educational software program, such as Kidspiration, according to the instructions. Create your own project. Take notes about what students will need to know about using the program. Share your project with students in a classroom as a model on which they can base their own projects.

2. Visit a library media center and ask to preview several children's films for your present or future grade level. Start a resource file of film titles that you feel would enhance the literacy curriculum for that grade level. Alternatively, research various online video sites and preview clips to create a list of titles.

3. Browse online sites created specifically for using technology to scaffold instruction for English learners and to help them learn English. Take notes on ideas that would be useful for your own classroom.

4. Create an online scavenger hunt for students at a specific grade level, based on a topic the students may study, such as spiders. Try it out with students of that grade and report the results back to your class.

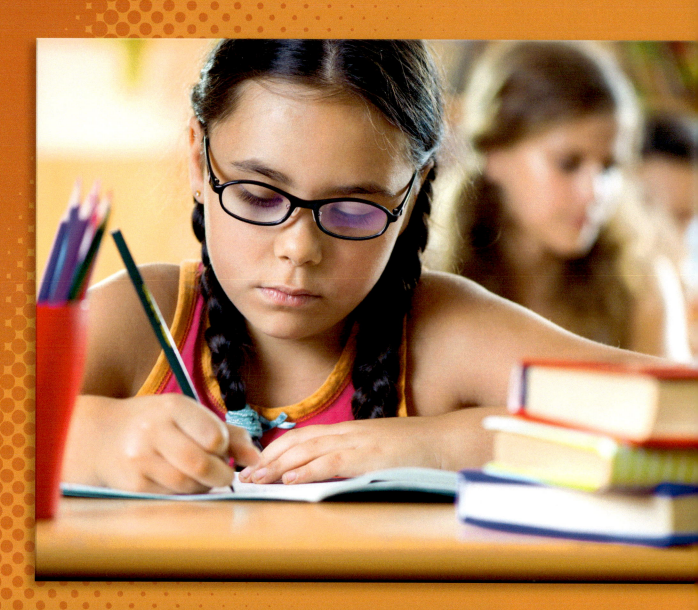

INFORMING INSTRUCTION

focus questions

What are the appropriate types of assessment for early literacy?

How can literacy assessment be used to inform instruction?

How does a balance of formal and informal assessment offer a more accurate picture of progress in literacy?

How can assessment be aligned with state standards?

milio and his first-grade teacher, Mr. Steel, are discussing which version of his illustrated report to put in his *showcase portfolio*—his "favorite" or the one he proudly considers his "best." During this conference, the child's teacher takes *anecdotal notes* or written observations to guide Emilio in the self-assessment and reflection he will be expected to attach to his report. In an upcoming end-of-year parent–teacher conference, Mr. Steel and Emilio will show the boy's parents his showcase portfolio, filled with samples of Emilio's written work and Emilio's personal reflections about it. Mr. Steel will also share with the parents the teacher *observational portfolio* he has compiled over the past few months to show Emilio's literacy progress. By explaining some informal assessment data he has collected, Mr. Steel will be able to inform Emilio's parents of his current reading and comprehension levels, which phonics elements he has mastered, and which he still needs help with; Mr. Steel will suggest that they can also help reinforce these at home. Finally, Mr. Steel gathers data from a standardized reading test that compares Emilio's reading with that of other students his age. The assessment device, administered in the fall and the spring, also shows numerically how much Emilio has grown as a reader over the school year. Mr. Steel will end the parent–teacher conference by offering to lend several books at Emilio's independent reading level, based on a *reading interest inventory* he recently administered to discover the child's reading preferences.

INTRODUCTION

ngoing assessment of literacy development refers to the use of various instruments, daily observation, and many work samples to measure progress. It also refers to the ongoing analysis of the data from these instruments and observations concerning individuals, small groups, and the entire class so that the teacher can customize instruction and, when necessary, plan appropriate interventions. The assessment in Mr. Steel's classroom is ongoing and dynamic; he bases all of his instructional decisions on it. In an effective primary classroom such as his, all instruction is based on information acquired through valid assessment procedures. Moreover, students in the class, like Emilio, recognize their own strengths and limitations and are encouraged to use strategies designed to increase their literacy competence. Finally, in a strong primary classroom, the teacher uses and interprets the results from a variety of informal and formal assessment tools and effectively communicates those results to students, their parents or caregivers, and relevant school personnel. Students know how well they are doing, and so does everyone who cares about them.

WHY ASSESS?

ssessment is more than merely gathering a range of information about a child's literacy progress; it must be data collection with a distinct instructional purpose (Salvia & Yesseldyke, 2000). Effective use of classroom-based assessments depends on the teacher's ability to select assessments based on instructional goals, frequent and systematic collection and analysis of data, and immediate instructional interventions based on analysis of that data (Risko & Walker-Dahlhouse, 2010). The major reason to spend precious classroom time assessing the competencies students are displaying is to determine how well they are progressing with respect to a specific aspect of learning; for example: What blends can this student recognize? How well can she retell a story? What is her attitude toward writing (Sulzby, 1990)? Equally important is to adapt instruction based on assessment that shows that learning is not taking place. Other information that can be gained from literacy-related assessments includes the following (Cheek, Flippo, & Lindsey, 1997):

- determining a child's overall reading ability
- examining a child's ability to use graphophonic, semantic, and syntactic cues in reading
- analyzing a child's ability to construct meaning from text
- determining a child's experiential background for content-area material
- determining a child's overall literacy strengths and needs

This basic information can then be used for classroom program planning and decision making, to ensure that classroom instruction and activities are responsive to and appropriate for the current class level. Assessment information indicates who might benefit from differentiation or need more academic challenge (Afflerbach, 2007).

A second major reason for assessment is to help students take ownership of their learning by allowing them to see how they are doing and to establish equal partnership in fostering literacy growth. By keeping individual progress charts and writing samples over time, for example, students can observe their own growth, begin to set their own goals, and self-assess these personal goals. This leads to a potent feeling of intrinsic accomplishment. When young students are taught to think about and reflect on their own learning, they become more active partners in the whole endeavor.

Finally, it is important to keep careful progress records for the class as well as each individual student to demonstrate to other school personnel, parents, and the outside community that teachers are doing an effective job teaching children to read and write. The education of children has always been on local, statewide, and national political agendas, perhaps because every community member has been through the school system and is, therefore, a self-proclaimed "expert" on all subjects related to schools. Hence, teachers must inform others and document progress, especially when new programs and ideas are being initiated.

PRINCIPLES OF ASSESSMENT

effective teaching requires a reciprocal, synergistic relationship between assessment and teaching. In other words, teaching and assessing should continually inform one another. The teacher finds out what needs to be assessed by observing lessons; reciprocally, the assessment tells the teacher what to teach or, in some cases, reteach. For example, a first-grade class has been discussing the difference between "telling" and "asking" or between a statement and a question. An observer examining the teacher's lesson plans on the sentence activities should be able to expect that the ending assessment for the lessons will be very closely aligned with the teacher's learning objectives for those lessons.

Following is a discussion of other assessment principles that can help you determine if your assessment plan will complement your instruction (adapted from Cooper, 1997).

The Core of Assessment Is Daily Observation

Teachers who frequently observe and take anecdotal notes on each aspect of literacy development know much more about the status of their students than can be obtained from any formal testing, no matter how reliable the testing is purported to be. Assessment should be a daily event, occurring every time the student reads and writes. Through observing patterns of growth over time, you are in an ideal position to get a clear picture of how each student is progressing.

Students Are Actively Engaged in the Assessment Process

Although young children cannot be involved in every aspect of literacy assessment, sometimes asking for input when evaluating their work can be a key factor in encouraging students to take charge of their own learning and inviting ownership of their successes. Because teaching and learning are ideally collaborative process-es, you do not want students to view assessment as an uncomfortable practice that you "do" to them. On the other hand, when you and the students work and think together, assessment becomes a shared responsibility, with students participating enthusiastically as team players in their own learning.

Assessment Takes Many Different Forms

standardized test ■

Use different types of assessment tools for different purposes to ensure that each child's holistic literacy progress is measured. For example, writing samples, check-lists about retellings of stories, and anecdotal notes give insights that are not scientific but based solely on your judgment. Although data gathered with these tools are essential in effective planning and decision making, you also need **stan-dardized test** results that have accepted statistical reliability and validity (i.e., they consistently measure what they claim to be measuring). Standardized assessments are generally developed by a publisher or by the school district to allow an objec-tive determination of whether grade-level standards developed by the district or state have been met. To get a truly multidimensional overview of a child's perfor-mance in any aspect of literacy, you need to analyze the data from both sources.

Assessment Avoids Cultural Bias

Children from various cultures, linguistic groups, and backgrounds may have dif-ferent language issues as well as varied experiences and styles of learning. When planning assessment procedures, and particularly when interpreting and reporting them to others, consider these factors judiciously.

An example of the importance of considering cultural bias can be found in the case of a little girl in a second-grade class in the Virgin Islands who was diagnosed with a severe reading disability. Upon examining the test, her perceptive teach-er realized that the student was certainly *not* reading-disabled. She had scored poorly because she had not known many vocabulary words, such as *chimney* and *caboose*—words that have little meaning for residents of a tiny tropical island!

Assessment should mainly attempt to determine what students *can* do—not what they *cannot* do. When you understand the literacy abilities of your learn-ers, it becomes much easier to decide which new literacy experiences to offer to help them develop further. Not only is this a more constructive way of looking at learning, but students benefit in other crucial ways. Students simply progress more readily in an atmosphere where mistakes are viewed as ways to learn rather than failures to be avoided at all cost.

Traditional summative biannual reading achievement tests, conducted in whole-class settings, may encounter problems when attempting to glean any use-ful information about the literacy skills of students for whom English is a second language. Even the academic language used in the instructions, for example, may cause confusion and render the test results invalid. To remedy this problem, some researchers suggest that either the test or test procedures be modified to provide increased accessibility to what the instrument is actually testing (Lindholm-Leary & Borsato, 2006), or that teachers incorporate informal assessments that are adaptable to students who are culturally and linguistic diverse (Spinelli, 2008). Such tests could include simplified instructional language or easier syntax, with perhaps shorter sentences and fewer clauses. Another possible strategy would be to translate the assessment into the child's home language or give the student more time to complete the test. Because such accommodations may not always be viable, balance the questionable test scores by supplementing them with classroom observations and work samples to provide more accurate conclusions about the child's literacy.

TYPES OF ASSESSMENT

You have at your disposal an almost overwhelming array of instruments to use as part of the assessment process. Many of these instruments blend naturally into instruction; others provide a separate means to assess literacy progress, either formally or informally. Because so many assessment tools are available, it is impossible to discuss each one in this chapter. Therefore, a sampling of some of the most pervasive assessment devices that are compatible with a balanced early literacy program are explored here. An example of a comprehensive framework for guiding the assessment process is presented in Figure 13.1.

Assessment can be thought of as informal or formal. **Formal assessments** use standardized tests that are given under controlled conditions so that groups with similar backgrounds can be compared primarily for purposes of program evaluation. **Informal assessments** yield specific information that teachers can use to guide their teaching. Common informal instruments include anecdotal records, checklists, rubrics, portfolios, informal reading inventories, and running records.

- formal assessments

- informal assessments

Assessment can also be thought of as formative or summative. **Formative assessment,** sometimes referred to as assessment *for* learning, refers to the process of ongoing, usually informal, data gathering during instruction that both informs and guides teachers as they make instructional decisions; listening for miscues as a student reads and taking anecdotal notes or making a checklist of all students who can generate rhyming words are examples of formative assessment. Formative assessment is closely related to the ongoing direct assessment measures that teachers use; it is also referred to as *classroom assessment* (although not all forms of classroom assessment are formative). Information from formative assessment helps teachers provide the level of quality feedback learners need and to quickly adjust their instruction if learning is not taking place.

- formative assessment

Summative assessment, sometimes referred to as assessment *of* learning and usually more formal, refers to the evaluative assessment or tests that result in a grade or ranking (e.g., a final unit test, end-of-chapter test, weekly spelling test, or standardized achievement test). Large-scale, high-stakes testing that is prominent in most schools today is also an example of summative assessment. Summative assessments are generally more comprehensive than formative assessments and are designed to include a degree of objectivity and accountability. I (Nancy Cecil) offer the following analogy from my own life to describe the difference between formative and summative assessment: When I write a chapter for this text, I subjectively include what I think is appropriate and then reread it and revise it; that is like *formative* assessment. When the editor and reviewers read what I have written, they compare what I have written with their objective standards for what they think the chapter should contain relative to other books they have read or published; this process is analogous to *summative* assessment.

- summative assessment

| figure | 13.1 | A framework for guiding the assessment process. |

WHAT DO I WANT TO KNOW?	HOW AM I GOING TO FIND OUT?		
	Informal		Formal
	Formative	Summative	
Concepts about print	Observations of book handling & tracking	Checklist of orthographic knowledge	M. Clay's "Concepts About Print"
Phonemic awareness	Observation of songs, rhymes, repetitions Word games	Checklist of phonemic awareness skills	Standardized tests (Torgeson's "Test of Phonemic Awareness")
Phonics	IRI Observation of ability to generate/identify sound–letter relationships	Running records Shared reading	Miscue analysis Botel phonics survey
Oral reading (fluency)	One-to-one observation Paired reading	Mediated reading Anecdotal notes Running records	DIBELS IRI Miscue analysis
Spelling	Writing samples Pretests	Daily writing Journals	Weekly tests Dictations
Reading comprehension	Retellings QARs Discussions	Paraphrasing Summarizing Class contributions Cloze tests	Standardized tests PARCC, SBAC
Vocabulary	Writing samples Journals Oral discussions	Formal writing Essays	Word Writing CAFÉ PARCC, SBAC Standardized tests
Writing	Writing samples Journals Quickwrites	Formal writing Writing samples Daily work Journals	PARCC, SBAC Rubrics (scaled scores) Editing checklist
Reading/writing attitudes	Questionnaire Number of books read/written	Conferences Interest inventories Reading response journals	
Student views of own literacy	Books chosen Attitude survey Reading survey	Portfolio choices Reflection log Dialogue journals	Self-reports Interviews

Most of the techniques discussed in the rest of this chapter can be used easily on the basis of the information given; others require reviewing an examiner's handbook. Appropriate references are given for those that require more detailed study, and samples of others are presented in Appendices D and E.

see appendix D
see appendix E

Three basic types of formative assessments are used in primary classrooms, and each offers a unique perspective for a balanced early literacy program: skills-based assessment, curriculum-based assessment, and process-oriented assessment.

Skills-Based Assessment

Skills-based assessment focuses on the use of tests to measure reading and spelling skills and subskills. These tests are administered by the teacher or reading specialist and sometimes provide numerical scores that represent a child's rank relative to the performance of other students at the same age or grade. The data obtained from these tests can be, but are not always, related to the content of instruction. Examples of skills-based assessments would be systematic appraisals of a child's ability to name letters, the child's knowledge of concepts of print, or the number of vocabulary words the student knows compared with others his age.

■ skills-based assessment

Curriculum-Based Assessment

Curriculum-based assessment ties evaluation directly to the teacher's literacy curriculum to identify instructional needs and to determine what is needed for a student to "master" a concept. Such assessment may include criterion-based assessment, in which the child's performance is compared against standards deemed appropriate for mastery in a particular area. Scores from such a tool typically offer a number or percentage for the amount of material each student has mastered. These tools are usually administered in the classroom using items and materials derived from the curriculum. Examples of curriculum-based assessment include asking a student to read a passage aloud from the child's basal reader and counting the number of words read correctly per minute, or culminating a thematic unit on dinosaurs by asking students to quickly write down (or tell, for preliterate children) everything they know about dinosaurs.

■ curriculum-based assessment

Process-Oriented Assessment

Process-oriented assessment refers to a teacher's observations of the child's actual reading and writing abilities. Measures used for such assessment are informal and subjective and are, therefore, usually supplemented by norm-referenced testing that objectively compares a student with others of the same age or grade. In process-oriented assessment, the literacy behavior being examined is documented in the learning context in which it normally occurs. For example, a process-oriented assessment tool could be an informal checklist designed by the teacher to answer such questions as, "Are the child's letters in the proper sequence?" or "Can the student spell words correctly in isolation but not in context?" The assessment takes place while the student does a self-selected writing task, such as writing in a journal (see Chapter 9). An *informal reading inventory* (to be discussed later in this chapter) with miscue analyses also falls under this category.

■ process-oriented assessment

FORMAL ASSESSMENT PROCEDURES

Using formal assessment devices in the classroom has both advantages and disadvantages. Although formal group tests can be used broadly to compare a

An assessment program

Mr. Steel, the teacher we met at the beginning of this chapter, has created an assessment program that incorporates data from a wide variety of assessment tools to evaluate the literacy growth of Emilio and the other students in his class. Those tools are listed here and are further discussed in this chapter.

- Twice a year the students take a norm-referenced achievement test called the *Stanford Achievement Test* (The Psychological Corporation) to allow Mr. Steel to obtain general literacy information about his class and an indication of how well the students in his school are doing compared with other students of the same age and grade across the nation. (Although Mr. Steel's school uses the Stanford test, many schools have implemented other tests, including tests developed by SMARTER Balanced Test Assessment Consortium (SBAC) or Partnership for Assessment of Readiness for College and Careers (PARCC), assessments that are aligned with the CCSS.)

- At the beginning of the year, students are given an *informal reading inventory (IRI)* to evaluate each student's reading progress, determine at which level she is reading, and identify specific strengths and needs in comprehension and decoding (process-oriented assessment).

- Once a week, Mr. Steel listens to each student read from basal readers and takes *running records* to check their reading fluency (curriculum-based assessment).

- Every day Mr. Steel observes each student and takes *anecdotal notes* monitoring anything he considers significant in their struggles, their successes, and their attitudes; he sometimes uses checklists to make his observations more formal when documenting students' knowledge of sight words, ability to answer a range of comprehension questions, or other skills (process-oriented assessment).

- At the end of each basal reader unit, students are given an oral or written *cloze* test to determine their comprehension and understanding of grammar (process-oriented assessment).

- Once a week, Mr. Steel listens as students *retell stories* to evaluate their English language fluency, knowledge of story structure, and comprehension skills (process-oriented assessment).

- Once or twice a week, Mr. Steel and his students examine together and briefly discuss the work in their *writing portfolios* (process-oriented assessment).

- Every six to eight weeks, Mr. Steel administers a *phonics survey test* to those students who need it, to measure growth in phonics elements; he also gives a quick *survey of sight words* to determine which words students still need to master (skills-based assessment).

student's performance with the performance of a cross-section of students in other areas of the country, such tests provide little or no usable information about the diagnostic needs of individual students. As with any assessment device, you must first determine what information you seek and then decide if the instrument is appropriate to those goals.

Achievement Tests

norm-referenced tests ■

grade-level equivalency score ■

Norm-referenced tests, often called "surveys" or achievement tests, are formal tests, usually administered in a group, that offer you a "ballpark" estimate of students' reading performance. The results are more helpful in comparing groups than in making judgments about individual students. They provide a **grade-level equivalency score** (e.g., 3.7), which supposedly indicates that the student is performing as well as a student in the seventh month of the third grade on the subskills tested, although such a figure should be considered only a rough estimate of the child's true ability.

Most of these tests, such as the *Gates–MacGinitie Reading Tests* (Riverside Publishing), are general and sample the child's overall literacy achievement. They provide little specific information on a child's literacy strengths and needs, and they can be culturally and linguistically biased. Most reading achievement tests for older children include subscores on vocabulary and comprehension, as well as a total reading score. Readiness tests, such as those normally administered at the end of kindergarten and/or at the beginning of first grade, frequently measure phonemic awareness skills, letter recognition, visual–motor coordination, listening comprehension, and auditory and visual discrimination. The *Test of Early Reading Ability* (PRO-ED), for example, measures knowledge of the alphabet, comprehension, and reading conventions. Clay (1979) offers a more process-oriented tool to assess the emergent literacy development of a young child with her *Concepts About Print Test: Stones* (Heinemann).

One widely used norm-referenced achievement test, *Dynamic Indicators of Basic Early Literacy Skills* (DIBELS; Good & Kaminski, 2002), includes subtests that cover aspects of phonemic awareness and oral reading fluency (including a retelling component) (see Figure 13.2). The Oral Reading Fluency subtest is standardized and individually administered. Students read a passage aloud for one minute, and then the number of correct words per minute is determined to attain the oral-reading fluency rate. The retell fluency section is a measure of the child's comprehension, working along with the Oral Reading Fluency assessment. The use of DIBELS to assess English learners has increased (Hagans, 2008; Richards-Tutor, Solari, & Leafstedt, 2013; Scheffel, Lefly, & Houser, 2012) and the same is true for students with special needs (Burke, Hagan-Burke, Kwok, & Parker, 2009; Johnson, Jenkins, Petscher, & Catts, 2009; Lembke & Stichter, 2006; Puhalla, 2011; Ricci, 2011; Yurick, Cartledge, Kourea, & Keyes, 2012). A list of additional formal reading and reading readiness tests can be found in Appendix D.

Norm-referenced tests compare a child's performance with that of a sample group of students, called the **norming group**. This sample group has taken the test under controlled conditions, and their average performance determines the norms,

DIBELS

https://dibels.org
https://dibels.uoregon.edu

> **see appendix D**

■ norming group

| figure | **13.2** | Components of DIBELS. |

COMPONENT	GRADES	DESCRIPTION
Initial Sounds Fluency	Pre-K and K	The student must select a picture of an object whose name begins with a given phoneme. The teacher monitors both fluency and accuracy.
Letter Naming Fluency	K and 1	The student must identify as many uppercase and lowercase letters as possible within one minute.
Phoneme Segmentation Fluency	K and 1	The teacher says a word aloud, and the student must quickly repeat that word, inserting a clear pause between each phoneme. The student must do this for as many words as possible within one minute.
Nonsense Word Fluency	K and 1	The student must correctly pronounce as many nonsense words as possible in one minute.
Oral Reading Fluency	1, 2, 3	The student must read aloud as much of a passage of text as possible in one minute. After reading aloud, the student must also describe or retell the content of the passage of text.
Word Use Fluency	K, 1, 2, 3	The student is given a word to use in a sentence or to define, and the teacher monitors both the accuracy of the use or definition as well as the number of words the student uses in his or her response.

Source: DIBELS, University of Oregon.

or average performance, for other students who take the test. As mentioned earlier, from a norm-referenced test, teachers receive a numerical grade-level equivalent score for every child. Thus, a score of 2.3 suggests that the child's score was equivalent to that of the average student in the norming group in the third month of second grade. These tests also allow for a percentile rank, enabling the teacher to quickly see how each student's score compares with that of the norming group. Finally, these

stanines ■ tests show the range of classroom scores through the use of **stanines,** which distribute all scores into nine sections, the first three being "below average," the middle three "average," and the top three "above average." Teachers usually find these types of scores more useful for assessment because they represent a wider range of achievement and are better suited to fluctuations that may occur in children's scores.

Scores on norm-referenced tests should be interpreted cautiously, however. Although such tests may compare groups adequately and give a fair sketch of how a class is doing, they can be problematic for making major instructional decisions for individual students. Because these tests are administered in groups, and because they are timed, a student who is a powerful but plodding reader may appear less able than she actually is; similarly, an impulsive guesser may do well on a multiple-choice exam and appear to be more skilled than is actually the case. Children from diverse cultural and/or linguistic groups may not have the background to answer the questions at all, though they may be highly literate in their own languages or do well when the context of the question items matches their own experiences.

Standardized norm-referenced tests are administered in a highly circumscribed manner. A teacher's manual, or technical manual, accompanies such tests and describes in detail the procedures for giving and interpreting the test. Included in the manual are the following (adapted from Rupley & Blair, 1990):

1. *Overview and purpose.* This information details the purpose and levels of the test, tells how to select the appropriate level for the child's grade placement, and provides specific information on the literacy areas that are included.

2. *Administration.* This section tells the teacher about time limits for each subtest and exactly what to say to students about how to complete each portion of the test. It also provides sample questions to answer jointly with students to get them familiar with the test's format.

3. *Directions for scoring.* Specific scoring information varies, but most norm-referenced tests now offer the option of either hand-scoring or machine-scoring. The procedures for both are usually provided.

4. *Interpreting the results.* Most norm-referenced literacy tests provide general information for planning literacy instruction based on students' strengths and needs, and such tests suggest specific activities to enhance specific literacy areas. There is often information on how to report classroom scores for administrative purposes.

5. *Technical data.* Selection and characteristics of the norming group, information on how reliable and valid the test is, scaled scores, and test item difficulty are usually described in this section.

Criterion-Referenced Tests

criterion-referenced
tests (CRTs) ■ Other standardized tests frequently used to assess children's literacy development are **criterion-referenced tests (CRTs).** Whereas a norm-referenced test compares a child's performance relative to other children's performances, a commercial criterion-referenced test, such as *Woodcock Reading Mastery Tests* (American Guidance Services), measures specific literacy skills in terms of mastery of those skills.

Performance standards are identified as *mastery, review, reteach*, or *lack of mastery*. Many states, and sometimes districts, develop their own CRTs, which are *not* standardized. These tests are created to determine "minimum competency," or the lowest acceptable performance level, and they are considered "mastery tests," designed to test specific district or state standards. As mentioned earlier, the tests developed by SBAC and PARCC, which are aligned to the CCSS, are additional examples of criterion-referenced assessments used in many states.

A large number of *behavioral objectives* are often found in commercially published, standardized CRTs; for example, phonics analysis may result in as many as 20 to 25 specific behavioral objectives. Such objectives often focus on reading sub-skill behaviors such as the following:

- Recognizes the sound represented by the letter *b*
- Recognizes the sound represented by the letter *a* in the medial position in a word
- Knows the sound represented by the letter *o* in the initial position of a one-syllable word

The major benefit of CRTs is that they are instruction-specific; that is, they reflect children's capabilities with regard to stated objectives, allowing you to assess the varying levels of performance in your class and then tailor programs to meet those needs. For example, a CRT might suggest that all but four students in the class can identify all the consonants when they are found in the beginning of words. Two of the remaining students need further help identifying the beginning consonants *p, d*, and *b*; the other two students need help identifying only the initial *r*.

Diagnostic Reading Tests

Many school districts use group **diagnostic reading tests.** They are popular not only because they are easy to administer and interpret but also because, unlike norm-referenced tests, they provide valuable diagnostic information about the strengths and needs of each student in the class. Because more diagnostic information is gained from these tools than from norm-referenced tests, some school districts prefer these formal tests, even though they generally cost more and take longer to administer. Districts appreciate the fact that such tests often have subtest scores in areas other than vocabulary and comprehension. The *Stanford Diagnostic Reading Test* (The Psychological Corporation), or SDRT, is one of the most widely used group diagnostic reading tests currently available.

■ diagnostic reading tests

Teachers who need more detailed information often give individual diagnostic tests. These typically are administered by reading specialists trained to provide a more thorough assessment and analysis of a variety of severe reading disorders. Two individual diagnostic reading tests currently being used in school districts are the *Diagnostic Reading Scales* (CTB McGraw-Hill) and the *Durrell Analysis of Reading Difficulties* (The Psychological Corporation). The Gray Oral Reading Test (GORT) and Test of Reading Comprehension (TORC) are additional tests focused on students with special needs.

INFORMAL ASSESSMENT PROCEDURES

meaningful instruction based on the needs of students in a classroom can best be provided by combining standardized assessment with various informal assessment measures. Informal assessment demands greater teacher knowledge in terms of test administration and interpretation, but the specificity of the information gained makes the assessment well worth the effort.

The IRI helps teachers assess each child's reading progress and diagnose possible problems.

Informal assessment devices are numerous and include informal reading inventories; interest and attitude inventories; reading, spelling, and writing placement tests; story retelling tasks; phonemic awareness and phonics survey tests; and written teacher observation procedures such as checklists and other anecdotal notes.

Informal Reading Inventory

An **informal reading inventory (IRI)** is one of the most valuable tools for evaluating the reading progress of each student in the class and for diagnosing specific reading strengths and needs. Because they actually hear the student reading aloud, observant teachers are offered a kind of window into the child's brain to see the child's strategies for decoding and constructing meaning. The IRI is an individual diagnostic reading test composed of lists of leveled sight words or sometimes sentences and a set of graded reading passages from preprimer through grade 8 or even 12, with accompanying comprehension questions

informal reading inventory ■

for each passage. Most basal reading series include their own IRI (sometimes called a student placement test) as part of their evaluation program, but such devices as the *Basic Reading Inventory (BRI), Flynt–Cooter Reading Inventory for the Classroom,* and Burns and Roe's *Informal Reading Inventory* are also commercially available. In addition, the Texas Education Agency in collaboration with the Center for Academic and Reading Skills developed the *Texas Primary Reading Inventory* to assess a child's early literacy development, including print awareness, phonemic awareness, graphophonemic knowledge, and listening and reading comprehension. You can design your own informal reading inventory by compiling a series of graded passages and using readability formulas and taxonomies for developing appropriate questions.

The IRI is an invaluable tool because it enables you to do the following:

1. Identify each child's instructional, frustration, and independent reading levels as well as their listening comprehension level.

2. Determine strengths and needs in decoding and comprehension abilities.

3. Understand how students are using syntactic (structure), graphophonic (visual–sound), and semantic (meaning) cues to make sense of reading.

4. Compare how a student decodes words in isolation with how that student decodes words in the context of meaningful sentences.

The IRI takes about 20 to 30 minutes to administer and is often recorded; the student reads orally while the teacher notes the child's miscues, or deviations from the actual text, by using a kind of shorthand. After the oral reading, the teacher asks a series of comprehension questions. When the student falls below about 90 percent in word recognition, achieves less than 50 percent in comprehension, or appears frustrated, the test is terminated; the passage level at which this occurs

frustration level ■

is called the **frustration level.** After the student reaches the frustration level, the teacher reads aloud passages at succeedingly higher grade levels until the student is unable to answer 75 percent of the comprehension questions (this percentage may vary depending on the IRI being used). The purpose of this last step is to deter-

reading capacity level ■

mine the child's **reading capacity level,** also called *listening comprehension level.* A reading capacity level is the highest level of material the student can understand when the passage is read to him or her.

Material is at the child's **independent level** (i.e., appropriate for recreational reading) when that student can read the passage without stress and correctly pronounce 95 percent of the words or higher and answers at least 90 percent of the comprehension questions. A passage at which the student can correctly pronounce between 90 to 95 percent of the words and answer at least 75 percent of the comprehension questions is the child's **instructional level,** the appropriate level of difficulty for classroom instruction in reading. As stated earlier, material is at a child's *frustration level* if the student reads less than 90 percent of the words correctly (see Figure 13.3).

■ independent level

■ instructional level

After analyzing decoding and comprehension miscues to establish what instruction is needed in these skill areas, you will do a **miscue analysis** to determine how the student is using clues to think about reading. Look for patterns of miscues, such as those that retain the meaning (e.g., *Dad* for *father*), miscues that retain the syntactic pattern (e.g., *being* for *beginning*), or those that simply retain the visual/sound similarities (e.g., *further* for *feather*). Miscues such as repetitions of words or phrases usually do not signify errors but indicate that the student may be rereading to try to rework a word or passage that didn't seem to make sense.

■ miscue analysis

Choose a commercial IRI that corresponds as closely as possible to the instructional materials used in the classroom and to what you consider a text deviation (e.g., a *repetition* is usually considered a positive second search for meaning). Also, by noting the types of comprehension questions, the number asked, and how scoring is handled, you can examine how the inventory evaluates comprehension. Also, look at the clarity of instructions for administration, scoring, and interpretation as another basis for selecting the IRI with which you feel most comfortable.

Running Record

Another method for analyzing a child's miscues is the **running record** (Clay, 1985), which is comparable to the miscue analysis that often accompanies the IRI but is easier to administer and much more expedient. The IRI is the more thorough evaluation, however, as it generally requires the student to read more than one passage and then compares the child's reading of words in isolation with the reading of words in context. Multiple samples always offer a clearer picture of the child's "true" reading ability, but at times the expediency of the running record makes it more appealing.

■ running record

With the running record, students orally read a passage of text ranging from easy to difficult. Although comprehension is not formally measured, you may ask students to do a retelling after the passage is read to check for understanding. Document students' strengths and limitations in the use of various decoding strategies

figure   13.3   Summary of informal reading inventory percentages.*

	WORD RECOGNITION	COMPREHENSION
Independent level	95% or above	90% or above
Instructional level	90 to 95%	75% or above
Frustration level	below 90%	below 50%
Listening comprehension level	N/A	75% or above

*Percentages may vary among inventories.

by making a check mark on a piece of paper as the student reads each word correctly and by writing the word diacritically to denote substitutions, repetitions, mispronunciations, or unknown words. Alternatively, you can duplicate the pages the student will read and then record errors next to or on top of the text copy (see Figure 13.4).

figure   13.4   An example of a running record.

The first thing you must do when you ✓ ✓ ✓ ✓ ✓ ✓ what/when ✓

wash your dog is to find him. Some ✓ ✓ ✓ ✓ ✓ ✓ ✓ ✓

dogs do not like to take baths. Use a ✓ ✓ ✓ ✓ ✓ ✓ bats/baths ✓ ✓

hose. Get the dog very wet. Then put horse/hose ✓ ✓ ✓ ✓ ✓ ✓ ✓

some doggy shampoo on him. Rinse ✓ ✓ shan–/shampoo ✓ Ring/Rinse ✓

him really well. Then dry him off. That ✓ ✓ will/well ✓ ✓ ✓ ✓ ✓

is the part your dog will like the best! ✓ ✓ ✓ ✓ ✓ ✓ ✓ ✓ ✓

Give him a reward for letting you give ✓ ✓ ✓ roar/reward ✓ let/letting ✓ ✓

him the bath. ✓ ✓ ✓

ANALYSIS

Total words:	67	Chelsea H.
		Name of student
Deviations from text:	8	
Accuracy level:	84%	67
	(frustration level)	*WPM (words per minute)*

This child read the text in a halting, word-by-word manner. After reading, the child was able to give the main idea of the text, but was unable to recall details due to the errors in decoding of key words. Her errors were:

Substitutions:	what/when	roar/reward	ring/rinse	let/letting
	horse/hose	will/well	bats/baths	

Mispronunciations: shan–/shampoo

Most of her errors affected comprehension because they made no sense, semantically or syntactically, in the sentences. A series of minilessons on using the context to help decode unfamiliar words is recommended.

After identifying the words the student read incorrectly, calculate the percentage of the words the student read correctly. Use the percentage of words read correctly to determine whether the material is too easy, too difficult, or at the appropriate instructional level for the student at that time, following the same percentages discussed for the IRI determination of reading levels. Additionally, time the student to determine the child's reading rate.

As with the IRI, you can then do a miscue analysis, categorizing the child's miscues according to the graphophonic, semantic, and syntactic cueing systems (see Chapter 1), in order to examine what word identification strategies are being used. Errors can then be classified and charted, and instructional decisions can be made accordingly.

Anecdotal Notes

Many teachers incorrectly assume that their own observations about a child's literacy status are not as important as the results of formalized tests. Researchers strongly dispute this belief (Cambourne & Turbill, 1990). One of the most powerful and reliable parts of any teacher's assessment and evaluation process, researchers claim, is her daily, systematic observation of the students, using either a clipboard, a tablet or other mobile device, or a recording device. Ideally, schedule some observation time every day to focus on particular students and to make brief logs or **anecdotal notes** about those students' involvement in literacy events (Rhodes & Nathenson–Mejia, 1992). Teachers should observe students in every possible literacy context: one-to-one interactions, small-group discussions, and large-class settings. The focus should always be on what students *do* as they read and write; the most useful notes describe specific events, report rather than evaluate, and relate the events to other information about the student. Teachers can make observations about a preliterate learner's concepts about print or an older child's reading and writing activities—the questions they ask, the books they are reading, what they seem to like and dislike in reading, and whether they use strategies and skills fluently or display some confusion.

■ anecdotal notes

Studies have shown that anecdotal notes are instrumental for helping teachers assess students with special needs (Bourke, Mentis, & Todd, 2011; Schleper, 1996). By using anecdotal notes, teachers of these students can document evidence of learning that is often not captured on standardized tests. This informal assessment also allows teachers to make modifications to their instruction based on their student observations. Specific notes can be organized around the literacy areas shown in the box on the following page.

Anecdotal notes dynamically document students' growth over time; they also direct teachers' attention to problem areas needing explicit instruction for individuals and to possible minilesson topics for small groups.

Sight Words

You may wish to make informal, periodic assessments of students' recognition of **sight words** or sight vocabulary and keep a running tally for each child. To accomplish this, number 3 × 5 index cards and arrange them in the same order as the words from a list of sight words or high-frequency words, such as Fry's list of "instant words," that are appropriate for the student (see Appendix G). While holding up the cards for the student to respond to, use the list to note which words the student recognizes and reads successfully. The student must say the word immediately, with no hesitation or sounding out. For each correct response, make a check mark next to the corresponding word on the word list. For incorrect

■ sight words

▶ **see appendix G**

Observable behaviors for anecdotal notes

BOOK HANDLING SKILLS

1. Holds the book appropriately.
2. "Reads" from front to back.
3. Knows the difference between the pictures and the words.
4. Understands the terms "beginning of" and "end of" the book.
5. Understands the term "cover of the book."

CONCEPTS ABOUT PRINT

1. Points to the words and not the pictures while being read to.
2. Is able to touch each word as it is read (one-to-one correspondence).
3. Knows that we read from left to right and top to bottom.
4. Knows that we read a book from front to back.
5. Knows the difference between a letter, a word, and a sentence.

PHONEMIC AWARENESS

1. Can hear and pronounce the sounds of English correctly.
2. Can "stretch" a word out to hear the sounds.
3. Can hear the distinctions between words in continuous speech.

PHONICS: LETTER AND SOUND RELATIONSHIPS

1. Can recognize the visual form and name the letters of the alphabet.
2. Can identify initial consonants in context.
3. Can identify rhyming words.
4. Can recognize spelling patterns and use conventional spelling in writing.
5. Can recognize some high-frequency words (list).

FLUENCY

1. Reads grade-level material with accuracy.
2. Reads at reading rate commensurate with grade level.
3. Varies reading rate according to the type of text and reading purpose.
4. Reads with appropriate expression.
5. Reads with appropriate phrasing, attending to punctuation features in text.

VOCABULARY

1. Uses grade-level-appropriate vocabulary in written work.
2. Uses grade-level-appropriate vocabulary when speaking.
3. Uses available resources to seek meaning of unfamiliar words.
4. Demonstrates curiosity about and interest in unknown words.
5. Incorporates newly taught content-area words into writing assignments and oral discussions.

COMPREHENSION

1. Answers literal and open-ended questions about text.
2. Paraphrases text when asked what it was about.
3. Can give the main idea of a story or informational piece.
4. Can answer critical questions about text.
5. Asks questions when meaning is not clear.

responses, write the mispronunciation or substitution above the word, for later analysis. The child's score is the number of words checked.

Cloze Tests

Cloze is an easy-to-use device that uses a short passage from the basal reader or other reading material, with certain words deleted (and replaced with blanks), to determine a child's ability to comprehend the ideas in the sentences and in the entire passage. Besides establishing whether the basal reader or other text is at the appropriate instructional level for a child, the procedure can also diagnose the child's ability to use context clues in reading. By listing each incorrect response made by the child, you can determine if the response makes sense syntactically or semantically. Often, a response may be semantically and syntactically correct without being the exact keyed response (e.g., for "The boy *stroked* the dog" the student substitutes "The boy *petted* the dog"), which would be considered acceptable. The cloze can be designed in written form or orally, in a recording, for preliterate learners.

Interest and Attitude Inventories

Children's interests and attitudes about reading, writing, and school in general have been found to be highly correlated with success in literacy. The **interest and attitude inventory** assesses these factors and should therefore be included in any comprehensive assessment program. Given the importance of these factors, they should be assessed and monitored both incidentally (using anecdotal notes) and deliberately (through an informal questionnaire, administered orally or in writing, to the whole class or to individuals). A sample *reading interest inventory* and *attitude survey* are found in Appendix E. You can design your own inventory, appropriate to the age and developmental level of your learners, or use a survey such as the *Primary Reading Attitude Survey* (Appendix E) or the *Elementary Reading Attitude Survey* (McKenna & Kear, 1990). Students are asked questions and respond by circling a picture that shows how they feel about aspects of reading or free-time activities in general. The questions should be designed to solicit at least the following key information, which can be used to determine possible reading and writing interests:

■ interest and attitude inventory

> see appendix E

- the subject areas that are motivating to the child
- the child's favorite story or text
- what the student does in his or her spare time
- what sports or hobbies the student enjoys
- the child's favorite television program
- the child's preferred instructional arrangements—for example, teacher-directed, working alone, with a small group, or with one other child
- the child's attitudes toward reading and writing
- what reading materials and experiences the student has been exposed to

Story Retelling

By listening to the **retelling** of a story or informational piece, you can gain diagnostic information about the child's use of language, the child's knowledge of narrative or expository structure, and how the student comprehends or constructs meaning from text. Therefore, a series of retellings over time assesses progress in these areas and provides important information about each child.

■ retelling

To use this strategy, have the student read a passage aloud or silently (or read the text to a preliterate child). After the reading, ask the student to retell the passage. If needed, provide gentle prompts, such as "Tell me more," or "Keep going; you're doing great." If the student requires further prompting, ask questions about specific parts of the passage that the student did not mention. If retellings are recorded, use the recording to observe the child's oral language and determine how well the student comprehends the passage and organizes ideas. This sample can later be compared with past or subsequent retellings. You can also review and discuss the retelling with the child, using the procedure to develop the same skills that were assessed.

ASSESSING SPECIFIC COMPONENTS OF LITERACY

m any other tools are used for informal assessment of specific literacy components, ranging from a variety of structured, skills-based tools to less-structured observational procedures. It is not possible to mention all the assessment devices available, nor is it necessary or possible to use every device contained in this chapter. Because you have limited instructional time, choose tools based on the literacy needs of your class.

Assessing Phonemic Awareness

Although several norm-referenced phonemic awareness tests are available, such as the *Test of Phonological Awareness* (PRO-ED), you can informally measure phonemic awareness at frequent intervals to determine which sounds need to be taught or reinforced. In the informal assessment of these important abilities, you give the student several examples of what he is expected to do in the testing of each skill (see Chapter 4). For example, if a class or specific students have difficulty with matching beginning sounds, you can assign specific sound activities, such as the What's the Sound? activity in Chapter 4. The phonemic awareness skills appear in order in the following box (adapted from *Phonemic Awareness Assessment*, Peddy, 1995, unpublished). Examples are provided for each skill, although you may need to create additional examples to ensure that the student completely understands the task; for example, what it means to "rhyme."

Assessing Phonics Skills

The phonic analysis abilities of individual students in the class can be assessed formally, using norm-referenced instruments such as the *Botel Phonics Survey*, but

Assessing phonemic awareness

Rhyming: "I'll say two words, and you tell me if they rhyme."

EXAMPLES: *boy, toy; go, help; we, me*

Word-to-word match: "I'll say two words, and you tell me if they begin with the same sound."

EXAMPLES: *bat, boy; day, can; run, hop*

Odd word out: "I'll say four words, and you tell me which word ends with a different sound."

EXAMPLES: *bat, hit, make, wet*

(Do the same with beginning sounds.)

Blending: "Tell me what word we would make if we put these sounds together."

EXAMPLES: /a/ /t/; /g/ /o/; /w/ /i/ /n/; /r/ /a/ /n/

Phoneme segmentation: "Tell me what sounds you hear in the words I tell you."

EXAMPLES: *be, pat, got, fish*

Phoneme counting: "Tell me how many sounds you hear in the words I tell you."

EXAMPLES: *in, cat, ship, lake*

Sound-to-word matching: "Answer these questions about what sounds you hear."

EXAMPLES: Is there a /p/ in *pat*? Is there a /n/ in *sun*? Is there a /sh/ in *wash*?

Sound isolation: "See if you can hear these sounds."

EXAMPLES: What is the first sound in *tug*? What is the ending sound in *bat*? What is the middle sound in *cane*?

Phoneme deletion: "Tell me what word would be left if I take away these sounds."

EXAMPLES: Say *cat* without the /c/. Say *hit* without the /h/. Say *bean* without the /n/.

progress in these skills can also be assessed by using an informal inventory of phonics skills (see Chapter 5). As in the phonemic awareness assessment described in the previous section, this procedure also requires that you offer as many examples as necessary for the student to understand what is being asked and that you create lessons based on the evidence from the assessment. For instance, a phonics skills test may indicate that a student has trouble reading a specific long vowel sound, such as the –ai pattern. Knowing this, you can teach subsequent lessons that target –ai words, use activities such as Sound Switch (Chapter 5, p. 82), have students read decodable text with the pattern, and follow up with writing exercises using –ai words. The inventory in the following box can be given to the whole class as a pretest or post-test to discover what skills need to be taught, or given individually by having a student read each word orally so you can check knowledge of letter–sound correspondence. Give students an answer form with categories and numbers on it to use in recording their responses. Phonics elements mastered, as well as those yet to be learned, can be recorded and analyzed for each student for the purpose of future instructional planning.

Assessing Fluency

In order to assess reading fluency, listen to students read aloud and make more formal judgments about their progress in the three areas of fluency: rate of reading, reading accuracy, and prosody. The most widely used method to assess and increase a child's reading rate is to ask a student to read a specified passage and determine how much of the passage can be read in one minute (Samuels, 1979). Timed readings differ from traditional silent reading time: in timed reading, you select the passages, and the students read them and then answer comprehension questions about what they have read (Fox, 2003). The purpose of such an instruc-

---

Phonics assessment inventory

Consonant sounds (beginning): "Write the beginning letter of each word I say."

    EXAMPLES: *hit, bat, name, just, game, pond*

Consonant sounds (final): "Write the last letter of each word I say."

    EXAMPLES: *man, soft, jam, rub, grass, talk*

Consonant blends (initial): "Write the first two letters of each word I say."

    EXAMPLES: *truck, crab, star, grin, drown, blame*

Consonant blends (final): "Write the last two letters of each word I say."

    EXAMPLES: *back, first, cart, jump, hand, perk*

Consonant digraphs (initial): "Write the first two letters of each word I say."

    EXAMPLES: *shout, child, that, photo, those, chin*

Consonant digraphs (final): "Write the last two letters of each word I say."

    EXAMPLES: *much, ring, cash, moth, sang, luck*

Long and short vowels: "If the vowel in the word I say is short, write short and the vowel. If the vowel in the word I say is long, write long and the vowel."

    EXAMPLES: *sat, hike, same, bone, bless, cot, rug, feet, tin, cube*

Vowel digraphs and diphthongs: "Write the two vowels that go together to form a team—such as /ow/, /oi/, /oy/, and /oo/—in the words I say."

    EXAMPLES: *how, look, oil, ought, boy, mood*

tional strategy is that students work on increasing their fluency and reading rate, though never at the expense of comprehension.

When assessing accuracy, determine whether each student can decode words accurately and has a large store of words that he can recognize automatically, by sight. For determining how a student reads words in context, simply listening to each child's oral reading and counting the number of errors per 100 words can provide valuable information about the child's reading accuracy. This information is helpful for selecting texts for individual or small-group instruction. In addition, the results can show you what to do next to help a student progress. For example, a fluency test may show that a student is not reading with accuracy. You can follow up with a phonics assessment to learn what orthographic patterns are difficult for the student and devise solid lessons based on the evidence. Once you know the pattern that is causing difficulty, you can use the assessment evidence to create targeted lessons. Fluency assessments may also indicate that other students are reading accurately but too slowly to comprehend a text fully and would benefit from repeated readings to increase their reading rate. A more thorough assessment providing more detailed information about why a student lacks reading accuracy can be obtained through a running record (refer back to Figure 13.4).

Finally, assess students to consider the following question about prosody: Is each of my students able to chunk words into phrases, heed punctuation, and read with appropriate expression that approximates conversational speech? The best way to assess a student's prosody is to listen to the student read aloud and use a checklist to determine if the reading contains the qualities that comprise fluent, expressive reading.

The National Assessment of Educational Progress (NAEP) used four levels to distinguish fluent from disfluent reading (see Figure 13.5). You can use these four levels to determine the reading prosody level of each learner in your class. By the end of second grade, students should have reached Level 4. Although most students can benefit from prosody instruction, such instruction is imperative for students scoring below Level 4 after second grade (U.S. Department of Education,

| figure | 13.5 | Oral reading prosody scale. |

Level 4 Reads primarily in larger, meaningful phrase groups. Although some regressions, repetitions, and deviations from text may be present, these do not appear to detract from the overall structure of the story. Preservation of the author's syntax is consistent. Some or most of the story is read with expressive interpretation.

Level 3 Reads primarily in three- or four-word phrase groups. Some smaller groupings may be present. However, the majority of phrasing seems appropriate and preserves the syntax of the author. Little or no expressive interpretation is present.

Level 2 Reads primarily in two-word phrases with some three or four-word groupings. Some word-by-word reading may be present. Word groupings may seem awkward and unrelated to larger context of sentence or passage.

Level 1 Reads primarily word-by-word. Occasional two-word or three-word phrases may occur—but these are infrequent and/or they do not preserve meaningful syntax.

Source: U.S. Department of Education, Institute of Education Sciences, National Center for Education Statistics, National Assessment of Educational Progress (NAEP), 2002 Oral Reading Study.

2002). Teachers need to be cautioned not to overinterpret the reading-rate norms, however, especially with students for whom English is a second language.

Besides the assessment procedures mentioned earlier that involve the teacher, students can be taught to ask their own questions about their reading (see Appendix E). To use these questions, first discuss each of them with the students. Then allow students to record a passage as they read and play it back, listening reflectively to their reading and answering each of the questions.

> see appendix E

Assessing Vocabulary and Writing

Word Writing CAFÉ

Evaluating the complexity of a child's writing can provide an insight into the level of difficult words that a student feels comfortable using when composing, but until recently, no objective assessment of students' word-writing skills could be given to a whole class at one time (Cecil, 2007). Moreover, no assessment device was available that considered students' accuracy, complexity, and fluency in their ability to generate words. The tool Word Writing CAFÉ (Leal, 2005; CAFÉ stands for complexity, accuracy, fluency, and evaluation) was developed to allow teachers to objectively evaluate their students' word-writing ability in terms of fluency, accuracy, and complexity in grades 1–6. Through scoring and tracking their students' progress over the school year, teachers can use the assessment data to understand and improve students' word-writing capabilities through explicit instruction.

To administer the Word Writing CAFÉ, give each student a piece of paper on which three columns of 10 boxes are drawn. Ask the students to write down as many words as they can think of in 10 minutes (see Figure 13.6 for an example of a completed form). The words are then scored according to the following steps:

- To determine word *fluency:* Count the total number of boxes with any writing in them. Anything counts as a word, except scribbles or pictures. This is the TW (total words) figure.

- To determine *accuracy:* Cross out misspelled words, duplicated words, proper names, and numbers that are not spelled out. This is the CW (correct words) figure.

- To determine the *complexity:* Count the number of syllables in each correctly spelled word. Using the blanks provided, fill in the number of one-syllable words (1s) and so on.

Dorothy Leal, the creator of the Word Writing CAFÉ, offers the following important suggestions to consider when administering this helpful assessment tool:

- Use the device to track student progress, not to assign student grade-level abilities.

- Be sure the assessment is administered in a nonprint environment where students cannot copy from word walls or other print displays.

- Use *only* the following prompts to give students ideas of what they can write:
  - "Write words that tell what you like to do and where you like to go."
  - "Write words that describe what you can see, hear, smell, taste, and feel."
  - "Write words that tell what is in your house or school."
  - "Write any word that you know how to read or write."

As national benchmarks have not yet been completed for this pilot assessment device, it can be used as a criterion-referenced test, to determine progress over time in each of the three areas assessed. National benchmarks are forthcoming.

figure **13.6**   Complete CAFÉ form.

1st/2nd

Name   Skylar   Date   Oct. 15   Teacher   Mr. Nuan

The	I	dad	I	sun	I
see	I	mom	I	mun	
They	I	two	I	your	I
Then	I	too	I	six	I
Thes		to	I	ran	I
you	I	grandma	2	~~playd~~	
yes	I	grandpa	2	play	I
no	I	cat hat	I	sally bally	
on	I	day hog	I		
can	I	Boo!	I		

TW: ___28___   CW: ___24___   1S: ___22___   2S: ___2___
3S: _____   4S: _____   5S: _____   6S: _____

Observation/anecdotal notes

The Word Writing CAFÉ is one way to evaluate fluency, accuracy, and word complexity. However, word writing is not the only goal of a writing program. Teachers should evaluate for *authentic* writing for *authentic* purposes. As important as it is to listen to students as they read, it is equally imperative to observe students as they write, in order to provide immediate feedback while students are writing and while they can use it to improve their writing. Take anecdotal notes during writing workshop to determine which students easily settle to the task of writing and which students struggle with ideas and writing conventions. In addition to monitoring for students who spend a great deal of time sounding out words and asking for spelling assistance, note how easily a student is able to think of writing ideas and complete the writing tasks and how willing he is to share written products.

Rubrics

Rubrics are a tool that teachers often use to assess writing. Rubrics often rate each element on a scale from 1 (low) to 4 or 5 (high) and can be more informative than the traditional marking of errors that many students receive. For example, using the 6 + 1 Trait® Rubric: 5-Point Beginning Writer's Rubric (see Appendix E), you can score students on specific writing traits or elements such as voice or organization (see Chapter 9) and use this data to inform subsequent writing instruction.

see appendix E

Most districts have adopted rubrics that cover the types of writing being taught in classrooms; you can also create your own rubrics using web-based sites such as Rubistar or teAchnology.

Wolf and Gearhart (1993) provide a variation on the rubric in assessing student writing using a two-pronged approach (which can be modified to fit other writing genres). First, you fill out a *narrative feedback form* that contains writing elements of a story (theme, setting, communication, character, plot, convention, and writing process). Provide students with one commendation and one recommendation in each area (although it is not necessary to fill out every component). Second, complete a *narrative rubric*, which evaluates aspects of the piece along a scale. For instance, a student's narrative may be judged on whether the characters are presented as flat and static (on one end of the scale), as opposed to round and dynamic (on the other end). You can set specific criteria to focus on aspects of subgenres that may need to be addressed.

Writing folders

The writing folder, whether in printed or electronic form, is where students keep their rough drafts in various stages of the writing process, along with other daily compositions, topics for future pieces they might like to write, and, for older students, notes from minilessons (see Chapter 9). Students also include their own assessments and reflections about any piece they have completed. Material from their writing folders is the basis for teacher–student conferences on individual instructional needs, and minilesson topics are chosen from observations during these sessions.

In preparing for special displays, publications, or parent–teacher meetings, you and the student might meet and select pieces to put in a special "showcase portfolio" to be shown to parents. Writing folders are often proudly decorated and personalized by students and kept in a special place in the classroom where they are easily accessible. Anecdotal notes regarding this folder can be important assessment data on the child's writing progress.

RESPONSE TO INTERVENTION: BLENDING ASSESSMENT AND INTERVENTION

The 2004 reauthorization of federal legislation, IDEA (Individuals with Disabilities Education Act), formalized the process of assessing and teaching struggling learners, but more recently it has gained the interest of reading educators (Fuchs, Fuchs, & Vaughn, 2008). The purpose of **Response to Intervention (RTI)** is not only to provide early intervention for students who are at risk for school failure but also to develop more valid procedures for identifying students with reading disabilities. RTI allows teachers to determine which students need special education instruction in reading, based on whether the student can respond to either typical classroom instruction or the more intensive type of support that is also possible in a typical classroom (e.g., brief but intensive small-group intervention on key skills).

RTI is a framework that incorporates both assessment and intervention so that immediate benefits come to the student. Assessment data are used to inform interventions and determine their effectiveness. As a result of the intervention-focused nature of RTI, eligibility services shift toward a supportive rather than a sorting function. The purpose of the formalized routine in RTI is to help teachers do what good teachers have always done—make instructional decisions based on their students' needs.

Although RTI is not limited to identifying literacy needs, I will discuss its specific characteristics in relation to literacy. To implement RTI, the following must first be in place:

WWW
Web-Based Rubric Sites
www.rubistar.com
www.teach-nology.com/web_tools/rubrics/
6 + 1 Trait Rubric
http://educationnorthwest.org/traits

■ Response to Intervention (RTI)

valid ■
reliable ■

1. Ways to measure reading proficiency that are **valid** *(does it measure what it purports to measure?)* and **reliable** *(are the results consistent over time?)* so that students can receive the appropriate type and level of reading instruction for their needs.

2. An assessment program that monitors the students' progress in reading as a result of the instruction they are receiving.

3. Various levels, or tiers, of instruction available to students to meet their instructional needs.

4. A data-driven decision-making process in which, once students' level of reading development and instructional needs have been determined, they are placed in the appropriate level and offered the type of scientifically validated literacy instruction that will address their specific needs.

Progress should be monitored regularly to ensure that the instruction students receive is yielding the desired results. Successful RTI schools then routinely transform progress-monitoring data into visual displays such as time-series graphs to share with teachers, intervention team members, parents, and others. These displays demonstrate whether the student is benefiting from the intervention.

In some classrooms, RTI instruction has three tiers, although in others it can have five or six tiers. Following is an example of a three-tier plan. Tier 1 instruction is the common core curriculum given to all the students in the class. Most children (typically, around 80 percent) should make adequate progress in reading as a result of Tier 1 instruction. The routine progress monitoring allows teachers to determine who is and who is not progressing with the core curriculum. Students who are not progressing are placed in Tier 2 instruction, which supplements—but does not replace—Tier 1 instruction. Tier 3 adds an additional layer of instruction as well as instructional intensity for students who have not progressed with Tier 2 instruction according to assessment results. If this new layer of intensive instruction does not then yield results, individual instruction follows, usually with a reading specialist. If that extra instruction does not prove successful for the student and every other avenue has been exhausted, a decision is made for a special education placement, as deemed necessary.

On the face of it, RTI makes perfect sense in that it strives to meet the needs of all students; however, in order to work efficiently, RTI assumes that the time, the staff, and the financial resources are all available for both the routine assessments and the increasingly complex layers of instructional interventions. Despite these concerns, a growing body of evidence indicates that RTI can work (Gerzel-Short & Wilkins, 2009; Haager, Klingner, & Vaughn, 2007; Jimerson, Burns, & VanDerHeyden, 2007), including with English learners (Rinaldi & Samson, 2008), if committed teachers, reading specialists, and administrators think creatively about how to implement it.

COMPILING AND SUMMARIZING ASSESSMENT INFORMATION

The acts of compiling and summarizing the variety of assessment data help teachers manage this data and access it when needed. In literacy assessment, information about students is gathered from various formal, informal, and observational sources, with many of the same behaviors appearing in several different appraisals. For example, Mr. Steel has information from writing folders, journal entries, phonics tests, story retellings, IRIs, reading achievement tests, cloze tests, and many anecdotal observations, to name just a few sources. These primary data must be put together to get the big picture of each student's capabilities. Teachers can compile this information into a student profile (see Appendix E). Moreover, as

see appendix E ◄

CASE EXAMPLE

RTI in action: Literacy success for Landon
(ADAPTED FROM MESMER & MESMER, 2009)

To illustrate how RTI might work, we look at a second-grader, Landon, and follow his progress in literacy. This vignette shows how a team, including Joan, a reading teacher; Steve, a special educator; and Anthony, Landon's second-grade teacher, worked collaboratively within the RTI framework to foster the literacy progress of one child. Figure 13.7 presents the literacy screening assessments the team used to monitor Landon's needs and progress.

Step 1: Evidence-based literacy practices are established

In September, Landon was given the Phonics Mastery Survey (Appendix E), which assesses a child's ability to identify letters, consonant sounds, rhyming words, more complex consonant and vowel sounds, syllables, and a list of grade 2 words. He was also given a spelling assessment, The Monster Test (Gentry, 1985). These are the measures from which an entry benchmark score is formed. If the benchmark score does not meet the grade-level minimum, then additional, lower diagnostics are administered (preprimer and primer lists, letter naming, letter sounds, concepts about print, phonological awareness). Students also read passages through which accuracy, reading rate, phrasing, and comprehension scores are determined.

In the fall, Landon received a benchmark score of 22 on the first-grade word list and fell below the expected stage of spelling development on the spelling assessment. An expected benchmark score of 30, based on 15 words on the first-grade list, and at least a phonetic stage of spelling development are expected for the beginning of second grade. Specifically, Landon had trouble with all except short vowel sounds, and knew no consonant blends or digraphs. On the Qualitative Reading Inventory (QRI), Landon read instructionally at the primer level (1.1) with appropriate phrasing and expression and answered five of six comprehension questions correctly, missing only the critical evaluative question. He read the 120 words in the primer story in 4 minutes and 20 seconds, a rate of about 28 words correct per minute (WCPM) and 20 words below the 50th percentile for second-graders in the fall. When follow-up diagnostic assessments were administered, data showed that Landon had mastered alphabetic skills such as phonemic awareness and letters. Anthony wrote in his initial analysis: "Landon seemed to have mastered some basic concepts of reading and his low-level comprehension is good, but he needs more practice at his independent reading level to become fluent and to progress." To begin with, Landon received small-group classroom instruction, including reading daily in on-level materials and working with Anthony on critical comprehension and decoding. In September, October, and November, Anthony took running records on the books that Landon and the other students had been reading. Although the accuracy and book levels of other students were steadily increasing, Landon's accuracy was averaging 90 percent, but only in less difficult books. Anthony explained, "I felt like Landon needed still more help, or he would continue to fall behind."

Step 2: Scientifically based interventions are implemented

The team discussed Landon's needs and designed an appropriate intervention. Based on its review of the data, the team determined that accurate, fluent reading in text seemed to

figure 13.7	
Literacy screening assessments used by Landon's team.	

SCREENING DEVICE	AUTHOR(S)
Dynamic Indicators of Basic Early Literacy Skills (DIBELS)	Good & Kaminski
Assessments for Phonological Awareness (see Appendix E)	Beilby
Qualitative Reading Inventory (QRI)	Leslie & Caldwell
Phonics Mastery Survey (see Appendix E)	Cecil
The Monster Test (see Appendix E)	Gentry

be the problem. Landon could easily understand books above his reading level, but his progress was impeded by slow rate and lack of word-recognition skills. The group decided that an intervention increasing the amount of reading practice for Landon would build his reading level. The designed intervention comprised the following components: modeling of fluent reading, repeated readings, error correction, comprehension questions, and self-monitoring. They decided that Joan would implement the intervention with three other students in the classroom in 20-minute sessions, three times per week. In addition, Anthony would continue to work with Landon in the classroom during small-group literacy instruction. He had Landon read from the same materials used by Joan to further increase practice opportunities, and she set a daily goal for Landon on comprehension questions. Landon checked his answers each day and provided the results to his teacher at the end of the reading time.

Step 3: Progress of student receiving intervention is monitored

While the intervention was implemented, Joan monitored Landon's accuracy and fluency in reading passages at the primer through second-grade levels, because the goal was to understand Landon's progress toward grade-level norms. As Landon read these passages weekly, Joan kept track of his accuracy (percentage of words correct) and reading rate (WCPM). Landon demonstrated some gains in accuracy and fluency, but his progress was not increasing at a rate that would allow him to meet the second-grade literacy goals.

In addition to review of Landon's progress during the six weeks of intervention instruction, Landon's midyear Phonics Mastery Survey and QRI scores were evaluated by the team. He was found to be reading independently at the primer (1.1) level; barely instructional at the first-grade level, with 14 errors and a reading rate of 42 WCPM; and still unable to read words with consonant blends and digraphs correctly—nor did he fare any better with complex vowel sounds. Despite the increase in Landon's instructional level and fluency, the team remained concerned about the lack of reduction in the number of errors that Landon was making and his lack of knowledge of all but rudimentary vowel and consonant sounds. The team decided that these concerns would ultimately become detrimental to Landon's fluency and comprehension, particularly as texts increased in difficulty. The team determined that individualized intervention was needed.

Step 4: Individualized interventions are implemented when the student continues to struggle

Results from the Phonics Mastery Survey further revealed that Landon was having difficulty decoding words with more than one syllable and words that contained difficult vowel patterns. This resulted in reduced accuracy and fluency. The team enhanced the intervention by adding practice with problem words. Landon practiced incorrectly read words, received instruction in how to analyze word parts and extend analytic skills to similar words, and practiced through word sorts. Following word sorts, Landon read each word within a sentence. Joan implemented this individualized intervention for 10 minutes each day following the reading practice intervention (discussed earlier).

Joan continued to monitor Landon's reading accuracy and fluency weekly. The team determined that the intervention would be implemented for at least 6 weeks, as this time frame would correspond with the end of the school year, although the team recognized that interventions in early literacy often need to run longer—between 10 and 20 weeks. Moreover, Landon's progress was measured each week so that the intervention could be modified if he failed to make adequate gains. Landon quickly responded to the decoding intervention. Data were collected once per week on the percentage of words read correctly from second-grade passages. Landon's response to the intervention contrasted dramatically with his performance when reading unknown words prior to the intervention. By the sixth week, Landon correctly read 100 percent of words presented; before the intervention he was reading only 55 percent to 60 percent accurately. Landon improved in reading fluency as well. Prior to word attack intervention, the effects of the fluency intervention had leveled off. With the addition of the decoding intervention, Landon's fluency steadily improved until he met the second-grade goal. By the end of May, Landon met the grade-level goals: he was reading instructionally at second-grade level with comprehension at a rate of about 60 WCPM, according to the latest administration of the QRI.

A graph of Landon's progress was created using Power Point so that the team, parents, administrators, and others could have a visual display of the results of all assessments and interventions.

Step 5: Decisions are made to determine eligibility for special education services

Despite falling below the second-grade benchmark in September, Landon demonstrated growth in accuracy, fluency, and decoding as a result of the efforts of school personnel. The team reviewed Landon's intervention data and determined that special education services were not necessary. However, Anthony voiced concerns about Landon and the continued need for support. Although Anthony could see that Landon had made great progress with the extra interventions in addition to the regular curriculum, he was concerned about regression during the summer. He suggested that a meeting be held with Landon's parents to discuss specific summer literacy activities that they could encourage at home. Additionally, Anthony insisted that a meeting with the team be scheduled immediately in September to talk about his needs for his third-grade year.

Landon's progress was significant, considering his skills at the beginning of the year. If the interventions had not met Landon's needs, the team would have been charged with determining whether the lack of response was indicative of a learning disability.

the year progresses, the amount of information proliferates, resulting in far more data than anyone could possibly commit to memory. Two other ways to compile and summarize information are *teacher observational portfolios* for each student and *group profiles* for the entire class.

Portfolios

Artists use portfolios to demonstrate their skills and achievements; teachers can use portfolios in a similar manner to portray the literacy work and progress of each student in their class over an extended period of time (Porter & Cleland, 1995; Valencia, 1990).

There are many options for the contents of portfolios whether they are in hard copy or electronic form; they can be organized in any way that is helpful to you, students, parents, and families. Typically, you will select appropriate data, based on observations and informal assessments of students' reading and writing behaviors and accomplishments, and put these data into a progress file, or a **teacher observational portfolio.** In some cases, you and the student make a collaborative decision about which materials will be assembled to go into a showcase portfolio.

■ teacher observational portfolio

An alternative vehicle for showcasing students' work is a *video portfolio,* a representation of a child's ongoing reading prowess. Students can be recorded reading aloud during various intervals during the year, or they can be videoed during reading discussion groups. Writing workshop and special projects such as readers theater can also be videoed to record progress.

Group Profiles

Group profiles are compilations of individual performances of all the students in the class on one or more assessments. They focus on the range of class literacy behavior and identify clusters or subgroups of students with similar strengths and needs. They also condense information about the whole class's performance onto several worksheets. Unlike individual teacher observational portfolios, student profiles do not cut across different areas but summarize one literacy area for the entire class (see Appendix E).

■ group profiles

▶ **see appendix E**

Group profiles are primarily planning tools that convey the strengths and needs of the entire class so that appropriate activities can be planned to meet them. Instead of generalizing about what the class knows and can do, the group profile graphically shows, for example, that only two students need more direct instruction in phonemic awareness, whereas most of the class is ready for formal phonics instruction or, for example, that four students need no phonics instruction but could use specific comprehension strategies (see Chapter 8) to enrich their advanced reading abilities.

USING ASSESSMENT TO INFORM INSTRUCTION

the principles of assessment presented at the beginning of this chapter suggest that there must be a reciprocal, synergistic relationship between assessment and teaching; in other words, teaching and assessing must continually inform one another. Putting this into practice, however, takes intentional and focused observation on the part of the classroom teacher. Assessing students with no clear plan as to what will be done with the testing results wastes valuable instructional time. The remainder of this chapter consists of practical information, in the form of answers to frequently asked questions, about the choice of assessment tools and what to do with assessment results.

1. When and why might a teacher decide to use a specific assessment tool? Certain assessment tools are mandated by the state or district where you work. So-called **high-stakes assessments** must be administered usually once or twice a year. These assessments are often used to determine how well students are doing compared with other students in the area, the state, and/or the nation. The funding of certain programs often depends on how well students do on these tests—hence the moniker "high stakes."

high-stakes
assessments ■

Other, more specific diagnostic assessments may be used when you wonder why a student is not progressing as well as expected in a certain area. For example, you may decide to administer a test of phonological awareness (see Appendix E) when you discover, through observation, that a student is not learning to decode, and you fear he may not possess the prerequisite ability to hear discrete sounds in words. You might decide to use the same assessment when a standardized reading test shows that the student is weak in decoding and you are interested in determining the underlying cause. Such time-consuming assessment devices need not be administered to every student in the class, but only to those about whom you require more specific information.

see appendix E ◄

End-of-chapter and unit tests are examples of assessments that you would use to find out if all students have attained the learning objectives you identified at the beginning of the chapter or unit (e.g., criterion-referenced tests). Other classroom assessments, such as Quick Writes and random quizzes, are administered during instruction to measure student progress. Such assessments give feedback about students and offer fodder for reflection about areas that might require alternative teaching strategies or different pacing.

Sometimes an assessment tool tells you what not to teach or to whom not to teach a specific concept or skill. For example, a phonics assessment device administered to all the students in a class might reveal that five students have mastered all the phonics skills and, instead of sitting through lessons on the letters and their corresponding sounds, would be better served by reading material to comprehend and respond to in written form. Similarly, a Quick Write at the beginning of a social science unit might reveal that the students in the class already know a great deal about habitats, requiring you to revise and enhance your plans for the unit.

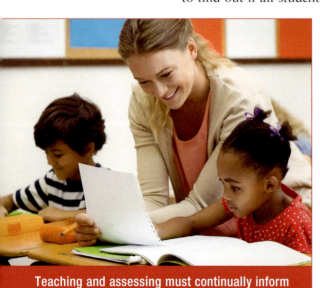

Teaching and assessing must continually inform one another.

2. When can informal assessments be administered? We've discussed a number of informal literacy assessments, such as observing behaviors for anecdotal notes. One question that many teachers (especially new teachers) have is *when* these assessments can take place. Guided reading (Chapter 11), which is done with small groups, is an excellent time to observe student reading and take anecdotal notes or fill out checklists on specific skills such as *concepts about print* (see Appendix E). During guided reading is also a good time because assessment should be *ongoing:* you can listen to and evaluate a student's needs, use guided reading sessions to teach that skill, and then reassess in a later guided reading session to see if the student has progressed. Some assessments, such as running records, informal reading inventories, and sight word recognition tests, need to be administered to a single student. Guided reading also can allow you to assess individual students by reading with only one student at a time instead of with a small group. A variation many teachers use is to assign the class an activity (e.g., essay writing or partner reading) to allow the teacher one-on-one time with each student to administer a running record or IRI individually.

see appendix E

3. If a need is identified, when and how might that need be addressed? When observations or specific assessments show that a large number of students have a specific need, that area can be addressed by reteaching the skill or concept through the vehicle of a minilesson (see Chapter 9) or through explicit instruction during shared or guided reading (see Chapter 11). When several students have the same need, a temporary group can be formed to differentiate instruction and focus on that need; for example, students who need reinforcement in finding the answers to inferential questions, as determined by an informal reading inventory, can become a temporary group working directly with you. Through this type of flexible grouping, individual students can be helped directly through reading conferences, or specific assignments designed to rectify the problem can be sent home with the student if the parents or caregivers are able to help at home. (See the Case Example on p. 305 describing Chelsea's journey.)

Cross-age tutoring, a program in which older students work with younger ones on specific subject areas such as reading and writing, can be a successful alternative to classroom intervention if tutors are wisely chosen and given some minimal training in the strategy needed. For example, fifth-grade students at Fruitridge Elementary School in Sacramento paired up with first-grade students and were successful in helping the younger children improve their comprehension scores when they listened to the students read stories at their independent reading levels and had discussions afterward that emanated from critical and creative questions designed collaboratively with the fifth-grade teacher.

4. How can assessment and instruction be aligned with standards? Standards provide a systematic way for educators to ask themselves, "What do we want our students to know, and what do we want them to be able to do?" Standards are also an attempt to do away with the often sporadic nature and uncertainty of testing, grading, accountability, and instructional planning. Teachers in nearly every state are now committing time and effort to redesigning curriculum, resequencing courses, aligning materials and resources, redesigning instructional practices, and evaluating and reporting student progress—all in response to standards.

The alignment of curriculum and assessment with standards is illustrated by a teacher in New Jersey who is teaching her second-grade English learners a unit on farm animals. Although the standards she follows are the CCSS, the standards adopted by her state, the process of aligning curriculum with the standards is the same with every set of standards. This teacher first familiarizes herself with

cumulative progress
indicators ■

the standards for her grade level and then looks for innovative teaching methods and materials to help her meet those standards. For example, CCSS.ELA.Literacy.SL.2.2 states: "Recount or describe key ideas or details from a text read aloud or information presented orally or through other media" (NGACBP & CCSSO, 2010, p. 23). Each such standard has accompanying **cumulative progress indicators** that help the teacher put the standard in place so that it can be observed when it is demonstrated by the students (see Figure 13.8).

In this unit, the teacher's major objective is to have students identify animals found in Latin America, identify the sounds they make, and compare them with farm animals found in the United States. To fulfill this objective, she reads them a story, *The Day the Dog Said Cock-a-Doodle-Doo!* by David McPhail. Students then compare sounds animals make in both languages, Spanish and English. Using two hula hoops, the students identify and discuss the similarities and differences in animal sounds in Latin America and the United States. The right side of one hoop represents sounds animals make in Latin America; the left side of the other hoop represents sounds animals make in the United States. The middle, where the two hula hoops overlap, represents sounds animals make in both places. Later, together as a class, the students put symbols to the sounds the animals make, using a Venn diagram on an interactive whiteboard and three different colors.

After this lesson, the teacher creates a checklist of the progress indicators for each skill and ability contained in the standard covered by the lesson (see Figure 13.8). Through observation of the participation and discussion inherent in the lesson, she then determines whether individual students are making progress in meeting this standard.

figure	13.8	Correlating standards with instruction.

UNIT: "FARM ANIMALS IN TWO COUNTRIES"

Standards Addressed in the Unit

Name: _____   Date: _____

Cumulative Progress Indicators:

CCSS.ELA-Literacy.SL.2.1 Participate in collaborative conversations with diverse partners about *grade 2 topics and texts* with peers and adults in small and larger groups.	NEVER	SOMETIMES	FREQUENTLY	ALWAYS
CCSS.ELA-Literacy.SL.2.2 Recount or describe key ideas or details from a text read aloud or information presented orally or through other media.	NEVER	SOMETIMES	FREQUENTLY	ALWAYS
CCSS.ELA-Literacy.RL.2.2 Recount stories, including fables and folktales from diverse cultures, and determine their central message, lesson, or moral.	NEVER	SOMETIMES	FREQUENTLY	ALWAYS
CCSS.ELA-Literacy.L2.1.1 Demonstrate command of the conventions of standard English grammar and usage when writing or speaking.	NEVER	SOMETIMES	FREQUENTLY	ALWAYS

Source: NGACBP & CCSSO, 2010.

CASE EXAMPLE

From diagnosis to intervention to avid reader: Chelsea's journey

Diagnosis

Chelsea is a second-grade student in a suburban middle-class school just outside Sacramento. English is her native language. When she began falling behind in the second month of the school year, her teacher, Mr. Green, reviewed his anecdotal notes about Chelsea's literacy progress. He noticed she seemed distracted in free reading time and resisted reading aloud when asked. Mr. Green administered a running record and determined that Chelsea was reading word by word and made many errors that changed the meaning of the text. Her accuracy level (84 percent) on the second-grade passage revealed that it was at her frustration level. Specifically, Chelsea appeared to have trouble decoding multisyllabic words. Also, a retelling of the passage showed that while Chelsea got the main idea of the passage, she was not able to recall any details. This retelling supported many earlier observations, suggesting that Chelsea paid little attention to the details of what she read.

From Fry's group of instant words (Appendix G) that Mr. Green flashed on index cards, Chelsea recognized 120 of 162 words on the first-grade list and fewer than half on the second-grade list. Chelsea also demonstrated consistent problems with spelling. Although she does surprisingly well on weekly spelling tests, she has trouble, mostly with multisyllabic words,

with writing assignments, and in her dialogue journal.

An Interest Inventory given at the beginning of the year suggested that Chelsea did not enjoy reading, but liked being read to. When asked how she felt about herself as a reader, Chelsea replied, "I don't care much for reading. I've never read a book I liked. It's hard for me. I can do it when I try, but I'd rather watch television." When Mr. Green asked Chelsea who she thought was a good reader and what good readers do, Chelsea mentioned her 10-year-old sister, Brooke. "Brooke is a really good reader," the little girl mused. "She reads all the time and she reads fast. She read a Harry Potter book in three days!"

Intervention

Mr. Green first spent time with Chelsea during library time. From Chelsea's Interest Inventory, he noticed that she liked the program *Jane and the Dragon.* He selected several similar fantasies on Chelsea's independent reading level and asked her to leaf through them to see if she might like them. She became entranced with these books and soon had read four in the series. Mr. Green made provisions for her to read one to the kindergarten class once a week.

To help Chelsea begin to read more purposefully, Mr. Green paired her with another student and encouraged the two girls to do dyad reading with passages on a daily basis (see Chapter 8). Using this strategy, the two students took turns summarizing the paragraphs the other student read, and both began to pay more attention to details in the passages.

Mr. Green also did explicit instruction of question–answer relationships (QARs; see Chapter 8) with Chelsea, teaching her and several other students with the same need how to find the answers to specific kinds of questions in the text.

Mr. Green created an individual progress chart so that Chelsea could keep track of the growth she made in both reading comprehension and accuracy. He also gave her a Sight Word Bingo game to take home to play with her younger brother and older sister. (Chapter 6 in DeVries, 2015, contains a description of this activity, and Appendix D in that book contains sample bingo cards.)

Finally, Mr. Green used the strategy of Spelling in Parts (SIP; see Chapter 6) to help Chelsea break words into chunks in order to decode them and spell them more successfully.

Avid reader

The dyad reading has helped Chelsea to continually be aware of the details of what she is reading, as she now knows she will be accountable for summarizing what she has read.

QARs have helped Chelsea see reading in a new light. She is now able to go back in a text and find answers to different kinds of questions and has integrated the four kinds of comprehension (see Chapter 8) into her understanding of the kinds of information she should be gleaning as she reads. Today, when she does a retelling of a passage, she automatically includes the answers to all four kinds of questions.

The SIP strategy has helped Chelsea to both spell and decode multisyllabic words more quickly and effectively. Though she still has problems with "hidden" syllables, like schwas, she is able to break words into pronounceable parts, or chunk them, in order to decode them.

By June, Chelsea was reading at grade level according to a recent running record. As a result of a newly sparked inter-est in reading (*anything* about dragons!), Chelsea is reading voraciously and looks forward to her sojourns with the kinder-garten class. The volume of reading she is now doing, coupled with the repeated readings necessary to prepare for reading to the kindergarten class, has improved her reading rate, accu-racy, and prosody. Additionally, Chelsea admits she now loves to read.

SUMMARY

The major goal for literacy assessment in a primary classroom is to find out how each student is progressing in a particular area at a given time and to make instructional adjustments more closely attuned to the children's changing needs. The best way to achieve this assessment goal is by using a balance of for-mal, informal, and observational assessment tools.

The use of formalized reading achievement tests provides important compar-ative data designed to be valid and reliable, but results do not always provide accurate and specific information for individual students, in context. Data from such tests should therefore be interpreted with caution, especially when the test-takers are culturally diverse learners or students whose first language is not English. Moreover, collaboration is vital when addressing students with special needs; their instruction must be viewed more in terms of a team effort (Harp & Brewer, 2005).

Informal assessments and anecdotal information derived from careful obser-vation, though nonscientific, can support or question standardized test results. Informal assessments, if resulting data are compiled frequently and interpreted wisely, can be an excellent method of continually informing instruction.

see appendix E

The value of the assessment devices discussed in this chapter and those con-tained in Appendix E depends largely on reflective analysis and how the devices are used for communicating about literacy progress and resultant instructional plans with the child, his parents, and others. By recognizing the strengths and limitations of different types of assessment devices, you can maximize their value for creating a comprehensive literacy program.

questions FOR JOURNAL WRITING AND DISCUSSION

1. Interview a local primary-grade teacher to determine what assessment strate-gies he uses, or, if you are already teaching, interview a teacher from another school. What and how does the teacher assess? How does the teacher balance formal and informal assessments? Discuss your findings with others in your class to see if similarities, differences, and/or conclusions can be drawn.

2. It is no longer enough to simply give children the opportunity to learn; news-papers and current education journals say that schools must now provide proof that learning has actually taken place. Discuss this pervasive feeling in terms of its implications for literacy assessment.

3. Imagine that at a parent–teacher meeting, a parent confronts you about your assessment program, complaining that you spend too much time assessing

and too little time teaching, considering the brief school day. Role-play the confrontation, defending your position.

4. The SBAC and PARCC have developed assessments aligned to the CCSS. If your state has adopted the standards and uses one of the assessments, how have the schools/districts in your area prepared teachers and students for the assessment?

suggestions   FOR PROJECTS AND FIELD ACTIVITIES

1. Select one of the informal assessment instruments discussed in this chapter and prepare to use it with first- or second-grade students to measure a literacy-related area or skill. Summarize the results and share them with your class. *Note:* Blank copies of some of the assessments are available in Appendix E.

> see appendix E

2. Observe a classroom teacher or reading specialist as she administers an IRI or a running record to a young child. Discuss the interpretation of results with the teacher. Why was the assessment given? What was learned? How will the teacher adapt instruction as a result of the information gained?

3. Examine a standardized reading achievement test that is routinely administered to beginning readers in your area. Review the teacher's manual and technical manual for information about administering and scoring the test. Evaluate the instructions and test items for clarity, and compare the norming population with the students in your area. Examine the items for illustrations of cultural stereotypes and/or bias. Interview school authorities to determine how the information is reported and used to make classroom, school, and district decisions about reading instruction. Finally, peruse Buros's *Mental Measurements Yearbook*, available in the reference section of libraries, for more information on this test and how it compares with others of its kind.

Home as Partner

14

focus questions

How can teachers help heighten parents' or caregivers' awareness of their critical role in the literacy development of their children?

What are examples of appropriate literacy activities that teachers can share with families to help promote literacy development?

How can teachers best keep families informed about their child's progress in literacy?

rs. Nguyen teaches first grade in inner-city Los Angeles. Early in the school year, Mrs. Nguyen collects the personal literacy histories of every student in her class to inform her later instructional decisions. Much as physicians gather the medical history of children they treat, this teacher knows she must learn about the literacy experiences the students have already had, including the kind of literacy materials to which they have been exposed, to get a clear picture of where to begin instruction. She knows that every child has had rich experiences upon which to build, although these experiences may differ from those that middle-class youngsters commonly encounter. Over the years, contrary to what she originally expected, she has found that parents are eager to share information about their children and are usually willing to be active participants in their children's reading development.

Because formal and informal reading measures suggest that many of her students may be at risk for reading failure, Mrs. Nguyen uses their own community materials as "fodder" for early literacy instruction. For example, she scours the neighborhood for letters on stores and signs with which the students will be familiar, takes pictures of the letters, and brings them into the classroom for instruction. She uses the *M* in McDonald's, the *T* in Taco Bell, the *W* in Walmart, and so forth, to reinforce these letters. Students, then, are encouraged to look for other environmental print when they go home at the end of the day. Parents are invited to share in this literacy scavenger hunt, and many express gratitude that they have been able to help.

INTRODUCTION

he preceding vignette illustrates a primary aspect of the home–school connection. The example from Mrs. Nguyen's classroom demonstrates the integration of literacies from the children's homes and communities with classroom literacy instruction. It shows a profound regard for parents as partners in the literacy process who have already laid the foundation and are interested in helping in any way they can. *Note:* For the sake of readability, the term "parent" is used throughout this chapter. This term should be understood to encompass the concept of caregiver as well—a family member or other committed adult who may have primary responsibility for the care of a child.

It is often said, and will be echoed throughout this chapter, that parents are their children's first teachers. Consider: all the experiences children amass, beginning at birth, affect their success in literacy. Moreover, the success of the school literacy program depends, in large part, on the quality of the opportunities for literacy development that occur in the home (Fan & Chen, 2001). Because some students come to school already knowing how to read and write, researchers have extensively studied such children and their home environments (Briggs & Elkind, 1973; Morrow, 1983; Teale, 1978). Although the parents often claim the children began reading and writing "naturally," investigators are now convinced that there is more to it than that, and that much can be done through adult–child interaction and the home environment to enhance the literacy program that exists at school.

Parents can influence their children's literacy development in several ways. The first is through interpersonal interaction with them. This includes the various ways in which all members of the household converse, work, and play with one another. The second is through the climate of the household. When family members hold literacy in high esteem and retain high academic expectations for their children, the motivational climate in the household is favorable to literacy development. Finally, the physical environment in the home also has a direct impact on literacy development. Having the tools of literacy easily accessible—books, magazines, newspapers, writing materials, online resources, and so forth—makes a subtle yet profound statement about the importance of literacy activities.

While collecting information about home literacy practices is often done with the intent of helping families increase student achievement, Grant and Potter (2011) remind us that parent program models should not be viewed as top-down, with only school literacy practices viewed as "correct." In order for a solid home–literacy connection to succeed, Ms. Nguyen and her colleagues must remember not to judge what parents do or not do at home, but rather work *with* families, especially families from diverse cultural, linguistic, or socioeconomic backgrounds whose children historically have not done well in school.

The following sections offer more specific information, synthesized from current research, on exactly how reading development is enhanced in the home.

RESEARCH ON HOME LITERACY

every teacher hopes for a class full of students whose parents care about and support their literacy growth at home. Teachers know, intuitively and through research, that such children will have a much easier road to becoming readers and writers than those who do not have this background. Indeed, research from the 1970s and 1980s consistently identified strong correlations between parents reading to and with their children and children's later success in literacy (Anderson et al., 1985; Chomsky, 1972; Laosa, 1982; Teale & Sulzby, 1986b). Later research attempted to identify the essential nature of what transpires during parent–child reading interactions to make them so beneficial. Lancy and Bergin (1992) found that children who are most fluent and positive about reading came from parent–child pairs who viewed reading as fun, kept stories moving with a "meaning-seeking" rather than a purely "decoding" orientation, and encouraged questions and humor while reading together.

Positive home practices can be beneficial; survey results in *The Condition of Education* (National Center for Education Statistics, 2003) indicate that early reading success is enhanced by literacy activity in the home, while Nord, Lennon, Liu, and Chandler (1999) concluded that when children are read to three or more times a week, they are more likely to learn their letters. Teachers have long been telling parents to simply read to their children, but some research suggests this exhortation has been misguided. For example, Lancy, Draper, and Boyce (1989) describe the parents of good readers as using expansionist strategies, such as adding personal information and explanations, or "scaffolding," as their children grapple to understand stories. For example, the parent might start reading a story with the child and then make guesses as to what will happen next, thereby modeling the comprehension strategy of making predictions. Over time, the parent takes a less active role and encourages the child to use expansionist strategies herself when reading. These are especially useful with a story that has been read multiple times. When the child experiences difficulty, parents of a good reader tend to make a mild joke of it, thus defusing anxiety, whereas parents of a poor reader treat a decoding error as a serious infraction, sometimes even covering up an illustration to prevent "cheating," according to Lancy and colleagues.

Tracy and Young (1994) studied the home reading behaviors of struggling and more advanced readers and their college-educated mothers. They found no difference in the frequency of children's oral reading during first grade and found that struggling readers actually did *more* oral reading in second and third grades than did the more proficient readers. Tracy (1995), in a later analysis of videotaped reading sessions with struggling and more advanced readers, noted a striking contrast in the degree to which advanced readers received more physical and verbal attention, support, and extended feedback from their families. In a more in-depth study of more than 40 families, Baker and colleagues (1994) analyzed differences between literacy activities of low- and middle-income families. Low-income families reported doing more reading practices and homework (e.g., flash cards, letter practice) with their kindergarten-aged children than did middle-income parents; middle-income parents reported only slightly more book reading with their children than did low-income parents. The middle-income parents reported more enjoyable activities with print, however, as well as more recreational reading on the part of their children. From these studies, it appears that the nature of what actually takes place during literacy events matters a great deal—perhaps more than the mere fact that the parent–child literacy activity occurs.

Although most research focuses on parents reading to and with children, additional studies indicate that such practices as subscribing to magazines and newspapers and using the library support vocabulary growth and word recognition skills (Griffin & Morrison, 1997; Leseman & de Jong, 1998); rhyming games, telling stories, and singing songs have also been shown to improve literacy outcomes (Baker, Scher, & Makler, 1997). Moreover, research on the use of home–school journals (Kay, Neher, & Lush, 2010) and repeated reading (Hindin & Paratore, 2007) provide more evidence for the benefits of solid parent–child literacy interactions.

UNDERSTANDING DIFFERENCES IN HOME PRACTICES

because many teachers come from middle-class backgrounds, they may view the home literacy practices they experienced in their own homes as the most effective ones. The image that comes to mind for many teachers is a young child sitting on the lap of a parent—usually a young female—while a large storybook is being read. As a result, educators may undervalue many of the literacy experiences that occur in the homes and communities of non-middle-class students (Heath, 1983; Moll, Amanti, Neff, & Gonzalez, 1992; Rogers, 2001), including those of homes having a student with special needs (González, 2006). However, teachers should consider the wide range of literacy practices that may occur, so as to more effectively build upon the literacy experiences that children from a host of backgrounds bring with them to school (Thomas, Fazio, & Stiefelmeyer, 1999).

Bear in mind that most parents—regardless of income level or cultural or ethnic background—value education for their children. However, different parents may have differing perceptions of what it means to be literate, and they may not always be aware of the most effective tactics for fostering literacy with their children. Several researchers have reported the high value that many low-income families place on literacy. For example, Delgado-Gaitan (1987) found that the possibility of a better education for their children was cited as a major reason for Hispanic immigration to the United States. Taylor and Dorsey-Gaines (1988), in studying low-income parents whose children succeed in school, noted extraordinary sacrifices and efforts made in the interest of the child's education, despite the parents' limited educational levels. Finally, Fitzgerald, Spiegel, and Cunningham (1991), in a study of low- and high-income parents, reported that low-income families rated the value of education higher than the high-income families.

Another important difference among parents concerns their concepts of literacy. Goldenberg, Reese, and Gallimore (1992) found that low-income Hispanic parents help their children acquire literacy mainly by emphasizing letter names and spelling–sound correspondences. Similarly, Baker and colleagues (1994) reported that low-income parents spend much time explicitly instructing their children in the work and practice elements of reading, whereas middle-income parents use a more playful approach involving stories and play. Literacy is presented and modeled as an enjoyable pastime and an important lens through which to understand the world. Knowing that this difference may exist, teachers should emphasize to all parents that children for whom literacy learning is painful tend to avoid books and reading, whereas children who learn to enjoy reading for its own sake are more likely to ask for books and to read recreationally, thus becoming more successful readers (Baker, Serpell, & Sonnenschein, 1995).

Be aware that nearly all parents participate in some literacy activities with their children. True, some parents may have problems reading and writing, or English may not be their first language, but nearly all engage in a wide range of literacy activities in the course of their daily lives. One question that parents who are not native English speakers ask teachers is what language they should be using at home with their children. Research indicates that the development of literacy skills in a student's home language will assist his English literacy development (August & Shanahan, 2006; Chavez-Reyes, 2010; Gold-

Every teacher hopes for a class full of students whose parents have fostered literacy growth at home.

enberg, 2008; Thomas & Collier, 2002). Thus, parents of English learners should be encouraged to play rhyming games, sing songs, and read to and with their children in their primary language. Sanchez, Plata, Grosso, and Leird (2010) describe how Spanish-speaking parents can incorporate *dichos,* sayings in Spanish (such as "*Donde hay gana, hay maña,*" "Where there is the desire, there is the ability"), as a method of supporting literacy development. Haneda (2006) describes how English learners use literacy in both English and their native language in their home and communities with siblings, in formal heritage language classes, on personal websites (blogs), in instant messaging, and in other ways. Although referring to Spanish speakers, Rodríguez-Brown's (2011) assertions are applicable to parents from all linguistic backgrounds. She writes: "Parents who are not fully proficient in English may be able to read more fluently, ask more questions, and extend the stories when they do shared-reading in Spanish. . . . Access to reading materials in the language that parents know best and the type of interaction between parent and child during shared readings is critical in supporting the richness of the home literacy environment" (pp. 746–747).

In his research on family literacy practices, Barton (1997) found many examples of parents who experience difficulties with written communication who nonetheless kept diaries, maintained household accounts, wrote poetry, took phone messages, and sent letters. These parents dealt with shopping lists, bills, forms, recipes, junk mail, and TV schedules. Such parents should not be perceived as unintelligent people living in barren homes "waiting to be filled up by literacy," as the media might lead us to believe. For the most part, adults who admit having problems with reading and writing are ordinary people leading ordinary lives, and if they have children, like everyone else, they are deeply concerned about their children's education.

Key partners in literacy with the schools include mothers, fathers, siblings, and other relations and family friends that children cite as important in their literacy lives. In addition, focusing exclusively on parent–child relations excludes important social agencies and community resources that may enhance literacy behaviors. Educators have also moved beyond the notion that parents should read only to young children and have recognized that children of all ages—from infancy up to the teenage years—can benefit significantly from literacy practices carried out at home. Parents can learn from their children, too! Literacy learning can be a symbiotic event within families. Finally, rather than asking parents to replicate what is done in school, educators are now trying to support the practices parents are already doing in their homes to promote literacy (Barton, 1997).

HELPING PARENTS WHO CANNOT READ

ore than 44 million adults lack sufficient literacy skills to read a food label, fill out a job application, or even read a simple storybook to their child (National Center for Education Statistics, 2008). The obvious proactive response to this statistic would be to invite illiterate parents to functional literacy classes to prepare them to foster literacy skills in their own children. However, given the life situations of most illiterate parents, who often also are the "working poor"—long hours at work, time restrictions, lack of resources and reliable transportation, to name a few—most parents enrolled in literacy programs never complete the course. Given the difficulty for these parents of becoming literate in a timely manner, are there still strategies you can share with parents so that they can help their children in their own quests for literacy?

Following are some suggestions that you can offer to parents who, though they may have limited English literacy skills, want to help their own children succeed at becoming proficient readers (Cooter, 2006).

dialogic reading ■

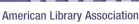

American Library Association

www.ala.org

Introduce them to dialogic reading. In **dialogic reading,** the child selects a picture storybook he or she can read independently. The child then leads a discussion about the pictures in the book. The parent merely listens and uses "what" or "why" questions, elaborates on what the child says, points, and gestures at items on the printed page but takes the position of "follower" in the book conversation (American Library Association, 2005). Ideally, parents should be taught to use a book in this language-rich way. Fortunately, the American Library Association holds parent training sessions and can assist teachers in locating trainers through the Every Child Ready to Read@Your Library program. For more information, visit their website.

Create make-believe-alouds. If parents cannot read aloud to their children, they can still foster a love for reading and language using this cross between story reading and storytelling. A parent needn't even know the words on a page to take a picture storybook or wordless book and, using the illustrations as a guide, create an imaginative tale that captivates the young reader's attention. Morgan and Goldstein (2004) found that inviting illiterate parents to create stories to accompany picture books in this fashion significantly increased the quality of the language interactions.

Build on what the parent can do: talk. Whether they speak in English or the parent's home language, encourage parents to share songs, family stories, oral traditions, and so forth. Simply by talking and listening, parents can do much to help their children with literacy. Also, urge parents to speak in longer sentences in any conversation with their children and to use complex or uncommon words, explaining their meaning through demonstrations or pictures. Indeed, the mother's *mean length of utterance* (MLU), or the average words spoken together to the child, has been found to be predictive of that child's later language development (Murray, 1990).

Teachers may offer these suggestions to parents during parent–teacher conferences or workshops. Often these parents, who need the additional support, cannot attend conferences and workshops at school. However, you can get this information to parents in several ways, the most straightforward being via a home visit (see p. 323). During such a visit, you can describe and demonstrate dialogic reading and make-believe-alouds discussed earlier, as well as explain the positive benefits of talk. If a home visit is not possible, you do not have to demonstrate these activities in person. You can create videos and upload them to a school website, or simply put demonstrations on DVDs and send them home with students so parents can watch these activities in their homes. Finally, you can teach your students these activities and assign them as a regular homework activity. Because the child is coaching his parents, these activities may be more inviting to parents who have not had positive experiences with schools in the past.

Nearly all caregivers, even those who experience difficulties with literacy themselves, participate in some literacy activities with their children.

COMMUNICATING WITH PARENTS

good communication between the home and the school right from the start of the school year is essential to any comprehensive literacy program for the early grades. Home–school communication must be established early so that families and schools can work collaboratively to benefit the children most effectively. Edwards (2004) suggests that such strong collaborations "involve rethinking the relationship between home and school such that students' opportunities to learn are expanded" (p. 77). This occurs when you accept that parents define literacy and their role in supporting it in varying ways. Moreover, such collaborations depend on your becoming knowledgeable about the cultural diversity of the families of each of the students you teach and considering how such variations affect parent–teacher relationships.

Conferences

Because most educators are aware of the need for effective communication with parents, many schools schedule several parent–teacher conference days when teachers are available to talk with parents about the progress of their children. The parent–teacher conference can be a fruitful time during which you explain to the parent, in clear terms, the components of the literacy program and how the child is progressing within the program. Moreover, it is the ideal time to communicate to parents that their partnership is needed to reinforce the notion on which a comprehensive literacy program is based: that literacy activities are important in the world and are enjoyable. After hearing about the literacy program, parents typically want to know how they can help their child at home.

What brings the parent to school? When both the school district and individual schools make a concerted effort to let parents know that "We want you, we need you, and we have valuable information to share with you about your child's literacy needs," they will come, if flexible scheduling makes attendance possible. Therefore, schools must take a positive approach and work with the strengths and needs of the families involved.

Guidelines for effective parent-teacher conferences

Parents are concerned about their children, but they may need reassurance that their concern is appropriate and that they are capable of taking part in the partnership. Consider the following points in this regard:

1. Set up the conference with the comfort of the parents in mind. Rather than sitting behind a desk as an authority figure, create an arrangement in which all adults can sit side by side.

2. Understand that parents and caregivers have a right to their anxiety. It is quite normal for them to wonder how their child compares with his or her peers.

3. Inform parents about their child's strengths and limitations while sympathizing with their concerns. "Don't worry" is a phrase that has little value and should be avoided.

4. Refrain from being judgmental; listen actively to parents, and always seek common ground. Instead of blaming them for what may not have occurred in the home,

praise them for their concern and desire to help. This will engender a feeling of true partnership.

5. Focus on specific constructive suggestions rather than vague generalities. "Your child needs help hearing beginning sounds in words" is much more helpful than "Your child is not ready to learn to read."

6. Discuss the child's progress using examples such as progress forms, test results, or samples of the child's work.

7. Accept the parents' questions and provide clear, honest responses.

8. Suggest to the parents specific activities they can do at home, such as those described in a later section of this chapter, to help the child with any deficiencies or to enhance reading interest and proficiency.

9. Thank the parents for attending and let the parents know that you are available for additional conferences if there are further concerns.

Scheduling the conference

Conference scheduling is vitally important. Scheduling strategies should include not only a variety of options for parents but flexibility for teachers as well. Offer some conference times early in the day, and some late, to accommodate parents who cannot come to school during the regular school day. For this arrangement to be successful, the district's administrative unit must be fully committed to the partnership concept and arrange for you to receive compensation for your efforts.

Conducting the conference

Conferences can be productive and pleasant for both the teacher and the parent if the teacher follows a few simple procedures. Begin the conference with a friendly and relaxed greeting to the parent. Adopt a tone of friendly acquaintance with the parent, reinforcing the idea that you are both on the same team. If the parent speaks little or no English, arrange to have an aide or community member present who can translate, or invite an older English-speaking sibling to perform this important task. In advance, ask the student to teach you a few polite phrases ("How are you?" or "I am very pleased to meet you") in her home language, so that you can make the parent feel welcome. This is also a great time to identify specific goals for the child, as well as an action plan that both you and the parent can implement to increase the child's literacy. For example, at the conference, you and the parent might decide on a goal of increasing the child's decoding skills by reading a decodable text out loud at home every night for 20 minutes. Begin and end the conference on a positive note, addressing what is positive and unique about the child.

What parents should know about reading in the early grades

The most common query from parents during conferences crosses all ethnic, cultural, and socioeconomic levels: "What can I do to help my child become a good reader?" You can offer general advice based on practices that research has found helpful (as presented in the Research on Home Literacy section earlier in this chapter), but parents are most interested in specific activities they can do with their children to help them succeed. In the past, teachers often suggested that parents drill children on the alphabet or help them with the sounds of letters. Many well-meaning parents became convinced that formal teaching of skills would help their children get a head start. As mentioned earlier, newer research on literacy suggests otherwise. When parents provide a rich literacy environment at home, instruction in literacy becomes easier for both the teacher and the child at school. Therefore, this becomes the most important message to deliver to parents. Because most children do not enter public school before age 5 and preschool before age 3, if at all, schools need to take the responsibility of disseminating information in the community so that parents can put it into practice at home.

Parent Workshops

Parents able to attend workshops can benefit from information about activities they can undertake with their children to help build decoding and comprehension skills—and most important, to enjoy reading. Many teachers have had great success conducting two or three workshops during the academic year, each focusing on one activity. (See the following three activities for sample workshop activities.) Some schools require that parents who enroll their children in prekindergarten and preschool programs attend workshops in order for their child to participate in the programs. Refreshments or a parent potluck draws many parents, and a format of simple instructions for the activity followed by practice in small groups bolsters parents' confidence to try the activity at home with their children.

Questioning

ACTIVITY

Encourage parents to follow up on critical-thinking strategies introduced in class by exploring at home the kinds of questions that extend and provoke critical and creative thinking. When children read at home, instruct parents to follow every paragraph or so with a thought-provoking question that cannot be answered with simply "yes" or "no." "Why do you think . . . ?" and "What if . . . ?" questions almost always fulfill these purposes. In a parent workshop, you might begin by brainstorming with parents a list of the kinds of questions that will be the most useful for expanding comprehension and then discuss the kind of responses they are likely to generate. Follow this preparation by giving each attendee a copy of a short story containing several paragraphs. Have parents contribute appropriate questions for each paragraph. Praise correct choices. If a contributed response is not appropriate, accept it, and then rework it into a useful question. For example, if a parent offers, "Did the boy go into the woods?" (and the answer is given in the paragraph), you can accept the answer and then slightly modify it to, "Why do you think the boy went into the woods?" The latter question requires the child to consider the data, compare them with what he or she knows of the world, and create an answer.

Parent Think-Aloud

ACTIVITY

Parents who already read with their children can extend the reading activity to become a comprehension-modeling practice by utilizing think-alouds. In a parent workshop, explain to parents that in this activity, as its name implies, the parent shares aloud everything he is thinking as a paragraph is read, including the following:

- making predictions *("I bet Jerry will ask for his dog back.")*

- imaging *("Ooh—that meadow reminds me of the field behind Mr. Darrow's farm where we used to hike, remember?")*

- generalizing *("So I guess these polar bears hibernate like the grizzlies we were reading about.")*

- using context to figure out the meaning of unknown words *("It says the pancakes were huge and Tiny had a hard time finishing them. Since Tiny had a hard time eating them, I'll bet 'huge' means really big.")*

Using adult passages, model how a parent might do a think-aloud, slowing your thinking way down and offering a window to the brain for the benefit of the child. Invite parents to add their observations about the passages; praise comments that might lead to think-alouds that would be particularly helpful for children.

Pass out a passage to each attendee and have pairs of parents practice reading a paragraph out loud, sharing their meaning-gaining thought processes as they do so. Have them switch roles after each paragraph so that both parents get a chance to practice the technique. Finally, encourage parents to try this activity at home as part of shared reading. Explain that children can be invited to add their thoughts to those of their parents as they get the gist of the activity.

Dyad Reading

ACTIVITY

A third activity for parents is one that is especially effective for informational text and, thus, will help parents to be of assistance when their child has reading to do in content areas such as science and social studies. Dyad reading can be explained to parents as a way to have their children read aloud and be sure they are understanding what they are reading. If only one text is available, as is often the case with content area textbooks, the parent and child sit side by side and take turns reading aloud, rotating after every paragraph. When the reader has finished the paragraph, the reader summarizes it for the listener, who then adds any material that may have been overlooked by the reader. They then switch roles. To introduce this activity to parents, explain the steps as you model them with a partner or attendee who has been briefed in advance. You may model the activity using one text, as this is the way it will be used at home. However, for the purpose of the demonstration, you may reproduce the passage for the attendees. It may also be helpful to explain to parents that an effective summary is a shortened version of the original—no more than a third in length—that contains the main idea as well as important details. When you have answered questions about the steps of the procedure, hand out new informational passages to pairs of parents and have them practice dyad reading, rotating roles after each paragraph. Encourage them to use this technique at home whenever their child brings home homework in the content areas that requires reading. A variation on dyad reading that is also helpful is to engage in the same activity but discuss the pictures that are found in the text. Not only is using pictures, graphs, and photos a good way to increase comprehension (see Chapter 10), but it also allows parents who cannot read or do not speak English to engage with their children in meaningful ways that promote high levels of literacy.

Other Communication with Parents

Besides regularly scheduled conferences and workshops, teachers can keep parents informed in a variety of other ways, including newsletters, notes, and reading festivals.

Newsletters

A monthly, or even weekly, newsletter, perhaps in the form of an attractive, simply written electronic document or printed flyer, can help explain the school's literacy program and help avoid misunderstanding and confusion that can be brought about by a zealous media that sometimes provides negative press about what goes on in the schools. The newsletter can also be a vehicle for conveying or reiterating suggestions for home reading. Newsletters can also include student contributions, such as drawings, poems, and student-written reports and opinion pieces, that can increase interest from parents who want to read what their students are producing. Students who want to contribute, of course, will also be motivated to write! Additionally, any frequently asked questions can be addressed in the letter.

Progress notes

Progress notes are a more individualized way to keep parents informed about their child. At frequent intervals, you can write short notes about individual children, using a positive, congratulatory tone. You might write a note when a student has completed a book, asked an incisive question, or written an especially interesting piece. Such notes might also include a few open-ended questions for the parent to ask the child about a story that has been read in class or some vocabulary words to review with the child. You might also ask the parent to listen to the child read a passage from a recently finished book so the parent can share in the enjoyable experience of completing a book and celebrating success.

Reading festivals

Reading festivals provide a special opportunity, other than the formal parent–teacher conference, to bring parents to the school. Parents, children, and invited community members come together to share favorite books, articles, and stories. Any number of activities can be planned. You can ask parents to bring in their favorite children's book to read with the class. Community members—especially role models that youngsters do not ordinarily associate with reading, such as firefighters, sports figures, or police officers—can be invited to read with small groups of students. Choral reading can be done, with adults and students taking appropriate or reverse roles. Art activities, such as making and playing reading games or constructing dioramas or murals in connection with a favorite text, can be offered.

Reading festivals work well in collaboration with book fairs or book swaps. A book fair can be organized with the help of a local bookstore or a children's paperback book company, such as Scholastic. A book swap, on the other hand, requires less advance planning and can be arranged simply by asking students to bring in old books and magazines from home. Students can then take turns reading aloud the blurbs on the back covers before swapping the books. Teachers work with parents to match books to readers by interest and reading levels.

Family literacy night

Families can come together for a special night of reading and writing together in a variation of the reading festival (Hutchins, Greenfeld, & Epstein, 2008). At a **family literacy night,** parents, relatives, and children read books together and participate in all sorts of reading-related activities. Children can perform readers theater scripts or their original drama, or they can dress up as their favorite book characters and answer questions about the book from the character's perspective. They can give book talks about their favorite texts or read poems, do choral readings, or present puppet shows. You can arrange to give away books through

■ family literacy night

programs such as Reading Is Fundamental (RIF) for students to add to their home libraries. Finally, parents and children can write together, with paper products, computers, and other resources provided by the school or local libraries. You can also use the opportunity at such an event to demonstrate one of the three workshop activities described earlier in the chapter.

READING ALOUD TO AND WITH CHILDREN

How to "Raise a Reader"

www.randomhouse.com/
kids/parents

Parents can best help children develop reading literacy by reading to and with them. Research has shown that children who read early generally come from homes where reading materials are readily accessible (Sulzby & Teale, 2010) and that shared reading in the home is beneficial to children (Gallimore & Reese, 1999; Goldenberg, 2004; Roberts, Jurgens, & Buchinal, 2005; Van Steensel, 2006). Additionally, early reading experiences provide children with at least three major concepts about text. These concepts—ultimate reasons for parents to read aloud to their children—should be shared with parents in a straightforward way. First, children come to see reading as pleasurable as they associate it with warm quality time with parents. Second, they learn about language and how it works. Through hearing common language patterns, children imitate new ways of communicating. Finally, children begin to understand that the purpose of reading is to make personal meaning from text and that a message is communicated through each sentence, story or passage, and book. All these concepts are important foundations for literacy.

Suggest to parents that they provide library corners for their children, preferably in their bedrooms. Books needn't be new—they can be purchased at garage sales or borrowed from the public library. The reading corner doesn't need to be large; it can even be made from cinder blocks and old wood. Virtually every room can hold reading material that is visible and accessible. Even before children are crawling or walking, books can be brought to their cribs and playpens; waterproof books are available for bath time.

Parents often need information about texts that are appropriate to read to their children. Figure 14.1 offers suggestions of reading materials for every age from birth to third grade. Additional suitable texts for parents to share with their children are listed in Appendix A.

see appendix A

OTHER SUGGESTIONS FOR PARENTS

most of the information and activities presented so far in this chapter focus on books. But books are not the only tools that can encourage children to read, nor do students have to read only books to be considered literate. Following are other ways parents can help promote reading at home:

- Read cereal boxes, menus, place mats, street signs, coupons, junk mail, and other forms of print together.
- Point out and read familiar signs such as "Walmart," "Yield," "Exit," and "Beware of Dog!"
- Play guessing games such as "I spy with my little eye something beginning with a *b* or a /b/ sound."
- Sing songs, nursery rhymes, raps, and chants.
- Share newspapers, magazines, and websites of an appropriate level, and encourage children to pick out certain words from advertisements.
- Provide a quiet time each evening, when TV and video games are not allowed and the child is encouraged to read.

figure	14.1	Age-appropriate reading materials.

AGE	TYPE OF READING MATERIAL
Birth–1 year old	Vinyl or cardboard books; colorful, large pictures; rhymes. Suggestion: *Mother Goose* (Candlewick, 1996).
1–2 years old	Washable cloth; animals and familiar objects; let child turn pages. Suggestion: *Pat the Bunny* (Childs Play, 1995).
2–3 years old	Nonsense, funny books; simple informational books; encourage child to pretend to read. Suggestion: *Henny Penny* (Galdone, 1984).
3–4 years old	Longer stories, fairy tales, folktales; how things work; repeated readings. Suggestion: *Mike Mulligan and His Steam Shovel* (Houghton Mifflin, 1977).
4–5 years old	Variety of books, informational, alphabet, predictable, wordless that tell a story. Suggestions: *Time Flies* (Crown, 1994), *Plant a Little Seed* (Christensen, 2012).
5–6 years old	Predictable books where child can chime in; language play. Suggestion: *I'm a Caterpillar* (Scholastic, 1997).
7–9 years old	More plot development; informational; take turns reading. Suggestions: *Hattie and the Fox* (Bradbury, 1987), *The Animal Book: A Collection of the Fastest, Fiercest, Toughest, Cleverest, Shyest—and Most Surprising Animals* (Jenkins, 2013).

Adapted from Neuman and Celano, 2001.

FAMILY LITERACY PROGRAMS

The ways in which parents interact with their child are paramount to fostering the child's literacy abilities, but some parents may require more assistance than teachers can offer in a traditional school-based workshop. Research increasingly supports the notion that the necessary parent–child interactions are often more complex than just reading together and the parent providing the child with literacy materials. In fact, simply telling a parent to read to a child may be counterproductive and lead to behavior quite different from what the teacher intended, depending on the background of the parent (Mikulecky, 1996).

To address this growing concern, the federal government has begun to set up various family literacy programs, such as Even Start, designed both to increase the literacy skills of the parents and to provide positive strategies and attitudes for fostering their child's literacy at home. Projects involve participants who are speakers of English as a first or second language and are located in a variety of settings, such as libraries, schools, universities, or family centers. A wide variety of activities takes place, ranging from discussions to training in positive parent–child interactions, as well as direct teaching of literacy skills for the parent, leading to the attainment of a high school diploma. Moreover, other family literacy programs have increased student motivation and achievement (Morrow & Young, 1997) and have had a positive effect on students' writing ability (Saint-Laurent & Giasson, 2005). Finally, positive results have also been attributed to family literacy programs such as Project FLAME, a program that engages Head Start parents in interactive workshops to help them become literacy educators at home (Rodríguez-

Reading aloud to infants and toddlers

Parents often ask teachers, early childhood educators, and librarians, "When should I begin reading aloud to my child?" The answer is: "From birth!" Parents should be told that reading with their child builds language skills and stimulates the imagination. It introduces children to art through the illustrations, and it instills positive associations with reading. Infants and toddlers who have been read to typically become proficient readers earlier and thus perform better in school.

The following are suggested guidelines preschool educators can give parents for reading with children of various ages. Parents should be aware, however, that each child has his or her own personality and rate of development.

Infant: 0–6 Months

- Talk to your baby as you go about your day.
- Share lullabies, songs, and rhythmic activities.
- Read aloud with the baby on your lap, in a high chair, or even while the child is lying on the floor.
- Stories should focus on sounds and bold pictures.

Infant: 6–12 Months

- Select vinyl or sturdy cardboard books. At this age, babies are teething and put everything into their mouths.
- Select books with built-in sound effects, or make your own sound effects. Vary your tone of voice.

- The tactile sense becomes important at this age. Select books with a variety of textures.
- Babies this age like to look at pictures of other babies and familiar objects.
- As the baby can now focus, help guide her hand to point to pictures as you read about them.

Toddler: 12–18 Months

- Choose participatory texts where the child can chime in with a refrain or help make animal noises.
- Toddlers may be beginning to make the connection between words and what they represent. Label objects and pictures.
- The child can begin to help turn the pages.
- Keep some durable books in a special place where the child can reach them on his own.

Toddler: 18–24 Months

- Select texts that require more and more participation from the child.
- Point to pictures in books and invite the child to label what she sees.
- Praise correct responses and quickly tell the child a word that she needs or doesn't seem to be able to say.
- Read a favorite book again and again if it is requested.

Family Literacy Programs

http://cfl.uic.edu/programs/ parent-engagement- programs-2/parent- engagement-programs/ flame-family-literacy/

Family and Community Literacy Engagement

www.ed.gov/family-and- community-engagement

www.familieslearning.org/

Brown, 2004, 2009), and Project Early Access to Success in Education (EASE) (Jordan, Snow, & Porche, 2000). More opportunities for family and community engagement are provided by the U.S. Department of Education and the National Center for Families Learning.

Literacy programs aimed at both children and adults have varying perspectives on what family literacy should be. Most initiatives reflect what most adult participants feel they need to help their children become literate, and many also stress the vital role of the community in education. Family literacy can help adults in a way that isn't constrained by intimidating traditions of formal education; instead, it draws on the knowledge the family already possesses. Most educators working with families realize that there is no single road to becoming literate and that they must seek the help of the parents to ascertain what positive practices already occur in the home. Moreover, family literacy programs must be constructed with more than test scores in mind. A study by Auerbach and Collier (2012) illustrates how a family literacy project intended to supplant home literacy practices in favor of activities aligned with standardized testing failed to increase student achievement.

Long-term, community-based family literacy programs can be an important adjunct to the relationship the classroom teacher builds with the parent. The classroom teacher can support such programs by acknowledging that literacy's domain is not exclusively in the public schools.

TROUBLESHOOTING

family literacy programs aim to get parents the help they need to develop general literacy interactions at home. But what about parents with whom the teacher has been totally unable to communicate? Certainly, the value of the parent–teacher conference as a venue for discussing specific issues related to the progress of pupils' literacy cannot be underestimated. Therefore, the means for addressing several factors that preclude some parents' attendance at school functions are discussed in the following sections.

Flexible Scheduling

Most schools have several parent–teacher days, during which teachers are available to talk with parents about their child's progress. Although this can be an ideal opportunity to focus on the child's literacy, some parents work during the day and for various compelling reasons are not able to take time off to attend these sessions. Because it is inappropriate—and impossible—for teachers to evaluate parents' priorities and work responsibilities, some schools respond to the problem with flexible scheduling. As mentioned earlier, scheduling some conference slots later in the day or in the evening (with teachers having the morning to prepare) has been helpful in many schools; these schools report success in reaching parents who had previously not attended conferences because of job conflicts.

Home Visits

Some parents may be reluctant to attend school functions because they feel uncomfortable in the school environment. They themselves may not have done well in school, and for them anything related to school holds unpleasant memories—much as the dentist's office does for those who suffered painful extractions as a child. Also, parents from certain cultural groups may hold the teacher in such high esteem that they may feel ashamed of being unfamiliar with the language and customs associated with the formal academic environment and fear embarrassing themselves. Because parents in these situations are most often the ones teachers most want to see with regard to their child's literacy habits and attitudes, it can be helpful for the teacher initially to go to the family's home. Several national organizations (e.g., Parent Teacher Home Visit Project and Harvard Family Research Project) can serve as excellent resources to help schools learn about conducting home visits. A handwritten note or brief telephone call saying the teacher will be in the area on a certain day and requesting permission to stop by for a chat is rarely refused. During this visit, nothing educational need be discussed; the teacher should look for common ground with the parent, often found in the adults' common care and concern for the child. A teacher's warm and down-to-earth attitude often forges an initial rapport that makes the parents' attendance at the next conference more likely. If the parents are non–English speakers, a teacher may take along a speaker of the parents' language if available.

Home Visit Resources

www.pthvp.org

www.hfrp.org

Common Language

A third possible barrier for parents is the tendency of many teachers to use the technical "jargon" of literacy with parents. Parents may refrain from attending meetings

Today's parents need to be involved in the technologies that play a large role in literacy learning.

about their child because they believe they would not be astute enough to understand the teacher's "educated language." In an effort to position the field of education as a "true" profession, educators have acquired a vocabulary of very specific literacy terminology. Lack of "phonemic awareness," for instance, could be replaced in discussions with parents by "a problem hearing sounds in words." Then a clear explanation of the child's problem, how it is being corrected in class, and how the parent might best help the child at home, will ensure the parents' comprehension. Other literacy terms can also be discussed in laymen's terms, of course, with the same result—that the parents understand what the teacher is talking about and feel more able to help. Inviting parents to be true partners in the education of their child requires communication between parents and teachers as equals.

SUMMARY

There is a pressing need for primary classrooms to use children's home literacies as the foundation for literacy instruction. We also need to communicate to parents how much they are needed as valuable partners in their children's literacy growth. Teachers do not always appreciate just how much communication and sensitivity is required to make this relationship work so that there is true synergy between home and school. Teachers often need to be the primary movers, envisioning innovative ways to get parents—from all cultural and linguistic backgrounds—to school. In some cases, a home visit is more appropriate.

Strive to help parents feel at ease by talking to them in clear terms about the progress of their child and explaining the most effective ways to reinforce the goals of a comprehensive literacy program at home. Be aware of current research that indicates that parents, regardless of income level or educational background, care deeply about their children's success in literacy and need only to be guided to the best practices for augmenting the school's literacy program. Finally, explore family literacy programs in your community that teach parents both to help their children read and write and to further their own educational achievement. Such programs add another dimension to the parent–school partnership, demonstrating for parents and students that the entire community sees literacy as a positive and worthwhile goal.

questions FOR JOURNAL WRITING AND DISCUSSION

1. Develop an argument to counter that of someone who believes that children from poor families always come to school with fewer literacy experiences than middle-class youngsters. Cite research contained in this chapter to bolster your argument.

2. Using the memories of your own family life as a young child, discuss some activities that you feel helped your literacy development. Include any books or materials that you especially remember.

suggestions FOR PROJECTS AND FIELD ACTIVITIES

1. Interview members of your family or friends who are raising young children. Ask them to discuss specific activities they have done on a daily basis with their children to promote literacy. Collect ideas from other members of your class and put them together in a pamphlet. If possible, arrange to have this pamphlet available at your field placement school to hand out to parents.

2. Obtain permission to sit in on one or more conferences between a parent and a teacher in your field experience. Note the following:

   - How did the teacher make the parent feel welcome?
   - What did the teacher tell the parent about the child's literacy progress?
   - What, if anything, did the teacher share with the parent about activities that could be undertaken at home to enhance the child's literacy development?
   - What specific questions, if any, did the parent have about her child's literacy development? How were these questions addressed?

3. Online, search for a parents and literacy website, or use one suggested in Appendix C. Evaluate the contents of the website as to how helpful you think the information might be to parents who wish to help their child with literacy.

see appendix C

The Early Literacy Classroom

ORCHESTRATING A COMPREHENSIVE PROGRAM

focus questions

What are the most important considerations when planning a comprehensive early literacy program?

What is the best classroom climate for a comprehensive literacy program?

How can the schedule be arranged so that time for literacy instruction is maximized?

I t is the first week of September, and Mrs. Ramon is just getting to know her new class. The 26 students are from four diverse language groups and have entered her first-grade class with an overwhelming array of linguistic, cultural, and socioeconomic backgrounds and emotional needs. For example, Hoa comes from a Vietnamese-speaking home, having arrived in California with her family when she was 13 months old. Her father is deceased, and her mother is currently unemployed and speaks very little English, although she has recently begun attending English classes. Hoa's personal linguistic and cultural data pool is Vietnamese—totally different from most of the class. Responsible for two younger siblings, Hoa has grown up quickly. Although she interacts verbally to a small extent with her mother, her invalid grandmother, and her church community in Vietnamese, the time she spends engaging in language activities in her home language is limited.

On the other hand, Cody, a native English speaker, has been classified as mildly emotionally disturbed and as having a learning disability that comes across as a lack of linguistic sophistication. He comes to Mrs. Ramon with an individual education plan (IEP), created by a team of educators and psychologists to help him to thrive in a regular classroom. Each week Mrs. Ramon is in contact with Cody's grandmother, who is raising him, to coordinate what goes on in the home with what is happening at school. Since Cody's grandmother works seven days a week at a grocery store to provide food and housing for her family, she has little extra time to work with Cody on his schoolwork.

Finally, Lisa comes from an English-speaking home, and her parents are both professionals in the field of education. She attended a neighborhood preschool for two years before entering public school. Lisa has had a wealth of encounters with English, listening to and interacting with her parents and older brother, singing nursery rhymes at preschool, learning to spell her name, listening to a variety of stories read to her every night, and having all her questions patiently answered and elaborated upon by the many indulgent adults around her.

These three students are representative of the heterogeneous garden of children who provide a positive challenge for Mrs. Ramon—one that she meets by equipping herself with plenty of current information as well as a repertoire of effective strategies to help each learner reach his or her potential.

INTRODUCTION

I t is three weeks later, and we reenter Mrs. Ramon's class. During math and science, where hands-on activities are taking place, Hoa sits in the middle of a small group of English-speaking students who chatter to her about the task at hand—observing air pressure in a balloon. Hoa still knows very little English, but there are three other Vietnamese-speaking students in the class, and during journal writing time, they sit together, conversing in Vietnamese as they draw pictures.

The book *Stone Soup* was the focus of the classroom last week. The teacher read the story several times with much miming and dramatization, once using a flannel board to demonstrate the key events in the story. Even Hoa shyly chimed in on the repetitive refrain, "Soup from a stone? Fancy *that!*" Hoa has picked up the words *stone* and *soup* and the names of an assortment of common vegetables from the repetition afforded by this engaging tale, and these words are showing up in the pictures in her journal, as evidenced when she colors a large purple turnip. When Mrs. Ramon asks Hoa about her pictures, she names some items in English as well as Vietnamese. The entire class stops what they are doing to celebrate Hoa's initial spoken words in English. Mrs. Ramon smiles warmly at the little girl and writes some abbreviated anecdotal notes about her amazing progress on her tablet.

Cody has listened intently to the story and written in his journal about a time he helped his grandmother make soup. Mrs. Ramon praises his creativity, but when another student asks to look at his work, Cody becomes angry and agitated. Mrs. Ramone escorts Cody to the "time out" area of the classroom, gives him the book to look through, and invites him to return to the class when he has calmed himself down. She later engages Cody with three other students in a role-playing activity that Cody especially enjoys based on the story. This verbal reenactment of the story provides oral language that helps to expand Cody's language skills.

Lisa, in another corner of the room, prefers to labor alone, following her unique writing agenda. She pens the words *cat, mat,* and *hat* very neatly in her journal. When asked if she can write a story using some new words on the word wall, she does not answer but begins a second column, chirping to no one in particular, "I'll do *et* words now," as she begins to write the words *wet, get, met,* and *set.* Then she begins to write a story about a man who met a cat, spelling these words correctly and using the sounding-out strategies she knows to spell mostly the surface sounds of others. When the teacher comes around, Lisa is able to read all the words of her story upon request. Mrs. Ramon grins as she jots anecdotal notes on her tablet about Lisa's current successes, but she also notes that Lisa seems overly concerned that everything she writes must be neat and spelled correctly, thus reducing the growth that occurs when children explore and feel free to take risks.

Hoa, Cody, and Lisa are developing literacy skills at very different yet appropriate rates, because Mrs. Ramon is supporting their individual growth patterns with self-selection of literacy activities, wise grouping, and careful attention to their unique needs. This teacher knows that Hoa is developing her oral comprehension in English by listening to a group of fluent English speakers discuss what they are doing with concrete objects. Also, she recognizes that drawing instead of writing allows Hoa to talk about what she knows in two languages. Seeing her participate in the refrain of a story, Mrs. Ramon understands that the student is also learning that writing can tell a story—one that she can access because of the entertaining visuals. On the other hand, Cody writes in spurts about a red Camaro, but frequently gets up and walks around the room, expending excess energy and then coming back to his piece, much better able to focus after the physical break. By contrast, the teacher is trying to encourage Lisa to move beyond what she can do perfectly and to grow as a writer by taking some risks.

The remainder of this final chapter explores how Mrs. Ramon provides a balanced, comprehensive, literacy program for *all* of her students by creating a climate conducive to learning, using literacy materials appropriate for her learners, and maximizing the limited available instructional time.

A CLASSROOM CLIMATE CONDUCIVE TO LITERACY

m rs. Ramon is the most requested teacher at the elementary school where she teaches, partly because the students all seem to love her, but mostly because parents are certain their children will learn to read and write by the end of the school year. Although education never comes with a guarantee, Mrs. Ramon stops just short of a promise to teach every student in her class to read and write by June. How does she do it?

Teachers are challenged to create a classroom climate that fosters the joy of literacy and learning.

The answer to that question lies, at least in part, in the way she makes decisions about classroom instruction. Mrs. Ramon has spent the past few years developing a comprehensive literacy program that includes systematic, explicit development of decoding skills yet manages to retain the exploration, engagement, and joy of a more child-centered, holistic approach to instruction. Any changes in her classroom are usually precipitated by a combination of three factors: (1) her ongoing assessment of her learners tells her when change is in order; (2) she reads about a strategy or observes an activity that she feels would be beneficial in her class; (3) she has read research in respected literacy journals such as *The Reading Teacher* that provides convincing evidence that a literacy practice she is considering is effective and should be tried. As an example of her responsiveness to research, Mrs. Ramon explains to us that she studiously avoids the following practices that experts say make learning to read more difficult for children.

PRACTICES TO AVOID

1. Emphasizing only phonics instruction
2. Drilling students endlessly on isolated letters or sounds
3. Making sure that students perform correctly or not at all
4. Focusing on the one "best" answer
5. Making perfect oral reading the most important literacy goal
6. Focusing on skills at the expense of comprehension
7. Using workbooks with every reading lesson
8. Always grouping according to ability
9. Following the basal without making adjustments
10. Expecting students to spell perfectly all the words they read

Another reason Mrs. Ramon is so successful undoubtedly has much to do with the positive classroom climate she has achieved. Five environmental factors immediately stand out when one enters her classroom. Let's examine them.

Print Saturation

The factory-like school building in this urban neighborhood is in desperate need of repair, but the visitor entering Mrs. Ramon's first-grade classroom is struck at once by how enticing it is—in sharp contrast to the grim environment outside. Both bulletin boards in the room are colorfully adorned with the written work and art of the students, and lively mobiles extending from the ceiling attest, in bold print, to the attributes of each learner in the class. Glancing around the room, the visitor observes a wide variety of print, including labels on the arts and crafts work, labels on each item in the room, charts, several word walls, written questions about objects the children have brought in, a diversity of commercially produced books, and even more texts written and published by the students. Visitors are struck, also, by how students converse about the tasks at hand at frequent intervals throughout the day. It seems that all day long the students are immersed in reading, writing, listening, speaking, viewing, and visually representing—offering all students an abundance of opportunity to fill their personal linguistic data pools. Mrs. Ramon knows that to be a culturally relevant teacher, she must use knowledge about the social, cultural, and language backgrounds of her students to support their success (Ladson-Billings, 2009; Morrison, Robbins, & Rose, 2008).

Demonstrations

Showing students the intricacies of literacy is a tenet of comprehensive instruction and is far more potent than merely *telling* them about it. Mrs. Ramon's classroom presents many opportunities for demonstrations of how language and print work. When Mrs. Ramon writes a label in front of the students to accompany their latest craft work, she sounds out the word for them, asking them to volunteer sounds they know, and offering explanations about new sounds and sound combinations. When she writes a short story summary in front of the students, thinking aloud as she decides what to say and how to spell the words, she demonstrates how drafts are written, how to deal with unknown spellings, how to scour the environment for words, and how reading, writing, and spelling are interrelated. When she rereads her writing, she shows the students how to edit and proofread and why it is sometimes necessary to rewrite. When Mrs. Ramon conducts a shared reading lesson, she demonstrates how written language is read, what punctuation marks are for, what to do when you don't know a word, what sounds the various symbols make, and so forth. Finally, by reading daily to students, Mrs. Ramon shows that she thinks reading is enjoyable and worth setting aside time for. By selecting informational texts as well as storybooks, she introduces students to different purposes for reading.

High Expectations

Teachers who allow students to make decisions about their own learning are usually more successful than those who make all the decisions autocratically. Mrs. Ramon expects all of her students to learn and to take responsibility for many decisions about their own learning. To enable students to meet her high expectations, Mrs. Ramon gives the students plenty of opportunities to take risks and experiment without fear of failure. She encourages them to be confident and to use the decoding strategies they know to take calculated guesses at unknown words when reading. She often allows them to choose their own writing topics and texts to read during free reading time. She expects them to formulate hypotheses about written language through trial and error and make many mistakes as they experiment with spelling. Although she expects students to be conscientious about checking the spelling of words they have been taught, Mrs. Ramon does *not* presume that students' writing should always be perfect—especially in initial drafts.

Teacher Feedback

Successful teacher–student interactions are probably the key to literacy learning for children from diverse backgrounds. Mrs. Ramon interacts with all her students about their reading, writing, speaking, listening, viewing, and visually representing in such a way that her feedback is both supportive and instructive to her learners; she also insists that students respond to each other's work in this positive and respectful way. Moreover, she is careful never to communicate that some tasks are achievable by certain students but not others. To that end, Mrs. Ramon uses a flexible grouping system so that students do not feel stigmatized by consistent placement in low-ability groups. At various times during the day, she may have

Teacher feedback to children about their reading and writing should be positive and supportive.

students arranged into skill groups, literature circles, reading buddies, peer-editing groups, cooperative groups, and other group structures (see Chapter 11).

Mrs. Ramon's interactions with her students may take the form of a whole-class lesson, a minilesson, a small group activity, or a one-to-one conference. Whatever form the interaction takes, Mrs. Ramon's response is immediate and always emanates from her careful observation of her students.

Instructional Modifications and Differentiation

Mrs. Ramon is a mindful kid watcher. She considers the goals she has set for all the students in her class, children as diverse as Hoa, Lisa, and Cody. Each week she spends time reflecting on the progress made by each of her students. If a student is not making expected progress, she modifies her instructional approaches and differentiates her instruction. For example, a student may be moved to a lower level of text for independent reading, or phonics instruction may be conducted in the context of known words rather than by isolating sounds and then blending those sounds. Or learning more about a child's cultural background may cause Mrs. Ramon to modify her approach to disciplining a child's behavior, as when she discovers that Danny, her student who is Native American, comes from a culture where it is deemed disrespectful to make eye contact with a teacher.

Mrs. Ramon carefully assesses and evaluates each individual modification she makes. If progress is not made with these modifications, she then explores avenues available within her school to collaborate with others to build success for each student. This may entail talking with the principal to discover processes and procedures already in place, contacting other staff resources, or if necessary, making referrals to the intervention assistance team. With the help of the parents, this team recommends instructional or behavioral management interventions that Mrs. Ramon can implement immediately to ensure that her students are progressing and experiencing success.

ORGANIZING THE CLASSROOM ENVIRONMENT

The quality of the classroom environment has received considerable attention in recent years as teachers have become increasingly aware of the need to *invite* students to learn in an organized fashion. The physical arrangement of the classroom is crucial because children must have plenty of room and a range of appropriate materials to be able to experiment with literacy, independently and in small groups. Thus, one of the most immediate concerns of beginning and experienced teachers before their learners ever arrive in September should be the arrangement of the classroom space, so that it is conducive to effective and enjoyable learning. As teachers plan layouts that will suit their classroom activities, they often begin very simply and cautiously. Later, as the need arises, they tend to subdivide the classroom into functional work areas for accomplishing specific literacy tasks and to make more detailed instructional plans.

Room Arrangement

Mrs. Ramon, the first-grade teacher we have been visiting, has several useful areas in her classroom. The largest is a whole-class learning and sharing area. Mrs. Ramon has just brought in a slightly threadbare but brightly colored carpet for students to sit on when they use this area; this new feature has created quite a stir during shared reading time. Other areas in this teacher's classroom are quiet writing and publishing areas, a silent reading area with an overstuffed couch and beanbag chairs, reading conference areas in both corners, appealing display areas for books and artwork, a "time out" area for emotional disruptions, and ample storage areas. Mrs. Ramon sees to it that areas for storing books, magazines, and other reading materials are attractive and well lit. Each area in the classroom is clearly labeled with neatly printed signs. Mrs. Ramon has learned, through experience, that neatness is important, because these labels become models for students' written products and provide an opportunity for environmental reading.

Mrs. Ramon spends several weeks at the end of each summer considering how best to rearrange her classroom. A major objective of the physical design in her classroom has always been to create the optimal physical surroundings for children to learn from the environment and from each other. Each year she makes physical adjustments in her classroom as she reflects on a grouping arrangement that didn't work well or as she decides to borrow a learning center idea from another teacher. For Mrs. Ramon, the flow of traffic seemed to be a problem last year. Therefore, classroom furnishings in her room this year are expressly chosen and positioned to facilitate easy movement between classroom areas, provide access to necessary materials and a clear view of the whiteboards, and create specific areas for demonstrations and small-group work. (See Figure 15.1 for this room layout.)

Literacy Materials

If teachers make wise choices in the selection of literacy materials, literacy instruction can be made easier. Over the 11 years that she has been teaching, Mrs. Ramon

figure 15.1 Mrs. Ramon's classroom.

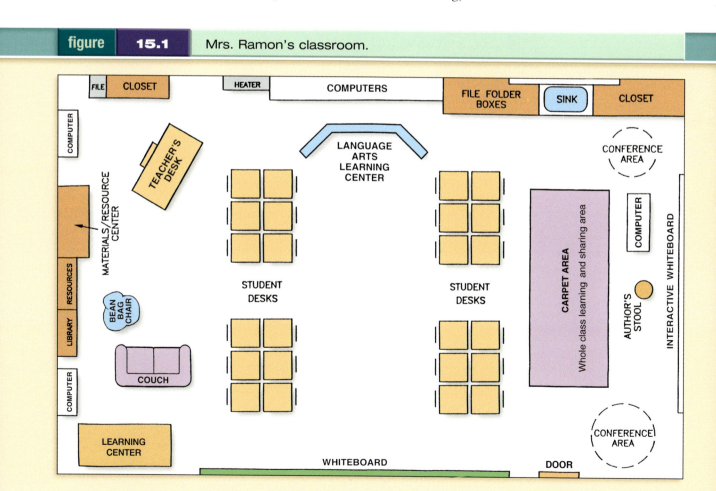

Children thrive on language play, drama, puppetry, and other oral and receptive language activities.

has amassed a rich variety of materials, supplies, tablets, and books, and she has carefully organized and stored them so that they are readily accessible to her students. *Manipulative,* or *hands-on, materials* are a standard feature in her classroom, as in most primary classrooms, but in this classroom literacy materials are viewed with equal respect because Mrs. Ramon knows that manipulating the tools of literacy production—pencils, paper, books, e-books, and the like—is a valuable part of children's early sound-to-symbol learning. Therefore, to motivate students to write, Mrs. Ramon provides the following:

- a variety of writing utensils, such as gel pens, colored pencils, and felt-tip pens
- various kinds of paper—bordered, colored, lined, and unlined
- access to computers and tablets

The materials listed in Figure 15.2 are what Mrs. Ramon considers the "bare essentials" for an emergent literacy classroom.

DEVISING AN INSTRUCTIONAL PLAN

Perhaps the most determinative decisions in setting up the classroom relate to wise use of the limited amount of time available. Mrs. Ramon admits that she feels more and more pressured each year to cover the vast amount of material and topics she believes are vital for her learners. This year, for example, she must see that her literacy curriculum addresses the Common Core State Standards for the first grade, and she must learn how to evaluate the students' progress using computer assessments. Thus, each year she, like most teachers, must adjust her instructional schedule and decide what information to discard and what to add to an already overcrowded curriculum.

When making these decisions, Mrs. Ramon keeps in mind the four components of an emergent literacy curriculum that she believes are key to her students' success in learning about print; each supports her learners' continued growth in reading, writing, listening, and speaking. Mrs. Ramon will not compromise on any of the following components:

1. direct systematic instruction in phonics and other supportive reading group activities
2. frequent exposure to language experience approach stories and informational pieces
3. extensive writing, listening, viewing, and composing experiences
4. a variety of opportunities for oral discussions, language play, drama, puppetry, and other oral and receptive language activities

With these essentials firmly in mind, Mrs. Ramon sets up a schedule of daily instructional activities. Although unplanned events (fire drills, assemblies, absences, guest speakers, parties) often interfere with this plan, an observer in the room could expect to see a day similar to the one described in the box beginning on the following page. Let's make a hypothetical visit. Some of the strategies and tools discussed previously are boldfaced.

figure **15.2** Essentials for an emergent literacy classroom.

FURNITURE

Teacher's desk and chair and a table
   at which to work privately with the students

Desks or tables and chairs for each student

READING MATERIAL

Trade books at various reading levels
Wordless books and picture storybooks
Multicultural and multiethnic trade books
Phonemic awareness materials
Connected texts at different reading levels
Predictable and patterned texts
Student-authored books

Informational texts
E-books
Song books
Magazines
Other printed material (e.g., catalogs, brochures, menus)
Diagnostic tools
Comic books

ENVIRONMENTAL PRINT/DISPLAY SPACE

Calendar
Teacher- and student-produced charts
Commercially produced charts
Signs and labels designating areas of the classroom
Notices to students and parents

Samples of children's work
Artwork with dictation or written comments
Letter charts with graphic reference material
Rules, class helper assignments, fire drill information,
   and so forth

WRITING SUPPLIES

Many kinds and colors of paper
Old envelopes and stationery
Many kinds of writing utensils
Alphabet stamps
Letter stencils

Staples, tape, and glue for bookmaking
Manipulative letters and letter stencils
Mini-chalkboards or whiteboards
Pocket charts and sentence strips
Computers/tablets

STORAGE SPACES

Storage space for supplies, accessible to students
Storage space just for teacher
Book storage spaces
- bookcases
- revolving book racks for paperbacks
- crates

Cubbies for students' belongings
Storage space for students' work
- crates for file folders and learning center materials
- teacher file cabinet
- homework cubbies

OTHER SUPPLIES/EQUIPMENT

Objects to observe and write about
Materials for experimentation, observation,
   and writing
Art supplies
Puppets
Flannel board
Digital camera/video camera
Computers/tablets

Globes, maps, atlases
Science and math equipment
Easels to hold chart paper, big books
Bulletin boards to display students' work
Educational games and software
TV, DVD player
Whiteboard/interactive whiteboard
Microphone and speakers

CASE EXAMPLE

A day in Mrs. Ramon's classroom

Mrs. Ramon's class is self-contained and heterogeneously grouped. The instructional day begins at 8:30 and ends at 3:00. No specific time was assigned during our visit for pull-out or special programs such as art, music, physical education, or recess.

8:30–8:40 As we enter the room, we notice the students going about their daily business of communicating with one another and writing notes to each other and to the teacher, which they put in each other's mailboxes designed expressly for this purpose. They also eagerly listen to the digital morning message playing on the interactive whiteboard, written and recorded by Mrs. Ramon before they arrived. Then they read the message chorally. This message tells them about some enjoyable activity they can look forward to during the day or asks them a thought question. This morning's message asks, "Are you more like the sun or the rain?" Students immediately begin discussing this with partners. While these activities are going on, Mrs. Ramon takes a few moments to do a **running record** and **story retelling** with individual students, using a daily rotation.

8:40–9:00 The whole class now congregates on the carpet to discuss the oversized calendar. Using this prop, they discuss the weather; mark in a symbol for rain; and chant the month, the day of the week, and the date. They pledge allegiance to the flag and sing a favorite song of the children's choosing. This day the choice is "Hooray for the World!" by Red Grammer. Every student seems to know the words, but Mrs. Ramon has them written on the whiteboard and points to each one as it is sung, to reinforce the connection between written and spoken language. As the teacher takes attendance, she features the beginning sound of the day—/fr/—and applies it to every child's first name, **"the name game."** For example, *Nancy* becomes *Francy, Jennifer* becomes *Frennifer,* and so forth. This lively language game is followed by a brief session of **interactive writing.**

9:00–9:05 Before their **shared reading** lesson, Mrs. Ramon does a brief review of the **phonics** components introduced yesterday, two different ways to represent /j/ (*j* and *dge*). The teacher holds up the **word cards** for *jam, badge, jump, ledge, fudge,* and *jar.* She asks for volunteers to say each word. When a student says the word correctly, that student puts the word in the **pocket chart** and then helps Mrs. Ramon

sound out (**segment**) the word on the board. Finally, the teacher reads the nursery rhyme "Jack be nimble, Jack be quick," asking them to chant it with her, raising a quiet hand every time they hear a word with a /j/.

Tomorrow Mrs. Ramon will have some students do a closed **word sort,** asking partners to sort a series of pictures representing words containing either *j* or *dge.* Other students will look in magazines for pictures containing these two sound representations. After much discussion of the words that have been found and how they fit in the children's chosen pattern, students will then be invited to put their discoveries on the **word wall** under the appropriate column.

9:05–9:55 For the **shared reading** lesson, students in Mrs. Ramon's room move into three different groups; these groups are flexible and change frequently, depending on the activity. Today the teacher is ready to do the first rereading of the **big book** *My Friends* by Taro Gomi, from the first-grade **basal reader** (Macmillan/McGraw-Hill). Four students who need extra reinforcement will be tracking the text as they listen to a recording of *My Friends* at one of the computers; several other students need no further work with this story and are provided with a more challenging trade book that comes with the basal series, *Grandfather Bear Is Hungry,* a Russian folktale retold by Margaret Read MacDonald. These students will **dyad read,** taking turns reading or summarizing a page of text. The remaining 14 students participate in a **shared rereading** of the text in which Mrs. Ramon demonstrates left-to-right orientation as she reads and points out punctuation marks at the end of sentences. Since this group is preparing to learn the *ap* rime, Mrs. Ramon stops at the page that says, "I learned to nap from my friend the crocodile." She frames the word *nap* with a **word mask,** calling the children's attention to it. They orally stretch out the word and say it several times together. She asks a variety of **comprehension questions** during this rereading, asking how the

girl feels about learning to walk from a cat, what they think the girl likes to do best, and so forth.

After finishing the rereading of this book, the students are asked to act out different action words in the book, such as jumping like a dog, marching like a rooster, and napping like a crocodile. This activity not only lends enjoyment and appreciation to the story but also adds new words to the vocabulary of the English learners in the class.

Tomorrow students will be given a small **decodable text** containing many of the same phonic elements, such as the *ap* rime, to read independently and then **partner read.** Such a successful experience with the already introduced phonic elements will help reinforce these sounds in a real reading context, providing valuable practice with easily decoded text.

9:55–10:00 The preceding lesson ends with a five-minute (usually less) **phonics** lesson on *ap.* The teacher models sounding out several words with the same rime—*nap, map, cap, rap,* and *tap*—stretching out the sounds so the students can easily identify them. After doing this several times, individual students are encouraged to try it.

Tomorrow Mrs. Ramon plans to pass out individual whiteboards on which the students will write the letters as they stretch them out, holding up the whiteboards as they finish, so she can immediately assess how individuals are doing.

10:00–10:35 Writing workshop is a natural extension of the reading lesson. After students procure their **writing folders** from their cubbies, Mrs. Ramon takes five minutes to do a **minilesson** on the use of capital letters at the beginning of sentences, as this is an area she has observed to be a concern with almost every child. She conducts this minilesson with the entire class, although such a lesson is often conducted for only the small group who has shown a particular need for it.

Mrs. Ramon then puts a writing prompt on the board: "A friend is _____ but a friend is not _____." This sentence stem is not an assignment but only a writing option for those who are searching for a topic. After a brief discussion about this topic, the students begin the writing process. Several students are in the **prewriting** stage and are researching their topic online from the list of sites provided by Mrs. Ramon. Some students begin **drafting;** others are illustrating previously written pieces. Some students are writing their pieces using word processing software and inserting clip art that Mrs. Ramon helps them to download from the Internet, while other students are using Kidspiration to organize their ideas.

Some students are sharing their ideas with a partner; others are offering feedback. **Peer-editing conferences** and **teacher–student conferences**

Kidspiration
www.inspiration.com/Kidspiration

are occurring at tables set aside for this purpose. Mrs. Ramon, when she is not conferencing with individual students about their work, walks around helping others sound out words, observing, and taking **anecdotal notes** on their progress.

What amazes the observer in this classroom is how engaged the students are and how well they know the boundaries of the activities in which they may participate during writers' workshop. They know they are free to schedule their own time as long as they show progress toward their own goals.

10:35–11:35 This period covers math instruction and practice activities. Language is involved in even this content area. Mrs. Ramon has a student do an addition problem on the board and then queries the other youngsters, "What is another way to think about that?" Four students respond by telling the others their differing ways of thinking about and solving the math problem. Mrs. Ramon shares with us that later in the year students will keep learning logs that summarize, in words, the concept that has been introduced, such as "Tell what you do when you add two numbers."

11:35–12:15 Lunch.

12:15–12:35 After lunch Mrs. Ramon always looks forward to **reading aloud** to her students. For this activity, she selects quality **children's literature** from a variety of genres, cultures, and styles, balancing informational and narrative text. Today the teacher shares the beautifully illustrated Caldecott medal winner *Officer Buckle and Gloria* (1995) by Peggy Rathmann. Mrs. Ramon feels this is one of the most important times in the day. She is engaging students in a positive experience with literature, introducing new vocabulary, and often thinking aloud about many of her comprehension strategies as she reads. The children clearly enjoy this time too, and they are encouraged to draw as they listen, later sharing how their sketches tell about what is happening in the story.

12:35–1:35 This is the time for social studies, science, computer skills, health, or other content-area and instructional activities. Much speaking, listening, reading, writing, viewing, and visually representing are naturally integrated into these content areas. Today, following on the theme of friendship in the morning's story, Mrs. Ramon leads a multi-cultural social studies lesson, teaching the students, with the help of her linguistically diverse learners, to say "my friend" in the four different languages represented in the class-room. Children chant these words in the different tongues and then work on a poster showing themselves and a friend involved in an activity that portrays friendship. Finally, Mrs. Ramon shows students pictures taken from online resources showing scenes from cities in each of the four countries. Tomorrow Mrs. Ramon will have the students create a **word web** on friendship, brainstorming ideas and, perhaps, using those ideas in their journals.

1:35–1:45 Independent reading time is a critical time in each day. Students quickly and quietly get trade books, magazines, or other reading material from their desks or from the classroom library and begin reading silently. As this is a schoolwide program, everyone in the school—from the principal to the janitor—stops what they are doing to read. Afterward, the teacher often invites the students to talk about what they are reading and encourages them to explain what they do when they read.

1:45–2:15 Mrs. Ramon works on **spelling** and other literacy-related activities. These activities include **drama, word sorts,** word-building activities, small- and large-group sharing of writing, learning center activities, or a combination of these experiences. This day, pairs of students give each other a **post-test** on their spelling words for the first 15 minutes. Then students correct their own errors by consulting their primary dictionaries. Many of the students then become involved in a **readers theater** production of *The Boy Who Cried Wolf*, a story the students had very much enjoyed and wish to act out. The students, having heard the story several times for the purpose of acting it out, have now created roles for everyone. Besides the boy, the wolf, the townspeople, the sheep, and the wise man, they have added parents, siblings, and a talking bird that tells the shepherd what to do. Every student has a speaking part that the teacher helps them write down so they have a rough "script" to memorize.

Other students choose to go to the table that has been turned into a **learning center,** with the theme "What is a friend?" In this physically appealing, specialized setting, students work on a series of tasks integrating a content area, such as social studies, with the language arts of reading, writing, listening, speaking, viewing, and visually representing.

Through self-selected, individualized activities, the students seek answers to questions independently, such as "What does a friend do?" Each of the activities has been introduced by the teacher, yet the step-by-step instructions are also written on cards next to the individual activities. For example, one gives students the directions for making finger puppet friends. It asks them to create a dialogue with a partner to resolve a problem between two friends. Students later share their product with the larger group.

2:15–2:40 Students write in their **dialogue journals** while Mrs. Ramon goes around the room transcribing text for the few children who are still primarily drawing pictures. She encourages others to sound out the words they are attempting to spell. Mrs. Ramon always carries her tablet to take **anecdotal notes** on children's progress, in this case their understanding of the **alphabetic principle.** The students who finish early love to review previous entries and to revisit their teacher's responses. Mrs. Ramon gives written feedback in each child's journal at least once a week.

2:40–2:50 Mrs. Ramon again **reads aloud** to her students, often finishing a story from the earlier session. Since she completed the early afternoon story, she chooses to read a short informational piece from *Cricket* magazine containing new information about why dinosaurs disappeared from the Earth. She tries to offer a variety of read-aloud materials, both informational and narrative, including genres from science fiction to folktales, to whet the appetite of these burgeoning readers and expose them to many types of material. To conclude, the teacher asks students to turn to a neighbor and tell one thing they learned about dinosaurs from listening to the piece.

2:50–3:00 Mrs. Ramon calls these final few moments in the school day "the day in review." She asks volunteers to share with the class what they consider to be the highlights of the day. She gains much insight into their young minds and sees, from their perspectives, what worked and what didn't. The students get a final oral language opportunity as Mrs. Ramon observes their comments. Students then do cleanup as necessary and receive their weekly **parent packets,** which contain material corresponding to what they have studied this day. The parents are asked to review the material with their children, sign the packet, and send it back with their children the following day. Sometimes the parents are asked to view a video that Mrs. Ramon has posted on the school's website. These brief videos help parents with activities such as teaching sight words, reading with their children and making predictions, and teaching their student a new vocabulary word. This communication with parents enhances the literacy growth of the students, lets parents know what is happening in the classroom, and allows parents to assist in a positive way. The parent packet taken home by most of Mrs. Ramon's students this day is presented in Figure 15.3. Other students may have more or less advanced assignments, according to their needs.

After the students have left, we notice that Mrs. Ramon immediately puts anecdotal notes in her students' work portfolios. She reflects on how she might offer interventions for the students who need them and how she might provide more challenge to others. Then she approaches to debrief us on her day of teaching, which, she intimates, has been physically and emotionally exhausting, as always. However, this remarkable teacher confesses, "I cannot imagine a profession that is more personally rewarding and more fun than turning children on to the joys of literacy."

WWW

Videos to Share with Parents

www.earlyliteracylearning. org/ta_pract_videos1.php

---

figure	15.3

An example of a first-grade homework packet.

Help your child practice the vocabulary words from *The Cat Has a Nap,* using the cards in this packet. This can be done in any of the following ways, whichever is most enjoyable for you and your child:

- Show your child the word cards and give them to him/her when they are said correctly.
- Have your child make sentences using the words on the cards.
- Have your child write a story with the words.
- Ask your child to spell the words as you say them.
- Put the cards on the table. Say a word and ask the child to identify the card with that word on it.

Then, please listen as your child reads from the book *The Cat Has a Nap.* Be sure your child's finger is under each word as it is read. Ask the child to read the story twice. Make sure the reading is a "treat," not a "treatment."

As always, please read daily to your child, preferably a text that your child has chosen. Please initial as completed.

Monday   _____

Tuesday   _____

Wednesday _____

Thursday   _____

SUMMARY

throughout this book we have explored ways to teach literacy to early readers and writers. The approach described has been a comprehensive one, in which students receive the explicit, systematic instruction in phonics necessary to help them become automatic decoders. This phonics instruction, however, was presented as a means to an end that allowed students to quickly concentrate on more vital tasks—what reading can mean and how it can make them feel. To that end, many strategies for making text meaningful and using text as a springboard to substantive writing activities were introduced. Yet reading about specific strategies, seeing only individual pieces of the big picture, is not completely satisfactory. Particularly if one has never taught, it is important to see how a real teacher manages to orchestrate all of these elements in a total program for a heterogeneous garden of children with varying strengths and needs. With this in mind, we observed one of the finest teachers we know and invited you, the reader, to see for yourself what such a program might look like.

Though Mrs. Ramon has a challenging situation with a first-grade class composed of a wide range of learners, she will most likely succeed—as she does year after year—at teaching every student in her class not only to read and write, but to enjoy these activities. How does she manage to achieve such lofty goals? Besides creating a comprehensive program of skills-based and holistic methods of teaching literacy, Mrs. Ramon has set up her class in a caring way that is respectful of all the individuals who are in her charge. Her instructional plans emanate from a program of ongoing observation and assessment and are adjusted according to her students' changing needs. She has gathered a host of inviting literacy materials and arranged them in a classroom designed to facilitate the various activities that she plans each day. She has saturated the room with print, so that students are constantly encountering the idea that *print* and *talk* are integrally connected. Additionally, Mrs. Ramon sincerely expects each of her learners to read and write—and they rise to the occasion; her confidence bolsters them when they face a challenging instructional situation. Above all, this teacher's interaction with her learners is continually constructive and positive; she is the consummate cheerleader and encourages the students to offer similar support to one another.

Perhaps the most crucial personal ingredient in Mrs. Ramon's success—and that of so many teachers like her—is her love of and enthusiasm for all aspects of literacy and learning in general. Outside the classroom, Mrs. Ramon is constantly keeping up with new developments in literacy through journals, conferences, and in-service presentations. In her classroom, this teacher often shares her personal writing with students, delightedly looks up words she does not know in front of her students, and has been known to shed a tear or two, unabashedly, while sharing *The Velveteen Rabbit* with her first-graders.

Balance in literacy is possible when a competent and caring teacher creates a comprehensive program of explicit instruction, writing, speaking, listening, viewing, visually representing, and literature-rich experiences. Mrs. Ramon's classroom is a working example of the achievement of these goals.

questions FOR JOURNAL WRITING AND DISCUSSION

1. Reflect on a teacher you know who seems to be highly effective in teaching literacy to young children. In light of this chapter, what would you say makes this teacher impressive? What do you believe made Mrs. Ramon such an effective teacher of early literacy? What are their similarities? Differences?

2. Brainstorm a list of ways you will ensure that the students in your classroom not only *can* read but do read. Share and discuss this list with others in your class.

3. Discuss the provisions that must be made in a classroom so that learners who are linguistically and culturally diverse succeed. How do you believe such provisions affect native English-speaking students in the class?

suggestions FOR PROJECTS AND FIELD ACTIVITIES

1. Arrange to observe an early childhood classroom. Make notes about the environment, the classroom climate, and the literacy activities in which the students engage. Your observation summary should be as objective as possible. Compare your experience with those of others in your class, and include in your discussion your personal reactions to the classroom you observed.

2. Interview an early childhood educator. Ask this teacher how she decides on changes in curriculum she needs to make. Which is the most potent factor in changing a classroom practice for this teacher: (1) what research says; (2) what other teachers say; or (3) what the teacher observes?

3. Make a sketch of an ideal classroom, showing the arrangement of furniture, equipment, materials, and storage space that best suits what you believe to be a comprehensive literacy environment. Compare your sketch with the diagram of a literacy classroom in this chapter. How is yours different? Why? Share your sketch with others in your class, discussing the benefits and drawbacks of each design.

APPENDIX

A

Children's Literature Resources

BOOKS FOR DEVELOPING PHONEMIC AWARENESS

The following books are suitable for use in reinforcing particular letter sounds, patterns, and letter combinations.

Agee, J. (2009). *Orangutan tongs: Poems to tangle your tongue.*

Alborough, J. (1992). *Where's my teddy?*

Alda, A. (1992). *Sheep, sheep, help me fall asleep.*

Alda, A. (1994). *Pig, horse, cow, don't wake me now.*

Andreas, G. (2009). *K is for kissing a cool kangaroo.*

Brown, M. (1994). *Pickle things.*

Brown, M. W. (1983). *Four fur feet.*

Carlstrom, N. W. (1986). *Jesse bear, what will you wear?*

Carter, D. (1990). *More bugs in boxes.*

deRegniers, B., Moore, E., & Carr, J. (1988). *Sing a song of popcorn.*

Dewdney, A. (2005). *Llama, llama, red pajama.*

Feldman, E. (2009). *Billy and Milly, short and silly!*

Fox, M. (1993). *Time for bed.*

Galdone, P. (1973). *The three billy goats gruff.*

Geraghty, J. (1992). *Stop that noise!*

Gordon, J. (1991). *Six sleepy sheep.*

Grossman, B. (1995). *My little sister ate one hare.*

Hague, M. (1993). *Teddy bear, teddy bear: A classic action rhyme.*

Hale, B. (2013). *Clark the shark.*

Hawkins, C., & Hawkins, J. (1986). *Tog the dog.* (See also other books in this series.)

Hoberman, M. A. (2004). *The eensy-weensy spider.*

Hutchins, P. (1976). *Don't forget the bacon.*

Johnston, T. (1991). *Little bear sleeping.*

Jorgensen, G. (1988). *Crocodile beat.*

Komaiko, L. (1987). *Annie bananie.*

Krauss, R. (1985). *I can fly.*

Kushkin, K. (1990). *Roar and more.*

Leedy, L. (1988). *Pingo the plaid panda.*

Lewison, W. (1992). *Buzz said the bee.*

Lindbergh, R. (1990). *The day the goose got loose.*

Marzollo, J. (1989). *The teddy bear book.*

Marzollo, J. (1994). *Ten cats have hats.*

Most, B. (1991). *A dinosaur named after me.*

Ochs, C. P. (1991). *Moose on the loose.*

Oppenheim, J. (1989). *Not now! said the cow.*

Otto, C. (1991). *Dinosaur chase.*

Parry, C. (1991). *Zoomerang-a-boomerang: Poems to make your belly laugh.*

Patz, N. (1983). *Moses supposes his toeses are roses.*

Philpot, L., & Philpot, G. (1993). *Amazing Anthony ant.*

Pomerantz, C. (1993). *If I had a paka.*

Prelutsky, J. (1989). *Poems of A. Nonny Mouse.*

Raffi. (1987). *Down by the bay.*

Root, P. (2003). *One duck stuck.*

Ruzzier, S. (2013). *Bear and bee.*

Ryan, C. (2012) *Moo hoo.*

Seeger, L. V. (2006). *Walter worried.*

Serfozo, M. (1988). *Who said red?*

Seuss, Dr. (1957). *The cat in the hat.*

Seuss, Dr. (1963). *Hop on pop.*

Seuss, Dr. (1965). *Fox in sox.*

Seuss, Dr. (1974). *There's a wocket in my pocket.*

Shaw, N. (2006). *Sheep in a jeep.* (See also other books in this series.)

Singer, M. (2010*). Mirror, mirror: A book of reversible verse.*

Sowers, P. (1991). *The listening walk.*

Speed, T. (1995). *Two cool cows.*

Thomas, J. (2009). *Rhyming dust bunnies.*

Van Allsburg, C. (1987). *The Z was zapped.*

Van Laan, N. (1990). *A mouse in my house.*

Wadsworth, O. A. (1985). *Over in the meadow.*

Winthrop, E. (1986). *Shoes.*

Wood, A. (1999). *Silly Sally.*

Ziefert, H., & Brown, H. (1996). *What rhymes with eel?*

PREDICTABLE BOOKS

The following books are suitable for increasing the listening comprehension of young learners, as they contain rhymes, rhythm, and/or repetition. Children are therefore able to anticipate certain key words and phrases.

Baker, K. (2007). *Hickory dickory dock.*

Carle, E. (2005). *A house for hermit crab.*

Carlstrom, N. W. (1986). *Jesse Bear, what will you wear?*

Fox, M. (1986). *Hattie and the fox.*

Fleming, D. (2006). *The cow who clucked.*

Galdone, P. (1975). *Henny Penny.*

Gibbs, E. (2013). *I spy pets.*

Kent, J. (1971). *The fat cat.*

Martin, B., Jr. (2007). *Baby bear, baby bear, what do you see?* (See also other books in this series.)

Mesler, J., & Cowley, J. (1980). *In a dark, dark wood.*

Pinkney, J. (2006). *The little red hen.*

Rosen, M. (2004). *We're going on a bear hunt.*

Taback, S. (2004). *The house that Jack built.*

Tafuri, N. (1984). *Have you seen my duckling?*

Underwood, D. (2013). *Good bye, bad bye.*

Wood, A. (1999). *Silly Sally.*

EASY-TO-READ BOOKS

These books are appropriate for early readers to read independently, as they are written with a controlled vocabulary of limited sight words and easily decodable words.

Bang-Campbell, M. (2002). *Little rat sets sail.*

Bateman, D. M. (2007). *Deep in the swamp.*

Benchley, N. (1966). *Oscar otter.*

Byars, B. (1996). *My brother, Ant.*

Cazet, D. (1998). *Minnie and Moo go dancing.*

Christelow, E. (2007). *Five little monkeys go shopping.*

Cole, J., & Calmenson, S. (1990). *Ready . . . set . . . read!*

Donnio, S. (2007). *I'd really like to eat a child.*

Eaton, M. (2007). *The adventures of Max and Pinky, best buds.*

Friend, C. (2007). *The perfect nest.*

Geist, K. (2007). *The three little fish and the bad shark.*

George, J. C. (2008). *Goose and duck.*

Gran, J. (2007). *Big bug surprise.*

Grant, J. A. (2008). *Chicken said, "Cluck!"*

Grey, M. (2007). *Ginger bear.*

Henry, J. (2013). *Cheer up, Mouse!*

Hills, T. (2007). *Duck, duck, goose.*

Lin, G. (2009). *Ling & Ting: Not exactly the same!*

Little, J. (2003). *Emma's strange pet* (An I can read book).

Lloyd-Jones, S. (2007). *How to be a baby, by me the big sister.*

Lobel, A. (1976). *Frog and toad all year* (and others in the series).

Manning, M., & Granstrom, B. (2007). *Dino-dinners.*

Milgrim, D. (2003). *See Pip point* (Ready-to Read).

Parish, H. (2013). *Amelia Bedelia's first library card.*

Pearce, P. (2013). *Amy's three best things.*

Pomerantz, C. (1993). *Outside dog.*

Seeger, L. V. (2008). *One boy.*

Seuss, Dr. (1957). *The cat in the hat.*

Seuss, Dr. (1960). *Green eggs and ham.*

Seuss, Dr. (1963). *Hop on pop.*

Steffensmeier, A. (2007). *Millie waits for the mail.*

Tankard, J. (2007). *Grumpy bird.*

Van Laan, N. (2003). *Busy, busy mouse.*

Wheeler, L. (2007). *Dino-Hockey.*

Willems, M. (2013). *A big guy took my ball!*

WORDLESS BOOKS

These books have no words, as the name suggests, and are useful for encouraging language development as children tell the story that goes with the pictures, reinforcing an understanding of story structure. The books are also ideal for English learners, who can share the story in their own language.

Alborough, J. (2009). *Hug.*

Baker, J. (2010). *Mirror.*

Berner, R. S. (2008). *In the town all year 'round.*

Day, A. (1985). *Good dog, Carl.*

Faller, R. (2007). *Polo: The runaway book.*

Geisert, A. (2006). *Oops.*

Hyewon, Y. (2008). *Last night.*

Idle, M. (2013). *Flora the Flamingo.*

Khing, T. T. (2007). *Where is the cake?*

Lehman, B. (2007). *Rainstorm.*

Lehman, B. (2008). *Trainstop.*

Martin, R. (1989). *Will's mammoth.*

Meyer, M. (2007). *A boy, a dog and a frog.*

Rathman, P. (2002). *Good night, Gorilla.*

Thomson, B. (2010). *Chalk.*

Turkle, B. (1991). *Deep in the forest.*

Wiesner, D. (2007). *Flotsam.*

Van Ommen, S. (2007). *The surprise.*

Wiesner, D. (1991). *Tuesday.*

ALPHABET BOOKS

The following books are useful in introducing the letters and corresponding sounds of the alphabet in an enjoyable and whimsical way.

Brent, I. (1993). *An alphabet of animals.*

Brown, M. W. (2010). *Goodnight moon ABC.*

Brown, M. W. (2009). *Sleepy ABC.*

Crowther, R. (2010). *Most amazing hide-and-seek alphabet book.*

Ehlert, L. (1989). *Eating the alphabet: Fruits and vegetables from A to Z.*

Frazier, D. (2010). *A fabulous fair alphabet.*

Gerstein, M. (2001). *The absolutely awful alphabet.*

Hague, K. (1983). *Alphabears.*

Hoban, T. (1982). *A, B, See.*

Hoban, T. (1987). *26 letters and 99 cents.*

Isadora, R. (1983). *City seen from A to Z.*

Kellogg, S. (1987). *Aster Aardvark's alphabet adventure.*

Kitchen, B. (1984). *Animal alphabet.*

MacDonald, S. (1986). *Alphabatics.*

Martin, B., Jr., & Archaumbault, J. (1989). *Chicka, chicka, boom, boom.*

Patience, J. (1993). *An amazing alphabet.*

Sendak, M. (1990). *Alligators all around: An alphabet.*

Seuss, Dr. (1991). *Dr. Seuss's ABCs* (2nd ed.).

Sierra, J. (2009). *The sleepy little alphabet.*

Tallon, R. (1979). *Zoophabets.*

Vamos, S. R. (2013). *Alphabet truck.*

INFORMATIONAL BOOKS

Informational books—that is, nonfiction—can be a valuable part of a young child's reading diet and are often used by teachers to supplement textbooks in the content areas. Informational books are readily available for primary-aged youngsters and are becoming increasingly popular; in fact, in the past few years, publishers' lists have contained nearly as many informational books as fictional titles.

Anderson, S. (2009). *America Ferrera: Latina superstar (Hot celebrity biographies)*.

Aston, D. H. (2015). *A butterfly is patient*. Illus. by S. Long.

Barry, F. (2010). *Let's save the animals*.

Bishop, N. (2008). *Frogs*. Photog. by N. Bishop.

Bullard, L. (2011). *Power up to fight pollution*. Illus. by W. Thomas.

Cerullo, M. M. (2000). *The truth about great white sharks*. Illus. by J. L. Rotman.

Christelow, E. (2013). *What do authors and illustrators do?*

Christensen, B. (2012). *Plant a little seed*.

Cole, J. (2000). *The new baby at your house*.

Davies, N. (2013). *Deadly! The truth about the most dangerous creatures on earth*. Illus. by N. Layton.

Doubilet, D. & Hayes, J. (2009). *Face to face with sharks (Face to face with animals)*.

Drummond, A. (2011). *Energy Island: How one community harnessed the wind and changed their world*. Illus by A. Drummond.

Floca, B. (2013). *Locomotive*.

Fox, K. C. (2011). *Older than the stars*.

Gibbons, G. (2006). *Groundhog Day! Shadow or no shadow?*

Gibbons, G. (2006). *Valentine's Day is . . .*

Gibbons, G. (2009). *Dinosaurs!*

Gibbs, E. (2013). *I spy pets*. Illus. by E. Gibbs.

Goldish, M. (2012). *Dolphins in the Navy*.

Goldish, M. (2013). *Soldiers' dogs*.

Hamilton, K. (2001). *This is the ocean*. Illus. by L. Siomades.

Harlow, R. (2002). *Garbage and recycling: Environmental facts and experiments*.

Jenkins, S. & Page, R. (2008). *What do you do with a tail like this?*

Jenkins, S. (2010). *Bones: Skeletons and how they work*.

Jenkins, S. (2012). *The beetle book*. Illus. by S. Jenkins.

Jenkins, S. (2013). *The animal book: A collection of the fastest, fiercest, toughest, cleverest, shyest—and most surprising—animals*. Illus. by S. Jenkins.

Jocelyn, M. (2013). *Sneaky art: Crafty surprises to hide in plain sight*.

Kalman, M. (2012). *Looking at Lincoln*.

Kelly, I. (2011). *Even an octopus needs a home*. Illus. by I. Kelly.

Koontz, R. (2009). *What's the difference between a butterfly and a moth?* Illus. by D. Bandelin & B. Dacey.

Lunis, N. (2009). *Miniature horses (Peculiar pets)*.

Lunis, N. (2011). *Glow-in-the-dark animals (Animals with super powers)*.

Lyon, G. E. (2011). *All the water in the world*. Illus. by K. Tillotson.

Markle, S. (2005). *Army ants*.

Markle, S. (2011). *How many baby pandas?*

Markle, S. (2013). *What if you had animal teeth?* Illus. by H. McWilliam.

McNamara, M. (2008). *How many seeds in a pumpkin?* Illus. by G. B. Karas.

McNulty, F. (2005). *If you decide to go to the moon*.

Micklethwait, L. (2009). *A child's book of art*.

National Geographic Kids. (2011). *Weird but true! 3: 300 outrageous facts*.

National Geographic Kids. (2012). *5,000 awesome facts (About everything!)*.

National Geographic Kids. (2012). *Quiz whiz: 1,000 super fun, mind-bending, totally awesome trivia questions*.

Nivola, C. A. (2008). *Planting the trees of Kenya: The story of Wangari Maathai*.

Patent, D. H. (2008). *When the wolves returned: The restoring of nature's balance in Yellowstone*.

Person, S. (2012). *Cougar: A cat with many names*.

Peterson, C. (2012). *Seed, soil, sun: Earth's recipe for food*. Photog. by D. R. Lundquist.

Posada, M. (2007). *Guess what is growing inside this egg*.

Rappaport, D. (2002/2007). *Martin's big words: The life of Dr. Martin Luther King, Jr.* Illus. by B. Collier.

Robbins, K. (2005). *Seeds*.

Rotner, S. (2012). *Body actions.* Illus. by S. Rotner & D. A. White.

Sandler, M. (2011). *Freaky-strange buildings.*

Schulte, J. (2005). *Can you find it inside?*

Serafini, F. (2008). *Looking closely along the shore.* Photog. by F. Serafini.

Shange, N. (2011). *Coretta Scott.* Illus. by K. Nelson.

Simon, S. (2000). *Seymour Simon's book of trucks.*

Simon, S. (2006). *Weather.*

Winter, J., III. (2014). *You never heard of Willie Mays?* Illus. by T. Widener.

BOOKS FOR INCREASING READING COMPREHENSION

The following books have interesting themes or relatively complex plots and are suitable for developing the comprehension skills of summarizing, visualizing, predicting, connecting to prior knowledge, or getting the main idea when used in small group discussion.

Avi. (2008). *The end of the beginning: Being the adventures of a small snail (and an even smaller ant).*

Bang, M. (2004). *When Sophie gets angry.*

Bercaw, E. C. (2000). *Halmoni's day.*

Brodsky, K. (2013). *A catfish tale.*

Bunting, E. (1997). *A day's work.*

Bunting, E. (1999). *Smoky night.*

Calmenson, S. (1989). *The principal's new clothes.*

Demi. (1999). *The donkey and the rock.*

Hall, D. (1994). *I am the dog, I am the cat.*

Hoffman, M. (1991). *Amazing grace.*

Janezcko, P. (2001). *Stone bench in an empty park.*

Long, E. (2013). *Chamelia and the new kid in class.*

Paladino, C. (1999). *One good apple: Growing our food for the sake of the earth.*

Rabinowitz, A. (2014). *A boy and a jaguar.*

Ringgold, F. (2003). *If a bus could talk: The story of Rosa Parks.*

Scotton, R. (2013). *Splat and the cool school trip.*

Steig, W. (1990). *Doctor Desoto.*

Uchida, Y. (1996). *The bracelet.*

Winter, J. (2008). *Wangari's trees of peace: A true story from Africa.*

Woodson, J. (2001). *The other side.*

Youme, S. (2005). *That is life: A Haitian story of hope.*

BOOKS FOR DEVELOPING CONCEPTS AND VOCABULARY

These books use some words and concepts unfamiliar to young children, but through context and with scaffolding by the teacher, the words can be discussed and incorporated into the children's speaking vocabulary.

Asch, F. (2000). *The sun is my favorite star.*

Asper-Smith, S. (2011). *Have you ever seen a smack of jellyfish?*

Baker, K. (2010). *LMNO peas.*

Cleary, B. F. (2003). *Dearly, nearly, and insincerely: What is an adverb?*

Cooney, B. (1982). *Miss Rumphius.*

Cumpiano, I. (2008). *Quinito, day and night, Quinito, dia y noche.*

Fleischman, P. (1999). *Mind's eye.*

Gravett, E. (2007). *Wolves.*

Hall, M. (2009). *My heart is like a zoo.*

Hatkoff, I. (2006). *Owen and Mzee: The true story of a remarkable friendship.*

Heller, R. (1987). *A cache of jewels and other collective nouns.*

Heller, R. (1989). *Many luscious lollipops: A book about adjectives.*

Heos, B. (2013). *Mustache baby.*

Jonas, A. (1989). *Color dance.*

Lyon, G. E. (1990). *Come a tide.*

McMillan, B. (1989). *Super, super, superwords.*

Seeger, L. V. (2007). *First the egg.*

Steinberg, L. (2005). *Thesaurus Rex.*

Terban, M. (1986). *I think I thought and other tricky verbs.*

Yankovic, A. (2013). *My new teacher and me.*

Ziefert, H. (1997). *Night knight: A word play flap book.*

MULTICULTURAL BOOKS

The following books will help young students better understand various cultures from around the world. Most of these are picture books.

Baker, J. (2010). *Mirror.* (Australia, Morocco)

Cohn, D. (2009). *Namaste!* (Nepal)

Figueredo, D. (2003). *The road to Santiago.* (Cuba)

Germein, K. (1999). *Big rain coming.* (Australia)

Gonzalez, L. (2008). *The storyteller's candle.* (Puerto Rico)

Gower, C. (2005). *Long-Long's New Year: A story about the Chinese spring festival.* (China)

Graber, J. (2009). *Muktar and the camels.* (Kenya)

Javaherbin, M. (2010). *Goal!* (South Africa)

Malaspina, A. (2010). *Yasmin's hammer.* (Bangladesh)

Matze, C. (1999). *The stars in my Geddoh's sky.* (Middle East)

Onyefulu, I. (1998). *Grandfather's work: A traditional healer in Nigeria.* (Nigeria)

Rumford, J. (2010). *Rain school.* (Chad)

Say, A. (1999). *Tea with milk.* (Japan)

Stanley, S. (1998). *Monkey Sunday: A story from a Congolese village.* (Congo)

Stuve-Bodeen, S. (2003). *Babu's song.* (Tanzania)

Tonatiuh, D. (2010). *Dear Primo: A letter to my cousin.* (Mexico)

Williams, K. L. (2005). *Circles of hope.* (Pakistan)

*List adapted from David & Lorraine Cheng Library, William Paterson University.

BOOKS TO INSPIRE WRITING

The books in this section are about writers or writing issues, and the formats in these books can also be used for rhetorical imitation, or "copycatting." After reading them aloud, the teacher can point out the structure of the story so that children can use this structure to write their own story.

Ada, A. F. (1998). *Yours truly, Goldilocks.*

Barrett, J. (2001). *Things that are the most in the world.*

Brown, M. W. (2006). *Another important book.*

Cameron, A. (1996). *The stories Julian tells.*

Carle, E. (2013). *Friends.*

Clements, A. (2007). *Dogku.*

Fox, M. (1990). *I went walking.*

Lawlor, L. (2010). *Muddy as a duck puddle and other American similes.*

Numeroff, L. J. (1985). *If you give a mouse a cookie.*

Oakley, G. (1987). *The diary of a churchmouse.*

Pulver, R. (2003). *Punctuation takes a vacation.*

Raschka, C. (2007). *Yo! Yes?*

Rylant, C. (2000). *In November.*

Shannon, G. (1999). *Tomorrow's alphabet.*

Shulevitz, U. (2003). *One Monday morning.*

Viorst, J. (1972). *Alexander and the horrible, terrible, no good, very bad day.*

Recommended Books for Teachers

Adams, M. J. (1990). *Beginning to read: Thinking and learning about print.*

Allington, R. L., Cunningham, P. M., & Cunningham, J. W. (2009). *What really matters in response to intervention: Research-based designs.*

Allington, R. L., Cunningham, P. M., & Cunningham, J. W. (2009). *What really matters in vocabulary: Research-based practices across the curriculum.*

Beaty, J. J., & Pratt, L. (2011). *Early literacy in preschool and kindergarten* (3rd ed.).

Beauchat, K. A., Blamey, K. L., & Walpole, S. (2010). *The building blocks of preschool success.*

Beck, I. L. (2005). *Making sense of phonics: The hows and whys.*

Cecil, N. L. (2007). *Focus on fluency: A meaning-based approach.*

Cecil, N. L., & McCormick, C. W. (2009). *A feast of rhyme, rhythm, and song: Developing phonemic awareness through music.*

Collins, K. (2008). *Reading for real: Teach students to read with power, intention, and joy in K–3 classrooms.*

Columba, L., Kim, C., & Moe, A. J. (2009). *The power of picture books in teaching math, science, and social studies, grades preK–8.*

Combs, M. (2010). *Readers and writers in the primary grades: A balanced and integrated approach, K–3* (4th ed.).

Corgill, A. M. (2008). *Of primary importance: What's essential in teaching young writers.*

Cunningham, P. M., & Allington, R. L. (2011). *Classrooms that work: They can all read and write* (5th ed.).

Cunningham, P. M., & Cunningham, J. W. (2010). *What really matters in writing: Research-based practices across the curriculum.*

DeVries, B. (2014). *Literacy assessment and intervention for classroom teachers* (4th ed.).

Dickenson, D. K., & Neuman, S. B. (2005). *Handbook of early literacy research.*

Enz, B. J., & Morrow, L. M. (2009). *Assessing preschool literacy development: Informal and formal measures to guide instruction.*

Flippo, R. F. (2005). *Personal reading: How to match children to books.*

Fuhrken, C. (2009). *What every elementary teacher needs to know about reading tests (From someone who has written them).*

Graves, M. F., Juel, C., Graves, B. B., Calfee, R., & Dewitz, P. (2011). *Teaching reading in the 21st Century* (5th ed.).

Gregory, E. (Ed.) (1997). *One child, many worlds: Early learning in multicultural communities.*

Hale, E. (2008). *Crafting writers, K–6.*

Hayes, K., & Creange, R. (2000). *Classroom routines that really work for preK and kindergarten.*

Heard, G., & McDonough, J. (2009). *A place for wonder: Reading and writing nonfiction in the primary grades.*

Herrera, S., Perez, D. R., & Escamilla, K. (2010). *Teaching reading to English language learners: Differentiated literacies.*

Hiebert, E. H., & Raphael, T. E. (1998). *Early literacy instruction.*

Hughes, M., & Searle, D. (1997). *The violent E and other tricky sounds: Learning to spell from kindergarten through grade 6.*

Jalongo, M. R. (2011). *Early childhood language arts* (5th ed.).

Johnston, P. H. (Ed.) (2010). *RTI in literacy—responsive and comprehensive.*

Kristo, J. V., & Bamford, R. A. (2004). *Nonfiction in focus: A comprehensive framework for helping* students become independent readers and writers of nonfiction, K–6.

Lapp, D., Flood, J., Moore, K., & Nichols, M. (2005). *Teaching literacy in first grade.*

McGee, L. M., & Morrow, L. M. (2005). *Teaching literacy in kindergarten.*

McGee, L. M., & Richgels, D. (2004). *Literacy's beginnings: Supporting young readers and writers* (4th ed.).

McKenna, M. C., Walpole, S., & Conradi, K. (2010). *Promoting early reading: Research, resources, and best practices.*

McLaughlin, M. (2010). *Guided comprehension in the primary grades.*

McLaughlin, M., & Fisher, L. (2005). *Research-based reading lessons for K–3.*

Meier, D. R. (Ed.) (2009). *Here's the story: Using narrative to promote young children's language and literacy learning.*

Moore, P., & Lyon, A. (2005). *New essentials for teaching reading in pre-K–2: Comprehension, vocabulary, fluency.*

Moore-Hart, M. A. (2010). *Teaching writing in diverse classrooms K–8: Enhancing writing through literature, real-life experiences and technology.*

Morrow, L. M. (2005). *Literacy development in the early years: Helping children read and write* (5th ed.).

Podhajski, B., Varricchio, M., Mather, N., & Sammons, J. (2010). *Mastering the alphabetic principle (MAP): How to map speech to print for reading and spelling.*

Morrow, L. M., Freitag, E., & Gambrell, L. B. (2009). *Using children's literature in preschool to develop comprehension: Understanding and enjoying books* (2nd ed.).

Moss, B., & Lapp, D. (2010). *Teaching new literacies in grades K–3.*

Moss, B., & Young, T. A. (2010). *Creating lifelong readers through independent reading.*

Paratore, J. R., & McCormack, R. L. (2005). *Teaching literacy in second grade.*

Preece, A., & Cowden, D. (1993). *Young writers in the making: Sharing the process with parents.*

Raphael, T. E., Highfield, K., & Au, K. H. (2006). *QAR now: A powerful and practical framework that develops comprehension and higher-level thinking in all students.*

Rasinski, T. V., Padak, N. D., & Fawcett, G. (2010). *Teaching children who find reading difficult.*

Richards, C., & Leafstedt, J. (2010). *Early reading intervention: Strategies and methods for struggling readers.*

Riddle, J. (2009). *Engaging the eye generation: Visual literacy strategies for the K–5 classroom.*

Rog, L. J. (2007). *Marvelous minilessons for teaching beginning writing.*

Roskos, K. A., Tabors, P. O., & Lenhart, L. A. (2009). *Oral language and early literacy in preschool: Talking, reading, and writing* (2nd ed.).

Samuels, S. J., & Farstrup, A. E. (Eds.) (2006). *What research has to say about fluency instruction.*

Strickland, D. S., & Schickedanz, J. A. (2009). *Learning about print in preschool: Working with letters, words, and beginning links with phonemic awareness* (2nd ed.).

Szymusiak, K., Sibberson, F, & Koch, L. (2008). *Beyond leveled books: Supporting early and transitional readers in grades K–5.*

Temple, C. A., Ogle, D., Crawford, A. N., & Freppon, P. (2011). *All children read: Teaching literacy in today's diverse classrooms* (3rd ed.).

Tompkins, G. E. (2011). *Literacy in the early grades: A successful start for preK–4 readers and writers.*

Vukelich, C., & Christie, J. (2009). *Building a foundation for preschool literacy: Effective instruction for children's reading and writing development* (2nd ed.).

Walpole, S., & McKenna, M. C. (2009). *How to plan differentiated reading instruction: Resources for grades K–3.*

Websites for Early Literacy

Please note that although we have made every effort to use current information, website addresses change frequently. Websites are identified using the following categories to indicate the site's primary focus, but many sites offer a great variety of tools!

C	=	Comprehension	**T**	=	Teachers/lesson plans
P	=	Parents	**PH**	=	Phonics
PA	=	Phonemic awareness	**G**	=	Group reading
F	=	Fluency	**E**	=	Emergent literacy
W	=	Writing	**I**	=	Informational text
V	=	Vocabulary			

T 6+1 Trait Rubric, http://educationnorthwest.org/traits ■ The creators of 6 + 1 Trait Writing® offer an overview of their models with research that supports the program, lesson plans, writing prompts, and rubrics. They also give information on how to score students on elements such as 'voice' and 'organization' and use this data to inform subsequent writing instruction.

T A to Z Teacher Stuff, www.atozteacherstuff.com ■ This site for teachers offers online lesson plans, thematic units, teacher tips, discussion boards, educational articles and sites, as well as literature activities.

C ABCteach, www.abcteach.com ■ Great site with much free printable material. Some of the materials work at developing higher-level thinking skills.

PH Adrian Bruce's Reading Stuff, www.adrianbruce.com/reading/games.htm ■ A reading resources website offering free and printable word games, phonics games, reading games, comprehension strategies, and phonics posters.

T, P American Library Association, www.ala.org ■ Provides information on parent training sessions and assists teachers in locating trainers through the Every Child Ready to Read@Your Library program.

V Angelfire, www.angelfire.com/ill/monte/findacognate.html ■ Tool that provides cognates for Spanish or English words.

G Author sites: www.eric-carle.com, www.tomiedepaola.com, www.janbrett.com ■ These sites contain information about the authors of popular picture books and are helpful in planning author studies. Children will enjoy browsing, too.

I Awesome Library, www.awesomelibrary.org/student.html ■ This site contains over 26,000 resources. A must-see for information across content areas for teacher and student use. The Talking Library is perfect for English learners, and many sites are available in various languages.

PH BBC, www.bbc.co.uk/schools/wordsandpictures ■ Words and picture activities and games for phonics, CVC words, consonant clusters, long vowel sounds, and others.

W Bellingham Schools, bellinghamschools.org/sites/default/files/BIO/Biomaker.htm ■ A webpage that provides steps for students to write comprehensive, interesting biographies.

T, P Best Kids Websites, http://bestkidswebsites.com ■ A list of helpful websites and resources for teachers, children, and parents.

W Biography Maker, The, bellinghamschools.org/sites/default/files/BIO/Biomaker.htm ■ This site provides the structure to guide children to write a biography by asking the right questions to draw out a person's life story.

C Book Adventure, www.bookadventure.com ■ This site is designed to encourage children from K–8 to read more often, for longer periods of time, and with greater comprehension.

W Book Creator, www.redjumper.net/bookcreator ■ This app can be used to build stories using text, images, video, music, and narration, and to share the finished product.

C, G BookPALS Storyline, www.storylineonline.net ■ An online series of streaming videos where children of all ages can find and appreciate wonderful stories read by famous actors.

T Book Wizard, www.scholastic.com/bookwizard ■ A website devoted to helping classroom teachers level the books in their classroom libraries, find resources to extend books, and create reading lists. The site also includes a feature to help teachers select books with an easier, similar, or more difficult reading level than ones they are using.

W Bravenet, www.bravenet.com ■ A tool that can help teachers create a classroom website with student-created video presentations and math projects.

T Case Technologies to Enhance Literacy Learning, http://ctell.uconn.edu/home.htm ■ This case-based site aids anchored instruction using multimedia cases delivered online.

I Children's Book Council (CBC), www.cbcbooks.org ■ Provides lists of outstanding social studies and science trade books for young people.

C, W Children's Story Online, www.childrenstory.com/stories ■ Allows children to collaborate with peers around the world to develop positive reading and writing connections through the Internet.

T Choosing Children's Literature, www.dawcl.com ■ Database for award-winning children's literature.

I, G Cleveland Rock & Roll Hall of Fame, www.rockhall.com/education ■ Offers lesson plans that integrate music with history and literature. Older children can explore the site independently.

PA, V, I, T Colorín Colorado, www.colorincolorado.org ■ A bilingual Spanish–English website that provides information to teachers on how to teach phonemic awareness to English learners; also offers vocabulary resources and excellent resources for helping English learners with information text, with specific connection to the CCSS.

T Common Core State Standards Initiative, www.corestandards.org ■ This overview of the Common Core State Standards provides a thoughtful look at how the standards were determined and what teachers can expect of their students at various grade levels.

I Cradle of Aviation, www.cradleofaviation.org/education ■ At this site, simply click on the links on the sidebar. The screen will emerge with information and activities about planes, aviation, and related topics.

T Crayola, www.crayola.com ■ This site includes both a teacher area concerned with integrating art across the curriculum and a site for children. The children's site has an ongoing story with a new chapter every week.

I Defenders of Wildlife, www.defenders.org ▪ The programs addressed on this website focus on the extinction of animal species and the destruction of their environment. The website is committed to protecting endangered plants and wild animals.

PH Developmental Studies Center Scope and Sequence Chart, www.devstu.org/sites/default/files/media/pdfs/ sipps/sipps_beg_sands_3rd_ed.pdf ▪ Offers a beginning level scope and sequence chart for teaching phonics.

T Disney Educational Online, http://Disney.go.com/educational ▪ Part of the Classroom Connect family of online education community resources, this site offers lesson plans for K–12 teachers.

T Dynamic Indicators of Basic Early Literacy Skills (DIBELS), www.voyagersopris.com ▪ A site that provides achievement tests including subtest of Oral Reading Fluency, Phonemic Awareness, and Retell Fluency.

T Early Childhood Literacy Technology Project, www.montgomeryschoolsmd.org/departments/earlychildhood ▪ Site evaluates early literacy software. Good place for teachers to find out what is available and worthwhile.

W Edublog, www.edublogs.org ▪ A site focused on classroom blogging that provides free blog creation tools for teachers and students with helpful video tutorials.

I Education World's Scavenger Hunt, www.education-world.com/a_curr/curr113.shtml ▪ A child appropriate website that uses a scavenger hunt as a way for students to research a wide variety of topics including wild and domestic animals, cars, other countries, volcanoes, and planets.

T Educational Technology and Mobile Learning, www.educatorstechnology.com/2012/07/15-free-awesome-drawing-and-painting.html ▪ A free drawing program that allows students to add words to their pictures, which can be used as an activity to create a digital dictionary.

T Educational Technology Network, www.edtechnetwork.com/document_cameras.html ▪ Provides ideas on how to use a document reader in the elementary classroom.

I Eisenhower National Clearinghouse, www.goenc.com ▪ This clearinghouse is dedicated to identifying superior curriculum resources, creating high-quality professional development materials, and improving science and math learning in K–12 classrooms.

I Endangered Species Coalition, www.stopextinction.org ▪ This group is the watchdog for the Endangered Species Act of 1973. The website disseminates information and provides discussions about environmental, scientific, and conservation issues related to the ESA Act.

C, T EPals Book Club, www.epals.com/#!/main ▪ This site connects children with other learners. Children may establish free accounts and collaborate on projects and inventions.

C ERIC, www.askeric.org ▪ This is an excellent website for listening and reading comprehension. Many activities and lessons for beginning readers are offered.

P Families Learning, www.familieslearning.org ▪ A federal government family literacy program designed to provide activities and strategies for teaching literacy skills.

P Family and Community Literacy Engagement, www.ed.gov/family-and-community-engagement ▪ A federal government family literacy program designed to provide activities and strategies for teaching literacy skills.

I Fish America Foundation, www.fishamerica.org ▪ This organization has assisted over 700 grassroots organizations to enhance fish production and increase water quality throughout North America.

T Folger Shakespeare Library, www.folger.edu/teach-learn ▪ Resources, teaching ideas, and lesson plans for teaching Shakespeare through performance with young children.

w **Fotobabble, www.fotobabble.com/** ■ An app that can be used to add audio and images to text stories.

v **Free Dictionary, The, www.thefreedictionary.com/add2ie.htm#addon.** ■ A free online word reference tool that students can access while reading online text.

T, PA **Get Ready to Read!, www.getreadytoread.org** ■ Early literacy screening, tools, and activities to help with skill-building and to improve communication between children and adults.

I **Global Exchange, http://globalexchange.org** ■ Founded in 1988, this is the site for a human rights organization focused on promoting environmental rights and political awareness around the world.

w **Glogster, www.glogster.com** ■ Can be used to create research project presentations incorporating multimedia.

I **Graphics Soft, http://graphicssoft.about.com/od/softwareforkids/** ■ Provides information on drawing and graphics software for children.

I **Greenpeace, www.greenpeace.org** ■ This activist organization is dedicated to achieving change in environmental and conservationist issues through direct action and international conferences.

P **Harvard Family Research Project, www.hfrp.org** ■ An organization that provides resources about conducting home visits.

I **History Place, The, www.historyplace.com** ■ This site provides information about history that can be used as resources for any social studies unit, especially good for World War II.

F, PH, PA **Idea Box, www.theideabox.com** ■ This is a site for young children that includes online stories as well as song and craft activities for teachers. Lots of activities for teaching the alphabet, phonics, and phonemic awareness.

w **Inspiration, www.inspiration.com** ■ Software that can be used to brainstorm writing processes.

G **Jan Brett (author), www.janbrett.com** ■ Author's site includes lesson plans and reproducible materials to supplement them. These can be used to enhance guided reading, shared reading, and learning centers.

I **Journey North, www.learner.org/jnorth** ■ This site includes information about an Internet project and resources for the study of seasonal change. Children from all fifty states and Canada have taken part in the project.

I **JumpStart, www.jumpstart.com** ■ This site offers activities for teachers, games for students, and links to Knowledge Adventure, for more teaching tools and activities.

P, T **K–12.com, http://eprcontent.k12.com/placement/placement/placement_langarts_2.html** ■ This site includes placement tests for phonics assessment.

w **Kid Pix, http://kid-pix.soft112.com/** ■ Child friendly software that can be used to create presentations and incorporate multimedia into a student's writing to aid comprehension.

w **Kid Pub, www.kidpub.org/kidpub** ■ Children can publish their original work on this site.

w **Kidblog, http://kidblog.org** ■ A site focused on classroom blogging that provides free blogs for teachers and students with helpful video tutorials.

P **Kiddyhouse.com, www.kiddyhouse.com** ■ Resource for parents, children, and teachers. Includes a discussion board and has free worksheets, clip art, and lesson plans.

w **Kidpix, www.mackiev.com/kidpix** ■ Software that allows students to create multimedia works of art by pasting, drawing, altering, and animating them with easy-to-use tools. This software is useful for the creation of projects, charts, and presentations.

I   Kids Web Japan, web-jpn.org/kidsweb   ■   Introduces children to Japan, including Japanese lifestyle, pictures, and legends. Managed by the Japan Center for Intercultural Communications.

G, I   KidsClick!, www.kidsclick.org   ■   This site offers more than 4,000 links for children on subjects such as literature, machines, and mythology. The reading level of each linked site is designated.

W   Kidspiration, www.inspiration.com/Kidspiration   ■   A program designed to help students organize their writing and ideas into stages.

W   Klein Inspiration, www.kleinspiration.com   ■   Provides information on using technology in reading and writing workshops.

W   Launchpad, www.launchpadmag.com   ■   Allows students to create and present their writing online, as well as read the books of other children from around the world.

C, T   Laura Candler, www.lauracandler.com   ■   This teacher's site offers literary lessons and related tools.

V, T   Lesson Plan Central, http://lessonplancentral.com/lessons/Language_Arts/Vocabulary   ■   This site includes vocabulary lesson plans.

T   Livescribe, www.livescribe.com/en-us/solutions/learningdisabilities/   ■   Speech recognition software that has been found to be especially useful in supporting students with special needs.

F   Lois Walker's site, www.scriptsforschools.com   ■   For teachers interested in drama, this site offers script packages for beginning readers for a small price.

W   Lucidpress, www.lucidpress.com   ■   An app that can be used to create a layout for writing and photos and adding multimedia to print and digital documents.

I   Magic School Bus, http://scholastic.com/MagicSchoolBus/index.htm   ■   This site includes content area materials and activities for children, as well as a resource area for teachers.

C, I   Miss Maggie, www.missmaggie.org   ■   Miss Maggie's earth adventures uses puzzles, activities, and games to teach children about environmental issues. The site includes weekly lesson plans, cross-curricular activities, and companion books and articles.

E, P, PH, G   MoJo's Musical Mouseum, www.kididdles.com/lyrics/index.html   ■   Click on the musical notes displayed by the song titles in this site and hear a music box play the tune while you read the lyrics. Song lyrics may be accessed through a subject index or a searchable database.

W, I   Montgomery County Teacher Websites, www.montgomery.k12.ky.us   ■   Teachers and students will find many informational links to sound and photo displays of Western subjects (e.g., cowboys and rodeos).

E, PA, PH, P   MotherGoose.com, www.mothergoose.com   ■   Free preschool games, crafts, letter-play, and rhyming activities. Over 360 Mother Goose rhymes.

P   Mr. Rogers' Neighborhood Online, www.pbskids.org/rogers   ■   This site offers the same quality learning experiences as the television show.

I   My Hero Project, www.myhero.com   ■   This site allows children to read about many heroes and heroines around the world as they come to understand what it means to make a difference.

W   My Town Is Important, www.mrsmcgowan.com/projects.html   ■   Mrs. McGowan's project allows students to work collaboratively and create projects about their own cities.

G   National Geographic Kids, kids.nationalgeographic.com/kids   ■   An online magazine that provides a number of interesting science and nature related articles for children.

P, E Net-Mom's Internet Safehouse, www.netmom.com ■ Great site for preschoolers and their parents. Lots of activities to get young children excited about reading.

I New Literacies, http://ctell.uconn.edu/cases.htm ■ Multimedia cases focused on literacy instruction; created to help teachers improve children's reading achievement.

I New York Philharmonic Kidzone, www.nyphilkids.org/main.phtml ■ Activities on this site include videos about instruments, composing music, games and puzzles.

T Nuance, www.nuance.com/dragon/index.htm ■ Speech recognition software that has been found to be especially useful in supporting students with special needs.

P Parent Teacher Home Visit Project, www.pthvp.org ■ An excellent resource for helping schools learn about conducting home visits.

P, E PBS Kids, www.pbskids.org ■ Lots of early literacy activities and great information to help parents foster their young children's literacy development.

T Picture This, picturethis.sdcoe.net ■ Provides in depth tips for teachers on how to incorporate the making of videos into the curriculum.

F Poetry for Kids, www.poetry4kids.com/index.php ■ This site helps teachers use poetry to teach fluency.

T Preschool Rainbow, www.preschoolrainbow.org ■ Site is billed as the place where "early childhood teachers find their ideas." Thematically arranged curricula, games, and so forth.

P Project FLAME, http://cfl.uic.edu/programs/parent-engagement-programs-2/parent-engagement-programs/flame-family-literacy/ ■ A program that engages Head Start parents in interactive workshops to help them become literacy educators at home.

W Read Along Stories, www.rif.org/kids/readingplanet/bookzone/read_aloud_stories.htm ■ Fun, interactive online stories that have animated illustrations.

PA, T, C, W Read, Write, Think, www.readwritethink.org ■ This site offers phonemic awareness games and activities and options allowing children to respond to literature.

F, T Readers theater sites: www.aaronshep.com/rt/index.html, www.teachingheart.net/readerstheater.htm ■ These sites offer scripts and other tools for readers theater programs.

T, E Reading Is Fundamental, www.rif.org ■ By visiting this site, teachers will get involved with one of the nation's best-known reading initiatives. It includes practical information on books to bring to the classroom and has a program for early readers designed to get child-care providers involved in early literacy.

C, W Reading Planet, www.rif.org/readingplanet/content/read_aloud_stories.mspx ■ This Reading Is Fundamental site offers ideas and activities to incorporate into the curriculum and keep students interested and motivated.

V Reading Rainbow, www.readingrainbow.com/classic-series ■ Provides videos with captions, allowing children to see the words contextualized by the actions being performed on screen.

PA Reading Rockets, www.readingrockets.org/reading-topics/english-language-learners ■ Provides information for teachers on ways to teach phonemic awareness to English learners.

W Reading Rockets, www.readingrockets.org/article/48589 ■ Provides students with ideas on how to use dialogue journals, as well as a list of recommended children's literature that simulates the journal format.

C, W, T Reading Rubrics, www.mrsmcgowan.com/reading/writing_resources.html ■ This portion of Mrs. McGowan's site includes rubrics for comprehension, poetry writing, and holistic writing.

T   Resources & Tools, www.scholastic.com/teachers/teaching-resources ▪ Here teachers can find teaching ideas for reading, writing, and spelling, as well as lesson plans, extension activities, and other teaching resources for all grade levels.

C   Rethinking Schools, www.rethinkingschools.org/index.shtml. ▪ Offers lesson plans using critical literacy practices.

T   Rubistar, www.rubistar.com ▪ A website that allows teachers to create their own rubrics for writing instruction.

P, T   Scholastic, www.scholastic.com/teachers/article/teach-phonics-skills-chart ▪ This Scholastic site offers a "teaching with phonics" skills chart for teachers.

F, T   Scholastic, http://teacher.scholastic.com/reading/bestpractices/assessment/3t4oralcalc.htm ▪ This Scholastic site offers an oral fluency calculator.

P, T   Scholastic, http://teacher.scholastic.com/reading/bestpractices/phonics/nonsensewordtest.pdf ▪ This Scholastic site offers a PDF printout of the Nonsense Word Test.

G   Science News for Kids, www.sciencenewsforkids.org ▪ An online magazine that provides a number of interesting science-related articles for children.

I   Smithsonian Education, www.smithsonianeducation.org ▪ This is an extraordinary museum site. Click on History & Culture on the left-hand side under Topics. There you will learn about the Wright Brothers, Black Wing, and World War II aviators.

G, I   Smithsonian Education, www.smithsonianeducation.org/students ▪ The younger children's version of the Smithsonian Institution website. Includes a picture of the day, activity ideas, and information about all the subjects the 14-museum network encompasses.

PA, T Songs for Teaching, www.songsforteaching.com/avni/alliterativebooks.htm ▪ Children's books for teaching phonemic awareness with rhyme, alliteration, and other word play.

G, F   Stacks, The, www.scholastic.com/stacks ▪ At The Stacks, students can post book reviews, get reading recommendations, play games associated with their favorite reading series, and watch "meet the author" videos.

E, PH Starfall, www.starfall.com/n/level-k/index/play.htm?f ▪ An adult narrator pronounces the name of each capital letter as the child clicks on it, reinforcing letter names. A child narrator says the name of the lowercase letters. Activities and animations are brief, motivational, and support letter recognition and beginning phonics.

T   Superkids, www.superkids.com ▪ Provides reviews of educational software.

W   SurveyMonkey, www.surveymonkey.com ▪ A free online survey creator that can be used to create blank checklists students can use to share feedback on each other's writing.

T   Teacher Created Resources, www.teachercreated.com ▪ Teacher Created Resources is a publisher of educational materials and classroom supplies for preschool through middle school. The site includes literature units, language arts ideas, and free literacy materials.

T   Teach-nology, www.teach-nology.com/web_tools/rubrics/ ▪ A website that allows teachers to create their own rubrics for writing instruction.

PA, T TEAMS Educational Resources, http://teams.lacoe.edu/teachers/index.asp ▪ Rhyming word activities and a wide variety of other phonemic awareness activities.

V, T   Tech Teachers, www.techteachers.com ▪ This site offers many links to sites focusing on vocabulary development using digital tools.

T   The Teachers Corner, www.theteacherscorner.net ▪ This helpful site offers a collection of educational worksheets, lesson plans, and activities for literacy and other content areas.

T   The Teaching Channel, www.teachingchannel.org ▪ A site that offers teachers lesson plans and videos of effective teaching in literacy.

G   Time for Kids, www.timeforkids.com/TFK/kids/news ▪ An online magazine that provides a wide range of reading with high-interest articles for children.

I   Treasure Hunts for ESL Students, http://iteslj.org/th ▪ A child-appropriate website that uses a scavenger hunt as a way for students to research for a wide variety of topics including wild and domestic animals, cars, other countries, volcanoes, and planets.

I   U.S. Library of Congress, www.americaslibrary.gov/cgi-bin/page.cgi ▪ A place where kids can learn about the history of America in a fun, interactive way.

I   U.S. Library of Congress, http://lcweb.loc.gov/homepage/lchp.html ▪ Here teachers will find a wealth of information for learners of all ages about virtually any informational topic. Click on Kids, Families. Then click on Jump Back in Time to explore any historical era.

C   University of Calgary, http://people.ucalgary.ca/~dkbrown ▪ Children's literature web guide that provides resources such as author websites, children's bestsellers, book award winners, and other literature resources for teachers and parents.

P   Videos to Share with Parents, www.sanjuan.edu/howe ▪ This district website contains various videos that can be shared with parents to help them encourage children's literacy.

V   Vocabulary.co.il, www.vocabulary.co.il ▪ Provides numerous vocabulary building games for children to learn new vocabulary and build background.

V, T   Vocabulary.com, www.vocabulary.com ▪ Learning activities and lesson plans to help teachers plan effective vocabulary instruction.

W   Weebly, www.weebly.com ▪ A tool that can help teachers create a classroom website with student-created video presentations and math projects.

I   When They Were Young, www.loc.gov/exhibits/young/young-exhibit.html ▪ This virtual tour of an exhibit at the U.S. Library of Congress shows engrossing photographs of children that cross generations and cultures.

W   Wikihow, www.wikihow.com/Create-a-Free-Website-(for-Kids) ▪ Step-by step article that shows kids how to create a website.

V   Word Wizard, www.wordwizard.com ▪ At this amazing site, children can find anything at all pertaining to words.

I   Zoobooks series, www.zoobooks.com ▪ This series has a website with pictures, sound effects, games, and information about wild animals.

F   Zoodles, www.zoodles.com/free-online-kids-games/funschool ▪ Set up for children from preschool to grade 6. Primarily includes games that make learning fun.

Commercial Assessment Instruments

CRITERION-REFERENCED READING TESTS

Basic Inventory of Natural Language. San Bernardino, CA: CHECpoint Systems. (Grades K–12)

The Lollipop Test: A Diagnostic Screening Test of School Readiness. Atlanta, GA: Humanistics Limited. (First half of K to grade 1 entrants)

PRI Reading Systems. Monterey, CA: CTB/McGraw-Hill. (Grades K–9)

Reading Yardsticks. Chicago: Riverside Publishing Company. (Grades K–8)

Woodcock Reading Mastery Tests. Woodcock, R. W. Circle Pines, MN: American Guidance Services. (Grades K–12)

FORMAL READING TESTS

Biemiller Test of Reading Processes. Biemiller, A. Toronto, Ontario, Canada: Guidance Centre. (Grades 2–6)

California Achievement Test, Forms C and D. Monterey, CA: CTB/McGraw-Hill. (Grades K–12.9)

Gates–MacGinitie Reading Tests. MacGinitie, W. H. Chicago: Riverside Publishing. (Ages 6 1/2–17)

Iowa Test of Basic Skills: Primary Battery. Chicago: Riverside Publishing. (Grades K–3.2)

Metropolitan Achievement Test. San Antonio, TX: The Psychological Corporation. (Grades K–12.9)

Stanford Achievement Test. San Antonio, TX: The Psychological Corporation. (Grades 1.5–9.9)

Test of Reading Comprehension (TORC). Brown, V., Hammill, J., and Wiederholt, J. L. Austin, TX: PRO-ED. (Grades 2–6)

FORMAL TESTS FOR EMERGENT READERS

Clymer Barrett Reading Test. Santa Barbara, CA: Chapman, Brook, & Kent. (Grades K and beginning 1)

CTBS Readiness Test. Monterey, CA: CTB/ McGraw-Hill. (Grades K.0 to 1.3)

Metropolitan Readiness Test. Nurss, J. R., and McGauvran, M. E. San Antonio, TX: The Psychological Corporation. (First half of K to beginning Grade 1)

The Primary Language Record: Handbook for Teachers. Portsmouth, NH: Heinemann. (Preschool to Grade 2)

"Sand: Concepts about Print" Tests. Clay, M. M. Portsmouth, NH: Heinemann. (Pre-K to end of K)

Stanford Early School Achievement Test (SESAT). Madden, R., Gardner, E. F., and Collins, C. S. San Antonio, TX: The Psychological Corporation. (Grades K–1.9)

"Stone: Concepts about Print" Tests. Clay, M. M. Portsmouth, NH: Heinemann. (Pre-K to end of K)

Test of Basic Experiences 2 (TOBE2). Moss, M. H. Monterey, CA: CTB/McGraw-Hill. (Pre-K to end of Grade 1)

The Test of Early Reading Ability (TERA). Reid, D. K., Hresko, W. P., and Hammill, D. D. Austin, TX: PRO-ED. (Ages 3 to 7)

INFORMAL READING INVENTORIES

Analytical Reading Inventory. Woods, M. L., and Moe, A. J. Boston: Pearson.

Bader Reading and Language Inventory. Bader, L. A. New York: Macmillan.

Basic Reading Inventory Pre-Primer–Grade Twelve. Johns, J. L. Dubuque, IA: Kendall/Hunt.

Burns/Roe Informal Reading Inventory. Roe, B. D. Boston: Houghton Mifflin.

Classroom Reading Inventory. Silvaroli, N. J., and Wheelock, W. H. New York: McGraw-Hill.

Diagnostic Reading Inventory. Jacobs, H. D., and Searfoss, L. W. Dubuque, IA: Kendall/Hunt.

Ekwall/Shanker Reading Inventory. Shanker, J. L., and Cockrum, W. E. Boston: Pearson.

The Flynt–Cooter Reading Inventory for the Classroom. Flynt, E. S., and Cooter, R. B., Jr. Columbus, OH: Merrill/Prentice Hall.

Qualitative Reading Inventory. Leslie, L., and Caldwell, J. S. Boston: Allyn & Bacon.

Reading Miscue Inventory: Alternative Procedures. Goodman, Y., Watson, D. J., and Burke, C. L. Katonah, NY: Richard C. Owens.

Reading Placement Inventory. Sucher, F., and Allred, R. A. Oklahoma City: The Economy Company.

Retrospective Miscue Analysis: Revaluing Readers and Reading. Goodman, Y., and Marek, A. M. Katonah, NY: Richard C. Owens.

Texas Primary Reading Inventory. Austin, TX: Texas Education Agency.

PHONEMIC AWARENESS TESTS

Auditory Discrimination Test. Wepman, J. Los Angeles: Western Psychological Services.

Comprehensive Test of Reading Related Phonological Processes. Torgeson, J., and Wagner, W. Austin, TX: PRO-ED. 512-451-3246.

Lindamood Auditory Conceptualization Test. Lindamood, C., and Lindamood, P. Austin, TX: PRO-ED. 512-451-3246.

The Phonological Awareness Profile. Robertson, C., and Salter, W. East Moline, IL: LinguiSystems. 800-PRO-IDEA.

Scholastic Ready-to-Use Primary Reading Assessment Kit. Fiderer, A. New York: Scholastic, 1998. 800-724-6527.

Test of Awareness of Language Segments. Sawyer, D. J. Austin, TX: PRO-ED. 512-451-3246.

Test of Phonological Awareness. Torgeson, J., and Bryant, B. Austin, TX: PRO-ED. 512-451-3246.

Informal Checklists and Assessment Devices

HOW THE TOOLS IN THIS APPENDIX ARE ORGANIZED

Knowledge of Print

Name _____ Date _____

Interest in Writing

○ Very motivated (enjoys writing)

○ Moderate (writes with prompting)

○ Minimal (only writes if asked to do so)

Awareness of Directionality

○ Consistently writes from left to right and top to bottom

○ Sometimes writes from left to right and top to bottom

○ No awareness of directionality evident

Word Representation

○ Includes a vowel when representing a word

○ Uses several letters to represent a word; not always a vowel

○ Uses a phonetically correct initial consonant for words

○ Can write own name

○ Uses random shapes, letters, and numbers for writing

○ Uses drawings alone to represent writing

Concepts About Print Assessment

Name _____   Date _____

Book Orientation

- ○ Can point to front of book
- ○ Can point to back of book
- ○ Can point to title

Difference Between Illustrations and Print

- ○ Can point to illustrations
- ○ Can point to print
- ○ Can point to where text begins

Directionality of Print

- ○ Can show directionality of print on page
- ○ Can point to beginning of text
- ○ Can point to end of text
- ○ Can show beginning and end of words on page (knows word boundaries)

Print Terminology

- ○ Can identify top and bottom of page
- ○ Can point to a letter
- ○ Can point to a word
- ○ Can point to a specific word on request
- ○ Can point to a specific letter on request
- ○ Can point to a lowercase letter
- ○ Can point to an uppercase letter
- ○ Can identify different punctuation marks on request

Interest Inventory

Name _____ Age _____ Date _____

1. What do you like to do most when you have spare time?
   _____

2. What do you usually do after school?
   _____

   in the evenings?
   _____

   on Sundays?
   _____

   on Saturdays?
   _____

3. How old are your brothers and sisters? _____
   How do you get along with them? _____
   What do you like to do with them?
   _____

4. Do you take any special lessons?
   _____

5. Are your parents/grandparents from another country? _____
   Which one? _____ What language do they speak? _____

6. What kind of food do you like?
   _____

7. Have you ever been to a(n): *(circle all that apply)*
   airport?   circus?   library?   museum?   farm?
   amusement park?   concert?   picnic?   ball game?   zoo?
   swimming pool?   beach?   dairy?   firehouse?

8. Have you ever taken a trip by: *(circle all that apply)*
   airplane?   train?   bus?   boat?
   Where did you go? _____

9. What types of work do you think you would like to do to earn money?
   _____

10. What television programs do you like best?

    _____

    videos or movies?

    _____

    computer programs or apps?

    _____

    video games?

    _____

11. Do you ever listen to the news on TV? _____

12. What songs do you like?

    _____

13. Do you have any pets? _____ What kind? _____

    _____

    What kind of pet would you like to have?

    _____

14. Do you have books you read for fun at home? _____

15. Do you like to have someone read aloud to you? _____

16. Do you ever use the Internet by yourself or with your family? If so, what kind of sites do you like to visit?

    _____

17. What is your favorite type of book?

    _____

18. Are there any books you would like to own?

    _____

19. What book is your all-time favorite? *(only one title, please)*

    _____

20. Do you enjoy shopping alone or with friends best? _____

21. Would you rather spend your relaxation time alone or with others?

    _____

An Early Reader's View of the Reading Process

Name _____   Age _____   Date _____

1. Name someone you know who is a good reader. _____
   What makes him/her a good reader?
   _____

2. Do you think (person named in #1) ever comes to a word they don't know
   or an idea they don't understand when they are reading? _____

3. (If yes for #2) When they come to a word they don't know or an idea they
   don't understand, what do you think they do about it?
   _____

4. When *you* are reading and you come to a word you don't know, what do
   you do?
   _____

5. If you knew that someone was having trouble in reading, how would you
   help that person?
   _____

6. What do you think a teacher would do to help that person?
   _____

7. Who helped you learn to read? _____
   How did they help you?
   _____

8. What would you like to be able to do better when you read?
   _____

9. Do you think that you are a good reader? _____
   Why or why not?
   _____

10. What do you like/dislike about reading?
    _____

    Additional notes or comments:
    _____

Response to Literature Checklist

Name _____ Date _____

Responds to teacher's questions

| Never | Sometimes | Frequently | Always |

Comments on or interprets text

| Never | Sometimes | Frequently | Always |

Connects text to own life

| Never | Sometimes | Frequently | Always |

Asks questions about text

| Never | Sometimes | Frequently | Always |

Makes predictions

| Never | Sometimes | Frequently | Always |

Shares own background information related to text

| Never | Sometimes | Frequently | Always |

Strays from topic of text

| Never | Sometimes | Frequently | Always |

Primary Reading Attitude Survey

Name _____   Date _____

How Do You Feel . . .

1. When you read?
2. About reading in your free time?
3. About going to the library?
4. About reading instead of watching TV or playing a video game?
5. About reading to your family?
6. About reading independently at your desk in school?
7. About how important reading is?
8. About reading at bedtime?
9. About reading on an elecronic device?
10. About writing your own stories?
11. About school?
12. About reading to try to learn something?
13. When someone else reads to you?
14. When you come to a new word in a story?
15. About reading in your favorite subject in school?
16. About your reading group in school?
17. About reading out loud?
18. About checking out books from the library?
19. About reading with your teacher?
20. About answering questions about what you read?
21. About taking reading tests?

Primary Reading Attitude Survey Scoring Sheet

Student _____ Grade _____

Teacher _____ Administration Date _____

Scoring guide

☺ 3 points   😐 2 points   ☹ 1 point

Recreational Reading	Academic Reading
1. _____	11. _____
2. _____	12. _____
3. _____	13. _____
4. _____	14. _____
5. _____	15. _____
6. _____	16. _____
7. _____	17. _____
8. _____	18. _____
9. _____	19. _____
10. _____	20. _____
	21. _____

Raw score _____   Raw score _____

Full scale raw score (Recreational + Academic) _____

Percentile Ranks

Recreational _____

Academic _____

Full scale _____

Quick Phonemic Awareness Assessment Device

A high correlation exists between the ability to recognize spoken words as a sequence of individual sounds and reading achievement. Explicit instruction can increase the phonemic awareness of children. To assist in determining the level of phonemic awareness of each child in your class, the following assessment items may be utilized. *Use as many samples as necessary to determine mastery.*

Assessment 1. Isolation of beginning sounds. Ask the child what the first sound of selected words is.

"What is the first sound in *dog?*"

Assessment 2. Deletion of initial sound. Read a word and ask the child to say it without the first sound.

"Say the word *cat.* Say *cat* without the /k/."

Assessment 3. Segmentation of phonemes. Ask the child to say the separate sounds of the word being read.

"What are the two sounds in the word *go?*"

Assessment 4. Blending of phonemes. Slowly read the individual sounds of a word and ask the child to tell what the word is.

"What word am I saying? /d/ /o/ /g/"

Assessment 5. Phoneme manipulation. Read a word and ask the child to replace the initial sound with another. Have the child say the new word.

"In the word *fan,* the first sound is an /f/. If you replace the /f/ with an /m/, how would you say the new word?"

Assessments for Phonological Awareness*

DIRECTIONS FOR USE

Teachers: You will probably not need to complete these assessments for all of your students. Teacher observation and anecdotal records for each child in your class will determine which students need to acquire skills. Description of students to use assessment with:

- difficulty identifying sound elements
- difficulty recognizing when sounds rhyme
- unable to recognize familiar sight words
- nonreaders or emergent readers

For accurate results, follow the guidelines listed here. When completing assessments:

- Make sure children understand concepts being used, such as *beginning, end, first, last, same, sound,* and so on. Use terms they are familiar with.
- Always reinforce task to be completed by modeling or teaching, if necessary, during practice only. Continue until concept is clear or it is apparent the student cannot perform the task. Record practice responses to refer to later.
- Require students to pronounce only sounds asked for, without adding extra sounds.
- A letter between two slash marks, for example /m/, represents the sound that letter stands for. Use during assessment to record student responses.
- A capital letter represents the name of the letter as a response. Record student response, but remind student to say the sounds, not the letter names.
- Put a check ✔ when student responds correctly, or record incorrect response. If an incorrect response is made before correct response, record error first, then put a check.
- When the student waits or hesitates more than 3 seconds, record with a W. Then, record the response, if any, and continue on to the next word.
- If no response is given, say "Try it" and record with a T. Then record the response, if any, and continue on to the next word.

A score of 4/5 or greater on each assessment task generally demonstrates adequate knowledge in this task. Lower scores reflect a need for some instruction in the task. Teach identified tasks using Phonological Awareness Activity Guide at appropriate levels based on results.

*Developed by Katherine Beilby. Used with permission.

Assessments for Phonological Awareness, *continued*

Name _____   Grade _____   Date _____

Phonological Awareness: Rhyme

Directions: Responses to rhymes must include more than the ending of the given word (e.g., jam, am is not acceptable). Nonsense words are an acceptable response. Record all responses on the line following each prompt given by teacher, including practice responses. Explain and model tasks during practice only.

Practice: Say "Rhyming words sound the same at the end. I can rhyme with dad: mad, sad. Tell me a word that rhymes with: pin, (_____), fat, (_____), tie, (_____)."

Assessment:

   1. sick _____   2. jam _____   3. dog _____   4. wet _____   5. cup _____

   SCORE _____

Phonological Awareness: Matching Beginning Sound to Word

Directions: Require student to pronounce only the beginning consonant sound (not letter names). Reinforce correct responses during practice only.

Practice: Say "I'm going to say a sound that you hear at the beginning of a word. I can say the first sound in mug, /m/; the first sound in rug, /r/. Listen closely and tell me the first sound in: man, (_____), sing, (_____), late, (_____)."

Assessment:

   1. sun _____   2. not _____   3. like _____   4. five _____   5. mat _____

   SCORE _____

Phonological Awareness: Blending Onset–Rimes

Directions: This task demonstrates how sounds can be put together to make words. Onset is the part of the word that precedes the vowel, while rime would include everything from the vowel on.

Practice: Say "Now I will say the first sound and then the rest of the word to make a whole word. I can put these sounds together: /r/ un, run; /s/ et, set. Listen closely and tell me the word I have when I put these sounds together: /m/ op, (_____), /w/ eek, (_____), /s/ ome, (_____)."

Assessment:

   1. /m/ ut _____   2. /f/ it _____   3. /n/ ap _____   4. /l/ et _____   5. /s/ ock _____

   SCORE _____

Comments:

_____

_____

_____

_____

Phonological Awareness: Segmenting Onset–Rimes

Directions: This task requires the student to take words apart by saying the first sound and then the rest of the word. Reinforce tasks during practice only.

Practice: Say "I can say the sounds in a word: name, /n/ ame; let, /l/ et. Tell me the sounds in coat, (_____), let, (_____), hip, (_____)."

Assessment:

1. lap _____   2. jet _____   3. fun _____   4. mom _____ 5. sit _____

SCORE _____

Phonological Awareness: Blending Phonemes

Directions: This task requires the student to synthesize or blend each sound in a word. The teacher must pronounce the sounds in a word and have the students say the word quickly. Blending and segmenting tasks require very stretched pronunciation of words without stopping between sounds.

Practice: Say "I'm going to say a word very slowly, and then I'll say it fast: /s/ /a/ /t/, sat. I'll say a word slowly. You say it fast. /h/ /i/ /de/ (_____), /b/ /i/ /g/ (_____)."

Assessment:

1. /f/ /a/ /t/ _____   2. /k/ /ee/ /p/ _____   3. /t/ /i/ /me/ _____
4. /p/ /e/ /t/ _____   5. /h/ /o/ /pe/ _____

SCORE _____

Phonological Awareness: Segmenting Phonemes

Directions: This task requires the student to analyze or segment each sound in a word. Segmenting is the opposite of blending. Each sound must be clearly articulated to receive full credit.

Practice: Say "I can say each sound in a word: came, /c/ /a/ /me/. Tell me each sound in the word sad, (_____), deer, (_____)."

Assessment:

1. red _____   2. pig _____   3. home _____   4. bus _____ 5. cake _____

SCORE _____

Comments:

_____

_____

_____

_____

_____

Knowledge of Sounds and Letters Checklist

First say to the child "Read letter names." Then say "Give letter sounds."

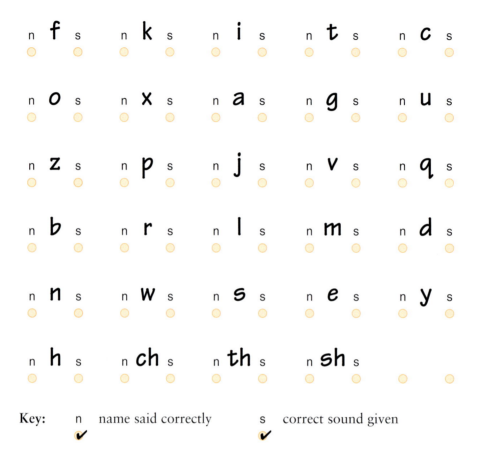

Key: n   name said correctly   s   correct sound given
        ✔   ✔

Note: If only the long sounds of a, e, i, o, u are given, ask for "another" sound. (Also true of c and g, which also have alternate sounds.) If given, add another check beside circle.

Phonics Mastery Survey

Instructions: Before administering this survey, reproduce letters and words on 3 × 5-inch cards in large, lowercase letters, so the child can see them with ease. This survey should be administered to one child at a time. Use a separate sheet to document each child's progress. In the first section, stop if the child makes more than ten errors. For every other section, stop when child makes five or more errors. When sounds are incorrect, write the sound the child makes above the word.

1. Consonant Sounds

Show the child one card at a time, featuring lowercase consonant letters. Ask the child to tell you what sound the letter makes. On the assessment sheet, circle the letter if an incorrect sound is given. Write the incorrect sound the child gives on top of the letter.

p b m w f v t s d r j h z n l y k c g

If the child is not able to identify at least ten sounds, terminate this assessment and administer the Knowledge of Sounds and Letters Checklist (p. 374).

2. Rhyming Words

Ask the child to read the following words and to say three words that rhyme with each of them. Nonsense words are acceptable.

1. be _____

2. go _____

3. say _____

4. do _____

5. make _____

6. will _____

7. get _____

8. blink _____

9. tan _____

10. bug _____

3. CVC Words

Ask the child to read the following short-vowel, CVC nonsense words. There are four examples of each short vowel sound. Indicate which vowel sounds were read correctly and which were not.

1. nid _____		11. wat _____	
2. gat _____		12. vin _____	
3. bul _____		13. lom _____	
4. rup _____		14. hap _____	
5. sen _____		15. yub _____	
6. nat _____		16. pem _____	
7. det _____		17. dom _____	
8. rit _____		18. kud _____	
9. nup _____		19. wom _____	
10. nop _____		20. zet _____	

4. Consonant Blends

Ask the child to read the following words and nonsense words that contain beginning or ending consonant blends (or both). Indicate any blends the child says incorrectly.

1. blithe _____		11. trink _____	
2. clog _____		12. brind _____	
3. plush _____		13. scup _____	
4. flounce _____		14. stint _____	
5. frisk _____		15. smeat _____	
6. dwelt _____		16. spole _____	
7. skig _____		17. gluck _____	
8. crass _____		18. brame _____	
9. trek _____		19. dredge _____	
10. swap _____		20. lasp _____	

5. Consonant Digraphs

Have the child read the following nonsense words containing consonant digraphs. Indicate any digraphs the child says incorrectly.

1. shan	_____	11. scord	_____
2. thort	_____	12. squean	_____
3. phrat	_____	13. sling	_____
4. chib	_____	14. sprill	_____
5. phant	_____	15. strug	_____
6. yeth	_____	16. splom	_____
7. rosh	_____	17. shred	_____
8. lotch	_____	18. squim	_____
9. gresh	_____	19. throbe	_____
10. chass	_____		

6. Long Vowel Sounds

Ask children to read the following nonsense words that contain long vowel sounds. There are four examples of each long vowel sound. Indicate which vowels are read correctly and which are not.

1. stope	_____	11. ploan	_____
2. kade	_____	12. tayne	_____
3. fede	_____	13. sheed	_____
4. gride	_____	14. vied	_____
5. blude	_____	15. trewd	_____
6. kroan	_____	16. whade	_____
7. jaike	_____	17. strean	_____
8. theade	_____	18. blipe	_____
9. smight	_____	19. roke	_____
10. dreud	_____	20. krume	_____

7. Other Vowel Sounds

Have the child read the following words and nonsense words that contain variant vowel sounds. Indicate vowel sounds the child reads incorrectly.

1. nook (oo) _____
2. krouse (ou, ow) _____
3. sar (ar) _____
4. moil (oi) _____
5. noy (oy) _____
6. thirl (ir, er, ur) _____
7. floom (oo) _____
8. gorn (or) _____
9. chaw (aw, au) _____
10. zout (ou) _____
11. larm (ar) _____
12. groil (oi) _____
13. nirl (ir, er, ur) _____

8. Number of Word Parts (Syllables)

Ask the child to read the following words and count the number of word parts or syllables in each word. (Correct answers are in parentheses.)

1. retention (3) _____
2. ride (1) _____
3. panic (2) _____
4. carnival (3) _____
5. monster (2) _____
6. contaminate (4) _____
7. computer (3) _____
8. antagonist (4) _____
9. guess (1) _____
10. consider (3) _____

Peer Editor's Feedback for Writing

Author: _____   Editor: _____

Editor: Please answer these questions about my writing.

1. Do you think the opening grabs you?
   ○ Yes   ○ No
   What would you change?

   _____

   _____

   _____

2. Is there a part I should throw away?
   ○ Yes   ○ No
   Which part?

   _____

   _____

   _____

3. Did I use any tired words?
   ○ Yes   ○ No
   Which ones?

   _____

   _____

   _____

4. What is the best part of my writing?

   _____

   _____

   _____

5. Is there any part you didn't understand?
   ○ Yes   ○ No
   Which part?

   _____

   _____

   _____

6. Do I need a different ending?

   ○ Yes   ○ No

   What would you change?

   _____

   _____

   _____

7. Do I provide enough details to tell my story or to inform readers about my topic?

8. Are there any sentences I should combine or separate? If yes, put the sentence numbers in the box. If no, leave the box blank.

   Combine [_____]

   Separate [_____]

9. What do you like best? Why?

   _____

   _____

   _____

Praise, Question, and Polish (PQP) Form

Title of piece: _____ Date: _____

Author: _____

Peer Editor: _____

Praise: What do you like about the piece? Be specific.

_____

_____

_____

_____

_____

_____

Question: What questions do you have about things you don't understand in the piece?

_____

_____

_____

_____

_____

_____

Polish: What suggestions do you have to make the piece even better?

_____

_____

_____

_____

_____

_____

Beginning Writer's Checklist

Name _____   Date _____

Key: 3   Almost always   2   Sometimes   1   Rarely

Book Orientation

_____ Draws pictures most of the time

_____ Tells about pictures

_____ Draws pictures to accompany writing

Composing/Writing

_____ Generates story ideas orally

_____ Thinks of own ideas and writes them

_____ Uses models or themes in stories

_____ Uses patterns (scaffolds) for writing

Writing Fluency

_____ Uses one- or two-word patterns

_____ Writes two to four lines

_____ Writes easy pattern texts

_____ Writes two to four paragraphs

_____ Writes chapter books

Use of Writing Process

_____ Prewrites (maps, webs, orally rehearses ideas)

_____ Reads writing to others

_____ Does multiple drafts

_____ Offers constructive feedback to others

_____ Makes changes based on feedback

6 + 1 Trait® Rubric: 5-Point Beginning Writer's Rubric

	1. Experimenting	*2. Emerging*	*3. Developing*	*4. Capable*	*5. Experienced*
	IDEAS	**IDEAS**	**IDEAS**	**IDEAS**	**IDEAS**
	Big Idea is unclear; print sense is just beginning	Big Idea is conveyed in a general way through text, labels, symbols	Big Idea is stated in text	Big Idea is clear, but general—a simple story or explanation	Big Idea is clear; topic is narrow, fresh, and original
A	Details are missing, or if present, are unclear	Few details are present	Details are relevant to topic and support Big Idea	Details are telling, and sometimes specific to Big Idea	Details are accurate, relevant, high-quality, and support or enrich Big Idea
B	Experience with topic is unclear	Some experience with topic is demonstrated	Experience with topic is obvious	Experience with topic is supported by text	Experience with topic is demonstrated clearly
C	Pictures, if present, are unclear	Pictures, if present, connect to a few words	Pictures, if present, support topic	Pictures, if present, add descriptive details to topic	Pictures, if present, clarify, enrich, and enhance topic

Key question: Does the writer stay focused and share original and fresh information or perspective about the topic?

	ORGANIZATION	**ORGANIZATION**	**ORGANIZATION**	**ORGANIZATION**	**ORGANIZATION**
	Beginning/ending is absent	A bare beginning is present	Beginning and middle are present, but no ending	Beginning, middle, and predictable ending are present	Beginning attracts, middle works, ending is present
A	Transitions are not present	Transitions are starting to emerge	Transitions rely on connective "and"	Transitions work in predictable fashion	Transitions are somewhat varied
B	Sequencing is not present	Sequencing is limited or confusing	Sequencing is adequate	Sequencing is sound	Sequencing is purposeful from start to finish
C	Pacing is not evident	Pacing is predictable, monotonous	Pacing is adequate	Pacing moves reader through piece	Pacing is purposeful
D	Title (if required) is missing	Title (if required) is attempted	Simple title (if required) works	Title (if required) fits content	Title (if required) is engaging
E	Structure is random	Structure is unclear or only starting to emerge	Structure is present and works	Structure matches purpose	Structure clarifies topic

Key question: Does the organizational structure enhance the ideas and make the piece easier to understand?

	VOICE	**VOICE**	**VOICE**	**VOICE**	**VOICE**
	Individual expression is not present	Individual expression is emerging	Individual expression is present	Individual expression is supported by text	Individual expression reflects unique tone
A	Writing for audience is not evident	Writing starts to address audience	Writing addresses audience in a general way	Writing connects to audience	Writing clearly engages audience
B	Voice is not discernible	Voice is emerging in pictures and/or text	Voice is present	Voice supports writer's purpose	Voice is engaging and enthusiastic for purpose
C	Risk-taking is not evident	Risk-taking is limited to "safe" choices	Risk-taking reveals moments of sparkle	Risk-taking uncovers individual perspective	Risk-taking reveals person behind words

Key question: Would you keep reading this piece if it were longer?

6 + 1 Trait® Rubric: 5-Point Beginning Writer's Rubric, *continued*

	1. Experimenting	2. Emerging	3. Developing	4. Capable	5. Experienced
	WORD CHOICE	**WORD CHOICE**	**WORD CHOICE**	**WORD CHOICE**	**WORD CHOICE**
	No words are present—only letters strung together or scribbles	Words are difficult to decode; some are recognizable	General or ordinary words convey message	Favorite words are used correctly	Specific, accurate words are used well
A	Word patters are imitated	Environmental words are used correctly	New words are attempted but don't always fit	New and different words are used with some success	Precise, fresh, original words linger in reader's mind
B	Vocabulary relies upon environmental print	Vocabulary includes phrases, clichés	Vocabulary is limited to safe, known words	Vocabulary is expanding	Vocabulary is natural, effective, and targets audience
C	No awareness of parts of speech exists	Nouns emerge as main word choice	Basic verbs and nouns dominate piece	Modifiers add to mix of words	Variety of parts of speech adds depth
D	Words do not convey meaning of piece	Words begin to convey single idea or topic	Words are mundane, normal, generic for topic	Words clarify topic and convey meaning	Words enhance, enrich, and/or showcase meaning
E	Words do not create mental imagery	Words begin to create mental imagery	Words are grouped in ways that create general mental imagery	Phrases, word groups create specific mental imagery	Strong attempts at figurative language create clear mental imagery

Key question: Do the words and phrases create vivid pictures and linger in your mind?

	SENTENCE FLUENCY	**SENTENCE FLUENCY**	**SENTENCE FLUENCY**	**SENTENCE FLUENCY**	**SENTENCE FLUENCY**
	Letters and words are scribbled across page	Words are strung together into phrases	Simple sentences are used to convey meaning	Simple and compound sentences strengthen piece	Consistently varied sentence construction enhances piece
A	Sentences are not used, but instead random words or marks	Sentence parts are present, but not complete	Most simple sentence parts are present; variety in beginnings or length exists	Sentence structure varies; variety in beginnings and length exists	Sentences vary in structure as well as beginnings and length
B	Connective words do not exist	Connective words may appear in sentence parts	Connective words, mostly "and," serve as links between phrases	Connective words are more varied	Connective words work smoothly and enrich fluency
C	Rhythm is not evident	Rhythm is choppy and repetitive	Rhythm is more mechanical than fluid	Rhythm is more fluid than mechanical and is easy to read aloud	Rhythm is fluid and pleasant to read aloud

Key question: Can you feel the words and phrases flow together as you read it aloud?

6 + 1 Trait® Rubric: 5-Point Beginning Writer's Rubric, *continued*

	1. Experimenting	2. Emerging	3. Developing	4. Capable	5. Experienced
	CONVENTIONS	**CONVENTIONS**	**CONVENTIONS**	**CONVENTIONS**	**CONVENTIONS**
	Nearly every convention requires editing	Some conventions are correct, most are not	Half of conventions are correct and half need editing	More conventions are correct than not	Conventions require little editing to be published
A	Spelling is not evident, only strings of letters	Semiphonetic spelling is attempted	Phonetic spelling is used; high-frequency words are still spotty	Spelling is usually accurate for grade-level words	High-frequency words are spelled correctly; spelling is very close on others
B	No sense of punctuation exists	Random punctuation exists	End punctuation is usually correct; experiments with other punctuation	End punctuation is correct; some other punctuation is correct	Punctuation is usually correct and/or sometimes even creative
C	Print sense is still emerging	Upper and lowercase letters are randomly used	Capitals are inconsistent but begin most sentences and some proper nouns	Capitals are more consistent and begin sentences and most proper nouns	Capitals are consistently accurate for sentence beginnings, proper nouns, and title
D	No awareness of grammar and/or usage exists	Part of a grammatical construction is present	A grammatical construction is present	Subject/verb agreement, proper tense are present but the rest is still spotty	Some control is shown over basic grade-level grammar

Key question: How much editing would have to be done to be ready to share with an outside source? (Expectations should be based on grade level and include only skills that have been taught.)

	PRESENTATION	PRESENTATION	PRESENTATION	PRESENTATION	PRESENTATION
	No formatting clues are present; placement of text and pictures is totally random	Formatting of text and pictures is starting to come together	Formatting of text and pictures is generally correct	Formatting of text and pictures is clear and thoughtful	Formatting of text and pictures assists comprehension
A	Only scribbles are present	Handwriting shows letters beginning to take shape, though random in placement	Handwriting includes few discrepancies in letter shape; shapes are easily identifiable	Handwriting reveals proper manuscript, spaced and written appropriately	Handwriting is neat and easy to read; proper manuscript or cursive is used
B	Letters and/or words are strung together with no spacing	Spacing between letters and words is attempted	Spacing of words is mostly correct	Words, sentences, and paragraphs have proper spacing	White space is used well within piece and to frame text
C	If pictures are present, they are randomly placed	Pictures are placed appropriately	Pictures fit with text	Pictures add detail, support piece, and are appropriate	Pictures are "balanced" with text and match content
D	No identifiable markers (title, heading, bullets, page numbers) exist	Markers are present but not connected to text	Some markers match some text	Markers clarify, organize, and define text	Markers enrich, enhance, and/or help showcase text
E	No charts, tables, graphs are evident	Charts, tables, graphs are attempted but randomly placed	Charts, tables, graphs match text and are placed properly	Charts, tables, graphs match and clarify text; are placed together properly	Charts, tables, graphs match, clarify, and enrich text and are placed properly

Key question: Is the finished piece easy to read, polished in presentation, and pleasing to the eye?

This abbreviated version of the 6 + 1 Trait® Writing Model of Instruction & Assessment Scoring Guide is used with permission of Education Northwest, Portland, OR. Copyright © Education Northwest.

Fluency Questions for Student Self-Assessment

Name _____   Date _____

- Did my reading sound the way people really talk?
- Would someone understand what the author meant from listening to me read?
- Did I have to work hard to pronounce the words right?
- Did I make many mistakes in my reading?
- When I made a mistake that changed the meaning, did I go back and change it?
- Did I read with good expression?
- Did I change the loudness and softness to show the meaning?
- Did I change the speed when I needed to, to stress certain parts?
- Did I read too slowly?
- Did I read too quickly?
- Did I group the words right as I read?
- Did I make my voice go down for periods?
- Did I make my voice go up for question marks?
- Did I stop a little bit for commas?
- Did I sound excited for exclamation marks?
- Did I stress any words that needed to be stressed?

What is the best thing about my reading?

_____

_____

_____

What should I work on to make my reading better?

_____

_____

_____

Developmental Spelling Test (The "Monster Test")

An easily administered 10-word checklist, such as the following developmental test devised by Gentry (1985), makes it possible for teachers to assess young children's developmental stages of spelling ability.

	WORDS	PRECOMMUNICATIVE SPELLINGS	SEMI-PHONETIC SPELLINGS	PHONETIC SPELLINGS	TRANSITIONAL SPELLINGS	CORRECT SPELLINGS
1.	monster	random letters	mtr	mostr	monstur	monster
2.	united	random letters	u	unitid	younighted	united
3.	dress	random letters	jrs	jras	dres	dress
4.	bottom	random letters	bt	bodm	bottum	bottom
5.	hiked	random letters	h	hikt	hicked	hiked
6.	human	random letters	um	humm	humin	human
7.	eagle	random letters	el	egl	egul	eagle
8.	closed	random letters	kd	klosd	clossed	closed
9.	bumped	random letters	b	bopt	bumpt	bumped
10.	type	random letters	tp	tip	tipe	type

From Gentry, J. Richard (1985). "You Can Analyze Developmental Spelling." *The Early Years (9),* 44–45. Reprinted with permission of the author.

Beginning Speller Checklist

Name _____   Date _____

Identification of Words in Context

- ○ Guesses at words
- ○ Looks at pictures and then guesses
- ○ Looks at beginning of word
- ○ Tries to figure out first sound
- ○ Uses strategies to sound out word

Pictures and Word Sorts

- ○ Can sort pictures accurately
- ○ Can explain why he or she sorted pictures that way
- ○ Can sort words accurately
- ○ Can explain why he or she sorted words that way
- ○ Can sort pictures/words independently
- ○ Can sort words quickly

Spelling Lists and Tests

- ○ Recognizes misspelled words
- ○ Can find words with the same patterns as spelling list words
- ○ Achieves 80% or better accuracy on spelling post-tests

Spelling in Writing

- ○ Shows appropriate concern about accuracy
- ○ Experiments with spelling when needed
- ○ Spells learned words correctly
- ○ Writes with spaces between words
- ○ "Chunks" syllables and sounds in words
- ○ Segments (sounds out) words

Running Record Form

Student _____   Date _____

Teacher _____   Reading Level _____

Text _____

Number of Errors _____   Percentage _____

Running Words _____   Level for student: Easy, Instructional, Frustration

Text	Analysis			
	Number		System Used	
	E	SC	E	SC

Website Credibility, Accuracy, Reasonableness, and Support (CARS) Checklist

Name _____   Date _____

Credibility

1. What is the authority of the author?

   _____

   _____

   _____

2. What are his/her credentials?

   _____

   _____

   _____

3. Is there evidence that peers have judged the site positively?

   ○ Yes   ○ No

   Evidence: _____

4. Does the piece exhibit correct grammar and spelling?

   ○ Yes   ○ No

Accuracy

5. Is the site current, with updated information?

   ○ Yes   ○ No

   Evidence: _____

6. Is the information easy to understand and complete?

   ○ Yes   ○ No

   Evidence: _____

7. Does the author acknowledge other viewpoints of possible controversies?

   ○ Yes   ○ No

   Evidence: _____

Website Credibility, Accuracy, Reasonableness, and Support (CARS) Checklist, *continued*

Reasonableness

8. Does the author present a fair and objective point of view?

   ○ Yes   ○ No

   Evidence: _____

9. Does the author appear concerned with the truth?

   ○ Yes   ○ No

   Evidence: _____

Support

10. Does the author provide documentation for his or her ideas?

    ○ Yes   ○ No

    Evidence: _____

11. Are all sources listed?

    ○ Yes   ○ No

12. Are there other resources on this topic with similar information?

    ○ Yes   ○ No

    Other resources: _____

13. Are these sites mentioned or linked?

    ○ Yes   ○ No

    Example: _____

Adapted from Harris, R. *Evaluating Internet Research Sources,* www.virtualsalt.comevalu8it.htm.

Evaluating Technology Applications

Application _____   Date _____

- Does it serve the intended purpose? For example, if it claims to improve fluency, can you see that children's fluency is actually improving?
  ○ Yes   ○ No

- Can it be used independently by your students, or will you need to work with them to facilitate?
  ○ Independently   ○ Teacher help

- Are there so many sight and sound distractions that children will become overstimulated and lose the literacy focus?
  ○ Yes   ○ No

- Does it offer children an opportunity for free choice? (This can be part of the motivation for using technology.)
  ○ Yes   ○ No

  How? _____

  _____

- Does it use humor? Children tend to prefer these programs and use them more frequently.
  ○ Yes   ○ No

- Does it align with conventional literacy goals, district benchmarks, and/or state standards for literacy?
  ○ Yes   ○ No

  Which ones? _____

  _____

- Does it address your students' individual literacy needs?
  ○ Yes   ○ No

  Which ones? _____

  _____

- Does it contribute to an overall unit theme or project?
  ○ Yes   ○ No

  Which ones? _____

  _____

Adapted from Labbo, Lelu, Kinzer, et al., 2003.

Student Profile

Name _____   Date _____

Reading

- ○ Letter names
- ○ Letter sounds
- ○ Decodes words
- ○ Reads words
- ○ Reads sentences
- ○ Reads fluently/comprehends

Writing

- ○ Writes letters
- ○ Copies writing from board
- ○ Writes words using phonics
- ○ Writes sentences
- ○ Writes simple stories
- ○ Writes stories with structure

Speaking

- ○ No verbal response
- ○ Single word responses
- ○ Responds with phrases
- ○ Responds with sentences
- ○ Questions and answers
- ○ Gets in class discussions

Comments:

_____

_____

_____

_____

_____

By Rita Lehmann and Janet Rodgers. Used with permission.

Vocabulary Growth Group Profile

For First/Second Grade

Teacher _____   Date _____

+ = always   x = sometimes   o = seldom/never

Criteria	Students															
1. Uses sentence-level context as a clue to the meaning of a word or phrase.																
2. Uses frequently occurring affixes as a clue to the meaning of a word.																
3. Identifies frequently occurring root words and their inflectional forms.																
4. Defines words by category and by one or more key attributes (e.g., a *duck* is a bird that swims; a *tiger* is a large cat with stripes).																
5. Identifies real-life connections between words and their use (e.g., "Look for places at home that are *cozy*").																
6. Distinguishes shades of meaning among verbs differing in manner (e.g., *look, peek, glance, stare, glare, scowl*) and adjectives differing in intensity (e.g., *large, gigantic*) by defining or choosing them or by acting out the meanings.																
7. Uses glossaries and beginning dictionaries, both print and digital, to determine or clarify the meaning of words.																
8. Uses words and phrases acquired through conversations, reading and being read to, and responding to texts, including using frequently occurring conjunctions to signal simple relationships (e.g., *because*).																

Criteria based on standard for first and second grades (NBACBP & CCSSO, 2010, p. 27).

Kid Graph

Directions: Color in the squares for the amount of minutes you spend in recreational reading each day. Ask your parent to sign on the line below, showing that they have checked the amount of time you have spent reading.

	Sun.	Mon.	Tue.	Wed.	Thur.	Fri.	Sat.
15 min.							
14 min.							
13 min.							
12 min.							
11 min.							
10 min.							
9 min.							
8 min.							
7 min.							
6 min.							
5 min.							
4 min.							
3 min.							
2 min.							
1 min.							

My child has read for the actual amount of time noted on the graph.

_____

Rimes and Common Words Containing Them

ack: lack, back, Jack, stack, sack, pack, quack, tack

ail: tail, pail, mail, quail, fail, wail, sail

ain: pain, main, stain, gain, rain, vain

ake: sake, take, bake, lake, wake, fake, rake, cake, make

ale: pale, gale, dale, sale, bale, hale, male

ame: name, game, same, tame, lame, came, dame, fame

an: ran, pan, can, Nan, fan, tan, man, than

ank: sank, thank, bank, tank, stank, dank, shrank

ap: cap, map, lap, sap, gap, nap, zap, tap

ash: dash, cash, stash, lash, mash, gash, trash, crash, flash

at: cat, bat, Nat, mat, pat, sat, at, tat, rat, that, scat

ate: gate, hate, late, sate, plate, slate, crate, fate

aw: saw, paw, claw, law, jaw, straw, raw, flaw

ay: day, play, stay, say, gray, ray, lay, gay, jay, way

eal: seal, meal, steal, heal, deal

eat: meat, beat, heat, cheat, feat, wheat

ell: tell, smell, sell, well, swell, bell, fell, shell

est: test, best, west, vest, jest, nest, pest, chest

ice: nice, mice, rice, lice, spice, twice, vice

ick: pick, Nick, tick, lick, stick, thick, Dick, brick, sick

ide: side, bride, tide, bide, pride, hide, ride

ite: kite, bite, sprite

ight: right, night, tight, flight, might, bright

ill: bill, hill, kill, thrill, fill, shrill, drill, sill, pill, will, Jill, dill, Lill, mill, quill

in: chin, fin, bin, win, sin, twin, din, grin, pin, tin

ine: fine, mine, twine, wine, vine, nine, line

ing: king, string, sing, thing, ring, wing, bring, swing

ink: link, think, rink, mink, drink, wink, sink, blink, stink, kink

ig: big, wig, twig, jig, pig

ip: lip, skip, sip, flip, whip, dip, drip, trip, tip, hip, ship

ir: sir, whir, stir, fir

ock: rock, lock, sock, mock, knock, block, clock

oke: poke, broke, stroke, Coke, joke, woke, choke

oil: boil, toil, soil

ook: book, look, took, hook, crook

op: chop, mop, crop, top, stop, flop, plop, drop, hop, shop

ore: sore, tore, more, core, bore, wore, snore, chore, shore, store

uck: stuck, truck, buck, suck, pluck, struck, duck, luck

ug: bug, plug, rug, dug, hug, drug

ump: bump, clump, jump, dump, hump, lump, pump

unk: junk, bunk, sunk, hunk, stunk, dunk

Fry's List of "Instant Words"

FIRST 100 WORDS (Approx. 1st Grade)

Group 1A

the	a	is	you	to	and	we
that	in	not	for	at	with	it
on	can	will	are	of	this	your
as	but	be	have			

Group 1B

he	I	they	one	good	me	about
had	if	some	up	her	do	when
so	my	very	all	would	any	been
out	there	from	day			

Group 1C

go	we	then	us	no	him	by
was	come	get	or	two	man	little
has	them	how	like	our	what	know
make	which	much	his			

Group 1D

who	an	their	she	new	said	did
boy	three	down	work	put	were	before
just	long	here	other	old	take	cat
again	give	after	many			

SECOND 100 WORDS   (Approx. 2nd Grade)

Group 2A

saw	home	soon	stand	box	upon	first
came	girl	house	find	because	made	could
book	look	mother	run	school	people	night
into	say	think	back			

Group 2B

big	where	am	ball	morning	live	four
last	color	away	red	friend	pretty	eat
want	year	went	got	play	found	left
men	bring	wish	black			

Group 2C

may	let	use	these	right	present	tell
next	please	leave	hand	more	why	better
under	while	should	never	each	best	another
seem	tree	name	dear			

Group 2D

fan	five	read	over	such	way	too
shall	own	most	sure	thing	only	near
than	open	kind	must	high	far	both
end	also	until	call			

THIRD 100 WORDS   (Approx. 3rd Grade)

Group 3A

ask	small	yellow	show	goes	clean	buy
thank	sleep	letter	jump	help	fly	don't
fast	cold	today	does	face	green	every
brown	coat	six	gave			

Group 3B

hat	car	write	try	myself	longer	those
hold	full	carry	eight	sing	warm	sit
dog	ride	hot	grow	cut	seven	woman
funny	yes	ate	stop			

Group 3C

off	sister	happy	once	didn't	set	round
dress	tell	wash	start	always	anything	around
close	walk	money	turn	might	hard	along
bed	fine	sat	hope			

Group 3D

fire	ten	order	part	early	fat	third
same	love	hear	yesterday	eyes	door	clothes
through	o'clock	second	water	town	took	pair
now	keep	head	food			

Phonics Terms and Orthography Chart

COMMON PHONICS TERMS

accent (primary) The syllable in a word that receives the strongest and loudest emphasis.

analytic phonics A whole-to-part phonics approach that emphasizes starting with whole words and identifying individual sounds as part of those words. Efforts are generally made to avoid pronouncing the sounds in isolation. Also known as *implicit phonics.*

auditory discrimination The ability to hear similarities and differences between sounds as they appear in spoken words.

base word A word to which prefixes and/or suffixes are added to create new but related words. The simplest member of a word family.

breve An orthographic symbol (˘) placed above vowel graphemes to indicate pronunciation of a short vowel.

circumflex An orthographic symbol (^) placed above vowel graphemes to indicate pronunciation.

closed syllable Any syllable ending with a consonant phoneme. *Examples:* come /m/; love /v/; ran /n/.

compound word A word made up of two or more base words. *Example:* football.

consonant blend Sounds in a syllable represented by two or more letters that are blended together without losing their own identities. *Examples:* green /g/ /r/; swing /s/ /w/; clap /c/ /l/.

consonant cluster Two or more consonant letters appearing together, which when sounded, represent a blend. *Examples:* gr, cr, str.

consonants Sounds represented by any letter of the English alphabet except *a, e, i, o,* and *u.* Consonants are *sounds* that are made by restricting the breath channel.

decoding The process of determining the pronunciation of an unknown word.

deductive instruction Instructional procedure that centers on telling children about generalizations and having them apply those generalizations to specific words. A general-to-specific analysis.

digraph Two letters that stand for a single phoneme or sound. *Examples:* shout /sh/; what /wh/; rang /ng/; meat /ea/. A digraph is a grapheme containing two letters and one sound.

dipthong A single sound made up of two vowel sounds in immediate sequence and pronounced in one syllable. *Examples:* oil /oi/; toy /oy/.

grapheme A letter or combination of letters that represents a phoneme. *Examples:* The phoneme /b/ in *bat* is represented by the grapheme (letter) *b;* the phoneme /f/ in *phone* is represented by the graphemes *p* and *h.*

macron An orthographic symbol, (–), placed over a vowel to show that it is pronounced as a long sound.

onset The consonant sound(s) of a syllable that come before the vowel sound. (See the definition of *rime* for examples of onsets.)

open syllable Any syllable ending with a vowel phoneme. *Examples:* see /e/; may /a/; auto /o/.

phoneme The smallest sound unit of a language that distinguishes one word from another. *Examples:* the phoneme /h/ distinguishes *hat* from *at;* the words *man* and *fan* are distinguished by their initial phonemes /m/ and /f/, respectively.

phoneme blending The process of recognizing isolated speech sounds and the ability to pronounce the word for which they stand.

phoneme segmentation The ability to isolate all the sounds within a word.

phonemic awareness The ability to recognize spoken words as a sequence of individual sounds.

phonetics The scientific study of human speech sounds.

phonics A method in which basic phonetics, the study of human speech sounds, is used to teach beginning reading.

phonogram A letter sequence composed of a vowel grapheme and an ending consonant grapheme(s). *Examples:* -it in *bit, lit,* and *sit,* or -ain in *pain, gain,* and *rain.*

r-controlled vowel When a vowel is followed by the letter *r*, it makes the vowel sound neither long nor short. *Example:* in the word *car*, the vowel sound becomes /a/; in the word *more*, it becomes /ô/.

rime The part of a syllable that includes the vowel sound as well as any consonant sound(s) that come after it. The graphic representation of a rime is referred to as a *phonogram. Example:* in the word *cat*, the onset is /c/ and the rime is /at/.

root Often used as a synonym for *base word.*

schwa sound An unstressed sound commonly occurring in unstressed syllables. It is represented by the symbol, ə, and closely resembles the short sound for *u. Examples: i* in *April; io* in *station; u* in *circus.*

silent letter A name given to a letter that appears in a written word but is not heard in the spoken word. *Example: knight* has six written letters but only three are heard; *k, g,* and *h* are "silent."

slash marks Slanting lines (/ /) enclosing a grapheme(s) indicate that the reference is to the sound and not to the letters.

syllable A unit of pronunciation consisting of a vowel alone or a vowel with one or more consonants. There can be only one vowel phoneme (sound) in each syllable.

synthetic phonics A part-to-whole phonics approach that emphasizes the learning of individual sounds, often in isolation, and combining them to form words. Also known as *explicit phonics.*

umlaut An orthographic symbol (¨) placed above vowel graphemes to indicate pronunciation.

visual discrimination The ability to visually perceive similarities and differences. In reading, this means to perceive similarities and differences in written letters and words.

vowels Sounds represented by the graphemes (letters) *a, e, i, o, u,* and sometimes *y* and *w*, in the English alphabet. Vowels are sounds that are made without closing or restricting the breath channel.

An Introduction to English Orthography.

CONSONANTS

b	ball
d	dust
f	fast
h	hat
j	jar
k	kite
l	last
m	man
n	near
p	put
qu	quack
r	ran
t	tack
v	vase
w	wall
x	x-ray
z	zoo

VARIANT CONSONANTS

c, g	
	cot
	cent
	get
	giraffe

DIGRAPHS WITH h

ch	chin
	school
	charade
gh	ghost
ph	phone
sh	shine
th	thin
	then
wh	whale
	whom

DIGRAPHS WITH FIRST SILENT LETTER

ck	neck
gn	gnat
kn	know
wr	wren

DIGRAPH CLUSTER FOLLOWING A SHORT VOWEL

dge	ledge
tch	match

ADDITIONAL DIGRAPH

ng	song

BLENDS—INITIAL

r	green
l	clear
s	spine
	strap
tw	twine

BLENDS—FINAL

ld	held
lk	talk
nd	pond
nk	sink
nt	want

SPECIAL COMBINATION OF CONSONANT AND VOWEL

ci	crucial
si	pension
ti	nation

VOWELS

SINGLE—SHORT

a	ă	apple
e	ĕ	elephant
i	ĭ	itch
o	ŏ	octopus
u	ŭ	umbrella

SINGLE—LONG

a	ā	ape
e	ē	event
i	ī	ivy
o	ō	open
u and	ū	uniform
oo	ōō	crude

SINGLE—THIRD SOUND

a	ä	father (fäther)
o	ōo	move (mōove)
u	ŏo	bush (bŏosh)

SCHWA ə IN UNACCENTED SYLLABLES

a	əmong
e	blankət
i	Aprəl
o	bacən

DIGRAPHS/DIPHTHONGS WITH a

ai as /ā/	pain
ay as /ā/	play
au as /aw/	caution
aw as /aw/	straw

DIGRAPHS WITH e

ee as	/ē/	weed
ea as	/ē/	meat
	/ĕ/	dead
	/ā/	great
ie as	/ē/	belief
	/ī/	tie
ei as	/ē/ (after c)	receive
	/ā/	rein
ey as	/ē/	monkey
	/ā/	prey

DIGRAPHS AND DIPHTHONGS WITH o

oa as	/ō/	bloat
oi as	/oy/	noise
oy as	/oy/	toy
oo as	/ōō/	soon
	/ŏŏ/	took
ou as	/ow/	trout
	/ŭ/	young
	/ō/	soul
	/ōō/	troupe
ow as	/ow/	owl
	/ō/	blow

Glossary

academic language Words commonly used in educational contexts across the disciplines.

accuracy In fluency, the ability to recognize and read words correctly.

achievement test A formalized test that measures the extent to which a person has assimilated a body of information or possesses a certain skill after instruction has taken place.

affixes Meaning units (prefixes and suffixes) that are added to root or base words.

alliteration A pattern in which several words begin with the same sound.

alphabetic principle The principle that there is a one-to-one correspondence between phonemes (or sounds) and graphemes (or letters); letters represent sounds.

analog A strategy of comparing patterns in words to ones already known.

anecdotal notes Written observations made by the teacher of literacy-related behaviors in an authentic literacy context.

antonyms A pair of words that have opposite meanings.

assessment The process of gathering information about a learner's growth and progress through the use of any of a variety of formal and informal assessment tools and devices; assessments may be formative or summative. See Ch. 13 for more information and the chart on p. 280 of this book for an overview of the assessment process.

authentic assessment Ongoing assessment that is used to guide instruction and uses tasks that resemble real-world reading and writing; can be interpreted by a teacher who evaluates the performance in light of *all* the child's strengths.

automaticity Fluent performance without the conscious deployment of attention.

basal readers A coordinated, graded set of textbooks, teacher's guides, and supplementary materials from which to teach reading.

big book An enlarged version of a book used by the teacher for mediated reading instruction so that students can track the print and attention can be focused on particular phonemic elements.

blend A consonant sequence before or after a vowel within a syllable, such as *cl*, *st*, or *br*; the written language equivalent of a consonant cluster.

camouflage A vocabulary-enriching activity in which learners must try to disguise a chosen word by creating an oral story using several words above their normal speaking vocabulary. The other students must try to guess the hidden word.

closed sort A word sort that classifies words into predetermined categories.

cloze procedure An instructional technique in which certain words are deleted from a passage by the teacher, with blanks left in their places for students to fill in by using the context of the sentence or paragraph.

code-switch The use of English for known words and the home language for words not yet acquired in English.

cognates Words with similar spellings and meanings across languages.

compound word A word made up of two or more base words, such as *football*.

comprehension The cognitive process of interpreting text into a meaningful message that is dependent on the reader's decoding abilities, prior knowledge, cultural and social background, and monitoring strategies.

concepts about print Concepts about the way print works, including directionality, spacing, identification of words and letters, connection between written and spoken language, and the function of punctuation.

constructivist model of learning A learning theory suggesting that children are active learners who organize and relate new information to their prior knowledge.

context The surrounding information in a sentence or text.

context–relationship procedure A strategy used to help students integrate new words into their meaning vocabularies.

contextual clues The syntactic and semantic information in the surrounding words, phrases, sentences, and paragraphs in a text.

contract spelling A method in which students have a written agreement with the teacher each week to learn specific words.

controlled vocabulary A system of introducing only a certain number of grade-level-appropriate words before the reading of each story, with periodic review.

conventional spelling stage The final stage of spelling development, in which the student has mastered the basic principles of English orthography and most words are spelled correctly.

correct spelling stage *See* conventional spelling stage.

criterion-referenced test A test for which scores are interpreted by comparing the test taker's score to a specified performance level rather than with the scores of other students.

critical literacy Encourages readers to actively analyze texts and connect what they read to the real world; evaluate common assumptions and stereotypes present in the text; interpret and understand author point of view, motives, and possible biases; and take action to address a social justice issue.

critical reading Reading to evaluate the material.

cueing systems The four language systems that readers rely upon for cues as they seek meaning from text: graphophonic (based on letter–sound relationships), syntactic (based on grammar or structure), semantic (based on meaning), and pragmatic.

cumulative progress indicators A description of specific activities that accompany curriculum standards to help the teacher observe when students demonstrate such standards.

curriculum-based assessment Assessment that ties evaluation directly to the literacy curriculum to identify instructional needs.

decodable text Beginner-oriented books that contain the same letters or word patterns currently being studied, or those previously taught.

decoding The translation of written words into verbal speech for oral reading or mental speech for silent reading.

developmental spelling stages Stagelike progressions that children advance through when learning to spell, characterized by increasingly complex understandings about the organizational patterns of words, including precom-

municative, prephonetic, phonetic, transitional, and conventional spelling stages.

developmentally appropriate practice (DAP) According to NAEYC, "a framework of principles and guidelines for best practice in the care and education of young children, birth through age 8."

diagnostic reading tests Age-related, norm-referenced assessment of specific skills and behaviors that children have acquired compared with other children of the same chronological age.

dialogic reading A strategy in which a child leads the discussion about the pictures in a picture storybook with the parent or teacher taking the position of follower in the book conversation.

dialogue journals Journals that provide a means of two-way written communication between learners and their teachers, in which learners share their thoughts with teachers, including personal comments and descriptions of life experiences, and the teachers, in turn, write reactions to the learners' messages.

direct instruction Teacher control of the learning environment through structured, systematic lessons, goal setting, choice of activities, and feedback.

directionality of print The concept that in English, writing goes from left to right and from top to bottom. Directionality of print varies among languages.

domain-specific vocabulary Vocabulary specific to a discipline or content area.

dramatic play Simulating real experiences with no set plot or goal.

drop everything and read (DEAR) A time set aside each day during which children quickly and quietly get trade books, magazines, or other reading material from their desks or from the classroom library and begin reading silently.

DRTA (directed reading–thinking activity) A time-honored format for guiding students as they read selections, usually from basal reading programs.

dyad reading A paired reading activity in which students alternately read aloud or listen and summarize what their partner has read.

early readers/writers Moving from emergent literacy to the first stage of conventional literacy, early readers are able to independently read text that is selected as being at an appropriate level. These readers use early reading strategies; for example, they begin to attend to print and apply the one-to-one correspondence of matching sounds to letters in order to read, and they commonly look at beginning and ending letters in order to decode unfamiliar words. Early writers typically progress through five stages of invented spelling, ranging from writing the initial consonant sound through phonetic and transitional phases.

echo reading A strategy where a lead reader reads aloud a section of text and others follow immediately after it or echo the leader's reading.

emergent literacy Behaviors seen in young children when they use texts (both traditional and electronic) and writing tools to imitate reading and writing activities, even though the children cannot actually read and write in the conventional sense.

encoding Transferring oral language into written language.

English learner (EL) A person who is in the process of acquiring English as a second language.

environmental print Print that is encountered outside books and that is a pervasive part of everyday living.

ESL (English as a second language) A program for teaching English language skills to those whose native language is not English.

experience–text relationship A lesson format designed to enhance comprehension by helping students to develop prior knowledge and relate it to what they read.

experiential background The fund of total experiences that aid a reader in finding meaning in printed symbols.

experimental spellings Unconventional spellings, or approximations, resulting from an emergent writer's initial attempts to associate sounds with letters.

explicit instruction Teacher control of the learning environment through structured, systematic lessons, goal setting, choice of activities, and feedback.

expository frame A basic structure for expository text designed to help students organize their thoughts for writing or responding to text.

expository structures Organizational structures or patterns that authors use when writing informational text.

expository text Nonfiction text providing factual information about a topic; also called *informational text.*

expressive writing Personal writing that expresses emotion such as diaries or letters.

false cognates Words that sound alike and may seem to be related but have quite different meanings.

family literacy night An event where relatives and children read books together and participate in a variety of literacy-related activities.

fluency Achieving speed, accuracy, expression, and prosody in reading; merging word recognition and comprehension. *See also the next entry.*

fluent readers/writers Fluent readers use multiple sources of information flexibly to accurately read a variety of unknown texts with appropriate expression and phrasing. Fluent readers are able to read for meaning with less attention to decoding and can independently solve problems encountered in the text. Fluent writing uses mostly conventional spelling, and children are able to write expressively using increasingly rich vocabulary and more complex sentences.

formal assessments Standardized tests given under controlled conditions so that specific groups can be compared primarily for purposes of program evaluation.

formal (standardized) test A testing instrument for which readability and validity can be verified; the results of these tests are based on right or wrong answers, and individual scores are interpreted against national norms.

formative assessment During instruction, the process of ongoing data-gathering, usually informal, that informs and guides teachers as they make instructional decisions.

frustration level A level of reading difficulty at which a reader is unable to cope; when reading is at the frustration level, the reader recognizes approximately 90 percent or fewer of the words encountered and comprehends 50 percent or fewer.

grade-level equivalency score A conversion of a score on a test into one that tells how a child compares with others in the same grade; e.g., a grade equivalent score of 4.5 on a reading test would suggest that the child is reading as well as children in the normative sample who are in the fifth month of fourth grade.

graded word list A list of words at successive reading levels.

gradual release of responsibility An approach to teaching that shifts the responsibility for thorough learning from the teacher to the student in steps ("I do," "we do," "you do").

grand conversation A response to text strategy whereby students share personal connections to the text, make predictions, ask questions, and show individual appreciation.

grapheme A written symbol that represents a phoneme.

graphophonic information Cues based on sound or visual similarities.

group profile A listing of scores on a specific reading or writing skill that allows the teacher to view the strengths and weaknesses of the whole class for purposes of reteaching and reporting to parents and others.

guided reading A teacher-mediated instructional method designed to help readers improve skills, comprehension, recall, and appreciation of text.

high-frequency words Words common in reading material that are often difficult to learn because they cannot be easily decoded.

high-stakes assessments Assessment tools mandated by a state or district, often used to determine how well children are doing compared with other children in the area, state, or nation and whether certain programs will be funded.

holistic approach A whole-to-parts approach in which acquiring meaning is considered more critical than the underlying skills of reading.

holographic stage The earliest language acquisition stage, in which one word is used to represent a concept or idea.

homonyms Words that are pronounced the same but have different spellings.

hypermedia projects Presentations and projects that combine text, graphics, audio, and video, as well as hyperlinks. Because the presentation includes links, it may not be viewed in a linear sequence.

independent level A level of reading difficulty low enough that the reader can progress without noticeable obstructions; the reader can recognize approximately 98 percent of the words and comprehend at least 90 percent of what is read.

individual dictation A strategy in which the student dictates a message while the teacher writes it down, sounding out the words in front of the child.

informal assessments Assessments, often teacher-administered in the classroom, that yield specific information that teachers can use to guide their teaching; these include tools such as checklists, rubrics, portfolios, and informal reading inventories.

informal reading inventory (IRI) An informal assessment instrument offering a series of text passages designed to help the teacher determine a student's independent, instructional, and frustration reading levels as well as listening comprehension level.

informational texts Nonfiction texts that provide factual information about a topic; expository text.

instructional level A level of difficulty low enough that the reader can be instructed by the teacher during the process; in order for the material to be at this level, the reader should be able to read approximately 95 percent of the words in a passage and comprehend at least 75 percent.

interactive story writing A mediated writing experience used to help emergent readers learn to read and write. With help from the teacher, children dictate sentences, and the teacher verbally stretches each word so children can distinguish sounds and letters. Children use chart paper to write the letter while repeating the sound.

interest and attitude inventory An informal tool that allows teachers to discover information about their students; for example, how they feel about reading and about themselves as readers.

interest inventory A list of questions used to assess a person's preferences in a particular area.

intervention The corrective instructional program the teacher devises as a result of assessment.

jigsaw grouping A collaborative learning technique in which each member of a small group becomes an expert on a different part of the text and shares his or her new knowledge with the group so that all group members get a sense of the whole text.

journals Students keep journals in the same way artists keep sketch books. Students write in them regularly to record life events of their choosing or, for very beginning writers, to complete sentence stems offered by the teacher. At the beginning reader stage, journals are often accompanied by illustrations and are rarely corrected.

knowledge chart (also known as K-W-L) A process intended to be used before and after the reading of an expository selection to document what students already know, what they wish to find out, and then what they have learned after reading the selection.

language arts The global term for reading, writing, listening, speaking, viewing, and visually representing.

language experience approach (LEA) An approach in which reading and the other language arts are interrelated and the experiences of children are used as the basis for the material that is written in conjunction with the teacher and then used for reading.

learning center A location within the classroom in which children are presented with instructional materials, specific directions, clearly defined objectives, and/or provisions for self-evaluation.

learning logs Journals that students use to summarize a day's lesson and to react to what they have learned.

letter-name stage *See* phonetic stage.

leveled books Books that are assigned levels with subtler differences in the difficulty between levels than more traditional "grade-leveled" texts.

literacy The competence to carry out the complex reading and writing tasks in a functionally useful way necessary to the world of work and life outside the school.

literacy scaffolds Structures that provide a template for a writing idea; scaffolds allow the learner to achieve at a higher level than would be attainable without the scaffolds.

literal comprehension Understanding ideas that are directly stated.

literary sociogram A diagram used to help students understand the complexity of the relationships among characters in a story or chapter.

long vowels Vowels that represent the sounds in words that are heard in letter names, such as the /a/ in *ape,* /e/ in *feet,* /i/ in *ice,* /o/ in *road,* and /u/ in *mule.*

look–say method An early meaning-based method of reading instruction requiring children to use the context alone to figure out words they do not know.

masking Using a sliding frame or other device to help students focus on a particular word or part of a word.

Matthew effect The phenomenon that suggests that skilled decoders get better at reading while poor decoders tend to fall further behind.

meaning vocabulary The body of words whose meanings one understands and can use.

mediated reading Large- or small-group instruction in which the teacher guides the students in selected reading skills.

metacognition A person's awareness of his or her own thinking and the conscious efforts to monitor this awareness.

metacognitive strategies Techniques for monitoring one's own thinking.

metalinguistic ability The conscious awareness of sound, meaning, and the practical nuances of language.

minilesson A short lesson on procedures, concepts, strategies, or skills taught based on teacher observation of the need for it.

mirror blogs Blogs that allow children to reflect on their thinking or about lessons or content that has been introduced.

miscue An unexpected reading response that may change or disrupt the meaning of a text (deviation from text).

miscue analysis A procedure that lets the teacher gather important instructional information; it provides a framework for observing students' oral reading and their ability to construct meaning.

morning message Students observe as the teacher writes a meaningful morning message addressed to all the children on the board about a specific event that is planned for the day or about an interesting question. The morning message is used as an instructional tool for discussing skills that students are learning, such as conventions of writing or phonic elements.

morpheme The smallest meaning-bearing linguistic unit in a language.

morphology The aspects of language structure related to the ways words are formed from prefixes, roots, and suffixes (e.g., "re-heat-ing") and are related to each other.

motivation The incentive to do something; a stimulus to act.

multicultural Classrooms are multicultural settings when children from a variety of cultures learn together daily, making it necessary to know how children's perceptions, knowledge, and demeanor are shaped by their experiences at home and in their own community.

multimodal literacy A form of literacy requiring today's students to be literate in multiple modes of communication, including the ability to read, produce, and interpret text, graphics, images, sound, and videos.

narrative text Text that contains the structural features of a story.

new literacies Ways to read and write texts, and also to view and visually represent texts in new and exciting ways, often including enhancements such as video and audio; often in electronic rather than traditional print format and available for viewing on various devices.

nonstage theory A theory that suggests that unskilled and skilled readers use the same strategies to figure out unknown words.

norm-referenced test A test designed to yield results interpretable in terms of the average results of a sample population.

norming (normative) group A large number of students chosen to represent the kinds of students for whom an assessment device is designed.

norms Statistics or data that summarize the test performance of specified groups, such as test takers of various ages or grades.

one-to-one correspondence An awareness that letters or combinations of letters correspond directly to certain sounds in the English language.

onset All the sounds of a word that come before the first vowel.

open sort A type of picture or word sort in which the categories for sorting are left up to the child.

oral recitation lessons (ORL) Three-part lessons designed to increase oral reading fluency.

oral synthesis Hearing sounds in sequence and blending them together to make a word; sounding out.

orthographic knowledge Understanding of the writing system of a language, specifically the correct sequence of letters, characters, or symbols.

parent packets Folders containing early reading and writing reinforcement activities that can be completed at home with a child's parents or caregivers.

partner reading A joint reading event in which a fluent reader is paired with a less fluent reader.

patterned stories Narrative pieces written by students based on books with clear patterns that can be emulated.

percentile Raw scores are converted to percentiles so that comparisons can be made. Percentiles range from 1 to 99 with 1 being the lowest and 99 being the highest.

phoneme The smallest unit of sound in a language.

phoneme blending Blending individual sounds to form a word.

phoneme counting Counting the number of sounds in a word.

phoneme deletion Omitting the beginning, middle, or ending sounds of a word.

phoneme isolation Identifying the beginning, middle, and/or ending sounds in a word.

phoneme substitution Substituting the beginning, middle, or ending sounds of a word.

phonemic awareness A division of phonological awareness that refers to a child's ability to manipulate, classify, and listen to each speech unit, or phoneme, in order to distinguish words with different meanings made from them.

phonemic segmentation The process of separating sounds within a word.

phonetic stage The third stage of spelling development, in which consonants and vowels are used for each spoken syllable.

phonics Instruction in the association of speech sounds with printed symbols.

phonics generalizations Rules that help to clarify English spelling patterns.

phonological awareness The recognition that speech is made up of a variety of sound units that can be segmented into larger "chunks" known as syllables.

phonological sensitivity (PS) A term used to describe the dual components of phonological processing: phonological awareness and phonemic awareness.

phonology The study of the sound system of language.

picture sort A precursor to the word sort activity in which children categorize pictures according to their common sounds.

picture walk An instructional strategy in which the teacher guides the children through the text by looking at and discussing the pictures before reading the story.

play centers Areas of the classroom containing inviting props and set aside for spontaneous dramatic play.

polysemantic A word having multiple meanings, such as the word *fast*.

portfolio A place to collect evidence of a child's literacy development. It may include artifacts collected by the child, the teacher, or both.

precommunicative stage The initial stage of spelling development, in which the child scribbles random letters with little concept of which letter makes which sound.

predictable books, predictable texts Books or texts that use repetition, rhythmic language patterns, and familiar patterns; sometimes called *pattern books*.

predictive questions Questions designed to activate students' prior knowledge before they read in order to focus their attention on key ideas as they read.

prefixes Meaningful chunks attached to the beginnings of words, such as *re + play = replay*.

preliterate stage *See* prephonetic stage.

prephonetic stage The second stage of spelling development, in which the child becomes aware of the alphabetic principle.

primary language The home language of a child or the first language a child learns to speak.

process-oriented assessment Assessment that relies on the teacher's observation of the child's actual reading and writing abilities.

prosody Appropriate expression in oral reading that sounds much like conversational speaking.

QARs (question–answer relationships) A strategy in which students become aware of their own comprehension processes, particularly the importance of the knowledge they bring to text and their role as active seekers rather than passive receivers of information through reading.

r-controlled vowels Vowels that occur in a syllable preceding an *r* and the vowel sound is modified, such as the /r/ in *car*.

readability An objective measure of the difficulty of written material.

readers theater A form of drama in which participants read aloud from scripts adapted from stories and convey ideas and emotions through vocal expression. This oral interpretation strategy helps children to see that reading is an active process of constructing meaning. Unlike a play, there is no costuming, movement, stage sets, or memorizing of lines.

reading The construction of meaning from coded messages through symbol decoding, vocabulary awareness, comprehension, and reflection.

reading buddies A social reading activity in which students read and reread books with a partner who may help them with unfamiliar words and encourage them to continue reading.

reading capacity level The highest level of material children understand when the passage is read to them.

reading interest inventory An informal assessment device used to determine a child's interests so that the teacher can match appropriate reading material to her or him.

reading process The steps a reader goes through to construct meaning from what the author has written.

reading product Some form of communication that results from the reading process.

reading rate Speed of reading, often reported in words per minute.

reading readiness The level of preparedness for formal reading instruction.

reading response journal A journal in which readers record their first reactions to something they have read.

realia Pictures, brief video clips, or objects introduced in tandem with a new word or concept to build new associations with the words, especially used for the benefit of English learners, to provide accessibility to the associated print.

reciprocal teaching A technique to develop comprehension and metacognition in which the teacher and students take turns predicting, generating questions, summarizing, and clarifying ideas in a passage.

recreational reading An independent reading activity for motivating voluntary reading interest and appreciation rather than instruction.

reliability A measure of consistency; a test or an assessment is a reliable measure, or possesses reliability, if that assessment produces similar results when given more than once over a short period of time.

reliable Yielding consistent assessment results over time.

repeated readings Students reread a selection for a different purpose and think again about what they have read. Rereading helps improve a young reader's speed, accuracy, expression, comprehension, and linguistic growth.

Response to Intervention (RTI) A framework that incorporates both assessment and intervention with the goal of yielding immediate benefits to the student. Assessment data are used to inform interventions and determine their effectiveness. Using RTI, instruction and intervention shift toward a supportive function that allows teachers to make instructional decisions based on their students' needs.

retelling Teachers analyze students' retellings of text to gauge their level of comprehension and use of language. In examining the retellings, teachers look for the number of events recalled, how children interpret the message, and how children use details or make inferences to substantiate ideas.

rime Words with rime have two parts: onset (the consonant or consonant blend at the beginning of the word), and rime (the ending letters that are shared). Thus, rime is the vowel and any letter that follows the beginning consonant or consonant blend. (Example: *am* in *Sam*.)

root word A word to which prefixes and/or suffixes are added to create new, but related, words.

rubber-banding The process in which the teacher stretches out all the sounds in a word so learners can pay attention to each phoneme or sound.

running records An assessment procedure for analyzing a student's oral reading; the teacher uses a chart showing the text broken down line-by-line and notes substitutions, repetitions, mispronunciations, and unknown words as the student reads.

scaffolding An instructional support mechanism by which the teacher enables students to accomplish more difficult tasks than they could without assistance.

schema A preexisting knowledge structure developed about a thing, a place, or an idea; a framework of expectations based on previous knowledge.

semantic cues Meaning clues.

semantic gradient A vocabulary-enriching activity that allows children to discuss the many shades of meaning of words, beginning with a word and ending with its opposite.

semantic map A graphic representation of the relationship among words and phrases in written material.

sentence stems The first two or three words of a sentence followed by blank spaces offered to students to support initial attempts at writing.

sentence strips Rectangular pieces of tag board or construction paper on which are written individual sentences from a story students have read.

shared reading A mediated technique whereby the teacher reads aloud while students follow along using individual copies of the book, a class chart, or a big book.

sheltered instruction When teaching English learners, efforts by the teacher to bridge the language gap by providing meaningful contexts for words and concepts being introduced. In providing sheltered instruction, the teacher may use pictures, film clips, charts, and graphs as well as gestures, charades, and pantomime to get concepts across.

short vowels Vowels that represent the sound of /a/ in *apple*, /e/ in *end*, /i/ in *igloo*, /o/ in *frog*, and /u/ in *bus*.

sight words Words that are recognized by the reader immediately, without having to resort to decoding.

signal words Those transitional words that signify sequence, such as *first*, *next*, and *finally*.

silent period The initial stage in second-language acquisition when a learner is increasing receptive vocabulary but not able to express ideas orally.

skills-based approach A parts-to-whole approach to reading instruction in which all the reading skills are taught sequentially.

skills-based assessment Assessment focusing on the use of tests to measure reading and spelling skills as well as the subskills of these areas.

sound boxes Placeholders for sounds used by children during phonemic awareness exercises.

sound mapping Matching letters and letter combinations with sound (sound–symbol association).

spelling conscience A desire to spell correctly as evidenced by a student's proofreading material or using resources to find out how to spell unknown words.

spelling consciousness The ability to recognize that a word that has been written down is spelled correctly or incorrectly.

SSR *See* sustained silent reading.

stage theory A theory that suggests that children go through three stages in acquiring literacy: the "selective cue stage," the "spelling–sound stage," and the "automatic stage."

standardized reading tests Achievement tests that are published, norm-referenced, group-administered, survey tests of reading ability.

standards Broad curricular goals containing specific grade-level targets or benchmarks. They represent systematic ways for educators to ask themselves, "What do we want our students to know and what do we want them to be able to do?"

stanine A way of reporting test scores that distributes them into nine groups, with 1 being the lowest and 9 the highest.

story frame A basic outline for a story designed to help students organize their ideas about what they have read.

story grammar A set of rules that define story structures.

story retelling *See* retelling.

structured listening activity An activity in which students listen to a story accompanied by visuals that support the action in the story and then retell the story with the help of the visuals.

suffixes Meaningful chunks attached to the ends of words, such as *play + ing = playing.*

summative assessment Evaluative assessment or testing that results in a grade or ranking.

sustained silent reading (SSR) A program for setting aside a certain period of time daily for self-selected, silent reading. During SSR time, each child chooses material to read for a designated period of time, typically 10–15 minutes for beginning readers. Everyone, including the teacher, reads without interruption.

syllabication Breaking words into syllables; "chunking."

syllable juncture stage *See* conventional spelling stage.

syllables The units of pronunciation that include a vowel sound.

synonyms Groups of words that have the same, or very similar, meanings.

syntactic cues Clues derived from the word order or grammar of the sentence.

talk-to-yourself chart A chart to help children self-assess their ability to read and spell new words.

teachable moments The spontaneous, indirect teaching that occurs when teachers respond to students' questions or when students otherwise demonstrate the need to know something.

teacher observational portfolio A progress file containing observations and informal assessments of children's reading and writing behaviors and accomplishments.

telegraphic stage The language acquisition stage in which an idea or concept is represented by the addition of a second word, as in "bad doggie."

text talk An approach to read-alouds that is designed to enhance young children's ability to construct meaning from decontextualized language to promote text comprehension and further language development.

think-aloud A strategy in which the teacher models aloud for students the thinking processes used when reading or writing.

think, pair, and share A cooperative learning strategy in which children listen to a question, think of a response, pair to discuss with a partner, and then share their collaboration with the whole class.

tracking Indicating understanding of the one-to-one correspondence of spoken and written words by finger-pointing.

trade books A book designed to be sold to the public through a book dealer, as opposed to, say, a textbook intended for a specific audience.

transactional model A perspective of early reading instruction from cognitive psychology and psycholinguistic learning that views children as bringing a rich prior knowledge background to literacy learning.

transitional readers/writers Transitional readers read unfamiliar text with more independence than early readers. Transitional readers use meaning, grammatical, and letter cues more fully. They recognize a large number of frequently used words on sight and use illustrations in a limited way while reading. Transitional writers may use phonetic or invented spelling, but the spelling is easily readable; writing also begins to demonstrate characteristics of the transitional speller, able to apply spelling rules, patterns, and other strategies.

transitional stage The fourth stage of spelling development, in which the child can approximate the spelling of various English words.

transition words Words that help connect one idea to the next; for example they may relate ideas *(however, in addition)* and define organization *(first, second).*

transmission model A perspective of early reading instruction from behavioral psychology that views children as empty vessels into which knowledge is poured.

twin texts Books that lead children from fiction into nonfiction by pairing related fiction and nonfiction books to form a bridge from reading stories to understanding factual content.

validity The degree to which a test measures what it purports to measure.

Venn diagram A set of overlapping circles used to graphically illustrate the similarities and differences of two concepts, ideas, stories, or other items.

vicarious experiences Indirect experiences, not involving the senses.

visual literacy Ability to interpret and understand images, icons, video, photographs, graphs, charts, maps, and any other form of visual representation of ideas.

vocabulary The knowledge and use of words.

whole language philosophy A pedagogy that moved from a narrow focus on isolated subskills to one that encouraged teachers to look at reading more holistically, as part of the total communication process.

within-word stage *See* transitional stage.

word attack An aspect of reading instruction that includes intentional strategies for learning to decode, sight-read, and recognize written words.

word bank A collection of sight words that have been mastered, usually recorded in some manner, such as on index cards or electronically.

word building An activity in which children arrange letter cards to spell words, practicing phonics and spelling concepts.

word hunt An activity in which children search for words that correspond to a certain pattern that has been identified by them or by the teacher.

word map A visual illustration of a word, showing its meaning by offering examples and explaining what it is and what it is not.

word play A learner's manipulation of sounds and words for purposes of language exploration, practice, and pleasure.

word sort An activity in which students sort a collection of words into two or more categories.

word wall A chart or bulletin board on which are placed, alphabetically, important vocabulary to be referred to during word study activities.

wordless books Picture books without words.

writing process A set of recursive stages in which a writer engages in activities designed to solve certain problems unique to a particular stage. For early writers, as with more experienced writers, the writing process typically includes prewriting, drafting, sharing, revising, editing, proofreading, and publishing stages.

writing prompts Motivational ideas or structures that are offered by the teacher to inspire students to write.

writing workshop A regular writing session with the goal of building students' fluency in writing through continuous, repeated exposure to the process of writing. Writing workshop usually includes a minilesson, writing time, peer editing, student–teacher conferences, and sharing. Students may be encouraged to choose a topic or the teacher may use writing prompts.

References

Abadiano, H. R., & Turner, J. (2004). Expanding the writing process to accommodate students with learning disabilities. *NERA Journal, 40*(1), 75–79.

Adams, C. (2009). Digital storytelling. *Instructor, 119*(3), 35–37.

Adams, M. J. (1990). *Beginning to Read: Thinking and Learning About Print*. Cambridge, MA: MIT Press.

Adams, M. J. (1991). Why not phonics and whole language? In W. Ellis (Ed.), *All Language and the Creation of Literacy*. Baltimore: Orton Dyslexia Society.

Adams, M. J., & Bruck, M. (1995). Resolving the great debate. *American Educator, 19*(7), 10–20.

Adams, M. J., Foorman, B. R., Lundberg, I., & Beeler, T. (1998). *Phonemic Awareness in Young Children*. Baltimore: Brookes.

Adams, M. J., Treiman, R., & Pressley, M. (1997). Reading, writing and literacy. In I. Sigel and A. Renninger (Eds.), *Handbook of Child Psychology, Vol. 4: Child Psychology in Practice*. New York: Wiley.

Afflerbach, P. (2007). *Understanding and Using Reading Assessment, K–12*. Newark, DE: International Reading Association.

Afflerbach, P., Pearson, P. D., & Paris, S. G. (2008). Clarifying the difference between reading skills and strategies. *The Reading Teacher, 6*, 364–373.

Al Otaiba, S., Puranik, C. S., Ziolkowski, R. A., & Montgomery, T. M. (2009). Effectiveness of early phonological awareness interventions for students with speech or language impairments. *Journal of Special Education, 43*(2), 107–128.

Alegria, J., Pignot, E., & Morais, J. (1982). Phonetic analysis of speech and memory codes in beginning readers. *Memory and Cognition, 10*, 451–456.

Allen, J. (2012). Teaching tips: What should be common in the common core state standards? *Reading Today Online*. Newark, DE: International Reading Association.

Allen, R. V. (1976). *Language Experiences in Communication*. Boston: Houghton Mifflin.

Allington, R. L. (2004). Setting the record straight. *Educational Leadership, 61*, 22–25.

Allington, R. L. (2009). *What Really Matters in Fluency: Research-Based Best Practices Across the Curriculum*. Boston: Allyn & Bacon/Pearson.

Allyn, P. (2013). Top 10: Teaching writing in the Common Core era. Pearson: Research and Innovation Network. Retrieved from http://research network. pearson.com/college-career-success/top-10-teaching-writing-in-the-common-core-era

American Library Association (2005). Background research: Dialogic reading for two- and three-year-olds. Retrieved from www.ala.org/ala/pla/plaissues/earlylit/researchandeval/dialogicreading.htm/

Anderson, C. (2000). *How's It Going? A Practical Guide to Conferencing with Student Writers*. Portsmouth, NH: Heinemann.

Anderson, N. L., & Briggs, C. (2011, April). Reciprocity between reading and writing: Strategic processing as common ground. *The Reading Teacher, 64*, 546–549.

Anderson, R. C., Hilbert, E. H., Scott, J. A., & Wilkinson, I. (1985). *Becoming a Nation of Readers: The Report of the Commission on Reading*. Washington, DC: National Institute of Education.

Anderson, R. C., Wilson, P. T., & Fielding, L. G. (1988). Growth in reading and how children spend their time outside of school. *Reading Research Quarterly, 23*, 285–303.

Anderson, V., & Roit, M. (1998). Reading as a gateway to language proficiency for language-minority students in the elementary grades. In *Promoting Learning for Culturally and Linguistically Diverse Students: Classroom Applications*. New York: Wadsworth.

Anthony, J. L., Lonigan, C. J., Burgess, S. R., Driscoll, K., Phillips, B. M., & Cantor, B. G. (2002). Structure of preschool rhyme, words, syllables, and phonemes.

Journal of Experimental Child Psychology, 82, 65–92.

Anthony, J. L., Lonigan, C. J., Driscoll, K., Phillips, B. M., & Burgess, S. R. (2003). Phonological sensitivity: A quasi-parallel progression of word structure units and cognitive operations. *Reading Research Quarterly, 38,* 470–487.

Armbruster, B. B., Lehr, E., & Osborn, J. (2001). *Put Reading First: The Research Building Blocks for Teaching Children to Read. Kindergarten Through Grade 3.* Washington, DC: National Institute for Literacy.

Ashton-Warner, S. (1965). *Teacher.* New York: Simon & Schuster.

Au, K. H. (1979). Using the experience–text–relationship with minority children. *The Reading Teacher, 32,* 478–479.

Au, K. H. (1991, June 25). Paper presented at the Notre Dame Reading Conference, South Bend, IN, sponsored by Houghton Mifflin, Boston.

Au, K. H. (1997). *Literacy Instruction in Multicultural Settings.* Orlando, FL: Harcourt Brace.

Auerbach, S., & Collier, S. (2012). Bringing high stakes from the classroom to the parent center: Lessons from an intervention program for immigrant families. *Teachers College Record, 114*(3), 1–40.

August, D., McCardle, P., Shanahan, T., & Burns, M. (2014). Developing literacy in English language learners: Findings from a review of the experimental research. *School Psychology Review, 43*(4), 490–498.

August, D., & Shanahan, T. (Eds.). (2006). *Developing Literacy in Second Language Learners: Report of the National Reading Panel on Language Minority Children and Youth.* Mahwah, NJ: Erlbaum.

August, D., & Shanahan, T. (2010, September). Response to a review and update on *Developing Literacy in Second-Language Learners: Report of the National Literacy Panel on Language Minority Children and Youth. Journal of Literacy Research, 42,* 341–348.

Aulls, M. W., & Graves, M. F. (1985). *Quest: New Roads to Literacy.* New York: Scholastic.

Ausubel, D. P. (1959). Viewpoints from related disciplines: Human growth and development. *Teachers College Record, 60,* 245–254.

Baer, G. T., & Dow, R. S. (2013). *Self-Paced Phonics: A Text for Educators* (5th ed.). Upper Saddle River, NJ: Prentice Hall.

Baghban, M. (1984). *Our Daughter Learns to Read and Write: A Case Study from Birth to Three.* Newark, DE: International Reading Association.

Baker, L., Scher, D., & Makler, K. (1997). Home and family influences on motivation for reading. *Education Psychology, 32,* 69–82.

Baker, L., Serpell, R., & Sonnenschein, S. (1995). Opportunities for literacy learning in the homes of urban preschoolers. In L. Morrow (Ed.), *Family Literacy: Connections in Schools and Communities* (pp. 236–252). Newark, DE: International Reading Association.

Baker, L., Sonnenschein, S., Serpell, R., Fernandez-Fein, S., & Scher, D. (1994). *Contexts of Emergent Literacy: Everyday Home Experiences of Urban Pre-kindergarten Children.* Research report. Athens, GA: National Reading Research Center, University of Georgia and University of Maryland.

Ball, E. W., & Blachman, B. A. (1991). Does phonemic awareness training in kindergarten make a difference in early word recognition and developmental spelling? *Reading Research Quarterly, 26*(1), 49–66.

Barclay, K., & Coffman, T. (1990). I know an old lady: Linking literacy and lyrics. *Teaching K–8, 6,* 28–29.

Barone, D., & Wright, R. (2009). Literacy instruction with digital and media technology. *The Reading Teacher, 62,* 292–302.

Barton, D. (1997). Family literacy programmes and home literacy practices. In D. Taylor (Ed.), *Many Families, Many Literacies: An International Declaration of Principles.* Portsmouth, NH: Heinemann.

Baumann, J. F., Kame'enui, E. J., & Ash, G. E. (2003). Research on vocabulary instruction: Voltaire redux. In J. Flood, D. Lapp, J. R. Squire, & J. M. Jensen (Eds.), *Handbook of Research on Teaching the English Language Arts* (2nd ed., pp. 752–785). Mahwah, NJ: Erlbaum.

Bear, D., Invernizzi, M., Templeton, S., & Johnston, F. (2003, 2004). *Words Their Way: Word Study for Phonics, Vocabulary, and Spelling Instruction* (3rd ed.). Upper Saddle River, NJ: Pearson.

Bear, D. R., Invernizzi, M., Templeton, S., & Johnston, F. (2012). *Words Their Way: Word Study for Phonics, Vocabulary, and Spelling Instruction* (5th ed.). Upper Saddle River, NJ: Merrill/Prentice Hall.

Beaty, J. J., & Pratt, L. (2011). *Early Literacy in Preschool and Kindergarten* (3rd ed.). Boston: Pearson.

Beck, I. (1984). Developing comprehension: The impact of the directed reading lesson. In R. C. Anderson, J. Osborn, & R. J. Tierney (Eds.), *Learning to Read in American Schools: Basal Readers and Content Texts.* Hillsdale, NJ: Erlbaum.

Beck, I. L. (2006). *Making Sense of Phonics: The Hows and Whys.* New York: Guilford Press.

Beck, I. L., & Juel, C. (1995). The role of decoding in learning to read. *American Educator, 3.*

Beck, I. L., & McKeown, M. G. (2007). Increasing young low-income children's oral vocabularies through rich and focused instruction. *Elementary School Journal, 108,* 97–113.

Beck, I. L., McKeown, M. G., & Kucan, L. (2002). *Bringing Words to Life: Robust Vocabulary Instruction.* New York: Guilford Press.

Beck, I. L., McKeown, M. G., & Kucan, L. (2008). *Creating Robust Vocabulary: Frequently Asked Questions and Extended Examples.* New York: Guilford Press.

Beck, I. L., McKeown, M. G., & Kucan, L. (2013). *Bringing Words to Life: Robust Vocabulary Instruction* (2nd ed.). New York: Guilford Press.

Benjamin, R. G., & Schwanenflugel, P. J. (2010, October–December). Text complexity and oral reading prosody in young readers. *Reading Research Quarterly, 45*(4), 388–404.

Bernhardt, E., Destino, T., Kamil, M., & Rodriguez-Munoz, M. (1995). Assessing science knowledge in an English/Spanish bilingual elementary school. *Cognosos, 4,* 4–6.

Berninger, V., Vaughn, K., Abbott, R., Brooks, A., Abbott, S., Reed, E., Rogan, L., & Graham, S. (1998). Early intervention for spelling problems: Teaching spelling units of varying size within a multiple connections framework. *Journal of Educational Psychology, 90,* 587–605.

Bialostok, S. (1997). Offering the olive branch: The rhetoric of insincerity. *Language Arts, 74*(8), 618–627.

Biemiller, A., & Boote, C. (2006). An effective method for building meaning vocabulary in primary grades. *Journal of Educational Psychology, 98,* 44–62.

Bissex, G. L. (2004). *Gnys at Wrk: A Child Learns to Read and Write* (repr. ed.). Cambridge, MA: Harvard University Press.

Blachman, B. (2000). Phonological awareness. In M. L. Kamil, P. B. Mosenthal, P. D. Pearson, & R. Barr (Eds.), *Handbook of Reading Research*, Vol. 3 (pp. 483–502). Mahwah, NJ: Erlbaum.

Blachman, B. A. (1991). Getting ready to read: Learning how print maps to speech. In J. F. Kavanagh (Ed.), *The Language Continuum: From Infancy to Literacy.* Timonium, MD: York Press.

Blachowicz, C., & Fisher, P. (2010). *Teaching Vocabulary in All Classrooms* (4th ed.). Upper Saddle River, NJ: Prentice Hall.

Blachowicz, C. E. (1987). Vocabulary instruction: What goes on in the classroom? *The Reading Teacher, 2,* 132–137.

Blachowicz, C. E., & Lee, J. J. (1991). Vocabulary development in the whole literacy classroom. *The Reading Teacher, 45,* 188–195.

Blachowicz, C. L. Z., & Ogle, D. (2008). *Reading Comprehension: Strategies for Independent Learners* (2nd ed.). New York: Guilford Press.

Blevins, W. (2006). *Phonics from A to Z: A Practical Guide* (2nd ed.). Jefferson City, MO: Scholastic.

Block, C. C., & Pressley, M. (2007). Best practices in teaching comprehension. In L. B. Gambrell, L. M. Morrow, & M. Pressley (Eds.), *Best Practices in Literacy Instruction* (3rd ed., pp. 220–242). New York: Guilford Press.

Bond, G., & Dykstra, R. (1967). The cooperative research program in first-grade reading instruction. *Reading Research Quarterly, 2,* 5–142.

Bortnem, G. M. (2008). Teacher use of interactive read alouds using nonfiction in early childhood classrooms. *Journal of College Teaching and Learning, 5*(12), 29–44.

Boulware-Gooden, R., Carreker, S. M., Thornhill, A., & Malatesha, J. (2007). Instruction in metacognitive strategies enhances comprehension and vocabulary achievement of third grade students. *The Reading Teacher, 61,* 70–77.

Bourke, R., Mentis, M., & Todd, L. (2011). Visibly learning: Teachers' assessment practices for students with high and very high needs. *International Journal of Inclusive Education, 15*(4), 405–419.

Boyles, N. (December 2012/January 2013). Closing in on close reading. *Educational Leadership, 70*(4). Retrieved from http://www.ascd.org/publications/educational-leadership/dec12/vol70/num04/Closing-in-on-Close-Reading.aspx

Bridge, C., Winograd, P. N., & Haley, D. (1983). Using predictable materials vs. preprimers to teach beginning sight words. *The Reading Teacher, 36*(9), 884–891.

Briggs, C., & Elkind, D. (1973). Cognitive development in early readers. *Developmental Psychology, 9,* 279–280.

Brown, T. H. (2010). Learning to read: The unofficial scripts of succeeders and strugglers. *The Reading Teacher, 64,* 261–271.

Bryant, P. E., MacLean, M., Bradley, L. L., & Crossland, J. (1990). Rhyme and alliteration, phoneme detection, and learning to read. *Developmental Psychology, 26,* 429–438.

Bryce, N. (2011). Meeting the reading challenges of science textbooks in the primary grades. *The Reading Teacher, 64,* 474–485.

Buckley, M. H. (1986). When teachers decide to integrate the language arts. *Language Arts, 63,* 369–377.

Burke, M. D., Hagan-Burke, S., Kwok, O., & Parker, R. (2009). Predictive validity of early literacy indicators from the middle of kindergarten to second grade. *Journal of Special Education, 42*(4), 209–226.

Burns, P., Roe, B., & Ross, E. (1999). *Word Recognition and Meaning Vocabulary: A Literacy Skills Primer.* Boston: Houghton Mifflin.

Butler, A., & Turbil, J. (1986). *Towards a Reading and Writing Classroom.* Portsmouth, NH: Heinemann.

Byrne, B., & Fielding-Barnsley, R. (1989). Phonemic awareness and letter knowledge in the child's acquisition of the alphabetic principle. *Journal of Educational Psychology, 81,* 313–321.

Byrnes, J. P., & Wasik, B. A. (2009). *Language and Literacy Development: What Educators Need to Know.* New York: Guilford Press.

Calderón, M., August, D., Slavin, R., Duran, D., Madden, N., & Cheung, A. (2005). Bringing words to life in classrooms with English-language learners. In E. H. Hiebert and M. L. Kamil (Eds.), *Teaching and Learning Vocabulary: Bringing Research to Practice* (pp. 115–136). Mahwah, NJ: Erlbaum.

Calderón, M., Slavin, R., & Sanchez, M. (2011, Spring). Effective instruction for English learners. *Future of Children, 21*(1), pp. 103–127. Retrieved from http://www.jstor.org/stable/41229013

California Department of Education (1996). *Teaching Reading: A Balanced Comprehensive Approach to Teaching Reading in Prekindergarten Through Grade Three.* Sacramento: Author.

California Reading Association (1996). *Building Literacy: Making Every Child a Reader.* Sacramento: Author.

California State Board of Education (2014). *ELA/ELD Framework, 2–3 Grade Span.* Retrieved from http://www.cde.ca.gov/ci/rl/cf/documents/chapter4s-beadopted.pdf

Calkins, L., Ehrenworth, M., & Lehman, C. (2012). *Pathways to the Common Core: Accelerating Achievement.* Portsmouth, NH: Heinemann.

Calkins, L. M. (2000). *The Art of Teaching Writing.* Boston: Allyn & Bacon.

Calo, K. M. (2011). Incorporating informational texts in the primary grades: A research-based rationale, practical strategies, and two teachers' experiences. *Early Childhood Education Journal, 39*(4), 291–295.

Cambourne, B., & Turbill, J. (1990). Assessment in whole language classrooms: Theory into practice. *Elementary School Journal, 90,* 337–349.

Camp, D. (2000). It takes two: Teaching with twin texts of fact and fiction. *The Reading Teacher, 53,* 400–408.

Cardoso-Martins, C. (1995). Sensitivity to rhymes, syllables, and phonemes in literacy acquisition in Portuguese. *Reading Research Quarterly, 30,* 808–828.

Carnine, D., Silbert, J., Kameenui, E., & Tarver, S. (2003). *Direct Instruction Reading,* 4th ed. Upper Saddle River, NJ: Prentice Hall.

Carnine, L., Carnine, D., & Gersten, R. (1984). Analysis of oral reading errors made by economically disadvantaged students taught with a synthetic phonics approach. *Reading Research Quarterly, 19,* 343–356.

Carroll, J. M., Snowling, M. J., Hulme, C., & Stevenson, J. (2003). The development of phonological awareness in preschool children. *Developmental Psychology, 39,* 913–923.

Castek, J., Bevans-Mangelson, J., & Goldstone, B. (2006). Reading adventure online: Five ways to introduce the new literacies of the Internet through children's literature. *The Reading Teacher, 59,* 714–728.

Caswell, L. J., & Duke, N. K. (1998). Non-narrative as a catalyst for literacy development. *Language Arts, 75,* 108–117.

Cazden, C. B. (1993, May). *A Report on Reports: Two Dilemmas of Genre Teaching.* Paper presented at the Working with Genre Conference, Sydney, Australia. ERIC No. ED363593.

Cecil, N. L. (1994a). *Freedom Fighters: Affective Teaching of the Language Arts.* Salem, WI: Sheffield.

Cecil, N. L. (1994b). *Teaching to the Heart: An Affective Approach to Reading Instruction.* Salem, WI: Sheffield.

Cecil, N. L. (2007). *Focus on Fluency: A Meaning-Based Approach.* Scottsdale, AZ: Holcomb Hathaway.

Cecil, N. L., & Lauritzen, P. (1994). *Literacy and the Arts in the Integrated Classroom: Alternative Ways of Knowing.* White Plains, NY: Longman.

Cecil, N. L., & Pfeifer, J. E. (2011). *The Art of Inquiry: Questioning Strategies for K–6 Classrooms.* Winnipeg, MB: Portage & Main.

Chaaya, D., & Ghosn, I. K. (2010). Supporting young second language learners' reading through guided reading and strategy instruction in a second grade classroom in Lebanon. *Educational Research and Reviews, 5*(6), 329–337.

Chapman, L., Greenfield, R., & Rinaldi, C. (2010). "Drawing is a frame of mind": An evaluation of students' perceptions about reading instruction within a response to intervention model. *Literacy Research and Instruction, 49*(2), 113–128.

Chard, D. J., Vaughn, S., & Tyler, B. J. (2002). A synthesis of research on effective interventions for building reading fluency with elementary students with learning disabilities. *Journal of Learning Disabilities, 35*, 386–486.

Chavez-Reyes, C. (2010). Inclusive approaches to parent engagement for young English language learners and their families. *Yearbook of the National Society for the Study of Education, 109*(2), 474–504.

Cheek, E. H., Flippo, R. F., & Lindsey, J. D. (1997). *Reading for Success in Elementary School.* Madison, WI: Brown & Benchmark.

Chomsky, C. (1972). Stages in language development and reading exposure. *Harvard Educational Review, 42*, 1–33.

Christie, J. F., Enz, B. J., & Vukelich, C. (2011). *Teaching Language and Literacy: Preschool Through the Elementary Grades.* Boston: Pearson.

Cisero, C. A., & Royer, J. M. (1995). The development and cross-language transfer of phonological awareness. *Contemporary Educational Psychology, 20*, 275–303.

Clark, C. H. (1995). Teaching students about reading: A fluency example. *Reading Horizons, 35*, 251–265.

Clark, K. F. (2004). What can I say besides "sound it out"? Coaching word recognition in beginning reading. *The Reading Teacher, 57*, 440–449.

Clay, M. (2000). *Concepts About Print: What Have Children Learned About the Way We Print Language?* Portsmouth, NH: Heinemann.

Clay, M. M. (1972). *Reading: The Patterning of Complex Behavior.* Portsmouth, NH: Heinemann.

Clay, M. M. (1979). *Stones: The Concepts About Print Test.* Auckland, New Zealand: Heinemann.

Clay, M. M. (1985). *The Early Detection of Reading Difficulties* (3rd ed.). Auckland, New Zealand: Heinemann.

Clay, M. M. (1990). What is and what might be in evaluation. *Language Arts, 67*(3), 288–298.

Clay, M. M. (1991). *Becoming Literate: The Construction of Inner Control.* Portsmouth, NH: Heinemann.

Clay, M. M. (1993). *An Observation Survey.* Portsmouth, NH: Heinemann.

Clymer, T. (1963). The utility of phonic generalizations in the primary grades. *The Reading Teacher, 16*, 252–258.

Cohen, L., & Spenciner, L. J. (2008). *Teaching Students with Mild and Moderate Disabilities: Research-Based Practices* (2nd ed.). Upper Saddle River, NJ: Pearson.

Coiro, J., & Dobler, E. (2007). Exploring the online reading comprehension strategies used by sixth-grade skilled readers to search for and locate information on the Internet. *Reading Research Quarterly, 42*, 214–257.

Cole, A. D. (1998). Beginner-oriented texts in literature-based classrooms: The segue for a few struggling readers. *The Reading Teacher, 51*, 488–500.

Combs, M. (2010). *Readers and Writers in the Primary Grades: A Balanced and Integrated Approach, K–3* (4th ed.). Boston: Pearson.

Comeau, L., Cormier, P., Grandmaison, E., & Lacroix, D. (1999). A longitudinal study of phonological processing skills in children learning to read in a second language. *Journal of Educational Psychology, 91*, 29–43.

Common Sense Media (2011). *Zero to Eight: Children's Media Use In America.* San Francisco: Author. Retrieved from http://www.commonsensemedia.org/research/zero-eight-childrens-media-use-america

Connor, C., Morrison, F., & Petrella, J. (2004). Effective comprehension instruction: Examining child x instruction interactions. *Journal of Educational Psychology, 96*, 419–427.

Connor, C. M., Morrison, F. J., Fishman, B., Giuliani, S., Luck, M., Underwood, P., . . . Schatschneider, C. (2011). Classroom instruction, child X instruction interactions and the impact of differentiating student instruction on third graders' reading comprehension. *Reading Research Quarterly, 46*(3), 189–221.

Cooper, J. D. (1997). *Literacy: Helping Children Construct Meaning.* Boston: Houghton Mifflin.

Cooter, K. S. (2006). When mama can't read: Counteracting intergenerational illiteracy. *The Reading Teacher, 59*, 698–702.

Core Damages Poetry Instruction. *A Pioneer White Paper.* Boston: Pioneer Institute.

Corgill, A. M. (2008). *Of Primary Importance: What's Essential in Teaching Young Writers.* Portland, ME: Stenhouse.

Cornett, C. (2010). *Comprehension First: Inquiry into Big Ideas Using Important Questions.* Scottsdale, AZ: Holcomb Hathaway.

Cossu, G., Shankweiler, D., Liberman, I. Y., Tola, G., & Katz, L. (1988). Awareness of phonological segments and reading ability in Italian children. *Applied Psycholinguistics, 9*, 1–16.

Council of Chief State School Officers (CCSSO) and the National Governors Association (NGA) (2010).

Common Core State Standards for English Language Arts and Literacy in History/Social Studies, Science, and Technical Subjects. Washington, DC: CCSSO and NGA.

Cowan, K., & Sandefur, S. (2013). Building on the linguistic and cultural strengths of EL students. *Voices from the Middle, 20*(4), 22–27.

Cox, C. (2008). *Teaching Language Arts: A Student-Centered Classroom.* Boston: Allyn & Bacon.

Cox, C. (n.d.). Journal writing. ReadingRockets.org. Retrieved from http://www.readingrockets.org/article/48589

Crosson, A. C., & Lesaux, N. K. (2009). Revisiting assumptions about the relationship of fluent reading to comprehension: Spanish-speakers' text-reading fluency in English. *Reading and Writing, 23*(5), 475–494.

Cudd, E. (1990). The paragraph frame: A bridge from narrative to expository text. In N. L. Cecil (Ed.), *Literacy in the '90s: Readings in the Language Arts.* Dubuque, IA: Kendall/Hunt.

Culatta, B., Hall, K., Kovarsky, D., & Theadore, G. (2007). Contextualized Approach to Language and Literacy (Project CALL): Capitalizing on varied activities and contexts to teach early literacy skills. *Communication Disorders Quarterly, 28*(4), 216–235.

Cummins, J., Brown, K., & Sayers, D. (2007). *Literacy, Technology, and Diversity.* Boston: Pearson.

Cummins, S., & Stallmeyer-Gerard, C. (2011). Teaching for synthesis of informational texts with read-alouds. *The Reading Teacher, 64,* 394–405.

Cunningham, P. (2012). *Phonics They Use: Words for Reading and Writing* (5th ed.). New York: Pearson.

Cunningham, P. M. (2007). Best practices in teaching phonological awareness and phonics. In L. B. Gambrell, L. M. Morrow, & M. Pressley (Eds.), *Best Practices in Literacy Instruction* (pp. 159–177). New York: Guilford Press.

Cunningham, P. M. (2013). *Phonics They Use: Words for Reading and Writing* (6th ed.). Boston: Allyn & Bacon.

Cunningham, P. M., & Allington, R. L. (2010). *Classrooms That Work: They Can All Read and Write* (5th ed.). Boston: Allyn & Bacon.

Cunningham, P. M., & Cunningham, D. P. (1997). *Making More Words.* Carthage, IL: Good Apple.

Cunningham, P. M., & Cunningham, J. W. (2002). What we know about how to teach phonics. In A. E. Farstrup and S. J. Samuels (Eds.), *What Research Has to Say About Reading Instruction* (3rd ed., pp. 87–109). Newark, DE: International Reading Association.

Dalton, B., & Grisham, D. L. (2011). eVoc strategies: 10 ways to use technology to build vocabulary. *The Reading Teacher, 64,* 306–317.

Daniels, H., & Steineke, N. (2004). *Mini-Lessons for Literature Circles.* Portsmouth, NH: Heinemann.

Dechant, E. V. (1982). *Improving the Teaching of Reading* (3rd ed.). Englewood Cliffs, NJ: Prentice Hall.

Delgado-Gaitan, C. (1987). Mexican adult literacy: New directions for immigrants. In S. R. Goldman and H. Trueba (Eds.), *Becoming Literate in a Second Language* (pp. 9–32. Norwood, NJ: Ablex.

deManrique, A. M. B., & Gramigna, S. (1984). La segmentacion fonologica y silabica en ninos de pre-escolar y primer grado [The phonological segmentation of syllables of children in preschool and first grade]. *Lectura y Vida, 5,* 4–13.

DeVries, B. A. (2015). *Literacy Assessment and Intervention for Classroom Teachers* (4th ed.). Scottsdale, AZ: Holcomb Hathaway.

Dexter, D. D., Park, Y. J., & Hughes, C. A. (2011). A meta-analytic review of graphic organizers and science instruction for adolescents with learning disabilities: Implications for the intermediate and secondary science classroom. *Learning Disabilities Research and Practice, 26,* 204–213.

Dickenson, D., Hao, Z., & He, W. (1995). Pedagogical and classroom factors related to how teachers read to 3- and 4-year-old children. In K. A. Hinchman, C. K. Kinzer, & D. J. Leu (Eds.), *Perspectives on Literacy Research and Practice.* Chicago: Chicago Reading Conference.

Dixon-Krauss, L. (2002). Using literature as a context for teaching vocabulary. *Journal of Adolescent and Adult Literacy, 45,* 310–318.

Donnelly, W. B., & Roe, C. J. (2010). Using sentence frames to develop academic vocabulary for English learners. *The Reading Teacher, 64,* 131–136.

Dowhower, S. L. (1991). Speaking of prosody: Fluency's unattended bedfellow. *The Reading Teacher, 42,* 502–507.

Downing, J., & Thomson, D. (1977). Sex role stereotypes in learning how to read. *Research in the Teaching of English, 11,* 149–155.

Duffelmeyer, F. A., & Banwart, B. H. (1993). Word maps for adjectives and verbs. *The Reading Teacher, 46,* 351–353.

Duffy, G., Roehler, L., & Hermann, B. (1988). Modeling mental processes helps poor readers become strategic readers. *The Reading Teacher, 41,* 762–767.

Duke, N. K. (2000). 3.6 minutes per day: The scarcity of informational texts in first grade. *Reading Research Quarterly, 35,* 202–224.

Duke, N. K., & Bennett-Armistead, V. S. (2003). *Reading and Writing Informational Text in the Primary Grades: Research-Based Practices.* New York: Scholastic.

Duke, N. K., Bennett-Armistead, V. S., & Roberts, E. M. (2003). Bridging the gap between learning to read and reading to learn. In D. M. Barone and L. M. Morrow (Eds.), *Literacy and Young Children: Research-Based Practices* (pp. 226–242). New York: Guilford Press.

Duke, N. K., & Block, M. K. (2012). Improving reading in the primary grades. *Future of Children, 22(2),* 55–72.

Durán, E. (2006). *Teaching English Learners in Inclusive Classrooms.* Springfield, IL: Thomas.

Durán, E. (2012). *Systematic Instruction in Reading for Spanish-Speaking Students* (2nd ed.). Springfield, IL: Thomas.

Durgunoglu, A., Nagy, W. E., & Hancin-Bhatt, B. J. (1993). Cross-language transfer of phonological awareness. *Journal of Educational Psychology, 85,* 453–465.

Durkin, D. (1966). *Children Who Read Early.* New York: Teachers College Press.

Durkin, D. (1990). Dolores Durkin speaks on instruction. *The Reading Teacher, 43,* 472–476.

Ebbers, S. M., & Denton, C. A. (2008). A root awakening: Vocabulary instruction for older students with reading disabilities. *Learning Disabilities Research and Practice, 23,* 90–102.

Echevarria, J., Vogt, M. E., & Short, D. (2010). *Making Content Comprehensible for Elementary English Learners: The SIOP Model.* Boston: Allyn & Bacon.

Edwards, P. A. (2004). *Children's Literacy Development: Making It Happen Through School, Family, and Community Involvement.* Boston: Allyn & Bacon/Pearson.

Eeds, M., & Wells, D. (1989). Grand conversations: An exploration of meaning construction in literature study groups. *Research in the Teaching of English, 23,* 4–29.

Ehri, L., & Robbins, C. (1992). Beginners need some decoding skills to read words by analogy. *Reading Research Quarterly, 27,* 13–29.

Eldredge, J. L. (1995). *Teaching Decoding in Holistic Classrooms.* Englewood Cliffs, NJ: Merrill/Prentice Hall.

Elkonin, D. B. (1973). USSR. In J. Downing (Ed.), *Comparative Reading: Cross-National Studies of Behavior and Processes in Reading and Writing* (pp. 551–579). New York: Macmillan.

Ellermeyer, D. A., & Chick, K. A. (2007). *Activities for Standards-Based, Integrated Language Arts Instruction.* Scottsdale, AZ: Holcomb Hathaway.

Engel, T., & Streich, R. (2009). Yes, there *is* room for soup in the curriculum: Achieving accountability in a collaboratively planned writing program. *The Reading Teacher, 59,* 660–679.

Englert, C. S., & Hiebert, E. H. (1984). Children's developing awareness of text structures in expository materials. *Journal of Educational Psychology, 76,* 65–74.

Esolen, A., Highfill, J., & Stotsky, S. (2014, April). *The dying of the light: How Common Core damages poetry instruction.* White Paper 113. Pioneer Public Policy Research.

Every Child a Reader: The Report of the California Reading Task Force. (2000). Sacramento: California Department of Education.

Factoid Books. (1999). *The Big Book of Grimm, by the Brothers Grimm as Channeled by J. Vankin and over 50 Top Comic Artists!* New York: Paradox Press.

Fan, X. T., & Chen, M. (2001). Parental involvement and students' academic achievement: A meta-analysis. *Educational Psychology Review, 13,* 1–22.

Farnan, N., Lapp, D., & Flood, J. (1992). Changing perspectives in writing instruction. *The Reading Teacher, 35,* 550–556.

Felvegi, E., & Matthew, K. I. (2012). Ebooks and literacy in K–12 schools. *Computers in the Schools, 29(1–2),* 40–52.

Fielding, L. G., & Pearson, P. D. (1994). Reading comprehension: What works. *Educational Leadership, 2,* 62–68.

Fisher, D., & Frey, N. (2007). Implementing a schoolwide literacy framework: Improving achievement in an urban elementary school. *The Reading Teacher, 61,* 32–43.

Fisher, D., & Frey, N. (2012). Engaging the adolescent learner: Text complexity and close readings. Retrieved from http://education.ucf.edu/mirc/docs/Fisher_and_Frey_January_2012.pdf

Fisher, D., & Frey, N. (2015). *Text-Dependent Questions, Grades K–5: Pathways to Close and Critical Reading.* Thousand Oaks, CA: Corwin Literacy.

Fisher, D., Flood, J., Lapp, D., & Frey, N. (2004). Interactive read-alouds: Is there a common set of implementation practices? *The Reading Teacher, 58,* 8–17.

Fitzgerald, J., Spiegel, D. L., & Cunningham, J. W. (1991). The relationship between parental literacy level and perceptions of emergent literacy. *Journal of Reading Behavior, 13*(2), 191–212.

Fitzpatrick, J. (1997). *Phonemic Awareness: Playing with Sounds to Strengthen Beginning Reading Skills.* Cypress, CA: Creative Teaching Press.

Flesch, R. (1955, repr. 1993). *Why Johnny Can't Read.* Cutchogue, NY: Buccaneer Books.

Fletcher, J., Shaywitz, S., Shankweiler, D., Katz, L., Liberman, I., Stuebing, K., Francis, D., Fowler, A., & Shaywitz, B. (1994). Cognitive profiles of reading disability: Comparisons of discrepancy and low achievement definitions. *Journal of Educational Psychology, 86*(1), 6–23.

Fletcher, J. M., & Lyon, G. R. (2002). *Reading: A Research-Based Approach.* Palo Alto, CA: Hoover Institute.

Flynt, E. S., & Cooter, R. B. (2005). Improving middle grades reading in urban schools: The Memphis comprehension framework. *The Reading Teacher, 58,* 774–780.

Foorman, B., Francis, D., Beeler, T., Winikates, D., & Fletcher, J. (1998). Early interventions for children with reading problems: Study designs and preliminary findings. *Learning Disabilities: A Multi-Disciplinary Journal.*

Forseth, C. A., & Avery, C. (2002). *And with a Light Touch: Learning About Reading, Writing, and Teaching with First Graders* (2nd ed.). Portsmouth, NH: Heinemann.

Fountas, I., & Pinnell, G. (2006). *Teaching for Comprehending and Fluency: Thinking, Talking, and Writing About Reading, K–8.* Portsmouth, NH: Heinemann.

Fountas, I., & Pinnell, G. S. (2001). *Guiding readers and writers, Grades 3–6: Teaching comprehension, genre, and content literacy.* Portsmouth, NH: Heinemann.

Fountas, I. C., & Pinnell, G. S. (1996). *Guided Reading: Good First Teaching for All Children.* Portsmouth, NH: Heinemann.

Fountas, I. C., & Pinnell, G. S. (1999). *Matching Books to Readers: Using Leveled Books in Guided Reading, K–3.* Portsmouth, NH: Heinemann.

Fountas, I. C., & Pinnell, G. S. (2013). Guided reading: The romance and the reality. *The Reading Teacher, 66,* 268–284.

Fox, B. J. (2003). *Word Recognition Activities: Patterns and Strategies for Developing Fluency.* Upper Saddle River, NJ: Merrill.

Freedmon, B. (2003, April). *Boys and Literacy: Why Boys? Which Boys? Why now?* Paper presented at the meeting of the American Educational Research Association, Chicago, Illinois. Retrieved from ERIC database. [ED477857]

Freppon, P. A., & Dahl, K. L. (1991). Learning about phonics in a whole language classroom. *Language Arts, 68,* 190–197.

Fresch, M. J., & Wheaton, A. (1997). Sort, search, and discover: Spelling in the child-centered classroom. *The Reading Teacher, 51,* 20–31.

Fu, D., & Shelton, N. R. (2007, March). Including students with special needs in a writing workshop. *Language Arts, 84*(4), 325–336.

Fuchs, D., Fuchs, L. S., & Vaughn, S. (2008). *Response to Intervention: A Framework for Reading Educators.* Newark, DE: International Reading Association.

Gajria, M., Jitendra, A. K., Sood, S., & Sacks, G. (2007). Improving comprehension of expository text in students with LD: A research synthesis. *Journal of Learning Disabilities, 40*(3), 210–225.

Gallimore, R., & Reese, L. J. (1999). Mexican immigrants in urban California: Forging adaptations from familiar and new cultural resources. In M. C. Foblets and C. I. Pang (Eds.), *Culture, Ethnicity, and Immigration* (pp. 245–263). Leuven, Belgium: ACCO.

Garan, E. M. (2004). *In Defense of Our Children: When Politics, Profit, and Education Collide.* Portsmouth, NH: Heinemann.

García, G. E. (1998). Mexican-American bilingual students' metacognitive reading strategies: What's transferred, unique, problematic? *National Reading Conference Yearbook, 47,* 253–263.

Garthwait, A. (2001). Hypermedia composing: Questions arising from writing in three dimensions. *Language Arts, 78,* 237–244.

Gaskins, I. W., Ehri, L. C., Cress, C., O'Hara, C., & Donnelly, K. (1997). Procedures for word learning: Making discoveries about words. *The Reading Teacher, 50,* 312–327.

Gately, S. E. (2008). Facilitating reading comprehension for students on the autism spectrum. *Teaching Exceptional Children, 40*(3), 40–45.

Genesee, F., Lindholm-Leary, K., Saunders, W., & Christian, D. 2006. *Educating English Language Learners.* New York: Cambridge University Press.

Gentry, J. R. (1981). Learning to spell developmentally. *The Reading Teacher, 34,* 378–381.

Gentry, J. R. (1985). You can analyze developmental spelling. *Early Years, 9,* 44–45.

Gentry, J. R. (2004). *The Science of Spelling: The Explicit Specifics That Make Great Readers and Writers (and Spellers!).* Portsmouth, NH: Heinemann.

Gentry, J. R. (2006). *Breaking the Code: The New Science of Beginning Reading and Writing.* Portsmouth, NH: Heinemann.

Gentry, J. R. (2008). *Breakthrough in Beginning Reading and Writing: The Evidence-Based Approach to Pinpointing Students' Needs and Delivering Targeted Instruction.* New York: Scholastic.

Gentry, J. R., & Gillet, J. W. (1993). *Teaching Kids to Spell.* Portsmouth, NH: Heinemann.

Gerzel-Short, L., & Wilkins, E. A. (2009). Response to Intervention: Helping all students learn. *Kappa Delta Pi Record, 45*(3), 106–110.

Gibbons, G. (1994). *Frogs.* New York: Holiday House.

Gibbons, P. (2002). *Scaffolding Language, Scaffolding Learning: Teaching Second Language Learners in the Mainstream Classroom.* Portsmouth, NH: Heinemann.

Gillam, S. L., Fargo, J. D., & St. Robertson, K. (2009). Comprehension of expository text: Insights gained from think-aloud data. *American Journal of Speech-Language Pathology, 18*(1), 82–94.

Gillon, G. T. (2007). *Phonological Awareness: From Research to Practice. Challenges in Language and Literacy.* New York: Guilford Press.

Goldenberg, C. (2008). Teaching English language learners; What the research does—and does not—say. *American Educator, 32*(2), 8–11, 14–23, 42–44.

Goldenberg, C., Reese, L., & Gallimore, R. (1992). Effects of school literacy materials on Latino children's home experiences and early reading achievement. *American Journal of Education, 100,* 497–536.

Goldenberg, C. N. (2004). Literacy for low-income children in the 21st century. In N. Unrau and R. Ruddell (Eds.), *Theoretical Models and Processes of Reading* (pp. 1636–1666). Newark, DE: International Reading Association.

Goldman, J. (2014). Research-based writing practices for English learners. *In the STARlight: San Bernadino County.* Retrieved from http://en.elresearch.org/uploads/Starlight_JGoldman_English_BW.pdf

González, R. A. (2006). Culturally and linguistically diverse families. In E. Durán (Ed.), *Teaching English Learners in Inclusive Classrooms* (pp. 194–236). Springfield, IL: Thomas.

Good, R. H., & Kaminski, R. A. (Eds.) (2002). Dynamic Indicators of Basic Early Literacy Skills (6th ed.). Eugene, OR: Institute for the Development of Educational Achievement. Available: http://dibels.uoregon.edu/

Goodman, K. S. (1986). *What's Whole in Whole Language?* Portsmouth, NH: Heinemann.

Goodman, K. S. (1997). Putting theory and research in the context of history. *Language Arts, 74*(8), 595–599.

Graham, S., Berninger, V., Abbott, R., Abbott, S., & Whitaker, D. (1997). The role of mechanics in composing of elementary school students: A new methodological approach. *Journal of Educational Psychology, 89,* 170–182.

Graham, S., Bollinger, A., Booth Olson, C., D'Aoust, C., MacArthur, C., McCutchen, D., & Ollinghouse, N. (2012). *Teaching Elementary School Students to Be Effective Writers: A Practice Guide.* NCEE 2012–4058. Washington, DC: National Center for Education Evaluation and Regional Assistance, U.S. Department of Education. Retrieved from http://ies.ed.gov/ncee/wwc/publications_reviews.aspx#pubsearch

Graham, S., & Hebert, M. A. (2010). *Writing to Read: Evidence for How Writing Can Improve Reading. A Carnegie Corporation Time to Act Report.* Washington, DC: Alliance for Excellent Education.

Grant, C. A., & Potter, A. A. (2011). Models of parent–teacher/school engagement in a time of educational reform, increased diversity, and globalization. In E. M. Olivos, O. Castellanos, & A. Ochoa (Eds.), *Bicultural Parent Engagement: Advocacy and Empowerment* (pp. 120–142). New York: Teachers College Press.

Graves, D. H., & Hansen, J. (1983). The author's chair. *Language Arts, 60,* 176–183.

Graves, M. F. (1986). Vocabulary learning and instruction. *Review of Research in Education, 13,* 91–128.

Graves, M. F. (2006). *The Vocabulary Book: Learning and Instruction.* New York: Teachers College Press.

Graves, M. F., Watts, S., & Graves, B. (1998). *Essentials of Classroom Teaching: Elementary Reading* (2nd ed.). Upper Saddle River, NJ: Prentice Hall.

Griffin, E. A., & Morrison, F. J. (1997). The unique contributions of home literacy environment to differences in early literacy learning. *Early Child Development and Care, 127/128,* 233–243.

Griffith, L. W., & Rasinski, T. V. (2004). A focus on fluency: How one teacher incorporated fluency with her reading curriculum. *The Reading Teacher, 58,* 126–137.

Griffith, P. L., & Olson, M. W. (1992). Phonemic awareness helps beginning readers break the code. *The Reading Teacher, 15,* 516–523.

Grossen, B. (1997). *30 Years of Research: What We Now Know About How Children Learn to Read.* New York: Center for the Future of Teaching and Learning.

Guastello, E. F., & Lenz, C. (2005). Student accountability: Guided reading kid stations. *The Reading Teacher, 59,* 144–156.

Guillaume, A. M. (1998). Learning with text in the primary grades. *The Reading Teacher, 51,* 476–486.

Gunn, B. K., Simmons, D. C., & Kame'enui, E. J. (2004). *Emergent Literacy: Synthesis of the Research.* Retrieved from http://www.researchconnections. org/childcare/resources/2776/pdf

Gurian, M. (2009). *The Purpose of Boys: Helping Our Sons Find Meaning, Significance, and Direction in Their Lives.* San Francisco: Jossey-Bass.

Guthrie, J. T., McRae, A., Coddington, C. S., Klauda, S. L., Wigfield, A., & Barbosa, P. (2009). Impacts of comprehensive reading instruction on diverse outcomes of low- and high-achieving readers. *Journal of Learning Disabilities, 42*(3), 195–214.

Haager, D., Klingner, J., & Vaughn, S. (2007). *Evidence-Based Reading Practices for Response to Intervention.* Baltimore, MD: Brookes.

Hagans, K. S. (2008). A response-to-intervention approach to decreasing early literacy differences in first graders from different socioeconomic backgrounds. Evidence for the intervention validity of the DIBELS. *Assessment for Effective Intervention, 34*(1), 35–42.

Hall, M. A. (1981). *Teaching Reading as a Language Experience* (3rd ed.). Columbus, OH: Merrill.

Halladay, J. L., & Neumann, M. D. (2012). Connecting reading and mathematical strategies. *The Reading Teacher, 65,* 471–476.

Halliday, M. (1975). *Learning How to Mean: Explorations in the Development of Language.* New York: Arnold.

Hamilton, E. R., & Cherniavsky, J. (2006). Issues in synchronous versus asynchronous e-learning platforms. In H. F. O'Neil and S. R. Perez (Eds.), *Web-Based Learning: Theory, Research, and Practice* (pp. 87–106). Mahwah, NJ: Erlbaum.

Hancock, M. R. (2008). The status of reader response research: Sustaining the reader's voice in challenging times. In S. Lehr (Ed.), *Shattering the Looking Glass: Challenge, Risk, & Controversy in Children's Literature* (pp. 97–116). Norwood, MA: Gordon.

Haneda, M. (2006). Becoming literate in a second language: Connecting home, community, and school literacy practices. *Theory into Practice, 45*(4), 337–345.

Hansen, B. D., Wadsworth, J. P., Roberts, M. R., & Poole, T. N. (2014). Effects of naturalistic instruction on phonological awareness skills of children with intellectual and developmental disabilities. *Research in Developmental Disabilities, 35*(11), 2790–2801.

Hansen, J. (2001). *When Writers Read* (2nd ed.). Portsmouth, NH: Heinemann.

Harlin, R. P. (1990). *Effects of Whole Language on Low SES Children.* Paper presented at the National Reading Conference, Austin, TX, December.

Harp, B., & Brewer, J. A. (2005). *The Informed Reading Teacher: Research-Based Practice.* Upper Saddle River, NJ: Pearson.

Harris, A. J., & Sipay, E. R. (1990). *How to Increase Reading Ability: A Guide to Developmental and Remedial Methods* (9th ed.). New York: Longman.

Harris, R. (2010). Evaluating Internet research sources. Retrieved from www.virtualsalt.com/evalu8it.htm

Hartman, D., Fogarty, E., Coiro, J., Leu, Jr., D. J. Castek, J., & Henry, L. A. (2005, December). *New Literacies for Learning.* Symposium presented at the 55th annual meeting of the National Reading Conference, Miami, FL.

Hasbrouck, J., & Tindal, G. (2006). Oral reading fluency norms: A valuable assessment tool for reading teachers. *The Reading Teacher, 59,* 636–644.

Hayes, H. (2013) How technology is helping special-needs students excel. EDTECH. Retrieved from http:// www.edtechmagazine.com/k12/article/2013/03/how-technology-helping-special-needs-students-excel

Hayes, K., & Creange, R. (2001). *Classroom Routines That Really Work for Pre-K and Kindergarten.* New York: Scholastic.

Heath, S. B. (1983). *Ways with Words: Language, Life and Work in Community and Classrooms.* Cambridge, England: Cambridge University Press.

Heilman, A. W. (2005). *Phonics in Proper Perspective* (10th ed.). Upper Saddle River, NJ: Prentice Hall.

Helman, L., & Burns, M. (2008, September). What does oral language have to do with it? Helping young English-language learners acquire a sight word vocabulary. *The Reading Teacher, 62,* 14–19.

Henderson, E. H. (1995). *Teaching Spelling* (3rd ed.). Boston: Houghton Mifflin.

Hendricks, C., & Rinsky, L. A. (2007). *Teaching Word Recognition Skills* (7th ed.). Columbus, OH: Pearson Merrill Prentice Hall.

Hennings, D. G. (1992). *Beyond the Read Aloud: Learning to Read Through Listening to and Reflecting on Literature.* Bloomington, IN: Phi Delta Kappan Educational Foundation.

Henry, L. A. (2006). SEARCHing for an answer: The critical role of new literacies while reading on the Internet. *The Reading Teacher, 59,* 614–627.

Hernandez, D. J. (2012). *Double Jeopardy: How Third Grade Reading Skills and Poverty Influence High School Graduation.* Baltimore: Casey Foundation. Retrieved from http://www.aecf.org/m/resourcedoc/AECF-DoubleJeopardy-2012-Full.pdf

Herrell, A. L., & Jordan, M. (2006). *50 Strategies for Improving Vocabulary, Comprehension, and Fluency* (2nd ed.). Upper Saddle River, NJ: Pearson.

Hindin, A., & Paratore, J. R. (2007). Supporting young children's literacy learning through home-school partnerships: The effectiveness of a home repeated-reading intervention. *Journal of Literacy Research, 39*(3), 307–333.

Hoffman, J. V. (1985). *The Oral Recitation Lesson: A Teacher's Guide.* Austin, TX: Academic Resource Consultants.

Hohn, W., & Ehri, L. (1984). Do alphabet letters help pre-readers acquire phonemic segmentation skill? *Journal of Educational Psychology, 78,* 752–762.

Holdaway, D. (1979). *The Foundation of Literacy.* Portsmouth, NH: Ashton Scholastic.

Holdaway, D. (1986). The structure of natural language as a basis for literacy instruction. In M. L. Sampson (Ed.), *The Pursuit of Literacy: Early Reading and Writing.* Dubuque, IA: Kendall/Hunt.

Hong, M., & Stafford, P. (1999). *Spelling Strategies That Work: Quick Lessons That Help Students Become Effective Writers.* Jefferson City, NJ: Scholastic.

Hoskisson, K., & Tompkins, G. E. (2001). *Language Arts: Content and Teaching Strategies* (5th ed.). Upper Saddle River, NJ: Prentice Hall.

Hsu, C. (2010). Writing partnerships. *The Reading Teacher, 63,* 153–158.

Hudson, R. F., Lane, H. B., & Pullen, P. C. (2005). Reading fluency and assessment: What, why and how? *The Reading Teacher, 58,* 702–714.

Hui-Tzu, M. (2008). EFL vocabulary acquisition and retention: Reading plus vocabulary enhancement and narrow reading. *Language Learning, 58,* 73–115.

Hutchins, D., Greenfeld, M., & Epstein, J. (2008). *Family Reading Night.* Larchmont, NY: Eye on Education.

HW 21 Community (2012). Written-language production standards for handwriting and keyboarding (Grades K–8). Retrieved from https://www.hw21summit.com/media/zb/hw21/Written-Language_Production Standards.pdf

Individuals with Disabilities Education Act (IDEA). (1997). PL No. 105–117.

International Dyslexia Association (2012). What is dyslexia? Retrieved from http://www.interdys.org/FAQ.htm

International Reading Association (2002). *Integrating Literacy and Technology into the Classroom: A Position Statement of the International Reading Association.* Newark, DE: Author.

International Reading Association (IRA) (2012). Literacy implementation guidance for the ELA Common Core State Standards. Retrieved from http:www.reading.org/Libraries/association_documents/ira_ccss_guidelines_pdf

International Society for Technology in Education (2007). ISTE's educational technology standards for students. Retrieved from www.iste.org/Content/Navigationmenu/NETS/For Students/2007standards/NETS_for_students_2007.htm

Invernizzi, M., Abouzeid, M., & Gill, J. T. (1994). Using students' invented spellings as a guide for spelling instruction that emphasizes word study. *Elementary School Journal, 95,* 155–167.

IRA Board (1998). IRA Board issues position statement on phonemic awareness. *Reading Today, 26,* June/July.

Irujo, S. (n.d). What does research tell us about teaching reading to English language learners? In *Teaching English Learners: The Best of the ELL Outlook.* Amesbury, MA: Course Crafters.

Isabell, V. (2010). Dialogue journals: A way to encourage emergent writers. *Senior Honors Theses,* Paper 239.

Israel, S., & G. G. Duffy (Eds.). 2008. *Handbook of Research on Reading Comprehension.* New York: Routledge Education/Erlbaum.

Jalongo, M. R. (1988). *Young Children and Picture Books: Literacy from Infancy to Six.* Washington, DC: National Association for the Education of Young Children.

Jalongo, M. R. (2013). *Early Childhood Language Arts* (6th ed.). Boston: Pearson.

Jiménez, R. T. (1997). The strategic reading abilities of five low literacy Latina/o readers in middle school. *Reading Research Quarterly, 32*(3), 224–243.

Jiménez, R. T., García, G. E., & Pearson, P. D. (1996). The reading strategies of bilingual Latina/o students who are successful English readers: Opportunities and obstacles. *Reading Research Quarterly, 31*(1), 90–112.

Jimerson, S. R., Burns, M. K., & VanDerHeyden, A. M. (2007). *The Handbook of Response to Intervention: The Science and Practice of Assessment and Intervention.* New York: Springer.

Johnson, D. D. (1973). Sex differences in reading across cultures. *Reading Research Quarterly, 9*(1), 67–86.

Johnson, D. D., & Pearson, P. D. (1984). *Teaching Reading Vocabulary* (2nd ed.). New York: Holt, Rinehart, & Winston.

Johnson, E. S., Jenkins, J. R., Petscher, Y., & Catts, H. W. (2009). How can we improve the accuracy of screening instruments? *Learning Disabilities Research and Practice, 24*(4), 174–185.

Jones, J. (2005). Priority male: If we want boys to love books, it's important to recognize what they want. *School Library Journal, 51*(3), 37.

Jordan, C. E., Snow, C. E., & Porche, M. V. (2000). Project EASE: The effects of a family literacy project on kindergarten students' early literacy skills. *Reading Research Quarterly, 34*, 524–546.

Juel, C. (1991). Beginning reading. In R. Barr, M. L. Kamil, P. B. Mosenthal, & P. D. Pearson (Eds.), *Handbook of Reading Research*, Vol. 2 (pp. 759–788). New York: Longman.

Juel, C. (1994). *Learning to Read and Write in One Elementary School.* New York: Springer-Verlag.

Justice, L. M., & Pullen, P. C. (2003). Promising interventions for promoting emergent literacy skills: Three evidence-based approaches. *Topics in Early Childhood Special Education, 23*, 99–113.

Kajder, S., & Bull, G. (2003). Scaffolding for struggling students: Reading and writing with blogs. *Learning and Leading with Technology, 31*, 32–35.

Kamil, M. (1994, April). Matches between reading instruction and reading task demands. Presentation at the Educational Research Association, New Orleans.

Kamil, M. L. (2004). Vocabulary and comprehension instruction: Summary and implications of the National Reading Panel findings. In P. McCardle and V. Chabra (Eds.), *The Voice of Evidence in Reading Research* (pp. 213–234). Baltimore: Brookes.

Kay, A. M., Neher, A., & Lush, L. H. (2010). Writing a relationship: Home-school journals. *Language Arts, 87*(6), 417–426.

Kemper, L. W., & Brody, S. B. (2001). Advanced decoding and fluency. In S. B. Brody (Ed.), *Teaching Reading: Language, Letters, and Thought.* Milford, NH: LARC.

Kendall, J. S. (2011). *Understanding Common Core State Standards (Professional Development).* Alexandria, VA: Association for Supervision and Curriculum Development.

Kennedy, M., Lloyd, J., Cole, M., & Ely, E. (2012, September/October). Specially designed vocabulary instruction in the content areas. *Teaching Exceptional Children, 45*(1). Retrieved from http://tecplus.org/articles/article/1

Kervin, L. and Mantei, J. (2010). Incorporating technology within classroom literacy experiences, *Journal of Literacy and Technology, 11*(3), 77–100.

Kindle, K. J. (2009). Vocabulary development during read-alouds: Primary practices. *The Reading Teacher, 63*, 202–211.

Kinniburgh, L. H., & Baxter, A. (2012). Asking question answer relationships in science instruction to increase the reading achievement of struggling readers and students with reading disabilities. *Current Issues in Education, 15*(2), 1–10.

Kist, W. (2005). *New Literacies in Action: Teaching and Learning in Multiple Media.* New York: Teacher's College Press.

Klein, P. D., & Olson, D. R. (2001). Texts, technology, and thinking: Lessons from the Great Divide. *Language Arts, 78*, 227–236.

Klenk, L., & Kibby, M. W. (2000). Re-mediating reading difficulties: Appraising the past, reconciling the present, constructing the future. In M. L. Kamil, P. B. Mosenthal, P. D. Pearson, & R. Barr (Eds.), *Handbook of Reading Research*, Vol. 3. Mahwah, NJ: Erlbaum.

Koskinen, P. S., Blum, I. H., Bisson, S. A., Phillips, S. M., Creamer, T. S., & Baker, T. K. (2000). Book access, shared reading, and audio models: The effects of supporting the literacy learning of linguistically diverse students in school and at home. *Journal of Educational Psychology, 92*, 23–36.

Kraemer, L., McCabe, P., & Sinatra, R. (2012). The effects of read-alouds of expository text on first graders' listening comprehension and book choice. *Literacy Research and Instruction, 51*(2), 165–178.

Krashen, S. D. (2004). False claims about literacy development. *Educational Leadership, 61*, 18–21.

Kress, G. (2003). *Literacy in the New Media Age.* London: Routledge.

Kucer, Stephen B. Associate Professor of Language and Literacy, Washington State University, Vancouver. Personal correspondence, September 15, 2010.

Kuhn, M. R., Schwanenflugel, P. J., Meisinger, E. B., Levy, B. A., & Rasinski, T. V. (2010, April–June). Aligning theory and assessment of reading fluency: Automaticity, prosody, and definitions of fluency. *Reading Research Quarterly (45)*2, 230–251.

Kuhn, M. R. and Stahl, S. A. (2003). Fluency: A Review of developmental and remedial practices. *Journal of Educational Psychology, 95*, 3–21.

Labadie, M., Wetzel, M., & Rogers, R. (2012). Opening spaces for critical literacy: Introducing books to young readers. *The Reading Teacher, 66*(2), 117–127.

Labbo, L. D. (2005). From morning message to digital morning message: Moving from the tried and true to the new. *The Reading Teacher, 58*, 782–785.

Labbo, L. D., Eakle, A. J., & Montero, M. K. (2002, May). Digital language experience approach: Using digital photographs and software as a language experience approach innovation. *Reading Online, 5*(8). Retrieved from http://www.readingonline.org/electronic/elecindex.asp?HREF=labbo2/Back

Labbo, L. D., Leu, D. J., Kinzer, C. J., Teale, W. H., Cammack, D., Kara-Soteriou, J., & Sanny, R. (2003). Teacher wisdom stories: Cautions and recommendations for using computer-related technologies for literacy instruction. *The Reading Teacher, 57,* 300–304.

LaBerge, D., & Samuels, S. J. (1974). Toward a theory of automatic information processing in reading. *Cognitive Psychology, 6*, 293–323.

LaBerge, D., & Samuels, S. J. (1976). Toward a theory of automatic processing in reading. In H. Singer and R. Ruddell (Eds.), *Theoretical Models and Processes of Reading* (pp. 548–579). Newark, DE: International Reading Association.

Ladson-Billings, G. (2009). *The Dreamkeepers: Successful Teachers of African American Children* (2nd ed.). San Francisco: Wiley.

Lancy, D. F., & Bergin, C. (1992). The role of parents in supporting beginning reading. Paper presented at the annual meeting of the American Educational Research Association, San Francisco, CA.

Lancy, D. F., Draper, K. D., & Boyce, G. (1989). Parental influence on children's acquisition of reading. *Contemporary Issues in Reading, 4*(1), 83–93.

Landauer, T. (1995). *The Trouble with Computers.* Cambridge, MA: MIT Press.

Lane, H. B., & Allen, S. A. (2010). The vocabulary rich classroom: Modeling sophisticated word use to promote word consciousness and vocabulary growth. *The Reading Teacher, 63*, 362–370.

Langer, J. A., Bartolomé, L., Vásquez, O., & Lucas, T. (1990). Meaning construction in school literacy tasks: A study of bilingual students. *American Educational Research Journal, 27*(3), 427–471.

Langer, J. A., & Flihan, S. (2000). Writing and reading relationships: Constructive tasks. In R. Indrisa-no and J. R. Squire (Eds.), *Writing: Research/Theory/Practice.* Newark, DE: International Reading Association.

Laosa, L. M. (1982). School, occupation, culture, and family: The impact of parental schooling on the parent–child relationship. *Journal of Educational Psychology, 74*(6), 791–827.

Larson, L. C. (2008). Electronic reading workshop: Beyond books with new literacies and instructional technologies. *Journal of Adolescent and Adult Literacy, 52*, 121–131.

Lasaux, N., & Siegel, L. (2003). The development of reading in children who speak English as a second language (ESL). *Developmental Psychology, 39*, 1005–1019.

Leal, D. J. (2005). The Word Writing CAFÉ: Assessing student writing for complexity, accuracy, and fluency. *The Reading Teacher, 59*, 340–350.

Lee, D. M., & Allen, R. V. (1963). *Learning to Read Through Language Experience* (2nd ed.). New York: Meredith.

Lefever-Davis, S., & Pearman, C. (2005). Early readers and electronic texts: CD-ROM storybook features that influence reading behaviors. *The Reading Teacher, 58*, 446–454.

LeLoup, J. W., & Ponterio, R. (2003, December). Second language acquisition and technology: A review of the research. *CAL Digest.* Washington, DC: Center for Applied Linguistics.

Lembke, E. S., & Stichter, J. P. (2006). Utilizing a system of screening and progress monitoring within a three-tiered model of instruction: Implications for students with emotional and behavioral disorders. *Beyond Behavior, 15*(3), 3–9.

Leseman, P. P., & de Jong, P. F. (1998). Home literacy: Opportunity, instruction, cooperation and socio-emotional quality predicting early literacy development. *Reading Research Quarterly, 33*, 294–319.

Lesgold, A. M., & Curtis, M. E. (1981). Learning to read words efficiently. In A. M. Lesgold and C. A. Perfetti (Eds.), *Interactive Processes in Reading.* Hillsdale, NJ: Erlbaum.

Leu, D. J. (1997). Caity's question: Literacy as deixis on the Internet. *The Reading Teacher, 23*, 62–67.

Leu, D. J. (2007). *Teaching with the Internet K–12: New Literacies for New Times.* Norwood, MA: Gordon.

Leu, D. J., Jr., Castek, J., Coiro, J., Gort, M., Henry, L. A., & Lima, C. O. (2005). *Developing New Literacies Among Multilingual Learners in the Elementary Grades.* Paper prepared as part of the Technology in Support of Young Second Language

Learners Project at the University of California Office of the President, under a grant from the William and Flora Hewlett Foundation.

Lewison, M., Leland, C., & Harste, J. (2008). *Creating critical classrooms: K-8 reading and writing with an edge*. New York: Lawrence Erlbaum Associates.

Liang, L. A., Peterson, C. A., & Graves. M. F. (2005). Investigating two approaches to fostering children's comprehension of literature. *Reading Psychology, 26*, 4–5.

Liberman, I., Shankweiler, D., Fischer, F., & Carter, B. (1974). Explicit syllable and phoneme segmentation in the young child. *Journal of Experimental Child Psychology, 18*, 201–212.

Lindholm-Leary, K., & Borsato, G. (2006). Academic achievement. In F. Genesee, K. Lindholm-Leary, W. M. Saunders, & D. Christian (Eds.), *Educating English Language Learners: A Synthesis of Research Evidence* (pp. 176–222). New York: Cambridge University Press.

Lindsey, K., Manis, F., & Bailey, C. (2003). Prediction of first-grade reading in Spanish-speaking English-language learners. *Journal of Educational Psychology, 95*, 482–494.

Literacy GAINS (2009). Connecting practice and research: A critical literacy guide.

Locke, J. L. (1993). *The Child's Path to Spoken Language*. Cambridge, MA: Harvard University Press.

Logsdon, A. (2013). Strategies that help learning disabilities: Helpful strategies for teaching children with learning disability. Retrieved from http://learning disabilities.about.com/od/instructionalmaterials/qt/Learning-Disability-Strategies-scope-and-sequence.htm

Lonigan, C. J. (2006). Conceptualizing phonological processing skills in prereaders. In D. K. Dickinson & S. B. Newman (Eds.), *Handbook of early literacy research* (pp. 77–89). New York: Guilford.

Loo, J. H. Y., Bamiou, D., Campbell, N., & Luxon, L. M. (2010). Computer-based auditory training (CBAT): Benefits for children with language- and reading-related learning difficulties. *Developmental Medicine and Child Neurology, 52*(8), 708–717.

Lovett, M. W., Steinbach, K. A., & Frijters, J. C. (2000). Remediating the core deficits of developmental reading disability: A double deficit perspective. *Journal of Learning Disabilities, 33*(4), 334–358.

Luckner, J., & Handley, C. (2008). A summary of the reading comprehension research undertaken with students who are deaf or hard of hearing. *American Annals of the Deaf, 153*(1), 6–36.

Lundberg, I., Olofsson, A., & Wall, S. (1980). Reading and spelling skills in the first school years predicted from phonetic awareness skills in kindergarten. *Scandinavian Journal of Psychology, 21*, 159–173.

Malloy, J., & Gambrell, L. (2006). Approaching the unavoidable: Literacy instruction and the Internet. *The Reading Teacher, 59*, 482–484.

Mantzicopoulos, P., & Patrick, H. (2011). Reading picture books and learning science: Engaging young children with informational text. *Theory into Practice, 50*(4), 269–276.

Marinak, B. A., & Gambrell, L. B. (2009). Ways to teach about informational text. *Social Studies and the Young Learner, 22*(1), 19–22.

Martin, Jr., B., & Archambault, J. (1997). *Knots on a Counting Rope*. Illus. T. Rand. New York: Holt.

Mathews, M. M. (1966). *Teaching to Read: Historically Considered*. Chicago: University of Chicago Press.

May, L. (2011). Animating talk and texts: Culturally relevant teacher read-alouds of informational texts. *Journal of Literacy Research, 43*(1), 3–38.

McCracken, M. J., & McCracken, R. A. (1996). *Spelling Through Phonics*. Winnipeg, MB: Peguis.

McCracken, R. A., & McCracken, M. J. (1986). *Stories, Songs, and Poetry to Teach Reading and Writing: Literacy Through Language*. Chicago: American Library Association.

McGee, L. M. (1998). How do we teach literature to young children? In S. Neuman and K. Roskos (Eds.), *Children Achieving: Best Practices in Beginning Literacy*. Newark, DE: International Reading Association.

McGee, L. M., & Richgels, D. J. (2011). *Literacy's Beginnings: Supporting Young Readers and Writers* (6th ed.). Boston: Allyn & Bacon.

McGill-Franzen, A. (2005). *Kindergarten Literacy*. New York: Scholastic.

McIntyre, E., & Freppon, P. A. (1994). A comparison of children's development of alphabetic knowledge in a skill-based and whole language classroom. *Research in the Teaching of English, 28*, 391–417.

McIntyre, E., Hulan, N., & Layne, V. (2010). *Reading Instruction for Diverse Classrooms: Research-Based, Culturally Responsive Practice*. New York: Guilford Press.

McKenna, M. C. (1998). Electronic texts and the transformation of beginning reading. In D. Reinking, M. Mckenna, L. D. Labbo, & R. Kieffer (Eds.), *Handbook of Literacy and Technology: Transformations in a Post-Typographic World* (pp. 45–59). Mahwah, NJ: Erlbaum.

McKenna, M. C., & Kear, D. J. 1990. Measuring attitude toward reading: A new tool for teachers. *The Reading Teacher, 43* (9), 626–639.

McKeown, M. G. (1985). The acquisition of word meaning from context by children of high and low ability. *Reading Research Quarterly, 20,* 482–496.

McLaughlin, M. (2012). Reading comprehension: What every teacher needs to know. *The Reading Teacher, 65,* 432–440.

McMath, J., King, M., & Smith, W. (1998). Young children, questions and nonfiction books. *Early Childhood Education Journal, 26,* 19–27.

Meskill, C., & Mossop, J. (2000). Electronic texts in ESOL classrooms. *TESOL Quarterly, 34,* 585–592.

Mesmer, E. M., & Mesmer, A. E. (2009). Response to intervention: What teachers of reading need to know. *The Reading Teacher, 62,* 114–121.

Mesmer, H. E., & Griffith, P. L. (2005). Everybody's selling it—But just what is explicit, systematic phonics instruction? *The Reading Teacher, 59,* 366–376.

Mikulecky, L. (1996). *Family Literacy: Directions in Research and Implications for Practice.* Retrieved from http://www.ed.gov/pubs/famLit/appendb

Miller, M. A., Fenty, N., Scott, T. M., & Park, K. L. (2011). An examination of social skills instruction in the context of small-group reading. *Remedial and Special Education, 32*(5), 371–381.

Mitchell, A., & Brady, S. (2013). The effect of vocabulary knowledge on novel word identification. *Annals of Dyslexia, 63*(3–4), 201–216.

Mitchell, D. R. (2008). *What Really Works in Special and Inclusive Education: Using Evidence-Based Teaching Strategies.* New York: Routledge.

Moats, L. C. (1995). *Spelling: Development, Disabilities, and Instruction.* Timonium, MD: York Press.

Mohr, K. A. (2006). Children's choices for recreational reading: A three-part investigation of selection preferences, rationales, and processes. *Journal of Literacy Research, 38*(1), 81–104.

Moll, L. C., Amanti, C., Neff, D., & Gonzalez, N. (1992). Funds of knowledge for teaching: Using a qualitative approach to connect homes and classrooms. *Theory into Practice, 31,* 132–141.

Montelongo, J. A., Hernández, A. C., Herter, R. J., & Cuello, J. (2011). Using cognates to scaffold context clue strategies for Latino ELs. *The Reading Teacher, 64,* 429–434.

Morgan, L., & Goldstein, H. (2004). Teaching mothers of low socioeconomic status to use decontextualized language during storybook reading. *Journal of Early Intervention, 26,* 235–252.

Morphett, M. V., & Washburn, C. (1931). When should children begin to read? *Elementary School Journal, 31,* 496–503.

Morrison, K., Robbins, H., & Rose, D. G. (2008). Operationalizing culturally relevant pedagogy: A synthesis of classroom-based research. *Equity and Excellence in Education, 41,* 433–452.

Morrow, L. M. (1983). Home and school correlates of early interest in literature. *Journal of Educational Research, 76,* 221–230.

Morrow, L. M., & Gambrell, L. B. (2011). Best practices in early literacy in preschool, kindergarten, and first grade. In L. B. Gambrell, L. M. Morrow, & M. Pressley (Eds.), *Best Practices in Literacy Instruction* (4th ed.). New York: Guilford Press.

Morrow, L. M., & Young, J. (1997). A family literacy program connecting school and home: Effects on attitude, motivation, and literacy achievement. *Journal of Educational Psychology, 89*(2), 736–742.

Moss, B. (2004). Teaching expository text structures through information and book retellings. *The Reading Teacher, 57,* 710–718.

Moss, B. (2005). Making a case and a place for effective content area literacy instruction in the elementary grades. *The Reading Teacher, 59,* 46–55.

Moss, B., Leone, S., & Depillo, M. (1997). Exploring the literature of fact: Linking reading and writing through information trade books. *Language Arts, 74,* 418–429.

Mott, M. S., & Rutherford, A. S. (2012). Technical examination of a measure of phonological sensitivity. *SAGE Open* (April–June), 1–14.

Mullis, I. V. S., Martin, M. O., Kennedy, A. M., & Foy, P. (2007). *IEA's Progress in International Reading Literacy Study in Primary School in 40 Countries.* Chestnut Hill, MA: TIMSS and PIRLS International Study Center, Boston College.

Murray, A. D. (1990). Fine-tuning of utterance length to preverbal infants: Effects on later language development. *Journal of Child Language, 17,* 511–525.

NAEYC (2009). Position statement on developmentally appropriate practice. Retrieved from http://www.naeyc.org/files/naeyc/file/positions/position statement Web.pdf

NAEYC (2011). Developmentally appropriate practice. Retrieved from http://www.naeyc.org/DAP

NAEYC (2013). *The Common Core State Standards: Caution and opportunity for early childhood education.* Washington, DC: NAEYC.

Nagy, W. E. (1988). *Teaching Vocabulary to Improve Reading Comprehension.* Clearinghouse on Reading and Communication Skills and the National Council of Teachers of English and the International Reading Association. Urbana, IL: ERIC.

Nagy, W. E., & Herman, P. (1985). Incidental vs. instructional approaches to increasing reading vocabulary. *Educational Perspectives, 23,* 16–21.

Nagy, W. E., Herman, P., & Anderson, R. (1985). Learning words from context. *Reading Research Quarterly, 19,* 304–330.

Narkon, D. E., Wells, J. C., & Segal, L. S. (2011). E-word wall. *Teaching Exceptional Children, 43*(4), 38–45.

National Assessment Governing Board. (2002). Reading Framework for the 2003 National Assessment of Educational Progress. Retrieved from http://www.nagb/pubs/reading_framework/tok.html

National Assessment Governing Board (2007). *Writing Framework for the 2011 National Assessment of Educational Progress, Pre-Publication Edition.* Iowa City, IA: ACT.

National Association for the Education of Young Children and the Fred Rogers Center for Early Learning and Children's Media at Saint Vincent College (2012). Technology and interactive media as tools in early childhood programs serving children from birth through age 8. Retrieved from http://www.naeyc.org/files/naeyc/PS_technology_WEB.pdf

National Center for Education Statistics (2003). Societal support for learning: Family support (Indicator 37). *The Condition of Education, 2003.* Washington, DC: Author. Retrieved from http://nces.ed.gov/pubs2003/2003067_6.pdf

National Center for Education Statistics (2008). *The National Adult Literacy Survey.* Washington, DC: Author.

National Endowment for the Arts (2004). *Reading at Risk: A Survey of Literary Reading in America* (Rep. No. 46). Washington, DC: Author.

National Governors Association (2013). *A Governor's Guide to Early Literacy: Getting All Students Reading by Third Grade.* Washington, DC: NGACBP. Retrieved from http://www.nga.org/files/live/sites/NGA/files/pdf/2013/1310NGAEarlyLiteracyReportWeb.pdf

National Governors Association Center for Best Practices (NGACBP) and Council of Chief State School Officers (CCSSO) (2010). *Common Core State Standards.* Washington, DC: NGACBP and CCSSO.

National Governors Association Center for Best Practices (NGACBP) and Council of Chief State School Officers (CCSSO) (2010). *English Language Arts Standards, Language, Grade K.* Washington, DC: NGACBP and CCSSO.

National Institute for Literacy (2001). *Put Reading First: The Research Building Blocks for Teaching Children to Read Kindergarten Through Grade 3.* Washington, DC: Author.

National Institute for Literacy (2008). *Developing Early Literacy: Report of the National Early Literacy Panel. A Scientific Synthesis of Early Literacy Development and Implications for Intervention.* T. Shanahan, Chair. Louisville, KY: National Center for Family Literacy.

National Institute of Child Health and Human Development (2000). *Report of the National Reading Panel. Teaching Children to Read: An Evidence-Based Assessment of the Scientific Research Literature on Reading and Its Implications for Reading Instruction.* NIH Publication No. 00-4769. Washington, DC: National Academies Press.

National Reading Panel (2000). *Report of the National Reading Panel: Teaching Children to Read: An Evidence-Based Assessment of the Scientific Research Literature on Reading and Its Implications for Reading Instruction.* Washington, DC: National Institute of Child Health and Human Development, National Institutes of Health.

Nelson, J. R., & Stage, S. A. (2007). Fostering the development of vocabulary knowledge and reading comprehension through contextually-based multiple meaning vocabulary instruction. *Education and Treatment of Children, 30,* 1–22.

Neuman, S. B., & Celano, D. (2001). Books aloud: A campaign to "put books into children's hands." *The Reading Teacher, 54,* 550–557.

Nilsen, A., & Nilsen, D. (2003). A new spin on teaching vocabulary: A source-based approach. *The Reading Teacher, 56,* 436–439.

Nord, C. W., Lennon, J., Liu, B., & Chandler, K. (1999). *Home Literacy Activities and Signs of Children's Emerging Literacy: 1993 and 1999.* NCES No. 2000-026. Washington, DC: U.S. Department of Education. Retrieved from http://nces.ed.gov/pubs2000/2000026.pdf

NYSED (2011). *New York State P–12 Common Core Learning Standards for English Language Arts and Literacy.* Retrieved from http://www.p12.nysed.gov/ciai/common_core_standards/

Ogle, D. (1986). K-W-L: A teaching model that develops active reading of expository text. *The Reading Teacher, 39,* 564–570.

Ogle, D., & Correa-Kovtun, A. (2010). Supporting English-language learners and struggling readers in content literacy with the "partner reading and content, too" routine. *The Reading Teacher, 63,* 532–542.

Ollila, L. O., & Mayfield, M. (Eds.) (1992). *Emerging Literacy*. Needham Heights, MA: Allyn & Bacon.

Opitz, M., & Guccione, L. (2009). *Comprehension and English Language Learners: 25 Oral Reading Strategies That Cross Proficiency Levels*. Portsmouth, NH: Heinemann.

Opitz, M. F., & Rasinski, T. (1998). *Good-Bye Round Robin: 25 Effective Oral Reading Strategies*. Portsmouth, NH: Heinemann.

Ozmen, R. G. (2011). Comparison of two different presentations of graphic organizers in recalling information in expository texts with intellectually disabled students. *Educational Sciences: Theory and Practice, 11*(2), 785–793.

Pages, J. M. (2002, April). Using an author's style and text patterns to support the reading of information. Retrieved from http://www.kidbibs.com/learning tips/lt39.htm

Paige, R. (2004). Key policy letters signed by the education secretary or the deputy secretary. Retrieved from http://www.ed.gov/policy/elsec/guid/secletter/040701.html

Palincsar, A. S., & Brown, A. L. (1986). Interactive teaching to promote independent learning from text. *The Reading Teacher, 39*, 771–777.

Palincsar, A. S., Brown, A. L., & Martin, S. M. (1987). Peer interaction in reading comprehension instruction. *Educational Psychologist, 22*, 231–253.

Palmer, R. (2013). The top 10 iPad apps for special education. *The Journal*. Retrieved from http://online.qmags.com/TJL0613/default.aspx?pg=10&mode=1#pg10&mode1

Palmer, R. G., & Stewart, R. A. (2003). Nonfiction trade book use in primary grades. *The Reading Teacher, 57*, 38–48.

Palumbo, A., & Loiacono, V. (2009). Understanding the causes of intermediate and middle school comprehension problems. *International Journal of Special Education, 24*(1), 75–81.

Pappas, C. C. (1993). Is narrative "primary"? Some insights from kindergarteners' pretend readings of stories and information books. *Journal of Reading Behavior, 25*, 97–129.

Pappas, C. C., Varelas, M., Patton, S. K., Ye, L., & Ortiz, I. (2012). Dialogic strategies in read-alouds of English-language information books in a second-grade bilingual classroom. *Theory into Practice, 51*(4), 263–272.

Parkes, B. (2003). The power of informational texts in developing readers and writers. In L. Hoyt, M. Mooney, & B. Parkes (Eds.), *Exploring Informational Texts: From Theory to Practice* (pp. 2–7). Portsmouth, NH: Heinemann.

Pearson, P. D. (1985). Changing the face of reading comprehension instruction. *The Reading Teacher, 38*, 724–738.

Pearson, P. D. (1993). Teaching and learning reading: A research perspective. *Language Arts, 70*, 502–511.

Pearson, P. D., Raphael, T. E., Benson, V. L., & Madda, C. (2007, 2014). Balance in comprehensive literacy instruction: Then and now. In L. B. Gambrell, L. M. Morrow, & M. Pressley (Eds.), *Best Practices in Literacy Instruction* (3rd ed., pp. 31–54). New York: Guilford Press.

Peetoom, A. (1986). *Shared Reading: Safe Risks with Whole Books*. Richmond Hill, ON: TAB.

Peha, S. (1996). *Where the Writing Happens: Welcome to Writer's Workshop*. Unpublished manuscript.

Peregoy, S. F., & Boyle, O. F. (2013). *Reading, Writing, and Learning in ESL: A Resource Book for Teaching K–12 English Learners* (6th ed.). Boston: Allyn & Bacon/Pearson.

Perfetti, C. (1985). *Reading Ability*. New York: Oxford University Press.

Pflaum, S. W. (1990). *The Development of Language and Literacy in Young Children* (3rd ed.). Upper Saddle River, NJ: Prentice Hall.

Pierce, M. E., & Fontaine, L. (2009). Designing vocabulary instruction in mathematics. *The Reading Teacher, 63*, 239–243.

Polacco, P. (1998). *Thank You, Mr. Falker*. New York: Philomel.

Porter, C., & Cleland, J. (1995). *The Portfolio as a Learning Strategy*. Portsmouth, NH: Heinemann.

Powel, D. A., & Aram, R. (2008). Spelling in parts: A strategy for spelling and decoding polysyllabic words. *The Reading Teacher, 61*, 567–570.

Pressley, M. (2005). *Reading Instruction That Works*. New York: Guilford Press.

Pressley, M., Duke, N. K., & Boling, E. C. (2004). The educational science and scientifically-based instruction we need: Lessons from reading research and policy making. *Harvard Educational Review, 16*, 1–62.

Proctor, P. C., Dalton, B., & Grisham, D. L. (2007). Scaffolding English language learners and struggling readers in a universal literacy environment with embedded strategy instruction and vocabulary support. *Journal of Literacy Research, 39*(1), 71–93.

Project RED (2011). The technology factor: Nine keys to student achievement and cost-effectiveness. Retrieved from http://www.pearsonfoundation.org/downloads/ProjectRED_TheTechnolgyFactor.pdf

Pufpaff, L. A. (2009). A developmental continuum of phonological sensitivity skills. *Psychology in the Schools, 46*(7), 679–691.

Puhalla, E. M. (2011). Enhancing the vocabulary knowledge of first-grade children with supplemental booster instruction. *Remedial and Special Education, 32*(6), 471–481.

Quiroga, T., Lemos-Britton, Z., Mostafapour, E., & Beringer, V. (2002). Phonological awareness and beginning reading in Spanish-speaking ESL first graders: Research into practice. *Journal of School Psychology, 40,* 85–111.

Raphael, T. E. (1984). Question-answering strategies for children. *The Reading Teacher, 36,* 186–190.

Raphael, T. E., Highfield, K., & Au, K. H. (2006). *QAR Now.* New York: Scholastic.

Rasinski, T. (2003a). Beyond speed: Reading fluency is more than reading fast. *California Reader, 2,* 5–11.

Rasinski, T. (2003b). *The Fluent Reader.* New York: Scholastic.

Rasinski, T., Samuels, S. J., Hiebert, E. H., Petscher, Y., & Feller, K. (2011). The relationship between a silent reading fluency instructional protocol on students' reading comprehension and achievement in an urban school setting. *Reading Psychology, 32*(1), 75–97.

Rasinski, T. V. (2000). Speed does matter. *The Reading Teacher, 54,* 146–151.

Rasinski, T. V., & Padak, N. (1996). Five lessons to increase reading fluency. In L. R. Putnam (Ed.), *How to Become a Better Reading Teacher: Strategies for Assessment and Intervention.* Columbus, OH: Merrill/Prentice Hall.

Rasinski, T. V., Padak, N. D., & Fawcett, C. (2010). Developing comprehension with informational text. In T. V. Rasinski, N. D. Padak, & C. Fawcett (Eds.), *Teaching Children Who Find Reading Difficult* (pp. 187–205). Boston: Allyn & Bacon.

Rasinski, T. V., Padak, N., Newton, J., & Newton, E. (2011). The Latin-Greek connection. *The Reading Teacher, 65,* 133–141.

Read, C. (1986). *Children's Creative Spelling.* London: Routledge and Kegan Paul.

Read, S. (2005). First and second graders writing informational text. *The Reading Teacher, 59,* 36–44.

Reading and Writing Project (2010). *Position statements on the common core and pathways to achieving the standards.* New York: Teachers College Press. Retrieved from http://readingandwritingproject.com/about/common-core-standards.html

Reed, D. K. (2012). *Why Teach Spelling?* Portsmouth, NH: RMC Research Corporation, Center on Instruction.

Reutzel, D. R. (1992). Breaking the letter a week tradition: Conveying the alphabetic principle to young children. *Childhood Education, 69*(1), 20–23.

Reutzel, D. R. (1995). Fingerpoint-reading and beyond: Learning about print strategies (LAPS). *Reading Horizons, 35,* 4.

Reutzel, D. R., & Cooter, R. B. (2003). *Strategies for Reading Assessment and Instruction* (2nd ed.). Upper Saddle River, NJ: Merrill.

Reutzel, D. R., & Cooter, R. B., Jr. (2014). *Teaching Children to Read: The Teacher Makes the Difference* (7th ed.). Upper Saddle River, NJ: Merrill/Prentice Hall.

Reutzel, D. R., & Hollingsworth, P. M. (1993). Effects of fluency training on second-graders' reading comprehension. *Journal of Educational Research, 86*(6), 325–331.

Reutzel, D. R., Petscher, Y., & Spichtig, A. N. (2012). Exploring the value added of a guided, silent reading intervention: Effects on struggling third-grade readers' achievement. *Journal of Educational Research, 105*(6), 404–415.

Rhoades, J. (2013). Resources for teaching critical evaluation of online information. *Reading Today Online.* Retrieved from http://www.reading.org/General/Publications/blog/BlogSinglePost/reading-today-online/2013/03/22/tile-sig-feature-resources-for-teaching-critical-evaluation-of-online-information

Rhodes, L. K., & Nathenson–Mejia, S. (1992). Anecdotal records: A powerful tool for ongoing literacy assessment. *The Reading Teacher, 45,* 502–511.

Ricci, L. A. (2011). Exploration of reading interest and emergent literacy skills of children with Down syndrome. *International Journal of Special Education, 26*(3), 80–91.

Richards, M. (2000). Be a good detective: Solve the case of oral fluency. *The Reading Teacher, 53,* 534–539.

Richards-Tutor, C., Solari, E. J., Leafstedt, J. M., Gerber, M. M., Filippini, A. et al. (2013). Response to Intervention for English learners: Examining models for determining response and nonresponse. *Assessment for Effective Intervention, 38*(3), 172–184.

Riches, C., & Genesee, F. (2006). Literacy: Crosslinguistic and crossmodal issues. In F. Genesee, K. Lindholm-Leary, W. M. Saunders, & D. Christian (Eds.), *Educating English Language Learners: A Synthesis of Research Evidence* (pp. 64–108). New York: Cambridge University Press.

Richgels, D. J. (1995). Invented spelling ability and printed word learning in kindergarten. *Reading Research Quarterly, 30,* 96–109.

Richgels, D. J. (2002). Informational texts in kindergarten. *The Reading Teacher, 55,* 586–595.

Rinaldi, C., & Samson, J. (2008). English language learners and Response to Intervention: Referral considerations. *Teaching Exceptional Children, 40*(5), 6–14.

Risko, V. J., & Walker-Dahlhouse, D. (2010). Making the most of assessments to inform instruction. *The Reading Teacher, 63,* 420–422.

Rizzo, J. (2010). *Oceans: Dolphins, Sharks, Penguins, and More! Meet 60 Cool Sea Creatures and Explore Their Amazing Watery World.* Washington, DC: National Geographic (Kids) Society.

Roberts, J., Jurgens, J., & Buchinal, M. (2005). The role of literacy practices in preschool children's language and emergent literacy skills. *Journal of Speech, Language, and Hearing Research, 48,* 345–359.

Roberts, T. (1975). Skills of analysis and synthesis in the early stages of reading. *British Journal of Educational Psychology, 45,* 3–9.

Roberts, T., & Neal, H. (2004). Relationships among preschool English language learners' oral proficiency in English, instructional experience and literacy development. *Contemporary Educational Psychology, 29,* 283–311.

Rodríguez-Brown, F. V. (2004). Project FLAME: A parent support family literacy model. In B. Wasik (Ed.), *Handbook of Family Literacy* (pp. 213–229). Mahwah, NJ: Erlbaum.

Rodríguez-Brown, F. V. (2009). *The Home–School Connection: Lessons Learned in a Culturally and Linguistically Diverse Community.* New York: Routledge.

Rodríguez-Brown, F. V. (2011). Family literacy: A current view of research on parents and children learning together. In M. L. Kamil, P. D. Pearson, E. B. Moje, & P. P. Afflerbach (Eds.), *Handbook of Reading Research,* Vol. 4. (pp. 726–753). Mahwah, NJ: Erlbaum.

Rogers, K. (2008). Selecting books for your child: Finding "just right" books. *Reading Rockets.* Retrieved from http://www.readingtogether.org

Rogers, R. (2001). Family literacy and cultural models. *National Reading Conference Yearbook, 50,* 96–114.

Rosenbaum, C. (2001). A world map for middle school: A tool for effective vocabulary instruction. *Journal of Adolescent and Adult Literacy, 45,* 44–48.

Rosenblatt, L. (2005). *Making Meaning with Text: Selected Essays.* Portsmouth, NH: Heinemann.

Rosenshine, B., Meister, C., & Chapman, S. (1996). Reciprocal teaching: A review of the research. *Review of Educational Research, 64,* 479–530.

Roskos, K., Brueck, J., & Widman, S. (2009). Investigating analytic tools for e-book design in early literacy learning. *Journal of Interactive Online Learning, 8.* Retrieved from http://www.ncolr.org/jiol/issues/PDF/8.3.3.pdf

Rothstein-Fisch, C., & Trumbull, E. (2008). *Managing Diverse Classrooms: How to Build on Students' Cultural Strengths.* Alexandria, VA: Association for Supervision and Curriculum Development.

Routman, R. (1995). *Invitations: Changing as Teachers and Learners K–12* (2nd ed.). Portsmouth, NH: Heinemann.

Routman, R. (2000). *Conversations.* Portsmouth, NH: Heinemann.

Rupley, W. H., & Blair, T. R. (1990). *Teaching Reading: Diagnosis, Direct Instruction, and Practice* (2nd ed.). Upper Saddle River, NJ: Prentice Hall.

Sacramento Bee (2010). Big step for level school standards. Editorial. June 14, p. A21.

Saint-Laurent, L., & Giasson, J. (2005). Effects of a family literacy program adapting parental intervention to first graders' evolution of reading and writing abilities. *Journal of Early Childhood Literacy, 5*(3), 253–278.

Salinger, T. (1993). *Models of Literacy Instruction.* New York: Macmillan.

Salvia, J., Yesseldyke, J. E, & Bolt, S. (2012). *Assessment: In Special and Inclusive Education* (12th ed.). Boston: Houghton Mifflin.

Samuels, J. S., Schermer, N., & Reinking, D. (1992). Reading fluency: Techniques for making decoding automatic. In J. S. Samuels and A. E. Farstrup (Eds.), *What Research Has to Say About Reading Instruction* (pp. 124–144). Newark, DE: International Reading Association.

Samuels, S. J. (1979). The method of repeated readings. *The Reading Teacher, 32,* 403–408.

Sanchez, C., Plata, V., Grosso, L., & Leird, B. (2010). Encouraging Spanish-speaking families' involvement through dichos. *Journal of Latinos and Education, 9*(3), 239–248.

Saunders, W. M., & Goldenberg, C. (1999). Effects of instructional conversations and literature logs on limited-and fluent-English proficient students' story comprehension and thematic understanding. *Elementary School Journal, 99,* 277–301.

Schaffer, L. M., & Schirmer, B. R. (2010). The guided reading approach: A practical method to address diverse needs in the classroom. *Odyssey: New Directions in Deaf Education, 11*(1), 40–43.

Scheffel, D., Lefly, D., & Houser, J. (2012). The predictive utility of DIBELS reading assessment for reading comprehension among third grade English language learners and English speaking children. *Reading Improvement, 49*(3), 75–92.

Schickedanz, J., & Casbergue, R. (2007). *Writing in Preschool: Learning to Orchestrate Meaning and Marks*. Newark, DE: International Reading Association.

Schiefele, U., Schaffner, E., Möller, J., Wigfield, A., Nolen, S., & Baker, L. (2012). Dimensions of reading motivation and their relation to reading behavior and competence. *Reading Research Quarterly, 47*, 427–463.

Schlagel, R., & Schlagel, J. (1992). The integrated character of spelling: Teaching strategies for multiple purposes. *Language Arts, 69*, 418–424.

Schleper, D. R. (1996). Write that one down! Using anecdotal records to inform our teaching. *Volta Review, 98*(1), 201–208.

Schmar-Dobler, E. (2003). Reading on the Internet: The link between literacy and technology. *Journal of Adolescent and Adult Literacy, 47*, 80–85.

Schmitt, N. (2008). Instructed second language vocabulary learning. *Language Teaching Research, 12*, 329–363.

Schnorr, R. F. (2011). Intensive reading instruction for learners with developmental disabilities. *The Reading Teacher, 65*(1), 35–45.

Schulman, M. B., & Payne, C. D. (2000). *Guided Reading: Making It Work*. New York: Scholastic.

Schwartz, R. M. (2005). Decisions, decisions: Responding to primary students during guided reading. *The Reading Teacher, 58*, 436–443.

Serafini, F. (Dec. 2011/Jan. 2012). When bad things happen to good books. *The Reading Teacher, 64*, 2238–2241.

Shanahan, T. (2005). *The National Reading Panel Report: Practical Advice for Teachers*. Naperville, IL: Learning Point Associates.

Shanahan, T. (2008). Relations among oral language, reading, and writing development. In C. A. MacArthur, S. Graham, & J. Fitzgerald, *Handbook of Writing Research*. New York: Guilford Press.

Shanahan, T. (2012). Close reading PowerPoint. Retrieved from https://docs.google.com/viewer?a=v&pid=sites-&srcid=ZGVmYXVsdGRvbWFpbnx0c2NvbW1vbmNvcmV8Z3g6NDMzYWUyOWNmNWEzNTU0Mg

Shaywitz, S., Escobar, M., Shaywitz, B., Fletcher, J., & Makuch, R. (1992). Evidence that dyslexia may represent the lower tail of a normal distribution of reading disability. *New England Journal of Medicine, 326*(3), 145–150.

Shefelbine, J. (1995). Learning and using phonics in beginning reading. *Scholastic Literacy Paper, 10*.

Shepard, M. J., & Uhry, J. K. (1997). Teaching phonological recoding to young children with phonological processing deficits: The effect on sight-vocabulary acquisition. *Learning Disability Quarterly, 20*(2), 104–125.

Shokouhi, H., & Maniati, M. (2009). Learners' incidental vocabulary acquisition: A case on narrative and expository texts. *English Language Teaching, 2*(1). Retrieved from http://www.ccsenet.org/journal/index.php/elt/article/view/330

Silverman, R., & Hines, S. (2009). The effects of multimedia-enhanced instruction on the vocabulary of English-language learners and non-English-language learners in pre-kindergarten through second grade. *Journal of Educational Psychology, 101*(2), 305–314.

Simpson, C. G., Spencer, V. G., Button, R., & Rendon, S. (2007). Using guided reading with students with autism spectrum disorders. *Teaching Exceptional Children Plus, 4*(1), 1–9.

Sipe, R., Walsh, J., Reed-Norwall, K., Putnam, D., & Rosewarne, T. (2002). Supporting challenged spellers. *Voices from the Middle, 9*, 21–31.

Slepian, J., & Seidler, A. (1985). *The Hungry Thing*. New York: Scholastic.

Smith, L. A. (2006). Think Aloud Mysteries: Using structured, sentence-by-sentence text passages to teach comprehension strategies. *The Reading Teacher, 59*, 764–773.

Snowling, M. J., & Hulme, C. (2012). Annual research review: The nature and classification of reading disorders—a commentary on proposals for DSM-5. *Journal of Child Psychology and Psychiatry, 53*(5), 593–607.

Soto Huerta, M. E. (2012). Guiding biliteracy development: Appropriating cross-linguistic and conceptual knowledge to sustain second-language reading comprehension. *Bilingual Research Journal, 35*(2), 179–196.

Spache, G., & Spache, E. (1985). *Reading in the Elementary School* (5th ed.). Boston: Allyn & Bacon.

Spiegel, D. L., & Fitzgerald, J. (1986). Improving reading comprehension through instruction about story parts. *The Reading Teacher, 39*, 676–682.

Spiegelman, A., & Mouly, F. (Eds.). (2000). *Little Lit: Folklore and Fairy Tale Funnies*. New York: RAW Junior.

Spinelli, C. G. (2008). Addressing the issue of cultural and linguistic diversity and assessment: informal evaluation measures for English language learners. *Reading and Writing Quarterly, 24*(1), 101–118.

Stahl, S. A. (1983). Differential word knowledge and reading comprehension. *Journal of Reading Behavior, 15*, 33–50.

Stahl, S. A. (1992). Saying the "P" word: Nine guidelines for exemplary phonics instruction. *The Reading Teacher, 45,* 618–624.

Stahl, S. A. (2001). Teaching phonics and phonological awareness. In S. B. Neuman and P. K. Dickinson (Eds.), *Handbook of Early Literacy Research,* Vol. 1 (pp. 333–347). New York: Guilford.

Stahl, S. A., & Fairbanks, M. M. (1986). The effects of vocabulary instruction: A model-based meta-analysis. *Review of Educational Research, 56,* 72–110.

Stahl, S. A., & Kapinus, B. (1991). Possible sentences: Predicting word meanings to teach content area vocabulary. *The Reading Teacher, 45,* 36–43.

Stanberry, K., & Swanson, L. (2009). Effective reading interventions for kids with learning disabilities. LD Online. Retrieved from http://www.ldonline.org/article/33084#research

Stanovich, K., & Stanovich, P. (1995). How research might inform the debate about early reading acquisition. *Journal of Research in Reading, 18*(2), 87–105.

Stanovich, K. E. (1980). Toward an interactive-compensatory model of individual differences in the development of reading fluency. *Reading Research Quarterly, 16,* 32–71.

Stanovich, K. E. (1986). Matthew effects in reading: Some consequences of individual differences in the acquisition of reading. *Reading Research Quarterly, 22,* 360–407.

Stanovich, K. E. (1992). Speculations on the causes and consequences of individual differences in early reading acquisition. In P. B. Gough, L. C. Ehri, & R. Treiman (Eds.), *Reading Acquisition* (pp. 307–342). Hillsdale, NJ: Erlbaum.

Stanovich, K. E. (1994). Romance and reality. *The Reading Teacher, 47,* 280–291.

Stanovich, K. E., & Siegel, L. S. (1994). The phenotypic performance profile of reading-disabled children: A regression-based test of the phonological-core variable-difference model. *Journal of Educational Psychology, 86*(1), 24–53.

Stauffer, R. G. (1969). *Teaching Reading as a Thinking Process.* New York: Harper & Row.

Stauffer, R. G. (1980). *The Language Experience Approach to the Teaching of Reading* (2nd ed.). New York: Harper & Row.

Steptoe, J. (1987). *Mufaro's Beautiful Daughters: An African Tale.* New York: Lothrop, Lee & Shepard.

Stetter, M., & Hughes, M. (2010, February). Using story grammar to assist students with learning disabilities and reading difficulties improve their comprehension. *Education and Treatment of Children, (33)*1, 115–151.

Stevens, R. J., Van Meter, P. N., Garner, J., Warcholak, N., & Bochna, C. (2008). Reading and Integrated Literacy Strategies (RAILS): An integrated approach to early reading. *Journal of Education for Students Placed at Risk, 13*(4), 357–380.

Stimson, J. (1993). *The Three Billy Goats Gruff.* Illus. C. Russell. Loughborough, UK: Ladybird Books.

Stricklin, K. (2011). Hands-on reciprocal teaching: A comprehension technique. *The Reading Teacher, 64,* 620–625.

Struiksma, T., & Zuno, N. (2003). Roll call variation. In N. T. Ruiz, J. Cintrón, & R. Figueroa (Chairs), *Migrant/OLE Project.* Symposium conducted at the meeting of the Migrant/OLE Project, in collaboration with the California Department of Education—Migrant Educational International Office and California State University, Sacramento. San Francisco: State Literacy Academy.

Sulzby, E. (1990). Assessment of writing and children's language while writing. In W. H. Teale and E. Sulzby (Eds.), *Emergent Literacy: Writing and Reading.* Norwood, NJ: Ablex.

Sulzby, E., & Teale, W. H. (2010). The development of the young child and the emergence of literacy. In J. Flood, D. Lapp, M. E. Squire, & J. M. Jensen (Eds.), *Handbook of Research on Teaching the English Language Arts* (5th ed.). Sponsored by the International Reading Association/National Council of Teachers of English. Mahwah, NJ: Erlbaum.

Swanson, E., Edmonds, M. S., Hairrell, A., Vaughn, S., & Simmons, D. C. (2011). Applying a cohesive set of comprehension strategies to content-area instruction. *Intervention in School and Clinic, 46*(5), 266–272.

Sweeney, J., & Peterson, S. (1996). *350 Fabulous Writing Prompts: Thought-Provoking Springboards for Creative, Expository, and Journal Writing.* New York: Scholastic.

Sweet, A. P., & Snow, C. E. (2003a). Reading for comprehension. In A. P. Sweet and C. E. Snow (Eds.), *Rethinking Reading Comprehension* (pp. 1–11). New York: Guilford Press.

Sweet, A., & Snow, C. (2003b). *Understanding Comprehension: RAND Report on Comprehension.* Washington, DC: RAND.

Tangel, D., & Blachman, B. A. (1992). Effect of phoneme awareness instruction on kindergarten children's invented spelling. *Journal of Reading Behavior, 24,* 233–261.

Tangel, D., & Blachman, B. A. (1995). Effect of phoneme awareness on the invented spelling of first-grade children: A one year follow-up. *Journal of Reading Behavior, 27,* 153–185.

Taylor, D., & Dorsey-Gaines, C. (1988). *Growing Up Literate: Learning from Inner-City Families.* Portsmouth, NH: Heinemann.

Teague, M. (1997). *How I Spent My Summer Vacation.* New York: Dragonfly Books.

Teale, W. H. (1978). Positive environments for learning to read: What studies of early readers tell us. *Language Arts, 55,* 922–932.

Teale, W. H., & Sulzby, E. (1986a). *Emergent Literacy.* Norwood, NJ: Ablex.

Teale, W. H., & Sulzby, E. (1986b). Home background and young children's literacy development. In *Emergent Literacy: Writing and Reading.* Norwood, NJ: Ablex.

Temple, C., Martinez, M., & Yokota, J. (2011). *Children's Books in Children's Hands: An Introduction to Their Literature* (4th ed.). Boston: Pearson.

Thomas, A., Fazio, L., & Stiefelmeyer, B. L. (1999). *Families at School: A Guide for Educators.* Newark, DE: International Reading Association.

Thomas, W. P., & Collier, V. P. (2002). *A National Study of School Effectiveness for Language Minority Students' Long-Term Academic Achievement.* Santa Cruz, CA: Center for Research on Education, Diversity and Excellence. Retrieved from http://www.crede.ucsc.edu/research/llaa/1.1_final.html

Tierney, R. J., Readence, J. E., & Dishner, E. K. (2005). *Reading Strategies and Practices: A Compendium* (6th ed.). Boston: Allyn & Bacon.

Tompkins, G. (2002). *Language Arts: Content and Teaching Strategies* (5th ed.). Upper Saddle River, NJ: Merrill/Prentice Hall.

Tompkins, G. (2014). *Literacy for the 21st century* (6th ed.). Boston: Allyn & Bacon.

Tompkins, G. E. (1997). *Best Teaching Practices* (video). Boston: Allyn & Bacon.

Tompkins, G. E. (2006). *Literacy for the 21st Century: A Balanced Approach* (4th ed.). Upper Saddle River, NJ: Merrill/Prentice Hall.

Tompkins, G. E. (2015). *Literacy in the Early Grades: A Successful Start for PreK–4 Readers and Writers* (4th ed.). Boston: Pearson.

Tompkins, G. E., & Collom, S. (2004). *Sharing the Pen: Interactive Writing with Young Children.* Upper Saddle River, NJ: Merrill/Prentice Hall.

Torrey, J. W. (1979). Reading that comes naturally. In G. Waller and G. E. MacKinnon (Eds.), *Reading Research: Advance in Theory and Practice,* Vol. 1 (pp. 115–144). New York: Academic Press.

Trachtenburg, P. (1990). Using children's literature to enhance phonics instruction. *The Reading Teacher, 43,* 648–654.

Tracy, D. H. (1995). Children practicing reading at home: What we know about how parents help. In L. Morrow (Ed.), *Family Literacy: Connections in Schools and Communities.* Newark, DE: International Reading Association.

Tracy, D. H., & Young, J. W. (1994). Mother–child interactions during children's oral reading at home. In D. Leu and C. Kinzer (Eds.), *Multidimensional Aspects of Literacy Research, Theory, and Practice* (Forty-Third Yearbook of the National Reading Conference). Chicago: National Reading Conference.

Trelease, J. (2006). *The New Read Aloud Handbook* (6th ed.). New York: Penguin.

U.S. Department of Education, Institute of Education Sciences, National Center for Education Statistics, National Assessment of Educational Progress (NAEP) (2002). Oral Reading Study. Washington, DC: Author.

Vacca, R. T., & Vacca, J. L. (2010). *Content Area Reading* (10th ed.). Boston: Allyn & Bacon.

Vadasy, P. F., Sanders, E. A., & Peyton, J. A. (2006). Code-oriented instruction for kindergarten students at risk for reading difficulties: A randomized field trial with paraeducator implementers. *Journal of Educational Psychology, 98,* 508–528.

Valencia, S. (1990). A portfolio approach to classroom reading assessment: The whys, whats, and hows. *The Reading Teacher, 43,* 338–340.

Van Allsburg, C. (1985). *The Polar Express.* New York: Houghton Mifflin.

Van Scoter, J. V. (2008). The potential of IT to foster literacy development in kindergarten. In J. V. Knezek (Ed.), *International Handbook of Informational Technology in Education* (pp. 149–161). London: Springer.

Van Steensel, R. (2006). Relations between socio-cultural factors, the home literacy environment and children's literacy development. *Journal of Research in Reading, 29,* 367–382.

Vardell, S. M., Hadaway, N. L., & Young, T. A. (2006). Matching books and readers: Selecting literature for English learners. *The Reading Teacher, 59,* 734–741.

Vaughn, S., & Edmonds, M. (2006). Reading comprehension for older readers. *Intervention in School and Clinic, 41*(3), 131–137.

Vaughn, S., & Linan-Thompson, S. (2007). *Research-Based Methods of Reading Instruction for English Language Learners, Grades K–4.* Alexandria,

VA: Association for Supervision and Curriculum Development.

Vellutino, F. R. (1991). Introduction to three studies on reading acquisition: Convergent findings on theoretical foundations of code-oriented versus whole-language approaches to reading instruction. *Journal of Educational Psychology, 83*(4), 437–443.

Viorst, J. (1987). *Alexander and the Terrible, Horrible, No Good, Very Bad Day.* New York: Atheneum.

Vogt, M. E. (2004, August/September). Book reading drops, says new survey. *Reading Today, 22,* 6.

Vygotsky, L. S. (1986). *Thought and Language.* Trans. A. Kosulin. Cambridge, MA: MIT Press. (Original work published 1934.)

Wagner, R. K., Torgeson, J. K., & Rashotte, C. A. (1994). Development of reading-related phonological processing abilities: New evidence of bidirectional causality from a latent variable longitudinal study. *Developmental Psychology, 30,* 73–87.

Walsh, M., Asha, J., & Sprainger, N. (2007). Reading digital texts. *Australian Journal of Language and Literacy, 30*(1), 40–53.

Warschauer, M. (2008). Laptops and literacy: A multi-site case study. *Pedagogies: An International Journal, 3,* 52–67.

Warschauer, M., Grant, D., Del Real, G., & Rousseau, M. (2004). Promoting academic literacy and technology: Successful laptop programs in K–12 schools. *System, 32,* 525–537.

Watson, D. (1987). Reader-selected miscues. In D. Watson (Ed.), *Ideas and Insights: Language Arts in the Elementary School.* Urbana, IL: National Council of Teachers of English.

Wetzel, M., Peterson, K., Weber, N., & Steinback, E. (2013) Public voices: Critical literacy and newspaper writing in a fourth grade classroom. *Critical Literacy: Theories and Practices* 7(1).

White, T. G. (2005). Effects of systematic and strategic analogy-based phonics on grade 2 students' word reading and reading comprehension. *Reading Research Quarterly, 40*(2), 234–255.

Wilde, S. (1992). *You Ken Red This! Spelling and Punctuation for Whole Language Classrooms.* Portsmouth, NH: Heinemann.

Willingham, D., & Lovette, G. (2014). Can reading comprehension be taught? *Teachers College Record.*

Wilson, D. (2012). Training the mind's eye: 'Brain movies' support comprehension and recall. *The Reading Teacher, 66,* 189–194.

Wilson, P. (2012). Four things all educators should understand about the dyslexic brain. Edutopia. Retrieved from http://www.edutopia.org/blog/4-things-about-dyslexic-brain-patrick-wilson

Wink, J. (2005). *Critical Pedagogy: Notes from the Real World* (3rd ed.). Boston: Allyn & Bacon/Pearson.

Wiseman, D. L. (1992). *Learning to Read with Literature.* Boston: Allyn & Bacon.

Wolbers, K. A. (2008). Using balanced and interactive writing instruction to improve the higher order and lower order writing skills of deaf students. *Journal of Deaf Studies and Deaf Education, 13*(2), 257–277.

Wolbers, K. A., Dostal, H. M., & Bowers, L. M. (2012, Winter). I was born full Deaf: Written language outcomes after 1 year of strategic and interactive writing instruction. *Journal of Deaf Studies and Deaf Education, 17*(1), 19–38.

Wolf, S. A., & Gearhart, M. (1993). Writing what you read: A guidebook for the assessment of children's narratives (CSE Resource Paper No. 10). Los Angeles: University of California, Center for Research on Evaluation, Standards, and Student Testing.

Wright, J. C., Huston, A. C., Murphy, K. C., et al. (2001). The relations of early television viewing to school readiness and vocabulary of children from low income families: The early window project. *Child Development, 72*(5), 1347–1366.

Yopp, H. K. (1995). Read-aloud books for developing phonemic awareness: An annotated bibliography. *The Reading Teacher, 48,* 538–543.

Yopp, H. K., & Stapleton, L. (2008). Conciencia Fonémica en Español (Phonemic Awareness in Spanish). *The Reading Teacher, 61*(5), 374–382.

Yopp, H. K., & Yopp, R. H. (2000). Supporting phonemic awareness development in the classroom. *The Reading Teacher, 43,* 22–28.

Yopp, R. H., & Yopp, H. K. (2006). Informational texts as read-alouds at school and home. *Journal of Literacy Research, 38*(1), 37–51.

Young, E. (1990). *Lon Po Po: A Red Riding Hood Story from China.* New York: Putnam.

Yurick, A., Cartledge, G., Kourea, L., & Keyes, S. (2012). Reducing reading failure for kindergarten urban students: A study of early literacy instruction, treatment quality, and treatment duration. *Remedial and Special Education, 33*(2), 89–102.

Zawilinski, L. (2009). HOT blogging: A framework for blogging to promote higher order thinking. *The Reading Teacher, 62,* 650–661.

Zucker, T., Moody, A., & McKenna, M. (2009). The effects of electronic books on pre-kindergarten-to-grade 5 students' literacy and language outcomes: A research synthesis. *Journal of Educational Computing Research, 40,* 47–87.

Zutell, J. (1996). The directed spelling teaching activity (DSTA): Providing an effective balance in word study instruction. *The Reading Teacher, 50,* 98–108.

Author Index

Subject Index